GRE

Graduate Record Examination

General Test

Thomas H. Martinson

Prentice Hall

New York • London • Toronto • Sydney • Tokyo • Singapore

Fifth Edition

 Prentice Hall General Reference
15 Columbus Circle
New York, NY 10023

An Arco Book

ARCO and PRENTICE HALL are registered trademarks
of Prentice-Hall, Inc.
Colophon is a trademark of Prentice-Hall, Inc.

Library of Congress Cataloging-in-Publication Data

Martinson, Thomas H.
   GRE : graduate record examination / Thomas H. Martinson. —5th
ed.
        p.   cm.
   At head of title: Arco
   ISBN 0-671-88823-4
   1. Graduate Record Examination—Study guides. I. Title. II. Title:
Arco GRE graduate record examination.
LB2367.4.M374   1994
378.1'.662   dc20   94-16422
                                                            CIP

Manufactured in the United States of America

1 2 3 4 5 6 7 8 9 10

LATE-BREAKING GRE NEWS

TWO NEW QUESTION TYPES ARE ANNOUNCED

A recent *GRE Information & Registration Bulletin* lists two new question types:

• Analysis of Explanations
• Pattern Identification

The *Bulletin's* "Sample Questions" section includes examples of both new question types, along with examples of the question types that have appeared on the GRE for years. However, as of this writing, the two new question types are still "experimental"; that is, they appear only in test sections that the testmakers use to "try out" new question types. There is usually one such section in a typical GRE, and it does not count toward a candidate's score.

However, candidates should bear in mind that these new question types may at some point be included in the GRE's regular scored sections. For a description of the two new types, see the section on Analytical Questions in the "Test Busters" portion of this book.

THE CAT HAS LANDED

The GRE's Computer-Based Testing (CBT) Program, launched in 1993 to give test-takers the option of taking a computerized version of the test, is using a new format. The computerized GRE was originally little more than a "test booklet on a computer screen." However, newer forms are constructed as Computer Adaptive Tests, or CATs.

In the CAT version of the GRE, the computer constructs a highly individualized test for each candidate based upon responses to previous questions. The process is interactive: after you answer a question, the computer uses information about your answer (and answers to previous questions as well) to select the next question for you. Since your exam is specifically constructed for you during the testing session, you will not waste time on questions that are either too easy or too hard.

The addition of the CAT version of the test represents the latest advance in the GRE Computer-Based Testing Program. The test-makers project that in the next few years the CAT version will completely supplant the old paper-and-pencil version of the test and that all testing will be interactive. This trend does not mean, however, that candidates should not continue to prepare for the GRE. The introduction of the CAT form of the GRE has not changed the *content* of the test—only the way the content is tested. Candidates can and should continue to use written materials to review for the test. For further information on the CAT form of the GRE, see the section on General Test-Taking Strategies in the "Test Busters" portion of this book.

About the Author

Thomas H. Martinson has nearly twenty years' experience preparing students for ETS exams. He has developed GRE, GMAT, and LSAT courses for several of the nation's leading test preparation centers. A graduate of Harvard Law School, Mr. Martinson is a member of the New York State and Washington, D.C. bars. He has also taught logic and argumentation at the university level.

CONTENTS

Part One
About the Graduate Record Examination General Test

Part Two
Test Busters

Bonus Section

The GRE Subject Tests and Financing Your Graduate Education

Part Three

GRE Math Review

Part Four
6 Full-Length Practice Examinations

Part One

ABOUT THE GRADUATE RECORD EXAMINATION GENERAL TEST

ORIENTATION

The letters G-R-E stand for Graduate Record Examinations. The GRE Program is sponsored by the Graduate Record Examinations Board, an independent committee affiliated with the Association of Graduate Schools and the Council of Graduate Schools in the United States. The GRE Program sponsors a General Test plus a battery of achievement tests in particular fields. The GRE Program is administered by Educational Testing Services (ETS). To obtain registration materials for the GRE, write:

Graduate Record Examinations Program
CN 6000
Princeton, NJ 08541-6000

This book treats the GRE General Test, so from this point on, we will use the term GRE to refer to the GRE General Test only (even though there are GRE Achievement Tests).

The purpose of the GRE is to provide a standard measure that will permit admission decisions to be based, at least in part, on an "objective" comparison of all candidates—no matter what their college or background.

The GRE generates three different scores: a verbal score, a math score and an analytical score. To learn how your scores will affect your application, you should study the informational bulletins published by the schools to which you are applying. In particular, you should try to determine what weight is given to which scores and what scores you will need to be a competitive applicant.

The Format of the GRE

The GRE consists of seven separately timed, thirty-minute sections. Each section is devoted to a particular type of question: verbal, math, or analytical.

Verbal questions test the extent of your vocabulary and your ability to read. Math questions test your knowledge of arithmetic, basic algebra, and elementary geometry. Analytical questions test your ability to think carefully and logically.

1

VERBAL QUESTIONS

The GRE uses four different types of verbal questions: antonyms, analogies, sentence completions, and reading comprehension.

Antonyms

An antonym item consists of a single, capitalized word followed by five answer choices. The basic idea is to pick the answer that has the meaning which is most nearly opposite that of the capitalized word.

Directions: The following question consists of a word printed in capital letters, followed by five (5) lettered words or phrases. Select the word or phrase which is most nearly opposite to the capitalized word in meaning.

WAIVE:

(A) repeat
(B) conclude
(C) insist upon
(D) improve on
(E) peruse

The best answer is **(C)**. To WAIVE means to forgo or to relinquish. A fairly precise opposite is "to insist upon."

Analogies

An analogy consists of one capitalized word pair followed by five answer choices (also word pairs). The idea is to select from among the choices a word pair that expresses a relationship similar to that expressed by the capitalized word pair.

Directions: The following question consists of a related pair of words or phrases in capital letters followed by five (5) lettered pairs of words or phrases. Choose the pair which best expresses a relationship similar to that expressed by the original pair.

MINISTER : PULPIT::

(A) doctor : patient
(B) student : teacher
(C) mechanic : engine
(D) programmer : logic
(E) judge : bench

The best choice is **(E)**. The PULPIT is the place where the MINISTER does his or her job, and the *bench* is the place where the *judge* does her or his job.

Sentence Completions

Sentence completion questions consist of a sentence, a part or parts of which have been omitted, followed by five letter choices that are possible substitutions for the omitted parts. The idea is to select the choice that best completes the sentence.

Directions: The sentence that follows contains one or more blank spaces indicating that something has been omitted. It is followed by five (5) lettered words or sets of words. Read and determine the general sense of the sentence. Then choose the word or set of words which, when inserted in the sentence, best fits the meaning of the sentence.

Her desire for _____ soon became apparent when she adamantly refused to answer questions about her identity or mission.

(A) assistance
(B) anonymity
(C) success
(D) publicity
(E) recognition

The best completion is offered by (**B**). The logic of the sentence requires that the missing element indicate a desire for something that can be achieved only by refusing to give information. If you don't give any information about your identity or your activities, you hope to insure that you remain *anonymous*.

Reading Comprehension

Reading comprehension questions, as the name implies, test your ability to understand the substance and logical structure of a written selection. The GRE uses reading passages of various lengths, ranging from 200 to 550 words. A long passage will be the basis for as many as seven or eight questions while a shorter passage might support only three or four questions. The questions ask about the main point of the passage, about what the author specifically states, about what can be logically inferred from the passage, and about the author's attitude or tone. Here is an example of a shorter reading comprehension selection. (To avoid getting mired in discussion of particular questions, the passage is followed by only two questions, rather than the usual three or four.)

Directions: Below is a reading selection followed by a number of questions. Read the selection. Then based on your understanding of the selection, select the best answer to each question.

The international software market represents a significant business opportunity for U.S. microcomputer software companies, but illegal copying of programs is limiting the growth of sales abroad. If not dealt with quickly, international piracy of software could become one of the most serious trade problems faced by the United States.

Software piracy is already the biggest barrier to U.S. software companies entering foreign markets. One reason is that software is extremely easy and inexpensive to duplicate compared to the cost of developing and marketing the software. The actual cost of duplicating a software program, which may have a retail value of $400 or more, can be as little as a dollar or two—the main component being the cost of the diskette. The cost of counterfeiting software is substantially less than the cost of duplicating watches, books, or blue jeans. Given that the difference between the true value of the original and the cost of the counterfeit is so great for software, international piracy has become big business. Unfortunately, many foreign governments view software piracy as an industry in and of itself and look the other way.

U.S. firms stand to lose millions of dollars in new business, and diminished U.S. sales not only harm individual firms but also adversely affect the entire U.S. economy.

1. In this passage, the author is primarily concerned to

(A) criticize foreign governments for stealing U.S. computer secrets
(B) describe the economic hazards software piracy poses to the United States
(C) demand that software pirates immediately cease their illegal operations
(D) present a comprehensive proposal to counteract the effects of international software piracy
(E) disparage the attempts of the U.S. government to control software piracy

2. The author's attitude toward international software piracy can best be described as

(A) concern
(B) rage
(C) disinterest
(D) pride
(E) condescension

The best answer to the first question is **(B)**. This question, typical of the GRE, asks about the main point of the selection. (A) is incorrect. Though the author implies criticism of foreign governments, their mistake, so far as we are told, is not stealing secrets but tacitly allowing the operation of a software black market. (C) is incorrect since this is not the main point of the selection. You can infer that the author would approve of such a demand, but issuing the demand is not the main point of the selection you just read. (D) can be eliminated for a similar reason. Though the author might elsewhere offer a specific proposal, he does not do so in the selection you just read. (E) also is wrong since no such attempts are ever discussed. Finally, notice how well (B) does describe the main issue. The author is concerned to identify a problem and to discuss its causes.

The best answer to the second question is **(A)**. This question asks about the tone of the passage, and concern very neatly captures that tone. You can eliminate (B) as an overstatement. Though the author condemns the piracy, the tone is not so violent as to qualify as rage. (C) must surely be incorrect since the author does express concern. He is not disinterested. (D) also is incorrect since the author specifically disapproves of the piracy. And finally, (E) is wrong because condescension is not the same thing as disapproval.

Although some minor variations in format are possible, the verbal sections of the GRE now have this structure:

Time—30 minutes

38 questions

1– 7	Sentence Completions
8-16	Analogies
17–27	Reading Comprehension
28–38	Antonyms

MATH QUESTIONS

The GRE uses three different kinds of math questions: problem solving, quantitative comparisons, and graphs. The math sections test your knowledge of arithmetic, basic algebra, elementary geometry, and common charts and graphs.

Problem Solving

If you have taken any other standardized exams that included math questions (such as the SAT), then you have probably already seen examples of problem solving questions. These are your typical word problem questions. Some test arithmetic.

Betty left home with $60 in her wallet. She spent 1/3 of that amount at the supermarket, and she spent 1/2 of what remained at the drugstore. If Betty made no other expenditures, how much money did she have when she returned home?

(A) $10
(B) $15
(C) $20
(D) $40
(E) $50

A quick calculation will show that the correct answer is (C). Betty spent 1/3 of $60, or $20, at the supermarket, leaving her with $40. Of the $40, she spent 1/2, or $20, at the drugstore, leaving her with $20 when she returned home.

Other problem-solving items test your knowledge of basic algebra.

If $2x + 3y = 8$ and $y = 2x$, then what is the value of x?

(A) –6
(B) –4
(C) 0
(D) 1
(E) 4

The best answer is **(D)**. To answer the question, you need to solve for x. Since $y = 2x$, you can substitute $2x$ for y in the first equation:

$$2x + 3(2x) = 8$$

Multiply: $2x + 6x = 8$

Add: $8x = 8$

Divide: $x = 1$

Problem-solving items also test your knowledge of elementary geometry.

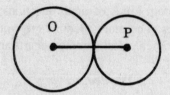

In the figure above, circle O and circle P are tangent to each other. If the circle with center O has a diameter of 8 and the circle with center P has a diameter 6, what is the length of segment OP?

(A) 7
(B) 10
(C) 14
(D) 20
(E) 28

The correct answer is **(A)**. The segment OP is made up of the radius of circle O and the radius of circle P. To find the length of OP, you need to know the lengths of the two radii. Since the length of the radius is one-half that of the diameter, the radius of circle O is 1/2(8) or 4, and the radius of circle P is 1/2(6) or 3. So the length of OP is $3 + 4 = 7$.

Quantitative Comparisons

The second type of math question on the GRE is quantitative comparison. Quantitative comparisons are presented in an unusual format with special instructions.

Without trying to understand all of the subtleties of the type, you can get the general idea of quantitative comparisons by reading a short summary of the instructions.

Directions: For each of the following questions two quantities are given, one in Column A and one in Column B. Compare the two quantities and mark your answer sheet with the correct lettered conclusion. These are your options:

A: If the quantity in Column A is the greater;
B: if the quantity in Column B is the greater;
C: if the two quantities are equal;
D: if the relationship cannot be determined from the information given.

Some quantitative comparisons test arithmetic, algebra, and geometry.

COLUMN A	COLUMN B
$6 - \frac{4}{2}$	$5 - \frac{4}{4}$

The correct answer is (**C**). Column A is just $6 - 2 = 4$, and Column B is $5 - 1 = 4$. Both columns have the value of 4, so they are equal. Other quantitative comparisons test algebra.

COLUMN A	COLUMN B
$x + 1$	$x - 1$

The correct answer is (**A**). Whatever the value of x, the expression $x + 1$ is one more than x, and the expression $x - 1$ is one less than x. So no matter what the value of x, Column A is 2 larger than Column B. And some quantitative comparisons test geometry.

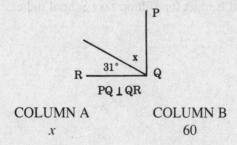

PQ ⊥ QR

COLUMN A	COLUMN B
x	60

The correct answer is (**B**). PQ is perpendicular to QR, so PQR is a 90 degree angle. Since one of the two angles making up the right angle is 31 degrees, the other must be 59 degrees. So $x = 59$, and column B (which is 60) is larger. Here is a final quantitative comparison to illustrate a relation that is indeterminable.

COLUMN A	COLUMN B
the price of a sweater that is marked 25% off	the price of a coat that is marked 20% off

The correct answer is (**D**). You are asked to compare the prices of the two articles. Although you know the percent discount taken on each, you have no way of knowing the actual cost of the item. Since the comparison cannot be made on the basis of what is given, the correct choice is (D).

Graphs

Graph questions are like problem-solving items except that the information to be used in solving the problem is presented in pictorial form.

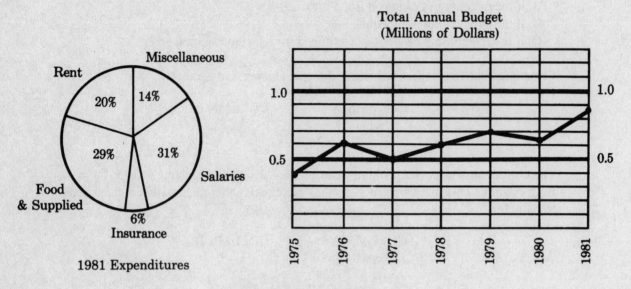

1981 Expenditures

HILLTOP DAY SCHOOL
FINANCIAL INFORMATION

1. The Total Annual Budget for Hilltop Day School increased by what percent from 1975 to 1981?

(A) 4%
(B) 8%
(C) 50%
(D) 125%
(E) 200%

2. How much money did Hilltop Day School spend for rent in 1981?

(A) $180,000
(B) $225,000
(C) $240,000
(D) $800,000
(E) $2,000,000

The two questions based on the graphs are essentially problem-solving questions, but the information needed to answer the questions is presented in graphic form.

The correct answer to the first question is **(D)**. The operating budget increased from

$0.4 million in 1975 to $0.9 million in 1981—an increase of $0.5 million. Expressed as a percentage increase: $(0.5/0.4) \times 100 = 1.25 \times 100 = 125\%$

The correct answer to the second question is (A). From the graph on the right, we learn that the total budget for 1981 was $0.9 million. The graph on the left breaks down the budget for 1981. It shows that 20% of the 1981 budget went for rent: 20% of $0.9 million = $180,000.

The usual format of the math sections is:

Time—30 minutes

30 Questions

1–15	Quantitative comparisons
16–20	Problem-solving items
21–25	Graph questions
26–30	Problem-solving items

ANALYTICAL QUESTIONS

The analytical sections use two different types of questions. One kind is called analytical reasoning and consists of logical games or puzzles; the other is called logical reasoning.

The analytical reasoning type involves a situation such as people standing in a row, or choosing items from a menu, or scheduling vacations. The questions then ask you to draw logical conclusions about the situation.

Questions 1-2

Five people, P, Q, R, S, and T, are standing single file in a ticket line. All are facing the ticket window.
Q is the second person behind P.
P is not the second person in the line.
R is somewhere ahead of S.

1. T could occupy all of the following positions in the line EXCEPT:

(A) 1
(B) 2
(C) 3
(D) 4
(E) 5

2. If R is the fourth person in line, which of the following must be true?

(A) T is the second person in line.
(B) Q is the second person in line.
(C) P is the third person in line.
(D) S is the third person in line.
(E) Q is the fifth person in line.

The correct answer to the first question is (C), as shown by the following reasoning. The initial conditions establish that Q is behind P separated by one person, an arrangement that can be shown as Q ? P. And since P cannot be the second person in line, only two arrangements are possible for Q and P:

	1	2	3	4	5
	P		Q		
OR			P		Q

Since these are the only two possibilities, either Q or P must be third in line, which means no one else can be third. Therefore, T cannot stand in the third position.

The correct answer to the second question is (A). Here we are given additional information to use in answering this item. Given that R is the fourth in line, since R is ahead of S, S must be fifth in line.

1	2	3	4	5
			R	S

This forces P and Q into positions 1 and 3:

1	2	3	4	5
P		Q	R	S

Finally, T must be second in line:

1	2	3	4	5
P	T	Q	R	S

The other type of analytical question is logical reasoning. A typical logical reasoning question presents an argument or an explanation which you are asked to analyze. You may be asked to describe the argument, draw further conclusions from it, attack or defend it, or just find the assumptions of the argument.

Wilfred commented, "Of all the musical instruments I have studied, the trombone is the most difficult instrument to play." Which of the following statements, if true, would most seriously weaken Wilfred's conclusion?

(A) The trombone is relatively easy for trumpet players to learn to play.
(B) Wilfred has not studied trombone as seriously as he has studied other instruments.
(C) Wilfred finds he can play the violin and the cello with equal facility.

(D) The trombone is easier to learn as a second instrument than as a first instrument.

(E) There are several instruments which Wilfred has not studied and which are very difficult to play.

The best choice is (**B**). The question asks you to identify a possible weakness in the argument. The conclusion of the argument is that the trombone is intrinsically more difficult to play than other instruments. The question asks you to find another explanation for Wilfred's impression. Choice (B) suggests the fault is not in the trombone but in Wilfred. The seeming difficulty of the trombone stems from the fact that Wilfred did not study it as diligently as he has studied other instruments.

Although some slight variation in the arrangement of questions occurs, the format of the analytical sections usually looks like this:

Time—30 minutes

25 Questions

1–6	Analytical reasoning
7–9	Logical reasoning
10–22	Analytical reasoning
23–25	Logical reasoning

THE MYSTERY SECTION

Each edition of the GRE includes two verbal sections, two math sections, two analytical sections plus a mystery section. The mystery section can be another verbal section, or another math section, or another analytical section, or something altogether different. The mystery section, however, is a non-counting section, that is, it does not affect your score.

The mystery section contains questions that are being tested for future use. It's not possible for the test writers to know in advance whether a particular question really fits the design specifications of the test. They can determine that only by having a large number of responses to a question. Then they can ascertain whether the question is of the correct level of difficulty, whether the right answer and wrong answers are clearly distinguishable, and so on. So they put new questions in the mystery section, testing their validity for future use.

The identity of the mystery section has to remain a mystery. Since the mystery section is not used in computing scores, if test-takers knew which was the mystery section, they might just take a thirty-minute break. In that case, the test-writers would learn nothing about the validity of the questions being tested. Can you guess which is the mystery section? Perhaps; perhaps not. And if you do think you've found it, what will you do? Put down your pencil and hope that it really is the mystery section? Obviously you do not want to take a chance that it will turn out to be one of the "live" sections that will determine your score.

The general rule to observe regarding the mystery section is to answer all sections to the best of your ability, but if you see something that is a total surprise while answering, don't let the presence of that section interfere with your performance on subsequent sections.

SCORING THE GRE

Your score report for the GRE will show three scores, a verbal score (based on the 76 questions in the two verbal sections), a math score (based on the 60 questions in the two math sections), and an analytical score (based on the 50 questions in the two analytical sections). Each of the three scores ranges from 200 (the minimum) to 800 (the maximum).

The scoring mechanism for the GRE is very simple. It consists of two steps. First, total the number of questions answered correctly; this is called the raw score. Then, using the appropriate conversion table, convert the raw score to its three-digit equivalent. The following is a partial conversion table:

RAW SCORES			SCALED SCORE
Verbal	Math	Analytical	
76	60	50	800
68	55	44	750
64	52	40	700
60	48	38	650
55	44	35	600
50	40	31	550
45	36	28	500
40	32	25	450
38	28	22	400
28	24	19	350
22	20	16	300
17	16	13	250

Part Two
TEST BUSTERS

GENERAL TEST-TAKING STRATEGIES

Even though the GRE uses several different question types, there are some tactics that are applicable to the test as a whole.

STARTING TO WORK

Take a brief overview of each section before beginning to work on it.

This is just a matter of caution. Some small adjustments in test format are always possible, so do not get caught off guard. When time is announced for you to begin work on a section, take five to ten seconds to look through the pages of that section. If there are unexpected changes, you can readily adjust your plan of attack.

Don't stop to ask directions.

Your allotted 30 minutes is all the time you get for a section. No additional time is given for reading instructions. If you spend 30 seconds reading directions each time you begin a new question type, you could lose 3 or 4 questions in each section.

The solution to this problem is to be thoroughly familiar with the directions for each question type and the format in which it is presented *before* the exam. Then you will recognize the format and already know what is required without having to review the directions for that part.

COVERING GROUND

The scoring mechanism for the GRE is the simple formula "score = correct answers." No points are awarded for near misses, and no extra points are given for accuracy. This means you have got to cover as much ground as possible.

Move as quickly as possible without unnecessarily sacrificing accuracy.

On the one hand, you have to answer as many questions as you can in the 30 minutes; on the other hand, you cannot afford to be so careful that you begin to beat yourself by not answering enough questions to get a good score. There is a trade-off between speed and accuracy, one that only you can find through practice.

To demonstrate the necessity of the trade-off, consider the cases of three hypothetical students: Timmy Toocareful, Carl Careless, and Terry Testwise. For purpose of discussion, let's study just the analytical sections, but the point when made will apply to the other four sections as well.

On his analytical sections, Timmy Toocareful attempted only 20 questions, but he was very accurate. Of the 20, Timmy answered 18 correctly, missing only 2. Additionally, he guessed at the remaining 30 questions, getting 1/5 of those right (as expected) for another 6 points.

Carl Careless used the opposite strategy. He worked very quickly to ensure that he attempted all 50 questions, and he paid the price. Of the 50, he answered only 30 correctly.

Terry Testwise used the proper strategy of working as quickly as possible without unnecessarily sacrificing accuracy. Of the 50, she attempted 40, missing 6. And she guessed at the other 10 questions, hitting 1/5 of them (as expected) for another 2 points.

The score reports would show:

Timmy Toocareful:
Analytical Score:	Raw Score 24	Scaled Score 420

Carl Careless:
Analytical Score:	Raw Score 30	Scaled Score 520

Terry Testwise:
Analytical Score:	Raw Score 36	Scaled Score 620

Most students are probably prone to err on the side of caution. In this case, Timmy, fearful of answering incorrectly, doesn't attempt enough questions to get his best score. Since there is no penalty for answering incorrectly, don't be overly worried about mistakes. Of course you don't want to be needlessly careless, but it's probably better to go too quickly than too slowly.

The following Test Buster will help you find the right trade-off:

Don't spend too much time on any question.

All questions are given equal weight. No extra credit is given for a difficult question. So there is no reason to keep working on a question after you have given it your best shot. Instead, once you realize that you are spinning your wheels, make the decision to make a guess and move on to the next question.

BEATING THE CLOCK

Many years ago, there was a program on television called "Beat the Clock." Contestants were given silly things to do within a certain time limit. For example, a contestant might be asked to stack 100 paper cups on top of each other in 30 seconds—while blindfolded! (The GRE is a lot like this.) On the television studio wall was a large clock with a single hand so contestants could keep track of the passing time. You need a similar device.

Bring your own watch to the test.

The proctors in charge of administering the test are supposed to keep you advised of the passing time, for example, by writing on a blackboard how many minutes remain. But you should not rely on their diligence. In the first place, it's easy for a proctor to forget to mark the passing time at exactly the right moment. So when you see the proctor write "5 minutes left," you might have only 4 minutes left or as much as 6 minutes left. Further, the proctor might mark the correct time at the right moment without your knowledge. When you look up from your work you see "5 minutes left," but when did the proctor write that down?

The solution is to have a watch with you. If you have a digital watch with a stopwatch function, you can use that. If your digital watch does not have a stopwatch function, write down the starting time for the section when you begin. Quickly add 30 minutes to that and write down the time you must finish. Circle that number for easy reference. If you have a watch with hands, adjust the minute hand to half-past any hour (the 6). The hour is irrelevant. If you begin work with the minute hand on the 6, your time will be up when the minute hand reaches the 12.

Keeping track of the time is not an end unto itself. You keep track of the time in order to use it to answer questions.

Concentrate intensely. If you find that your mind does begin to wander, stop briefly and regather your concentration.

The GRE is an arduous task. There is no way that you can maintain your concentration throughout all seven of the thirty-minute sections. There will be times when your attention begins to flag. Learn to recognize this. For example, if you find that you are reading and rereading the same line without understanding, put down your pencil, close your eyes, take a deep breath or two (or rub your eyes or whatever), and then get back to work.

Don't become obsessed with time.

Although time is an important part of the test, don't become preoccupied with the passing seconds. There are convenient points in each section to stop and check the remaining time, for example, as you turn a page.

BUSTING THE MULTIPLE-CHOICE FORMAT

Because of the multiple-choice format, you have a real advantage over the GRE. The correct answer is always right there on the page. To be sure, it's surrounded by wrong choices, but it may be possible to eliminate one or more of those other choices as non-answers. Look at the following reading comprehension question:

The author argues that the evidence supporting the new theory is

(A) hypothetical
(B) biased
(C) empirical
(D) speculative
(E) fragmentary

You might think that it is impossible to make any progress on a reading comprehension question without the reading selection, but you can eliminate three of the five answers in this question as non-answers.

Study the question stem. We can infer that the author of the selection has at least implicitly passed judgment on the evidence supporting the new theory. What kind of judgment might someone make about the evidence adduced to support a theory? (A), (C), and (D) all seem extremely unlikely. As for (A), while the theory is itself an hypothesis, the evidence supporting the theory would not be hypothetical. As for (C), evidence is empirical by definition. So it is unlikely that anyone would argue "This evidence is empirical." And (D) can be eliminated for the same reason as (A). Admittedly, this leaves you with a choice of (B) or (E), a choice that depends on the content of the reading selection; but at least you have a 50-50 chance of getting the question correct—even without reading the selection.

This brings us to the question of guessing.

Answer every question, and guess if you have to.

Unlike some other standardized exams you might have taken (such as the SAT), no points are deducted for incorrect answers. Since there is no penalty for taking a guess, and since there is always a chance you will hit on the right answer, don't leave any answer space blank. For those questions on which you can eliminate choices, make an educated guess. But even if you don't get to some questions, at least make a random guess on your answer sheet. You can't lose; you can only win.

The arrangement of answer choice letters is random. There is one exception to this general rule.

Strings of three letters are used, strings of four or more letters are not used.

Although strings of four or more of one letter are theoretically possible, they just don't occur. This is because the testwriters break them up. So you will not find a string of four (A)s in a row. If you do, at least one of your four answers will be wrong. Which one is it? There is no way of knowing for sure without checking your work.

CARE AND FEEDING OF THE ANSWER SHEET

Your test materials come in two parts. A booklet of thirty-odd pages containing the test questions and an answer sheet covered with lettered spaces for your responses. The space for marking your answers to a section will look something like this:

15 Ⓐ Ⓑ Ⓒ Ⓓ Ⓔ	22 Ⓐ Ⓑ Ⓒ Ⓓ Ⓔ	29 Ⓐ Ⓑ Ⓒ Ⓓ Ⓔ
16 Ⓐ Ⓑ Ⓒ Ⓓ Ⓔ	23 Ⓐ Ⓑ Ⓒ Ⓓ Ⓔ	30 Ⓐ Ⓑ Ⓒ Ⓓ Ⓔ
17 Ⓐ Ⓑ Ⓒ Ⓓ Ⓔ	24 Ⓐ Ⓑ Ⓒ Ⓓ Ⓔ	31 Ⓐ Ⓑ Ⓒ Ⓓ Ⓔ
18 Ⓐ Ⓑ Ⓒ Ⓓ Ⓔ	25 Ⓐ Ⓑ Ⓒ Ⓓ Ⓔ	32 Ⓐ Ⓑ Ⓒ Ⓓ Ⓔ
19 Ⓐ Ⓑ Ⓒ Ⓓ Ⓔ	26 Ⓐ Ⓑ Ⓒ Ⓓ Ⓔ	33 Ⓐ Ⓑ Ⓒ Ⓓ Ⓔ
20 Ⓐ Ⓑ Ⓒ Ⓓ Ⓔ	27 Ⓐ Ⓑ Ⓒ Ⓓ Ⓔ	34 Ⓐ Ⓑ Ⓒ Ⓓ Ⓔ
21 Ⓐ Ⓑ Ⓒ Ⓓ Ⓔ	28 Ⓐ Ⓑ Ⓒ Ⓓ Ⓔ	35 Ⓐ Ⓑ Ⓒ Ⓓ Ⓔ

Your answer sheet is graded by a machine that "reads" the marks you have made.

 Code your answers neatly, filling completely the answer space with a dark pencil mark. Leave no stray marks on the answer sheet. Enter one, and only one, answer per question. Don't worry if the answer sheet has more blanks than your booklet has questions. Leave the extra spaces blank.

Perhaps a visual aid will help explain the importance of this Test Buster:

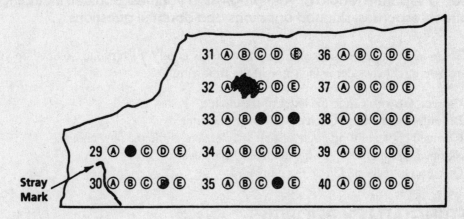

The answers to questions 29 and 35 are correctly entered. The answer to question 30, however, is incomplete; the machine might not see it. The answer to question 31 is too light; again, the machine might miss it. The mark for question 32 is messy; the machine might read (A), (B), or (C) as the intended response. Question 33 will be treated as incorrect since more than one space is darkened (no credit, no penalty). Question 34 will be treated in the same way since it has been left blank. (Leaving it blank was a mistake. It should have been answered even with a guess.)

The most common error in answer sheet management is misplacing an entire block of answers. This occurs when a test-taker skips a question in the test booklet but fails to skip a corresponding space on the answer sheet. The result is that the intended pattern of response is there, but it is displaced by one or more spaces. Unfortunately, the machine that grades the paper reads what actually is on the answer sheet—not what the test-taker intended. Here are some Test Busters to help you avoid this unpleasant problem.

Code your answers in groups.

Most test takers code their response to each question just after they have answered the question. They work in the rhythm: solve, code, solve, code, solve, code, and so on. It is this rhythm that can trip them up if they skip a question. Instead of coding your responses one by one, try coding them in groups.

Work problems for a while (noting your choices). Then find an appropriate moment to enter your responses on your answer sheet. You might wait until you have reached the end of a question type (for example, the sentence completions in the verbal sections or one of the logical puzzles in the analytical sections) or you might just wait until you reach the end of a page. As time for a section draws to a close, you should make sure you are current with your coding, so you will probably want to go to the one-by-one method. You don't want to run out of time on a section without the opportunity to enter answers to every question that you have worked.

Even if you are coding in groups, there is the ever present danger of an error. If you find that you have made a mistake, what do you do? You erase the wrong responses and enter the correct ones.

Keep a separate record of your progress in your test booklet, including correct responses, skipped questions and doubtful questions.

There is no single record keeping system that is good for everyone, so develop your own. You might consider using some of the following:

Correct Answer: Circle the letter of the choice.
Definitely Eliminated Choice: "X" over the letter.
Changed choice: Fill in circle of first answer, and circle the new choice.
Skipped Question: "?" by the number of the question.
Question to recheck: Circle the number.

SETTING ATTACK PRIORITIES

Although you have no choice about the order in which you must do the sections, you do have a choice about the order in which you do the questions within a section. There may be some advantage to doing the questions out of order.

The verbal sections contain sentence completions, analogies, reading comprehensions, and antonyms, in that order.

In the verbal sections, do the reading comprehension questions last.

Reading comprehension items come before antonyms, but they require that you invest a lot of time in reading a selection before you can answer a question. Antonyms, however, are very short. It may be better, therefore, to skip the reading comprehension part and go straight to the antonyms. After answering the shorter antonym items, you can return to reading comprehension.

The math sections contain quantitative comparisons, problem solving items, and graphs.

In a math section, the last few quantitative comparisons may be more difficult than the first few problem-solving items.

Questions within each type are arranged in ascending order of difficulty. This means that as you work through the fifteen quantitative comparisons at the beginning of a math section the going gets more difficult. But then you start a new type question, problem solving, and the first problem-solving item is likely to be easier than the last few quantitative comparisons. If you need to, skip the last three or four and go on to the problem-solving part.

It was suggested above that you might want to leave reading comprehension questions for last. A similar situation arises with regard to graphs. The graph on which the questions are based is like a long reading comprehension selection. Before you can begin to answer questions, you first have to study the graph—and that is time consuming.

In a math section, save the graph and its questions for last.

You might prefer to skip the graph (usually questions 21 through 25) and go to the second group of problem-solving questions. This is particularly true if you are running short of time. It makes no sense to spend two minutes studying a graph and run out of time before you get to answer even one question. You can better spend those two minutes more effectively on problem-solving items which are much shorter.

A similar situation arises in the analytical sections:

In an analytical section, do the logical reasoning problems first.

The basis for this suggestion is twofold. First, analytical reasoning questions (logical games) strike many people as strange and therefore exceptionally difficult, but logical reasoning problems (arguments) are more familiar and therefore easier. You always want to do the easiest material first, so you may want to do the six or seven logical reasoning questions before you tackle any logical games. Second, logical games are based upon an initial set of conditions which, like graphs, require time to read. So even if you are doing the analytical questions in the order in which they are presented, if time begins to run out, you may want to skip ahead and dispose of the last few logical reasoning questions first.

THE GRE COMPUTER ADAPTIVE TEST (CAT)

The first computerized version of the GRE, launched in 1993 as an optional alternative to the standard paper-and-pencil test, was little more than a "test booklet on the screen." The computer program simply displayed test items in the order in which they would have appeared in a regular test booklet. However, newer versions are constructed as Computer Adaptive Tests, or CATs. During a CAT, the computer controls the order in which test items appear, basing its selection on the candidate's responses to earlier items.

The basic concept behind Computer Adaptive Testing derives from a standard feature of the paper-and-pencil GRE: for most question types, items are arranged in ascending order of difficulty. But just as a coat tailored to the specifications of an "average" person would not actually fit very many people (because most people are not average), so too a GRE with questions of a wide range of difficulty does not precisely fit the needs of any single test-taker. Some candidates spend too much time trying to answer high-level questions that are just too difficult for them, while other candidates spend too much time disposing of low-level items that are simply too easy for them. But using the paper-and-pencil technology, it was just not feasible to create different versions—say, very easy, easy, average, difficult, and super-difficult—by altering the mix of questions; and in any event, how would anyone know in advance which version to take?

Computer Adaptive Testing provides a solution to this problem: the computer is able to create individualized tests based on each candidate's responses. At a grave risk of oversimplification, the testing procedure can be described as follows. The computer has access to a large number of test items classified according to question type (graphs, antonyms, reading comprehension, and so on) and arranged in order of difficulty. At the outset, the computer presents you with a couple of "seed" questions, items of average level of difficulty. If you answer those successfully, the program selects for the next question an item of greater difficulty; if you do not answer the "seed" questions correctly, the program lowers the level of difficulty. This process is repeated, with the program continuing to adjust the level of difficulty of questions, until you have provided all the answers that the computer needs to calculate your score. As you can imagine, your test will probably not look very much like the test of the person seated to your right nor that of the person seated to your left.

Although the CAT version differs from the paper-and-pencil version in *presentation* (it is both computerized and adaptive), the *content* of the CAT is still pure GRE. Consequently, you should prepare for the CAT in pretty much the same way that you would prepare for a paper-and-pencil version of the GRE. While the "adaptive" aspect of the CAT should have no effect on your preparation, it must have a great effect on your approach to the exam itself. On a CAT exam, you MUST ANSWER THE QUESTIONS IN THE ORDER PRESENTED. Since the exam adapts itself in response to your answers, you cannot skip and later return to any questions. And, you cannot rethink and change your answer at a later time. You cannot seek out and answer the easier question styles first. In other words, you must do the best you can to answer each question. Choose the answer that you have determined is best, or guess if necessary, confirm your choice, and move on to the next question.

Example:

Directions: Select the pair of words that best expresses a relationship similar to that expressed in the original pair.

BALLAD:SONG::

spire:church
ode:poem
novel:chapter
envelope:letter
leopard:jaguar

The correct answer to this analogy item is "ode:poem," regardless of whether it is found in the printed test booklet of a paper-and-pencil GRE or on the computer screen of a CAT.

Of course, the experience of taking a CAT—with its computerized display—does differ from that of taking a paper-and-pencil version in some fairly obvious ways. So here are some Test Busters that will help you cope with the electronic format.

Learn to use a mouse.

A mouse is a device that allows you to input information into the computer. Moving the mouse moves a "pointer" on the computer screen, and clicking a button on the mouse gives the computer instructions.

Example:

Indicate your response to an item as shown below. First choose the correct response.

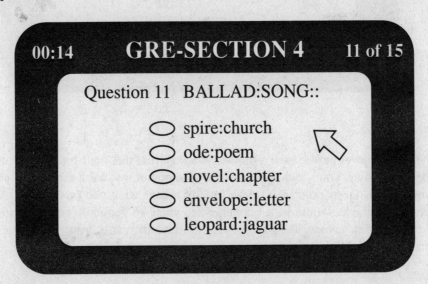

Next, position the pointer on the oval next to the response you have chosen.

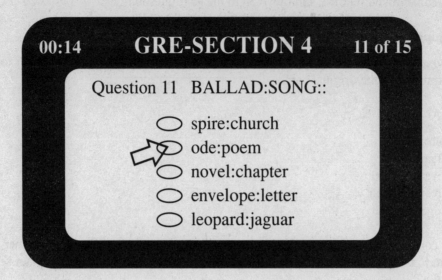

Click the button on the mouse. The oval will darken as shown below, indicating that the computer has registered your choice.

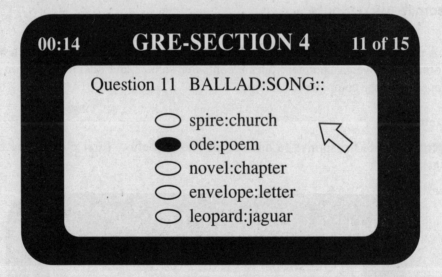

If you have never before used a mouse, you may find that your first efforts are a bit clumsy. If possible, you should get access to a computer that has a mouse and practice moving the on-screen pointer. It doesn't really matter what you practice on. A good choice, for example, would be a computerized game of "solitaire." By the time you have played a few games, using the pointer to move the cards around the screen, you will have mastered the use of the mouse.

Practice scrolling techniques.

In many computer programs, when a body of text is too long to be displayed in its entirety on the screen, you have the option of "scrolling" through the text. You can scroll up or down. The scroll function removes the top (or bottom) line and moves the other lines of text up (or down) one line on the screen, adding the next (or preceding) line of text. Your first experience with the scroll function may be a bit frustrating because it can be very sensitive. If you have the opportunity to play with a computer in advance of the test, you should also test a program that manipulates text, e.g., a word-processing program. Pay particular attention to the scrolling feature.

Take your time with the tutorials.

The computerized version of the GRE begins with these tutorials:

- How to Use a Mouse
- How to Select an Answer
- How to Use the Testing Tools
- How to Scroll

The program forces you to work through these tutorials, and you should pay careful attention to the directions. If you have never before worked with a mouse and a scroll bar, stay in the appropriate tutorials until you are comfortable with the mechanics of the computer. Time spent on the tutorials is not taken away from your time on the testing sections. And even if you are already "computer literate" and don't need to practice those techniques, you should nonetheless pay careful attention to the idiosyncrasies of the CAT program, e.g., how to indicate an answer, how to change an answer, how to move forward and backward, and what the various screen icons mean.

Do not waste time reading question-type directions.

While you can study the tutorials at leisure, you cannot afford to spend any of your testing time reading directions. And after you have finished your preparation, you shouldn't need to read them when they appear on the screen. You should know exactly what to do with each question type based just on its appearance. So don't waste time reading the directions for specific question types such as analogies or quantitative comparisons.

"Dismiss" test directions immediately.

Each section—and each new question type within a section—begins with a screen of directions. As noted above, you will not need to read them, but the directions do not disappear automatically. Instead, you have to "dismiss" them by pointing to the "Dismiss Directions" box on the screen and clicking the mouse. This procedure moves you into the body of the test. Do it immediately! Otherwise, you may find that you are passively staring at the directions screen waiting for the program to move on. (The directions screen is not like a logo or copyright screen of a program that is set to time out.)

Do not worry about how you are doing.

During a test, most of us have a tendency to worry about how we are doing. This is only natural. Of course, with a paper-and-pencil test, we don't get any feedback until the test is over.

But with the CAT form of the GRE, you get immediate feedback in the form of new questions. So you may have a tendency to wonder whether the level of difficulty of your questions is moving up or down, hoping to learn thereby whether you are doing well or not. You should avoid this type of speculation. It is a waste of time and mental energy, and it is doubtful whether you will really be able to make such a judgment about individual items.

TEST BUSTERS FOR VERBAL QUESTIONS

Sentence Completions

The basic idea of a sentence completion is "fill in the blank." The question type is a sort of hybrid, testing reading comprehension, word usage, and vocabulary. The question type is designed on the premise that it is possible to understand the gist of something even without hearing (or reading) every single word.

A little experiment will show you that this is true. Imagine that you are sitting in a lecture hall, listening to a professor, and someone sitting near you keeps rattling papers so you miss some words:

Tensions between the United States and Great Britain _____ even after the end of the War of 1812. One important _____ in Anglo-American relations during the nineteenth century was their _____ for one another, rather stronger on the side of the United States. "Twisting the lion's tail" was a favorite American political pastime, vestiges of which were still _____ even in the early part of the twentieth _____.

Even though you are missing some words, you should still be able to make sense of the lecture. In essence, based on the logic of the sentences, you are "automatically" filling in the blanks. There are several words which might be used to fill each blank such as:

Tensions between the United States and Great Britain *continued* even after the end of the War of 1812. One important *factor* in Anglo-American relations during the nineteenth century was their *antipathy* for one another, rather stronger on the side of the United States. "Twisting the lion's tail" was a favorite American political pastime, vestiges of which were still *evident* even in the early part of the twentieth *century*.

Of course, these words are not the only possible substitutions, but they will serve to show the general idea of a sentence completion.

This technique is the basic strategy for attacking sentence completions.

 Read the sentence through for meaning and try to anticipate words or phrases that might be used to complete its meaning.

Example:

There is no _____ for the United States to sign the treaty since there is every reason to believe no other nation intends to honor its provisions.

If you read this sentence, you should be able to anticipate that an appropriate completion would be something like "reason" or "incentive." In fact, the item reads:

There is no _____ for the United States to sign the treaty since there is every reason to believe no other nation intends to honor its provisions.

    (A) arrangement
    (B) continuation
    (C) incentive
    (D) procedure
    (E) importance

The correct answer is (**C**).

Occasionally, as just shown, you may actually anticipate the correct answer choice. More often, however, you will have to look for a choice that matches your anticipated substitution.

Examine the choices to find one that matches your anticipated completion.

Example:

Even though he is a leading authority on the French revolution, the chairperson of the department is a _____ speaker whose lectures on even the most exciting aspect of that historical period cause students to yawn and fidget.

The logic of the sentence prompts us to anticipate a completion such as "dull" or "uninteresting." As it turns out, however, the actual question reads:

Even though he is a leading authority on the French revolution, the chairperson of the department is a _____ speaker whose lectures on even the most exciting aspect of that historical period cause students to yawn and fidget.

    (A) sublime
    (B) confident
    (C) lackluster
    (D) honest
    (E) meritorious

The correct choice is (**C**). You must be prepared to match your anticipated response to an available choice.

Sometimes the structure of the sentence will make it impossible to anticipate a completion.

When you are unable to anticipate a possible completion, test each of the five answer choices to find the one that works best.

This Test Buster can be demonstrated using a different version of the sentence just examined:

The chairperson, who is a specialist in French history, is a _____ speaker whose lectures on the French Revolution completely _____ students.

Notice that many of the clues contained in the original, such as "yawn" and "fidget," are missing here. This makes it impossible to anticipate confidently any substitutions. It is possible to complete the sentence in the same spirit we did above using, say, "lackluster" and "bore." But the sentence might also have the following choices.

The chairperson, who is a specialist in French history, is a _____ speaker whose lectures on the French Revolution completely _____ students.

(A) lackluster . . . entertain
(B) moving . . . alienate
(C) dull . . . absorb
(D) forceful . . . require
(E) scintillating . . . enthrall

In situations such as this, where it is not possible to anticipate an answer confidently, you must test each choice by substitution until you find one that works.

The chairperson, who is a specialist in French history, is a *lackluster* speaker whose lectures on the French Revolution completely *entertain* students. (WRONG!)

The chairperson, who is a specialist in French history, is a *moving* speaker whose lectures on the French Revolution completely *alienate* students. (WRONG!)

The chairperson, who is a specialist in French history, is a *dull* speaker whose lectures on the French Revolution completely *absorb* students. (WRONG!)

The chairperson, who is a specialist in French history, is a *forceful* speaker whose lectures on the French Revolution completely *require* students. (WRONG!)

The chairperson, who is a specialist in French history, is a *scintillating* speaker whose lectures on the French Revolution completely *enthrall* students. (CORRECT!)

The technique of substitution shows choice (**E**) to be the best answer.
The technique of substitution has another use.

Test your answer choice by substituting it back into the sentence and reading it "aloud" in your mind.

This works as a failsafe device. By rereading the sentence to yourself in its entirety, you should be able to "hear" whether or not your chosen substitutions make sense.
Finally,

Don't worry about problems of grammar.

Although a substitution might be incorrect because it does not make a meaningful statement, a substitution will never make a meaningful statement that is grammatically incorrect.

STRUCTURAL CLUES

The logical structure of the sentence will often provide the clue to the correct answer.

Sometimes the substitution must be the parallel of some other thought in the sentence.

Often the blank must be filled by a word that will make one part of the sentence parallel to another part by continuing a thought or amplifying a thought.

Example:

The conductor's choice of tempo seemed entirely _____, so that each successive movement of the piece seemed to have no necessary connection to what had come before.

(A) musical
(B) believable
(C) arbitrary
(D) subtle
(E) cautious

The best choice is (**C**). The logical clue is the parallel that is required. What comes after the comma is intended to clarify or amplify what is contained in the blank. Which of the five choices has a meaning related to "no necessary connection"? Only (C), arbitrary, has such a meaning.

Example:

After a period of protracted disuse, a muscle will atrophy, _____ both its strength and the ability to perform its former function.

(A) regaining
(B) sustaining
(C) losing
(D) insuring
(E) aligning

The best choice is **(C)**. The logical structure requires a continuation of the idea of "atrophy."

A second important logical clue is the thought-reverser.

 Sometimes the substitution must be the reverse of some other thought in the sentence.

In such cases, the substitution must create a phrase that contrasts with some other element in the sentence.

Example:

Although the conditions in which she chooses to live suggest that she is miserly, her contributions to worthwhile charities show that she is _____.

(A) stingy
(B) thrifty
(C) frugal
(D) intolerant
(E) generous

The best choice is **(E)**. The "although" signals a thought-reverser. The idea that comes after the comma must contrast with the idea that comes before the comma. Only (E) sets up the needed contrast: miserly vs. generous.

Example:

There are many dialects of English with radically different pronunciations of the same word, but the spelling of these words is _____.

(A) inconstant
(B) uniform
(C) shortened
(D) contemplated
(E) abbreviated

The best choice is **(B)**. The "but" introduces a thought-reverser. The phrase completed by the substitution must create a contrast with the idea of difference expressed in the first clause. (B) does this nicely, contrasting "uniform" with "different."

There are many different ways of signaling a thought-reverser, such as: although, though, even though, but, despite, in spite of, and so. There are equally many ways of signaling a thought continuation, such as: since, because, and, therefore, so, and so on.

For this reason, you cannot hope to memorize a list of words or phrases and apply it in a purely mechanical fashion. Instead, you must always be looking for the inner logic of the sentence.

For some questions, it is not possible to describe the logical structure of the sentence as simply thought-continuation or thought-reversal.

 A sentence may contain both thought-continuers and thought-reversers.

Example:

The majority report issued by the committee was completely _____, extolling in great detail the plan's strengths but failing to mention at all its_____.

(A) comprehensive—proposal
(B) unbiased—weaknesses
(C) one-sided—shortcomings
(D) printed—good points
(E) skewed—defenders

The best choice is **(C)**. The logical structure of this sentence cannot be described as either a thought-reverser or a thought-continuer, for there are elements of both. First, the phrase following the comma, taken in isolation, expresses a contrast. The second blank must be filled by a word that is somehow the opposite of "strengths." Both (B) and (C) will provide the needed contrast. Second, the phrase following the comma, taken as a whole, is a continuer of the thought expressed before the comma. So the first blank must be filled by a word that describes something that covers only the good not the bad. "One-sided" will do the trick.

Here is another example of a sentence characterized by a complex logical structure:

Example:

The quarterback's injury was very painful but not _____, and he managed to _____ the game in spite of it.

(A) serious—interrupt
(B) incapacitating—finish
(C) harmful—abandon
(D) conclusive—enter
(E) excruciating—concede

The best answer is **(B)**. The first blank must complete the contrast set up by "but not." Only (A), (B), and (E) are possible choices on this basis. Then, the "in spite of" sets up a contrast between what comes before the comma and what follows. Only (B) provides the needed thought-reversal.

WORD CLUES

Some answer choices can be eliminated because, when substituted into the blanks, they would not create a meaningful English phrase.

Eliminate any answer choices that, when substituted, would not create a meaningful English phrase.

This Test Buster tells you to eliminate choices that would not result in an idiomatic construction.

Example:

The plot of the movie was extremely complicated and included many minor characters _____ to the central events.

(A) momentous
(B) tangential
(C) contemporary
(D) essential
(E) impervious

The best choice is (**B**). Two of the choices can be eliminated because they would not create a meaningful phrase:

(A) . . . momentous to . . . . (WRONG!)
(C) . . . contemporary to . . . . (WRONG!)

Then you would use the logic of the sentence to settle on (B). The blank must continue the idea of "minor characters," and (B) does this. The characters were only tangential to the main plot.

Example:

The governor's intolerance of _____ among his aides was intensified by his insistence upon total _____ from all.

(A) dissent—loyalty
(B) dishonesty—imagination
(C) flattery—communication
(D) compliance—commitment
(E) insight—familiarity

You can eliminate (D) and (E) on the basis of their first elements:

(D) . . . intolerance of compliance . . . . (WRONG!)
(E) . . . intolerance of insight . . . . (WRONG!)

It is almost impossible to construct an English sentence using these phrases. (And if you can come up with some bizarre sentence using them, that only proves the point.

Such a sentence would not appear on the GRE). You can eliminate (B) and (C) because the second substitution would not be idiomatic:

(B) . . . total imagination . . . . (WRONG!)
(C) . . . total communication . . . . (WRONG!)

GUESSING

The nice thing about this technique is that it can be used even when you don't understand the overall logic of the sentence.

Before guessing on a sentence completion, be sure to eliminate all choices that would fail to make a meaningful expression.

Doing this will improve your chances of a correct guess.

Example:

XXXXX XXXXXX XXXXXXX XXX X XXXXXXXXXX XX XXXXXXX, XXX XXXXXXX XXXX XXX
XXXXXXX XXXXX _____ our existing resources.

(A) squander
(B) conserve
(C) belie
(D) eliminate
(E) deny

The sentence above has been concealed from you to put you in the same position you would find yourself in if you were not able to penetrate the logic of a sentence. Still, you can eliminate some choices using the Test Buster we are discussing. Which of the following phrases are most likely to appear in an English sentence?

(A) . . . squander our existing resources.
(B) . . . conserve our existing resources.
(C) . . . belie our existing resources.
(D) . . . eliminate our existing resources.
(E) . . . deny our existing resources.

(A) and (B) are surely the most likely candidates, and this is a good basis for an educated guess.

Remember that in a sentence containing two blanks, both elements must work to complete the sentence:

When guessing, two blanks are better than one.

Use the technique of isolating phrases. If you can eliminate either of the two parts of a two-part answer choice, the entire choice should be eliminated. So a two-part substitution gives you twice as many chances of eliminating wrong answers.

Analogies

The basic idea of an analogy is to find pairs of words that express a similar relationship. Here is an example.

ACTOR:CAST::SINGER:CHORUS

The colons function as punctuation marks. The analogy reads

ACTOR	:	CAST	::	SINGER	:	CHORUS
ACTOR	is to	CAST	as	SINGER	is to	CHORUS

The most perfect example of an analogy is the mathematical proportion:

$$\frac{2}{3} = \frac{10}{15}$$

This mathematical proportion can be written as an analogy:

2:3::10:15

In a true mathematical proportion, there is also a mathematical relationship between the first and third elements and the second and fourth elements:

2:3::10:15

which can be written:

$$\frac{2}{10} = \frac{3}{15}$$

Verbal analogies are characterized by a similar feature:

ACTOR:CAST::SINGER:CHORUS

An actor and a singer are both performers, and a cast and a chorus are both performing groups. We will refer to this kind of connection as an indirect relation.

Verbal analogies differ from mathematical proportions in two important ways. First, while numbers are very precise, verbal analogies are not.

Example:

ELM:TREE::

(A) whale:mammal
(B) painting:artist

(C) diploma:graduation
(D) cart:horse
(E) cloud:rain

The best answer is (A). An elm is a type of tree, and a whale is a type of mammal. Admittedly, the analogy is not perfect, but that is the nature of verbal analogies. Some provide closer relations than others.

Additionally, there need be no detectable indirect relationship, as in the pairs above:

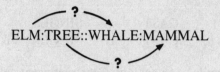

ELM:TREE::WHALE:MAMMAL

COMMON ANALOGY TYPES

Most GRE analogies fall into one of several categories.

Common Analogy Connection: *X* is the defining characteristic of *Y*.

Example:

CONDEMNATION:DISAPPROVAL::

(A) ignorance:patience
(B) optimism:insight
(C) blasphemy:irreverence
(D) sorrow:intention
(E) longing:hostility

The best choice is (C). Disapproval is the defining characteristic of condemnation, and irreverence is the defining characteristic of blasphemy.

Here are some other word pairs that fit this pattern:

FLUIDITY:LIQUID
HEROISM:EPIC
AGGRESSION:BELLICOSITY
HUMOR:COMEDIAN
RIDICULE:BURLESQUE
FAME:CELEBRITY
POVERTY:MONK
MISCHIEVOUSNESS:IMP
SOLEMNITY:DIRGE
DISORDER:ANARCHY

Common Analogy Connection: Lack of *X* is the defining characteristic of *Y*.

This is the mirror image of the analogy connection just discussed.

Example:

LOYALTY:TRAITOR::

(A) truthfulness:liar
(B) hope:optimist
(C) diligence:worker
(D) understanding:sage
(E) longevity:crone

The best choice is (A). Lack of loyalty is the defining characteristic of a traitor, and lack of truthfulness is the defining characteristic of a liar.

Here are some other word pairs that fit this pattern:

MATURITY:YOUTHFULNESS
WORDS:TACITURN
MEMORY:AMNESIA
MOVEMENT:PARALYSIS
FRICTION:LUBRICATION
PREMEDITATION:IMPULSE
ENERGY:LETHARGY
NOURISHMENT:STARVATION
HOPE:PESSIMISM
COMPANIONSHIP:HERMIT

 Common Analogy Connection: *X* is a spurious form of *Y*.

In these analogies, one word refers to an idea that is a defective form of some other idea.

Example:

MUMBLE:SPEAK::

(A) adorn:denude
(B) inflame:damage
(C) delimit:expand
(D) plagiarize:write
(E) convert:preach

The best answer is (D). Mumbling is a spurious (or defective) form of speaking, and plagiarizing is a spurious (or defective) form of writing.

Here are some more word pairs that fit this analogy pattern:

BRAVADO:COURAGE
QUACK:PHYSICIAN
POACHER:HUNTER
MINCE:WALK
SIMPER:SMILE
ALCHEMY:SCIENCE
EMBEZZLE:WITHDRAW
MALINGERING:ILLNESS
EXTORT:CHARGE
OFFICIOUS:IMPORTANT

 Common Analogy Connection: *X* **is the same thing as** *Y* **but more extreme.**

This analogy is based upon degree.

Example:

TOSS:HURL::

(A) speak:shout
(B) forget:learn
(C) consider:formulate
(D) sense:flourish
(E) prepare:emit

The best choice is (**A**). To hurl and toss are similar actions but one is more violent than the other; similarly, to shout and to speak are similar, but one is more violent than the other.

Here are some other word pairs that fit this analogy form:

DRIZZLE:POUR
COOL:FRIGID
DISAPPROVED:CONDEMNED
JOG:SPRINT
MERCHANT:MAGNATE
DEFEAT:ROUT
PARTY:ORGY
GIGGLE:LAUGH
TIFF:BATTLE
PROTEST:REVOLUTION
FRUGAL:MISERLY

 Common Analogy Connection: *X* **is a part of** *Y*.

In this type, one thing is a component of the other.

Example:

NOTE:SCALE::

(A) musician:instrument
(B) conductor:orchestra
(C) letter:alphabet
(D) book:cover
(E) singer:music

The best answer is **(C)**. A note is a part of a scale, and a letter is a part of an alphabet. Here are some other word pairs that fit this pattern:

PAGE:BOOK
CLIMAX:DRAMA
COLOR:SPECTRUM
VOLUME:LIBRARY
VERSE:SONG
LEG:JOURNEY
VERDICT:TRIAL
WICK:CANDLE
NOON:DAY

 Common Analogy Connection: *X* is a type of *Y*.

In this type of analogy, one thing is a particular kind of the more general idea.

Example:

BALLAD:SONG::

(A) credit:movie
(B) shutter:darkness
(C) novel:chapter
(D) portrait:painting
(E) melody:rhythm

The best answer is **(D)**. A ballad is a type of song, and a portrait is a type of painting. Here are some more word pairs that fit this pattern:

CARDIOLOGIST:PHYSICIAN
TIGER:CARNIVORE
BEER:BEVERAGE
SOPRANO:VOCALIST
SYNCOPATION:RHYTHM
THYME:SPICE
MONARCHY:GOVERNMENT
MEASLES:DISEASE
PROTESTANTISM:RELIGION
COURAGE:VIRTUE

Common Analogy Connection: *X* follows *Y* in sequence (either as a matter of logic or as a matter of cause and effect).

In this relation, one thing follows the other to create either a causal sequence or a logical sequence.

Example:

REHEARSAL:PERFORMANCE::

(A) entrapment:game
(B) engagement:marriage
(C) applause:audience
(D) antidote:illness
(E) satisfaction:appetite

The best answer is (**B**). A rehearsal precedes a performance, and an engagement precedes a marriage.

Here are other word pairs that fit this pattern. Notice that some are related as a matter of logical sequence while others form a causal sequence:

TADPOLE:FROG
STUMBLE:FALL
SWELL:BURST
CONVICT:SENTENCE
INFECTION:ILLNESS
PROSELYTIZE:CONVERT
APPETIZER:DESSERT
CROUCH:SPRING
SALUTATION:FAREWELL
CLIMAX:DENOUEMENT

 Common Analogy Connection: *X* is an interruption of *Y*.

This analogy form is the mirror image of the one just discussed.

Example:

RETIREMENT:SERVICE::

(A) employment:salary
(B) arrangement:flowers
(C) contract:agreement
(D) graduation:studies
(E) exchange:communication

The best choice is (**D**). Retirement represents the interruption of service, and graduation represents the interruption of studies.

Here are some other word pairs that fit this pattern:

RECESS:TRIAL
DISMISSAL:EMPLOYMENT
RELAPSE:RECOVERY
INCARCERATION:RELEASE
LUNCH BREAK:WORKDAY
DIVORCE:MARRIAGE
LAYOVER:JOURNEY
INTERMISSION:PERFORMANCE
DIGRESSION:SPEECH
DETOUR:TRAVEL

 Common Analogy Connection: *X* is the tool used by *Y* or *X* is the tool used to accomplish *Y*.

The central feature of this type of analogy is the tool.

Example:

SCALPEL:SURGEON::

(A) pen:reader
(B) bow:violinist
(C) bed:patient
(D) pistol:angler
(E) auto:soldier

The best answer is (**B**). The scalpel is the tool commonly associated with the surgeon, and the bow is the tool commonly associated with the violinist.
Here are some further examples:

TROWEL:BRICKLAYER
PALLET:PAINTER
FILTER:PURIFICATION
NEEDLE:SEW
PADDLE:CANOE
TACK:JOCKEY
TELESCOPE:ASTRONOMER
KNIFE:WHITTLE

 Common Analogy Connection: *X* is the place one would find *Y*.

There are many variations on this theme.

Example:

UMPIRE:PLAYING FIELD::

(A) carpenter:cabinet
(B) plumber:wrench
(C) judge:courtroom
(D) player:locker
(E) farmer:city

The best answer is (C). The umpire is found on the playing field, and the judge is found in the courtroom.

Here are some further examples:

WATER:RESERVOIR
PROFESSOR:CLASSROOM
COFFEE:MUG
SAILOR:SHIP
ROUSTABOUT:CIRCUS
HORSE:STABLE
PAINTING:MUSEUM
FARMER:FIELD
CHEF:KITCHEN
DOCTOR:HOSPITAL

 Common Analogy Connection: *X* is a sign of *Y*.

In this analogy type, one element functions as a symbol for or a sign of the other element.

Example:

YAWN:BOREDOM::

(A) smile:hatred
(B) blink:nausea
(C) sigh:hope
(D) grimace:joy
(E) wince:pain

The best choice is (E). A yawn is a sign of boredom, and a wince is a sign of pain.

Here are some further examples:

GRIMACE:PAIN
FIDGET:RESTLESSNESS
SNARL:ANGER
PURR:CONTENTMENT
STRUT:VANITY

GLOAT:SELF-SATISFACTION
SIGH:RELIEF
HISS:DISAPPROVAL
APPLAUSE:APPROBATION
SNEER:CONTEMPT

ANALYZING AN ANALOGY

The first step in attacking an analogy is to formulate a statement of the connection between the capitalized words.

Create a sentence that describes the relationship between the capitalized words.

You now have a list of the most common connections used on the GRE, but the list cannot be applied in a purely mechanical fashion. Your initial formulation may fit more than one answer choice.

Be prepared to refine your analogy description if necessary.

Example:

OVERTURE:OPERA::

(A) verdict:trial
(B) preface:book
(C) bedroom:apartment
(D) character:plot
(E) auto:garage

You might describe this analogy using one of the common connections as follows: An overture is part of an opera. This is a good start, but it's not enough. The initial formulation allows you to eliminate (E), but all the other answer choices fit the pattern you have proposed. At this point you need to refine your description and make it more precise.

Exactly what part of the opera is the overture? The overture is the opening part of the opera. This formulation will eliminate (A), (C), and (D), leaving only (B): The preface is the opening part of the book.

GUESSING

When you don't see a direct relation, look for an indirect relation.

The distinction between a direct and an indirect analogy relation was discussed above. The proper way to attack an analogy is to study the direct relationship, but there may be times when that is not enough. Sometimes the analogy relation may escape your notice. In such cases, you should look for an indirect relation.

Example:

DEFUNCT:LIFE::

(A) stagnant:motion
(B) arid:desert
(C) obese:weight
(D) orderly:pattern
(E) gracious:care

The correct choice is (**A**), as you might learn by using the common analogy connection "X is a lack of Y." But let us assume for the purpose of discussion that you did not see this connection. You would then have to look for a secondary relation. Which of the following words are most alike?

(A) DEFUNCT and stagnant
(B) DEFUNCT and arid
(C) DEFUNCT and weight
(D) DEFUNCT and orderly
(E) DEFUNCT and gracious

The closest connection is (**A**), since defunct means dead. And you can look for an indirect relation between the second element of each pair. Which of the following words are most closely associated?

(A) LIFE and motion
(B) LIFE and desert
(C) LIFE and weight
(D) LIFE and pattern
(E) LIFE and care

Since life is characterized by motion, you might be able to find the correct choice on the basis of this indirect relation.

Indirect relations are also useful when you have to make a difficult choice between two answers.

 When you have to make a choice between answers that are very close, look for an indirect relation.

Example:

SCROLL:BOOK::

(A) tome:library
(B) grave:tomb

(C) street:highway
(D) novel:fiction
(E) parchment:paper

This is not a difficult analogy, and you can probably find the proper direct relation to solve it. But let us assume for the purpose of discussion that you have eliminated (A), (C), and (D), but are undecided between (B) and (E). At this point it would be appropriate to look for an indirect relation to confirm one answer choice or the other. Which is more like a scroll, a grave or parchment? A scroll has a closer association with parchment, which makes it more likely that (E) rather than (B) is correct. In fact, **(E)** is the best answer.

A word of caution is in order.

 Do not use indirect relations as your first line of attack.

Some analogies have misleading indirect relations.

Example:

WICK:CANDLE::

(A) oil:lamp
(B) match:flame
(C) filament:bulb
(D) chapter:book
(E) worshipper:congregation

The best answer is **(C)**. If you try to skip the step of formulating a description of the analogy connection between the capitalized words by looking first for an indirect relation, you will be in trouble. The idea of candle is probably most closely associated with lamp or flame, but neither of these is the correct choice.

The correct technique is to formulate a sentence such as "A wick is a part of a candle." This eliminates both (A) and (B), even though it leaves you with (C), (D), and (E). Next, you should try to refine your sentence. If you cannot do this, then, and only then should you look for an indirect relation. In this case, the ideas of wick and candle are closely associated with those of filament and bulb, respectively. The indirect connection would reveal the correct choice.

Antonyms

The basic idea of an antonym question is to find an opposite for a word.

Example:

TRANSIENT:

(A) urgent
(B) youthful
(C) original
(D) eternal
(E) unfaithful

The best answer is (D). Transient means temporary or passing, so a good opposite would be "eternal."

Antonym items are first and foremost a test of vocabulary. This is both good and bad news. First the bad news: If you have no idea of the meaning of the capitalized word and the answer choices, there's not much you can do.

Example:

ACARPOUS:

(A) assiduous
(B) poignant
(C) fecund
(D) reticent
(E) prolix

The best answer is (C); but unless you know that acarpous means infertile and that fecund means fertile, there's not much you can do with the question except guess.

That's the bad news; now the good news.

When you don't know the meaning of an antonym, don't waste a lot of time trying to figure it out.

In other words, once you recognize that you are out of ammunition, just make a random guess and move on to the next item. This way you will free up time for other questions in the section.

The bad news is not quite as bad as it sounds. You will recognize most of the words, and there are some Test Busters that can help you out of tight spots.

SPECIAL ANTONYM SITUATIONS

Aside from the problem of word meaning, antonyms are made more difficult in several ways.

Antonym questions often test unusual meanings of a word that you know.

In other words, the test writer selects a word you are likely to be familiar with, but sets up the question to test a meaning you do not ordinarily associate with the word.

Example:

PRECIPITOUS:

(A) pleasantly sweet
(B) overly ambitious
(C) agreeably situated
(D) publicly known
(E) gently sloping

The best choice is (**E**). We most often use the word "precipitous" to mean rash or fool-hardy, but its central meaning is related to precipice, dropping off sharply.

Example:

AMPLIFY:

(A) announce
(B) entertain
(C) simplify
(D) covet
(E) require

The best answer is (**C**). One common meaning of the word "amplify" is to "make louder," for example, amplified sound. But the word means generally to increase, to enlarge, or to make fuller. Thus it can be used to mean "to describe something in increased detail." The best available opposite, therefore, is (C), simplify.

An antonym can also be more difficult because the part of speech of the capitalized word is not immediately clear. Many words can function as more than one part of speech, for example, free (verb and adjective), struggle (verb and noun), and design (verb and noun).

To resolve a question about part of speech check the answer choices.

Even though the capitalized word may be ambiguous in its part of speech, the answer choices will be unequivocal.

Example:

COUNTENANCE:

(A) procure
(B) insist
(C) disapprove
(D) forego
(E) interpret

The best answer is (**C**). The word "countenance" can be either a noun (meaning face) or a verb (meaning to approve of). Which meaning is intended? The answer choices are unequivocally verbs, which means the capitalized word must also be a verb. So the capitalized word means "approve of," and (C) is the best opposite.

Alter the part of speech of the capitalized words and answer choices.

Sometimes an antonym will use a word you know but as a part of speech that is unfamiliar to you.

Example:

SUBLIMITY:

(A) erosion
(B) baseness
(C) conciseness
(D) insistence
(E) partiality

The best choice is (**B**). You may know the word "sublimity" better as the adjective "sublime," meaning "lofty, high, or noble." So you may find it easier to think about the antonym by changing "sublimity" to the more familiar form, "sublime." As you think about each answer choice, you would then change it in your mind to an adjective. "Baseness," therefore, would become "base"; and "base" is an opposite of "sublime."

GUESSING

If you have only a vague idea of the meaning of the capitalized word, eliminate answer choices using positive or negative overtones.

Although you may not know the exact meaning of a word, you may have a vague recollection of the context in which you first encountered it. So you may know whether the word has positive overtones or negative ones. This recollection may be sufficient to get a correct answer.

Example:

RAFFISH:

(A) grotesque
(B) delinquent
(C) uncaring
(D) noble
(E) evil

The correct choice is (**D**). Let's assume that you do not know that "raffish" means "low, vulgar, and base." And let's further assume, however, that you have a vague knowledge of the word. You've seen it used to describe a character who is dishonest and not trustworthy. So even though you don't know the exact meaning of the word, you know that it has negative overtones. Since you are looking for the opposite of a word with negative overtones, you would eliminate every answer choice with negative overtones. As it turns out, this strategy works perfectly with this antonym, only one word is left. "Noble" is the only word with positive overtones.

 When the meaning of the capitalized word is unknown to you, try to determine its meaning by taking it apart.

Even when you encounter a word for the first time, you may be able to ascertain its meaning from its parts.

Example:

COGNOSCITIVE:

(A) courageous
(B) expensive
(C) unconscious
(D) redundant
(E) immature

The best answer is (C). This is a very unusual word, but you can probably figure out its meaning by looking at its root COG-. This is the same root found in words such as cognition and recognize, and it has to do with knowledge. So we infer that cognoscitive has something to do with awareness, and (C) looks like a good opposite.

A word of caution, however: Don't spend too much time trying to decipher the meaning of a word. Remember that each antonym counts for only one point. On a paper-and-pencil exam, skip the difficult antonym and come back to it if you have time. On a CAT exam, guess and go on.

VOCABULARY BUILDING

As was noted above, antonyms are largely a matter of vocabulary. Sentence completions and analogies are dependent on vocabulary too, though to a lesser extent. It stands to reason, therefore, that the more extensive your vocabulary, the more likely you will do well on the GRE.

Don't immediately get your dictionary, however, and start studying the a's. It is not possible to memorize a list of 10,000 words and hope to be able to use them on the GRE. Vocabulary is acquired through reading and study over a long period of time.

Still, there may be some value in reviewing a list of typical GRE words. The following words have all appeared on previous GREs (some on several tests) in antonyms, analogies, and sentence completions—sometimes as right answers, sometimes as wrong answers. It is clear, however, that these are words you are expected to know for the GRE.

You should review the list for two reasons. One, to make sure you do know the meaning of the entries; two, to see what kinds of words you should be adding to your vocabulary as you study and read.

Words from the GRE

ABEYANCE *(noun)* Temporary suspension of function or activity.

ABROGATE *(verb)* To repeal, annul, or abolish an authoritative act, for example, a law or decree.

ABSTEMIOUS *(adj.)* Refraining from pleasure, and from food or strong drink in particular.

ABSTRUSE *(adj.)* Difficult to comprehend; obscure.

ALACRITY *(noun)* Cheerfulness; a readiness or promptness to act or serve.

ALLOY *(verb)* To reduce the purity of (a metal) by mixing with one less valuable; to debase by mixing with something inferior.

AMALGAMATE *(verb)* To mix, blend, or unite; to alloy with mercury.

AMELIORATE *(verb)* To improve; to make better.

ANACHRONISTIC *(adj.)* Erroneous in date; characterized by being out of its historical time.

ANOMALOUS *(adj.)* Deviating from the general rule; unexpected.

APOCRYPHAL *(adj.)* False; spurious; of doubtful authenticity.

APOTHEOSIS *(noun)* A glorification to the point of godliness.

ARDUOUS *(adj.)* Steep and therefore difficult of ascent; difficult to do; requiring exertion; laborious.

ASSIDUOUS *(adj.)* Diligent; industrious.

ATTENUATION *(noun)* The act of making thin or fine.

AUDACIOUS *(adj.)* Bold or adventuresome.

AVER *(verb)* To confirm; to declare to be true.

BANE *(noun)* Poison; the cause of injury or mischief.

BEATIFY *(verb)* To make happy, to bless; to ascribe extraordinary virtue to; to regard as saintly or blessed.

BEDIZEN *(verb)* To adorn, especially in a cheap, showy manner.

BILGE *(noun)* A variant of bulge; the protuberance of a cask, usually around the middle.

BLANDISHMENT *(noun)* Flattery; enticement.

BREACH *(noun)* The act of breaking or state of being broken; a gap, break, or rupture.

BROACH *(verb)* To open up; to mention a subject.

BURNISH *(verb)* To polish, especially by friction; to make or become smooth or glossy.

CAJOLE *(verb)* To coax; to wheedle.

CALCIFY *(verb)* To change into a hard, stony condition.

CALUMNIATE *(verb)* To slander; to accuse a person falsely.

CAPITULATE *(verb)* To surrender; to give up; to stop resisting.

CAPRICIOUS *(adj.)* Whimsical; fickle; changeable.

CASTIGATE *(verb)* To chastise; to correct by punishing.

CHASTENED *(adj.)* Corrected; punished.

CODA *(noun)* A final passage in music bringing a composition to a formal close.

CODICIL *(noun)* An appendix or supplement; an addition to a will.

COEVAL *(adj.)* Of the same period; existing at the same time.

COGNIZANT *(adj.)* Having knowledge of something; informed.

CONJOIN *(verb)* To join together; to unite.

CONTEMN *(verb)* To scorn or despise.

CONTENTIOUS *(adj.)* Argumentative; quarrelsome.

CONTUMACIOUS *(adj.)* Insurbordinate; rebellious; disobedient.

CONUNDRUM *(noun)* A perplexing question; a riddle.

COUNTENANCE *(verb)* To favor; to approve; to give support to.

CRAVEN *(adj.)* Cowardly; base.

DAUNT *(verb)* To frighten or intimidate.

DEARTH *(noun)* Scarcity; lack.

DEBACLE *(noun)* A breakup; an overthrow; a sudden great disaster.

DEMUR *(verb)* To hesitate; to take exception; to object.

DENOUEMENT *(noun)* The outcome; the solution; the unraveling of a plot.

DESICCATE *(verb)* To dry completely; to preserve by drying.

DESUETUDE *(noun)* The cessation of use; disuse.

DESULTORY *(adj.)* Random; passing from one thing to another in a disorganized way.

DETUMESCENCE *(noun)* Diminution of swelling.

DIAPHANOUS *(adj.)* Transparent or translucent; gauzy.

DIFFIDENCE *(noun)* Modesty; humility; self-doubt.

DILATORY *(adj.)* Causing or tending to cause delay; procrastinating.

DISINGENUOUSNESS *(noun)* Insincerity; cunning; craftiness.

DISPARAGE *(verb)* To belittle; to show disrespect for.

DISSEMBLE *(verb)* To hide; to conceal; to disguise.

DISSOLUTE *(adj.)* Loose in behavior and morals; lewd; debauched.

DIVESTITURE *(noun)* The deprivation of rank, rights, etc.; the stripping of clothing, arms, etc.

DOGGEREL *(noun)* Trivial, poorly constructed verse.

DOGMATIC *(adj.)* Arrogant; dictatorial; authoritative.

DUCTILITY *(noun)* The quality of being easily molded or easily led.

DULCET *(adj.)* Melodious; harmonious.

ECLECTIC *(adj.)* Composed of materials or principles gathered together from several different places or fields.

EFFICACIOUS *(adj.)* Effective; capable of producing the desired result.

EFFLUVIA *(noun)* An outflow in the form of a vapor or stream of invisible particles; a noxious odor or vapor.

EFFRONTERY *(noun)* Boldness; impudence.

EMPIRICAL *(adj.)* Based solely on experiments or experience.

EMULATE *(verb)* To strive for equality; to compete with successfully.

ENERVATE *(verb)* To weaken; to enfeeble.

ENIGMA *(noun)* A puzzle; a perplexing statement; a riddle.

EPHEMERAL *(adj.)* Fleeting; short-lived; transitory.

EPITOME *(noun)* A part or thing that is representative of the characteristics of the whole; a brief summary or abstract.

EQUANIMITY *(noun)* Evenness of mind; calm; composure.

EQUIPOISE *(noun)* Equal distribution of weight; equilibrium.

EQUIVOCATE *(verb)* To make vague statements; to mislead intentionally by making an ambiguous remark.

ERUDITE *(adj.)* Learned; scholarly.

EUPHORIC *(adj.)* Feeling well; buoyant; vigorous.

EVINCE *(verb)* To show clearly; to indicate; to manifest.

EXCORIATE *(verb)* To flay, strip, or scratch; to denounce strongly.

EXCULPATE *(verb)* To clear from a charge of guilt or fault.

EXPATIATE *(verb)* To roam; to wander freely; in writing, to elaborate.

EXTRAPOLATE *(verb)* To estimate or infer on the basis of certain known variables.

EXTRICABLE *(adj.)* Capable of being released, set free, or disentangled.

FALLACIOUS *(adj.)* Faulty in logic; producing error or mistake; misleading and disappointing.

FATUOUS *(adj.)* Complacently stupid or inane.

FELICITOUS *(adj.)* Suitable to the occasion; apt.

FERVID *(adj.)* Intense; zealous; impassioned.

FLOUT *(verb)* To mock; to sneer.

FOMENT *(verb)* To stir up, arouse, or incite; to instigate.

FRENETIC *(adj.)* Frantic; frenzied.

FROWARD *(adj.)* Not willing to yield or comply with what is required.

FRUGAL *(adj.)* Economical; not spending freely.

FULSOME *(adj.)* Disgusting or offensive especially because of excess.

GAINSAY *(verb)* To deny; to contradict.

GARISH *(adj.)* Gaudy; too showy.

GARNER *(verb)* To store; to gather up and save.

GARRULOUS *(adj.)* Talkative; loquacious.

GERMINATE *(verb)* To sprout; to start developing or growing.

GIST *(noun)* The main point.

GOSSAMER *(adj.)* Light; thin; filmy.

GRATUITOUS *(adj.)* Free; voluntary; not required.

GROUSE *(verb)* To complain; to grumble.

HALLOW *(verb)* To consecrate; to make holy.

HAPLESS *(adj.)* Unlucky; unfortunate.

HEDONISTIC *(adj.)* Self-indulgent; living a life of pleasure.

HERMETIC *(adj.)* Completely sealed; magical.

HIRSUTE *(adj.)* Hairy; shaggy.

HONE *(verb)* To rub and sharpen.

IGNOMINIOUS *(adj.)* Shameful; dishonorable; disgraceful.

IMPERVIOUS *(adj.)* Incapable of being penetrated.

IMPRECATION *(noun)* An invoking of evil; a curse.

INCARCERATE *(verb)* To imprison.

INCURSION *(noun)* A running in; an invasion; a raid.

INDEFATIGABILITY *(noun)* The quality of not being easily exhausted.

INDOMITABLE *(adj.)* Not easily discouraged or subdued.

INELUCTABLE *(adj.)* Not to be avoided; certain; inevitable.

INGENUOUS *(adj.)* Frank; open; candid.

INSALUBRITY *(noun)* Unhealthfulness; unwholesomeness.

INSCRUTABLE *(adj.)* Incapable of being discovered or comprehended.

INSOLVENT *(adj.)* Unable to pay debts; bankrupt.

INSOUCIANT *(adj.)* Unconcerned; carefree.

INTEMPERANCE *(noun)* Lack of moderation or restraint; addiction to excessive amounts of alcoholic beverages.

INTRANSIGENCE *(noun)* Refusal to come to an agreement or compromise.

INTREPID *(adj.)* Fearless; brave; undaunted.

INVECTIVE *(noun)* A violent verbal attack; denunciation.

INVEIGH *(verb)* To attack verbally; to denounce.

JOCOSE *(adj.)* Merry; given to jesting.

LACHRYMOSE *(adj.)* Teary-eyed; mournful; sad.

LACONIC *(adj.)* Brief; short; pithy.

LASSITUDE *(noun)* Weakness; weariness; languor.

LAUDATORY *(adj.)* Praising.

LETHARGIC *(adj.)* Drowsy; completely indifferent.

LIONIZE *(verb)* To treat as a celebrity.

LOQUACIOUS *(adj.)* Talkative; garrulous.

LUGUBRIOUS *(adj.)* Mournful; very sad.

MALADROIT *(adj.)* Clumsy; awkward; bungling.

MALLEABLE *(adj.)* Yielding; amenable; adapting.

MELLIFLUOUS *(adj.)* Flowing sweetly (said of words).

MENDICANT *(noun)* A beggar.

METAMORPHOSE *(verb)* To change from one form into another.

MISANTHROPY *(noun)* Hatred or distrust of people.

MITIGATE *(verb)* To alleviate; to relieve; to soften.

MNEMONIC *(adj.)* Assisting the memory.

MOROSE *(adj.)* Gloomy; sullen.

MOTILITY *(noun)* The quality of having the inherent power of motion.

MULTIFARIOUS *(adj.)* Characterized by great variety or diversity.

MUNIFICENCE *(noun)* The quality of being extremely generous.

NADIR *(noun)* The lowest point; the time of greatest depression.

NEFARIOUS *(adj.)* Wicked; vile.

NEXUS *(noun)* A connection, tie, or link.

NOISOME *(adj.)* Noxious to health; harmful; hurtful.

OBDURATE *(adj.)* Hardened and unrepenting; stubborn; inflexible.

OBFUSCATE *(verb)* To darken; to obscure; to muddle.

OBSTREPEROUS *(adj.)* Noisy; vociferous.

OFFICIOUS *(adj.)* Unnecessarily accommodating; meddlesome.

OSSIFY *(verb)* To settle or fix rigidly into a practice; to become bone.

PAEAN *(noun)* A song of praise or triumph.

PALLIATE *(verb)* To make something (crime) appear less serious than it is; to alleviate; to ease.

PANEGYRIC *(noun)* A formal speech of praise; a eulogy.

PARADIGM *(noun)* A pattern; an example; a model.

PARADOX *(noun)* A statement that seems contradictory.

PARIAH *(noun)* An outcast; someone rejected and despised by others.

PAUCITY *(noun)* Dearth; scarcity; lack.

PEDAGOGY *(noun)* The profession or function of teaching.

PELLUCID *(adj.)* Transparent; easy to understand.

PEREGRINATION *(noun)* Traveling from one country to another; wandering.

PERFIDIOUS *(adj.)* Violating good faith; proceeding from treachery.

PERFUNCTORY *(adj.)* Performed without care or interest; automatic.

PERIPHERAL *(adj.)* Pertaining to the outer region of something as opposed to the center or core.

PETROUS *(adj.)* Like a rock; hard; stony.

PETULANT *(adj.)* Impatient or irritable.

PHLEGMATIC *(adj.)* Sluggish, dull, or apathetic.

PILLORY *(verb)* To punish; to hold up to public scorn.

PIQUANT *(adj.)* Agreeably pungent; stimulating.

PIQUE *(noun)* Resentment at being slighted.

PLACATE *(verb)* To appease or pacify.

PLETHORA *(noun)* Overabundance; excess.

PRECIPITOUS *(adj.)* Literally very steep, so by extension, hasty or rash.

PRECOCIOUS *(adj.)* Characterized by premature development, as a child who shows special talent earlier than usual.

PREDILECTION *(noun)* A preconceived liking; a preference.

PROCLIVITY *(noun)* A natural tendency to do something; an inclination; a leaning toward something.

PROFUSE *(adj.)* Poured forth; given or produced freely and abundantly.

PROLIFERATE *(verb)* To reproduce in quick succession.

PROLIX *(adj.)* Long and wordy.

PROPINQUITY *(noun)* Nearness in time, place or relationship; affinity of nature.

PROPITIATORY *(adj.)* Having the power to make atonement.

PROSAIC *(adj.)* Dull; tedious; commonplace.

PROSELYTIZE *(verb)* To make converts.

PROTUBERANCE *(noun)* The part of a thing that protrudes; a bulge.

PUNDIT *(noun)* A person of great learning; an authority.

QUAFF *(verb)* To drink or swallow in large quantities.

QUIXOTIC *(adj.)* Extravagantly chivalrous or romantically idealistic; impractical.

RAFFISH *(adj.)* Disreputable; tawdry.

RAMIFY *(verb)* To be divided or subdivided; to branch.

RAMPANT *(adj.)* Flourishing; spreading unchecked; violent and uncontrollable in action.

RAPACIOUS *(adj.)* Given to plunder; voracious; greedy.

RAUCOUS *(adj.)* Harsh; hoarse; rough-sounding.

RECIDIVISM *(noun)* A chronic relapse into antisocial behavior patterns.

RECONDITE *(adj.)* Profound; abstruse; concealed.

RECREANCY *(noun)* Cowardice; a cowardly giving up.

REDOUBTABLE *(adj.)* Formidable; to be feared or dreaded.

REFRACTORY *(adj.)* Stubborn; obstinate.

REFUTE *(verb)* To prove a person or argument wrong.

REPROBATE *(noun)* A depraved, vicious person.

RETICENT *(adj.)* Habitually silent; uncommunicative.

RIBALD *(adj.)* Characterized by coarse joking; vulgar.

RUBRIC *(noun)* Heading, title, or category.

SALIENT *(adj.)* Conspicuous; prominent; highly relevant.

SANGUINE *(adj.)* Cheerful; confident; optimistic.
SATURNINE *(adj.)* Gloomy; morose.
SAUCY *(adj.)* Impudent; rude.
SAVANT *(noun)* A knowledgeable or learned person.
SEDULOUS *(adj.)* Assiduous; diligent; persevering.
SEMINAL *(adj.)* Like seed, constituting a source; originative.
SENTENTIOUS *(adj.)* Short and pithy; often full of maxims and proverbs; trite.
SHARD *(noun)* A piece or fragment of an earthen vessel or of any brittle substance.
SINUOUS *(adj.)* Winding; serpentine; undulating.
SLAKE *(verb)* To assuage; to satisfy; to allay.
SLOTH *(noun)* Habitual indolence or laziness.
SOPHOMORIC *(adj.)* Self-assured although immature; affected; bombastic.
SOPORIFIC *(adj.)* Tending to cause sleep; characterized by sleepiness.
SPECIOUS *(adj.)* Simulating, resembling, or apparently corresponding with right or truth.
SPLENETIC *(adj.)* Bad-tempered; irritable.
SPURIOUS *(adj.)* Counterfeit; fraudulent.
SQUALID *(adj.)* Foul; filthy; extremely dirty.
STENTORIAN *(adj.)* Extremely loud or powerful.
STYMIE *(verb)* To hinder or obstruct; to check or block.
SUNDRY *(adj.)* Various; miscellaneous; separate.
SURREPTITIOUS *(adj.)* Secretive; clandestine.
SYCOPHANT *(noun)* A person who seeks favor through flattery; a parasite.
TACIT *(adj.)* Silent.
TAWDRY *(adj.)* Cheap; gaudy; showy.
TENACITY *(noun)* Persistence; firmness of hold.
TENUOUS *(adj.)* Unsubstantial; slight; flimsy; weak.
TIMOROUS *(adj.)* Fearful; timid.
TORPOR *(noun)* A state of dormancy; dullness; apathy.
TRACTABLE *(adj.)* Easily led, taught, or managed.
TRANSIENT *(adj.)* Temporary; fleeting.
TRENCHANT *(adj.)* Keen; penetrating; incisive.
TREPIDATION *(noun)* Fear; agitation.
TRUCULENCE *(noun)* The quality of being fierce; savage; cruel.
TURBID *(adj.)* Thick; dense; cloudy.
TURGID *(adj.)* Swollen; bloated; inflated.
TURPITUDE *(noun)* Wickedness; shamefulness.
UNTOWARD *(adj.)* Perverse; unruly; unseemly.
VACILLATE *(verb)* To hesitate; to waver.
VACUITY *(noun)* The quality of being empty; lack of intelligence; inanity.
VAPID *(adj.)* Tasteless; flavorless; dull; uninteresting.
VISCID *(adj.)* Thick; sticky; viscous.
VOLUBLE *(adj.)* Speaking glibly; talking with ease.
ZEAL *(noun)* Ardor; eager interest or enthusiasm.

Reading Comprehension

The reading selections that you will find on the GRE are unlike the material you are accustomed to reading in three respects: topic, format, and density. First, the selections are taken from many different disciplines such as science, medicine, philosophy, psychology, sociology, and literary criticism. Since you took most of your college courses in your major area of interest (with the obligatory survey courses in other areas), you are not likely to be familiar with the topics of all the reading selections.

The GRE assumes that you are not familiar with the content of the reading selections.

The test writers go out of their way to find material that test-takers will not have seen before, since they want to avoid giving anyone an advantage over other candidates. If you do encounter a topic you have studied before, that is an unusual stroke of luck. Rest assured, however, that everything you need to answer the questions is included in the selection itself.

GRE reading selections always begin in the middle of nowhere.

When you begin, you will have no advance warning of the topic discussed in the selection. As a result, the selection seems to begin in the middle of nowhere. Imagine that you encounter the following as the opening sentence of a reading comprehension selection on your GRE:

> Of the wide variety of opinions on which evolutionary factors were responsible for the growth of hominid intelligence, a theory currently receiving consideration is that intraspecific warfare played an important role by encouraging strategy sessions requiring a sort of verbal competition.

An appropriate reaction to this might be "What the . . . !" But in reality the topic introduced by the sentence above is not that bizarre. Let's give the sentence a context, say a scholarly journal.

PRIMITIVE BATTLE PLANS: A NEW THEORY
ABOUT THE GROWTH OF HUMAN INTELLIGENCE

> Of the wide variety of opinions on which evolutionary factors were responsible for the growth of hominid intelligence, a theory currently receiving consideration is that intraspecific warfare played an important role by encouraging strategy sessions requiring a sort of verbal competition.

The title summarizes the main point of the article and alerts you to the topic that will be introduced in the opening sentence. Unfortunately, on the GRE you will not be shown this courtesy. The selections will start rather abruptly, in the middle of nowhere.

The style of GRE reading comprehension selections is dry, compact, and often tedious.

To be suitable for the GRE, the selection must not be too long or too short. So the selections, which are taken from previously published material, are carefully edited. Even when the topic of the selection is itself interesting, the selection that emerges from the editing can be deadly boring.

These three features, unusual topic, abrupt beginning, and dense style, all work together to cause trouble for you.

 Don't let the reading comprehension selections intimidate you.

Many students are simply overawed by the reading selections. They begin to think "I've never even heard of this; I'll never be able to answer any questions." And when you start thinking like that, you're already beaten. Keep in mind that the passages are chosen so that you will be surprised, but remember that the selections are written so that they contain everything you need to answer the questions.

TYPES OF READING COMPREHENSION QUESTIONS

Every reading comprehension question asked on a GRE can be put into one of six categories.

Main Idea Questions

Every reading selection is edited so that it discusses some central theme, that is, it makes a main point. Main idea questions ask about this central theme or main point. They are most often phrased:

> The primary purpose of the passage is to . . .
> The author is primarily concerned with . . .
> Which of the following best describes the main point of the passage?
> Which of the following titles best summarizes the content of the passage?

Supporting Idea Questions

These questions ask not about the main point of the selection but about details included by the author to support or to develop the main theme of the selection. These questions may be worded as follows:

> According to the passage, . . .
> The author mentions. . . .
> Which of the following does the author discuss?

Implied Idea Questions

These questions ask about ideas that are not explicitly stated in the selection but are strongly implied. They are often worded as follows:

It can be inferred from the passage that . . .
The author implies that . . .
Which of the following can be inferred from the passage?

Logical Structure Questions

These questions ask about the organization of the passage. They may ask about the overall development of the selection, such as:

The author develops the thesis primarily by . . .
Which of the following best describes the author's method?

Or they may ask about the role played by a detail:

The author mentions . . . in order to . . .
The author introduces . . . primarily to . . .

Further Application Questions

These questions ask that you take what you have learned from the passage and apply it to a new situation. To answer this type of question you must go beyond what is explicitly stated or even strongly implied and comment on a situation not even discussed in the passage. These questions are phrased as:

With which of the following conclusions would the author most likely agree?
Which of the following statements, if true, would most weaken the conclusion . . . ?

Attitude Questions

These questions ask you to identify the overall tone of the passage or the author's attitude toward something discussed in the passage:

The tone of the passage can best be described as . . .
The author's attitude toward . . . is one of . . .

Later we will study specific examples of each type of question. For the present, you should just realize that reading selections are written in such a way as to be the vehicle for these six types of questions.

HOW TO READ A GRE READING COMPREHENSION SELECTION

Each GRE reading selection is in a sense an "excuse" to ask one of the six types of questions just mentioned. So the six types give you some idea of what the GRE thinks is good reading.

According to the GRE, good reading involves three levels of understanding and evaluation. Firstly, you must be able to grasp the overall idea or main point of the selection along with its general organization. Second, you must be able to subject the specific details to greater scrutiny and explain what something means and why it was introduced. Finally, you should be able to evaluate what the author has written, determining what further conclusions might be drawn and judging whether the argument is good or bad.

The first and most general level of understanding is the most important in a sense, for you cannot appreciate the details of a selection unless you understand the overall structure. And the second level must come before the third, because you will not be able to evaluate the selection unless you know exactly what it says. The priority of levels dictates the strategy you should follow in reading the selection.

Begin your attack on a selection by previewing the first sentence of each paragraph.

Your first task is to grasp the overall point of the selection. The first sentence of a paragraph is often the topic sentence, so a quick preview of the first sentences should give you a rough idea of the subject of the selection.

As you read, consciously ask yourself, "What is the main point of this discussion?"

Keeping in mind what you have learned by previewing topic sentences, begin your reading. As you read try to summarize the main topic of discussion. Once you can articulate the main point of the selection, it will be easier to place the specific details into the overall organization.

As you read, consciously ask yourself, "Why has the author introduced this idea?"

Once you have the main idea in mind, you must try to relate specific details to it, placing them in the overall framework.

Bracket, manually or mentally, material that is very technical or otherwise difficult to understand.

You don't need to have a full understanding of every single detail to appreciate the organization of the selection and most of its detail. If you encounter material that is overly technical and difficult to understand, draw a box around it with a pencil and leave it. You will already understand what "place" it occupies in the overall argument; having marked its location, you can easily find it if you need to study it more carefully in order to answer a question.

At the end of your reading, pause and quickly review the structure of the passage.

This does not mean you should try to recall all of the details you have read. However, you should be able to explain to yourself, at least vaguely, the main point of the selection and the most important features of the argument.

ANSWERING THE QUESTIONS

Main idea questions ask about the author's main point.

On a main idea question, choose an answer that refers to all of the important elements of the passage without going beyond the scope of the passage.

The correct answer to a main idea question will summarize the main point of the passage. The wrong answers are too broad or too narrow. Some will be too broad and attribute too much to the author. Others will be too narrow and focus on one small element of the selection, thereby ignoring the overall point.

With a main idea question in sentence completion form, be sure to test the suitability of the first word of each choice.

Example:

The author's primary purpose is to

(A) argue for . . .
(B) criticize . . .
(C) describe . . .
(D) persuade . . .
(E) denounce . . .

Make sure that the fist word or phrase is truly descriptive of the passage. In the example just given, if the selection is neutral in tone, providing nothing more than a description of some event or phenomenon, you could safely eliminate (A), (B), (D), and (E).

On a supporting idea question, find the part of the passage that is intended to be the basis for that question.

A supporting idea question basically asks "What did the author say?" This means that the answer to the question has to be stated explicitly in the passage. The best way to handle such a question is to make sure that you find the correct reference. Watch out! Wrong answers can refer you to other parts of the selection. In this way they do cite something specifically mentioned in the selection, but the citation is not an answer to the question asked. Wrong answers can also refer to things never mentioned in the selection.

On a supporting idea question, eliminate answer choices referring to something not mentioned in the passage or going beyond the scope of the passage.

One way the test writers have of preparing wrong answers is to mention things related to the general topic of the selection but not specifically discussed there. An answer to an explicit idea question will appear in the selection.

Sometimes the test writer will use a thought-reverser.

Example:

The author mentions all of the following *EXCEPT:*

If a supporting idea question contains a thought-reverser, the wrong answers can be found in the selection. The correct answer is not mentioned.

This is implicit in what was said above. Sometimes an explicit idea question will include a thought-reverser. In that case, it is asking for what is not mentioned in the selection. Out of the five choices, therefore, four will actually appear in the selection. The fifth, and correct, choice will not.

The correct answer to an implied idea question will be only a short step removed from what is explicitly stated in the text of the selection.

A question that asks about what can be inferred from a selection does not require a long chain of deductive reasoning. It is usually a one step inference. For example, the selection might make a statement to the effect that "X only occurs in the presence of

Y." The question might ask, "In the absence of Y, which should occur?" The correct answer would be: "X does not occur."

 The correct answer to a question that asks about the overall logical structure of a selection should correctly describe in general terms the overall development of the selection.

This kind of logical structure question is very much like a main idea question. Whereas a main idea question asks about the *content* of the selection, this type of question asks about the logical structure of the selection.

 On a question that asks about the logical function of a detail, find the appropriate reference and determine why the author introduced the detail at just that point.

This kind of question is related to the supporting details questions. Here, however the question stem states specifically that the detail has been mentioned but asks why. What role does it play in the overall argument?

Further application questions are the most difficult of all, for they require you to work in that third and most difficult level of reading comprehension.

 On a further application question, find the answer choice that has the most connection with the text of the selection.

You will see many examples of further application questions in the practice materials that follow. For the moment, accept the fact that the correct answer will be the one most clearly supported by the text.

 On an attitude or tone question, try to create a continuum of the answer choices and locate the author's attitude or tone on that continuum.

Example:

The tone of the passage is best described as one of

(A) outrage
(B) approval
(C) objectivity
(D) alarm
(E) enthusiasm

You might arrange these attitudes in a line, running from the most negative to the most positive.

(–) . . outrage . . alarm . . objectivity . . approval . . enthusiasm . . (+)

Example:

Directions: Read the passage below, and answer the questions that follow based on your understanding of the passage.

The need for solar electricity is clear. It is safe, ecologically sound, efficient, continuously available, and it has no moving parts. The basic problem with the use of solar photovoltaic devices is economics, but until recently very little progress had been made toward the development of low-cost photovoltaic devices. The larger part of research funding has been devoted to study of single-crystal silicon solar cells, despite the evidence, including that of the leading manufacturers of crystalline silicon, that the technique holds little promise. The reason for this pattern is understandable and historical. Crystalline silicon is the active element in the very successful semiconductor industry, and virtually all of the solid state devices contain silicon transistors and diodes. Crystalline silicon, however, is particularly unsuitable to terrestrial solar cells.

Crystalline silicon solar cells work well and are successfully used in the space program, where cost is not an issue. While single-crystal silicon has been proven in extraterrestrial use with efficiencies as high as 18 percent, and other more expensive and scarce materials such as gallium arsenide can have even higher efficiencies, costs must be reduced by a factor of more than 100 to make them practical for commercial use. Besides the fact that the starting crystalline silicon is expensive, 95 percent of it is wasted and does not appear in the final device. Recently, there have been some imaginative attempts to make polycrystalline and ribbon silicon, which are lower in cost than high-quality single crystals; but to date the efficiencies of these apparently lower-cost arrays have been unacceptably small. Moreover, these materials are cheaper only because of the introduction of disordering in crystalline semiconductors, and disorder degrades the efficiency of crystalline solar cells.

This dilemma can be avoided by preparing completely disordered or amorphous materials. Amorphous materials have disordered atomic structure as compared to crystalline materials: that is, they have only short-range order rather than the long-range periodicity of crystals. The advantages of amorphous solar cells are impressive. Whereas crystals can be grown as wafers about four inches in diameter, amorphous materials can be grown over large areas in a single process. Whereas crystalline silicon must be made 200 microns thick to absorb a sufficient amount of sunlight for efficient energy conversion, only 1 micron of the proper amorphous materials is necessary. Crystalline silicon solar cells cost in excess of $100 per square foot, but amorphous films can be created at a cost of about 50¢ per square foot.

Although many scientists were aware of the very low cost of amorphous solar cells, they felt that they could never be manufactured with the efficiencies necessary to contribute significantly to the demand for electric power. This was based on a misconception about the feature which determines efficiency. For example, it is not the conductivity of the materials in the dark which is relevant, but only the photoconductivity, that is, the conductivity in the presence of sunlight. Already, solar cells with efficiencies well above 6 percent have been developed using amorphous materials, and further research will doubtless find even less costly amorphous materials with higher efficiencies.

1. The author is primarily concerned with

(A) discussing the importance of solar energy
(B) explaining the functioning of solar cells
(C) presenting a history of research on energy sources
(D) describing a possible solution to the problem of the cost of photovoltaic cells.
(E) advocating increased government funding for research on alternative energy sources

2. According to the passage, which of the following encouraged use of silicon solar cells in the space program?

I. the higher cost of materials such as gallium arsenide
II. the fairly high extraterrestrial efficiency of the cells
III. the relative lack of cost limitations in the space program

(A) I only
(B) II only
(C) I and II only
(D) II and III only
(E) I, II, and III

3. In the second paragraph, the author mentions recent attempts to make polycrystalline and ribbon silicon primarily in order to

(A) minimize the importance of recent improvements in silicon solar cells
(B) demonstrate the superiority of amorphous materials over crystalline silicon
(C) explain why silicon solar cells have been the center of research
(D) contrast crystalline silicon with polycrystalline and ribbon silicon
(E) inform the reader that an alternative type of solar cell exists

4. Which of the following pairs of terms does the author regard as most nearly synonymous?

(A) solar and extraterrestrial
(B) photovoltaic devices and solar cells
(C) crystalline silicon and amorphous materials
(D) amorphous materials and higher efficiencies
(E) wafers and crystals

5. The material in the passage could best be used in an argument for

(A) discontinuing the space program
(B) increased funding for research on amorphous materials

(C) further study of the history of silicon crystals

(D) increased reliance on solar energy

(E) training more scientists to study energy problems

6. The author mentions which of the following as advantages of amorphous materials for solar cells over silicon crystals?

   I. the relative thinness of amorphous materials

  II. the cost of amorphous materials

 III. the size of solar cells which can be made of amorphous materials

(A) I only

(B) II only

(C) I and II only

(D) II and III only

(E) I, II, and III

7. The tone of the passage can best be described as

(A) analytical and optimistic

(B) biased and unprofessional

(C) critical and discouraged

(D) tentative and inconclusive

(E) concerned and conciliatory

Explained Answers

1. (D) This is a main idea question. The author begins by noting that solar energy is very important and, further, that the problem of the cost of solar cells, apparently an important part of solar energy technology, has not yet been solved. The author then discusses research on solar cells and the difficulties with silicon cells. In the third paragraph, the author states that there is a solution to this problem: amorphous materials. So the overall objective of the passage is to present amorphous materials as a possible solution to the problem of cost. This is neatly summarized by choice (D). (A) is incorrect since the author discusses the importance of solar energy only by way of introduction. (B) is incorrect because the author never explains how solar cells work. (C) is incorrect because the only reference to history is included to explain the bias in favor of silicon solar cells. (E) is incorrect because the author never mentions such funding. To be sure, the arguments contained in the passage might be very useful in making the further point suggested by (E), but then that is to admit that (E) is not the main point of the passage as written.

2. (D) This is an explicit idea question. In the second paragraph, the author discusses why silicon cells are used in the space program. The passage states that extraterrestrial efficiency is fairly high, so statement II is part of the correct answer choice. Moreover, the author mentions casually, but explicitly, that cost is not a factor in developing materials for the space program, so statement III is part of the correct choice. The extra cost of scarce materials, however, is not mentioned as a factor encouraging the use of silicon solar cells in the space program. Though it is stated that materials such as gallium arsenide are more efficient and more costly, these factors are not reasons why silicon cells are used in the space program. So the correct answer is II and III only.

3. (A) This is a logical structure question: Why does the author mention polycrystalline and ribbon silicon? In a way, the mention of these techniques could undermine the case for amorphous materials, since these are recent developments in crystalline substances which improve silicon solar cells. The author surely does not intend to weaken his argument. The logical move is to acknowledge the existence of a possible objection and to attempt to demonstrate that it is not really a very important objection. This is described by (A). (B) is incorrect, for though this is the general idea of the passage, it is not a proper response to the question asked. (C) is a point raised in the passage, but this is not the reason for the reference to polycrystalline and ribbon silicon. (D) is incorrect because the author never elaborates on the distinction between crystalline silicon and other forms of silicon. He only mentions that the latter are further developments on crystalline silicon. As for (E), though we infer from the mention of polycrystalline and ribbon silicon that other forms of solar cells exist, this is not the reason the author has introduced them into the discussion.

4. (B) This is an inference question. In the first paragraph, the author mentions that the basic problem with solar energy is the economics of solar photovoltaic devices. The rest of the passage discusses solar cells. We may infer from the juxtaposition of these terms that the author uses them synonymously. In any event, none of the other pairs are used interchangeably. As for (A), from the passage we may infer that "extraterrestrial" refers to space and that "solar" refers to the sun. As for (C), these terms are used as opposites. As for (D), though the author claims that amorphous materials are more efficient than silicon materials, he does not equate amorphous materials and efficiency. Finally, (E) is incorrect since a wafer is apparently a big crystal of silicon. But that means the terms are not used interchangeably.

5. (B) This is a further application question. We noted earlier, in question 1, that though the author does not specifically advocate greater funding for research on amorphous materials, the passage might be used in such an argument. Since there is an historical bias in favor of silicon cells, which have been the focus of most research, and amorphous materials offer an alternative, the natural conclusion is that further research should be done on amorphous materials. This is answer choice (B). (A) must be incorrect since the author never condemns the space program. He only notes that silicon cells were appropriate for the space program since cost was no object. (C) must be incorrect since the author advocates amorphous materials as opposed to silicon crystals for solar cells. (D) has some merit. To the extent that the entire passage advocates further research for solar energy, it could be used for the purpose suggested by (D). With an application question, however, the task is to find the answer choice most closely tied to the text, and that is (B). Logically then, there is nothing "wrong" with (D); it is just that it is not as closely related to the passage as (B). Finally, (E) is incorrect for the same reason: One could conceivably use the passage in the service of this goal, but (B) is a more obvious choice.

6. (E) This is an explicit idea question. All three statements are mentioned in the third paragraph as being advantages which amorphous materials have over silicon.

7. (A) This is a tone question. The tone of the passage is clearly analytical. The final paragraph is the warrant for the "optimistic" part of choice (A). The author implies that the problem of the cost of solar cells can be solved by further research on amorphous materials. (B) is incorrect since the position the passage advocates cannot, accurately be termed bias. (C) is correct insofar as the passage is critical, but the author does not seem to be discouraged. (D) is incorrect because the passage is argumentative and the author seems to be confident. Finally, (E) might be correct in that it states that the author is concerned, but there is nothing mentioned in the passage about which the author could be conciliatory.

GENERAL STRATEGIES

Here are some points that are generally applicable to the reading comprehension part of the GRE. Those marked with an asterisk apply only to the paper-and-pencil administered version.

 Reading comprehension is not an exercise in speed-reading.

Many people incorrectly think that the key to reading comprehension is speed, but even a fairly slow reading rate is adequate to handle the material on the GRE. The emphasis is on comprehension—not speed. (Of course, this does not mean you can afford to point at each word in the selection and move your lips as you read.)

It was mentioned above that it can be helpful to preview topic sentences to get an idea of the content of the passage. Here is a related idea.

 You may want to read the question stems before you begin reading the passage.*

This idea is that the question stems will also let you know in advance what the author will be discussing and can also alert you to look for certain key points. Two points of warning: First, while some test takers like this strategy, others find it a waste of time. As you work the practice tests in this book, try both methods and settle on the one that works better for you. Second, don't read the answer choice, just the question stems. The answer choices themselves are so long and involved that it would be a mistake to try to read them before reading the selection. Some question stems will not provide any useful information at all. For example, the stem "The author's main purpose is" is meaningless without the answer choices, so you would just skip it.

 Read every answer choice carefully.

This is something overlooked by most test takers. If you glance back at the sample reading comprehension exercise you just finished, you will see that many of the questions with their answer choices contain the equivalent of an entire paragraph of words. Reading comprehension does not end with the final sentence of the passage. Your ability to understand exactly what is said in an answer choice and your ability to distinguish among similar choices are also a part of this reading comprehension test.

TEST BUSTERS FOR ANALYTICAL QUESTIONS

Analytical Reasoning

In analytical reasoning questions, which consist of logical games or puzzles, each group of questions is based upon a series of statements that describe a situation; for example, seven children standing in a line at a movie theater, a host arranging a table seating for eight people, or a group of nine travelers to be divided into three tour groups. The questions ask about conclusions that can be deduced logically from the initial statement of the situation.

Example:

A group of six children—Mary, Frank, Ed, Dan, Sue, and Linda—took a series of tests. No two students received the same score on any given test.

Sue scored the highest on every test.
Mary scored higher than Frank on every test.
Ed scored higher than Dan on every test.
Linda's score on every test was somewhere between those of Dan and Frank.

1. Which of the following is a possible order, from highest to lowest, of student scores on a test?

(A) Sue, Frank, Mary, Linda, Ed, Dan
(B) Sue, Mary, Frank, Linda, Dan, Ed
(C) Sue, Mary, Linda, Frank, Ed, Dan
(D) Sue, Mary, Dan, Linda, Frank, Ed
(E) Sue, Mary, Ed, Dan, Linda, Frank

2. Which of the following *cannot* be the order of student scores, from highest to lowest?

(A) Sue, Mary, Frank, Linda, Ed, Dan
(B) Sue, Mary, Ed, Frank, Linda, Dan
(C) Sue, Mary, Ed, Linda, Frank, Dan
(D) Sue, Ed, Dan, Linda, Mary, Frank
(E) Sue, Ed, Mary, Frank, Linda, Dan

3. If Mary received the third highest score on a test, then which of the following must be true of that test?

(A) Dan received the second highest score.
(B) Frank received the second highest score.

66

(C) Dan received the fourth highest score.
(D) Linda received the fifth highest score.
(E) Frank received the sixth highest score.

4. If Ed received the fourth highest score on a test, then all of the following must be true of that test *except:*

(A) Mary received the second highest score.
(B) Frank received the third highest score.
(C) Dan received the fifth highest score.
(D) Ed received a higher score than Dan.
(E) Linda received a lower score than Frank.

5. If Linda received the fourth highest score on a test, the number of logically possible rank orderings of scores for all six children is

(A) 1
(B) 2
(C) 3
(D) 4
(E) 5

The first thing you will notice is that the rank ordering of the students (except for Sue) can change from test to test. This is a very important design feature of this question type. This flexibility or open-endedness allows the test writer to ask a series of questions, each of which is related to the initial situation but is different enough from the other questions in the group to require an independent solution.

This open-ended nature of the setup dictates in large part the kinds of questions that can be asked. If you review the five questions in the preceding group, you will observe that Questions 3 through 5 introduced additional information; for example, "If Mary received the third highest score..."

 Additional information provided in the form of a stipulation is to be used in answering that question only.

The questions can also be categorized according to the type of question asked and the type of answer choice that will satisfy the question:

(1) Which of the following could be true?
(2) Which of the following *cannot* be true?
(3) Which of the following must be true?
(4) All of the following must be true *except:*
(5) How many possibilities are there?

The five types are illustrated by questions 1 through 5, respectively.

1. (E) Answer choice (A) can be eliminated because Mary always scores higher than Frank. (B) is incorrect because Ed always scores higher than Dan. (C) can be eliminated because Linda's score must be somewhere between those of Frank and Dan. (D) is

incorrect because Ed always scores higher than Dan. (E) is the correct choice because that order is consistent with every condition governing the situation. This is not to say, of course, that (E) is the only possible rank ordering. Rather, (E) is the correct response to question 1 because it is an *acceptable* order: (E) *could be* the order.

2. (C) The second question type gives essentially the mirror image of the first type. This is because it contains a thought-reverser: *cannot*. The correct answer choice will be the one order that is not possible. Four of the choices will contain orders that are possible—and they will be incorrect choices. (C) cannot be the order because Linda's score must be between Franks's score and Dan's score. Each of the other choices is an order that is consistent with the situation as described.

3. (D) The third question type asks not about mere possibilities but about logical certainties. The correct answer to a question that asks "Which must be true?" will be a statement that can be logically deduced from the information given. The incorrect answer choices are wrong for either of two reasons. A statement that is logically inconsistent with the information supplied must be incorrect, and a statement that is merely possible, as opposed to logically necessary, is also incorrect. If Mary received the third highest score, then Frank scored fourth, fifth, or sixth. But Linda must have scored between Frank and Dan. Linda must be ranked fifth with Frank and Dan ranked fourth and sixth, though not necessarily in that order. Finally, Ed must have received the second highest score. So there are two possible orders:

1. Sue		1. Sue
2. Ed		2. Ed
3. Mary	or	3. Mary
4. Frank		4. Dan
5. Linda		5. Linda
6. Dan		6. Frank

Thus (D) is proved to be correct. (A) and (B) are contradicted by the diagram, so they cannot possibly be true. (C) and (E) are possible solutions, but they are not necessarily true. So neither (C) nor (E) can be the correct solution to a question that asks for a conclusion that is logically necessary.

4. (C) This question is the mirror image of Question 3. Four of the five choices make statements that are logically necessary. The incorrect choice will be incorrect either because it makes a necessarily false statement or because it makes a claim that is only possibly, though not necessarily, true. With Ed receiving the fourth highest score, Dan must rank either fifth or sixth. But Linda must be between Frank and Dan with Mary higher than Frank, so Linda must be fifth, with Dan sixth, Frank third, and Mary second: 1, Sue; 2, Mary; 3, Frank; 4, Ed; 5, Linda; and 6, Dan. (A), (B), (D), and (E) are all logically true, while (C) is logically false.

5. (B) This question asks about the number of possible solutions given a certain stipulation. With Linda ranked fourth, either Dan will be above Linda with Frank below or vice versa. If Dan scored higher than Linda, then Ed, who scored higher than Dan, must also have scored higher than Linda, which means that Mary and Frank scored lower than Linda. On the other hand, if Frank scored higher than Linda, then Mary, who scored higher than Frank, must also have scored higher than Linda, which means that Ed and Dan scored lower than Linda. So there are exactly two possible orderings if Linda ranks fourth:

<table>
<tr><td>1. Sue</td><td></td><td>1. Sue</td></tr>
<tr><td>2. Ed</td><td></td><td>2. Mary</td></tr>
<tr><td>3. Dan</td><td>or</td><td>3. Frank</td></tr>
<tr><td>4. Linda</td><td></td><td>4. Linda</td></tr>
<tr><td>5. Mary</td><td></td><td>5. Ed</td></tr>
<tr><td>6. Frank</td><td></td><td>6. Dan</td></tr>
</table>

The five main question types will be satisfied in the following ways:

A question that asks what *could be true* is answered by a statement that is logically *possible.* The incorrect choices are logically impossible.

A question that asks what *cannot be true* is answered by a statement that is logically *impossible.* The incorrect choices are either logically true or logically possible.

A question that asks what *must be true* is answered by a statement that is logically *necessary.* The incorrect choices are either logically possible or logically impossible.

A question that asks which of five statements is *not necessarily true* is answered by a statement that is either logically *false* or only *possibly true.*

A statement that asks for the number of *possible arrangements* is answered by a description of *all the possibilities.* The incorrect choices describe either *too few* or *too many* possibilities.

ANSWERING ANALYTICAL REASONING QUESTIONS

The first step in solving analytical reasoning questions is to preview the situation. Quickly read through the initial setup and the requirements without attempting to explore their significance or draw further conclusions. The preview step is included to provide a context for the more careful second reading.

Accept the situation at face value.

Test writers use familiar situations because these can be understood without lengthy explanation. There are no cheap tricks built into the situations. If the situation describes seven people standing in a ticket line, the line is a single-file line and one person is standing directly behind the other. Two people cannot have the same position in line; for example, no one is sitting on any one else's shoulders. If the situation might be misunderstood, then the test writer includes an explanatory note to clarify the ambiguity. For example, if the situation is a schedule of vacations for several employees and it is not otherwise clear whether employees can take vacations at the same time, the test writer will include a note to clarify the ambiguity, such as, "No employees take their vacations at the same time."

The second step is to read the description of the situation.

Read the description of the situation carefully.

This is absolutely critical. If you make an error at the beginning of your analysis, everything that is built on your initial reading will be affected by this error.

Pay particular attention to words such as *only, exactly, never, always, must be, can be, cannot be, some, all, no, none, entire, each, every, except, but, unless, if, more, less, before, after, possible, impossible, different, same, least, most, highest, lowest, first, last.*

There are two types of statements that are particularly subject to misinterpretation.

Be alert for connections that are asymmetrical.

A one-sided connection is one that imposes a condition on one individual vis-à-vis a second individual but does not impose that same condition on the second vis-à-vis the first.

Example:

If P is included in the tour, T must also be included.
S cannot eat at the Waffle Iron unless T does also.
Married men cannot attend on Sunday without their wives.

In each case, a one-sided condition is imposed. The first statement requires that T be included in the tour whenever P is included, that is, P cannot go without T; but the reverse is not true. So far as we know, T may be included without P. The second statement imposes a burden on T. T must accompany S. But the reverse is not true. S does not have to accompany T; T can eat alone. Finally, the third statement prevents married men from attending unless their wives also attend, but so far as we are told, the wives are free to attend without their husbands.

Do not confuse a "loose" connection with a "tight" connection.

Loose: Ed is sitting somewhere to Dan's left.
Tight: Ed is sitting immediately to the left of Dan.

Loose: Paul is in a grade ahead of Mary.
Tight: Paul is in the grade immediately ahead of Mary.

Loose:	Note X is higher on the scale than Note Y.
Tight:	Note X is two steps above Note Y on the scale.
Loose:	John is standing in the line somewhere between Paul and Mary.
Tight:	John is standing in the line immediately in front of Paul and immediately behind Mary.

Obviously, the tight connection in each pair provides more information than the loose connection.

As you are reading the description of the situation, you should take notes, jotting down the essence of the most important conditions and restrictions:

We recommend the following notational devices:

LOGICAL CONNECTIVE	SYMBOL
and	+
or	v
not	~
if, then	⊃
same as, next to	=
not same as, not next to	≠
greater than, older, before	>
if and only if	≡
less than, younger, after	<

Use capital letters for names and concepts.

To show how these devices could be used to summarize information, consider the following situation:

Example:

A teacher is setting up study groups for eight students—J, K, L, M, N, O, P, and Q. The groups must be formed in accordance with the following conditions.

If M is included in a study group, P and Q must also be included in the study group.
If P is included in a study group, then exactly two of the three students, L, M, and N, must also be included in that study group.
L cannot be included in a study group with P.
P can be included in a study group if and only if J is also included in that study group.
K, L, and M cannot all be included in the same study group.

This information could be summarized in the following way:

(1) M ⊃ (P+Q)
(2) P ⊃ (L + M) v (L+N) v (M + N)
(3) L ≠ P
(4) P = J
(5) ~ (K + L + M)

Statement 1 uses the horseshoe for "if, then." We place "P + Q" in parentheses. The parentheses function as punctuation. Had we not used them, the statement "M ⊃ P + Q" might be interpreted to mean "If M is included then P must be included, and Q must be included in any event." But that statement should be rendered as "(M ⊃ P) + Q."

Statement 2 shows us the logical structure of the second condition. If P is included, then either L and M must be included, or L and N must be included, or M and N must be included. Again, you will observe that we have used parentheses as punctuation marks.

Statement 3 uses "≠" to assert that L and P cannot both be included in a study group together. Statement 4 uses "=" to assert that P and J, when included in study groups, must be placed together. Finally, statement 5 says that it is not the case that K, L, and M are all included in the same study group.

The third step in the attack strategy is to digest the information.

Determine whether any further conclusions are readily deducible.

As we pointed out, most of the situations are characterized by extreme flexibility. If there are many possible solutions, it would be a mistake to attack the question set by trying to find them all. Such a strategy would be too time-consuming and wasteful. Since there will be only four to seven questions based on the situation, not every possible solution can be the basis for a question.

There are some situations in which it is possible to draw some further, fairly obvious conclusions. Clearly, you face a dilemma. You cannot afford to overlook conclusions that are required to answer questions, yet you cannot afford to spend precious minutes searching for further conclusions that either do not exist or are not needed. The solution to this dilemma is this: If you fail to make some further inferences that are required, when you approach the questions you will find them impossible to answer. That is the signal to try again. On the other hand, if you are able to find a correct answer to a question, that means you did all the work required for that question. Consider the following set:

Example:

A supervisor is scheduling flight crews for round-trip flights between City X and City Y. The trip is made once each day, Monday through Friday. Each flight must have a pilot and a copilot.

J and K can fly only as copilots.
L and M can fly only as pilots.
N can fly as either a pilot or a copilot.
No person may fly on two consecutive days.
On Tuesday, N will fly as pilot with J as copilot.
On Friday, L will fly as pilot.

1. Which of the following must be true?

(A) L will fly as pilot on Monday.
(B) M will fly as pilot on Wednesday.
(C) K will fly as copilot on Wednesday.
(D) N will fly as pilot on Thursday.
(E) J will fly as copilot on Friday.

2. If N flies as copilot on Friday, which of the following must be true?

(A) L will fly as pilot on Monday.
(B) L will fly as pilot on Wednesday.
(C) J will fly as pilot on Wednesday.
(D) K will fly as copilot on Thursday.
(E) N will fly as copilot on Thursday.

There are some further conclusions to be drawn:

	Monday	Tuesday	Wednesday	Thursday	Friday
Pilot		N			L
Copilot		J			

Since both N and J work on Tuesday, neither can work on Monday or Wednesday, which means that K must fly as copilot on both of those days:

	Monday	Tuesday	Wednesday	Thursday	Friday
Pilot		N			L
Copilot	K	J	K		

No further conclusions seem possible, but can we be sure of that? No, but we tackle the questions anyway.

1. **(C)** This question does not supply any additional information, so we should be able to answer it on the basis of our analysis of the original situation. Checking the choices against our second diagram, we see that (A), (B), (D), and (E) are possibly, though not necessarily, true. The diagram also shows that (C) is necessarily true. The fact that only one answer choice stands out as necessarily true means that we did all of the work necessary to answer this question.

Notice what would have happened had we neglected to draw the further conclusions. Had we attacked the questions on the basis of the first diagram, (C) too would have tested out as only possibly true. In that case, there would have been no choice that was necessarily true. That would have been the signal to return to the situation to look for those neglected inferences.

2. **(B)** This question supplies new information, and the first step toward answering is to digest the new information:

 When a question supplies new information, there will be additional conclusions to be drawn.

We enter the new information in the diagram:

	Monday	Tuesday	Wednesday	Thursday	Friday
Pilot		N			L
Copilot	K	J	K		N

With K flying on Wednesday and N flying on Friday, J must be the copilot on Thursday:

	Monday	Tuesday	Wednesday	Thursday	Friday
Pilot		N			L
Copilot	K	J	K	J	N

Is this all there is to it? Consult the choices. (D) and (E) are contradicted by the diagram, so they cannot be correct. (A), (B), and (C) all make statements that are possible, but none of them is necessary. In this situation, according to the attack strategy, we should try again with the new information. Since both L and N fly on Friday, M must be the pilot on Thursday, and this means that L will be the pilot on Wednesday.

	Monday	Tuesday	Wednesday	Thursday	Friday
Pilot		N	L	M	L
Copilot	K	J	K	J	N

Now we see that (C) is incorrect because it is contradicted by the diagram. (A) remains only possibly true. But (B) is shown to be necessarily true. Now we have a correct choice, so we know we did all the work necessary to answer the question.

IMPORTANT LOGICAL MOVES AND MANEUVERS

Analytical reasoning questions, like other thinking games such as chess and bridge, require the application of logical moves and maneuvers. In chess, the possibilities include the basic movements of the pieces (for example, a bishop moves on the diagonal of its color) and more advanced plays such as the knight fork. In bridge, the array of plays includes the finesse, the crossruff, and the end play. For analytical reasoning questions, we also have logical moves and maneuvers, some basic, others more complex. Although we could not possibly hope to investigate all of the complexities of human reasoning, we can offer a list of some of the most important logical plays.

"If, then" plays

Type 1:

If p, then q.
p.
Therefore, q.
Is a valid form of reasoning.

Example:

From

(1) If Paul attends the concert, then Quentin sees a play.

and

(2) Paul attends the concert.

we can validly conclude

Quentin sees a play.

But do not confuse this valid logical move with a similar, but invalid, logical move:

**If p, then q.
q.
Therefore, p.
Is not a valid form of reasoning.**

Example:
From

(1) If Paul attends the concert, then Quentin sees a play.

and

(2) Quentin sees a play.

we cannot validly conclude

Paul attends the concert.

One way of understanding the difference is as follows. The first statement in both lines of reasoning is the same, asserting that Paul's attending the concert entails (or requires) Quentin's seeing a play. In the first and valid form of reasoning, knowing that Paul attends the concert entitles us to conclude that Quentin sees a play, for the one event entails the other. But the first statement does not assert that Paul's attending the concert is the only event that leads to Quentin's seeing a play. Quentin may see a play even if Paul does not attend the concert.

Type 2:

**If p, then q.
Not-q.
Therefore, not-p.
Is a valid form of reasoning.**

Example:
From

(1) If Paul attends the concert, then Quentin sees a play.

and

(2) Quentin does not see a play.

we can validly conclude

Paul does not attend the concert.

Again, do not confuse this valid form of reasoning with a similar, but invalid, logical move:

If p, then q,
Not-p.
Therefore, not-q.
Is not a valid form of reasoning.

Example:
From

(1) If Paul attends the concert, then Quentin sees a play.

and

(2) Paul does not attend the concert.

we cannot validly conclude

Quentin does not see a play.

In the first and valid form of reasoning, knowing that Quentin does not see a play entitles us to conclude that Paul does not attend the concert, for had Paul attended the concert, Quentin would have seen the play. On the other hand, since statement 1 does not assert that the only reason for Quentin's seeing a play is Paul's attending the concert, we may not conclude that Paul's not attending the concert necessarily results in Quentin's not seeing a play.

Type 3:

If and only if p, then q.
p.
Therefore, q.
Is a valid form of reasoning.

Example:
From

(1) If and only if Paul attends the concert, then Quentin sees a play.

and

    (2) Paul attends the concert.

we can validly conclude

    Quentin sees a play.

Additionally,

If and only if p, then q.
q.
Therefore, p.
Is a valid form of reasoning.

Example:
From

    (1) If and only if Paul atttends the concert, then Quentin sees a play.

and

    (2) Quentin sees a play.

we can validly conclude

    Paul attends the concert.

You should observe that the situation here is different from that presented by the first type of "If, then" move described above. The critical distinction between the two is the difference in wording of the first statement. Previously, we stated that

    If p, then q.
    q.
    Therefore, p.

was not a valid form of reasoning. Here we state that

    If and only if p, then q.
    q.
    Therefore, p.

is a valid form of reasoning. There is an important difference between

    If Paul attends the concert, Quentin sees a play.

and

    If and only if Paul attends the concert, Quentin sees a play.

The second statement asserts that the only reason for Quentin's seeing a play is Paul's attending the concert. So knowing that Quentin does see a play is sufficient to warrant the conclusion that Paul attends the concert.

If and only if p, then q.
Not-q.
Therefore, not-p.
Is a valid form of reasoning.

Example:

From

    (1) If and only if Paul attends the concert, then Quentin sees a play.

and

    (2) Quentin does not see a play.

we can validly conclude

    Paul does not attend the concert.

Additionally,

If and only if p, then q.
Not-p.
Therefore, not-q.
Is a valid form of reasoning.

Example:

From

    (1) If and only if Paul attends the concert, then Quentin sees a play.

and

    (2) Paul does not attend the concert.

we can validly conclude

    Quentin does not see a play.

Again, you will notice that this situation is different from that discussed in Type 2 "If, then" moves, because of the important difference between the first statements:

    If p, then q.

versus

    If and only if p, then q.

Here the statement, "If and only if Paul attends the concert, then Quentin sees a play" asserts that Paul's attending the concert is dependent upon Quentin's seeing a play. Once it is established that Quentin does not see a play, it follows logically that Paul does not attend the concert. On the other hand, the statement "If Paul attends the concert, then Quentin sees a play" does not assert that Paul's attending the concert is in any way dependent upon Quentin's seeing a play.

Another way of viewing the difference between the first two types of "If, then" moves and this third type is to see that a statement having the form "if and only if" is really two statements in one: "If and only if p, then q" is equivalent to "If p then q" *plus* "Only if p, then q." This last statement, "Only if p, then q" is equivalent to "If q, then p." For example, "Only if Paul attends the concert (then) does Quentin see a play" is equivalent to "If Quentin sees a play, Paul attends the concert."

If and only if p, then q = {
   (1) If p, then q.
   plus
   (2) If q, then p.

Type 4:

If p, then q.
If q, then r.
Therefore, if p, then r.
Is a valid form of reasoning.

Example:

From

   (1) If Paul attends the concert, then Quentin sees a play.

and

   (2) If Quentin sees a play, then Rachel visits her sister.

we can validly conclude

   If Paul attends the concert, then Rachel visits her sister.

   Further, this type of reasoning is valid for any number of steps. For example:

   If p, then q.
   If q, then r.
   If r, then s.
   If s, then t.
   Therefore, if p, then t.

is also a valid form of reasoning.

This type of reasoning should not, however, be confused with the following invalid form of reasoning:

If p, then q.
If q, then r.
Therefore, r.
Is not a valid form of reasoning.

Remember that the valid form of reasoning asserted the conclusion "*If* p, *then* r"; for example, "*If* Paul attends the concert, *then* Rachel visits her sister." The conclusion was not just "r," that is, we did not conclude that Rachel actually does visit her sister.

It is possible, however, to combine this type of "If, then" reasoning with other types of "If, then" reasoning:

If p, then q.
If q, then r.
p.
Therefore, r.
Is a valid form of reasoning.

Example:

From

(1) If Paul attends the concert, then Quentin sees a play.

and

(2) If Quentin sees a play, then Rachel visits her sister.

with

(3) Paul attends the concert.

we can validly conclude

Rachel visits her sister.

Using the Type 4, "If, then" move, statements 1 and 2 yield the conclusion "If Paul attends the concert, then Rachel visits her sister." This intermediate conclusion, coupled with 3, produces a Type 1 "If, then" conclusion, "Rachel visits her sister."

Similarly, the following is a valid form of reasoning:

If p, then q.
If q, then r.
Not-r.
Therefore, not-p.
Is a valid form of reasoning.

The valid form is a combination of Type 4 and Type 2 "If, then" moves.

Example:

From

(1) If Paul attends the concert, then Quentin sees a play.

and

(2) If Quentin sees a play, then Rachel visits her sister.

with

(3) Rachel does not visit her sister.

we can conclude

Paul does not attend the concert.

We have already seen that statements 1 and 2 combine in a Type 4 move to produce the conclusion "If Paul attends the concert, then Rachel visits her sister," and that intermediate conclusion, when coupled with "Rachel does not visit her sister" produces a Type 2 conclusion "Paul does not attend the concert."

Now we will see how these logical moves can be applied to a GRE Analytical Reasoning situation:

Example:

The coach of a soccer team is selecting players for the team. The candidates are Joan, Karla, Lisa, Myrna, Nan, and Opal.

Lisa must be selected for the team.
Joan can be selected for the team only if Karla is also selected.
Myrna and Nan can be selected for the team only if the other is also selected.
If Karla is selected for the team, then Nan cannot be selected for the team.
If Lisa is selected for the team, then Opal must also be selected.

1. Which of the following must be true?

(A) Myrna is selected for the team.
(B) Nan is selected for the team.
(C) Nan is not selected for the team.
(D) If Joan is selected for the team, Nan is not selected.
(E) If Karla is selected for the team, Nan is selected also.

2. If Joan is selected for the team, which of the following is a complete and accurate listing of the other candidates who must also be selected?

(A) Karla
(B) Karla and Lisa
(C) Karla, Lisa, and Opal
(D) Karla, Lisa, Opal, and Myrna
(E) Karla, Lisa, Opal, Myrna, and Nan

3. If Karla is not chosen for the team, then the largest number of candidates from the group who could be chosen is

(A) 1
(B) 2
(C) 3

(D) 4
(E) 5

Now let us use these rules of translation to attack a problem based on the team selection set previously.

(1) Lisa must be selected.	L
(2) Joan only if Karla.	J ⊃ K
(3) Myrna if and only if Nan.	M ≡ N
(4) If Karla, then not-Nan.	K ⊃ ~ N
(5) If Lisa, then Opal.	L ⊃ O

1. **(D)** From the information provided, we can draw only one further conclusion about the candidates who must be chosen: Opal must be chosen (using statements 1 and 5). (A), (B), and (C) are incorrect because they move from a hypothetical statement such as "If and only if M, then N" to an assertion such as "M" or "N." This form of reasoning was shown before to be invalid. Both (D) and (E) are hypothetical statements, but (E) directly contradicts statement 4 and must be incorrect. Finally, (D) is the correct choice.

(2) Joan only if Karla.	J ⊃ K
(4) If Karla, then not-Nan.	K ⊃ ~ N

Therefore,

if Joan, then not-Nan.	J ⊃ ~ N

Notice that this statement does not assert that Nan is not chosen for the team. Rather, it asserts that if Joan is chosen, then Nan is not chosen.

2. **(C)** We have already noted that both Lisa and Opal must be chosen for the team, so this eliminates (A) and (B) as incorrect. Further, using the stipulation provided in the question stem that Joan actually is selected, we reason

(2) Joan only if Karla.	J ⊃ K
Joan is chosen.	J
Therefore, Karla is chosen.	Therefore, K

Given that Karla is chosen, we reason

(4) If Karla, then not-Nan.	K ⊃ ~ N
Karla is chosen.	K
Therefore, Nan is not chosen.	Therefore, ~N.

This eliminates choice (E). Finally, statement 3 is really two assertions in one sentence.

If Myrna, then Nan *and* if Nan, then Myrna.

Focusing on the first half of that sentence, we reason

If Myrna, then Nan.	M ⊃ N
Nan is not chosen.	~ N
Therefore, Myrna is not chosen.	Therefore, ~ M.

With Myrna eliminated, the correct answer must be (C).

3. **(D)** We begin our analysis by recalling that both Lisa and Opal must be selected for the team. Then, we process the additional information included by stipulation in the stem: Karla is not chosen. Does Karla's not being chosen determine whether Nan is chosen? The answer is "no." To conclude anything about Nan on the basis of Karla's *not* being chosen would be to reason

> (4) If Karla, then not-Nan. $K \supset \sim N$
> Not Karla. $\sim K$
> Therefore, Nan.   Therefore, N

That is an invalid line of reasoning. Thus, even given that Karla is not chosen, Nan may or may not be chosen, which is to say, Nan is still eligible. Then, if Nan is still eligible, Myrna must also be eligible. So the largest number of candidates who *could* be selected is four: Lisa and Opal will be included, and Myrna and Nan could also be selected.

Translation Equivalents

Sometimes you will find it easier to appreciate the implications of a statement if you are able to translate it into a more convenient form.

A sentence using a negative verb can be translated into an affirmative sentence prefaced by "it is not the case that..."

For example, the restriction "Peter, Paul, and Mary cannot all serve on the committee together" is equivalent to "It is not the case that Peter, Paul, and Mary can all serve on the committee together." The condition "Chemicals X, Y, and Z cannot all be used in the same mixture" is equivalent to "It is not the case that the chemicals X, Y, and Z can all be used in the same mixture."

A double negative can be treated as an affirmative.

This principle is similar to the rule of arithmetic that states that when a negative number is subtracted, the positive equivalent of that number is actually being added. Thus, the statement, " It is not the case that John is not selected" really means "John is selected," and the awkward sentence "Mary is not not selected for the committee" is more easily rendered as simply "Mary is selected for the committee."

"If p, then q" is equivalent to "If not-q, then not-p."

Thus, the sentence "If John is selected for the committee, then Mary is also selected" is equivalent to "If Mary is not selected for the committee, then John is not selected." This principle can be particularly useful when combined with the preceding suggestion regarding double negatives. For example, the sentence "If John is not selected for the committee, then Mary is not selected for the committee" is first translated into the awkward statement "If Mary is not not selected for the committee, then John is not not selected for the committee," and simplified to "If Mary is selected for the committee, then John is selected for the committee."

"Not the case that p and q" is equivalent to "not-p or not-q," where the "or" is inclusive.

For example, the sentence "Mary and Peter are not both selected for the committee" means "It is not the case that Mary and Peter are both selected," which is equivalent, according to this principle of translation, to "Either Mary is not selected or Peter is not selected" (with the understanding that perhaps neither of them is selected). The principle also applies even when there are more than three elements involved, as in "Peter, Paul, and Mary cannot all serve on the committee." This is equivalent to "Peter does not serve, or Paul does not serve, or Mary does not serve" (with the understanding that maybe none of the three serves).

Now let us use these translational rules to attack a problem based on the team selection set from page 81:

4. If Myrna is selected to be on the team, which of the following statements is true?

    I. Joan is not selected for the team.
    II. Karla is not selected for the team.
    III. Joan and Karla are not both selected for the team.

    (A) I only
    (B) II only
    (C) III only
    (D) I and II only
    (E) I, II, and III

4. (E) All of the statements are true. From statement 3,

    Myrna if and only if Nan $M \equiv N$

and

    Myrna M

we conclude

    Therefore, Nan.   Therefore, N.

Statement 4 is equivalent to "If not not Nan, then not Karla" and that is equivalent to "If Nan, then not Karla." So we reason further

    If Nan, then not-Karla. $N \supset \sim K$
    Nan. N
    Therefore, not-Karla.   Therefore, $\sim K$.

Then statement 2 can be translated into "If Joan, then Karla" and that into "If not-Karla, then not-Joan." Now we have

If not Karla, then not-Joan.	~ K ⊃ ~ J
Not Karla.	~ K
Therefore, not-Joan.	Therefore, ~ J.

Our conclusion, then, is that neither Joan nor Karla can be selected if Myrna is selected. Thus statements I and II are true. What about III? III is equivalent to "It is not the case that both Joan and Karla are selected," and that in turn translates into "Either Joan is not selected or Karla is not selected, and maybe neither is selected." Since neither Joan nor Karla can be selected if Myrna is selected, III is also true. Therefore, all three statements are true.

The phrase "p only if q" means "If p, then q."

Some test takers misinterpret sentences having the structure "p only if q," taking them to mean "if q, then p," when the correct translation is "if p, then q." Consider the sentence "Paul will attend the lecture only if Sally also attends the lecture." This means that if Paul attends the lecture, Sally must also attend the lecture. So if we know that Paul attends the lecture, we can conclude that Sally also attends the lecture. But knowing that Sally attends the lecture does not entitle us to draw any conclusion about Paul's attendance. Sally may attend the lecture with or without Paul.

The statement "p unless q" means "if q, then not-p," and also "if p, then not-q."

For example, the sentence "Patty will be chosen for the team unless Mary is chosen for the team" means both "If Patty is chosen for the team, then Mary is not chosen for the team," and "If Mary is chosen for the team, then Patty is not chosen for the team." The two alternative sentences are logically equivalent.

Process of Elimination

p or q.
Not-p.
Therefore, q.
Is a valid line of reasoning.

This form of reasoning is often referred to as the process of elimination: It must be p or q; it cannot be p; therefore, it must be q. This line of attack can be used on statements considerably more complex: It must be p, q, r, s, or t; it is not p, q, r, or s; therefore, it must be t. Further, it can be used to narrow the available choices even where it does not yield a single, final result: It must be p, q, r, s, or t; it cannot be p, q, or r; therefore, it must be s or t.

The process of elimination is a very powerful tool. We can illustrate this by adding yet another question to the set we have been working with.

5. If Nan is not selected for the team, then which of the following is a complete and accurate listing of the candidates who could be selected?

(A) Lisa
(B) Lisa and Opal
(C) Lisa, Opal, and Myrna
(D) Lisa, Opal, and Joan
(E) Lisa, Opal, Joan, and Karla

5. (E) We begin by reasoning that the list of eligible candidates includes Joan, Karla, Lisa, Myrna, and Opal. On the assumption that Nan is not selected for the team, Myrna is eliminated from consideration, for Myrna can play on the team only if Nan also plays on the team. As for Karla, the fact that Nan is not selected means that Karla remains a possible choice. Since Karla cannot be eliminated, Joan cannot be eliminated. Finally, as for Lisa and Opal, their status is not affected by Nan's status, so they remain candidates (indeed, we know they must be chosen). So only Myrna is eliminated by Nan's elimination, and the candidates who remain are Lisa, Opal, Joan, and Karla: choice (E).

A question set may include more than six individuals, and with many individuals it may be difficult to keep track of all eliminations in your head:

Make a list of the cast of characters (by name or letter), and strike through those names or letters that you eliminate. The remaining names or letters will be the correct choice.

When dealing with a larger number of individuals, say eight or ten, there is a danger of overlooking someone. We recommend, therefore, that you make a list of the individuals in the question set:

J K L M N O P Q R

As you eliminate some of them as a matter of logic, eliminate them also on paper:

J̸ K L̸ M̸ N Ø P̸ Q̸ R̸

In this case, only K and N remain, and "K and N" would be the correct answer. This bookkeeping device minimizes the danger that you will forget to consider the status of one or more individuals in the question set.

Eliminating Logically Deficient Answer Choices

If a question stem supplies no additional information and does not contain a thought-reverser, attempt to eliminate four answer choices by comparing them to the initial description of the situation.

The test is constructed on the principle that one of the five choices is logically correct, while the other four choices are in some way logically deficient. If you can eliminate four choices as logically deficient then, by the process of elimination, you have proved the logical correctness of the remaining choice. Thus, in the context of the multiple-choice format, you prove the correctness of an answer choice in a negative way, without offering an affirmative proof of its correctness. Consider yet another question set:

Example:

Nine people, G, H, J, K, L, M, N, O, and P, are taking part in a parade. They will ride in three cars, the cars forming a line. Three people will sit in each car.

G and H must ride in the same car.
J must ride in the second car.
N and P must ride in the same car.
K and O must not ride in the same car.
M must ride in the same car with either O or J or both.

1. Which of the following groups of people could ride together in the same car?

(A) G, J, and N
(B) J, L, and O
(C) K, H, and L
(D) K, N, and O
(E) O, N, and P

First, we summarize the information for ready reference:

G and H together	$G = H$
J in second car.	$J = 2$
N and P together	$N = P$
K and O not together	$K \neq O$
M with O or J or both	$M = J \vee O \vee (J + O)$

1. (E) With a question of this sort, four of the choices are logically deficient because they are inconsistent with the initial requirements. (A) is incorrect because it includes G without H, in violation of the first requirement. (B) is incorrect because we have J and O riding with L, so M is riding in another car in violation of the final condition. (C) includes H without G and runs afoul of the first condition. Finally, (D) includes N without P and also places K and O in the same car, thereby violating two conditions. By elimination of (A), (B), (C), and (D), we prove that (E) is the correct choice.

 If a question stem supplies no additional information and does contain a thought-reverser, attempt to eliminate one answer choice on the grounds that it contradicts the initial description of the situation.

Consider another question for this set:

2. All of the following are possible arrangements for a car *except:*

(A) G, H, and J
(B) J, M, and O

(C) K, J, and O
(D) K, N, and P
(E) N, P, and L

2. (C) Begin by examining (A). The only restriction on G and H is that they be together, a restriction honored by (A). J must ride in the second car, and either O or J must ride with M. That makes it possible for J to ride with G and H, so (A) is consistent with the initial conditions. As for (B), J, M, and O are under the restriction that M ride with J or O *or* both, so (B) is an acceptable arrangement. As for (C), J must ride with either O or M, and that condition is honored; but another restriction requires that we separate K and O. Thus, (C) is not an acceptable arrangement. A quick check will show that (D) and (E) are consistent with the initial conditions.

At this point, you may want to ask whether, as a matter of strategy, you should not stop with (C). Why take the additional time to check (D) and (E) as well? Testing the remaining choices provides an additional check. For example, suppose that you had misread the final condition to require O or J but *not* both. You would have incorrectly concluded that (B) violates the initial conditions and would have selected (B) as the correct answer to the question. On the other hand, had you continued to check the remaining choices, you probably would have recognized that (C), too, was logically defective. Since only one of the four choices can be logically defective, the presence of two seemingly defective choices would have operated as an alarm, alerting you to recheck your work. A recheck, one would hope, would show that (B) was in fact an acceptable arrangement. Of course, this additional check for accuracy does consume time, so the question ultimately turns on whether you can afford to spend time for accuracy. If you are on or ahead of schedule, then you can probably afford the extra check; but if you are running late, then you should stop when you have eliminated the first possible choice, trusting that you have read the information correctly.

COMMON TYPES OF ANALYTICAL REASONING QUESTIONS

Analytical reasoning questions can be divided into certain common types, each based on a particular kind of situation. Moreover, certain question forms are associated with those situations, susceptible to attack strategies that you should be aware of. The following techniques, when used intelligently, will enable you to handle most, if not all, of the questions you will encounter on the exam.

Linear Order

Linear order is one of the most common situations used by the test writers. Such situations usually involve six to nine individuals arranged one behind the other. The situation may be described as seven people standing in a single file ticket line, or as seven people sitting in a row of chairs in a theater, or as a student scheduling seven one-hour courses in a day, or as a chef deciding which fish specialty to offer on each day of a seven-day week. Also, the situation described previously, the children taking a series of tests, was a linear ordering problem.

The situations just mentioned are very similar. Although the connections between individuals are "in front of" or "in back of" in one case and "before in time" and "after in time" in another, the concept of linear order is the same in each.

For any linear ordering problem use a diagram:
1 2 3 4 5 6 7 8

We will illustrate the use of the diagram with the following situation:

Example:

At a certain school, the school day is broken into six one-hour periods, first through sixth. A teacher is scheduling five subjects to be taught during a particular day. Each subject will be taught once during the day and will receive an entire period. One period during the day is a free period.

French must be taught earlier than the fourth period.
Geography is separated from French by the same number of periods that French is separated from History, though the number may be zero.
Science is taught at some time between Math and French.
History is taught either immediately before or immediately after Science.

1. Which of the following is a possible schedule of the five subjects from earliest in the day until latest in the day?

   (A) French, History, Science, Geography, Math
   (B) History, Science, Math, French, Geography
   (C) Geography, French, History, Science, Math
   (D) Geography, French, History, Math, Science
   (E) Science, Math, Geography, French, History

2. If Math is taught in the fifth period, which of the six periods is the free period?

   (A) first
   (B) second
   (C) third
   (D) fourth
   (E) sixth

3. If Science is taught in the fifth period, which of the six periods is the free period?

   (A) first
   (B) second
   (C) third
   (D) fourth
   (E) sixth

4. If the fifth period is a free period, which of the following must be true?

   (A) French is taught in the first period.
   (B) Geography is taught in the second period.
   (C) History is taught in the third period.

(D) Math is taught in the fourth period.
(E) Science is taught in the sixth period.

The first thing you should notice about the situation is that it is highly open-ended. It does not seem possible to establish any particular order for the schedule. Do not attempt to find a final solution to the problem. You would, however, want to make marginal notations of the statements about the situation:

(1) F < 4 (French before fourth)
(2) G – F = F – H (Separation of Geography/French equals that of French/History)
(3) (M/S/F) ∨ (F/S/M) (Science between Math and French)
(4) (H = S) (History and Science back-to-back)

1. (C) This question does not supply any additional information, so it must be possible to answer it with the information already available.

We proceed by testing for contradictions. First, French must be taught *before* the fourth period. (B) and (E) fail on this count and can be eliminated.

Next, we test each choice against the requirement that Geography be separated from French by the same number of periods that separate French and History. (A) can be eliminated on this ground.

Now we check to see that Science is taught between Math and French. (C) respects this requirement, but (D) does not. Thus, (D) can be eliminated as incorrect.

At this point we know that (C) must be correct. If you wish, you may check (C) again against each requirement just to satisfy yourself that it is an acceptable schedule. As test-taking strategy, however, this is a waste of time. Once you are able to eliminate four of the five choices on the ground of inconsistency with the requirements governing the situation, the remaining choice has to be correct.

In a linear ordering situation, if a question provides additional information, digest that information, using the process of elimination to generate further conclusions.

2. (E) This question does provide additional information. We begin by entering the new information on a diagram:

1	2	3	4	5	6
				M	

To respect conditions 1 and 2, Geography, French, and History must be taught in a row in periods 1, 2, and 3 or in periods 2, 3, and 4, though not necessarily in that order:

1	2	3	4	5	6
G/H	F	H/G		M	
	G/H	F	G/H	M	

Then, since Science is taught between Math and History, we know that Science is not taught in the sixth period, so the sixth period must be the free period.

This is sufficient to answer the question asked, but as a study exercise we will show that if Math is taught in the fifth period the schedule must be:

1	2	3	4	5	6
G	F	H	S	M	free

3. (A) This question is attacked similarly. If Science is taught in the fifth period, then Math must be taught in the sixth to respect condition 3:

1	2	3	4	5	6
				S	M

and History is required by condition 4 to be taught in the fourth period:

1	2	3	4	5	6
			H	S	M

Then condition 2 requires that Geography and French be taught in the second and third periods:

1	2	3	4	5	6
	G	F	H	S	M

4. (C) This question is attacked in the same manner. If the fifth period is free, then Geography, French, and History have to be taught in a row:

1	2	3	4	5	6
G/H	F	G/H		free	
	G/H	F	G/H	free	

But since History and Science are taught back-to-back, this leaves:

1	2	3	4	5	6
G	F	H	S	free	M
S	H	F	G	free	M

And since Science is taught between French and Math, we have only

1	2	3	4	5	6
G	F	H	S	free	M

(C) is proved correct by the diagram, and the other choices are shown to be incorrect by the diagram.

The process of elimination is very useful in handling question sets involving spatial orders:

Example:

Six individuals, J, K, L, M, N, and O, are standing in a single-file line. They are all facing forward.

J is either first or last in the line.
O is the fourth person in line.
M is standing either immediately in front of or immediately behind N.
K is standing neither immediately in front of nor immediately in back of N.

1. If K is second in the line, which of the following must be true?

(A) J is sixth in line.
(B) M is sixth in line.
(C) N is sixth in line.
(D) L is third in line.
(E) L is fifth in line.

2. If L and J are fifth and sixth in line, respectively, then which of the following must be true?

(A) K is first in line
(B) M is first in line.
(C) N is first in line.
(D) M is second in line.
(E) N is second in line.

3. If M is the second person behind L in the line, then which of the following is a complete and accurate listing of the positions in which K could be standing?

(A) first, second
(B) second, third
(C) second, fifth
(D) first, second, third, fifth
(E) first, second, third, fifth, sixth

Each of these questions is solved by a process of elimination. First, we summarize the information:

J is either first or last.	J = (1 or 6)
O is fourth.	O = 4
M is next to N.	M = N
K is not next to N.	K ≠ N

Be prepared to eliminate possible arrangements on the ground that two or more individuals must be placed together.

1. (D) With K second in line, we have the following:

1	2	3	4	5	6
	K		O		

M and N must be placed together, so this eliminates first and third as possible positions for M and N. So M and N will be fifth and sixth, though not necessarily in that order:

1	2	3	4	5	6
	K		O	M /	N

This means that J must be first in line, and by elimination, L is third:

1	2	3	4	5	6
J	K	L	O	M /	N

Be prepared to eliminate possible arrangements on the ground that two or more individuals cannot be placed together.

2. (D) On the assumption that L and J are fifth and sixth, respectively:

1	2	3	4	5	6
			O	L	J

Since M and N must be paired, this would seem to leave open four possible arrangements:

1	2	3	4	5	6
M	N		O	L	J
N	M		O	L	J
	M	N	O	L	J
	N	M	O	L	J

but the first and fourth of these can be eliminated on the ground that K would be placed in line next to N, in violation of one of the conditions. By elimination, then, there are only two possible orders:

1	2	3	4	5	6
N	M	K	O	L	J
K	M	N	O	L	J

The diagram confirms that M must be in second place, so (D) is correct. (A) and (C) are both possible, though not necessary. (B) and (E) are contradicted by the diagram.

Be prepared to eliminate possible arrangements on the ground that they fail to respect a condition that individuals be separated by a certain distance.

3. (C) Here we are asked to assume that M and L are in the order L, ?, M. Given that O is in the fourth position, where could L and M be placed?

1	2	3	4	5	6
			O		
L		M			
	L		M		
		L		M	
			L		M

But the second and fourth possibilities must be eliminated, because O is in the fourth position. This leaves two possible arrangements for L and M:

1	2	3	4	5	6
L		M	O		
		L	O	M	

Respecting the other conditions, we have:

1	2	3	4	5	6
L	N	M	O	K	J
J	K	L	O	M	N

So K could be only in the second or the fifth position.

Distributed Order

Another common situation is one in which there is an order, but more than one individual can be assigned to a particular position. For example, seven corporations have offices in a four-story building: three on one floor, two on another floor, and one on each of the remaining floors.

For a distributed order situation, pay careful attention to the distributional conditions.

Example:

A secretary is scheduling appointments for his boss during a certain week. There are exactly nine appointments open: one on Monday, three on Tuesday, one on Wednesday, two on Thursday, and two on Friday. He must schedule seven people, M, N, O, P, Q, R, and S:

Two people must have appointments on Thursday, and at least one person must be scheduled for an appointment on each of the other days.

N and Q must be scheduled on the same day.
M must be scheduled for Monday.
O cannot be scheduled for Friday.
S must be scheduled for Thursday.

1. Which of the following is *not* an acceptable schedule for the two appointments mentioned?

(A) R and S on Thursday.
(B) S and P on Thursday.
(C) S and O on Thursday.
(D) O and P on Wednesday.
(E) N and Q on Friday.

2. Which of the following must be true of the appointment schedule?

(A) R is scheduled for Tuesday.
(B) O is scheduled for Tuesday.
(C) P is scheduled for Thursday.
(D) N and Q are scheduled for Tuesday.
(E) Three days have exactly one appointment scheduled.

3. If N and Q are scheduled for Tuesday, how many different schedules are possible for the entire week?

(A) 1
(B) 2
(C) 3
(D) 4
(E) 5

1. (D) No additional information is provided, so the answer must be obtainable by comparing each choice to the requirements of the situation. Pay careful attention to the distributional conditions.

You might first test each choice against the requirements that govern the named individuals, for example, that N and Q must be seen on the same day. You will find that all are acceptable on those grounds. Then you would look to the distributional requirement: one open appointment on Wednesday. (D) is not an acceptable schedule, since it is not possible to schedule more than one appointment on Wednesday.

Note that we did not attack this question by trying to prove that the appointments mentioned in the other choices could be fitted into a week-long schedule consistent with the other requirements. That line of attack would have been very time-consuming as shown in this diagram for (A):

Mon.	Tues.	Wed.	Thurs.	Fri.
M	N+Q	O	R+S	P

This proves that (A) is an acceptable schedule, but to do this for each choice is inefficient. The better strategy is to look for a reason to disqualify an answer choice.

 Before working out a possibility in great detail, look at the other choices for an obvious answer.

2. (E) This question is the mirror image of the preceding one. (A) through (D) seem plausible enough, but for something like (A) to be correct (R must be scheduled Tuesday), the problem would have to be very difficult, that is, (A) could be necessarily true only by virtue of the subtle interaction of all the requirements. In general, the questions are just not that hard.

(E) is fairly obvious, given the distributional requirements. We must schedule at least one person each day of the week, so that takes care of five people. Thursday must have two people, so that takes care of six. Only one person remains, and he cannot be scheduled for Thursday. So exactly two days will have two appointments and three days will have one appointment.

3. (D) The question supplies additional information: If N and Q are scheduled for Tuesday, we know

Mon.	Tues.	Wed.	Thurs.	Fri.
M	N, Q		S	~ O

We know that Thursday must have one more appointment and that Wednesday and Friday must have an appointment. So the possibilities are:

Mon.	Tues.	Wed.	Thurs.	Fri.
M	N,Q		S	
		O	P	R
		O	R	P
		P	O	R
		R	O	P

Programs

A third common problem type we refer to as programs. In a program, a series of possible events is described.

Example:

A part-time college student is planning her curriculum for the first four semesters. She can choose only from the following:

In the first semester she will take course J or course K, but not both.

If she takes course J, then in the second semester she must take either course M or course P, but not both.

If she takes course K, then in the second semester she must take courses M and N.

If she takes M in the second semester, then she must take Q in the third semester and R in the fourth semester.

If she takes N in the second semester, she must take S in the third semester and T in the fourth semester.

If she takes P in the second semester, she must take N in the third semester and cannot take T in the fourth semester.

1. If the student takes T in her fourth semester, which of the following must be true?

   (A) She took J in her first semester.
   (B) She took K in her first semester.
   (C) She took P in her second semester.
   (D) She took P in her third semester.
   (E) She took N in her third semester.

2. If the student takes R in her fourth semester, which of the following must be true?

   (A) She took J in her first semester.
   (B) She took K in her first semester.
   (C) She took P in her second semester.
   (D) She took S in her third semester.
   (E) She took Q in her third semester.

With a program situation, use arrows to show the order of events.

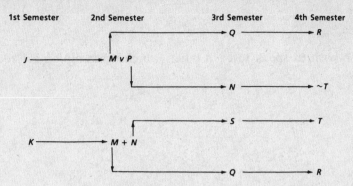

1. (B) As the diagram shows, if the student took T in the fourth semester, she must have taken K in the first semester. She could not have taken J in the first semester, so (A) is incorrect. Nor could she have taken P in the second semester, since that would have precluded her from taking T in the fourth semester; so (C) is incorrect. (D) is incorrect since P is a second-semester, not a third-semester, course. Finally, (E) is incorrect since that would have precluded her from taking T her fourth semester.

2. (E) If she took R in the fourth semester, she took Q in the third semester. (A) and (B) are both possible, but neither is necessary. She could have chosen either J or K. (C) is not possible, for the student could have taken M *or* P, not both. Similarly, (D) is only possible, for she could have taken J and then M, followed by Q and K.

Individual Characteristics

A fourth common type of situation provides information about characteristics that individuals may or may not have. Consider the following situation:

Example:

Five diplomats, P, Q, R, S, and T, are attending a conference.

P speaks only English and German.
Q speaks only French, Italian, and Spanish.
R speaks only German.
S speaks only English, Italian, and Spanish.
T speaks only French and German.

1. All of the following pairs of diplomats can speak to each other without a translator *except:*

(A) P and R
(B) P and T
(C) Q and S
(D) Q and R
(E) R and T

2. The language spoken by the most diplomats is

(A) English

(B) French
(C) German
(D) Italian
(E) Spanish

3. If S and T wish to speak to each other, which other diplomats could serve as translator?

I. P
II. Q
III. R

(A) I only
(B) II only
(C) III only
(D) I and II only
(E) I, II, and III

The most important thing with a situation such as this is organizing the information.

To keep track of individual characteristics, use an information table.

We would diagram the information as follows:

	English	French	German	Italian	Spanish
P	YES	NO	YES	NO	NO
Q	NO	YES	NO	YES	YES
R	NO	NO	YES	NO	NO
S	YES	NO	NO	YES	YES
T	NO	YES	YES	NO	NO

1. (D) The diagram shows that Q and R do not speak the same language. (A) is incorrect, for P and R both speak German. (B) is incorrect, P and T both speak German. (C) is incorrect, for Q and S both speak Italian and Spanish. (E) is incorrect, for R and T both speak German.

2. (C) The table shows that exactly three diplomats speak German, but only two diplomats speak the other languages.

3. (D) The table shows that S speaks English, Italian, and Spanish, and that T speaks French and German. P can serve as a translator since P can speak with S in English and T in German. Q can serve as a translator since Q can speak with S in either Italian or Spanish and with T in French. Finally, R cannot serve as a translator because R cannot speak with S at all.

Selection Situations

A fifth common situation is selecting individuals to be placed into groups. We used such a set to illustrate the use of common motivational devices.

If the situation requires selection of individuals from a single pool, use symbols to summarize the information.

The study-group selection situation requires the selection of individuals from a common pool. Contrast that situation with the following:

Example:

The president of a university is selecting a committee to study the university's grading policy. J, K, and L are members of the administration. M, N, and O are on the faculty. X, Y, and Z are students.

There must be at least as many faculty members on the committee as students.
If either J or M is selected to serve on the committee, the other must also be selected to serve on the committee.
N will not serve on the committee if L serves on the committee.
O will not serve on the committee if X is on the committee.

1. Which of the following is an acceptable committee?

(A) J, K, N, O, Y, Z
(B) J, K, M, O, X, Y
(C) J, L, M, O, Y, Z
(D) K, L, N, O, Y, Z
(E) J, K, L, M, Y, Z

2. If M is not selected for the committee, then the maximum number of people who could be appointed is

(A) 3
(B) 4
(C) 5
(D) 6
(E) 7

In this situation, the individuals are not all drawn from a common pool. There are three subgroups: administration, faculty, and students.

 If the situation requires selection of individuals from different pools, represent the information with connecting lines.

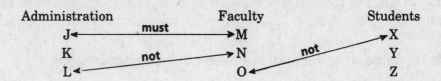

Here we use connecting lines with notations such as "must" or "not" to summarize the information.

1. (C) This question does not supply additional information. The first statement requires that there be at least as many faculty members as students, and (E) can be eliminated on that ground. The second statement requires that J and M be together, and (A) can be eliminated on that ground. The third statement requires that N and L not serve together, so (D) can be eliminated. The final statement requires that O and X not serve together, so (B) can be eliminated. This means that (C) must be the correct choice. If the question had read, "Which of the following is *not* an acceptable committee?" you would use the same process to find the impossible arrangement.

2. (C) Since M is not selected, J is not selected. K is under no restriction at all, so K can be included. Now we must decide whether to choose L or N. If we choose L, then N cannot serve, leaving O as the only faculty member. That would mean at most one student could serve. On the other hand, if we choose N over L, then a student can be appointed to match N. So we select N to get the maximum number. Now we have K, N, and a student, say Y. Next we choose between O and X. We cannot really choose X, for there is no faculty member to accompany X (other than N, who is paired with Y). So we choose O, and with O a second student, not X but Z. So the largest possible committee without M consists of K, N, O, Y, and Z, or five members.

Logical Reasoning

QUESTION STEMS

Logical reasoning questions ask you to analyze the structure of a statement or a verbal argument and to evaluate that structure. The arguments are fairly brief, usually no more than a single paragraph. The question stem will tell you what to do with the argument—for example, attack it, defend it, or describe it. You will select an answer choice in accordance with the instruction given in the stem.

The first step in attacking a logical reasoning item is to preview the problem. Take five to ten seconds to glance at the paragraph you are to analyze and at the question to see what is required.

 Read the question stem before thoroughly reading the paragraph.

The question stem will direct your reading. It will tell you what to look for; for example, an attack on the argument, a defense of the argument, or a description of the argument.

 (Circle) or jot down any thought-reversers in the question stem.

Thought-reversers are words such as *not, except,* and *but*. These words reverse the structure of the question. What would ordinarily be the correct answer choice, in the context of a thought-reverser, will be an incorrect choice; what ordinarily would have been an incorrect answer will be the correct choice in the context of the thought-reverser. While thought-reversers are ordinarily emphasized by the test writer in capitalization or italics, physically highlighting the word is a safety device.

Pay careful attention to any additional information provided by the question stem.

Some question stems include interpretive information, for example:

> The author criticizes the government's policies in which of the following ways?

The stem itself tells you that the structure of the argument is a critical analysis of government policies. Other stems alert the reader to possible misunderstandings:

> The author uses irony to make which of the following points?

The question stem informs us that the author is not to be taken literally, since the argument employs irony. Finally, the question stem will often instruct you to assume that factual assertions contained in the answer choices are in fact true.

Example:

Any truthful auto mechanic will tell you that your standard 5,000-mile checkup can detect only one-fifth of the problems that are likely to occur with your car. Therefore, such a checkup is virtually worthless and a waste of time and money.

Which of the following statements, if true, would weaken the above conclusion?

  I. Those problems which the 5,000-mile checkup will detect are the ten leading causes of major engine failure.
  II. For a new car, a 5,000-mile checkup is required to protect the owner's warranty.
  III. During a 5,000-mile checkup the mechanic also performs routine maintenance which is necessary to the proper functioning of the car.

(A) I only
(B) II only
(C) I and II only
(D) II and III only
(E) I, II, and III

Here you must be careful not to take issue with any of these statements in Roman numerals; you must answer the question by applying each statement to the initial argument as though it were proved conclusively to be true. With this in mind, the correct answer is **(E)**. The conclusion of the speaker is that the checkup has *no* value, so anything which suggests the checkup does have value will undermine the conclusion. Statement I shows a possible advantage of having the checkup. It says, in effect, while the checkup is not foolproof and will not catch everything, it does catch some fairly important things. Statement II also gives us a possible reason for visiting a mechanic for a 5000-mile checkup. Even if it won't keep your car in running order, it is necessary if you want to take advantage of your warranty. Finally, Statement III also gives us a good reason to have a checkup: The mechanic will make some routine adjustments. All three of these propositions, then, mention possible advantages of having a checkup. So all three weaken the author's conclusion that the checkup is *worthless* and a waste of money and time.

CAREFUL READING

You must read the initial paragraph more carefully than you read a textbook, a novel, a newspaper, a magazine, or other similar material.

Consider the kind of advertising you see every day:

Advertisement for Sugarless Chewing Gum K
Four out of five dentists surveyed recommend
sugarless gum for their patients who chew gum.

Does the advertisement claim that four out of five dentists recommend chewing gum K? Does the advertisement claim that four out of five dentists recommend sugarless gum? Does the advertisement claim that four out of five dentists recommend sugarless gum for their patients who already chew gum? The answer is "no" to each question. As for the first, the fact that a dentist endorses sugarless gum does not necessarily mean that the dentist endorses a particular brand of chewing gum. As for the second question, that a dentist recommends sugarless gum in general for patients who already chew gum does not amount to a general recommendation that patients chew gum. After all, the dentists in question may be firmly opposed to gum chewing but qualify that opposition by saying, "Well, if a patient of mine were going to chew gum in spite of my advice to the contrary, then I would urge that patient to chew sugarless gum." As for the third question, the advertisement does not even claim that four out of five dentists in general would endorse the qualified position just described. The advertisement said that four of five dentists *surveyed* gave this response. How many dentists were surveyed? Or again, how many times did the company conduct different surveys before it obtained the results it needed? The advertisement is consistent with the possibility that the company ran dozens of surveys of groups of five dentists before it got the result it required.

Consider another example:

Advertisement for Motor Oil L
No motor oil protects your car's engine better
than motor oil L. These other motor oils (showing pictures
of L's competitors) would like to make this claim.

Does the advertisement claim that motor oil L provides the best protection for your car's engine that you can obtain from a motor oil? Does it claim that L is better than all of the oils considered?

The answer to the first question is "yes," and this can be best understood in light of the fact that the answer to the second question is "no." The advertisement does not claim that L is any better than the others. There is a big difference between the following statements:

No other brand is better than L.
L is better than the other brands.

The first statement asserts only that L is second to none, and this is consistent with several brands, including L, all providing the same level of protection. The second statement asserts that L is better, but this is not the claim made in the advertisement as structured. This means, however, that L is claiming it provides the "best protection" available—even though the other motor oils may equally well provide the same quality, and therefore, the "best protection."

What about the second statement that L's competitors would also like to claim that they provide the best protection available? L company is probably correct in asserting that its competitors would like to make such a claim. Moreover, L's competitors are probably entitled to make such a claim, given the analysis of the claim above. So long as a competitor has a product that is not inferior to that sold by L, it too is entitled to make the claim that "No motor oil provides superior protection." L's competitors are probably sorry that they did not come up with the advertising claim first.

Recently we saw a placard in a bank window advertising the bank's IRA plan. The placard claimed, "Nine out of ten people cannot afford to retire." That seems to underscore the urgency for private retirement plans, until you realize that the claim is true because nine out of ten people are not yet of retirement age. It would not be surprising to learn that the 50 percent or so of the population under the age of 25 are not in a financial position to retire.

Finally, the following advertisement was used by a tax preparation firm during last year's tax preparation season:

Tax Preparation by M
Three out of four clients surveyed stated that they believed M
obtained larger refunds on their tax returns than they
would have had they prepared their returns themselves.

The implication intended is that the reader should purchase M's services in order to obtain a lager refund, but the evidence of the claim, when read carefully, does not provide very strong support for that conclusion. Even setting aside the ambiguity concealed behind the "three out of four clients surveyed," the fact that these people *believe* something does not prove that it is true.

ANALYZING LOGICAL ARGUMENTS

An argument consists of a conclusion, evidence for that conclusion, and an inference, that is, the connection between the evidence and the conclusion.

When we think of logical reasoning, we often think of "pure" logical arguments or constructions such as:

(1) All persons are mortal.
(2) Socrates is a person.
(3) Therefore, Socrates is mortal.

In this simple argument, (3) is the conclusion and (1) and (2) are the evidence for the conclusion. We also refer to (1) and (2) as the premises or the assumptions of the argument. The third element of the argument is the connection between the evidence or assumptions and the conclusion. This connection is often called an inference. The inference, however, is not found in writing. Rather, the inference is the "logic" of the argument, that is, the movement of thought from the evidence to the conclusion. In this case, we can see that the conclusion definitely follows from the premises or evidence strictly as a matter of the meanings of the terms.

Few of the arguments we use in our daily lives have such a simple and tidy structure. When we reason about real life concerns, we generally offer complex arguments in which there are arguments within arguments where the conclusions of subarguments function as evidence for the larger conclusions. Rarely does the evidence of the argument provide conclusive proof of the point we wish to make. Consider the following:

> Libertarians argue that laws making suicide a criminal act are both foolish and an unwarranted intrusion on individual conscience. With regard to the first, they point out that there is no penalty which the law can assess which inflicts greater injury than the crime itself. As for the second, they argue that it is no business of the state to prevent suicide, for whether it is right for a person to inflict fatal injury on himself as opposed to others is a matter between him and his God—one in which the state should not interfere. Such arguments, however, are ill-conceived.
>
> In the first place, the libertarian makes the mistaken assumption that the only goal of the law is deterrence. I maintain, however, that the laws we have proscribing suicide are not designed to deter but to educate us all to the value of human life. By making it a crime to take a life—even one's own—we make a public announcement of our shared conviction that each person is unique and valuable.
>
> In the second place, I do not concede that suicide is a crime without victims, and here I need not have recourse to the argument that a potential suicide might have later regretted the decision. Suicide does have victims, for it inflicts a cost upon us all: the emotional cost on those close to the suicide; an economic cost in the form of the loss of productive capacity of a mature and trained member of a society, a cost which we all bear since we share the cost of education and other benefits of production of each other; and a cost to humanity at large for the loss of a member of our human community.
>
> The fundamental difficulty with the libertarian position is that it assesses the implications of suicide only from the perspective of the individual, but our public laws are not structured to implement the vision of an individual. Rather, they are enacted to further the general welfare.

This argument is more representative of the arguments we make in real life. It is considerably more complex than the simple argument presented previously, and the conclusion does not follow from the evidence with the same degree of certainty. Still, the argument can be understood to have a logical structure:

(1) I. The libertarian position is that laws against suicide are wrong.
(2)   A. They are futile since no penalty is sufficient to deter a suicide.
(3)   B. They are illegitimate since suicide is a private matter.

(4) II. Point I-A is incorrect.

(5)   A. The libertarian assumes that the only function of the law is deterrence.

(6)   B. The function of laws against suicide is not deterrence but education.

(7) III. Point I-B is incorrect.

(8)   A. Suicide inflicts an emotional cost on others.

(9)   B. Suicide inflicts an economic cost on others.

(10)   C. Suicide inflicts a human cost on others.

(11) Therefore, the libertarian position is incorrect, and laws against suicides are legitimate because they protect the public.

This is a logical reconstruction of the argument; however, this is not the only way of interpreting the argument. Since the argument is fairly complex, and, in some instances ambiguous, the reconstruction may seem somewhat arbitrary. Still, it is a fairly reliable picture of the logic of the argument against the libertarian position on suicide.

First, note that the outline of the logical structure of the argument follows roughly, though not precisely, the order of presentation in the argument. We say roughly, though not precisely, because the logic of an argument is not dependent on the order in which the statements are presented. For example, we have positioned the overall conclusion of the argument last in our outline (statement 11), but that conclusion is also mentioned in the first paragraph. Nothing, however, turns on where we put the conclusion in our outline.

Second, the conclusion is supported by evidence, specifically, the three Roman-numeraled statements are evidence for the conclusion; that is, they are premises of the argument. Third, you should also see that each Roman-numeraled part of the argument is, in itself, a small argument: Statements 2 and 3 are the evidence for statement 1; statements 5 and 6 are the evidence for statement 4; and statements 8, 9, and 10 are evidence for statement 7.

Another way of rendering the logical structure of the argument is:

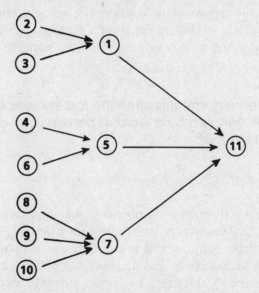

The diagram shows how the numbered statements function to support the conclusion. The arrows in the diagram are the inferences or connections between evidence and conclusions. For example, statements 8, 9, and 10 are the evidence for statement 7. The inference or connection there is a generalization: statement 7 is proven by the examples provided in statements 8, 9, and 10.

We are not recommending that you try to diagram arguments on the GRE in this fashion. Few, if any, GRE arguments are this complex, and many problems are very brief, consisting perhaps of only a single sentence. Additionally, you simply will not have time. Instead, we have introduced the diagrams to make you aware that any argument but the most simple should be analyzed into these parts: conclusion, evidence, and inference. To help you in the analysis, we recommend that you proceed in the following way:

 To analyze an argument: (1) locate the conclusion; (2) carefully define the claim made; (3) study the evidence offered and evaluate the strength of the inference.

Step 1

You begin by locating the conclusion, because you cannot begin to look for fallacies or other weaknesses in a line of reasoning or even find the line of reasoning until you have clearly identified the point the author wishes to prove. Any attempt to skip over this important step can only result in misunderstanding and confusion. We have all had the experience of discussing a point for some length of time only to say finally, "Oh, now I see what you were saying, and I agree with you." Of course, sometimes such misunderstandings are the fault of the speaker, who perhaps did not clearly state his position in the first place. This is particularly true in less formal discourse, such as conversation, where we have not carefully prepared our remarks before the discussion begins; but it can also occur in writing, though in the case of writing, the proponent of a claim generally has the opportunity to consider his words carefully and is therefore, one would hope, less likely to misstate his point. Often, however, the misunderstanding cannot be charged to the speaker or writer, and the blame must be placed on the listener or the reader.

 The conclusion of an argument is often the last sentence of the paragraph and may be signaled by a word or phrase such as *therefore, hence, so,* or *it follows that.*

This is the easiest of all cases. Consider an example:

> A new restaurant will open soon on the corner of Bleecker Street and Seventh Avenue, and the owners have applied for a license to operate a sidewalk cafe. Pedestrian traffic on that corner is heavy, particularly on Friday and Saturday nights. Moreover, that stretch of sidewalk is narrow due to the angle of intersection. A sidewalk cafe would seriously obstruct pedestrian traffic, causing inconvenience and even creating a safety hazard as pedestrians divert into the street. Therefore, the application should be rejected.

Here there is little or no problem identifying the conclusion of the argument—the application should be rejected. It is contained-in the final sentence of the paragraph and is clearly signaled by the transitional word "therefore."

The conclusion of an argument may be the first sentence of the paragraph.

One technique of good writing is to construct a paragraph so that the first sentence is a topic sentence. This alerts the reader to the point of the paragraph. But it hardly makes sense to introduce the very first sentence of a passage with the transitional word or phrase. After all, nothing preceded the opening sentence to require a transition. So when the conclusion is the first sentence of the argument, it is not likely to be adorned with any special signal. Rather, you must rely on the later development of the paragraph to help you recognize that the first sentence is the conclusion of the argument.

Find the conclusion of an argument by asking, "What is the author trying to prove?"

When the conclusion of the argument is not definitely signaled by an appropriate word or phrase, you may be in doubt as to what it is that the author hopes to prove. Here, you may need to examine each statement in the text and ask whether this is the ultimate point of the paragraph, or whether it serves only to support some other point. By the process of elimination, you should be able to locate the conclusion or main point of the paragraph. Consider an example:

> We must have a tax increase in this city. Right now, we are facing a dramatic rise in violent crime, and we need additional funds in order to hire more police officers.

The conclusion is contained in the first sentence, but how do we know that? We must ask, "What is the author trying to prove?" Is the author trying to *prove* that we are facing a dramatic rise in violent crime? No, because that statement is introduced only to prove something else, to wit, that we need money in order to hire more police officers. Perhaps that is the main point of the argument? Again, the answer is no. The author uses the statement that we need more money to prove something else, namely, that we must have a tax increase. Is that the conclusion of the argument? Yes. There is nothing else remaining in the argument that the author might be trying to prove.

Occasionally you will find GRE questions in which the initial paragraph or argument does not contain a conclusion; rather, the question stem directs you to draw the appropriate conclusion. In such situations, you obviously cannot begin your analysis by finding the conclusion, but this type of problem is a special case that we will handle when we discuss common types of questions.

Step 2

Once the main point of the argument has been isolated, it is necessary to take the second step of defining that point exactly. In particular, you must be attentive to any qualifications of the claim included by the author. Specifically, you may find it helpful to ask three questions: (1) How great (or how limited) a claim is the author making? (2) Precisely what is the author talking about? (3) What is the author's intention in making the claim?

Notice the ways in which the claim of the argument is delimited.

Authors frequently delimit their claims by using words such as *some, all, none, never, always, everywhere, usually, sometimes,* and *probably.* Thus, there is a big difference between the claims:

> *All* mammals live on land.
> *Most* mammals live on land.

The first is false, the second is true. Compare also:

> Women in the United States have *always* had the right to vote.
> *Since 1920*, women in the United States have had the right to vote.

Again, the first statement is false and the second is true. Finally, compare:

> It is raining and the temperature is predicted to drop below 32°F, therefore it will *surely* snow.
> It is raining and the temperature is predicted to drop below 32°F, therefore it will *probably* snow.

The first is a much less cautious claim than the second, and if it failed to snow the first claim would have been proved false, though not the second. The second statement claims only that it is probable that snow will follow, not that it definitely will. So someone could make the second claim and defend it when the snow failed to materialize by saying, "Well, I allowed for that in my original statement."

Notice the ways in which the claim is structured by the choice of descriptive words and phrases.

It is simply impossible to give an exhaustive list of the ways in which arguments might be delimited by descriptive words and phrases, but some examples will put you on the track:

> In nations which have a bicameral legislature, the speed with which legislation is passed is largely a function of the strength of executive leadership.

Notice here that the author makes a claim about "nations," so (at least without further information to license such an extension) it would be wrong to apply the author's reasoning to *states* (such as New York) which also have bicameral legislatures. Further, we would not want to conclude that the author believes that bicameral legislatures pass different laws from those passed by unicameral legislatures. The author mentions only the "speed" with which the laws are passed—not their content. Let us take another example:

All of the passenger automobiles manufactured by Detroit auto makers since 1975 have been equipped with seat belts.

We would not want to conclude from this statement that all *trucks* have also been equipped with seat belts since the author makes a claim only about "passenger automobiles," nor would we want to conclude that *imported cars* have seat belts, for the author mentions Detroit-made cars only. Finally, here is yet another example in which the descriptive terms in the claim are intended to restrict the claim:

No other major department store offers you a low price and a seventy-five-day warranty on parts and labor on this special edition of the XL-30 color television.

The tone of the ad is designed to create a very large impression on the hearer, but the precise claim made is fairly limited. First, the ad's claim is specifically restricted to a comparison of *department* stores, and *major* department stores at that. It is possible that some non-major department store offers a similar warranty and price; also it may be that another type of retail store, say an electronics store, makes a similar offer. Second, other stores, department or otherwise, may offer a better deal on the product, say a low price with a three-month warranty, and still the claim would stand—so long as no one else offered exactly a "seventy-five-day" warranty. Finally, the ad is restricted to a "special edition" of the television, so depending on what that means, the ad may be even more restrictive in its claim.

Try to determine the author's intention in making the claim.

Here we are not suggesting that you should try to read the mind of the author. Rather, we are urging you to be careful to distinguish between claims of fact and proposals of change. Do not assume that if an author claims to have found a problem, he also knows how to solve it. An author can make a claim about the cause of some event without believing that the event can be prevented or even that it ought to be prevented. For example, from the argument:

Since the fifth ward vote is crucial to Gordon's campaign, if Gordon fails to win over the ward leaders he will be defeated in the election.

you cannot conclude that the author believes Gordon should or should not be elected. The author gives only a factual analysis without endorsing or condemning either possible outcome. Also, from the argument:

Each year the rotation of Earth slows a few tenths of a second. In several million years, it will have stopped altogether, and life as we know it will no longer be able to survive on Earth.

you cannot conclude that the author wants to find a solution for the slowing of Earth's rotation. For all we know, the author thinks that the process is inevitable, or even desirable.

Some arguments do make a concrete recommendation; for example the argument against granting a license for a sidewalk cafe, introduced on page 106. There the author is not content to describe a problem, but intends to offer a very specific recommendation.

Step 3

Once you have located and precisely formulated the conclusion of an argument, you will probably need to go further and judge whether the evidence provided supports the conclusion as posed:

Be alert for the possibility that the conclusion rests upon an unstated premise.

Consider the following line of reasoning:

This animal has eight legs.
Therefore, this animal is a spider.

The conclusion is readily identifiable and easily understood, but does the evidence provide complete support for the conclusion? No. The conclusion follows from the evidence or single premise only on the assumption that spiders are the only animals with eight legs:

Only spiders have eight legs.
This animal has eight legs.
Therefore, this animal is a spider.

Now the conclusion does follow logically from the evidence, but the argument as originally presented contained an unstated premise.

There is nothing unusual in this. Most of the arguments we make are incomplete in one way or another. You might say, for example, to a dinner guest, "Pamela is not at her office, so she is on her way home." That is a form of reasoning that qualifies as an argument:

Pamela is not at her office.
Therefore, she is on her way home.

But the conclusion requires something else:

Either Pamela is at her office or on her way home.
Pamela is not at her office.
Therefore, she is on her way home.

Supported in this way, the argument is logically valid.

This is not to say, however, that the conclusion is *true* as a matter of fact. We say only that *if* our premises are true, then the conclusion must also be true, and one way to attack the argument is to object to one or the other, or even both premises; for example: "Perhaps some emergency required Pamela to leave the office for some destination other than home." This rebuttal objects that the unstated premise is open to question.

The unstated premise in the simple argument just discussed is easy to spot, but there will be times when you must look more carefully:

Example:

The notion of justice is not universally shared by all people. The tribespeople of Central Amaranda have no word for justice. The closest approximation to our word *justice* is *payyup*, a word that denotes the obligation to return that which has been borrowed. *Payyup* has only this limited meaning, and the language contains no other word to correspond to *justice*.

The author's conclusion rests on which of the following unstated premises?

(A) The tribespeople of Central Amaranda have no written language.
(B) A concept cannot exist unless there is a single word in a language to denote that concept.
(C) The language of the tribespeople of Central Amaranda is the only language without a word for justice.
(D) Although the notion of justice is not universally shared by all people, other values are universally shared.
(E) There are no other concepts for which the language of Central Amaranda lacks translational equivalents to the English language.

The first sentence of the argument contains the conclusion, and the evidence provided can be summarized by saying that the language studied has no single word for the concept of justice. Thus the argument would have the structure:

> The language has no single word for the concept of justice.
> Therefore, these people have no concept of justice.

Having rendered the argument in this way, we can see that something is indeed missing: A concept can exist only if denoted by a single word in a language. Thus, the unstated premise outlined in (B) is needed for the conclusion to follow, and none of the other choices provides a statement that will help draw the conclusion from the explicitly stated evidence.

One of the most interesting things about unstated premises is that they often conceal grave weaknesses in an argument. The argument just studied is open to attack on the ground that the unstated premise is incorrect; that is, a concept may exist even though no single word names it. Perhaps it is named by a cluster of terms of phrases.

An unstated premise is not the only way in which evidence of a conclusion might be deficient. Consider the following:

Example:

The harmful effects of marijuana and other drugs have been considerably overstated. Although parents and teachers have expressed much concern over the dangers which widespread usage of marijuana and other drugs pose for high school and junior high school students, a national survey of 5,000 students of ages 13 to 17 showed that fewer than 15 percent of those students thought such drug use was likely to be harmful.

Which of the following is the strongest criticism of the author's reasoning?

(A) The opinions of students in the age group surveyed are likely to vary with age.

(B) Alcohol use among students of ages 13 to 17 is on the rise, and is now considered by many to present greater dangers than marijuana usage.

(C) Marijuana and other drugs may be harmful to users even though the users are not themselves aware of the danger.

(D) A distinction must be drawn between victimless crimes and crimes in which an innocent person is likely to be involved.

(E) The fact that a student does not think a drug is harmful does not necessarily mean he will use it.

If you want to determine whether or not drug use is harmful to high school students, you surely would not conduct a survey of the students themselves. This is why (**C**) is correct. That a student does not *think* a drug is harmful does not mean that it is *not* actually harmful.

COMMON ARGUMENT FORMS

In the argument just analyzed, the evidence provides little, if any, support. We might call all such arguments *non sequiturs*, meaning that the conclusion does not follow from the evidence. It is useful, however, to identify certain argument forms that appear with a measure of frequency on the GRE: analogies, causal explanations, induction, circular arguments, and arguments containing ambiguities.

Arguments Based On Analogies

Some diplomats are assigned to countries where the political conditions are unstable and the risk of violent harm greater. Just as the government provides combat premiums as part of the pay to soldiers in war zones, so too the government should provide some sort of combat pay to diplomats working in politically unstable regions.

The argument relies on an analogy between diplomats and soldiers, and the comparison seems to have some merit. Of course, the analogy is not perfect—no analogy can be more than just that, an analogy. But some analogies are clearly so imperfect that they have no persuasive force. For example:

People should have to be licensed before they are allowed to have children. After all, we require people who operate automobiles to be licensed.

In this case, the two situations—driving and having children—are fairly dissimilar, and the argument seems to be very weak.

When analyzing an argument based on an analogy, focus on the most important dissimilarity between the situations or phenomena being compared.

Arguments Based on Causal Explanations

These questions ask that you evaluate the strength of an argument of the following sort:

> A recent survey by the Department of Labor revealed that increases in the salaries of ministers are accompanied by increases in the average consumption of rum. From 1975 to 1980, salaries of ministers increased on the average by 15 percent and rum sales grew by 14.5 percent. From 1970 to 1975, the average salary for ministers rose by only 8 percent, and rum sales grew by only 8 percent. This demonstrates that higher salaries for ministers cause an increase in the consumption of rum.

The causal connection asserted by the argument is very doubtful. Although the statistics may be accurate, there is probably some other causal explanation: Increases in ministers' salaries are the result of general economic conditions, and these general economic conditions also have an effect on the sale of liquor. So rather than increased rum consumption being caused by increased clergy salaries, both are effects of some third cause.

 When analyzing an argument that advances a causal explanation for some phenomenon, anticipate the existence of alternative causal linkages.

Arguments Based on Induction

 When evaluating an argument using induction (generalization or projection), seek to determine whether the sample is sufficiently representative to justify the conclusion.

An argument from induction uses generalization (basing a conclusion on a sample or examples):

> Every time I have visited the museum it has been mobbed with people. Therefore, the museum must always be filled with people.

or projection (predicting the future based on past events):

> Every time I have fished in the pond I have caught a large fish. Therefore, tomorrow when I fish in the pond, I will catch a large fish.

In each of these arguments, the conclusion is based on induction, that is, the use of samples of experience to support a broader conclusion about the world. And in each argument, the strength of the conclusion depends upon the representativeness of the sample of experience. As for the first, if the speaker has visited the museum only once or twice and then only at peak visiting times (Sunday afternoon), then the conclusion is fairly weak; but if he has visited the museum many times at various hours, then the conclusion is much stronger. As for the second, if the speaker has fished in the pond only once or twice, then her projection seems fairly weak. On the other hand, if she has fished in the pond often under a variety of circumstances, then the conclusion gains strength—provided, that is, that conditions have not changed, for example, the pond has been polluted or fished out.

Arguments Based on Circular Reasoning

 A circular argument (begging the question) is an argument in which the conclusion to be proved appears as one of the premises of the argument.

Let's look at an example:

> Beethoven was the greatest composer of all time. He wrote the greatest music of any composer, and he who composes the greatest music must be considered the greatest composer.

The argument hopes to prove the conclusion (stated in the first sentence) that Beethoven is the greatest of composers, but it can do this only by offering as evidence that Beethoven wrote the greatest music and that this qualifies him to be the greatest composer. For this reason, the argument is called "circular." A circular argument is logically defective, and there is really no way to strengthen it (except to offer an entirely new argument). So a GRE question based on a circular argument would most likely be one that asked you to recognize the deficiency in the attempted line of reasoning.

Arguments Containing Ambiguities

 An argument that uses a term in two different senses commits the fallacy of ambiguity.

An example of such an argument is:

> Man is only one million years old.
> John is a man.
> Therefore John is only one million years old.

The error of the argument is that it uses the word *man* in two different ways. In the first sentence, *man* refers to humanity, the group. In the second sentence, *man* refers to the individual, John. Consider another example:

Sin occurs only when man fails to follow the will of God. But since God is all-powerful, what He wills must actually be. Therefore, it is impossible to deviate from the will of God, so there can be no sin in the world.

The equivocation here involves the word *will*. The first time it is used, the author intends to say that the will of God is God's wish and implies that deviation from God's wish is possible. In the second instance, the author uses the word *will* in the way that implies that such deviation is not possible (God's will equals fact). The seemingly persuasive appeal of the argument depends upon this equivocation. Once you recognize that a key term of the argument is used in an ambiguous way, you see that the argument is fallacious.

A question based on an argument that commits this fallacy would probably ask only that you identify the offending term.

THE ANSWER CHOICES

Most test-takers make the mistake of assuming that once they have analyzed the argument, selecting an answer choice is pretty much pro forma. This assumption is naive.

Read the answer choices carefully.

A typical logical reasoning item will use as many words in the answer choices as in the initial argument, and the answer choices may be very similar in their wordings, requiring careful discrimination. (You may want to glance back at some of the questions we have studied to prove this to yourself.)

One of the most common errors of careless reading is the attempt to force an otherwise correct analysis of the problem to fit a wrong choice. Consider the following question:

> The idea that women should be police officers is absurd. After all, women are on the average three to five inches shorter than men and weigh 20 to 50 pounds less. It should be clear that a woman would be less effective than a man in those situations requiring the use of force to apprehend suspects.
>
> Which of the following, if true, would most weaken the argument?

The argument is open to attack along several lines. One obvious and quite promising attack would be to point out that the average size of a group says nothing about the size of any particular member of the group, that is, it would be wrong to disqualify all members of a group on size just because some members of the group might not qualify on size. It is quite possible that there would be female applicants equal in size to male applicants who would be accepted. Anticipating this attack as a possible choice, we might find:

> (A) Some of the female applicants are equal in size to male applicants whose applications were rejected.

With only a hurried reading, you might be prompted to select this answer. It does contain phrasing suggestive of the weakness noted previously; but when taken in its entirety, the choice really does not make the objection we anticipated. We wanted to object that some women might be equal in size to men who would be accepted—not to men who would be rejected.

Read all of the answer choices before making a final selection.

As you become familiar with logical reasoning items, you will begin to sense that there are identifiable patterns to the right and wrong choices. This is good, but do not become too rigid. Remember that the correct answer choice is correct only in context. A relatively weak attack on an argument, for example, might very well be the best answer, depending on the company it keeps. Suppose we add the following choice:

> (B) Police officers carry pistols and are given instruction in how to use them if necessary.

This is at least a partial answer to the initial argument. It says, in essence, that a firearm is a great equalizer. Still, it is not as powerful an attack as the one we anticipated. There may be situations requiring the use of force in which it is inadvisable or impossible to use a firearm. Yet, this choice could turn out to be the right answer if no better attack on the argument appears in the array of answer choices.

Discard unacceptable answer choices: the three out of five rule.

Consider yet another choice:

> (C) Some male applicants for the police force are rejected because they fail the written test even though their size is acceptable.

This is fairly clearly no attack on the argument at all. Many students report to us that in situations in which they are able to understand and analyze the initial argument three of five choices appear almost surely incorrect, while two of the choices have some plausibility. This varies somewhat, as students occasionally report they perceive only two obviously incorrect choices, while three choices have some plausibility. You should not be afraid to discard the three (or two) implausible choices. (Be prepared, however, to reconsider them if none of the remaining choices satisfies you.)

Contrast the remaining choices, articulating to yourself the difference between them, eliminating all but the best response.

Let us add two choices to our problem:

> (D) Some positions on the police force, such as public relations and desk jobs, never require the use of force.

> (E) Some of the female applicants for the police force are larger than many of the male officers presently on active police duty.

Answer (E) corresponds to the attack we anticipated above. Still, (D) does make an attempt to weaken the argument. On balance, however, (D) fails to come to grips with the logical error we first described. For that reason, (E) constitutes a better choice and would be regarded as the best of the five presented.

We stress that to be *best* does not mean to be *perfect*. You may be disappointed that your favorite line of attack does not appear as a choice or that the test writer did not phrase the attack in the way you expected. Still, you are forced to select the best available response.

COMMON TYPES OF LOGICAL REASONING QUESTIONS

We have already discussed the general skills needed for solving logical reasoning items, but there are some question types that deserve special comment.

Attack and Defense of Arguments

The correct answer to a question stem asking you to weaken or strengthen an argument is often a rebuttal of or a defense of an unstated premise.

See the discussion of unstated premises above.

Identification of Argument Forms

Some logical reasoning questions ask only that you identify or describe the form of the argument. The instructions for this section make it quite clear, however, that you do not need a specialized vocabulary. You would not, for example, be asked to specify that an argument commits the *post hoc, ergo propter hoc* fallacy, but you would be required to recognize that an argument is defective because it rests upon an incorrect causal explanation.

When responding to a form identification question, select the answer choice that most describes the form of the argument.

Because there are many different ways of presenting arguments and even more ways of describing them, this must be applied on a case-by-case basis. The following list is included to illustrate the answer choices that might be available to you:

Argues from Analogy

As we have seen, an argument from analogy introduces more or less similar situations. Then, a conclusion taken to apply to one situation is carried over to the other situation on the ground of the similarity between the two situations.

Generalizes

Again, as we have seen, a generalization is a broad conclusion based upon a sample of experience.

Uses Examples to Illustrate a Thesis

This form of argument is similar to generalization but can be distinguished in the way examples are used.

Compare argument 1, which generalizes, with argument 2, which illustrates a thesis:

1. Roosevelt, Truman, and Johnson, all Democrats, each got the U.S. involved in a war. Therefore, a characteristic of all Democratic presidents is that they involve our country in wars.

2. Because Republicans are overly concerned about business, they tend to control inflation by slowing the economy. This is exactly what happened during the administrations of Eisenhower, Nixon, and Reagan.

Ignoring the fact that the arguments are so overly simple as to be very weak, we can see the difference in form. The second argument offers an explanatory thesis illustrated by three examples. In the first argument, there is nothing but the generalization.

Suggests a New Causal Explanation

In the discussion of causal arguments, we noted that a powerful attack on such an argument is to find an alternative explanation for the event. Such an attack might be described as suggesting a new or alternative explanation.

Introduces a New Hypothesis

This description is somewhat broader than that just preceding. It might apply to a causal hypothesis, but it could also apply to the following:

The existence of natural evil, earthquakes, etc., creates serious difficulties for the theist. It is sometimes argued that natural evil proves that God is not entirely benevolent. Otherwise, He would not have introduced evil into the world. I suggest, however, that this is incorrect. God is omni-benevolent, but the existence of evil proves there is a force against which God is not entirely effective. Therefore, although God is omni-benevolent, he is not all powerful.

Introduces New Evidence

An argument of this type will introduce new evidence, say examples or statistics, to support a previously introduced theory:

General Smith believes that the enemy will attempt a sea invasion on the eastern front early next year, while General Jones thinks that they will try a land attack on the western front. Intelligence reports indicate increased hiring of skilled workers such as welders in the town of Gratz, where there is a large naval shipyard. This strongly indicates that General Smith is correct.

Uses a Key Term in an Ambiguous Manner

We have already studied arguments that are defective because they commit the fallacy of ambiguity.

Seeks to Question the Use of or to Redefine the Meaning of a Key Term

This description could apply to an objection to an argument committing the fallacy of ambiguity:

> Some theists argue that God introduced natural evil into the world in order that we might strengthen our immortal souls by facing adversity. Evil, however, exists only where there is a maleficent will, and since natural evil is the result of impersonal forces, it is not the product of evil intent. Therefore, natural evil is no evil at all.

Circular Argument

This, too, we have studied previously. Such arguments can also be described as tautologies, or as true by definition.

> Whiskey is a healthful elixir. If you are now 30 years of age and drink a glass of whiskey for breakfast every day for the next 25 years, you will live to be 55 years old.

The assertion is circular or tautologous. Since it is true that 30 plus 25 is equal to 55, doing anything for an additional 25 years will result in living to the age of 55.

Questions an Unstated Premise

We have discussed the importance of unstated premises. An argument that responds to a position by attacking an unstated premise of that position might be described in this way.

Draws a Conclusion Based on Opponent's Failure to Prove a Point

> Since Dr. Epstein's archaeological expedition failed to find any remains of prehistoric people in the region, we must conclude that the region was not inhabited during prehistoric times.

The weakness of the argument is that it takes the failure of proof of one proposition as proof for the opposite of that proposition. The failure of the expedition might be attributable to any number of reasons. So the failure to find evidence that the area was inhabited is not conclusive proof that the area was not inhabited.

Attempts to Discredit the Source of the Argument

> Professor Williams insists that the new drug will be useful in reducing inflammation in the joints caused by arthritis. That is unlikely. It is a well-known fact that Professor Williams interrupted his studies for a year to help campaign for the Communist party candidate for the state senate.

Such an attempt to discredit the source is obviously weak. A person's political views ordinarily have no direct relationship to his ability to see scientific truth.

Appeals to Authority

> The best treatment for a sore lower back is mild heat and bed rest. This is recommended by Dr. Farmer, who has treated over a thousand such cases.

The technique here is to appeal to an authority, Dr. Farmer, for support for the conclusion. The strength of such an appeal will depend on the nature of the authority. For example, is the authority truly an authority in the area? Does the authority have special knowledge that would make the conclusion more acceptable?

Appeals to the Emotions of the Listener

> In the upcoming election, cast your vote for the incumbent, Senator Jones, a person who believes in liberty, freedom, and the traditional moral values that made this nation great.

The semantic content of the argument is virtually nonexistent, but the statements contain strong emotional overtones. The appeal is to emotion rather than to reason.

Main Idea Questions

Main idea reading comprehension questions ask about the most important theme in a reading selection. Logical reasoning may also contain such questions. The reading selections are shorter in this section, but the task is similar:

 For a main idea question, select the answer choice that is most comprehensive without going beyond the passage.

Example:

The debate over economic policy during the past 40 years has focused on the role of competition. The socialists argue that competition is destructive. They rail against oppressive capitalism, giant corporations, and exorbitant profits, but they actually attack the lack of competition, not competition itself. It is only in those sectors where there is such a concentration of economic power that competition is impossible that exploitation is possible.

The author is making which of the following points?

(A) A capitalist economy allowing for competition is economically more efficient than a socialist economy.
(B) The evils of excessive concentrations of economic power should not be blamed on economic competition.
(C) A planned economy suffers from some of the same economic ills that afflict a free enterprise economy.
(D) The government should have a vigorous antitrust policy to ensure that excessive concentrations of corporate power cannot develop.
(E) Only in a completely competitive economy can economic efficiency be combined with political liberty.

The best choice is **(B)**. Notice that the author is making a fairly limited point: Economic oppression comes from concentration, not competition. (A) goes beyond the passage, for the author makes no mention of a socialist *economy*. (C) can be eliminated on the same ground. (A) and (C) are incorrect for the further reason that no comparison of a planned to a free enterprise economy is made. (D) goes far beyond the content of the passage by making a concrete recommendation of sweeping scope. Finally, (E) also exceeds the scope of the selection by introducing the idea of political liberty.

Further Inference Questions

Some logical reasoning questions test your ability to draw further conclusions from evidence presented. You may be asked to infer a further conclusion from a single statement:

If you are asked to draw a further conclusion from a single statement, look for an answer choice that is an exact restatement of the content of the initial statement.

Example:

If a student has not taken at least one semester of a foreign language, he cannot graduate.

Which of the following can be logically inferred from the statement above?

(A) If a student has taken at least one semester of a foreign language, he will graduate.
(B) If a student does not graduate, it is because he has not taken at least one semester of a foreign language.
(C) No student who has taken at least one semester of a foreign language can graduate.
(D) All students who have taken at least one semester of a foreign language are eligible for graduation.
(E) Only students who have taken at least one semester of a foreign language are eligible for graduation.

(E) is nothing more than a restatement of the content of the initial sentence. (A) is incorrect, for failing to meet the foreign language requirement may prevent a student from graduating, but the sentence does not say that meeting the requirement is, in and of itself, sufficient to qualify the student for graduation. (D) makes essentially the same assertion as (A), so it too is incorrect. (B) is incorrect since the failure to take a foreign language may not be the only reason for failing to graduate. Finally, (C) directly contradicts the initial statement.

Other questions of this type may provide evidence and ask you to find the most reliable conclusion that can be drawn from the evidence.

When asked to draw a further conclusion from evidence, prefer a choice that is limited. Avoid choices that go beyond the content of the selection.

Example:

Efficiency experts will attempt to improve the productivity of an office by analyzing production procedures into discrete work tasks. They then study the organization of those tasks and advise managers of techniques to speed production, such as rescheduling of employee breaks or relocating various equipment such as the copying machines. I have found a way to accomplish increases in efficiency with much less to do. Office workers grow increasingly productive as the temperature drops, so long as it does not fall below 68°F.

The passage leads most naturally to which of the following conclusions?

(A) Some efficiency gains will be short-term only.
(B) To maintain peak efficiency an office manager must occasionally restructure office tasks.
(C) Employees are most efficient when the temperature is 68°F.
(D) The temperature-efficiency formula is applicable to all kinds of work.
(E) Office workers will be equally efficient at 67°F and 68°F.

The best answer is **(C)**. The conclusion of the paragraph is so obvious that it is almost difficult to find. The author says office workers work better the cooler the temperature—provided the temperature does not drop below 68°. Therefore, we can conclude, the temperature at which workers will be most efficient will be precisely 68°. Notice that the author does not say what happens once the temperature drops below 68° except that workers are no longer as efficient. For all we know, efficiency may drop off slowly or quickly compared with improvements in efficiency as the temperature drops to 68°. So (E) goes beyond the information supplied in the passage. (D) also goes far beyond the scope of the the author's claim. His formula is specifically applicable to *office* workers. We have no reason to believe the author would extend his formula to nonoffice workers. (B) is probably not a conclusion the author would endorse since he claims to have found a way of achieving improvements in efficiency in a different and seemingly permanent way. Finally, (A) is not a conclusion the author seems likely to reach since nothing indicates that his formula yields only short-term gains which last as long as the temperature is kept constant. To be sure, the gains will not be repeatable, but then they will not be short-run either.

Logic Replication Questions

Some questions ask that you demonstrate your understanding of an argument by showing that you are able to find another argument that has a similar structure:

To answer a logic replication question, find the answer choice that best parallels the logical structure of the original argument.

Example:

The American buffalo is disappearing. This animal is an American buffalo. Therefore, this animal is disappearing.

The reasoning contained in the example above is most similar to that contained in which of the following?

(A) I am my nephew's favorite aunt, and I know this must be true since my nephew told me this; and no nephew would fib to his favorite aunt.

(B) Whales are an endangered species; all endangered species must be protected; therefore, whales must be protected.

(C) Wealthy people pay most of the taxes; this man is wealthy; therefore, this man pays most of the taxes.

(D) Caroline drove from Easton to New Meadows, a distance of 160 miles, in exactly four hours; therefore, Caroline averaged 40 miles per hour for the trip.

(E) An apple is a fruit; a pear is a fruit; therefore an apple is a pear.

The best answer is **(C)**. The error in the original argument is the attribution of a group characteristic (the buffalo as a group) to an individual member of the group (an individual animal is disappearing).

When analyzing the argument that is the basis for the logical replication, attempt to describe the structure of the argument in general terms, specifying any weakness or fallacy in the argument.

This Test Buster will help you avoid some of the incorrect choices. Once we have specified the nature of the fallacy in the argument, we are not tempted to pick (A). To be sure, (A) commits a fallacy, but that is the fallacy of circular reasoning.

Do not confuse content with structure, and even regard with disfavor an answer choice treating content similar to that of the original argument.

This Test Buster eliminates answer (B). The argument in (B) is not at all similar to the original argument, for (B) is a perfectly valid line of reasoning. Yet some test-takers will select (B) because of the similarity of content, since both arguments treat the notion of an endangered species. We can eliminate (D) also on the ground that it contains a valid, not an invalid, argument. If Caroline drove 160 miles in exactly four hours, then she did average 40 miles per hour. Notice that the conclusion does not assert that Caroline drove at exactly 40 miles per hour at all times during the trip, only that she averaged 40 miles per hour for the entire trip.

Represent the logical structure of an argument schematically.

Answer (E) is surely the second most tempting answer, and it is related to the original argument in that it too commits a fallacy of ambiguity. If we represent the arguments schematically, using capital letters to represent terms we will see that (C) is a better parallel of the original argument than (E). The original argument has a structure:

All B and D.	(All Buffalo are Disappearing.)
I is a B.	(This Individual is a Buffalo.)
Therefore, I is D.	(This Individual is Disappearing.)

choice (C) is schematized:

All W are T.	(All Wealthy people are people who pay the most Taxes.)
I is W.	(This Individual is a Wealthy person.)
Therefore, I is T.	(This Individual is a person who pays the most Taxes.)

but (E) is schematized:

All A are F.	(All Apples are Fruits.)
All P are F.	(All Pears are Fruits.)
Therefore, all A are P.	(All Apples are Pears.)

The distribution of the terms within the arguments show you that (E) is not similar to the original:

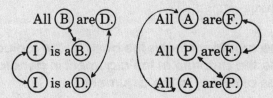

The New, Experimental Question Types

A recent *GRE Information & Registration Bulletin* lists two new analytical question types: Analysis of Explanations and Pattern Identification. The *Bulletin*'s "Sample Questions" section includes examples of both new types, along with examples of all the other question types that have appeared on the GRE for years. However, as of this writing, the two new types are still "experimental"; that is, the test-makers are still testing them to make sure that they fit the specifications of the test. For this reason, *as of this writing* the two types appear in the non-scored "Mystery Section" of the test. However, if you encounter these types of questions on *your* GRE, do not assume that you are necessarily in the "Mystery Section." You do not want to take a chance that the section will not be scored. It may instead turn out to be one of the "live" sections that will determine your score.

Even though "Analysis of Explanations" and "Pattern Identification" are still in the experimental stage, you may feel more comfortable with these new types if you have seen some examples of each and have learned some tips for answering them. Keep in mind, however, that the following discussion is based on the very limited information that has been made available thus far and also that the test writers have apparently not settled upon a final format for either type.

ANALYSIS OF EXPLANATIONS

"Analysis of Explanations" questions are designed to test your ability to generate and to evaluate causal explanations for phenomena. (The ability to formulate and to examine causal explanations is obviously a very large part of graduate study in many fields.) In "Analysis of Explanations," items are presented in sets. A set consists of a "Situation," a "Result," and "Statements" that provide additional information about the "Situation." You must classify the statements according to the type of information provided. The answer scheme for classifying the statements has not yet been settled, but here is a sample of an "Analysis of Explanations" problem set that reflects the current stage of development.

Example:

Situation: Over the past ten years, the population of Allen County has more than doubled. This increase in population has led to overcrowding at Peabody School. As a result, at the beginning of the most recent school year, 15 grammar school, 20 middle school, and 25 high school students were reassigned to Warren School, which has a larger building. Warren has seven more teachers than Peabody, but the average number of years of experience of the teachers is approximately equal for the two school systems. Both systems administer standardized achievement tests to all students at the end of each school year.

Result: At the end of the school year following the reassignment, scores achieved on the year-end achievement tests by Warren students were approximately 8 percent higher than those of the previous year.

Directions: Below you will find a series of statements which you are to assume are true. Answer A if the statement is relevant to some possible explanation of the result described above. Answer B if the statement is not relevant to some possible explanation of the result described above. In assessing the relationship of the assumed facts to the situation and the result, you should not consider explanations that are extremely unlikely or that require assumptions contrary to common sense.

1. A new computerized learning lab opened by Warren School at the beginning of the school year helped to improve the verbal and math skills of Warren students.

2. Most of the students reassigned to Warren School live as close to the Warren School as to the Peabody School.

3. All of the students who had been reassigned from Peabody School achieved scores on the year-end tests that were below the average of all students in the Warren School.

4. The dramatic growth in the population of Allen County can be explained by a rapid increase in the number of employers in the area that use advanced technologies.

Answers

1. (A) This Statement provides a possible explanation for the result: the computerized learning lab helped to boost scores.

2. (B) In order to make this Statement a part of an explanation for the Result, you would have to engage in wild speculation. And while it is not impossible to construct such an explanation, the directions for this type specifically caution against looking for possibilities that are farfetched.

3. (A) This Statement rules out a possible explanation for the Result: it is not the case that the transfer students scored very high and pulled up the Warren average. You will notice that this Statement provides "negative" information; that is, it eliminates a possible explanation. It is nonetheless *relevant* because it does cast some light on the relationship between the Result and the background situation.

4. (B) This Statement is irrelevant: events that occurred ten years earlier cannot possibly explain the Result identified.

Read the statements carefully.

A Statement that seems to be relevant may actually be irrelevant because it refers only to part of the background information given in the situation and not to any of the "active" factors.

Example:

5. During the school year following the reassignment of the students, Peabody School implemented an after-school tutoring service in order to raise student scores on the year-end achievement tests.

The correct answer is (B) because the statement is not relevant. Something that transpired at *Peabody* cannot explain what happened at *Warren*. To be sure, had this Statement specified *Warren*, it would have been relevant (in much the same way that Statement 2, above, is relevant). You can see that if you are not reading carefully, you may not make the distinction between Peabody and Warren and so get a wrong answer.

"Ancient History" is irrelevant.

The initial descriptive paragraph will likely include some information about past events that helped to create a present situation. Information about past events is likely to be "ancient history."

Example:

> **6.** The Allen County School Board chose to transfer students from Peabody to Warren rather than to expand classrooms at Warren because expansion was deemed too expensive.

The correct answer is (B). In this case, the explanation for the decision to transfer the students from Peabody to Warren is "ancient history" and cannot help to explain the increase in test scores at Warren. (Compare Statement 6 with Statement 4, above.)

Negative information can be relevant.

Statements providing additional information that *weakens* a possible explanation for the Result should be considered relevant.

Example:

> **7.** Except for the addition of the students reassigned from Peabody, the composition of the student body at Warren was substantially the same as the previous year.

The correct answer is (A). The facts established by this Statement tend to undermine a possible explanation for the Result: the increase in test scores was not due to a radical change in the makeup of the school's student body.

Let statements suggest explanations.

After reading the description of the Situation and the Result, you may immediately think of two or three possible explanations for the Result. But given the elliptical description of the Situation (in which some information is missing), there may be several more possible explanations that will not occur to you. So when you read a Statement, be open to the possibility that it suggests an explanation that did not occur to you.

Example:

> **8.** The teachers who administered the year-end achievement tests to the Warren students failed to follow proper testing procedures, so grades were higher than they should have been.

The correct answer is (A). This is a possible explanation for the Result that will probably not occur to most people. Yet, it clearly explains why the grades were higher than expected.

Do not engage in wild speculation.

Imagination knows no bounds! It is always possible to speculate about some causal chain that would connect one event with another.

Example:

   9. The principal at Warren resigned during the middle of the year.

The correct answer is (B). Now it is possible to speculate how this *might help* to explain the Result: the principal was not very effective; a new principal was hired who turned out to be very effective; because the new principal was very effective, the scores of students increased. But isn't the opposite equally as likely? Say that the old principal was very effective and the new principal was ineffective, yet the scores rose in spite of the change in principal. The fact that two equally plausible but contradictory conclusions can be drawn using Statement 9 is strong evidence that Statement 9 is not relevant.

   Although the answer scheme for Analysis of Explanations questions has not yet been finalized, the question type is similar to an experimental question type called "Weight of Evidence" that was unsuccessfully tested in the late 1970s for use on the Law School Admission Test (LSAT). Weight of Evidence questions also included an incomplete description of a factual situation with a conclusion about the situation followed by statements asserting facts assumed to be true. The statements were to be classified according to the following scheme:

   Mark answer:

   (A) if the additional information clearly proves the conclusion;
   (B) if the additional information tends to prove but does not clearly prove the conclusion;
   (C) if the additional information clearly disproves the conclusion;
   (D) if the additional information tends to disprove but does not clearly disprove the conclusion;
   (E) if the additional information makes the conclusion neither more nor less likely.

It would not be surprising to see the GRE test developers move toward a similar scheme for Analysis of Explanations, and if they do, the following Test Buster should prove useful.

When in doubt, choose the weaker category.

   The categories in the five-fold answer scheme can be ranked according to their explanatory power:

Powerful	(A) clearly proves and (C) clearly disproves
Less Powerful	(B) tends to prove and (D) tends to disprove
Least Powerful	(E) irrelevant

(A) and (C) are labeled "powerful" because they dispose of the conclusion one way or the other. (B) and (D) are labeled "less powerful" because they affect the conclusion but do not dispose of it. Finally, (E) is labeled "least powerful" because it does not affect the conclusion at all.

For the five-category answer scheme to work, the additional information provided in the Statements must *clearly* fall into one of the five categories. If there can be reasonable argument about whether a Statement should be classified as (A) versus (B) or (C) versus (D), then the item is defective. Similarly, if there can be reasonable argument about whether a Statement should be classified as (B) versus (E) or (D) versus (E), then the item is defective. In order for the answer scheme to work, Statements must not be ambiguous. Thus, if you are wavering between (A) and (B) or between (C) and (D), you probably aren't sure that the Statement completely disposes of the conclusion. In that case, enter (B) or (D) depending on whether you think that the Statement tends to prove or tends to disprove the conclusion. And if you are wavering between (B) and (E) or between (D) and (E), you are probably struggling to make a case for the relevance of the Statement. In that case, enter (E).

As noted, for this type of answer scheme to work, the additional information provided by the Statements must *clearly* fall into one category; but the more clearly the additional information is presented, the more obvious is the correct answer choice. In other words, the better the question type works as a matter of logic, the less effective it is as a testing device because the items become too easy. It is arguable that this was one of the defects of the Weight of Evidence question type on the LSAT, and it will be interesting to see whether Analysis of Explanations can avoid the problem.

PATTERN IDENTIFICATION

The second new type of question, Pattern Identification, is essentially a numbers puzzle. Each question consists of a series of numbers in which every number after the first is derived from the preceding number according to one or another mathematical formula. The task is to identify the formula or formulas that create the series. For example, if the first number in the series is 2 and the formula is "add 3 to the previous number," then the series is:

$$2 \ldots 5 \ldots 8 \ldots 11 \ldots 14$$

Or if the first number is 3 and the formula is "multiply the previous number by 2," then the series is:

$$3 \ldots 6 \ldots 12 \ldots 24 \ldots 48$$

As presently structured, Pattern Identification uses ten different operations:

Add 1	Subtract 1		
Add 2	Subtract 2	Multiply by 2	Divide by 2
Add 3	Subtract 3	Multiply by 3	Divide by 3

It is possible that a formula will combine two operations, *e.g.,* "subtract 1, then multiply by 3." (If a formula combines two operations, at least one of them must be either multiplication or division.)

Your task is to classify each series according to the following answer scheme:

Pattern A: number R number R number R number R number
Pattern B: number R number R number R number S number
Pattern C: number R number R number S number S number
Pattern D: number R number S number S number R number
Pattern E: number R number S number R number S number

Where R and S represent different mathematical formulas. For example, the series:

4 . . . 3 . . . 7 . . . 6 . . . 13

fits pattern E. For this series, R represents "subtract 1" and S represents "multiply by 2 and add 1":

4 R 3   S   7   R 6   S   13

$4 - 1 = 3$ $(3 \times 2) + 1 = 7$ $7 - 1 = 6$ $(6 \times 2) + 1 = 13$

(Although the second number can also be derived by the formulas "$(4 \div 2) + 1$" or "$(4 - 3) \times 3$", neither of those formulas will produce the fourth number.)

Example:

Operations				*Answer Choices*	
+1	−1			(A)	R R R R
+2	−2	×2	÷2	(B)	R R R S
+3	−3	×3	÷3	(C)	R R S S
				(D)	R R S R
				(E)	R S R S

1. 5 . . . 3 . . . 7 . . . 5 . . . 11

This is an example of Pattern E, where R is SUBTRACT 2 and S is MULTIPLY BY 2, THEN ADD 1. So the correct answer is **(E)**.

2. 4 . . . 6 . . . 8 . . . 4 . . . 2

This is an example of Pattern C, where R is ADD 2 and S is DIVIDE BY 2. So the correct answer is **(C)**.

3. 1 . . . 3 . . . 7 . . . 15 . . . 31

This is an example of Pattern A, where R is MULTIPLY BY 2, THEN ADD 1. So the correct answer is **(A)**.

Theoretically, 74 different formulas are available:
Ten single operations:

$m + 1$	$m + 2$	$m + 3$
$m - 1$	$m - 2$	$m - 3$
	$m \times 2$	$m \times 3$
	$m \div 2$	$m \div 2$

Forty-eight operations combining either addition or subtraction with either multiplication or division:

$$(m + 1) \times 2 \qquad (m + 2) \times 2 \qquad (m + 3) \times 2$$
$$(m + 1) \times 3 \qquad (m + 2) \times 3 \qquad (m + 3) \times 3$$
$$(m - 1) \times 2 \qquad (m - 2) \times 2 \qquad (m - 3) \times 2$$
$$(m - 1) \times 3 \qquad (m - 2) \times 3 \qquad (m - 3) \times 3$$

$$(m \times 2) + 1 \qquad (m \times 2) + 2 \qquad (m \times 2) + 3$$
$$(m \times 3) + 1 \qquad (m \times 3) + 2 \qquad (m \times 3) + 3$$
$$(m \times 2) - 1 \qquad (m \times 2) - 2 \qquad (m \times 2) - 3$$
$$(m \times 3) - 1 \qquad (m \times 3) - 2 \qquad (m \times 3) - 3$$

$$(m + 1) \div 2 \qquad (m + 2) \div 2 \qquad (m + 3) \div 2$$
$$(m + 1) \div 3 \qquad (m + 2) \div 3 \qquad (m + 3) \div 3$$
$$(m - 1) \div 2 \qquad (m - 2) \div 2 \qquad (m - 3) \div 2$$
$$(m - 1) \div 3 \qquad (m - 2) \div 3 \qquad (m - 3) \div 3$$

$$(m \div 2) + 1 \qquad (m \div 2) + 2 \qquad (m \div 2) + 3$$
$$(m \div 3) + 1 \qquad (m \div 3) + 2 \qquad (m \div 3) + 3$$
$$(m \div 2) - 1 \qquad (m \div 2) - 2 \qquad (m \div 2) - 3$$
$$(m \div 3) - 1 \qquad (m \div 3) - 2 \qquad (m \div 3) - 3$$

Another four using multiplication twice:

$$(m \times 2) \times 2 \qquad (m \times 3) \times 2$$
$$(m \times 3) \times 2 \qquad (m \times 3) \times 3$$

Another four using division twice:

$$(m \div 2) \div 2 \qquad (m \div 3) \div 2$$
$$(m \div 2) \div 3 \qquad (m \div 3) \div 3$$

And another eight using both multiplication and division:

$$(m \times 2) \div 2 \qquad (m \times 3) \div 2$$
$$(m \times 2) \div 3 \qquad (m \times 3) \div 3$$
$$(m \div 2) \times 2 \qquad (m \div 3) \times 2$$
$$(m \div 2) \times 3 \qquad (m \div 3) \times 3$$

Some formulas, however, produce the same results as others.

Examples:

ADD 1, THEN MULTIPLY BY 2 = MULTIPLY BY 2, THEN ADD 2
$$(m + 1) \times 2 = (m \times 2) + 2$$

DIVIDE BY 2, THEN DIVIDE BY 3 = DIVIDE BY 3, THEN DIVIDE BY 2
$$(m \div 2) \div 3 = (m \div 3) \div 2$$

Still, there are 60 different formulas.

The situation is further complicated because a single pair of numbers might fit more than one formula.

Examples:

m . . . n	*Possible Formulas*
2 . . . 4	ADD 2 MULTIPLY BY 2 MULTIPLY BY 3, THEN SUBTRACT 2
6 . . . 4	SUBTRACT 2 DIVIDE BY 2, THEN ADD 1 DIVIDE BY 3, THEN ADD 2

The task, then, is to devise an attack strategy that finds pairs of numbers that are joined by a unique formula.

Look first for a pair of numbers such that |*m*| – |*n*| is the greatest.

In this case, *m* is the first number in the pair and *n* is the second. This suggestion is based on the fact that larger differences are less likely to fit more than one formula.

Example:

m . . . n	*Unique Formula*
4 . . . 13	MULTIPLY BY 3, THEN ADD 1
12 . . . 23	MULTIPLY BY 2, THEN SUBTRACT 1
15 . . . 3	DIVIDE BY 3, THEN SUBTRACT 2

The larger the DIFFERENCE between the two numbers in the series, the less likely it is that difference can be explained by more than one formula.

Look for the largest number *m* such that *m* > *n*.

When the second number in a pair is smaller than the first number, try to define the relationship between those numbers in terms of subtraction, division, or both.

Example:

m . . . n	*Unique Formula*
10 . . . 2	DIVIDE BY 2, THEN SUBTRACT 3
21 . . . 6	DIVIDE BY 3, THEN SUBTRACT 1

Look for a pair of large numbers.

If a pair of large numbers are fairly close in value, then they cannot be linked by multiplication or division. And since a formula that combines more than one operation must include either multiplication or division, the formula connecting those two large numbers must use just addition or subtraction.

Example:

m . . . n	*Unique Formula*
33 . . . 35	ADD 2
12 . . . 11	SUBTRACT 1

Take advantage of the patterns listed as answer choices.

You do not have to create an answer pattern from scratch. Instead, your job is simply to identify which one of the five listed patterns fits the series—a much easier job. In fact, if you can identify a single pair that are connected by a unique formula (such as those pairs discussed above), you have all the information that you need to reach an answer.

Example:

2 . . . 6 . . . 14 . . . 5 . . . 12

The pair of numbers that show the greatest *difference* is 14, 5. The only formula that will generate 5 from the value 14 is DIVIDE BY 2, THEN SUBTRACT 2. That formula, however, does not fit the other pairs in the series: 2, 6; 6, 14; 4, 12. So even though we have not identified the formula that accounts for the other pairs, we know that the pattern is R R S R, or choice (D).

Note: A question type of this sort, with its extremely complex answer scheme, will very probably cause difficulties not just for the test-takers but also for the creators of the GRE. Therefore, it is highly unlikely that this particular question type will survive the experimental stage.

TEST BUSTERS FOR MATH QUESTIONS

Note: The math sections of the GRE test arithmetic, basic algebra, and elementary geometry—all material usually covered in high school courses. On page 163, you will find the start of a comprehensive review of these topics.

Don't automatically assume you need to spend hours in a lengthy review. Start by reading the Test Busters for math and refer to the math review only when you need a refresher on some point.

If, after a few pages, you find you really do need to review basic math before tackling the Test Busters, then do the comprehensive math review first.

Problem Solving

Each math section of the GRE normally contains ten problem-solving items divided into two groups of five. These are usually numbered 16 through 20 and 26 through 30 and are separated by a graph with five questions.

In order to attack this question kind, we can divide problem-solving items into three groups: manipulation problems, practical word problems, and geometry problems.

Manipulation problems, as the name implies, test your knowledge of arithmetic or algebraic manipulations.

Example:

$0.2 \times 0.005 =$

(A) 0.0001
(B) 0.001
(C) 0.01
(D) 0.1
(E) 1.0

The correct answer is **(B)**. The item tests whether or not you remember how to keep track of the decimal point in multiplication. Other manipulation problems involve algebra:

Example:

If $x + 5 = 8$, then $2x - 1 =$

(A) 25
(B) 12

(C) 5
(D) 4
(E) 0

The correct answer is (C). Since $x + 5 = 8$, $x = 3$. Then substitute 3 for x in the expression $2x - 1$: $2(3) - 1 = 5$.

Practical word problems go beyond simple manipulations. They require that you use your knowledge of manipulations in practical situations.

Example:

Joe works two part-time jobs. One week Joe worked 8 hours at one job, earning $150, and 4.5 hours at the other job, earning $90. What were his average hourly earnings for the week?

(A) $8.00
(B) $9.60
(C) $16.00
(D) $19.20
(E) $32.00

The correct choice is (D). To find Joe's average hourly earnings, we divide the total earnings by the number of hours worked:

$$\frac{\text{Earnings}}{\text{Hours}} = \frac{\$150 + \$90}{8 + 4.5} = \frac{\$240}{12.5} = \$19.20$$

Geometry problems involve the use of basic principles of geometry.

Example:

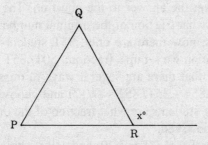

In the figure above, PQ = QR = PR. What is the value of x?

(A) 30
(B) 45
(C) 60
(D) 90
(E) 120

The correct answer is (E). This is an equilateral triangle (one having three equal sides), and equilateral triangles also have three equal angles, each 60 degrees. Then PR, as extended, forms a straight line. So $x + 60 = 180$, and $x = 120$.

Some of the problems you will encounter will be fairly simple, others will be more complex—particularly practical word problems and more difficult geometry problems. The more complex the question, the easier it is to misread and set off down a wrong track.

Read the questions very carefully.

The importance of this point is illustrated by the following very difficult, practical word problem.

Example:

The people eating in a certain cafeteria are either faculty members or students, and the number of faculty members is 15 percent of the total number of people in the cafeteria. After some of the students leave, the total number of persons remaining in the cafeteria is 50 percent of the original total. The number of students who left is what fractional part of the original number of students?

(A) $\frac{17}{20}$ (B) $\frac{10}{17}$ (C) $\frac{1}{2}$

(D) $\frac{1}{4}$ (E) $\frac{7}{20}$

The correct answer is **(B)**. Let T be the total number of people originally in the cafeteria. Faculty account for 15 percent of T, or .15T, and students account for the remaining 85 percent of T, or .85T. Then some students leave, reducing the total number of people in the cafeteria to half of what it was originally, or .5T. The number of faculty, however, does not change. So the difference between .5T and .15T must be students: .5T − .15T = .35T. But this is not yet the answer to the question. The question asks "The number of students who *left* is what fraction of the original number of students?" Originally there were .85T students; now there are only .35T students, so .50T students left. Now, to complete the solution we set up a fraction: .50T/.85T = 10/17.

By this point, you can appreciate that there are several ways to miss the question. Someone might just put .35T over .85T (.35T/.85T = 7/17) and choose (D). But this answers the question "The remaining students are what fraction of the original number of students?"—that is not the question asked.

Someone might also put .35T over T (.35T/T = 7/20) and select choice (E). But this too answers a different question: "The number of students who remain is what fractional part of the original number of people in the cafeteria?"

There are probably hundreds of other ways to miss the question, but it would be a shame to know how to answer the question and still miss it just because you did not read the question carefully.

A related error is answering in the wrong units.

Be sure to choose the answer that corresponds to the units specified in the question.

Example:

A certain copy machine produces 13 copies every 10 seconds. If the machine operates without interruption, how many copies will it produce in an hour?

(A) 78
(B) 468
(C) 1800
(D) 2,808
(E) 4,680

The correct answer is (**E**). The question stem gives information about copies per 10 seconds, but you must answer in terms of copies per hour. To solve the problem, first convert copies per 10 seconds to copies per minute. This can be done with a proportion:

$$\frac{13 \text{ copies}}{10 \text{ seconds}} = \frac{x \text{ copies}}{60 \text{ seconds}}$$

Solve by cross-multiplication: $13 \times 60 = 10x$
Solve for x: $x = 78$

The correct answer, however, is not 78. A machine that produces 78 copies per minute produces 60 times that in an hour: $60 \times 78 = 4,680$.

 If the question requires an answer to be expressed in certain units, draw a circle around that part of the question stem or jot down the units on your scratch paper.

 Take special note of any thought-reversers in the question stem.

A thought-reverser is any word such as *not, except,* or *but* which turns a question inside-out.

Example:

A survey of 100 persons revealed that 72 of them had eaten at restaurant P and that 52 of them had eaten at restaurant Q. Which of the following could *not* be the number of persons in the surveyed group who had eaten at both P and Q?

(A) 20
(B) 24
(C) 30
(D) 50
(E) 52

The correct answer is (**A**). Since there are only 100 people in the group, some of them must have eaten at both P and Q. The combined responses for P and Q equal 124, and 124 – 100 = 24. So 24 is the smallest possible number of people who could have eaten at both P and Q. (The largest possible number would be 52, which is possible if all of those who ate at Q had also eaten at P.) Thus far we have been concentrating on the question stem, but the answer choices also deserve special mention.

Answer choices to problem-solving items are generally arranged in a logical order.

Example:

Xxxx xxxxxxx xxxx xxxxxxxxxxxx xxxxxxx xxxxxxxxxx xxxx xxxxxxxxxxxx xxxx xxxxxxx xxxxxxxxxxx?

(A) 3,200
(B) 4,800
(C) 12,000
(D) 16,000
(E) 20,000

Notice that the choices in this dummy question are arranged from least to greatest. In other questions, choices are arranged from greatest to least. And in algebra questions, the choices are arranged logically according to powers and coefficients of variables.

Additionally, the wrong choices are not just picked at random. They are usually written to correspond to possible mistakes (misreadings, etc.). This actually helps you.

In a problem requiring some calculation, let the answer choices check your math.

To illustrate this technique, look at the dummy answers. Suppose that you worked a problem and your solution corresponded exactly to choice (B), 4800—not 3200 and not 12,000, nor anything else. In that case, you could be confident that your math was correct. To be sure, you might have a wrong answer because you set the solution up incorrectly, but there is no real possibility that you made a mistake in your number-pushing.

You can also turn this feature of the answer choices to your advantage in another way:

Eliminate any answer choice that cannot possibly be correct.

To illustrate this, here is an actual question to go with the dummy answers.

Example:

In a certain population, 40 percent of all people have biological characteristic X;

the others do not. If 8,000 people have characteristic X, how many people do not have X?

(A) 3200
(B) 4800
(C) 12,000
(D) 16,000
(E) 20,000

The correct choice is **(C)**. You can arrive at this conclusion by setting up a proportion:

$$\frac{\text{Percent with X}}{\text{Number with X}} = \frac{\text{Percent without X}}{\text{Number without X}}$$

Supplying the appropriate numbers:

$$\frac{40\%}{8000} = \frac{60\%}{x}$$

Cross-multiply: $.40x = .60(8000)$
Solve for x: $x = 12,000$

But you can avoid even this little bit of work. A little common sense, when applied to the answer choices, would have eliminated all but (C). In the first place, 40% of the people have X, so more people don't have X. If 8000 people have X, the correct choice has to be *greater than* 8000. This eliminates both (A) and (B). Next, we reason that if the correct answer were (D), 16,000, then only about 1/3 of the people would have X. But we know 40% have X. This allows us to eliminate (D) and also (E).

Manipulation Problems

Your approach to a manipulation problem depends upon the degree of difficulty of the manipulation.

For an easy arithmetic manipulation, perform the operation as indicated.

Example:

0.04 × 0.25 =

(A) 0.0001
(B) 0.001
(C) 0.01
(D) 0.1
(E) 1.0

The correct answer is **(C)**. The manipulation is very simple, so you should just do the indicated multiplication (keeping careful track of the decimal).

For a difficult arithmetic manipulation, look for a way to simplify, such as canceling, factoring, or approximating.

Example:

$$\frac{2}{3} \times \frac{3}{4} \times \frac{4}{5} \times \frac{5}{6} \times \frac{6}{7} \times \frac{7}{8} =$$

(A) $\frac{2}{33}$ (B) $\frac{1}{4}$ (C) $\frac{3}{8}$

(D) $\frac{1}{2}$ (E) $\frac{27}{33}$

The correct choice is **(B)**. Given enough time, you could work the problem out by multiplying all the numerators, multiplying all of the denominators, and then reducing. But the very fact that this would be time consuming should prompt you to look for an alternative. Try canceling:

$$\frac{2}{\cancel{3}} \times \frac{\cancel{3}}{\cancel{4}} \times \frac{\cancel{4}}{\cancel{5}} \times \frac{\cancel{5}}{\cancel{6}} \times \frac{\cancel{6}}{\cancel{7}} \times \frac{\cancel{7}}{8} = \frac{2}{8} = \frac{1}{4}$$

Example:

$$(27 \times 34) - (33 \times 27) =$$

(A) −1
(B) 1
(C) 27
(D) 33
(E) 918

The correct answer is **(C)**. Again, given the time, you could do the multiplication by hand; but that is not the point of the question. The question is included to see whether or not you understand that you can simplify matters considerably by factoring:

$$(27 \times 34) - (33 \times 27) = 27(34 - 33) = 27(1) = 27$$

Similarly, your approach to an algebraic manipulation will depend upon the manipulation to be performed.

If the manipulation consists of a single equation with just one variable, solve for the unknown.

Example:

If $3x - 5 = x + 11$, then $x =$

(A) 16
(B) 8

(C) 3
(D) 2
(E) 1

The correct answer is (B), and the appropriate method is to solve for x:

$$3x - 5 = x + 11$$

Combine terms: $\quad 2x = 16$

Solve for x: $\quad x = 8$

 If a manipulation includes two equations and two variables, solve by using the technique of simultaneous equations.

Example:

If $x + y = 8$ and $2x - y = 10$, then $x =$

(A) 16
(B) 8
(C) 6
(D) 4
(E) 2

The correct answer is (C), and the correct technique is to treat the two equations simultaneously. First, isolate y from the first equation:

$$x + y = 8$$

So: $\quad y = 8 - x$

Next, substitute $8 - x$ into the second equation in place of y:

$$2x - (8 - x) = 10$$

Combine terms: $\quad 3x = 18$

Solve for x: $\quad x = 6$

 For a question that asks you to find an answer choice that meets certain conditions, test each choice until you find the one that satisfies the conditions.

Example:

$5^3 \cdot 9 =$

(A) $5 \cdot 27$
(B) $15 \cdot 9$
(C) $15 \cdot 15 \cdot 5$
(D) $25 \cdot 27$
(E) $125 \cdot 27$

The correct choice is **(C)**, and you learn this by testing each choice to see which one is equivalent to $5^3 \cdot 9$. The expression $5^3 \cdot 9 = (5 \cdot 5 \cdot 5)(3 \cdot 3) = 15 \cdot 15 \cdot 5$.

PRACTICAL WORD PROBLEMS

Some practical word problems are fairly easy.

Example:

$2,000 is deposited into a savings account that earns interest at the rate of 10 percent per year, compounded semiannually. How much money will there be in the account at the end of one year?

(A) $2105
(B) $2200
(C) $2205
(D) $2400
(E) $2600

The best answer is **(C)**, and a simple calculation gets you the answer. First, calculate the interest earned on the first six months:

First Six Months

Principal	×	Rate	×	Time	=	Interest Earned
$2000	×	10%	×	0.5	=	$100

This $100 is then paid into the account. The new balance is $2100. Now you would calculate the interest earned during the second six months.

Second Six Months

Principal	×	Rate	×	Time	=	Interest Earned
$2100	×	10%	×	0.5	=	$105

This is then paid into the account. So the final balance is:

$$\$2100 + \$105 = \$2205$$

Other practical word problems are not so easy. For a difficult one, it will be necessary to break the solution into steps.

For a difficult manipulation problem, break down the solution process into steps. First, formulate a statement of what is needed; second, find the numbers you need; and third, perform the required arithmetic.

Example:

The enrollments at College X and College Y both grew by 8 percent from 1980 to 1985. If the enrollment at College X grew by 800 and the enrollment at College Y grew by 840, the enrollment at College Y was how much greater than the enroll-ment at College X in 1985?

(A) 400
(B) 460
(C) 500
(D) 540
(E) 580

The correct choice is **(D)**, but the solution is a good deal more involved than the one needed for the preceding problem, so take the solution step by step.

First, begin by isolating the simple question that must be answered:

> The enrollments at College X and College Y both grew by 8 percent from 1980 to 1985. If the enrollment at College X grew by 800 and the enroll-ment at College Y grew by 840, the enrollment at College Y was how much greater than the enrollment at College X in 1985?

This can be summarized as follows:

$$\text{College Y in 1985} - \text{College X in 1985}$$

So you know you must find the enrollments at both colleges in 1985. How can you do that? The numbers are there in the question, you just have to figure out how to use them. Take College Y first. You know that enrollments grew by 840 and that this repre-sents an increase of 8%. These numbers will allow you to find the enrollment in 1980:

$$8\% \text{ of 1980 Total} = 840$$
$$0.08 \times T = 840$$

Solve for T:
$$T = 10,500$$

This was the enrollment at College Y in 1980, but you need to know the enrollment at College Y in 1985. To do that, just add the increase:

$$1980 + \text{Increase} = 1985$$
$$10,500 + 840 = 11,340$$

Now do the same thing for College X:

$$8\% \text{ of 1980 Total} = 800$$
$$0.08 \times T = 800$$
$$T = 10,000$$
$$1980 + \text{Increase} = 1985$$
$$10,000 + 800 = 10,800$$

Now you have the numbers you were looking for. Substitute them back into your orig-inal solution statement:

$$\text{College Y in 1985} - \text{College X in 1985} = \text{Final Answer}$$
$$11,340 - 10,800 = 540$$

This is not the only way of reaching the correct solution, but it is the one most people would be likely to use. And it is very complex. A problem like this would be one of the last ones in a math section. It does illustrate nicely what you should do when you encounter a complex practical word problem.

Sometimes, however, you can avoid the necessity of going through the process above by using the answer choices.

Sometimes you can work backwards from the answer choices.

Example:

A car dealer gives a customer a 20 percent discount on the list price of a car, and he still realizes a net profit of 25 percent on his cost. If the dealer's cost is $4800, what is the usual list price of the car?

(A) $6000
(B) $6180
(C) $7200
(D) $7500
(E) $8001

You know that one of these five choices must be correct, so all you have to do is test each one until you find the correct one. Start with (C).

If the usual list price is $7200, what will be the actual selling price after the 20% discount?

Usual List Price	–	20% of Usual List Price	=	Final Selling Price
$7200	–	20% of $7200	=	Final Selling Price
$7200	–	$1440	=	$5760

On that assumption, the dealer's profit would be:

Final Selling Price	–	Cost	=	Profit
$5760	–	$4800	=	$960

Is that a profit of 25%?

$960/$4800 is less than 1/4 and so less than 25%. This proves that (C) is wrong.

Now you need to test another choice, logically either (B) or (D). But which one? Apply a little reasoning to the situation. Assuming a usual cost of $7200, the numbers worked out to a profit that was too small. Therefore, we need a larger price to generate a larger profit. So try (D).

$$\$7500 - (.20)(\$7500) = \$6000$$

If the final selling price is $6000, that means a profit for the dealer of $1200. And $1200/$4800 = 25%. So **(D)** must be the correct answer.

You might think this was a lucky guess. What if the answer choices had been arranged differently?

(A) $4000
(B) $6000
(C) $6180
(D) $7200
(E) $7500

In this case, you test (C) first and learn that it is incorrect. Then you go to (D) as above. Again, another wrong choice. Does this mean you have to do a third calculation? No! Since the choices are arranged in order, once you have eliminated (C) and (D), you *know* that (E) must be correct.

Some practical word problems give data in algebraic form rather than in number form, and then ask for an algebraic formula as an answer.

If the answer choices are algebraic formulas using unknowns from the question, substitute values to find the correct one.

Example:

At a certain printing plant, each of *m* machines prints 6 newspapers every *s* seconds. If all machines work together but independently without interruption, how many *minutes* will it take to print an entire run of 18,000 newspapers?

(A) $\dfrac{180s}{m}$ (B) $\dfrac{50s}{m}$ (C) ms

(D) $\dfrac{ms}{50}$ (E) $\dfrac{300m}{s}$

Since the information is given algebraically, the letters could stand for any numbers (so long as you don't divide by 0). Pick some values for *m* and *s* and see which answer choice works. For purpose of discussion, assume that the plant has 2 machines, so $m = 2$. Also assume that $s = 1$, that is, that each machine produces 6 newspapers each second. On this assumption, each machine prints 360 papers per minute; and with two such machines working, the plant capacity is 720 papers per minute. To find how long it will take the plant to do the work, divide 18,000 by 720.

$$18,000/720 = 25 \text{ minutes}$$

On the assumption that $m = 2$ and $s = 1$, the correct formula should produce the number 25. Test the choices:

(A) $\dfrac{180s}{m} = 180(1)/2$ is not equal to 25 (WRONG!)

(B) $\dfrac{50s}{m} = 50(1)/2$ is equal to 25 (CORRECT!)

(C) $50ms = 50(2)(1)$ is not equal to 25 (WRONG!)

(D) $\dfrac{ms}{50} = (2)(1)/50$ is not equal to 25 (WRONG!)

(E) $\dfrac{300m}{s} = 300(2)/(1)$ is not equal to 25 (WRONG!)

A similar technique can be used when no numbers or variables are supplied:

For questions with undefined quantities, assume arbitrary values.

Example:

If the value of a piece of property decreases by 10 percent while the tax rate on the property increases by 10 percent, what is the effect on the taxes?

(A) Taxes increase by 10 percent.
(B) Taxes increase by 1 percent.
(C) There is no change in taxes.
(D) Taxes decrease by 1 percent.
(E) Taxes decrease by 10 percent.

The correct answer is (**D**). Since no numbers are supplied you are free to supply your own. Assume the piece of property has a value of $1000, and assume further that the original tax rate is 10%. On the basis of those assumptions, the tax bill is originally 10% of $1000 or $100. Now make the specified adjustments. The value of the property drops by 10%, from $1000 to $900, but the tax rate goes up by 10%, from 10% to 11%. The new tax bill is 11% of $900, or $99. The original tax bill was $100; the new tax bill is $99; the net result is a decrease of $1 out of $100, or a 1% decrease.

GEOMETRY PROBLEMS

Geometry problems do require a knowledge of elementary geometry. You will need to know how to do things such as find the area of a triangle, a rectangle, and a circle. But this does not mean that you need to review the formal proofs that you had to go through when you first studied the subject. In fact, you probably remember what you need to know.

Trust your spatial intuition.

There is a difference between having an important piece of knowledge about geometry and being able to present a formal explanation of that knowledge.

Example:

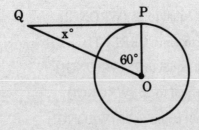

What is x?

(A) 15
(B) 30
(C) 45
(D) 60
(E) 90

The correct answer is (**B**). To solve the problem, you need to know that angle P is a right angle. Then you have a triangle with angles of 60°, 90°, and $x°$. Since there are 180 degrees in a triangle, x must be 30.

You probably did realize that angle P must be a right angle—and not just by looking at it and seeing that it seems to be 90 degrees. Rather your mind's eye probably told you that for some reason or other, angle P had to be 90 degrees.

In fact, angle P must be 90 degrees. PQ is a tangent, and PO is a radius. A tangent intersects a radius at a 90-degree angle. But you do not need to know the "official" justification to answer correctly. Just trust your spatial intuition.

Most geometry problems involve figures that are made up of two or more simple figures.

In a figure composed of two or more simple figures, a feature of one figure can be redefined as a feature of another figure.

Example:

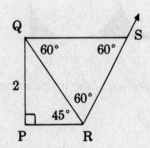

In the figure above, what is the perimeter of triangle QRS?

(A) 12
(B) 6 $\sqrt{2}$
(C) 6
(D) 3 $\sqrt{2}$
(E) 2 $\sqrt{3}$

The correct answer is (**B**). The trick is to see that QR is not only a side of triangle PQR, but is also a side of triangle QRS. Further, QRS is an equilateral triangle, so if you can find the length of one side, you know the length of the other sides as well.

How can you find the length of QR? PQR is a 45°-45°-90° triangle. Since QP is 2,

PR is also 2. Now you know two legs of the right triangle, and you can use the Pythagorean Theorem to find the hypotenuse:

$$QP^2 + PR^2 = QR^2$$
So: $$2^2 + 2^2 = QR^2$$
$$4 + 4 = QR^2$$
$$QR^2 = 8$$
$$QR = \sqrt{8}$$
$$QR = 2\sqrt{2}$$

Each of the three sides of QRS is equal to $2\sqrt{2}$, so the perimeter of QRS = 3 times $2\sqrt{2} = 6\sqrt{2}$.

Another common kind of geometry problem is the shaded area problem.

If a geometry question asks for the area of an irregular figure, the shaded area can be regarded as the difference between the areas of two common, regular figures.

Example:

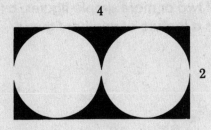

What is the area of the shaded portion of the figure above?

(A) $8 - 8\pi$
(B) $8 - 4\pi$
(C) $8 - 2\pi$
(D) $8 - \pi$
(E) π

The correct answer is (C). The shaded area is what's left over if you take the area of the two circles away from the area of the rectangle:

Rectangle minus Two Circles = Shaded Area

First, the area of the rectangle is just $2 \times 4 = 8$. Then, the diameter of the circles is equal to the width of the rectangle. So the diameter of the circles is 2, and the radius is 1. The formula for the area of a circle is πr^2, so each circle has an area of $\pi(1^2) = \pi$. Now we know the area of the shaded part of the diagram:

$$8 \text{ minus } 2(\pi) = 8 - 2\pi$$

BONUS SECTION
THE GRE SUBJECT TESTS
AND
FINANCING YOUR GRADUATE EDUCATION

Contents

The GRE Subject Tests

The GRE Subject Tests supplement the GRE General Test. Where the General Test operates as an aptitude test, the Subject Tests are achievement tests. A student's performance on a GRE Subject Test indicates his or her mastery of the content, skills, and processes of an undergraduate major field of study. As a standardized measure, scores and percentile rankings on the Subject Tests allow for comparison of students from different institutions and of students who have opted for very different undergraduate courses. The subscores, included within many of the exams, highlight special strengths and point out weaknesses and gaps.

Each GRE Subject Test is carefully tailored to its subject matter. Each is unique in length, format, and question style. However, the exams do have many features in common. While the number of questions ranges from 66 questions on the Mathematics test to 230 questions on the Literature in English test, testing time is a uniform 2 hours and 50 minutes. No test is administered in separately timed parts. This means that each student may set his or her own pace, working through the entire exam according to his or her own style. On all exams, each question is of equal weight. No question is any more important than any other question. All questions are multiple-choice, foiled from A to E. All carry a guessing correction. This means that one-fourth of a point is deducted for each wrong answer. This procedure eliminates any advantage that may be gained by random guessing; however, an educated guess raises the odds in the test-taker's favor and is certainly worthwhile.

The GRE Subject Tests are offered in the afternoon of dates on which the GRE General Test is offered in the morning. Since the Subject Tests are tests of competency in the major, few students take more than one. However, if a student wishes to take more than one Subject Test, a second date must be selected for the second exam. GRE Subject Tests cover far more material than any undergraduate can hope to be familiar with. No one should expect to answer every question. While all the tests are scored on a theoretical scale of 200 to 990, scores at the extremes are seldom represented. Scaled scores on one test are not comparable to scaled scores on another test. The score on each test must be interpreted only with respect to other scores on that same test. Percentile rankings are more readily meaningful than are scaled scores.

The fifteen GRE Subject Tests are offered in:

Biology	Literature in English
Chemistry	Mathematics
Computer Science	Music
Economics	Physics
Education	Political Science
Engineering	Psychology
Geology	Sociology
History	

There are Arco preparation books for six of these subject areas: Biology, Chemistry, Computer Science, Engineering, Mathematics, and Psychology. Each of these books includes test-taking assistance geared to the specific exam and a number of full-length model exams with every answer fully explained.

The following pages include illustrative excerpts from the Arco books.

GRE Biology Test

The GRE Biology Test is a 210-question examination. Some of the questions are grouped in sets based on diagrams or on experimental results. Most of the questions follow the familiar format of question stem followed by five choices. Other questions follow an inverted format in which five answer choices precede a series of statements. To answer these questions, choose the lettered answer choice that is most applicable to the statement.

The questions are drawn in about equal proportion from the broad fields of cellular and subcellular biology, organismal biology, and population biology, encompassing both ecology and evolution. The field of biology is far too broad for any student to have had exposure to all topics during an undergraduate career. You are not expected to be able to answer every question. However, outside specific knowledge in the various fields, you should be able to demonstrate an understanding of ideas, processes, and relationships, and of basic scientific research, tools, and procedures. You should be able to evaluate and draw conclusions from laboratory results and be familiar with the historical development of biological knowledge and the interconnections among biological fields and between biology and the other sciences.

The sample questions that follow are representative of the examination questions in content and in style. The correct answers, explained, appear directly after the questions. In answering these sample questions, circle the letter of your answer choice. For the inverted format questions, write the letter of your answer beside the question number.

Sample Questions

1. Which of the following characteristics do *not* describe the giraffe?

    (A) more cervical vertebrae than in most other mammals
    (B) long front legs
    (C) multiple "stomachs"
    (D) high systolic blood pressure
    (E) inhabitant of the veldt, which has relatively few trees

2. Quantitatively, the major pathway for energy flow in terrestrial food chains involves

    (A) detritus consumed by detritus feeders
    (B) perennial plants consumed by herbivores
    (C) herbivores consumed by carnivores and omnivores
    (D) secondary consumers such as carnivores consumed by tertiary consumers
    (E) animals in general affected by parasites

3. It has been stated that a balanced sex ratio is a result of optimizing the Darwinian fitness of individuals, but that it is not optimal for a typical population. Which of the following is *least* supportive of this statement?

    (A) Females are less fecund than males.
    (B) If males are in the minority, each passes his genes to a greater proportion of offspring than does each female.

    (C) Most human societies prize male offspring over female.
    (D) Sperm are much smaller and "cheaper" to produce than are ova.
    (E) In several species the male perishes soon after mating, but this is not seen in females.

4. Most of the seminal work on viruses used

    (A) the smallpox virus
    (B) large bacteriophages
    (C) plant RNA viruses
    (D) small bacteriophages
    (E) human DNA viruses

5. Which is true of RNA viruses?

    (A) They require reverse transcriptase to replicate.
    (B) They are not prominent among plant viruses
    (C) If double-stranded, they replicate in a symmetrical, conservative fashion.
    (D) They are not pathogenic to man.
    (E) They do not infect bacteria.

6. The bends involves the formation of nitrogen bubbles in the blood. It is most likely to be found in

    (A) a mountain climber going from sea level to 33,000 feet (¼ atm)
    (B) a diver going from 100 feet below sea level (4 atm) to the surface

(C) an aviator descending quickly from 33,000 feet to sea level

(D) any two of the above

(E) A, B, and C

7. Which of the following participates in and lowers the activation energy of cellular reactions, but is the same at the beginning of the reactions as at the end?

(A) retinol (vitamin A)

(B) FAD (flavin adenine dinucleotide)

(C) glucose

(D) acid phosphatase

(E) transfer RNA

8. A graduate student reports transplanting a pituitary gland from a tadpole under the skin of a light-adapted tadpole, whose skin color was appropriately light. The student states that the recipient turned dark even though there was no change in environmental conditions. The best response to this news is:

(A) Was the donor tadpole light-adapted or dark-adapted?

(B) Perhaps the recipient was turning color not in response to the new pituitary, but to endogenous circadian rhythms.

(C) Of course. Melanophore-stimulating hormone is always produced unless it is inhibited by the hypothalamus.

(D) You must be mistaken. A light-adapted tadpole will remain in that state no matter how much pituitary substance you put into it.

(E) Have you done a similar experiment on dark-adapted tadpoles?

9. Which characteristics of RNA distinguish it from DNA?

(A) RNA has uracil bases and a sugar moiety with less oxygen.

(B) RNA has thymine bases and a sugar moiety with less oxygen.

(C) RNA has an extra phosphodiester bond and a sugar moiety which has more oxygen and less hydrogen.

(D) RNA has uracil bases and a sugar moiety with more oxygen and as much hydrogen.

(E) RNA has thymine bases and a sugar moiety with more oxygen and as much hydrogen.

10. A major difference between meiosis and mitosis is that

(A) DNA is not replicated during meiosis

(B) DNA is replicated more in meiosis than in mitosis

(C) homologous chromosomes synapse during meiosis but not during mitosis

(D) meiosis immediately precedes fertilization

(E) meiosis occurs only in haploid organisms

11. In a frog embryo, an investigator separated the developing optic vesicle from the brain (point A) before the optic vesicle contacted the overlying epidermis. He transplanted the vesicle to a similar spot (B) in the opposite side of the embryo. As expected, the embryo developed

(A) a complete eye at B and no visual apparatus at A

(B) a complete visual apparatus at A and nothing at B

(C) only a lens at A and a complete eye with lens at B

(D) an optic cup only, at B, and a lens only, at A

(E) no optic cup or lens anywhere

12. In mammals, oogenesis differs from spermatogenesis in that

(A) the cytoplasm from the germ cell is unequally distributed

(B) each germ cell produces only one gamete

(C) yolk is accumulated

(D) A and B are correct

(E) A, B, and C are correct

13. Which base sequence could be from RNA but not from DNA?

(A) AGTA

(B) AUUT

(C) TGTG

(D) AAAA

(E) ACAT

14. Which is *false* with regard to Eumycetes, the fungi?

(A) They contain neither true roots, stems, or leaves.

(B) Yeasts are included in the phylum, along with ringworms and mushrooms.

(C) Haploid spores undergo asexual reproduction.

(D) They are either parasitic or saprophytic.

(E) Between 90 and 95 percent of all known species lack chlorophyll.

15. Other conditions being equal, which of the following would help an animal to survive in the Sahara Desert?

I. A small loop of Henle

II. A high constant body temperature

III. High circulating levels of antidiuretic hormone (ADH)

(A) I only

(B) III only

(C) I and II only

(D) II and III only

(E) I, II, and III

Directions: A set of five choices precedes a set of five questions. Choose the answer to each question from the choices directly above. An answer may be correct once, more than once, or not at all.

(A) liver
(B) pancreas
(C) esophagus
(D) stomach
(E) small intestine

16. Insulin decreases its free glucose concentration

17. Primarily receives nonarterial blood supply

18. Relatively small in carnivores

19. Gastrin receptors

20. Produces cholecystokinin

Questions 21 to 23 are based on the following chart which depicts a human pedigree. Squares represent males, circles females. Shaded symbols indicate people with a certain trait; empty symbols indicate the trait's absence.

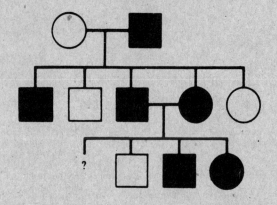

21. The trait appears to be
(A) sex linked dominant
(B) sex linked recessive
(C) autosomal dominant
(D) autosomal recessive
(E) extrachromosomally transmitted

22. What is the chance that the person indicated by the question mark exhibited the trait?
(A) 75 percent
(B) 66⅔ percent
(C) 50 percent
(D) 25 percent
(E) It cannot be determined from the information given.

23. Which of the following does the chart most clearly show?
(A) inbreeding
(B) outbreeding
(C) independent assortment
(D) linkage
(E) supergene

Explanatory Answers

1. (**A**) The giraffe, like virtually all mammals, has seven cervical vertebrae, massive though they are. A ruminant, the giraffe has several rumens ("stomachs"), and as an inhabitant of the relatively treeless veldt, has adapted to make the most of the situation by growing tall enough to reach most leaves. Longer front legs than back legs are part of this adaptation. Since the heart must pump blood to a great height, it must produce a high pressure.

2. (**A**) Detritus is any nonliving organic material that can be utilized by another organism for energy. This includes remains of dead organisms and fecal and urinary material. It is estimated that as much as 90 to 95 percent of the primary production of terrestrial plants is consumed not by herbivores but by detritus feeders. The most important detritus feeders are microorganisms such as bacteria and fungi and small arthropods; larger carrion feeders such as vultures play a much smaller role. In contrast to terrestrial systems, aquatic systems produce little detritus, since phytoplankton is highly digestible. In these systems, therefore, the bulk of energy flow is from primary producers (phytoplankton, primarily) to primary consumers.

3. (**C**) Since sperm are much smaller and "cheaper" to produce than ova, a given male can have many more offspring than a given female, meaning that males are more fecund. This observation supports the statement

that for a typical population, an *un*balanced sex ratio is optimal, since it does not waste resources in producing a large number of reproductively underutilized males. Observation (E), that males but not females sometimes perish after mating, is consistent with this view also. Choice (B), however, gives a Darwinian explanation for the general prevalence of balanced sex ratios: if there were few males and many females, the parent of a male would have a genetic advantage in terms of producing more descendants by producing male offspring; the situation would not stabilize until the number of males equalled the number of females.

In contrast to the above discussion, choice (C), that most human societies prize male over female offspring, is clearly inconsistent with the statement that population considerations should lead to favoritism toward females but that Darwinian factors should lead to no sex preference.

4. **(B)** Virology was originally an offshoot of bacteriology, and the larger viruses that interacted with bacteria were the most easily cultured and most accessible to study. The large bacteriophage *lambda* was, for instance, probably the first thoroughly studied virus, and it was on a bacteriophage that the Hershey-Chase experiment, showing that DNA is the basic genetic material, was performed.

5. **(C)** RNA viruses, which are double stranded, replicate in a symmetrical, conservative (*not* semi-conservative) fashion. In this manner, messenger RNA (mRNA) is produced from the viral RNA genome, and one strand is copied to great excess. On these strands, the complementary strand is directly produced. This method does not use reverse transcriptase, which allows for the synthesis of DNA from an RNA template.

RNA viruses are very prominent among plant viruses. They may be pathogenic to man, perhaps most prominently the poliovirus, which is in the class of picornaviruses (*pico*-, very small; *rna*-, RNA). RNA bacteriophages exist.

6. **(B)** The bends occur because the outside pressure suddenly becomes much less than the internal pressure. Gases dissolved in body fluids then tend to come out of solution. Nitrogen, which is dissolved in large amounts in all body fluids, including intracellular water, then forms potentially crippling or lethal bubbles in the bloodstream. Of the choices, only the example of the diver ascending too quickly involves a sudden lowering of outside pressure. Another case of the bends can occur in aviators who ascend too rapidly.

7. **(D)** The description is of an enzyme, which speeds reactions by lowering their activation energy and is regenerated at the end of the reaction. All biological names ending in *-ase* are enzymes (e.g., acid phosphatase, DNAase, and phosphofructokinase). Retinol, FAD, and transfer RNA participate in reactions but do not lower their activation energy and may be changed by the reactions.

8. **(C)** Melanophores are responsible for the observed skin color changes. They are under the control of melanophore-stimulating hormone (MSH). MSH is continuously produced by the pituitary gland unless the pituitary receives an inhibiting factor from the hypothalamus. Implanting a pituitary gland under the skin frees it from hypothalamic inhibition, leading to continuous production of MSH, which causes the tadpole to turn dark in all environmental situations.

9. **(D)** DNA and RNA each contain the bases guanine, cytosine, and adenine (G, C, A), but DNA contains thymine (T) where RNA contains uracil (U). RNA, ribonucleic acid, contains a ribose sugar attached to the base and to the phosphate linkage groups, whereas DNA, deoxyribonucleic acid, contains the sugar 2-deoxyribose. Where ribose bears a $2'$ hydroxyl group, deoxyribose bears a $2'$ hydrogen. RNA therefore contains more oxygen and as much hydrogen as DNA.

10. **(C)** During prophase of the first meiotic division, members of each chromosomal pair align themselves, forming a precise point-for-point association with regard to genes. Each chromosome is double stranded at this stage. This association is called synapsis and allows crossing over between chromatids. There is one genome duplication in both meiosis and mitosis; in mitosis, there is one division, but in meiosis, there are two divisions—hence the term *reduction division*.

11. **(A)** The optic cup induces differentiation of the overlying epidermis into the lens tissue. When transplanted, it produces a complete eye, including a lens, at its new location. As long as the optic cup never contacted the overlying skin at its original location, no part of the visual apparatus would be expected to develop there.

12. **(D)** Choices (A) and (B) are true. The primary spermatocyte produces four spermatozoa, each with as much cytoplasm of the primary germ cell as the others. The primary oocyte, however, leads to the production of one ovum, with almost all the cytoplasm coming from the primary germ cell. The ovum does not accumulate yolk in mammals; the yolk sac is formed in embryonic development.

13. **(B)** The distinguishing characteristic of RNA's base pattern is the presence of uracil (U), which is not found in DNA. Only choice (B) has uracil. The presence of thymine (T) in choice (B) does not exclude it from being representative of RNA. While thymine is not present during the transcription of RNA, it is often formed in transfer RNA due to modification of the uracil residues after transcription.

14. **(E)** By definition, fungi are thallophytes—plants lacking chlorophyll. *No* fungus species contains chlorophyll. The other statements give the most important characteristics of fungi.

15. **(D)** The loop of Henle, in the nephron of the kidney, actively reabsorbs sodium and chloride from the glomerular filtrate. Creation of an osmotic pressure gradient causes passive reabsorption of water. The larger (longer) the loop of Henle, the more water can be reabsorbed, and the less water will be lost in the urine. An organism that regulates its temperature at a high level will be able to avoid expending much water in keeping cool, as by sweating or panting. ADH, antidiuretic hormone, stimulates water reabsorption in the distal tubule of the nephron and the collecting duct of the kidney.

16. **(A)**

17. **(A)**

18. **(E)**

19. **(D)**

20. **(E)**

As the body's main metabolic organ, the **liver** performs a myriad of functions, including protein synthesis, detoxification of drugs, and lipoprotein formation and transformation. Under the stimulus of catecholamines, the liver produces glucose from smaller organic precursors and breaks down glycogen into glucose, releasing glucose into the blood to be transported to skeletal muscle. Insulin opposes this action; as the anabolic hormone, it stimulates hepatic glycogen production from glucose and thus tends to lower the liver's free glucose concentration. As the central metabolic organ, the liver receives blood directly from the gastrointestinal tract via the portal vein. Roughly two-thirds of the liver's blood supply comes from the portal vein; the rest comes from the hepatic artery.

The **pancreas** has both exocrine and endocrine functions. Under the influence of cholecystokinin and secretin, it releases bicarbonate-rich fluid and various digestive enzymes into the duodenum. Its endocrine functions primarily include insulin and glucagon production.

The **esophagus** is a muscular conduit between the oropharynx and the stomach. It has no digestive function other than transport.

The function of the **stomach** is to prepare food for digestion by the small intestine. To do this it physically macerates the food and hydrolyzes proteins into smaller peptides via pepsin, which is active at a pH so acidic that other proteins are denatured. An important stimulus for acid production is gastrin, which is produced in the stomach, duodenum, pancreas, and distal small intestine.

The **small intestine** digests and absorbs nutrients received from the stomach. It also produces the hormones cholecystokinin (cholecystokinin-pancreozymin, CCK-PZ), secretin, enterogastrone, gastrin, and others, all of which affect other digestive organs. Herbivores and omnivores have much longer intestines than do carnivores, which are able to digest and absorb their proteinaceous diet rapidly.

21. **(C)** The trait is autosomal dominant. That it is not recessive is seen by noting that the second mating shown produces one non-trait-bearing individual, and a cross between two recessives produces only more of the same. Knowing that the trait is dominant, it can be shown not to be sex linked by looking at the first parents. If it were sex linked, the male, who exhibits the trait, would pass it on his X-chromosome to all his daughters (XX), who would then exhibit it, since it is dominant. Since one of his daughters did not show the trait, it is not sex linked. It does in fact show the typical inheritance pattern of an autosomal dominant trait, and there is no reason to suspect that it is transmitted extra-chromosomally.

22. **(A)** Call the dominant allele A and its recessive allele a. Then the original mating must have involved aa (the double recessive mother) and Aa (the father) because double recessives were produced. Their affected offspring, two of whom mated, were Aa. Of their progeny, 25 percent would be AA, 50 percent Aa, and 25 percent aa; 75% would be A—, and would exhibit the trait.

23. **(A)** Inbreeding is mating between two closely related individuals, an occurrence clearly shown on the pedigree's second line. Independent assortment is not shown here, for that is a phenomenon between two different genes, not two alleles (which show segregation). A supergene is a set of different genes that undergo little recombination.

GRE Chemistry Test

The GRE Chemistry Test is a 150-question examination. Some of the questions appear in groups based upon descriptive paragraphs or experimental results.

The questions are drawn from the four fields of chemistry in the approximate proportions of analytical chemistry 15 percent, inorganic chemistry 25 percent, organic chemistry 30 percent, and physical chemistry 30 percent. The emphasis is upon knowledge of chemistry, so mathematical calculations are relatively simple. A periodic table is provided with the test booklet and values of logarithms are included with test questions as needed.

Since the variation in content of college chemistry courses is so great, no student is expected to have been exposed to all topics touched upon in the examination. It would be unrealistic to expect to be able to answer all of the questions. In fact, correct answers to 75 percent of the questions should yield a scaled score in the 900 range.

Your GRE Chemistry Test may include questions on many of the following:

- **Organic:** functional groups (alkanes, cycloalkanes, alkenes, alkynes, aromatics, halides, alcohols, ethers, phenols, aldehydes, ketones, acids, acid derivatives, and amines); stereochemistry; reaction mechanisms; polymerization; instrumentation for compound identification; biological substances; heterocyclic substances; history of organic chemistry.

- **Inorganic:** atomic structure; ionic bonding; covalent bonding; intermolecular forces; acids and bases; coordination chemistry; organometallic compounds; periodicity.

- **Analytical:** data analysis; stoichiometry; wet methods of analysis chromatography—a separation technique; instrumental analysis; electronics.

- **Physical:** gases—ideal and real; first law of thermodynamics; second and third laws of thermodynamics; free energy and equilibrium; quantum theory; symmetry; spectroscopy; statistical thermodynamics; solutions; solids; kinetics; phase rule—heterogeneous equilibria; surface chemistry; history of physical chemistry.

The sample questions that follow are representative of the examination questions. The correct answers, explained, appear directly after the questions. In answering these sample questions, circle the letter of your answer choice.

Sample Questions

1. A compound has a distribution coefficient (K_D) of 4.0. How much ether is needed to extract 1 g of compound from a solution containing 3 g of compound in 100 ml of water?

   (A) 5.0 ml

   (B) 8.3 ml

   (C) 50.0 ml

   (D) 12.5 ml

   (E) 10.0 ml

2. The gas that will liquefy with the most difficulty is

   (A) He

   (B) CO_2

   (C) NH_3

   (D) SO_2

   (E) H_2O

3. Of the following, the species that is not green or blue is

   (A) $Cu(H_2O)_4^{2+}$

   (B) $Cu(NH_3)_4^{2+}$

   (C) $CuCl_4^{2-}$

   (D) $CuSO_4 \cdot 5H_2O$

   (E) $Cu(NO_3)_2 \cdot 3H_2O$

4. Of the following, an important precaution to be observed in the storage of metallic sodium is to

   (A) leave the container uncovered.

   (B) store the sodium in kerosene.

   (C) store the sodium in water.

   (D) use an opaque container.

   (E) store the sodium in ethanol.

5. The formation of a purple or black color by a precipitate of silver chloride is due to

   (A) $AgCl \xrightarrow{\text{light}} Ag + Cl_2$

   (B) $AgCl + H_2O \longrightarrow AgOH + HCl$

   (C) $AgCl + H_2S \text{ (from air)} \longrightarrow Ag_2S + HCl$

   (D) $AgCl + Cl^- \longrightarrow AgCl_2^-$

   (E) $AgCl + NH_3 \longrightarrow AgNH_2Cl + Ag + NH_4Cl + H_2O$

6. Of the following, the compound that is not an amphoteric hydroxide is

   (A) zinc hydroxide.

   (B) lead hydroxide.

   (C) aluminum hydroxide.

   (D) magnesium hydroxide.

   (E) scandium hydroxide.

7. In the phase diagram of a one-component system like carbon dioxide, the solid-liquid line

   (A) usually slopes to the right.

   (B) usually slopes to the left.

   (C) is horizontal.

   (D) is vertical.

   (E) represents a metastable equilibrium.

8. A conductance cell, when filled with a 0.01-demal (mole/dm^3) KCl solution at 25°C, had a resistance of 155.00 Ω. The specific conductance of this 0.01-demal KCl solution at 25°C is 0.003244 Ω^{-1} cm^{-1}. This cell, when filled with a 0.01-demal solution of electrolyte A^+B^-, showed a resistance of 72.61 Ω at 25°C. Calculate the specific conductance of the A^+B^- solution.

   (A) 0.003244 Ω^{-1} cm^{-1}

   (B) 36.51 Ω^{-1} cm^{-1}

   (C) 0.001518 Ω^{-1} cm^{-1}

   (D) 0.006925 Ω^{-1} cm^{-1}

   (E) 0.004639 Ω^{-1} cm^{-1}

9. An important leaving group frequently used in the study of reaction mechanisms is

   (A) OH^-

   (B) NH_2^-

   (C) TsO^-

   (D) NH_3

   (E) F^-

10. Which of the following reagents does not react with cyclohexene?

    (A) Cl_2, H_2O

    (B) $NaOH$, H_2O

    (C) O_3, then Zn, H_2O

    (D) HCl

    (E) OsO_4, then Na_2SO_3

11. Consider the following synthesis:

    $$CH_2{=}CHCH_2{-}Br \xrightarrow{KCN}$$

    $$A \xrightarrow[H+]{H_2O} B \xrightarrow[\text{(2) Zn, }H_2O]{\text{(1) }O_3} C$$

    Compound C is

    (A)
    $$\overset{O}{\overset{\|}{H{-}C}}CH_2CH_2\overset{O}{\overset{\|}{C}}{-}H$$

    (B)
    $$HO{-}\overset{O}{\overset{\|}{C}}CH_2\overset{O}{\overset{\|}{C}}{-}OH$$

    (C)
    $$HO{-}\overset{O}{\overset{\|}{C}}{-}\overset{O}{\overset{\|}{C}}{-}OH$$

    (D)
    $$O{=}\overset{H}{\overset{|}{C}}CH_2\overset{O}{\overset{\|}{C}}{-}OH$$

    (E)
    $$O{=}\overset{H}{\overset{|}{C}}CH_2CH_2\overset{O}{\overset{\|}{C}}{-}OH$$

12. How many isomeric structures (containing a benzene ring) can be written for bromodichlorobenzene?

    (A) 3

    (B) 4

    (C) 5

    (D) 6

    (E) 7

13. In a standardization of hydrochloric acid with sodium carbonate, a student failed to dry the sodium carbonate completely. The resulting normality will be

    (A) too high.

    (B) too low.

    (C) independent of the amount of water present in the Na_2CO_3.

    (D) inversely proportional to the amount of water in Na_2CO_3.

    (E) the correct normality.

14. Chlorous acid can best be prepared by

    (A) $ClO_2 + OH^- \longrightarrow$

    (B) $Cl_2O_3 + H_2O \longrightarrow$

    (C) $Cl_2 + H_2O \longrightarrow$

    (D) $Cl_2O + H_2O \longrightarrow$

    (E) $Cl_2 + OH^- \longrightarrow$

Questions 15 and 16 make use of the following information:

$R = 1.987$ cal /mol K and $dG = V\,dP - S\,dT$

15. Calculate the change in Gibbs free energy during iso-thermal expansion of 1 mol of ideal gas from a pressure of 10 atm to a pressure of 1 atm at a temperature of 25°C.

   (A) 10 cal

   (B) −2980 cal

   (C) 298 cal

   (D) −1364 cal

   (E) 250 cal

16. To what extent does the Helmholtz (maximum work) function change during the conditions given in Question 15?

   (A) 0 cal

   (B) +250 cal

   (C) +1364 cal

   (D) −2980 cal

   (E) −1364 cal

Explanatory Answers

1. **(D)** The distribution coefficient is given by the equation

$$K_D = \frac{\text{concentration of compound in ether}}{\text{concentration of compound in water}}$$

So,

$$4.0 = \frac{(1\text{ g}) / (X\text{ ml})}{(3\text{ g} - 1\text{ g}) / (100\text{ ml})}$$

$$4.0 = \frac{100\,(1)}{2X}$$

$$8X = 100$$

$$X = 12.5\text{ ml}$$

2. **(A)** The critical temperature of He (5.3°K) is much lower than that of the other gases. Since the critical tempera-ture of a gas is the temperature above which a liquid will not condense, no matter how high the pressure, He must be cooled to 5.3°K before liquefaction will take place, a process representing much difficulty.

3. **(C)** $CuCl_4^{2-}$ is yellow, though solutions of it appear green because of the presence of the blue $Cu(H_2O)_4^{2+}$ complex. Upon further dilution, the solution turns blue as H_2O replaces Cl^- ions in the complex.

4. **(B)** Sodium is oxidized by air and reacts violently with water as follows:

$$6Na + 2O_2 \longrightarrow Na_2O_2 + 2Na_2O$$
$$\text{(major)} \quad \text{(minor)}$$
$$2Na + 2H_2O \longrightarrow 2NaOH + H_2$$

It does not, however, react with kerosene and is stored in kerosene because of the inert environment.

5. **(A)** The photosensitivity of silver chloride is well known. Once silver chloride is formed in a quantitative analysis, the precipitate should be digested in a dark drawer in order to keep the substance away from sunlight or artifi-cial light. The purple, grey, or black color of the silver chloride is due to the formation of metallic silver.

6. **(D)** Amphoteric hydroxides, which act as both acids and bases, are formed from metals in the IIIA and IVA groups and from higher atomic weight metals of the IIA group. Since magnesium is a light element of group IIA, response (D) is correct.

7. **(A)** The solid-liquid line usually slopes to the right. This means that as the pressure increases, the melting point of the solid increases. This increase of melting point with increasing pressure is common and occurs when the solid is denser than the liquid. In the system ice-water, how-ever, the solid-liquid line slopes to the left because the density of the solid is less than that of the liquid.

8. **(D)** The cell constant of the cell is calculated using the formula

$$K = L_S R$$

where K is the cell constant and L_S represents the spe-cific conductance corresponding to resistance R. Substi-tuting, we have

$$K = (0.003244)\,(155.00)$$
$$= 0.50282$$

Using this value of K and the resistance of the 0.01-demal AB solution, we can calculate the specific con-ductance of the A^+B^- solution:

$$L_S = \frac{K}{R} = \frac{0.50282}{72.61} = 0.006925\ \Omega^{-1}\ cm^{-1}$$

9. **(C)** $Ts\bar{O}$ is an abbreviation of the tosylate ion. Tosylate ion (*p*-toluensulfonate ion) is an excellent leaving group and is often used as a leaving group in mechanism stud-ies:

methyl tosylate

10. **(B)** Cyclohexene chemically combines with each of the other reagents listed as follows:

$$O=C-CH_2CH_2CH_2CH_2-C=O$$

(with H above each terminal C)

Cyclohexene does not combine with $NaOH, H_2O$.

11. **(D)** The synthesis proceeds as follows:

$$CH_2=CHCH_2-Br \xrightarrow{KCN}$$

$$CH_2=CHCH_2CN$$

$$\downarrow H_2O, H^+$$

$$CH_2=C-CH_2C-OH$$ (with H and O)

$$O=C-CH_2-C-OH$$

12. **(D)** There are only six structural isomers of bromodichlorobenzene:

13. **(A)** Since NV_{ml} = number of milliequivalents of sodium carbonate used, and the number of milliequivalents is equal to

$$\frac{\text{number of mg of sample}}{\text{equivalent weight of sample}}$$

So if the sample of sodium carbonate contains water, then the number of milliequivalents with water present is greater than the number when water is not. Since V_{ml} is the same for both samples, N must be greater for the sample with the water in it.

14. **(A)** $ClO_2 + OH^- \longrightarrow ClO_2^- + ClO_3^- + H_2O$

$$ClO_2^- + H^+ \longrightarrow HClO_2$$

The halogen oxide Cl_2O_3 does not exist.

Thus choice (B) can be rejected:

Choice (C) $Cl_2 + H_2O \rightarrow HOCl + H^+ + Cl^-$
Choice (D) $Cl_2O + H_2O \rightarrow 2HOCl$
Choice (E) $3Cl_2 + 6OH^- \rightarrow ClO_3^- + 5Cl^- + 3H_2O$

15. **(D)** For an ideal gas the change in Gibbs free energy is

$$\triangle G = \int_{P_1}^{P_2} V\, dP$$

$$= \int_{P_1}^{P_2} \frac{nRT\, dP}{P}$$

$$= nRT \ln (P_2 / P_1)$$

Therefore

$$\triangle G = -1(1.987)(298) \ln 10 = -1364 \text{ cal}$$

16. **(E)** By definition, $A = E - TS$. Therefore at constant T, $\triangle A = -T \triangle S$, where

$$\triangle S = nR \ln (V_2 / V_1)$$

For an ideal gas $V_2 / V_1 = P_1 / P_2$.
Thus $\triangle S = nR \ln(P_1 / P_2)$ and

$$\triangle s = (1)(1.987)(2.303)\log(10 / 1)$$
$$= (1)(1.987)(2.303)(+1)$$
$$= +4.576 \text{ eu}$$

Since $\triangle A = -T\triangle S$, substituting, we obtain

$$\triangle A = -298(+4.576)$$
$$= -1364 \text{ cal}$$

GRE Computer Science Test

The Gre Computer Science Test is an 80-question examination. Some of the questions are based on graphs, diagrams, program segments, grammars, and data structures. These questions may be grouped in sets.

The approximate distribution of questions is indicated below. The percentages provided for each subject matter are only approximate and may vary from one test to another slightly.

- **Software Systems and Methodology** (35 Percent): data types and organization; program control; programming languages; operating systems; compilers.

- **Computer Organization and Architecture** (20 Percent): computer logic design; processors and control units; memories; input/output and interface; networking.

- **Theory** (20 Percent): automata; language theory; algorithm analysis; analysis of program correctness.

- **Mathematical Structures for Computer Science** (20 Percent): discrete mathematics; abstract algebra; boolean algebra; set theory; graph theory; numerical mathematics.

- **Special Topics** (5 Percent): modeling; simulation; artificial intelligence; computer graphics; data communications.

The sample questions that follow are representative of the examination questions. The correct answers, explained, appear directly after the questions. In answering these sample questions, circle the letter of your answer choice.

Sample Questions

1. Suppose that a computer uses a floating-point representation comprising a signed magnitude fractional mantissa and an excess-16 base-8 exponent. What decimal number is being represented by the example below?

```
  ---Exponent---    ---Mantissa---
| 1 | 1 | 0 | 0 | 1 | 1 | 1 | 0 | 1 | 0 | 0 | 0 |
```

- (A) −6250
- (B) −20480
- (C) −320
- (D) −0.00122
- (E) −310

2. Consider the following program fragment:

```
read(a,b);
c:= 3.0*a + b;
if c=0 then a:=1 else a:=1.0/c + 1.0/b;
```

This program fragment will fault if given certain values for "a" and "b." Which is the weakest of the supplied conditions (least restrictive or *smallest*) which, if applied to the data, will prevent failure?

- (A) b>0
- (B) a>0 and b>0
- (C) a ≠ −b/3
- (D) b ≠ 0
- (E) 3.0*a ≠ 0 and b ≠ 0

3. Which of the following regular expressions denotes a language comprising all possible strings over the alphabet {a,b} *excluding* those of length 3?

- (A) {ε|0|1|00|01|11|10}{{0|1}{0|1}*}
- (B) ε|0|1|00|01|11|10|{0|1}{0|1}+
- (C) ε|0|1|{00|01|11|10}+{0|1}*
- (D) ε|0|1|{00|01|11|10}*
- (E) none of the above

4. Consider the following grammar, with start symbol E:

```
E→    E * E
   |  E / E
   |  E + E
   |  E - E
   |  (E)
   |  a|b|c|d|e|f.......x|y|z
```

The following strings are legal derivations from this grammar:

    I. a * b + c

    II. (a - b) * c

    III. a / (b - c)

Which of the above are rightmost sentential forms?

(A) I only

(B) II only

(C) III only

(D) I and III

(E) I, II, and III

5. Which of the following statements is incorrect?

(A) A collision in a pipelined architecture is an attempt by two different initiations to use the same stage at the same time.

(B) Latency is the number of time units between two initiations in a pipelined architecture.

(C) If initiations are of different but fixed reservation tables, the architecture is known as static pipelined configuration.

(D) Forbidden latency set is those latencies that cause collisions between initiations.

(E) none of the above

6. Consider the bit pattern 01010001. Which of the following has a *Hamming distance* of exactly 2 from this pattern?

(A) 01010000

(B) 01010010

(C) 01010011

(D) 01010110

(E) 01110001

7. A JK flip-flop has its J input connected to logic level 1 and its K input to the Q output. A clock pulse is fed to its clock input. The flip-flop will now

(A) change its state at each clock pulse.

(B) go to state 1 and stay there.

(C) go to state 0 and stay there.

(D) retain its previous state.

(E) none of the above.

8. A computer system stores floating-point numbers with a 16-bit mantissa and an 8-bit exponent, each in two's complement. The smallest and largest positive values which can be stored are

(A) 1×10^{-128} and $2^{15} \times 10^{128}$

(B) 1×10^{-256} and $2^{15} \times 10^{255}$

(C) 1×10^{-128} and $2^{15} \times 10^{127}$

(D) 1×10^{-128} and $(2^{15} - 1) \times 10^{127}$

(E) 1×10^{-256} and $(2^{15} - 1) \times 10^{255}$

9.

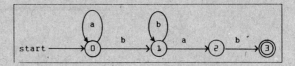

This finite state automaton recognizes:

(A) $a*b^+ab$

(B) $a*b*ab$

(C) $(a|b)*$

(D) $(a|b)^+$

(E) a^+b^+ab

Questions 10 and 11 refer to the following information:

A Finite State Machine, FSM, whose state table is shown below, has a single input, x, and a single output, z.

Present State	Next State, Z	
	X=0	X=1
A	B,0	E,0
B	C,1	B,1
C	D,1	B,0
D	C,0	B,1
E	C,1	D,0

10. The initial state of the FSM is unknown. Which is the shortest input sequence that will guarantee that the final state will be B?

(A) 00101

(B) 01

(C) 10

(D) 1011

(E) 11

11. Which of the following statements is true?

(A) The state table for the FSM is not in its minimal form.

(B) The state diagram can be drawn in plane without lines crossing.

(C) There exists an input sequence such that, for all initial states, it is possible to determine the initial state by observing the output sequence.

(D) If the initial state is E, it is possible to produce any arbitrary output sequence by applying the appropriate input sequence.

(E) All of the above are true.

12. Consider the following binary tree:

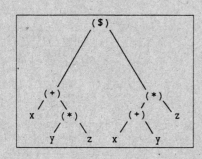

$ denotes exponentiation. If the tree is traversed in pre-order, which, if any, of the expressions below is formed?

(A) +x*z$+xy*z

(B) *yz+x$+xy*z

(C) $+*xyz*+xyz

(D) $+x*yz*+xyz

(E) none of the above

13. A node in a network forwards incoming packets by placing them on its shortest output queue. What *routing algorithm* is in operation?

(A) hot potato routing

(B) flooding

(C) static routing

(D) delta routing

(E) hierarchical routing

14. Which one of the *Boolean expressions* below is not logically equivalent to all of the rest?

(A) $A(B + C) + \overline{C} \oplus D$

(B) $AB + AC + \overline{C \oplus D}$

(C) $AB\overline{C}D + BC\overline{D} + CD + \overline{C}\ \overline{D}$

(D) $B\overline{D} + \overline{C}\ \overline{D} + AB + CD$

(E) $AB + \overline{CD} + CD + B\overline{D}$

15. What is the *Boolean expression* for the following circuit?

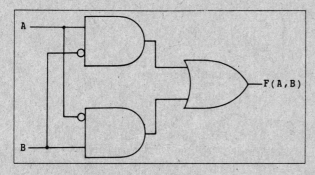

(A) $F(A,B) = A'B + A'B'$

(B) $F(A,B) = AB + A'B'$

(C) $F(A,B) = A \oplus B$

(D) $F(A,B) = A' + B'$

(E) $F(A,B) = A'B'$

16. Which of the following *Karnaugh maps* corresponds to the switching function:

$$F(x,y,z) = y' \ (x' + z')$$

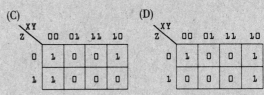

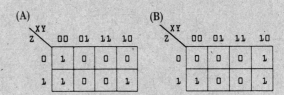

(E) none of the above

17. The binary tree below is to be *right in-threaded;* to which node would the successor pointer of "Q" point?

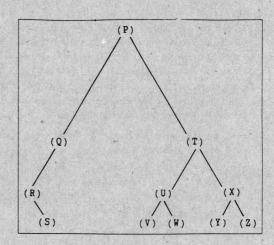

(A) R

(B) S

(C) T

(D) P

(E) V

18. A synchronous counter is depicted as follows. If it is currently in state $Q_aQ_bQ_c = 101$, what will be the next state?

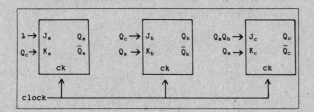

	Q_a	Q_b	Q_c
(A)	1	1	0
(B)	0	1	1
(C)	1	0	0
(D)	0	1	0
(E)	0	0	0

19. An excess-3 code is used to represent the integers 0 through 9, thus:

Number	Code (ABCD)
0	1100
1	0010
2	1010
3	0110
4	1110
5	0001
6	1001
7	0101
8	1101
9	0011

Which of the following expressions is the correct one for an *invalid* code?

(A) $\bar{B}.\bar{C}.\bar{D} + C.D$

(B) $B.C.D. + A.C.D$

(C) $\bar{B}.\bar{C}.\bar{D} + B.C.D + A.C.D + \bar{A}.\bar{C}.\bar{D}$

(D) $\bar{B}.\bar{C}.\bar{D} + A.C.D$

(E) $\bar{B}.\bar{C}.\bar{D} + B.C.D + A.C.D$

Explanatory Answers

1. (C)
The mantissa represents $\frac{1}{2} + \frac{1}{8}$.
The exponent represents $16 + 2 + 1 = 19$.
The number being shown is therefore

$$-0.625 \times 8^{(19-16)} = -0.625 \times 8^3$$
$$= -320$$

2. (D) If the *else* clause is invoked, the program will fault with a division by zero error *if either c or b is zero*. A first attempt to protect the program fragment might be to suppose that c (and therefore $3*a + b$) must not equal zero and also b must not equal zero. This is too "tight," however, because if $c = 0$, the else clause is not invoked. Consider each of the following alternatives:

(A) Too restrictive. Rules out $b = -3$ and $a = 1$, so $c := 0$ and $a := 1$, which is fine.

(B) Too restrictive. Rules out, say $a = -10$ and $b = 1$ (in fact, c can never be negative).

(C) Too restrictive. Rules out, say, $a = -1$ and $b = -3$ so $c = -6$, which is fine.

(E) Too restrictive. Rules out, say, $a = -1$ and $b = 3$ so $c = 0$ and $a := 1$, which is fine.

3. (E) Examining the alternatives in turn shows all of alternatives (A) through (D) to be inadequate.

(A) With the * operator providing no repeat, it is possible to take, say, 00 from the first subexpression, and, say, 0 from the second. The final string 000 has length 3.

(B) Considering only the last clause, $(0|1)(0|1)^+$, and with the + operator providing two repeats, this regular expression generates 0 followed by, say, 11. The result 011 is of length 3.

(C) One of the patterns from $(00|01|11|10)^+$ followed by, say, a 1 from $(0|1)*$ generates patterns of length 3.

(D) Examination of this last alternative also shows it to be faulty. Breaking the regular expression down into its parts reveals that we are permitted ϵ or 0 or 1 *and, as a distinct alternative* 00 or 01 or 11 or 10 repeated as many times as desired.

Thus, the expression generates:

```
0          first clause
1          first clause
ε          second clause with
              no repeats
00
01
11
10


000  second clause, with
001  one repeat
011
010
 :
```

This appears to be hopeful until we notice that *two* repeats of the parenthesized subexpression generates strings of length six. This regular expression will not generate any strings of length five at all. Since the definition only requires the exclusion of strings of length three, this alternative also fails to satisfy.

4. **(D)** A rightmost sentential form has the rightmost non-terminal replaced at each stage in a derivation. See the following derivations for confirmation of the answer.

```
I.  E
    E * E
    E * E + E
    E * E + c
    E * b + c
    a * b + c
II. E
    E + E
    (E) + E ← leftmost non-terminal re-
    placed
III. E
    E / E
    E / (E)
    E / (E - E)
    E / (E - c)
    E / (b - c)
    a / (b - c)
```

5. **(C)** Static pipeline configuration is one in which all initiations are of the same reservation table.

6. **(B)** The number of bits in which two code words differ is known as the *Hamming distance*. In this case, the only alternative with a Hamming distance of exactly 2 is (B).

7. **(A)** The characteristic table and the circuit for a JK flip-flop is given below:

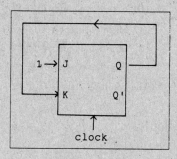

J	K	Q_{n+1}
0	0	Q_n
0	1	0
1	0	1
1	1	$Q_n{}'$

From the characteristic table it is clear that the flip-flop will change its state at each clock pulse.

8. **(D)** The possible positive 16-bit mantissa values are:

$$1 \text{ through } 2^{15} - 1.$$

The possible 8-bit exponent values are:

$$-2^7 \text{ through } 2^7 - 1$$
$$(\text{or } -128 \text{ through } 127).$$

Therefore, the smallest positive value is:

$$1 \times 10^{-128}$$

and the largest positive value is:

$$(2^{15} - 1) \times 10^{127}.$$

9. **(A)** The *fastest* way through the FSA accepts the string "bab." We may note, actually, that any string accepted by this automaton necessarily ends in "ab"; therefore, answer choices (C) and (D) are eliminated, since they both generate "aa" and "bbb."

Examination of the FSA shows that any number of a (including zero) may prefix an acceptable string. Alternative (E) is eliminated, therefore, since the + operator requires *at least one* a.

Considering the remaining candidates (A) and (B), the choice of (A) is correct because the + operator following b reflects the mandatory presence of a b forced by the transition from state 0 to state 1.

10. **(B)** The corresponding state diagram is given below.

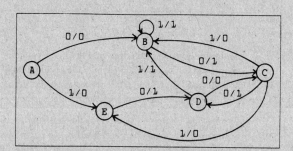

Observe from the state diagram that if the initial state is A,B,C,D, or E, the input sequence 01 will result in final state at B.

11. **(B)** Let us check each statement individually.

(A) The minimization table corresponding to the state table clearly indicates that the state table given is in its minimal form.

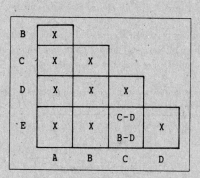

(B) The state diagram given in the solution to question 10 indicates that it lies in a plane with no lines crossing.

(C) First apply x = 0. If the initial state is B or E, we will have new state C and the output 1, so B and D are indistinguishable. Hence, the initial state cannot always be distinguished.

(D) By inspection of the given state table, it can be shown that statement (D) is not true.

12. (D) The (recursive) definition of preorder traversal is as follows:

```
visit the root, then
traverse the left subtree, then
traverse the right subtree.
```

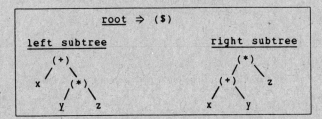

An initial division of the tree into the three components mentioned in the definition permits the elimination of all but alternatives (C) and (D) *since we are told to visit the root first, so the traversal must begin with $*.

We are now instructed to traverse the left subtree, presented in the figure underneath. Again, we begin by visiting the root, and continue with the left subtree. This tree is small enough to be able to see that, following the initial $, the preorder string continues with + , then x, *, y, z . . . , etc.

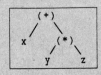

13. (A) When an IMP or node receives a packet, it tries to get rid of it as quickly as possible by placing it on its shortest output queue *without regard to where that line leads*.

14. (E) It can be shown algebraically, or by drawing a Vietch diagram or Karnaugh map, that answer choices (A), (B), (C), and (D) are logically equivalent.

15. (C) The outputs of each *gate* are indicated on the following circuit:

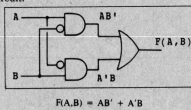

$$F(A,B) = AB' + A'B$$
$$= A \oplus B$$

16. (C) Convert the given switching function into sum-of-minterms form:

$$F(x,y,z) = y'(x'+z')$$
$$= x'y' + y'z'$$
$$= x'y'(z+z') + (x+x')y'z'$$
$$= x'y'z + x'y'z' + xy'z' + x'y'z'$$

or

$$F(x,y,z) = x'y'z' + xy'z' + x'y'z$$
$$= \Sigma m(0,1,4)$$

Hence the corresponding *Karnaugh map* is:

(C)

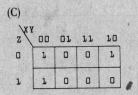

17. (D) To facilitate the efficient traversal of a binary tree, *threads* are sometimes used; terminal nodes, or nodes with missing descendents, are made to point to their successor. The successor node to Q in a right in-threaded binary tree is P.

18. (D) With the counter in state $Q_aQ_bQ_c = 101$, then:

1. Flip-flop a receives $J_a = 1$ and $K_a = 1$, and toggles.
2. Flip-flop b receives $J_b = 1$ and $K_b = 1$, and toggles.
3. Flip-flop c receives $J_c = 0$ and $K_c = 1$, and resets.

The resulting state is 010.

19. (C)

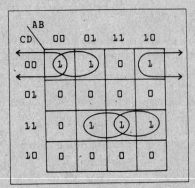

The function plotted above has a 1 output for all invalid codes. The looping shows alternative (C) to be correct.

GRE Engineering Test

The GRE Engineering Test consists of approximately 140 multiple-choice questions. There are five choices to each question with one correct or best answer. Some of the questions are based on tables, graphs, and figures; these questions are generally set up in groups.

There are two subscores provided in the test:

1. The engineering subscore, which is based on topics covered in an engineering undergraduate program in most colleges

2. The mathematical subscore, which gauges your ability to answer questions by recalling facts and intuitively approaching problems using calculus

There are approximately ninety engineering questions based on the following areas, about half based on the first four:

- Mechanics: statics, dynamics, kinematics
- Thermodynamics
- Transfer and rate mechanics: heat, mass, momentum
- Electricity
- Chemistry
- Nature and properties of matter, including the particulate
- Light and sound
- Computer fundamentals
- Properties of engineering materials
- Engineering economy
- Engineering judgment
- Fluid mechanics and hydraulics

There are about fifty questions leading to the mathematics subscore of the test. It is assumed that you have taken the following mathematics courses or studied the following topics in your undergraduate curriculum:

- Two courses in calculus
- Differential equations
- Linear algebra
- Numerical analysis
- Probability and statistics

The sample questions that follow are representative of the examination questions. The correct answers, explained, appear directly after the questions. In answering these sample questions, circle the letter of your answer choice.

Sample Questions

1. A bicycle of (standard) rear wheel drive has its wheels of diameter d replaced with wheels of diameter $d' < d$ in front and $d'' > d$ in the back. If the pedaling rate remains constant, the linear velocity of the bicycle changes by a factor of

   (A) $\dfrac{d''}{d}$

   (B) $\dfrac{d''}{d'}$

   (C) $\dfrac{(d'' - d)}{(d' - d)}$

   (D) $\dfrac{(d' - d)}{(d'' - d)}$

   (E) $\dfrac{(d' + d'')}{(2d)}$

2. The frictionless spring–mass system shown below oscillates once every 2 sec. If the mass m is 4 kg, what is the spring constant k?

   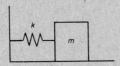

   (A) 2 N/m

   (B) 4 N/m

   (C) $\dfrac{\pi^2}{16}$ N/m

   (D) $4\pi^2$ N/m

   (E) π^2 N/m

3. For the circuit shown below, the voltage v_x is most nearly

   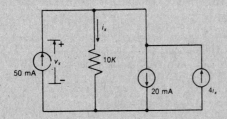

   (A) 1000 V

   (B) 100 V

   (C) 20 V

   (D) −20 V

   (E) −100 V

4. The critical point of water is reached at a critical temperature of 705°F, a critical pressure of 3206.2 lbf/in.^{2}, and a critical volume of 0.0503 ft^3/lbm. Which one of the following statements is true?

   (A) There is a constant-temperature vaporization process.

   (B) The saturated-liquid and saturated-vapor states are identical.

   (C) There is no definite change in phase from liquid to vapor.

   (D) There is no definite change in phase from solid to liquid.

   (E) There is no definite change in phase from solid to vapor.

5. Fifty grams of steam at 100°C are cooled to liquid water at 80°C. How much heat is transferred in the process (heat capacity of water is 1 cal/(g °C), heat of vaporization is 540 cal/g)?

   (A) 28,000 cal

   (B) 11,500 cal

   (C) 2,800 cal

   (D) 1,000 cal

   (E) none of the above

6. When sodium and chlorine are brought together each attains a rare gas configuration. This bond is

   (A) covalent

   (B) ionic

   (C) a hydrogen bond

   (D) a form of hybridization

   (E) magnetic in origin

Problems 7 to 9 are based on the following information.

Object A travels at constant speed on the edges of the top face of a cube—clockwise as viewed from above. Object B travels at the same speed on the bottom face of the cube—in the opposite sense. The graph below shows the straight-line distance between A and B as a function of time for $0 \le t \le 20$ sec.

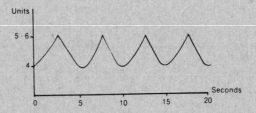

7. If the base of the cube is horizontal, how many times in the interval shown is one object directly above the other?

   (A) 0
   (B) 1
   (C) 2
   (D) 3
   (E) 5

8. What is the length of a side of the cube?

   (A) 2
   (B) 4
   (C) 6
   (D) 8
   (E) 12

9. In the time interval shown, how many times does the rate of change of distance between A and B change from positive to negative?

   (A) 0
   (B) 4
   (C) 8
   (D) 16
   (E) none of the above

10. Two new scales of temperature, called scale P and scale Q, are so chosen that the boiling point of water is calibrated to read $200°$ on both scales. A change of $10°$ on scale P represents the same change in temperature as a change of $20°$ on scale Q. It follows that

    (A) $0°$ on scale P corresponds to $-100°$ on scale Q
    (B) $50°$ on scale P corresponds to $-100°$ on scale Q
    (C) $100°$ on scale P corresponds to $-200°$ on scale Q
    (D) $0°$ on scale P represents the melting point of ice
    (E) neither scale P nor scale Q could be an absolute scale of temperature with zero point at absolute zero

11. A puck on a frictionless table is in pure translation when it strikes a meter stick, causing the latter to undergo both translation and rotation. It appears (incorrectly) that angular momentum is not conserved in the collision. The final angular momentum

    (A) was created during the puck–stick collision
    (B) arose from the friction between the stick and the table
    (C) must be zero, so the puck must end up rotating also
    (D) arose from friction between the puck and the stick
    (E) is due to none of the above

12. Which of the following is *not* true about polymers?

    (A) the local growth mechanism is linear
    (B) molecular weights can be 1,000,000 or more
    (C) the entire molecule is linear
    (D) polymers can make plastics and rubbers
    (E) polymers are macromolecules and not aggregates

13. $\int_a^b f(x)\ dx - \int_a^c f(x)\ dx$

    is equal to

    (A) $\int_a^c f(x)\ dx$

    (B) $\int_b^c f(x)\ dx$

    (C) $\int_c^b f(x)\ dx$

    (D) $-\int_a^c f(x)\ dx$

    (E) none of the above

14. Box A has three orange balls and two red balls. Box B has two orange balls and four red balls.

    If two balls are selected randomly (without replacement) from A and two more balls are selected randomly from B, what is the probability that all four balls are orange?

    (A) 12%
    (B) 10%
    (C) 4%
    (D) 2%
    (E) 1.2%

15. In the diagram below, the circuit on the left is magnetically coupled to the loop on the right. The induced current in the loop is

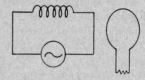

    (A) direct current
    (B) alternating current of the same frequency as the source
    (C) alternating current of twice the frequency of the source
    (D) alternating current of half the frequency of the source
    (E) zero

Explanatory Answers

1. **(A)** Pedaling drives the back wheel directly (in most bicycles) and since this rolls without slipping, we may ignore the front wheel. If we pedal at p revolutions per minute (rpm) and the wheel diameter is d, then our linear velocity is $p * \pi * d$ m/min. In other words, v is directly proportional to d and so an increase of d to d'' means the velocity increases by a factor of

$$\frac{d''}{d}$$

2. **(D)** The force on the mass (in the direction of its motion) is $-kx$ so the equation of motion is $-kx = ma$ or

$$\frac{d^2x}{dt^2} = -\frac{k}{m}x$$

If we look for an oscillatory solution of the form $x = A \cos(\omega t)$ then we find

$$\omega^2 = \frac{k}{m} \text{ or } \omega = 2\pi f = \sqrt{\frac{k}{m}}$$

$$k = 4\pi^2 f^2 m = 4\pi^2 (0.5)^2 4 = 4\pi^2 \frac{N}{m}$$

3. **(E)** Apply Kirchhoff's Current Law at the node indicated by dashed lines

$$50 - i_t - 20 + 4i_t = 0$$

$$i_t = -10 \text{ mA}$$

Hence,

$v_t = 10K \times i_t$
$v_t = -100$ V

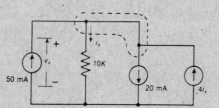

4. **(B)** At the critical point, the liquid changes to the vapor phase without undergoing a constant-temperature vaporization process. The temperature, pressure, and specific volume at the critical point are called the critical temperature, critical pressure, and critical volume, respectively.

   At a constant pressure greater than the critical pressure, there is no definite change in phase from liquid to vapor and no definite point at which there is a change from the liquid phase to the vapor phase. At a constant pressure lower than the critical point, there is a constant-temperature vaporization process, wherein the liquid phase and vapor phase coexist.

5. **(A)** The cooling process has two stages. First, steam at 100°C cools to liquid water at 100°C. The heat released in this condensation is (540 cal/g)(50 g) = 27,000 cal or

27 kcal. In the second stage, water at 100°C is cooled to water at 80°C. The heat released is

$$\Delta q = mc\Delta T = (50 \text{ g})(1 \text{ cal/g C°})(20\text{C°}) = 1000 \text{ cal}$$

In total 28,000 cal = 28 kcal of heat are transferred.

6. **(B)** Sodium is deficient in one electron and chlorine has a surplus of one electron. A stable configuration is possible if there is an outright transfer of the electron. Such bonds are called ionic or electrovalent.

7. **(E)** When one object is above the other, the distance between them is a minimum. There are five such minima in the figure.

8. **(B)** The distance between A and B is a minimum when one is on top of the other; their separation is then the side of the cube. From the figure, the minimum distance is 4 units.

9. **(B)** An equivalent question is, How often does the slope of this curve change from positive to negative? This happens at $t = 2.5$ sec, 7.5 sec, and so on, for a total of four times. Alternately, considering the case where A is initially above B on a corner, a few sketches reveal that twice each complete rotation around the cube the objects change their behavior from approaching to receding.

10. **(B)** The relationship between the two temperature scales is given by

$$Q = 2P - 200$$

Thus, when $P = 50°$, $Q = -100°$.

11. **(E)** Although conservation of kinetic energy is not always satisfied in two-particle collisions, conservation of linear and angular momentum is satisfied. The initial angular momentum of the system is not zero even though the sole moving object is in pure translation. $\vec{L} = \vec{r} \times \vec{p}$, $\vec{p}$ is not zero because there is straight line motion, and $\vec{r}$ is not zero for any choice of origin that does not lie along $\vec{p}$. This initial angular momentum is shared with the stick during the collision.

12. **(C)** Although the local growth mechanism for polymers is linear, the molecule as a whole has little motivation to remain linear—it may bend or twist or coil. There is no significant force tending to pull it along a line.

13. **(C)**

$$\int_a^b f(x)\, dx$$

is the area under the curve $f(x)$ from $x = a$ to $x = b$. Similarly, the second integral is the area under the curve from $x = a$ to $x = c$. By sketching these on a number line, we see that their difference is the area under the curve from $x = c$ to $x = b$, whether positive or negative. An alternative approach is to write the integrals in evaluated form as $F(b) - F(a)$ and $F(c) - F(a)$ (where F is the antiderivative of f), subtract, and go back to the unevaluated form.

14. **(D)** There are 10 distinct arrangements of the balls in A. In B there are

$$\frac{6!}{2!4!} = 15$$

such arrangements. In A the number of arrangements that results in two orange balls is

$$\binom{3}{2}\binom{2}{0} = 3$$

In B the number is

$$\binom{2}{2}\binom{4}{0} = 1$$

Thus, out of $10 \cdot 15$ possible arrangements in both boxes, there are $3 * 1 = 3$ arrangements of four orange balls.

$$\frac{3}{150} = 2\%$$

15. **(B)** The oscillating magnetic field in the solenoid means that the flux linkage to the loop oscillates at the same frequency as the oscillating magnetic field. As the flux linkage oscillates, the voltage across the loop changes phase just as rapidly according to Faraday's Law, $E = -d\Phi/dt$, where Φ is the magnetic flux. An oscillating voltage in the loop results in an oscillating current. All oscillations are at the same frequency because neither proportionalities nor derivatives change the frequency of a sinusoid.

GRE Mathematics Test

The GRE Mathematics Test is a 66-question examination. Some of the questions may be based on materials such as graphs and diagrams and may be grouped in sets.

The distribution of questions is roughly:

- **Calculus** (50 Percent): trigonometry, differential equations, coordinate geometry, applications;

- **Algebra** (25 Percent): elementary, linear (including matrices, eigenvectors, polynomials), and abstract (including number theory, and elementary theory of groups, rings, and fields);

- **Miscellaneous** (25 Percent): logic, set theory, topology, complex variables, probability and statistics, numerical analysis, combinatorial analysis, and the like.

Not all topics appear on every edition of the examination. Some topics may be included that are not mentioned here.

The sample questions that follow are representative of the examination questions. The correct answers, explained, appear directly after the questions. In answering these sample questions, circle the letter of your answer choice.

Sample Questions

1. A player rolls a die and receives a number of dollars corresponding to the number of dots on the face which turns up. What should the player pay for each roll if it is expected that he will break even in the long run?

   (A) $3.00
   (B) $3.25
   (C) $3.50
   (D) $3.75
   (E) $3.80

2. Find the value of $\int_0^{\pi/2} x^2 \sin x\, dx$.

   (A) π
   (B) $\dfrac{\pi}{2}$
   (C) $\pi - 1$
   (D) $\pi - 2$
   (E) $\dfrac{3\pi}{2}$

3. The function f is defined as $y = f(x) = \dfrac{2x + 1}{x - 3}$, where $x \neq 3$. Find the value of K so that the inverse of f will be $y = f_{(x)}^{-1} = \dfrac{3x + 1}{x - K}$.

   (A) 0
   (B) 1

   (C) 2
   (D) −1
   (E) −2

4. A point moves so that the square of its distance from a fixed point is proportional to its distance from a fixed line. Find its locus.

   (A) a circle
   (B) an ellipse
   (C) a parabola
   (D) a hyperbola
   (E) a straight line

5. The area from 0 to x under a certain graph is given by $A = (1 + 3x)^{1/2} - 1$, $x \geq 0$. Find the average value of the ordinate y, with respect to x, as x increases from 0 to 8.

   (A) $\dfrac{3}{7}$
   (B) $\dfrac{1}{2}$
   (C) $\dfrac{3}{8}$
   (D) $\dfrac{4}{7}$
   (E) $\dfrac{5}{8}$

6. The general solution of the differential equation
$$y'' + k^2 y = 0 \text{ is}$$

(A) $y = c_1 e^{kxi} + c_2 e^{-kxi}$

(B) $y = c_1 e^{kx} + c_2 e^{-kx}$

(C) $y = ke^{c_1 x} + ke^{c_2 x}$

(D) $y = c_1 xe^{kx} + c_2 e^{-kx}$

(E) $y = ke^{c_1 xi} + ke^{c_2 xi}$

7. Find the solution set of $\sin 2x < \sin x$ where $0 \le x \le 2\pi$.

(I) $\dfrac{\pi}{3} < x < \pi$

(II) $\dfrac{\pi}{3} < x < \dfrac{2\pi}{3}$

(III) $\dfrac{5\pi}{3} < x < 2\pi$

(IV) $\dfrac{\pi}{3} < x < \dfrac{5\pi}{3}$

(A) I only   (D) III only

(B) II and III only   (E) IV only

(C) I and III only

8. Find the volume of one of the two equal wedges cut from the cylinder $x^2 + y^2 = a^2$ by the planes $z = 0$ and $z = mx$.

(A) $m^2 a^2$

(B) $m\sqrt{a^2 + m^2}$

(C) $m^2 a^3$

(D) $\tfrac{2}{3} ma^3$

(E) $\dfrac{m^3 a^2}{3}$

9. A collection of objects, Group $G = \{p, q, r, s\}$ is given with the binary operation * defined by the table.

*	p	q	r	s
p	p	q	r	s
q	q	p	s	r
r	r	s	p	q
s	s	r	q	p

From the table, find the value of $(q*r)*(r*s)$

(A) p (B) q (C) r (D) s (E) none of these

10. What is the maximum number of digits in the period of the repeating decimal which is obtained from the rational number p/q, where q is prime number?

(A) q (B) $q + 1$ (C) $2q$ (D) $q - 1$ (E) $p + q$

11. Find the value of the continued fraction
$$1 + \cfrac{1}{1 + \cfrac{1}{1 + \cfrac{1}{1 + \dots}}}$$

(A) $\sqrt{5}$ (D) $\sqrt{3}$

(B) $\dfrac{1 - \sqrt{5}}{2}$ (E) ∞

(C) $\dfrac{1 + \sqrt{5}}{2}$

12. Find the interval of convergence for the series
$$x - \frac{x^2}{2} + \frac{x^3}{3} - \frac{x^4}{4} + \dots.$$

(A) $-1 < x < 1$ (D) $-1 < x \le 1$

(B) $-1 \le x < 1$ (E) none of these

(C) $0 \le x \le 2$

13. If the function $y = f(x)$ has an inverse function $y = f^{-1}(x)$, we may conclude that

(A) the graph of $y = f(x)$ is not symmetric with respect to the x-axis

(B) the graph of $y = f(x)$ is not symmetric with respect to the y-axis

(C) the graph of $y = f(x)$ is not symmetric with respect to the origin

(D) $y = f(x)$ is a continuous function

(E) none of the above are true

14. For the function $f(x) = x + \sin x$, we may infer which one of the following?

(A) It has no relative maxima or minima.

(B) It has one relative maximum and one relative minimum point for the interval $0 \le x \le 2\pi$.

(C) It has no points of inflection.

(D) It has one relative maximum but no minimum point in the interval $0 \le x \le 2\pi$.

(E) None of these.

15. Which system is an example of a group?

(A) The set of non-negative integers under ordinary multiplication.

(B) The set of non-negative reals under ordinary addition.

(C) The set of positive reals under ordinary multiplication.

(D) The set of non-negative rationals under multiplication.

(E) The set consisting of the four complex fourth roots of unity under ordinary addition.

16. The set of 2×2 matrices fails to satisfy the requirements of a group under matrix multiplication because

    (A) not every element has an inverse

    (B) the set lacks an identity element

    (C) the associative law is not satisfied

    (D) the commutative law is not satisfied

    (E) the closure law is not satisfied

17. Find the entire area of the limacon whose equation in polar coordinates, is $r = 2 + \cos \Theta$.

    (A) 4π (D) $11\pi/2$

    (B) $9\pi/2$ (E) 6π

    (C) 5π

Explanatory Answers

1. **(C)** The expected value

$$E = 1\left(\frac{1}{6}\right) + 2\left(\frac{1}{6}\right) + 3\left(\frac{1}{6}\right) + 4\left(\frac{1}{6}\right) + 5\left(\frac{1}{6}\right) + 6\left(\frac{1}{6}\right)$$

$$= 3\ 1/2 = \$3.50$$

2. **(D)** Let $u = x^2$, $dv = \sin x\, dx$

    then $du = 2x\, dx$, $v = -\cos x$

$$\int x^2 \sin x\, dx = -x^2 \cos x + \int 2x \cos x\, dx$$

Now let $U = 2x$ and $dV = \cos x\, dx$

       $dU = 2dx$ and $V = \sin x$

then $\displaystyle\int 2x \cos x\, dx = 2x \sin x - 2\int \sin x\, dx$

     $= 2x \sin x + 2 \cos x$

so that $\displaystyle\int_0^{\pi/2} x^2 \sin x\, dx =$

$$= \left| -x^2 \cos x + 2x \sin x + 2 \cos x \right|_0^{\pi/2}$$

$$= \left[(2 - x^2) \cos x + 2x \sin x \right]_0^{\pi/2}$$

$$= \pi - 2$$

3. **(C)** $y = \dfrac{2x + 1}{x - 3}$

      $xy - 3y = 2x + 1$

      $xy - 2x = 3y + 1$

      $x(y - 2) = 3y + 1$

      $x = \dfrac{3y + 1}{y - 2}$,   or as an inverse

function, $y = \dfrac{3x + 1}{x - 2}$

Hence $K = 2$

4. **(A)**

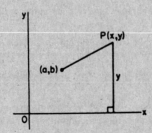

$$(y - b)^2 + (x - a)^2 = Ky$$

$$y^2 - 2by + b^2 - Ky + (x - a)^3 = 0$$

$$y^2 - (2b + K)y + \left(\frac{2b + K}{2}\right)^2 + (x - a)^2$$

$$= -b^2 + \left(\frac{2b + K}{2}\right)^2$$

$$(x - a)^2 + \left(y - \frac{2b + K}{2}\right)^2 = r^2$$

Eq. of a circle

5. **(B)** $y_{av} = \dfrac{1}{8 - 0}$

$$\int_0^8 y\, dx = \left[\frac{1}{8}(1 + 3x)^{1/2} - 1 \right]_0^8$$

Since $\displaystyle\int_0^8 y\, dx = A$

$$y_{av} = \frac{1}{8}[4] = \frac{1}{2}$$

6. **(A)**

The auxiliary equation is

$$m^2 + k^2 = 0$$

Solving, we get

$$m = \pm ki$$

Thus, e^{kxi} and e^{-kxi} are particular integrals, so that we may write the general solution in the form

$$y = c_1 e^{kxi} + c_2 e^{-kxi}$$

7. **(C)** $\sin 2x < \sin x$

       $2 \sin x \cos x < \sin x$

If $\sin x < 0$ or $\pi < x < 2\pi$,

then $2 \cos x > 1$ or $\cos x > 1/2$

thus $\dfrac{5\pi}{3} < x < 2\pi$

If $\sin x > 0$ or $0 < x < \pi$,

then $2 \cos x < 1$ or $\cos x < 1/2$

and $\pi/3 < x < \pi$

Hence I and III only.

8. **(D)**

$$V = 2\int_0^a \int_0^{\sqrt{a^2-y^2}} z\, dx\, dy$$

$$= 2\int_0^a \int_0^{\sqrt{a^2-y^2}} mx\, dx\, dy$$

$$= 2\int_0^a \left[\frac{mx^2}{2}\right]_0^{\sqrt{a^2-y^2}} dy$$

$$= 2\int_0^a \frac{m}{2}(a^2 - y^3)\, dy$$

$$= m\left[a^2 y - \frac{y^3}{3}\right]_0^a$$

$$= m\left[a^3 - \frac{a^3}{3}\right]$$

$$= \tfrac{2}{3}\, ma^3$$

9. **(C)** From the table $q*r = s$ and $r*s = q$ then $s*q = r$

10. **(D)** Since q is a prime number, the fraction cannot be reduced. Since the fraction becomes a repeating decimal, the number 0 cannot appear as a remainder in the division process. Thus the maximum number of possible digits in the period of the decimal is $q - 1$.

11. **(C)** Let $x = 1 + \cfrac{1}{1 + \cfrac{1}{1 + \dots}}$

then $x = 1 + \dfrac{1}{x}$

$x^2 - x - 1 = 0$

$x = \dfrac{1 \pm \sqrt{5}}{2}$

But the result must be positive.

Hence $X = \dfrac{1 + \sqrt{5}}{2}$.

12. **(D)**

$$\lim_{n \to \infty}\left|\frac{u_n + 1}{u_n}\right| = \lim_{n \to \infty}\left|\frac{x^{n+1}}{n + 1} \cdot \frac{n}{x^n}\right| < 1$$

$$\lim_{n \to \infty}\frac{n}{n + 1}\left|x\right| < 1 \quad \text{or} \quad \left|x\right| < 1$$

When $x = 1$, series is $1 - \frac{1}{2} + \frac{1}{3} - \frac{1}{4} + \dots$

(convergent)

When $x = -1$, series is $-1 - \frac{1}{2} - \frac{1}{3} - \frac{1}{4} + \dots$

(divergent)

Interval of convergence is $-1 < x \le 1$

13. **(B)** If the graph of $y = f(x)$ were symmetric with respect to the y-axis, then the relationship $y = f^{-1}(x)$ would be symmetric with respect to the x-axis, and it would not be a function because it lacks the single-valued criterion of function. Hence, we may infer (B).

14. **(A)**

$$y = x + \sin x$$
$$y' = 1 + \cos x = 0$$
$$\cos x = -1$$
$$x = \pi$$

$y'' = -\sin x$

when $x = \pi$, $y'' = 0$.

Since $y''' = -\cos x$, the value $x = \pi$ yields a point of inflection, and there are no maximum or minimum points.

15. **(C)** In (A), the inverse element of 0 does not exist. In (B), the inverse elements of the positive reals do not exist. In (D), there is no inverse of the 0 element. In (E), the identity element 0 is missing. (C) satisfies all requirements: inverse element, identity element, associative law and closure.

16. **(A)** The elements have inverses only when the determinant of the element $\neq 0$. All other requirements are satisfied except (D), and it is not necessary for a group. Hence, (A).

17. **(B)**

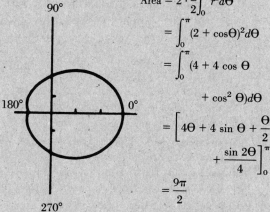

$$\text{Area} = 2 \cdot \frac{1}{2}\int_0^\pi r^2 d\Theta$$

$$= \int_0^\pi (2 + \cos\Theta)^2 d\Theta$$

$$= \int_0^\pi (4 + 4\cos\Theta + \cos^2\Theta) d\Theta$$

$$= \left[4\Theta + 4\sin\Theta + \frac{\Theta}{2} + \frac{\sin 2\Theta}{4}\right]_0^\pi$$

$$= \frac{9\pi}{2}$$

GRE Psychology Test

The GRE Psychology Test is a 220-question examination. Some of the questions appear in groups based upon descriptions of experiments or upon graphs of psychological functions.

The questions in the Psychology Test relate to courses of study offered to undergraduate psychology majors in colleges and universities throughout the United States. Questions may require students to recall information from the various psychology courses and to identify psychologists with the theories or conclusions with which they are associated. Some questions will require that students analyze relationships and apply principles. Others require drawing of conclusions from experimental data and evaluating experiments.

Although the GRE in Psychology yields two subscores—one in experimental psychology and one in social psychology—in addition to the total score, the test questions are usually drawn from three subject categories:

- **Questions of an experimental or natural science background:** This includes the areas of learning, cognition, and perception, ethology and comparative psychology, and sensation and physiology.

- **Questions of a social or social science background:** This includes the areas of personality, clinical and abnormal, and developmental and social psychology.

- **Questions of a general nature:** This includes historical and applied psychology, measurement, and statistics. It embraces information students should have acquired during their undergraduate studies in psychology.

The sample questions that follow are representative of the examination questions. The correct answers, explained, appear directly after the questions. In answering these sample questions, circle the letter of your answer choice.

Sample Questions

1. The idea that emotions have both physiological and cognitive components
   (A) was recognized by William James, who proposed that cognition precedes physiology
   (B) was recognized by Walter B. Cannon, who proposed that physiology precedes cognition
   (C) is the basis of modern psychophysiology
   (D) was recognized by Hans Selye, who proposed that stress precedes both cognition and physiology
   (E) was recognized by Stanley Schachter, who proposed that cognition mediates physiology

2. Two terms used to describe psychological disorders are *conversion reaction* and *psychosomatic illness*. Properly used,
   (A) *conversion reaction* refers to an essentially neurotic process, whereas an actual physical disorder is associated with *psychosomatic illness*
   (B) both terms mean the same thing
   (C) *conversion reaction* is a milder form of *psychosomatic illness*
   (D) *psychosomatic illness* is a phrase used by nontherapists, whereas *conversion reaction* has a technical meaning
   (E) *psychosomatic illness* refers to disorders associated with the central nervous system, whereas *conversion reaction* is associated with the peripheral nervous system

3. Independence vs. dependence, cooperation vs. competition, and impulse expression vs. moral standards are the most pervasive and difficult problems raised by
   (A) approach-approach conflicts
   (B) avoidance-avoidance conflicts
   (C) approach-avoidance conflicts
   (D) cognitive dissonance
   (E) experimental neurosis

4. You are a psychometrician assigned to evaluate a new culture-fair IQ test. Repeated administration of the test to a small sample leads to highly inconsistent results. You report that the test is

(A) reliable but not valid

(B) valid but not reliable

(C) valid and reliable

(D) of questionable value

(E) not culturally fair

5. Normative group influence is the influence to

(A) conform with the positive expectations of others

(B) accept as *normal* what most others report as normal

(C) work with others towards group goals

(D) conform with group leaders who are judged to be most *normal*

(E) join in discussions of group goals

6. An investigator reported a correlation coefficient of +.90 between a country's birth rate and the tendency of women in that country to sleep with the windows open. This can be interpreted to mean

(A) sleeping with the windows open causes an increase in the birth rate

(B) sleeping with the windows open can be hazardous to your health

(C) having many children causes one to sleep with the windows open

(D) when the birthrate is high, the women's tendency to sleep with the windows open is high

(E) men become more amorous in the heat

7. A researcher wishing to investigate whether a relationship exists between income and athletic ability asks the subjects to report their parents' incomes, and then tests all the subjects on a graded series of exercises. Given these data, the best statistical test to use to evaluate the hypothesis is

(A) the chi-square test

(B) the correlation coefficient

(C) the t-test

(D) the analysis of variance

(E) factor analysis

8. Immediately after a particular neuron has been fired, it is said to be in an absolute refractory period. This would lead one to suspect that for this period of time it

(A) cannot be excited

(B) will react paradoxically to excitation

(C) will react more globally to excitation

(D) will reverse polarity

(E) will temporarily decrease in size

9. An undesirable side effect of the frequent use of psychotropic drugs is

(A) invalidism

(B) Korsakoff's syndrome

(C) tardive dyskinesia

(D) violent outbursts

(E) infertility

10. Harlow's experiments on rhesus monkeys demonstrated that

(A) insight is an important part of problem solving

(B) the presence of food, regardless of its source, reduces anxiety

(C) fear is most easily overcome by the reduction of food drive

(D) cutaneous feedback plays an important role in reducing anxiety

(E) child-rearing among monkeys cannot be generalized to child-rearing among humans

11. A bimodal distribution would likely be found in a

(A) population but not a sample

(B) study in which the sample was not randomly drawn

(C) sample with two frequently occurring but separated values

(D) study of sex differences

(E) study of two correlated variables

12. Under what conditions of light stimulation is visual acuity best?

(A) in dim light

(B) in moderate light

(C) in bright light

(D) in light shifted to the red end of the spectrum

(E) in light shifted to the blue end of the spectrum

13. J. J. Gibson explains the persistence of perceptual constancies

(A) by citing innate perceptual structures

(B) as a ratio of the characteristics of the background in relation to those of the object

(C) as a function of previous experience with similar perceptual structures

(D) as a function of Gestalt principles

(E) as a function of their relationship with the personal equation

14. According to Ebbinghaus,

    (A) one-trial learning takes place only as a consequence of drive-reducing reinforcement

    (B) forgetting is directly proportional to the interval since the last learning trial

    (C) the meaningfulness of material to be learned has no effect on the learning curve

    (D) proportionally, the greatest amount of forgetting takes place immediately after learning

    (E) different experimental subjects retain material differently as a function of reinforcement schedules

15. Social psychologists have recently become interested in problems posed by shyness and fear of negative social evaluation. A treatment program set up by a therapist assumes that the underlying reason why shy people have difficulty is that when they are in challenging social situations their thoughts are preoccupied with fears about how others evaluate them. To counteract these preoccupations, the therapist places the *shy* person in simulated social situations and actively challenges any of the patient's fearful thoughts as they arise. This form of therapy is called

    (A) implosion therapy

    (B) behavioral therapy

    (C) psychoanalytically-oriented psychotherapy

    (D) psychodrama

    (E) cognitive therapy

16. The reticular activating system

    (A) alerts the brain that important information is on the way

    (B) treats all incoming information as equally important, but routes information to different parts of the brain

    (C) passes information through the front side of the brainstem

    (D) plays a less important role in brain functioning the higher on the evolutionary scale the organism is

    (E) is dormant during sleep

Explanatory Answers

1. **(E)** Schachter and Singer (1962) demonstrated that although physiological factors may influence the intensity of a response, cognitive factors, such as a belief about the causes of physiological reactions, also influence emotional arousal.

2. **(A)** According to the latest revision of the *Diagnostic and Statistical Manual* (*DSM-IIIR*), conversion disorder is a form of somatization disorder in which the symptoms are not adequately explained by the physical disorder or usual pathophysiological mechanisms, suggesting heavily involved psychological mechanisms. Although the term *psychosomatic disorder* is no longer used in the *DSM-IIIR*, it has generally come to mean one of seven or eight commonly diagnosed physical disorders, such as ulcers, in which there is an actual physical disorder that is likely to have a psychological component.

3. **(B)** According to group dynamics research, as pioneered by Lewin, avoidance-avoidance conflicts produce the greatest amount of discomfort, vacillation, and desire to *leave the field* or avoid the conflict by attempting to escape it entirely.

4. **(D)** Of the choices given, the most appropriate is that the test is of questionable value.

5. **(A)** Normative group influence is the influence to conform with the group norms.

6. **(D)** This answer alternative makes the fewest assumptions about causation, which avoids the most common error made in interpreting correlation coefficients.

7. **(B)** This investigation concerns the relationship between two sets of variables measured from the same subjects, which makes the data analyzable by the use of the Pearson Product Moment (PPM) coefficient of correlation.

8. **(A)** During the absolute refractory period, which lasts for a few milliseconds, the axon is unexcitable and cannot be fired. This is followed by a relative refractory period, during which the axon can be fired by a greater than usual excitation. After the relative refractory period, the level of excitability returns to normal.

9. **(C)** Tardive dyskinesia, which includes uncoordinated body movement, is a frequent negative side effect of the overuse of psychotropic drugs.

10. **(D)** By preferring the terry cloth *mother* to the wire *mother* when under stress, the rhesus monkeys in Harlow's experiments demonstrated that tactile sensation is an important part of attachment.

11. **(C)** Bimodal implies that there are two modes, or two frequently occurring values.

12. **(C)** Under bright light, the cones transmit the greatest amount of information. Since the cones are most centrally located, visual acuity or sharpness is greatest for objects directly in front of the eye when stimulated.

13. **(B)** Perceptual constancy refers to the apparent stability of a retinal image despite changes in size, shape, color, brightness, and location.

14. **(D)** Ebbinghaus' pioneering studies on learning, using himself as the main subject, used nonsense syllables as the main object of learning.

15. **(E)** Cognitive therapists, who have also done a great deal of work on depression, assume that psychological difficulties are the result of conflicting thought patterns (thus the term *cognitive*) that can be corrected by variations on conditioning techniques.

16. **(A)** Also called the reticular formation, the reticular activating system passes through the medulla in the hindbrain into parts of the forebrain. Its apparent function is to control wakefulness, attention, sleep, and some simple learning processes.

FINANCING YOUR GRADUATE EDUCATION

Education is expensive, and the higher the level of education, the greater the cost. As you contemplate going on to graduate or professional school, you must face the awesome question, "How am I going to pay for this?"

With the possible exceptions of a winning lottery ticket, a windfall inheritance or a very wealthy family, no single source of funds will be adequate to cover tuition, other educational costs, and living expenses during your years of graduate study. While the funding task is daunting, it is not impossible. With patience and hard work, you can piece together your own financial package.

CONSIDER DEFERRING YOUR APPLICATION

You might consider putting off applications for a few years while you work at the highest paying job you can find and accumulate some funds. A few years' savings will not cover the entire bill, but they can help. A real effort to earn your own way is a show of sincerity and good faith when you approach funders, too. You are probably better off delaying your applications altogether rather than applying and deferring your entry once you have been accepted. Deferral, if permitted, is generally limited to one year, and one year may not be sufficient to build your tuition fund.

If you cannot find a really high-paying job, you might seek a position or series of positions closely related to your field for the years between undergraduate and graduate or professional school. A year or more of exposure and involvement can help you to focus your interest. Experience in the field shows up as an asset on your graduate admissions applications and on your applications for fellowships. The more crystallized your interests, the better essays and personal statements you can write to support your requests.

Another benefit to deferral is the opportunity to establish residence. As you research the various graduate programs, you are likely to discover that some of the most exciting programs in your field of interest are being offered at state universities. State universities tend to have lower tuition rates than do private universities. Furthermore, the tuition charged to bona fide residents is considerably lower than that charged to out-of-state residents. The requirements for establishing residence vary from state to state; make it a point to inquire about the possibility of in-state tuition at each state university you are considering. The suggestion that you delay application until you are nearly ready to enter graduate school does not hold with regard to delay for purposes of establishing residence. Since you can only establish residence in one state, you want to apply and be accepted before you select your new home state. Most universities will cooperate and will allow you to move to the state, find employment, and defer enrollment until you qualify for in-state tuition.

WORKING PART-TIME

Another possible way to pay—this one hard on you but possible at many, though not at all, institutions—is to be a part-time student and a full- or part-time wage earner. Again, there are a number of options. You might find a totally unrelated but high-paying job. You will have to be creative in your search. Sanitation workers, for instance, tend to have hours like 7 am to 3 pm which leaves afternoon and evening for classes and study. The job of the sanitation worker is physically exhausting but makes no mental demands and in most localities is quite well paid. Another job which does not take too much thought is working for a courier service like United Parcel. Such delivery services operate twenty-four hours a day. During the night, packages are off-loaded from big interstate trucks and from bulk deliveries from individual shippers and are sorted and loaded onto delivery trucks for route drivers the next day. There is usually plenty of turnover among these night workers, and most parcel service employees are unionized, so the hourly rate is attractive. An alternative to physical labor might be seeking a job in a field related to your studies. Such a job could reinforce your learning and contribute to the job experience section of your resume. If you are earning a degree in computer science, you might find computer-related employment. If you are entering law school, you might work as a paralegal.

GETTING HELP FROM YOUR EMPLOYER

If you both defer application and enter a related field, you may be fortunate enough to find an employer who will pay for a part or even all of your graduate education. This option is most viable if the advanced degree is to be in business or law, but some corporations will finance a master's degree or even a doctorate if the further training will make the employee more valuable to them. Employers cannot require that you continue your employment for any specified number of years after earning your degree. Rather they rely on your gratitude and good will.

The programs under which employers help pay for education are as varied as the number of employers and the graduate programs. Many banks, insurance companies, and brokerage houses offer tuition rebates as part of their benefits packages. These companies rebate part or all of the tuition for courses successfully completed by their employees. Sometimes the rate of reimbursement is tied to the grade earned in the course. Some large law firms will advance part of the law school tuition for promising paralegals after a number of years of service. If these students successfully complete law school and return to the firm for summers and a certain number of years afterwards, the balance of the tuition may be reimbursed. And some industrial corporations will cover the cost of part-time study which enhances the skills of employees, thus making them still more useful to the organization. Such corporations may permit these employees to work a shortened work-week at full-time pay while they study. Some companies even give the employee a year's leave, without salary but with tuition paid, and with a guarantee that the employee will have a job at the end of the leave. This guaranteed position at the end of the leave is worth a lot. It offers peace of mind and freedom to concentrate on research and writing and assures that you will immediately begin earning money with which to repay supplementary graduate loans and leftover undergraduate loans.

If you have been working for the same employer for a year or more, you might do well to inquire about a tuition rebate program. If you are a valuable employee, your employer may be willing to make an investment in you.

THE MILITARY OPTION

If you are heavily burdened with loans from your undergraduate years and are willing to serve for three years in the armed forces, the government will pay off a large portion of your college loans for you. Without the undergraduate debt, you will be eligible for larger loans for your graduate study, and you will not have so many years of high repayment bills to face. After your three years of service, you will be eligible for GI Bill benefits so that you will not need to incur such hefty loans for graduate school. While you are actually in the service, you can attend graduate school part time and have 75% of the cost paid for you. Funding for medical school and law school is even more attractive. From the point of view of footing the bill for graduate studies, the military option sounds too good to be true. Of course there are strings attached. You must serve in the armed forces. You are subject to military rules and military discipline. You may find that a transfer of location totally disrupts your studies if you are trying to attend part time. And, in case of war or other military emergency, you must serve and quite possibly face physical danger. This is the trade-off. If the advantages of having the government pay your education bills outweigh the drawbacks in your eyes, by all means explore the military option. Check with more than one branch of the services; programs vary and change frequently. Ask lots of questions. Be certain that you fully understand all of your obligations, and insist that the funding commitment be in writing. You cannot change your mind and just quit the armed forces, so you must be certain that this route is right for you before you sign up.

If full-time military service is out of the question for you, but having the government underwrite your education is still attractive, consider the National Guard or the Reserves. The all-volunteer standing armed forces are not adequate for all national security needs, so efforts are constantly being made to increase the appeal of the Guard and the Reserves. The benefits offered are frequently readjusted, so you must make your own inquiries about loan repayments and funding of ongoing education while you are in service. Life in the Guard or the Reserves is not nearly so restrictive on a daily basis as life in the regular armed forces, but both Guard members and Reservists are subject to call-up in times of need, and if you are called, you must serve. Circumstances of a call-up may include dangerous assignment, severe economic difficulties, or service that you find morally repugnant (such as strike-breaking if you are a member of a Guard unit called by the governor). If these contingencies do not upset you, this form of long-term, part-time military service can relieve you of much of the cost of your advanced degree.

NEED-BASED FUNDING

The need-based funding picture for graduate studies is quite different from its counterpart at the undergraduate level. Most undergraduate funding is need-based; most graduate funding is not. All universities have a mechanism for distributing need-based funding, in grant/loan/self-help packages similar to undergraduate packages, but the funds are more limited. Your application information packet will tell you how to apply for need-based funding.

Basically you will have to fill out a university financial aid application, a U.S. Department of Education approved multi-data entry form (FFS, the family financial statement of American College Testing service; FAF, the financial aid form of the Educational Testing Service; or GAPS-FAS, the graduate and professional school financial aid service of the Educational Testing Service in California), and whatever other forms the university requires. The university will coordinate its need-based package with department sponsored merit funding and with any outside funding you can gather. Plan to look beyond university need-based funding. It will be top-heavy toward loans and will not be adequate for all your needs.

The following information distributed to all graduate school applicants by a leading large state university is specific to that university yet, at the same time, is representative of the need-based funding situation nationwide.

ASSISTANCE THROUGH THE OFFICE OF STUDENT FINANCIAL AID (OSFA)

You may be eligible for financial aid if you are enrolled at least half-time (five semester hours during the academic year, or three semester hours during the summer session) as a graduate student in a program leading to a degree. Students admitted as Special Nondegree Students may also be eligible for some of the programs listed below.

How to Apply

Specific information and application materials may be obtained from OSFA. To determine your eligibility for aid through the OSFA, you must provide information about your financial situation by submitting either the Financial Aid Form (FAF) to the College Scholarship Service (CSS) or the Family Financial Statement (FFS) to American College Testing (ACT). This University does not accept the Graduate and Professional School Financial Aid Service (GAPSFAS) form.

OSFA will process your financial aid application as soon as your file becomes complete. Some financial aid programs are subject to the availability of funds (first-come, first-served) and others are not. To be considered for all limited funds, be sure to submit your materials as soon as possible after January 1 for the upcoming academic year.

Financial need is an eligibility requirement for all of the following sources of assistance except the Supplemental Loans for Students (SLS) program and part-time jobs.

- Graduate Tuition Grants are based on exceptional need. These institutional grant funds are very limited. Approximately 200 students are awarded tuition grants early in the March prior to the academic year in which they plan to enroll.
- Educational Opportunity Program (EOP) Grants are institutional grants for minority students who demonstrate exceptional need.
- The College Work-Study Program is an employment program subsidized by the federal government and the state.
- Perkins Loans are long-term federal loans based on exceptional need.
- Stafford Loans (formerly Guaranteed Student Loans—GSL) are long-term federal loans based on need and arranged with a bank, credit union, or savings and loan.

- Supplemental Loans for Students (SLS) are arranged with a bank, credit union or savings and loan and are available to students with or without need.

  In addition, part-time jobs (not to be confused with College Work-Study jobs) available throughout the campus and community are posted daily on bulletin boards outside of the OSFA.

Special Note to Assistantship/Fellowship Recipients

Since most assistantship income is classified as "wages," it will not affect your academic year financial aid award (which is usually based on your previous year's income, according to the federal formula for determining financial aid eligibility). However, fellowship income classified as "scholarship" rather than "wages" will be treated as "scholarship resources" in your financial aid package, and thus may affect your eligibility for other financial aid programs.

Nonresident financial aid awardees who receive assistantships that allow resident classification for tuition purposes may have their need-based aid decreased due to the decrease in their educational cost.

Outside need-based funding in the form of grants is confined mainly to special populations. Since these grants are limited in number, they too are based on a combination of merit and need, not merely upon demonstrated need. Some of these special population grants are targeted toward bringing minority students into the professions, such as those sponsored by the Black Lawyers' Associations of various states. Others aim to develop academic talent among Native Americans and Hispanics. Others, such as Business and Professional Women's Foundation Scholarships, are earmarked for mature women reentering the academic world in search of advanced degrees. Grant and fellowship directories tend to index grants by specialty, by region of the country, by point in the studies and time span of funding, and by targeted population. When you consult these directories, you must consider your own identity along every possible dimension in order to locate all funding which could apply to you.

Much outside funding comes in the form of loans. Although helpful and often necessary, loans are still a last resort. For this reason, we shall defer our discussion of loans until the end of this chapter.

FELLOWSHIPS AND ASSISTANTSHIPS

By far the greatest source of funding for graduate study is the graduate department or program itself. Most departments dispense a mixed bag of fellowships, teaching assistantships and research assistantships. Some of these may be allocated to the department by the university; still others are foundation fellowships for which the department nominates its most promising candidates. In most cases, the amount of money attached to the various fellowships and assistantships varies greatly—from tuition abatement alone, to tuition abatement plus stipend (also of varying sums), to stipend alone. Some of the fellowships and assistantships are specifically earmarked for only the first year of graduate study. Others are annually renewable upon application and evidence of satisfactory work in the previous year. Still others are guaranteed for a specified number of years—through three years of coursework, for one year of research or fieldwork, or a stipend to pay living costs during the year of writing a dissertation, for example.

The information below describes graduate student funding only at the University of Iowa. It is presented here to open the array of possibilities. The information provided by other universities is similar, but each is unique.

SUPPORT FROM THE GRADUATE COLLEGE AND YOUR DEPARTMENT OR PROGRAM

The following awards and appointments are the primary sources of financial assistance available to graduate students through their department or program.

■ Teaching and Research Assistantships available in most departments, offer stipends typically ranging from $9,000 to $10,000 for half-time appointments. In accordance with general University policy, assistantship holders (quarter-time or more) are classified as residents for fee purposes for the terms during which their appointments are held and any adjacent summer sessions in which they are enrolled. Students on an appointment of half-time or more may have to carry a reduced academic load.

■ Iowa Fellowships for first-year graduate students entering doctoral programs carry a minimum stipend of $14,500 plus full tuition for four years on a year-round basis (academic year and summer session). For two of the four years and all summers, recipients have no assignments and are free to pursue their own studies, research and writing.

■ Graduate College Block Allocation Fellowships carry a stipend of $8,000 for the academic year.

■ Graduate Opportunity Fellowships for first-year graduate students from underrepresented ethnic minority groups carry a one-year stipend of $8,000 for the academic year.

■ Scholarships, traineeships, and part-time employment are offered by many graduate departments and programs. Funds are received from both public and private agencies, individuals, corporations, and philanthropic organizations. In general, submission of the *Application for Graduate Awards and Appointments* places eligible applicants in consideration for these awards.

How to Apply

Submit your *Application for Graduate Awards and Appointments* to your department or program by February 1 if you wish to be considered for the following fall. These non-need-based awards are made on the basis of academic merit. Only students admitted to a graduate department or program are eligible to apply. Fellowship and assistantship recipients are also eligible to apply for tuition scholarships awarded in amounts up to full-time tuition and fees. Contact your program or department for more specific information.

Surprisingly, the overall wealth of the institution is not necessarily reflected in the graduate funding it offers. Some universities choose to devote the bulk of their discretionary funds to undergraduate need-based aid. Others offer a greater share to graduate students. Some graduate departments in some universities have separate endowments apart from the university endowment as a whole. A department with its own source of funds can dispense these funds as it wishes, within the restrictions of the endowment, of course.

The case of Clark University in Worcester, Massachusetts, is illustrative of the ways a particular department funds its students. Clark is a relatively small, financially strapped institution. University-based funding for undergraduates is severely limited. Yet, every doctoral candidate in the geography department is equally funded; each receives tuition abatement and an equal stipend in return for teaching or research assistance. The funding is guaranteed for three years of course work. How can this be? The geography department at Clark has, over the years, developed an extremely high reputation. It is considered one of the premier geography departments in the United States. The university considers investment in its geography department to be one of its priorities because maintaining the reputation of its flagship department enhances the reputation of the university as a whole. Leading professors are eager to be associated with leading departments, so the Clark geography faculty includes some luminaries in its ranks. These faculty members in turn attract research funds. Research funds are used in part to pay for the services of research assistants. Publication of results of the research attracts further grants. These funds cover a number of graduate students. The reputation of the department also leads it to draw the best and the brightest among its doctoral candidates. These highly qualified students often draw outside fellowships on the basis of their own merit. Students who bring in their own funding release department funds for other students. And because of its reputation and the reputed caliber of its students, the department is often offered the opportunity to nominate its students to compete for private fellowships. Money entering the department in this way releases still more of the limited funds for student support. In a good year, there may even be funds to help some students at the beginning of their dissertation research. The situation at Clark, while it is Clark's alone, indicates that it may be possible to find funding even in a small, struggling school. Graduate aid is not monolithic. You must ask about the special features in each department and in each program. Do not limit your research to the overall university bulletin!

Sometimes a university will offer some departments the opportunity to nominate candidates for outside fellowships open to students of certain specified departments or to students of the university at large. For example, the MacArthur Foundation funds a number of interdisciplinary fellowships in peace studies at a few selected universities. Each participating university is allocated a number of fellowships to dispense at its discretion. The university then opens the competition to appropriate departments, and the departments in turn nominate candidates from among their most promising applicants. The departments choose nominees on the basis of personal statements submitted at the time of application and on the basis of those applicants' credentials and background experiences. They then solicit the nominees to prepare additional application materials and essays and supply additional recommendations to support application for the fellowship. Having MacArthur fellows among its students brings both money and prestige to the department. Each department studies credentials and statements carefully before soliciting applicants. However, the department could overlook someone. If you have not been invited to apply for a fellowship which you think you qualify for, you can suggest to the department— diplomatically, of course—that you consider yourself a likely candidate.

Few individuals are awarded any one fellowship, but each person who does win one is assured a comfortable source of funding. And someone has to win. It might as well be you. Those who win the named fellowships are removed from the competition for other merit-based or need-based funding, thus increasing the chance of other applicants to win any remaining funds.

Most foundation-funded fellowships, especially those for entering graduate students, are channelled through the department or program. To be considered for these fellowships you must be recommended by the department. There are some fellowships out there, however, for which you must apply as an individual. Some of these are regional, and some are targeted at a specific population. Some are tied to a field such as economics or philosophy, and others have a specific purpose in mind such as studies aimed at improving the welfare of the homeless. Of the privately funded fellowships some are for the first year only, some for the full graduate career, some for the last year of course work only, and still others to support the dissertation at a specific stage or throughout research and writing. Some are relatively small awards; others are so generous that they provide total financial security to the student. The sources of these fellowships range from your local Rotary Club to Rotary International, to AAUW (American Association of University Women) fellowships, to the prestigious Rhodes Scholarships.

FUNDING POSSIBILITIES FROM PRIVATE FOUNDATIONS

The names of some of the philanthropic foundations that give grants for graduate study are almost household words—Dana, Mellon, Ford, Sloan, Rockefeller, Guggenheim, MacArthur, Fulbright, Woodrow Wilson are but a few. These foundations, and others like them, offer funding at many levels of study and for a variety of purposes.

The National Science Foundation offers funding for the full graduate program in science and engineering for minority students as well as for the general population. Other National Science Foundation fellowships specifically fund the research and writing of doctoral dissertations. The U.S. Department of Education Jacob K. Javits Fellowships fund full doctoral programs in the arts, humanities and social sciences. The National Research Council Howard Hughes Medical Institute Doctoral Fellowships offer tuition and a $10,000 per year stipend for three to five years of doctoral work in biology or the health sciences. The Eisenhower Memorial Scholarship Foundation offers a number of $3,000 per year scholarships. The Mellon and Ford Foundations both fund ABD (all but dissertation) fellowships for minority Ph.D. candidates. Under the terms of the ABD fellowships, candidates teach one course per term at a liberal arts college and receive a healthy stipend while writing their dissertations. This program has the double-barreled purpose of assisting minority students while developing teaching talent.

The AAUW (American Association of University Women) is very active in disbursing funds to women for graduate study. Local units give small gifts to undergraduates. Larger grants are made by the AAUW through its Educational Foundation Programs office. In some years the AAUW supports as many as fifty women at the dissertation stage. The Business and Professional Women's Foundation gives scholarships to mature women entering graduate programs. Some of these scholarships are earmarked for women over the age of 35. The American Women in Selected Professions Fellowships fund women in their last year of law or graduate studies in sums ranging from $3,500 to $9,000 apiece.

Other funding for doctoral dissertations comes from the Woodrow Wilson National Fellowship Foundation (in social sciences and humanities), from the Social Science Research Council, and the Guggenheim Foundation. Some foundation funding is reserved for study abroad. Rhodes Scholarships, in particular, support students studying at Oxford. Various Fulbrights, Wilsons, Marshalls, and MacArthurs, among others, support research in foreign universities and at field sites.

The above listing is far from exhaustive. In fact, this is only a tiny sampling of the funding possibilities from private foundations. Even so, the number of grants available is far exceeded by the the number of graduate students who would like to have them. You must work hard to identify and to earn the grants for which you qualify.

FINDING SOURCES OF FINANCIAL AID

There are a number of directories that list these prizes, scholarships, and fellowships one by one. The directories give the name of the sponsor, who to contact, addresses, phone numbers, and deadlines. They also tell something of the purpose of the grants, the number of grants awarded, specific qualification requirements, and the dollar amounts. If the grants are awarded to support research, the directories may give representative titles of projects funded. One of the most useful features of the directories is their cross-indexing. When you consult a grants directory you can look up sources under ethnic designations, geographic designations, subject of study, purpose of research, duration of funding, etc. These directories are very useful as a starting point in the search for outside funding.

Consult the list of directories in the bibliography at the end of this chapter. With list in hand, go to a college library, large public library, or the financial aid office of your current institution and sit down with a directory and pad of paper. Give yourself many hours to find all the grants for which you qualify and to photocopy or write down the important details of each. Immediately call or write each sponsor requesting application materials. Do not rely on deadlines printed in the directories and put off requesting materials. Deadlines change. Do not discount grants or prizes with low dollar amounts attached. A small grant may not be adequate to see you through even a semester of study, but it will do much to enhance your resume. The fact that you were able to compete successfully for any prize makes you a more attractive candidate for the higher-tagged fellowships you apply for next year. If a grant cannot be combined, you may have to decline it, but the fact of having won is already in your favor. Most often, small grants can be combined with other sources of funding, so even small ones help.

APPLYING FOR A GRANT

The procedure for applying for grants and fellowships for your coursework years is similar for both university-administered and private foundation sources. The best advice is to start early. Everything takes longer than you expect, and deadlines tend to be inviolate. Everyone with money to give away is besieged by applicants. There is no need to extend deadlines.

Once you receive application material, begin immediately to accumulate the specified documentation. Each sponsor has different requirements, so read carefully. You will probably need official transcripts from every college you ever attended, even if you took only one course over the summer. You are likely to be asked for official copies of test scores, too. Letters of recommendation are always required. Think about them carefully. You want to request letters from people who have known you as a scholar—professors with whom you have worked closely or authors for whom you have done research or fact checking. You want your letters to be written by people whom you believe have admired your work and who express themselves well. And, consider the reliability of the people from whom you request letters of recommendation. Your application can be seriously jeopardized or even torpedoed if your recommendations do not come through on time. Choose carefully. Consider asking for one extra recommendation just in case someone lets you down. Having recommendations sent to you and then forwarding them in their sealed envelopes is the best way to keep track of what has come in if this procedure is permitted by the sponsor. Be aware that you may have to make a pest of yourself to get transcripts and letters in on time.

You are more in control of the other documents you are likely to be asked for in support of your application. The first of these is a "personal goals statement." This is a carefully reasoned, clear statement of your interests, the reasons for your choice of program, personal growth goals, and career goals. Ideally you should prepare this statement on a word processor so that you can retain the basic exposition but tailor each statement to the needs and interests of the specific sponsor. Try to tie in your statement with the special strengths of the program and with the advantages offered by a particular sponsor. Be sincere and enthusiastic. Adhere to the page limits or word count specified in the application instructions. And remember, neatness counts.

You may also be asked for your resume, samples of scholarly writing or summaries of research you have done. If the grant you seek is meant to finance research or dissertation, you may have to go into detail about the scope of your research, methodology, purpose, expected final results and even proposed budget. Give thought before you write. Then follow the sponsor's instructions, providing all the information that is requested, but not so much more as to overwhelm or bore the reader.

One caveat: Read the requirements carefully before you apply. If you do not fully qualify, do not apply. There are ample qualified applicants for every grant. Requirements will not be waived. The application process is an exacting one and requires you to impose upon others. Do not waste their time or your own.

EMPLOYMENT OPPORTUNITIES ON CAMPUS

While your department is clearly the best university-based source for fellowships, teaching assistantships, and research assistantships, do not totally discount the university as a whole. If you have an area of expertise outside of your own graduate department, by all means build upon it. If you are bilingual in a language taught at the university, you may be able to teach in the language department. Your best chance for a teaching assistantship outside of your department is in a university with relatively few graduate programs. Departments must favor their own graduate students, but if a department has no qualified students of its own, it may be delighted to acquire the services of a graduate student from another department. Some universities even have a formalized mechanism for allocating teaching assistants where they are needed. To return to the example of Clark, where all graduate students must serve as research or teaching assistants, often there are not as many openings for assistants in the undergraduate geography department as there are students. Clark has relatively few graduate programs, and geography students tend to have strong backgrounds in political science, economics and ecology. The graduate geography department and the undergraduate deans readily cooperate to place geography students where they are most needed. In universities with less defined needs for teaching assistants, you may have to be your own advocate. Regardless of your current department, if you can document your ability to assist in another department, you should pursue opportunities there. Do not be shy; let your area of special competence be well known.

Another possible source of university employment is as a residence advisor or freshman advisor. At some colleges and universities, residence advisors are undergraduates. At other institutions, older students—graduate students or students in one of the professional schools—are preferred. If you took peer- counseling training while in high school, consider yourself a candidate. If you were successful in a counseling function during your own undergraduate years, you should be a natural. In very large universities with big freshmen dormitories, a few graduate students with experience in residence advising may be taken on to coordinate and supervise the senior undergraduates who serve as floor or wing advisors. Obviously there are not many such coordinator positions available, but if you qualify, you may get the job.

There are a number of possible advantages to being appointed to a major university-based position such as teaching assistant or residence advisor. One is that, at a state university, you will become eligible instantly for in-state tuition. The reduced tuition is a valuable, non-taxable benefit. Another possibility is that you will be classified as an employee of the university. Policies vary, of course, but at many institutions employees of the university are eligible for reduced tuition or even for total remission of tuition. In addition, assistants generally receive a stipend which even if it does not totally cover living expenses is certainly a big help. Residence hall advisors may get free room along with tuition abatement, and residence hall advisors generally get choice accommodations.

If you were a member of a fraternity or sorority as an undergraduate, you may fulfill a role similar to that of residence advisor in your fraternity or sorority house. As an employee of the fraternity or sorority rather than of the university, you will not be eligible for employee-of-the-university benefits, but you will have free housing and, quite possibly, a salary or stipend as well. Fraternity employment will count toward self-help in a need-based package, but it should have no adverse effect on your winning a merit-based fellowship as well. Be aware, though, that if you are holding what is in effect two jobs, you may have to carry a lighter course load.

Students who work part time in the library, equipment and facilities departments, or in food service will probably not qualify for the perquisites of employees of the university (though depending on the institution and the number of hours worked they might). Campus-based hourly work tends not to be very well paid, but it does offer certain advantages such as elimination of travel time and costs and exemption from FICA (social security) deductions from your paycheck. Exemption from FICA is at the option of the institution, but is permitted by the federal tax code. The contribution which is not deducted has the effect of adding more than 7% to your salary.

ALL LOANS ARE NOT ALIKE

Finally loans come in to fill the financing gap. If you are already saddled with loans from your undergraduate education, you may cringe at the prospect of accumulating further debt. Don't panic. Not all loans are alike, and not all repayment schedules are equally onerous.

In particular, members of minority groups find creative financing routes available to them. The Consortium on the Financing of Higher Education (C.O.F.H.E.), a group of thirty-one universities and colleges including the Ivies and Sister colleges, is making a concerted effort to encourage minority students to pursue advanced degrees. The Kluge Foundation program at Columbia University is only one response to the funding problem. Because Columbia University is an expensive private university, its undergraduates often find themselves heavily indebted to the university by commencement. Under the terms of the Kluge grant, minority alumni of Columbia who successfully complete doctoral programs at accredited universities will have their undergraduate indebtedness wiped out by the Kluge funds. The Minority Issues Task Force of the Council of Graduate Schools is working on the funding problems of minority students, many of whom have very few resources. The funding picture is in constant flux. Be sure that you have the most current information at the moment you are ready to begin applying.

The loan forgiveness possibilities for members of the armed forces have already been touched upon. If military service is not for you, there are other loan forgiveness programs you may find attractive. With the shortage of highly-qualified, highly-motivated public school teachers, there has been a concerted effort to attract liberal arts graduates, even without full teaching credentials, into public school teaching. Liberal arts graduates who enter the public school teaching force under certain programs can have their undergraduate loans written off. If you enter public school teaching after receiving a graduate degree, you may still receive considerable help with those undergraduate loans. Paying off your own graduate school loans, then, will not be so overwhelming.

Most of the loan forgiveness programs for graduate loans apply to professional studies—medicine, dentistry, law, social work—rather than to straight academic disciplines. If your graduate studies will lead to a professional degree, you should not discount loan forgiveness programs out of hand.

A doctor who forgoes a lucrative suburban practice in favor of practicing for a number of years in an underserved area, be it poverty-ridden inner city or isolated rural community, may have a good portion of his or her loans paid off by the government or by private foundations or forgiven by the medical school itself. The doctor may find that the challenges of this practice and the gratitude of the population served are so satisfying that he or she will choose to make this practice a lifelong career. If not, the experience will certainly have been valuable as the doctor moves in new directions. Similarly, a number of prestigious law schools will wipe out the loans of their graduates who enter public service law instead of high-paying corporate law firms. And schools of social work or professional associations of social workers may help to pay off the loans of social workers who utilize their advanced degrees in certain aspects of social work or in highly underserved areas. If your ideals encourage using your educational opportunities to help others, you may find this assistance with your loan payments to give you the best of all possible worlds. The time commitment tends to only be a few years, after which you can move into the private sector with excellent experience to further your applications. Or, you may find that you really enjoy the work you have taken on and build a satisfying career in public service.

There are a number of other loan programs which, while they entail repayment, offer attractive features. The Hattie M. Strong Foundation, for instance, offers interest-free loans for the final year of graduate school or law school on the assumption that without money worries the student can earn higher grades in the final year and obtain a better position after graduation.

From your undergraduate days, you are probably aware of Stafford loans, formerly known as GSLs or Guaranteed Student Loans. At the graduate level the annual cap is $7,500 per year up to a borrowing limit of $54,750. The Stafford loan carries a lower rate of interest than most other loans. More important, repayment need not begin until six months after receipt of the degree, and the government pays the interest in the interim. There is a means test attached to the Stafford loan. Not every applicant is automatically eligible. However, many graduate students who are no longer dependent on parental income or assets do qualify for Stafford loans even though they did not as undergraduates.

University sponsored loans tend to be heavily need-based and to come as parts of total financial aid packages with grants, assistantships and jobs. And even need-based loans are often earmarked for specific underrepresented populations. If you think that you qualify, ask for the information and forms.

Everything that has been said about private foundation funding applies equally to loans as to grants and fellowships. The same directories which can lead you to grants and fellowships can lead you to foundation loans. Again, some of these require evidence of need; others are strictly merit-based. Some apply to the early years of graduate study; others are geared to the dissertation years. Some carry no or low rates of interest, and some have forgiveness provisions if certain conditions are met. In general, foundation loans are less painful than commercial loans. Do not limit your search through the grant directories to high-paying grants. Give equal attention to the smaller prizes and to the loan programs.

Most other loan programs are unrestricted as to income or assets but tend to have restrictions related to total debt with which the student is already burdened and to security or cosigners for the loan. The financial aid office of your current institution or the school to which you have been accepted can help you find your way through the maze of acronymic loan programs: SLS, PLUS, ALAS, TERI, Sallie Mae, Nellie Mae, and the Law Access Program administered by the Law School Admission Service. These last four are non-profit loan agencies which allow for greater flexibility than do the first three. In general the rates are tied to prime + 2 which is better than commercial rates. Repayment schedules, loan consolidation arrangements, co-signing requirements, etc. are all considered on a case-by-case basis.

GETTING INTO GRADUATE SCHOOL

Now that you know it is possible to pay for your graduate education, you must move toward securing admission and funding.

You have already taken a step toward graduate school because you have in hand a preparation book for a graduate school admission exam. Presumably you are about to take or have already taken one or more of these exams. A good score on the exam is an important component of the picture of competence and capability that you present to graduate programs and funding sponsors. If your grades and achievements have been impressive, a high score confirms you as an all-around good candidate. If either grades or achievements are mediocre, then high scores are imperative to bolster your cause. If you have not already taken the exam, study hard; prepare well. If you did not achieve a competitive score on a previous administration, it might be worthwhile to prepare further and try again.

The next thing to do is to begin to investigate which schools have the right programs for you. If you are still in college or out only a year or two, consult with professors who know you well, who are familiar not only with your interests but with your style of working. Professors may suggest programs that suit your needs, universities that offer emphasis in your areas of interest, and faculty members with whom you might work especially well. Your professors may have inside information about contemplated changes in program, focus or personnel at various institutions. This information can supplement the information in university bulletins and help you to decide which schools to apply to. If you have been out of school for several years, you may have to rely more on information bulletins. But do not stop there. Ask for advice and suggestions from people in the field, from present employers if your job is related to your career goals, and from the current faculty and advising staff at your undergraduate school. While the current personnel may not be familiar with you and your learning style, they will have up-to-date information on programs and faculties.

Send for university and departmental literature. Read everything you can about programs offered. Then study the statements on aid, both need-based and merit-based. Be sure that you are completely clear as to the process—criteria, forms required, other supporting documents, and deadlines. If any step of the process seems ambiguous, make phone calls. You can't afford to miss out on possible funding because you misinterpreted the application directions.

DON'T MISS DEADLINES

It's a good idea to prepare a master calendar dedicated to graduate school. Note the deadlines for each step of the process for every school, for every foundation, for every possible source of funds. Consult the master calendar daily. Anticipate deadlines, record actions taken by you and by others, follow up, keep on top of it. Do not just let events happen. Be proactive every step of the way.

The university, graduate school, and departmental bulletins will inform you about need-based aid and about any merit-based funding—teaching assistantships, research assistantships, no-strings fellowships, and private foundation fellowships—administered by the university or any of its divisions. This information will be complete for the funding to which it applies. It will include all procedures, documentation required, and deadlines. None of the literature you receive from the university, however, will tell you about fellowships or other funding for which you must apply directly. You must consult grants directories, foundation directories, and other source books to find the prizes, awards, scholarships, grants and fellowships for which you might qualify.

The following bibliography is an eclectic list of directories. The directories are listed by title and publisher without dates of publication. Most directories are updated frequently. Whenever you ask for a directory, look at the copyright date. If the directory appears to be more than a year old, ask the librarian if there is a newer edition available. Consult the most recent edition you can find. No matter how frequently a directory is updated, you should never rely on deadline dates given for grants. Write or call the sponsor of each grant that you are considering, and request the most current literature. Make certain that names and addresses have not changed. Verify dates for each step of the process. The information in the directory is a valuable starting point, but it is just that: a starting point.

Most of the directories listed below apply to more than one population. Use the index and the list of categories to find which portions of the book apply to you. Disregard any categories into which you do not fit. Concentrate in those areas where you do.

Aside from their copious cross-referencing, most directories also include bibliographies listing other information sources. Do not neglect these lists. One may send you to the perfect source for you.

BIBLIOGRAPHY

GENERAL DIRECTORIES

American Legion Education Program. Need a Lift? To Educational Opportunities, Careers, Loans, Scholarships, Employment. American Legion: Indianapolis, IN

Annual Register of Grant Support. Marquis: Chicago, IL

Catalog of Federal Domestic Assistance. U.S. Office of Management and Budget: Washington, D.C.

Chronicle Student Aid Annual. Chronicle Guidance Publication: Moravia, NY

*The College Blue Book,*Vol entitled *Scholarships, Fellowships, Grants & Loans.* Macmillan, NY

Directory of Financial Aids for Minorities. Reference Service Press: Santa Barbara, CA

Directory of Financial Aids for Women. Reference Service Press: Santa Barbara, CA

DRG: Directory of Research Grants. Oryx Press: Scottsdale, AZ

A Foreign Student's Selected Guide to Financial Assistance for Study and Research in the United States. Adelphi University Press: Garden City, NY

Foundation Directory. The Foundation Center: New York

Foundation Grants to Individuals. The Foundation Center: New York

The Graduate Scholarship Book, by Daniel J. Cassidy. Prentice Hall: New York.

Grants for Graduate Students, edited by John J. Wells and Amy J. Goldstein. Petersons: Princeton, NJ

The Grants Register. St. Martins: New York

Scholarships, Fellowships and Loans, Vols. VI-VIII. Bellman Publishing Co.: Arlington, MA

Selected List of Fellowship Opportunities and Aids to Advanced Education for United States Citizens and Foreign Nationals. National Science Foundation: Washington, D.C.

Taft Corporate Giving Directory: Comprehensive Profiles & Analyses of Major Corporate Philanthropic Programs. The Taft Group

FIELD AND SUBJECT DIRECTORIES

American Art Directory. R.R. Bowker: New York

American Mathematical Society Notices: "Assistantships and Fellowships in the Mathematical Sciences." December issue, each year.

American Philosophical Association. Proceedings and Addresses: "Grants and Fellowships of Interest to Philosophers." June each year.

Graduate Study in Psychology and Associated Fields. American Psychological Association: Washington, D.C.

Grants for the Arts, by Virginia P. White. Plenum Press: New York.

Grants and Awards Available to American Writers. PEN American Center: New York

Grants, Fellowships and Prizes of Interest to Historians. American Historical Association: Washington, D.C.

Grants in the Humanities: A Scholar's Guide to Funding Sources. Neal-Schuman: New York.

Journalism Career and Scholarship Guide. The Newspaper Fund: Princeton, NJ

Money for Artists: A Guide to Grants and Awards for Individual Artists. ACA Books: New York.

Music Industry Directory. Marquis: Chicago

Scholarships and Loans for Nursing Education. National League for Nursing: New York

WHERE TO LOOK

The best bibliography is of no use if you cannot locate the books that you seek. If you are in college, start with your college library and with the library of the office which promotes graduate study. The dean of the college may have a selection of directories on a bookshelf in the Dean's Office. Ask around. Financial aid offices may also have directories of foundation grants on their shelves. If your college is small or if you are no longer affiliated with a college, you might try the libraries of larger colleges and universities in your vicinity. Call before you go. The libraries of some large universities in major cities are restricted to students with ID cards and are closed to the public even for reference purposes. If the library is open to the public, a kind library assistant may tell you which directories are available so that you may make your trip to the most fruitful library.

One of the most helpful organizations in terms of well-stocked library of directories and general assistance in the search for grants is The Foundation Center. The Foundation Center is the publisher of a number of the directories listed. The Center also operates libraries and cooperating collections throughout the country. The center has four full scale libraries. These are at:

79 Fifth Avenue
(at 16th Street)
New York, NY 10003-3050
212-620-4230

312 Sutter St.
San Francisco, CA 94108
415-397-0902

1001 Connecticut Ave., N.W.
Suite 938
Washington, DC 20036
202-331-1400

1442 Hanna Building
1422 Euclid Ave.
Cleveland, OH 44115
216-861-1934

If any of these is convenient for you, call for current hours. The Center also operates a network of over 180 Cooperating Collections located in host nonprofit organizations in all 50 states, Australia, Canada, Mexico, Puerto Rico, the Virgin Islands, Great Britain and Japan. All contain a core collection of the Center's reference works and are staffed by professionals trained to direct grantseekers to appropriate funding information resources. Many host organizations also have other books and reports on funders and private foundations within their state.

Call toll-free 1-800-424-9836 for a complete address list.

If you have exhausted all other funding possibilities—need-based aid; university or department administered merit-based grants, fellowships and assistantships; privately sponsored grants, fellowships and loans; and government guaranteed loans—you may need to look into non-profit lending organizations. Start by contacting:

The Education Resources Institute
    (TERI)
330 Stuart Street
Boston, MA 02116
617-426-0681

New England Educational Loan Marketing Corp.
    (Nellie Mae)
25 Braintree Hill Park
Braintree, MA 02184
617-849-1325

Student Loan Marketing Association
    (Sallie Mae)
1050 Jefferson Street, NW
Washington, DC 20007
202-333-8000

Law School Admission Services
    (for law school loans, only)
P.O. Box 2000
Newtown, PA 18940-0998
215-968-1001

Most of the figures in this part of the GRE are drawn as accurately as possible. (*Note:* This is not true in the quantitative comparison section. See below.) If a figure is not drawn to scale, it will include the warning: "*Note:* Figure not drawn to scale."

For problem solving items, if a figure is drawn to scale, estimate quantities.

Example:

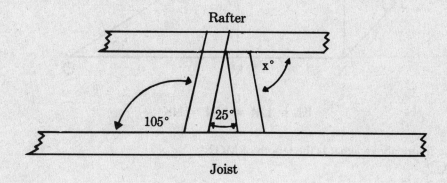

The figure above shows a cross section of a building. If the rafter is parallel to the joist, what is x?

    (A) 45
    (B) 60
    (C) 80
    (D) 90
    (E) 105

The correct choice is (**C**), and you can get that without a calculation. Look at the size of x. It is not quite a right angle, so you can eliminate both (D) and (E). Is it as small as 60 degrees? No, so you eliminate (B) and (A) as well. This means that (C) must be the correct answer.

In problem solving questions, when a figure is drawn to scale, you can measure lengths with the edge of your answer sheet or scratch paper.

Example:

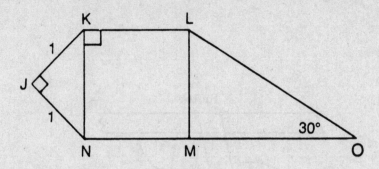

KL = LM = MN = NK

In the figure above, what is the length of MO?
   (A) 2
   (B) 2 $\sqrt{2}$
   (C) 2 $\sqrt{3}$
   (D) 4
   (E) 4 $\sqrt{2}$

The correct choice is **(B)**.

Take a piece of paper and mark on it the length of JK. This distance is 1. Now measure that distance against MO.

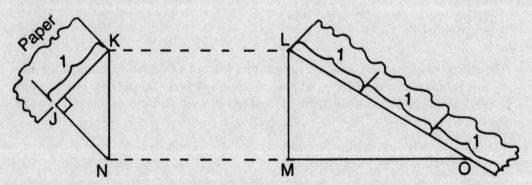

It appears that MO is slightly more than 2.5, make it about 2.8. Which answer is closest? The best approximation for the $\sqrt{2}$ is 1.4, so (B) is: 2 (1.4) = 2.8.

Quantitative Comparisons

For this type of question, you must compare two quantities, one shown in Column A and one shown in Column B. You must decide if one quantity is greater than the other, if the two quantities are the same, or if the relationship between the quantities cannot be determined from the information given.

Memorize the meaning of the four different answer choices.

For each question, you are given four answer choices as follows:

(A) if the quantity in Column A is the greater;
(B) if the quantity in Column B is the greater;
(C) if the two quantities are equal;
(D) if the relationship cannot be determined from the information given.

Examples:

Column A	Column B
$5 \times 6 \times 7 \times 8$	$5 + 6 + 7 + 8$

The correct answer to this quantitative comparison is (A). Column A is 1680 while Column B is 26.

Column A	Column B
$\frac{1}{7} - \frac{1}{8}$	$\frac{1}{8}$

The correct answer is (B). $\frac{1}{7} - \frac{1}{8} = \frac{1}{56}$. $\frac{1}{8}$ is greater than $\frac{1}{56}$.

Column A	Column B
3429	$3(10^3) + 4(10^2) + 2(10^1) + 9(10^0)$

The correct answer is (C):

$$3(10^3) = 3(1000) = 3000$$
$$4(10^2) = 4(100) = 400$$
$$2(10^1) = 2(10) = 20$$
$$9(10^0) = 9(1) = \underline{+\quad 9}$$
$$= 3429$$

So the two quantities are the same.

Column A	Column B
The product of three numbers between 3 and 4	The product of four numbers between 2 and 3

The correct answer is **(D)**. You don't know the value of any of the numbers. If the three numbers in Column A are almost 4, then Column A could be almost as large as 64. On the other hand, it could be almost as small as 27. As for Column B, if those four numbers are almost as large as 3, then Column B could be almost 81. On the other hand, if they are almost as small as 2, Column B could be almost as small as 16.

Information centered above the two columns applies to both columns.

Example:

Column A		Column B
	The price of a pound of cheese increased from $2.00 to $2.50.	
The percent increase in the price of cheese.		25%

The correct answer is **(C)**. The centered information applies to both columns. The percent increase in the price of cheese is 25%.

A symbol used more than once represents the same thing in each case.

Example:

Column A	Column B
$(x)(x)(x)(x)(x)$	x^5

The correct answer is **(C)**. $(x)(x)(x)(x)(x) = x^5$. Since the x on the left means the same thing as the x on the right, the two expressions are the same.

Figures in the quantitative comparison part are *not* necessarily drawn to scale.

This is very important. Although you can rely upon the arrangement of points, angles, lines, etc., you cannot trust the apparent magnitude of geometrical quantities.

Examples:

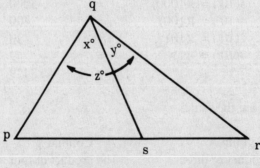

	Column A	Column B
1.	PS	PR
2.	PS	SR
3.	x	z
4.	x	y

	Column A	Column B
1.	PS	PR
2.	PS	SR
3.	x	z
4.	x	y

The answer to the first comparison is (**B**). Since point S lies between P and R, the entire length of PR must be longer than that part which is PS.

The answer to the second comparison is (**D**). You are not entitled to assume anything about the location of point S—other than that it is on PR somewhere between P and R. Thus, although it looks like PS is longer than SR, you cannot determine that as a matter of mathematics.

The answer to the third comparison is (**B**). Angle z is equal to $x + y$, so the entire angle z must be larger than just that part labeled x.

The answer to the fourth comparison is (**D**). The relative size of angles x and y is determined by the location of point S. Again, although S lies somewhere between P and R, its exact location cannot be mathematically determined. So the relative sizes of x and y remain an unknown.

When making a comparison, do only as much work as needed to determine whether one column is *always* larger than the other.

Example:

Column A	Column B
$(4.1)^{10}$	$(0.41)^{10}$

The correct answer is (**A**). At first glance, you might think that this comparison requires a lengthy calculation. In fact, it is very easy. Since 0.41 in Column B is less than 1, when it is raised to a power it gets smaller and smaller (multiplying the same fraction by itself again and again). On the other hand, since 4.1 in Column A is larger than 1, when it is raised to a power it keeps getting larger.

STRATEGIES FOR MAKING COMPARISIONS

Simplify complex arithmetic or algebraic expressions before trying to make a comparison.

Examples:

Column A	Column B
$\dfrac{2,000,000}{200,000}$	$\dfrac{1000}{100}$

$$x + y \neq 0$$

Column A	Column B
$\dfrac{6x + 6y}{x + y}$	6

The correct answer to both questions is (**C**). In the first problem, you should simplify the comparison by canceling. You wind up comparing $\frac{20}{2}$, which is 10, with $\frac{10}{1}$, which is also 10.

As for the second comparison, you should simplify first by factoring and then by canceling: $6x + 6y = 6(x + y)$. Then you can cancel the $x + y$ in both the numerator and the denominator of Column A, leaving just 6.

 If the arithmetic or algebra is manageable, go ahead and perform the indicated operations.

Examples:

Column A	Column B
$10,000,001 + 0.009$	$10,000,002 - 0.00199$
$(x^3)(x^2)(x^7)$	$(x^3)^4$

The correct answer to the first comparison is (**B**). The indicated addition and subtraction is not that difficult, so you won't lose much time doing it. Instead of trying to find an elegant logical solution to the comparison, use the crude method of adding and subtracting.

The correct answer to the second comparison is (**C**). Again, you should just do the operations that are indicated. Column A becomes x^{12}; so too does Column B.

 When the centered information contains unknowns, solve for the unknowns.

Example:

Column A	Column B
	$3x = 12$
	$4y = 20$
x	y

The correct answer is (**B**). You need values for x and y, so solve for both.

 Simplify the comparison by adding or subtracting the same value on each side.

Column A	Column B
$4x + 5$	$3x + 6$

The correct answer is (**D**). At first, however, you may not be able to see that the relationship is indeterminate. Start by subtracting 5 from both sides of the comparison. The result is:

Column A	Column B
$4x$	$3x + 1$

Now subtract $3x$ from both sides:

Column A	Column B
x	1

In this form, the comparison is fairly easy. Since you have no information about x, the answer must be **(D)**.

Simplify the comparison by multiplying or dividing each side by the same positive number.

Example:

Column A	Column B
$9^{99} - 9^{98}$	9^{98}

The correct answer is **(A)**. Divide both sides by 9^{98}:

Column A	Column B
$\dfrac{9^{99} - 9^{98}}{9^{98}}$	$\dfrac{9^{98}}{9^{98}}$
$9^1 - 9^0$	9^0
$9 - 1$	1
8	1

This proves that Column A is larger. (It doesn't prove how much larger since dividing changed the ratio between the two quantities, but we are only interested in which is larger—not how much larger.)

Warning!!! Do not try to simplify by multiplication or division unless you know the quantity you are using is *positive*.

Example:

Column A	Column B
$3x$	$4x$

The correct answer is **(D)**. But watch what happens if you try to divide both quantities by x:

Column A	Column B
$\dfrac{3x}{x} = 3$	$\dfrac{4x}{x} = 4$

This move is wrong since you do not know for certain that x is positive. As a result, you arrive at the erroneous conclusion that Column B is greater. You can prove this by trying a couple of different values for x. If x is a number like 2 or 5, it is true that Column B is greater. But if x is a negative number, then Column A is greater. Or if x is zero, the columns are equal. This technique only works when you know for certain that the term you are dividing or multiplying by is positive.

GUESSING

The explanation of our last example sets up our first guessing strategy.

If a comparison contains unknowns, try substituting numbers.

Example:

Column A	Column B
$(x - y)^2$	$(y - x)^2$

The correct answer to this comparison is **(C)**. You can solve the problem by doing the indicated algebraic manipulations. Both expressions turn out to be the same thing. But if you don't know how to do that, or if the technique does not occur to you, at least you can try a few random substitutions. Pick numbers for x and y. After two or three substitutions, when you see that the two columns keep turning out equal, go with **(C)**. Of course, there is no guarantee that this will always be true, but at least it gives you something to try.

Never Guess (E).

This is only common sense. There are only four possible choices, (A), (B), (C), and (D). So when you enter a random guess make sure you avoid the (E) column.

If a comparison contains neither a variable nor a geometric figure, do not guess (D).

Example:

Column A	Column B
$\dfrac{\pi^{14}(\sqrt{79} - .01)}{4071}$	$\dfrac{\sqrt{1,000,127} + 3^{16}}{\pi^6}$

The correct answer to this comparison must remain a mystery, but one thing is clear: The right answer is not **(D)**. Someone somewhere has a computer that can figure it out. So unless the comparison has a variable (unknown) or geometric figure (which might not be drawn to scale), don't guess **(D)**.

If the comparison does contain a variable or a figure, as a last resort guess (D).

This is a last-ditch guessing strategy. If you have a comparison that uses a variable or a figure and you can't figure out the relationship, go with your hunch—maybe it is indeterminate.

Graphs

In terms of total numbers, graphs are the least important part of the math sections of the GRE. You should have no more than five graph questions in each math section.

COMMON GRAPHS

Learning to read graphs is not that difficult once you understand the fundamental premise underlying all graphs:

One picture is worth a thousand words.

Graphs are useful because they communicate in picture form data that might take pages and pages to present.

The following paragraph summarizes in prose certain data about the national budget of country X:

> The national budget of country X is divided into three basic categories: domestic spending, military spending, and debt service. In 1991, domestic spending was $200 million, military spending was $400 million, and debt service was $300 million. In 1992, domestic spending was $300 million, military spending was $400 million, and debt service was $250 million. In 1993, domestic spending was $400 million, military spending was $300 million, and debt service was $350 million. In 1994, domestic spending was $500 million, military spending was $250 million, and debt service was $400 million. In 1995, domestic spending was $600 million, military spending was $500 million, and debt service was $400 million.

Obviously this method of presenting data is very cumbersome. It's much easier to absorb the information when it is presented in an organized manner such as a table or graph.

Common Graphs: The Table or Chart

Budget of Country X
(In millions of dollars)

	1991	1992	1993	1994	1995
Domestic	$200	$300	$400	$500	$600
Military	$400	$400	$300	$250	$500
Debt	$300	$250	$350	$400	$400

Another common graph that might be used to present this data is a bar graph.

Common Graph: The Bar Graph

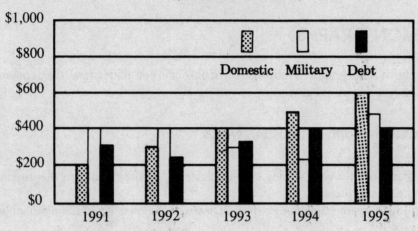

The same data might be presented in a line graph.

Common Graph: The Line Graph

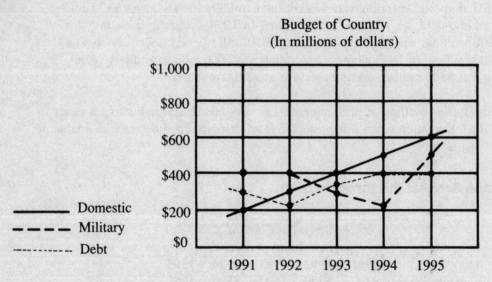

The information might also be presented in pie graphs.

Common Graph: The Pie Graph

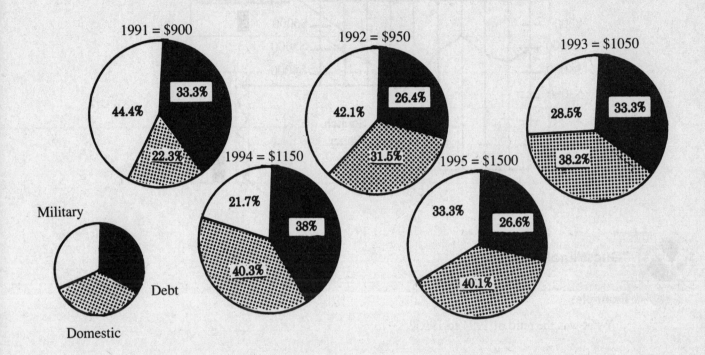

Budget of Country
(In millions of dollars)

ANSWERING QUESTIONS

Read the graph first for a general understanding, but when answering specific questions read it carefully.

To a certain extent, graph questions are like reading comprehension questions: Some test the most general level of understanding while others test subtle points. Your first reading of the graph should be for its main points. Then you can go back for details if you need them.

Use the edge of your scratch paper to make the graph easier to read.

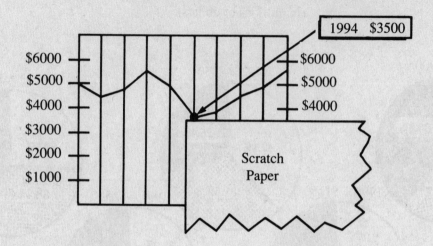

 "Guesstimate" quantities.

Example:

What was the ratio of 1994 to 1995?

(A) $\frac{1}{5}$

(B) $\frac{2}{5}$

(C) $\frac{1}{2}$

(D) $\frac{2}{3}$

(E) $\frac{3}{4}$

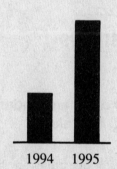

1994   1995

The correct choice is (**B**). You should be able to "guesstimate" this answer. The length of bar on the left is more than $\frac{1}{5}$ but less than $\frac{1}{2}$ the length of the bar on the right.

Part Three

GRE MATH REVIEW

MATHEMATICS REVIEW FOR THE GRE

In order to solve a mathematical problem, it is essential to know the mathematical meaning of the words used. There are many expressions having the same meaning in mathematics. These expressions may indicate a relationship between quantities or an operation (addition, subtraction, multiplication, division) to be performed. This chapter will help you to recognize some of the mathematical synonyms commonly found in word problems.

EXPRESSIONS

Equality

The following expressions all indicate that two quantities are equal (=):

> is equal to
> is the same as
> the result is
> yields
> gives

Also, the word "is" is often used to mean "equals," as in "8 *is* 5 more than 3," which translates to "8 = 5 + 3".

Addition

The following expressions all indicate that the numbers A and B are to be added:

A + B	2 + 3
the sum of A and B	the sum of 2 and 3
the total of A and B	the total of 2 and 3
A added to B	2 added to 3
A increased by B	2 increased by 3
A more than B	2 more than 3
A greater than B	2 greater than 3

Subtraction

The following expressions all indicate that the number B is to be subtracted from the number A:

A − B	10 − 3
A minus B	10 minus 3
A less B	10 less 3
the difference of A and B	the difference of 10 and 3
from A subtract B	from 10 subtract 3
A take away B	10 take away 3
A decreased by B	10 decreased by 3
A diminished by B	10 diminished by 3
B is subtracted from A	3 is subtracted from 10
B less than A	3 less than 10

Multiplication

If the numbers A and B are to be multiplied (A × B), the following expressions may be used:

A × B	2 × 3
A multiplied by B	2 multiplied by 3
the product of A and B	the product of 2 and 3

The parts of a multiplication problem are indicated in the example below:

$$\begin{array}{rl} 15 & \text{(multiplicand)} \\ \times\ 10 & \text{(multiplier)} \\ \hline 150 & \text{(product)} \end{array}$$

Other ways of indicating multiplication are:

Parentheses: A × B = (A)(B)
Dots: A × B = A · B
In algebra, letters next to each other: A × B = AB

A **coefficient** is a number by which to multiply a variable, such as in 3B, where 3 is the coefficient.

163

Inequalities

When two numbers are not necessarily equal to each other, this idea can be expressed by using the "greater than" symbol (>) or the "less than" symbol (<). The wider part of the wedge is always towards the greater number.

A is greater than B	A is less than B
A > B	A < B

A is greater than or equal to B	A is less than or equal to B
A ≥ B	A ≤ B

An **integer** can be defined informally as a whole number, either positive or negative, including zero, e.g., +5, −10, 0, +30, −62, etc.

A **prime number** can be defined informally as a whole number (positive only) that is evenly divisible only by itself and 1, e.g., 1, 2, 3, 5, 7, 11, 13, 17, 19, etc.

Division

Division of the numbers A and B (in the order A ÷ B) may be indicated in the following ways. (See also the discussion of fractions.)

A ÷ B	14 ÷ 2
A divided by B	14 divided by 2
the quotient of A and B	the quotient of 14 and 2

The parts of a division problem are indicated in the example below:

$$
\begin{array}{r}
5\tfrac{1}{7} \\
7\overline{)\,36} \\
35 \\
\hline
1
\end{array}
$$

(divisor) 7) 36 (dividend)

$5\tfrac{1}{7}$ (quotient)

35

1 (remainder)

Factors and Divisors

The relationship A × B = C, for any whole numbers A, B, and C, may be expressed as:

A × B = C	2 × 3 = 6
A and B are factors of C	2 and 3 are factors of 6
A and B are divisors of C	2 and 3 are divisors of 6
C is divisible by A and by B	6 is divisible by 2 and by 3
C is a multiple of A and of B	6 is a multiple of 2 and of 3

Symbols

Common symbols used on the exam are*:

≠	is not equal to
>	is greater than (3 > 2)
<	is less than (2 < 3)
≥	is greater than or equal to
≤	is less than or equal to
: and ::	is to; the ratio to (see also section on ratios)
$\sqrt{}$	radical sign—used without a number, it indicates the square root of ($\sqrt{9} = 3$) or with an index above the sign to indicate the root to be taken if the root is not a square root ($\sqrt[3]{8} = 2$) (see also section on powers and roots).
|x|	absolute value of (in this case x) (see section on basic properties of numbers, item 6).

BASIC PROPERTIES OF NUMBERS

1. A number greater than zero is called a **positive number.**

2. A number smaller than zero is called a **negative number.**

3. When a negative number is added to another number, this is the same as subtracting the equivalent positive number.

    Example: $2 + (−1) = 2 − 1 = 1$

4. When two numbers of the same sign are multiplied together, the result is a positive number.

    Example: $2 × 2 = 4$

    Example: $(−2)(−3) = +6$

*Geometric symbols are reviewed in the section on geometry.

5. When two numbers of different signs are multiplied together, the result is a negative number.

    Example: $(+5)(-10) = -50$

    Example: $(-6)(+8) = -48$

6. The **absolute value** of a number is the equivalent positive value.

    Example: $|+2| = +2$

    Example: $|-3| = +3$

7. An even number is an integer that is divisible evenly by two. Zero would be considered an even number for practical purposes.

8. An odd number is an integer that is not an even number.

9. An even number times any integer will yield an even number.

10. An odd number times an odd number will yield an odd number.

11. Two even numbers or two odd numbers added together will yield an even number.

12. An odd number added to an even number will yield an odd number.

FRACTIONS

Fractions and Mixed Numbers

1. A **fraction** is part of a unit.

    a. A fraction has a **numerator** and a **denominator.**

    Example: In the fraction $\frac{3}{4}$, 3 is the numerator and 4 is the denominator.

    b. In any fraction, the numerator is being divided by the denominator.

    Example: The fraction $\frac{2}{7}$ indicates that 2 is being divided by 7.

    c. The whole quantity 1 may be expressed by a fraction in which the numerator and denominator are the same number.

    Example: If the problem involves $\frac{1}{8}$ of a quantity, then the whole quantity is $\frac{8}{8}$, or 1.

2. A **mixed number** is an integer together with a fraction such as $2\frac{3}{5}$, $7\frac{3}{8}$, etc. The integer is the integral part, and the fraction is the fractional part.

3. An **improper fraction** is one in which the numerator is equal to or greater than the denominator, such as $\frac{19}{6}$, $\frac{25}{4}$, or $\frac{10}{10}$.

4. To change a mixed number to an improper fraction:

    a. Multiply the denominator of the fraction by the integer.

    b. Add the numerator to this product.

    c. Place this sum over the denominator of the fraction.

    Illustration: Change $3\frac{4}{7}$ to an improper fraction.

    SOLUTION: $7 \times 3 = 21$
    $$21 + 4 = 25$$
    $$3\tfrac{4}{7} = \tfrac{25}{7}$$

    Answer: $\frac{25}{7}$

5. To change an improper fraction to a mixed number:

    a. Divide the numerator by the denominator. The quotient, disregarding the remainder, is the integral part of the mixed number.

    b. Place the remainder, if any, over the denominator. This is the fractional part of the mixed number.

    Illustration: Change $\frac{36}{13}$ to a mixed number.

    SOLUTION:
    $$\begin{array}{r} 2 \\ 13\overline{)36} \\ 26 \\ \hline 10 \text{ remainder} \end{array}$$
    $$\tfrac{36}{13} = 2\tfrac{10}{13}$$

    Answer: $2\frac{10}{13}$

6. The numerator and denominator of a fraction may be changed, without affecting the

value of the fraction, by multiplying both by the same number.

Example: The value of the fraction $\frac{2}{5}$ will not be altered if the numerator and the denominator are multiplied by 2, to result in $\frac{4}{10}$.

7. The numerator and the denominator of a fraction may be changed, without affecting the value of the fraction, by dividing both by the same number. This process is called **reducing the fraction.** A fraction that has been reduced as much as possible is said to be in **lowest terms.**

Example: The value of the fraction $\frac{3}{12}$ will not be altered if the numerator and denominator are divided by 3, to result in $\frac{1}{4}$.

Example: If $\frac{6}{30}$ is reduced to lowest terms (by dividing both numerator and denominator by 6), the result is $\frac{1}{5}$.

8. As a final answer to an exam question, it may be necessary to:
   a. reduce a fraction to lowest terms
   b. convert an improper fraction to a mixed number
   c. convert a mixed number to an improper fraction

Addition of Fractions

9. **Fractions cannot be added unless the denominators are all the same.**
   a. If the denominators are the same, add all the numerators and place this sum over the common denominator. In the case of mixed numbers, follow the above rule for the fractions and then add the integers.
   Example: The sum of $2\frac{3}{8} + 3\frac{1}{8} + \frac{3}{8} = 5\frac{7}{8}$.
   b. If the denominators are not the same, the fractions, in order to be added, must be converted to ones having the same denominator. The lowest common denominator is often the most convenient common denominator to find, but any common denominator will work. You can cancel out the extra numbers after the addition.

10. The **lowest common denominator** (henceforth called the L.C.D.) is the lowest num-

ber that can be divided evenly by all the given denominators. If no two of the given denominators can be divided by the same number, then the L.C.D. is the product of all the denominators.

Example: The L.C.D. of $\frac{1}{2}$, $\frac{1}{3}$, and $\frac{1}{5}$ is $2 \times 3 \times 5 = 30$.

11. To find the L.C.D. when two or more of the given denominators can be divided by the same number:

   a. Write down the denominators, leaving plenty of space between the numbers.

   b. Select the smallest number (other than 1) by which one or more of the denominators can be divided evenly.

   c. Divide the denominators by this number, copying down those that cannot be divided evenly. Place this number to one side.

   d. Repeat this process, placing each divisor to one side until there are no longer any denominators that can be divided evenly by any selected number.

   e. Multiply all the divisors to find the L.C.D.

Illustration: Find the L.C.D. of $\frac{1}{5}$, $\frac{1}{7}$, $\frac{1}{10}$, and $\frac{1}{14}$.

SOLUTION:

$$
\begin{array}{r|cccc}
2 & 5 & 7 & 10 & 14 \\ \hline
5 & 5 & 7 & 5 & 7 \\ \hline
7 & 1 & 7 & 1 & 7 \\ \hline
 & 1 & 1 & 1 & 1 \\
\end{array}
$$

$$7 \times 5 \times 2 = 70$$

Answer: The L.C.D. is 70.

12. To add fractions having different denominators:

   a. Find the L.C.D. of the denominators.

   b. Change each fraction to an equivalent fraction having the L.C.D. as its denominator.

   c. When all of the fractions have the same denominator, they may be added, as in the example following item 9a.

Illustration: Add $\frac{1}{4}$, $\frac{3}{10}$, and $\frac{2}{5}$.

SOLUTION: Find the L.C.D.:

$$2 \overline{)\ 4 \qquad 10 \qquad 5}$$
$$2 \overline{)\ 2 \qquad 5 \qquad 5}$$
$$5 \overline{)\ 1 \qquad 5 \qquad 5}$$
$$\quad 1 \qquad 1 \qquad 1$$

L.C.D. $= 2 \times 2 \times 5 = 20$

$$\frac{1}{4} = \frac{5}{20}$$
$$\frac{3}{10} = \frac{6}{20}$$
$$+ \frac{2}{5} = + \frac{8}{20}$$
$$\frac{19}{20}$$

Answer: $\frac{19}{20}$

13. To add mixed numbers in which the fractions have different denominators, add the fractions by following the rules in item 12 above, then add the integers.

Illustration: Add $2\frac{5}{7}$, $5\frac{1}{2}$, and 8.

SOLUTION: L.C.D. $= 14$
$$2\frac{5}{7} = 2\frac{10}{14}$$
$$5\frac{1}{2} = 5\frac{7}{14}$$
$$+ 8 = + 8$$
$$15\frac{17}{14} = 16\frac{3}{14}$$

Answer: $16\frac{3}{14}$

Subtraction of Fractions

14. a. Unlike addition, which may involve adding more than two numbers at the same time, subtraction involves only two numbers.

b. In subtraction, as in addition, the denominators must be the same.

15. To subtract fractions:

a. Find the L.C.D.

b. Change both fractions so that each has the L.C.D. as the denominator.

c. Subtract the numerator of the second fraction from the numerator of the first, and place this difference over the L.C.D.

d. Reduce, if possible.

Illustration: Find the difference of $\frac{5}{8}$ and $\frac{1}{4}$.

SOLUTION: L.C.D. $= 8$
$$\frac{5}{8} = \frac{5}{8}$$
$$- \frac{1}{4} = - \frac{2}{8}$$
$$\frac{3}{8}$$

Answer: $\frac{3}{8}$

16. To subtract mixed numbers:

a. It may be necessary to "borrow," so that the fractional part of the first term is larger than the fractional part of the second term.

b. Subtract the fractional parts of the mixed numbers and reduce.

c. Subtract the integers.

Illustration: Subtract $16\frac{4}{5}$ from $29\frac{1}{3}$.

SOLUTION: L.C.D. $= 15$
$$29\frac{1}{3} = 29\frac{5}{15}$$
$$- 16\frac{4}{5} = - 16\frac{12}{15}$$

Note that $\frac{5}{15}$ is less than $\frac{12}{15}$. Borrow 1 from 29, and change to $\frac{15}{15}$.

$$29\frac{5}{15} = 28\frac{20}{15}$$
$$- 16\frac{12}{15} = - 16\frac{12}{15}$$
$$12\frac{8}{15}$$

Answer: $12\frac{8}{15}$

Multiplication of Fractions

17. a. To be multiplied, fractions need not have the same denominators.

b. A whole number can be thought of as having a denominator of 1: $3 = \frac{3}{1}$.

18. To multiply fractions:

a. Change the mixed numbers, if any, to improper fractions.

b. Multiply all the numerators, and place this product over the product of the denominators.

c. Reduce, if possible.

Illustration: Multiply $\frac{2}{3} \times 2\frac{4}{7} \times \frac{5}{9}$.

SOLUTION: $2\frac{4}{7} = \frac{18}{7}$
$$\frac{2}{3} \times \frac{18}{7} \times \frac{5}{9} = \frac{180}{189}$$
$$= \frac{20}{21}$$

Answer: $\frac{20}{21}$

19. a. **Cancellation** is a device to facilitate multiplication. To cancel means to divide a numerator and a denominator by the same number in a multiplication problem.

    Example: In the problem $\frac{4}{7} \times \frac{5}{6}$, the numerator 4 and the denominator 6 may be divided by 2.

    $$\frac{\overset{2}{4}}{7} \times \frac{5}{\underset{3}{6}} = \frac{10}{21}$$

    b. With fractions (and percentages), the word "of" is often used to mean "multiply."

    Example: $\frac{1}{2}$ of $\frac{1}{2} = \frac{1}{2} \times \frac{1}{2} = \frac{1}{4}$

20. To multiply a whole number by a mixed number:

    a. Multiply the whole number by the fractional part of the mixed number.

    b. Multiply the whole number by the integral part of the mixed number.

    c. Add both products.

    Illustration: Multiply $23\frac{3}{4}$ by 95.

    SOLUTION:
    $$\frac{95}{1} \times \frac{3}{4} = \frac{285}{4}$$
    $$= 71\frac{1}{4}$$
    $$95 \times 23 = 2185$$
    $$2185 + 71\frac{1}{4} = 2256\frac{1}{4}$$

    Answer: $2256\frac{1}{4}$

Division of Fractions

21. The **reciprocal** of a fraction is that fraction inverted.

    a. When a fraction is inverted, the numerator becomes the denominator and the denominator becomes the numerator.

    Example: The reciprocal of $\frac{3}{8}$ is $\frac{8}{3}$.

    Example: The reciprocal of $\frac{1}{3}$ is $\frac{3}{1}$, or simply 3.

    b. Since every whole number has the denominator 1 understood, the reciprocal of a whole number is a fraction having 1

as the numerator and the number itself as the denominator.

Example: The reciprocal of 5 (expressed fractionally as $\frac{5}{1}$) is $\frac{1}{5}$.

22. To divide fractions:

    a. Change all the mixed numbers, if any, to improper fractions.

    b. Invert the second fraction and multiply.

    c. Reduce, if possible.

    Illustration: Divide $\frac{2}{3}$ by $2\frac{1}{4}$.

    SOLUTION:
    $$2\frac{1}{4} = \frac{9}{4}$$
    $$\frac{2}{3} \div \frac{9}{4} = \frac{2}{3} \times \frac{4}{9}$$
    $$= \frac{8}{27}$$

    Answer: $\frac{8}{27}$

23. A **complex fraction** is one that has a fraction as the numerator, or as the denominator, or as both.

    Example: $\frac{\frac{2}{3}}{5}$ is a complex fraction.

24. To clear (simplify) a complex fraction:

    a. Divide the numerator by the denominator.

    b. Reduce, if possible.

    Illustration: Clear $\frac{\frac{3}{7}}{\frac{5}{14}}$.

    SOLUTION: $\frac{3}{7} \div \frac{5}{14} = \frac{3}{7} \times \frac{14}{5} = \frac{42}{35}$
    $$= \frac{6}{5}$$
    $$= 1\frac{1}{5}$$

    Answer: $1\frac{1}{5}$

Comparing Fractions

25. If two fractions have the same denominator, the one having the larger numerator is the greater fraction.

    Example: $\frac{3}{7}$ is greater than $\frac{2}{7}$.

26. If two fractions have the same numerator, the one having the larger denominator is the smaller fraction.

    Example: $\frac{5}{12}$ is smaller than $\frac{5}{11}$.

27. To compare two fractions having different numerators and different denominators:

 a. Change the fractions to equivalent fractions having their L.C.D. as their new denominator.

 b. Compare, as in the example following item 25, for the largest numerator.

Illustration: Compare $\frac{4}{7}$ and $\frac{5}{8}$.

SOLUTION: L.C.D. $= 7 \times 8 = 56$

$$\frac{4}{7} = \frac{32}{56}$$
$$\frac{5}{8} = \frac{35}{56}$$

Answer: Since $\frac{35}{56}$ is larger than $\frac{32}{56}$, $\frac{5}{8}$ is larger than $\frac{4}{7}$.

Note: Actually, any common denominator will work, not only the L.C.D.

28. To compare two fractions, multiply the denominator of the left fraction by the numerator of the right fraction and write the result above the right fraction. Then multiply the denominator of the right fraction by the numerator of the left fraction and write the result over the left fraction. If the number over the left fraction is larger than the number over the right fraction, the left fraction is larger. If the number over the right fraction is larger, the right fraction is larger. If the numbers over the two fractions are equal, the fractions are equal.

Illustration: Compare $\frac{5}{7}$ and $\frac{3}{4}$.

SOLUTION:

$$\overset{20}{\frac{5}{7}} \times \overset{21}{\frac{3}{4}}$$

$$3 \times 7 = 21$$
$$4 \times 5 = 20$$
$$20 < 21$$

Answer: $\frac{5}{7} < \frac{3}{4}$. This method will only determine which fraction is larger. It cannot be used to tell you the size of the difference.

Fraction Problems

29. Most fraction problems can be arranged in the form: "What fraction of a number is another number?" This form contains three important parts:

 • The fractional part
 • The number following "of"
 • The number following "is"

 a. If the fraction and the "of" number are given, multiply them to find the "is" number.

Illustration: What is $\frac{3}{4}$ of 20?

SOLUTION: Write the question as "$\frac{3}{4}$ of 20 is what number?" Then multiply the fraction $\frac{3}{4}$ by the "of" number, 20:

$$\frac{3}{4} \times \overset{5}{\underset{1}{20}} = 15$$

Answer: 15

 b. If the fractional part and the "is" number are given, divide the "is" number by the fraction to find the "of" number.

Illustration: $\frac{4}{5}$ of what number is 40?

SOLUTION: To find the "of" number, divide 40 by $\frac{4}{5}$:

$$40 \div \frac{4}{5} = \overset{10}{\underset{1}{\frac{40}{1}}} \times \frac{5}{4}$$
$$= 50$$

Answer: 50

 c. To find the fractional part when the other two numbers are known, divide the "is" number by the "of" number.

Illustration: What part of 12 is 9?

SOLUTION: $9 \div 12 = \frac{9}{12}$
$$= \frac{3}{4}$$

Answer: $\frac{3}{4}$

Practice Problems Involving Fractions

1. Reduce to lowest terms: $\frac{60}{108}$.
 (A) $\frac{1}{48}$
 (B) $\frac{1}{3}$
 (C) $\frac{5}{9}$
 (D) $\frac{10}{18}$
 (E) $\frac{15}{59}$

2. Change $\frac{27}{7}$ to a mixed number.
 (A) $2\frac{1}{7}$
 (B) $3\frac{6}{7}$
 (C) $6\frac{1}{3}$

(D) $7\frac{1}{2}$

(E) $8\frac{1}{7}$

3. Change $4\frac{2}{3}$ to an improper fraction.
   (A) $\frac{10}{3}$
   (B) $\frac{11}{3}$
   (C) $\frac{14}{3}$
   (D) $\frac{24}{3}$
   (E) $\frac{42}{3}$

4. Find the L.C.D. of $\frac{1}{6}$, $\frac{1}{10}$, $\frac{1}{18}$, and $\frac{1}{21}$.
   (A) 160
   (B) 330
   (C) 630
   (D) 890
   (E) 1260

5. Add $16\frac{3}{8}$, $4\frac{4}{5}$, $12\frac{3}{4}$, and $23\frac{5}{6}$.
   (A) $57\frac{91}{120}$
   (B) $57\frac{1}{4}$
   (C) 58
   (D) 59
   (E) $59\frac{91}{120}$

6. Subtract $27\frac{5}{14}$ from $43\frac{1}{6}$.
   (A) 15
   (B) $15\frac{5}{84}$
   (C) $15\frac{8}{21}$
   (D) $15\frac{15}{20}$
   (E) $15\frac{17}{21}$

7. Multiply $17\frac{5}{8}$ by 128.
   (A) 2256
   (B) 2305
   (C) 2356
   (D) 2368
   (E) 2394

8. Divide $1\frac{2}{3}$ by $1\frac{1}{9}$.
   (A) $\frac{2}{3}$
   (B) $1\frac{1}{2}$
   (C) $1\frac{23}{27}$
   (D) 4
   (E) 6

9. What is the value of $12\frac{1}{6} - 2\frac{3}{8} - 7\frac{2}{3} + 19\frac{3}{4}$?
   (A) 21
   (B) $21\frac{7}{8}$
   (C) $21\frac{1}{8}$
   (D) 22
   (E) $22\frac{7}{8}$

10. Simplify the complex fraction $\frac{\frac{4}{9}}{\frac{2}{5}}$.
    (A) $\frac{1}{2}$
    (B) $\frac{9}{10}$
    (C) $\frac{2}{5}$
    (D) 1
    (E) $1\frac{1}{9}$

11. Which fraction is largest?
    (A) $\frac{9}{16}$
    (B) $\frac{7}{10}$
    (C) $\frac{5}{8}$
    (D) $\frac{4}{5}$
    (E) $\frac{1}{2}$

12. One brass rod measures $3\frac{5}{16}$ inches long and another brass rod measures $2\frac{3}{4}$ inches long. Together their length is
    (A) $6\frac{9}{16}$ in.
    (B) $6\frac{1}{16}$ in.
    (C) $5\frac{1}{8}$ in.
    (D) $5\frac{1}{16}$ in.
    (E) $5\frac{1}{32}$ in.

13. The number of half-pound packages of tea that can be weighed out of a box that holds $10\frac{1}{2}$ lb. of tea is
    (A) 5
    (B) $10\frac{1}{2}$
    (C) 11
    (D) $20\frac{1}{2}$
    (E) 21

14. If each bag of tokens weighs $5\frac{3}{4}$ pounds, how many pounds do 3 bags weigh?
    (A) $7\frac{1}{4}$
    (B) $15\frac{3}{4}$
    (C) $16\frac{1}{2}$
    (D) $17\frac{1}{4}$
    (E) $17\frac{1}{2}$

15. During one week, a man traveled $3\frac{1}{2}$, $1\frac{1}{4}$, $1\frac{1}{6}$, and $2\frac{3}{8}$ miles. The next week he traveled $\frac{1}{4}$, $\frac{3}{8}$, $\frac{9}{16}$, $3\frac{1}{16}$, $2\frac{5}{8}$, and $3\frac{3}{16}$ miles. How many more miles did he travel the second week than the first week?
    (A) $1\frac{37}{48}$
    (B) $1\frac{1}{2}$
    (C) $1\frac{3}{4}$
    (D) 1
    (E) $\frac{47}{48}$

16. A certain type of board is sold only in lengths of multiples of 2 feet. The shortest board sold is 6 feet and the longest is 24 feet. A builder needs a large quantity of this type of board in $5\frac{1}{2}$-foot lengths. For minimum waste the lengths to be ordered should be
(A) 6 ft
(B) 12 ft
(C) 22 ft
(D) 24 ft
(E) 26 ft

17. A man spent $\frac{15}{16}$ of his entire fortune in buying a car for $7500. How much money did he possess?
(A) $6000
(B) $6500
(C) $7000
(D) $8000
(E) $8500

18. The population of a town was 54,000 in the last census. It has increased $\frac{2}{3}$ since then. Its present population is
(A) 18,000
(B) 36,000
(C) 72,000
(D) 90,000
(E) 108,000

19. If $\frac{1}{3}$ of the liquid contents of a can evaporates on the first day and $\frac{3}{4}$ of the remainder evaporates on the second day, the fractional part of the original contents remaining at the close of the second day is
(A) $\frac{5}{12}$
(B) $\frac{7}{12}$
(C) $\frac{1}{6}$
(D) $\frac{1}{2}$
(E) $\frac{4}{7}$

20. A car is run until the gas tank is $\frac{1}{8}$ full. The tank is then filled to capacity by putting in 14 gallons. The capacity of the gas tank of the car is
(A) 14 gal
(B) 15 gal
(C) 16 gal
(D) 17 gal
(E) 18 gal

Fraction Problems—Correct Answers

1. (C)   6. (E)   11. (D)   16. (C)
2. (B)   7. (A)   12. (B)   17. (D)
3. (C)   8. (B)   13. (E)   18. (D)
4. (C)   9. (B)   14. (D)   19. (C)
5. (A)   10. (E)   15. (A)   20. (C)

Problem Solutions—Fractions

1. Divide the numerator and denominator by 12:
$$\frac{60 \div 12}{108 \div 12} = \frac{5}{9}$$
One alternate method (there are several) is to divide the numerator and denominator by 6 and then by 2:
$$\frac{60 \div 6}{108 \div 6} = \frac{10}{18}$$
$$\frac{10 \div 2}{18 \div 2} = \frac{5}{9}$$
Answer: **(C)** $\frac{5}{9}$

2. Divide the numerator (27) by the denominator (7):
$$7\overline{)27}$$
$$\frac{21}{6} \text{ remainder}$$
$\frac{27}{7} = 3\frac{6}{7}$
Answer: **(B)** $3\frac{6}{7}$

3.
$$4 \times 3 = 12$$
$$12 + 2 = 14$$
$$4\frac{2}{3} = \frac{14}{3}$$
Answer: **(C)** $\frac{14}{3}$

4. 2$\overline{)6\quad10\quad18\quad21}$ (2 is a divisor of 6, 10, and 18)
3$\overline{)3\quad5\quad9\quad21}$ (3 is a divisor of 3, 9, and 21)
3$\overline{)1\quad5\quad3\quad7}$ (3 is a divisor of 3)
5$\overline{)1\quad5\quad1\quad7}$ (5 is a divisor of 5)
7$\overline{)1\quad1\quad1\quad7}$ (7 is a divisor of 7)
1   1   1   1
L.C.D. = $2 \times 3 \times 3 \times 5 \times 7 = 630$
Answer: **(C)** 630

5. L.C.D. = 120

$$16\frac{3}{8} = 16\frac{45}{120}$$
$$4\frac{4}{5} = 4\frac{96}{120}$$
$$12\frac{3}{4} = 12\frac{90}{120}$$
$$+ 23\frac{5}{6} = + 23\frac{100}{120}$$
$$55\frac{331}{120} = 57\frac{91}{120}$$

Answer: **(A)** $57\frac{91}{120}$

6. L.C.D. = 42

$$43\frac{1}{6} = 43\frac{7}{42} = 42\frac{49}{42}$$
$$- 27\frac{5}{14} = - 27\frac{15}{42} = - 27\frac{15}{42}$$
$$15\frac{34}{42} = 15\frac{17}{21}$$

Answer: **(E)** $15\frac{17}{21}$

7.

$$17\frac{5}{8} = \frac{141}{8}$$
$$\frac{141}{8} \times \frac{\overset{16}{\cancel{128}}}{1} = 2256$$

Answer: **(A)** 2256

8.

$$1\frac{2}{3} \div 1\frac{1}{9} = \frac{5}{3} \div \frac{10}{9}$$
$$= \frac{\overset{1}{\cancel{5}}}{\underset{1}{\cancel{3}}} \times \frac{\overset{3}{\cancel{9}}}{\underset{2}{\cancel{10}}}$$
$$= \frac{3}{2}$$
$$= 1\frac{1}{2}$$

Answer: **(B)** $1\frac{1}{2}$

9. L.C.D. = 24

$$12\frac{1}{6} = 12\frac{4}{24} = 11\frac{28}{24}$$
$$- 2\frac{3}{8} = - 2\frac{9}{24} = - 2\frac{9}{24}$$
$$9\frac{19}{24} = 9\frac{19}{24}$$
$$- 7\frac{2}{3} = - 7\frac{16}{24}$$
$$2\frac{3}{24} = 2\frac{3}{24}$$
$$+ 19\frac{3}{4} = + 19\frac{18}{24}$$
$$21\frac{21}{24}$$
$$21\frac{21}{24} = 21\frac{7}{8}$$

Answer: **(B)** $21\frac{7}{8}$

10. To simplify a complex fraction, divide the numerator by the denominator:

$$\frac{1}{9} \div \frac{2}{5} = \frac{2}{\cancel{9}} \times \frac{5}{\cancel{2}}$$
$$= \frac{10}{9}$$
$$= 1\frac{1}{9}$$

Answer: **(E)** $1\frac{1}{9}$

11. Write all of the fractions with the same denominator. L.C.D. = 80

$$\frac{9}{16} = \frac{45}{80}$$
$$\frac{7}{10} = \frac{56}{80}$$
$$\frac{5}{8} = \frac{50}{80}$$
$$\frac{4}{5} = \frac{64}{80}$$
$$\frac{1}{2} = \frac{40}{80}$$

Answer: **(D)** $\frac{4}{5}$

12.

$$3\frac{5}{16} = 3\frac{5}{16}$$
$$+ 2\frac{3}{4} = + 2\frac{12}{16}$$
$$5\frac{17}{16}$$
$$= 6\frac{1}{16}$$

Answer: **(B)** $6\frac{1}{16}$ in.

13.

$$10\frac{1}{2} \div \frac{1}{2} = \frac{21}{2} \div \frac{1}{2}$$
$$= \frac{21}{\cancel{2}} \times \frac{\cancel{2}}{1}$$
$$= 21$$

Answer: **(E)** 21

14.

$$5\frac{3}{4} \times 3 = \frac{23}{4} \times \frac{3}{1}$$
$$= \frac{69}{4}$$
$$= 17\frac{1}{4}$$

Answer: **(D)** $17\frac{1}{4}$

15. First week:
L.C.D. = 24

$$3\frac{1}{2} = 3\frac{12}{24} \text{ miles}$$
$$1\frac{1}{4} = 1\frac{6}{24}$$
$$1\frac{1}{6} = 1\frac{4}{24}$$
$$+ 2\frac{3}{8} = + 2\frac{9}{24}$$
$$7\frac{31}{24} = 8\frac{7}{24} \text{ miles}$$

Second week:
L.C.D. = 16

$$\frac{1}{4} = \frac{4}{16} \text{ miles}$$
$$\frac{3}{8} = \frac{6}{16}$$
$$\frac{9}{16} = \frac{9}{16}$$
$$3\frac{1}{16} = 3\frac{1}{16}$$
$$2\frac{5}{8} = 2\frac{10}{16}$$
$$+ 3\frac{3}{16} = + 3\frac{3}{16}$$
$$8\frac{33}{16} = 10\frac{1}{16} \text{ miles}$$

L.C.D. = 48

$$10\frac{1}{16} = 9\frac{51}{48} \text{ miles second week}$$
$$- 8\frac{7}{24} = - 8\frac{14}{48} \text{ miles first week}$$
$$1\frac{37}{48} \text{ more miles traveled}$$

Answer: **(A)** $1\frac{37}{48}$

16. Consider each choice:

Each 6-ft board yields one $5\frac{1}{2}$-ft board with $\frac{1}{2}$ ft waste.

Each 12-ft board yields two $5\frac{1}{2}$-ft boards with 1 ft waste ($2 \times 5\frac{1}{2} = 11$; $12 - 11 = 1$ ft waste).

Each 24-ft board yields four $5\frac{1}{2}$-ft boards with 2 ft waste ($4 \times 5\frac{1}{2} = 22$; $24 - 22 = 2$ ft waste).

Each 22 ft board may be divided into four $5\frac{1}{2}$-ft boards with no waste ($4 \times 5\frac{1}{2} = 22$ exactly).

Answer: **(C)** 22 ft

17. $\frac{15}{16}$ of fortune is $7500.

Therefore, his fortune $= 7500 \div \frac{15}{16}$

$$= \frac{\overset{500}{\cancel{7500}}}{1} \times \frac{16}{\cancel{15}}$$

$$= 8000$$

Answer: **(D)** $8000

18. $\frac{2}{3}$ of $54{,}000 =$ increase

$$\text{Increase} = \frac{2}{3} \times \overset{18{,}000}{\cancel{54{,}000}}$$

$$= 36{,}000$$

$$\text{Present population} = 54{,}000 + 36{,}000$$

$$= 90{,}000$$

Answer: **(D)** 90,000

19. First day: $\frac{1}{3}$ evaporates

$\frac{2}{3}$ remains

Second day: $\frac{3}{4}$ of $\frac{2}{3}$ evaporates

$\frac{1}{4}$ of $\frac{2}{3}$ remains

The amount remaining is

$$\frac{1}{\cancel{4}_2} \times \frac{\cancel{2}^1}{3} = \frac{1}{6} \text{ of original contents}$$

Answer: **(C)** $\frac{1}{6}$

20. $\frac{7}{8}$ of capacity $= 14$ gal

Therefore, capacity $= 14 \div \frac{7}{8}$

$$= \frac{\cancel{14}^2}{1} \times \frac{8}{\cancel{7}_1}$$

$$= 16 \text{ gal}$$

Answer: **(C)** 16 gal

DECIMALS

1. A **decimal,** which is a number with a decimal point (.), is actually a fraction, the denominator of which is understood to be 10 or some power of 10.

    a. The number of digits, or places, after a decimal point determines which power of 10 the denominator is. If there is one digit, the denominator is understood to be 10; if there are two digits, the denominator is understood to be 100, etc.

    Example: $.3 = \frac{3}{10}$, $.57 = \frac{57}{100}$, $.643 = \frac{643}{1000}$

    b. The addition of zeros after a decimal point does not change the value of the decimal. The zeros may be removed without changing the value of the decimal.

    Example: $.7 = .70 = .700$ and, vice versa, $.700 = .70 = .7$

    c. Since a decimal point is understood to exist after any whole number, the addition of any number of zeros after such a decimal point does not change the value of the number.

    Example: $2 = 2.0 = 2.00 = 2.000$

Addition of Decimals

2. Decimals are added in the same way that whole numbers are added, with the provision that the decimal points must be kept in a vertical line, one under the other. This determines the place of the decimal point in the answer.

Illustration: Add 2.31, .037, 4, and 5.0017

SOLUTION:

```
    2.3100
     .0370
    4.0000
 +  5.0017
   11.3487
```

Answer: 11.3487

Subtraction of Decimals

3. Decimals are subtracted in the same way that whole numbers are subtracted, with the provision that, as in addition, the decimal points must be kept in a vertical line, one under the other. This determines the place of the decimal point in the answer.

Illustration: Subtract 4.0037 from 15.3

SOLUTION:

$$\begin{array}{r} 15.3000 \\ -\ 4.0037 \\ \hline 11.2963 \end{array}$$

Answer: 11.2963

Multiplication of Decimals

4. Decimals are multiplied in the same way that whole numbers are multiplied.

   a. The number of decimal places in the product equals the sum of the decimal places in the multiplicand and in the multiplier.

   b. If there are fewer places in the product than this sum, then a sufficient number of zeros must be added in front of the product to equal the number of places required, and a decimal point is written in front of the zeros.

Illustration: Multiply 2.372 by .012

SOLUTION:

$$\begin{array}{r} 2.372 \quad \text{(3 decimal places)} \\ \times\ .012 \quad \text{(3 decimal places)} \\ \hline 4744 \\ 2372 \quad\quad\quad \\ \hline .028464 \quad \text{(6 decimal places)} \end{array}$$

Answer: .028464

5. A decimal can be multiplied by a power of 10 by moving the decimal point to the *right* as many places as indicated by the power. If multiplied by 10, the decimal point is moved one place to the right; if multiplied by 100, the decimal point is moved two places to the right; etc.

Example:
$$\begin{array}{l} .235 \times 10 \ = \ 2.35 \\ .235 \times 100 \ = \ 23.5 \\ .235 \times 1000 = 235 \end{array}$$

Division of Decimals

6. There are four types of division involving decimals:

   • When the dividend only is a decimal.
   • When the divisor only is a decimal.
   • When both are decimals.
   • When neither dividend nor divisor is a decimal.

   a. When the dividend only is a decimal, the division is the same as that of whole numbers, except that a decimal point must be placed in the quotient exactly above that in the dividend.

Illustration: Divide 12.864 by 32

SOLUTION:

$$\begin{array}{r} .402\quad\ \\ 32\ \overline{)\ 12.864} \\ \underline{12\ 8\quad\ \ } \\ 64 \\ \underline{64} \end{array}$$

Answer: .402

   b. When the divisor only is a decimal, the decimal point in the divisor is omitted and as many zeros are placed to the right of the dividend as there were decimal places in the divisor.

Illustration: Divide 211327 by 6.817

SOLUTION:

$$6.817\ \overline{)\ 211327}$$
(3 decimal places)

$$= 6817\ \overline{\smash{)}\ \begin{array}{r} 31000\quad\quad \\ 211327000 \end{array}}\quad \text{(3 zeros added)}$$
$$\begin{array}{r} 20451\quad\ \\ \underline{6817}\quad\ \\ 6817 \\ \underline{6817} \end{array}$$

Answer: 31000

   c. When both divisor and dividend are decimals, the decimal point in the divisor is omitted and the decimal point in the dividend must be moved to the right as many decimal places as there were in the divisor. If there are not enough places in the dividend, zeros must be added to make up the difference.

Illustration: Divide 2.62 by .131

SOLUTION: $.131 \overline{) \ 2.62} = 131 \overline{) \ 2620}$ $\overset{20}{}$
$\underline{262}$

Answer: 20

d. In instances when neither the divisor nor the dividend is a decimal, a problem may still involve decimals. This occurs in two cases: when the dividend is a smaller number than the divisor; and when it is required to work out a division to a certain number of decimal places. In either case, write in a decimal point after the dividend, add as many zeros as necessary, and place a decimal point in the quotient above that in the dividend.

Illustration: Divide 7 by 50.

SOLUTION: $50 \overline{) \ 7.00}$ $\overset{.14}{}$
$\underline{5 \ 0}$
$2 \ 00$
$\underline{2 \ 00}$

Answer: .14

Illustration: How much is 155 divided by 40, carried out to 3 decimal places?

SOLUTION: $40 \overline{) \ 155.000}$ $\overset{3.875}{}$
$\underline{120}$
$35 \ 0$
$\underline{32 \ 0}$
$3 \ 00$
$\underline{2 \ 80}$
200

Answer: 3.875

7. A decimal can be divided by a power of 10 by moving the decimal to the *left* as many places as indicated by the power. If divided by 10, the decimal point is moved one place to the left; if divided by 100, the decimal point is moved two places to the left; etc. If there are not enough places, add zeros in front of the number to make up the difference and add a decimal point.

Example: .4 divided by 10 = .04
.4 divided by 100 = .004

Rounding Decimals

8. To round a number to a given decimal place:

   a. Locate the given place.

   b. If the digit to the right is less than 5, omit all digits following the given place.

   c. If the digit to the right is 5 or more, raise the given place by 1 and omit all digits following the given place.

Examples:

   4.27   = 4.3 to the nearest tenth
   .71345 = .713 to the nearest thousandth

9. In problems involving money, answers are usually rounded to the nearest cent.

Conversion of Fractions to Decimals

10. A fraction can be changed to a decimal by dividing the numerator by the denominator and working out the division to as many decimal places as required.

Illustration: Change $\frac{5}{11}$ to a decimal of 2 places.

SOLUTION: $\frac{5}{11} = 11 \overline{) \ 5.00}$ $\overset{.45\frac{5}{11}}{}$
$\underline{4 \ 4}$
60
$\underline{55}$
5

Answer: $.45\frac{5}{11}$

11. To clear fractions containing a decimal in either the numerator or the denominator, or in both, divide the numerator by the denominator.

Illustration: What is the value of $\frac{2.34}{.6}$?

SOLUTION: $\frac{2.34}{.6} = .6 \overline{) \ 2.34} = 6 \overline{) \ 23.4}$ $\overset{3.9}{}$
$\underline{18}$
$5 \ 4$
$\underline{5 \ 4}$

Answer: 3.9

Conversion of Decimals to Fractions

12. Since a decimal point indicates a number having a denominator that is a power of 10, a decimal can be expressed as a fraction, the numerator of which is the number itself and the denominator of which is the power indicated by the number of decimal places in the decimal.

    Example: $.3 = \frac{3}{10}$, $.47 = \frac{47}{100}$

13. When the decimal is a mixed number, divide by the power of 10 indicated by its number of decimal places. The fraction does not count as a decimal place.

    Illustration: Change $.25\frac{1}{3}$ to a fraction.

    SOLUTION: $.25\frac{1}{3} = 25\frac{1}{3} \div 100$
    $= \frac{76}{3} \times \frac{1}{100}$
    $= \frac{76}{300} = \frac{19}{75}$

    Answer: $\frac{19}{75}$

14. When to change decimals to fractions:

    a. When dealing with whole numbers, do not change the decimal.

    Example: In the problem $12 \times .14$, it is better to keep the decimal:
    $$12 \times .14 = 1.68$$

    b. When dealing with fractions, change the decimal to a fraction.

    Example: In the problem $\frac{3}{5} \times .17$, it is best to change the decimal to a fraction:
    $$\frac{3}{5} \times .17 = \frac{3}{5} \times \frac{17}{100} = \frac{51}{500}$$

15. Because decimal equivalents of fractions are often used, it is helpful to be familiar with the most common conversions.

$\frac{1}{2}$	= .5	$\frac{1}{3}$	= .3333
$\frac{1}{4}$	= .25	$\frac{2}{3}$	= .6667
$\frac{3}{4}$	= .75	$\frac{1}{6}$	= .1667
$\frac{1}{5}$	= .2	$\frac{1}{7}$	= .1429
$\frac{1}{8}$	= .125	$\frac{1}{9}$	= .1111
$\frac{1}{16}$	= .0625	$\frac{1}{12}$	= .0833

    Note that the left column contains exact values. The values in the right column have been rounded to the nearest ten-thousandth.

Practice Problems Involving Decimals

1. Add 37.03, 11.5627, 3.4005, 3423, and 1.141. _____

2. Subtract 4.64324 from 7. _____

3. Multiply 27.34 by 16.943. _____

4. How much is 19.6 divided by 3.2, carried out to 3 decimal places? _____

5. What is $\frac{5}{11}$ in decimal form (to the nearest hundredth)? _____

6. What is $.64\frac{2}{3}$ in fraction form? _____

7. What is the difference between $\frac{3}{5}$ and $\frac{9}{8}$ expressed decimally? _____

8. A boy saved up $4.56 the first month, $3.82 the second month, and $5.06 the third month. How much did he save altogether?

    _____

9. The diameter of a certain rod is required to be 1.51 ± .015 inches. The rod's diameter must be between _____ and _____ .

10. After an employer figures out an employee's salary of $190.57, he deducts $3.05 for social security and $5.68 for pension. What is the amount of the check after these deductions?

    _____

11. If the outer radius of a metal pipe is 2.84 inches and the inner radius is 1.94 inches, the thickness of the metal is _____ .

12. A boy earns $20.56 on Monday, $32.90 on Tuesday, $20.78 on Wednesday. He spends half of all that he earned during the three days. How much has he left? _____

13. The total cost of $3\frac{1}{2}$ pounds of meat at $1.69 a pound and 20 lemons at $.60 a dozen will be

    _____ .

14. A reel of cable weighs 1279 lb. If the empty reel weighs 285 lb and the cable weighs 7.1

lb per foot, the number of feet of cable on the reel is _____.

15. 345 fasteners at $4.15 per hundred will cost _____.

Problem Solutions—Decimals

1. Line up all the decimal points one under the other. Then add:

$$
\begin{array}{r}
37.03 \\
11.5627 \\
3.4005 \\
3423.0000 \\
+\quad 1.141 \\
\hline
3476.1342
\end{array}
$$

   Answer: 3476.1342

2. Add a decimal point and five zeros to the 7. Then subtract:

$$
\begin{array}{r}
7.00000 \\
-\;4.64324 \\
\hline
2.35676
\end{array}
$$

   Answer: 2.35676

3. Since there are two decimal places in the multiplicand and three decimal places in the multiplier, there will be 2 + 3 = 5 decimal places in the product.

$$
\begin{array}{r}
27.34 \\
\times\; 16.943 \\
\hline
8202 \\
1\;0936 \\
24\;606 \\
164\;04 \\
273\;4 \\
\hline
463.22162
\end{array}
$$

   Answer: 463.22162

4. Omit the decimal point in the divisor by moving it one place to the right. Move the decimal point in the dividend one place to the right and add three zeros in order to carry your answer out to three decimal places, as instructed in the problem.

$$
\begin{array}{r}
6.125 \\
3.2\overline{)\;19.6.000} \\
19\;2 \\
\hline
4\;0 \\
3\;2 \\
\hline
80 \\
64 \\
\hline
160 \\
160
\end{array}
$$

   Answer: 6.125

5. To convert a fraction to a decimal, divide the numerator by the denominator:

$$
\begin{array}{r}
.454 \\
11\overline{)\;5.000} \\
4\;4 \\
\hline
60 \\
55 \\
\hline
50 \\
44 \\
\hline
6
\end{array}
$$

   Answer: .45 to the nearest hundredth

6. To convert a decimal to a fraction, divide by the power of 10 indicated by the number of decimal places. (The fraction does not count as a decimal place.)

$$
\begin{aligned}
64\tfrac{2}{3} \div 100 &= \tfrac{194}{3} \div \tfrac{100}{1} \\
&= \tfrac{194}{3} \times \tfrac{1}{100} \\
&= \tfrac{194}{300} \\
&= \tfrac{97}{150}
\end{aligned}
$$

   Answer: $\tfrac{97}{150}$

7. Convert each fraction to a decimal and subtract to find the difference:

   $\tfrac{9}{8} = 1.125 \qquad \tfrac{3}{5} = .60$

$$
\begin{array}{r}
1.125 \\
-\;.60 \\
\hline
.525
\end{array}
$$

   Answer: .525

8. Add the savings for each month:

$$
\begin{array}{r}
\$4.56 \\
3.82 \\
+\;5.06 \\
\hline
\$13.44
\end{array}
$$

   Answer: $13.44

9.
$$
\begin{array}{r}
1.51 \\
+ \ \ .015 \\
\hline
1.525
\end{array}
\qquad
\begin{array}{r}
1.510 \\
- \ \ .015 \\
\hline
1.495
\end{array}
$$

Answer: The rod may have a diameter of from 1.495 inches to 1.525 inches inclusive.

10. Add to find total deductions:

$$
\begin{array}{r}
\$3.05 \\
+ \ 5.68 \\
\hline
\$8.73
\end{array}
$$

Subtract total deductions from salary to find amount of check:

$$
\begin{array}{r}
\$190.57 \\
- \ \ \ 8.73 \\
\hline
\$181.84
\end{array}
$$

Answer: $181.84

11. Outer radius minus inner radius equals thickness of metal:

$$
\begin{array}{r}
2.84 \\
- \ 1.94 \\
\hline
.90
\end{array}
$$

Answer: .90 in.

12. Add daily earnings to find total earnings:

$$
\begin{array}{r}
\$20.56 \\
32.90 \\
+ \ 20.78 \\
\hline
\$74.24
\end{array}
$$

Divide total earnings by 2 to find out what he has left:

$$
2 \overline{\smash{)}\ \$74.24} \quad \$37.12
$$

Answer: $37.12

13. Find cost of $3\frac{1}{2}$ pounds of meat:

$$
\begin{array}{r}
\$1.69 \\
\times \ \ \ 3.5 \\
\hline
845 \\
5 \ 07 \\
\hline
\$5.915
\end{array} = \$5.92 \text{ to the nearest cent}
$$

Find cost of 20 lemons:
$.60 \div 12 = \$.05$ (for 1 lemon)
$.05 \times 20 = \$1.00$ (for 20 lemons)

Add cost of meat and cost of lemons:

$$
\begin{array}{r}
\$5.92 \\
+ \ 1.00 \\
\hline
\$6.92
\end{array}
$$

Answer: $6.92

14. Subtract weight of empty reel from total weight to find weight of cable:

$$
\begin{array}{r}
1279 \text{ lb} \\
- \ \ 285 \text{ lb} \\
\hline
994 \text{ lb}
\end{array}
$$

Each foot of cable weighs 7.1 lb. Therefore, to find the number of feet of cable on the reel, divide 994 by 7.1:

$$
\begin{array}{r}
14 \ 0. \\
7.1 \overline{\smash{)}\ 994.0.} \\
71 \ \ \ \ \ \\
\hline
284 \ \ \\
284 \ \ \\
\hline
0 \ 0
\end{array}
$$

Answer: 140

15. Each fastener costs:

$$\$4.15 \div 100 = \$.0415$$

345 fasteners cost:

$$
\begin{array}{r}
345 \\
\times \ .0415 \\
\hline
1725 \\
345 \ \ \\
13 \ 80 \ \ \ \\
\hline
14.3175
\end{array}
$$

Answer: $14.32

PERCENTS

1. The **percent symbol (%)** means "parts out of a hundred." Thus a percent is really a fraction—25% is 25 parts out of a hundred, or $\frac{25}{100}$, which reduces or simplifies to $\frac{1}{4}$, or one part out of four. Some problems involve expressing a fraction or a decimal as a percent. In other problems it is necessary to express a percent as a fraction or decimal in order to perform the calculations efficiently. When you have a percent (or decimal) which

converts to a common fraction (25% = .25 = $\frac{1}{4}$), it is usually best to do any multiplying or dividing by first converting the percent or decimal to the common fraction, since the numbers are usually smaller and will work better. For adding and subtracting, percentages and decimals are often easier.

2. To change a whole number or a decimal to a percent:

   a. Multiply the number by 100.

   b. Affix a % sign.

Illustration: Change 3 to a percent.

SOLUTION: $3 \times 100 = 300$
$$3 = 300\%$$

Answer: 300%

Illustration: Change .67 to a percent.

SOLUTION: $.67 \times 100 = 67$
$$.67 = 67\%$$

Answer: 67%

3. To change a fraction or a mixed number to a percent:

   a. Multiply the fraction or mixed number by 100.

   b. Reduce, if possible.

   c. Affix a % sign.

Illustration: Change $\frac{1}{7}$ to a percent.

SOLUTION: $\frac{1}{7} \times 100 = \frac{100}{7}$
$$= 14\frac{2}{7}$$
$$\frac{1}{7} = 14\frac{2}{7}\%$$

Answer: $14\frac{2}{7}\%$

Illustration: Change $4\frac{2}{3}$ to a percent.

SOLUTION: $4\frac{2}{3} \times 100 = \frac{14}{3} \times 100 = \frac{1400}{3}$
$$= 466\frac{2}{3}$$
$$4\frac{2}{3} = 466\frac{2}{3}\%$$

Answer: $466\frac{2}{3}\%$

4. To remove a % sign attached to a decimal, divide the decimal by 100. If necessary, the resulting decimal may then be changed to a fraction.

Illustration: Change .5% to a decimal and to a fraction.

SOLUTION: $.5\% = .5 \div 100 = .005$
$$.005 = \frac{5}{1000} = \frac{1}{200}$$

Answer: $.5\% = .005$
$$.5\% = \frac{1}{200}$$

5. To remove a % sign attached to a fraction or mixed number, divide the fraction or mixed number by 100, and reduce, if possible. If necessary, the resulting fraction may then be changed to a decimal.

Illustration: Change $\frac{3}{4}\%$ to a fraction and to a decimal.

SOLUTION: $\frac{3}{4}\% = \frac{3}{4} \div 100 = \frac{3}{4} \times \frac{1}{100}$
$$= \frac{3}{400}$$

$$\frac{3}{400} = 400 \overline{)3.0000}^{\;.0075}$$

Answer: $\frac{3}{4}\% = \frac{3}{400}$
$$\frac{3}{4}\% = .0075$$

6. To remove a % sign attached to a decimal that includes a fraction, divide the decimal by 100. If necessary, the resulting number may then be changed to a fraction.

Illustration: Change $.5\frac{1}{3}\%$ to a fraction.

SOLUTION: $.5\frac{1}{3}\% = .005\frac{1}{3}$
$$= \frac{5\frac{1}{3}}{1000}$$
$$= 5\frac{1}{3} \div 1000$$
$$= \frac{16}{3} \times \frac{1}{1000}$$
$$= \frac{16}{3000}$$
$$= \frac{2}{375}$$

Answer: $.5\frac{1}{3}\% = \frac{2}{375}$

7. Some fraction-percent equivalents are used so frequently that it is helpful to be familiar with them.

$\frac{1}{25} = 4\%$	$\frac{1}{5} = 20\%$
$\frac{1}{20} = 5\%$	$\frac{1}{4} = 25\%$
$\frac{1}{12} = 8\frac{1}{3}\%$	$\frac{1}{3} = 33\frac{1}{3}\%$
$\frac{1}{10} = 10\%$	$\frac{1}{2} = 50\%$
$\frac{1}{8} = 12\frac{1}{2}\%$	$\frac{2}{3} = 66\frac{2}{3}\%$
$\frac{1}{6} = 16\frac{2}{3}\%$	$\frac{3}{4} = 75\%$

Solving Percent Problems

8. Most percent problems involve three quantities:

    • The rate, R, which is followed by a % sign.
    • The base, B, which follows the word "of."
    • The amount of percentage, P, which usually follows the word "is."

    a. If the rate (R) and the base (B) are known, then the percentage (P) = R × B.

    Illustration: Find 15% of 50.

    SOLUTION: Rate = 15%
    $$\text{Base} = 50$$
    $$P = R \times B$$
    $$P = 15\% \times 50$$
    $$= .15 \times 50$$
    $$= 7.5$$

    Answer: 15% of 50 is 7.5.

    b. If the rate (R) and the percentage (P) are known, then the base (B) = $\frac{P}{R}$.

    Illustration: 7% of what number is 35?

    SOLUTION: Rate = 7%
    $$\text{Percentage} = 35$$
    $$B = \frac{P}{R}$$
    $$B = \frac{35}{7\%}$$
    $$= 35 \div .07$$
    $$= 500$$

    Answer: 7% of 500 is 35.

    c. If the percentage (P) and the base (B) are known, the rate (R) = $\frac{P}{B}$.

    Illustration: There are 96 men in a group of 150 people. What percent of the group is men?

    SOLUTION: Base = 150
    $$\text{Percentage (amount)} = 96$$
    $$\text{Rate} = \tfrac{96}{150}$$
    $$= .64$$
    $$= 64\%$$

    Answer: 64% of the group are men.

Illustration: In a tank holding 20 gallons of solution, 1 gallon is alcohol. What is the strength of the solution in percent?

SOLUTION:

$$\text{Percentage (amount)} = 1 \text{ gallon}$$
$$\text{Base} = 20 \text{ gallons}$$
$$\text{Rate} = \tfrac{1}{20}$$
$$= .05$$
$$= 5\%$$

Answer: The solution is 5% alcohol.

9. In a percent problem, the whole is 100%.

    Example: If a problem involves 10% of a quantity, the rest of the quantity is 90%.

    Example: If a quantity has been increased by 5%, the new amount is 105% of the original quantity.

    Example: If a quantity has been decreased by 15%, the new amount is 85% of the original quantity.

10. Percent change, percent increase, and percent decrease are special types of percent problems in which the difficulty is in making sure to use the right numbers to calculate the percent. The full formula is:

    $$\frac{(\text{New Amount}) - (\text{Original Amount})}{(\text{Original Amount})} \times 100 = \text{percent change}$$

    Where the new amount is less than the original amount, the number on top will be a negative number and the result will be a **percent decrease.** When a percent decrease is asked for, the negative sign is omitted. Where the new amount is greater than the original amount, the percent change is positive and is called a **percent increase.**

    The percent of increase or decrease is found by putting the amount of increase or decrease over the original amount and changing this fraction to a percent by multiplying by 100.

    Illustration: The number of automobiles sold by the Cadcoln Dealership increased from 300 one year to 400 the following year. What was the percent of increase?

SOLUTION: There was an increase of 100, which must be compared to the original 300.

$$\tfrac{100}{300} = \tfrac{1}{3} = 33\tfrac{1}{3}\%$$

Answer: $33\tfrac{1}{3}\%$

Practice Problems Involving Percents

1. 10% written as a decimal is
   (A) 1.0
   (B) 0.1
   (C) 0.01
   (D) 0.010
   (E) 0.001

2. What is 5.37% in fraction form?
   (A) $\tfrac{537}{10,000}$
   (B) $\tfrac{537}{1000}$
   (C) $5\tfrac{37}{10,000}$
   (D) $5\tfrac{37}{100}$
   (E) $\tfrac{537}{10}$

3. What percent is $\tfrac{3}{4}$ of $\tfrac{5}{6}$?
   (A) 60%
   (B) 75%
   (C) 80%
   (D) 90%
   (E) 111%

4. What percent is 14 of 24?
   (A) $62\tfrac{1}{2}\%$
   (B) $58\tfrac{1}{3}\%$
   (C) $41\tfrac{2}{3}\%$
   (D) $33\tfrac{3}{5}\%$
   (E) 14%

5. 200% of 800 equals
   (A) 4
   (B) 16
   (C) 200
   (D) 800
   (E) 1600

6. If John must have a mark of 80% to pass a test of 35 items, the number of items he may miss and still pass the test is
   (A) 7
   (B) 8
   (C) 11
   (D) 28
   (E) 35

7. The regular price of a TV set that sold for $118.80 at a 20% reduction sale is
   (A) $158.60
   (B) $148.50
   (C) $138.84
   (D) $95.04
   (E) $29.70

8. A circle graph of a budget shows the expenditure of 26.2% for housing, 28.4% for food, 12% for clothing, 12.7% for taxes, and the balance for miscellaneous items. The percent for miscellaneous items is
   (A) 79.3
   (B) 70.3
   (C) 68.5
   (D) 29.7
   (E) 20.7

9. Two dozen shuttlecocks and four badminton rackets are to be purchased for a playground. The shuttlecocks are priced at $.35 each and the rackets at $2.75 each. The playground receives a discount of 30% from these prices. The total cost of this equipment is
   (A) $7.29
   (B) $11.43
   (C) $13.58
   (D) $18.60
   (E) $19.40

10. A piece of wood weighing 10 ounces is found to have a weight of 8 ounces after drying. The moisture content was
    (A) 80%
    (B) 40%
    (C) $33\tfrac{1}{3}\%$
    (D) 25%
    (E) 20%

11. A bag contains 800 coins. Of these, 10 percent are dimes, 30 percent are nickels, and the rest are quarters. The amount of money in the bag is
    (A) less than $150
    (B) between $150 and $300

(C) between $301 and $450

(D) between $450 and $800

(E) more than $800

12. Six quarts of a 20% solution of alcohol in water are mixed with 4 quarts of a 60% solution of alcohol in water. The alcoholic strength of the mixture is

(A) 80%

(B) 40%

(C) 36%

(D) $33\frac{1}{3}$%

(E) 10%

13. A man insures 80% of his property and pays a $2\frac{1}{2}$% premium amounting to $348. What is the total value of his property?

(A) $19,000

(B) $18,000

(C) $18,400

(D) $17,400

(E) $13,920

14. A clerk divided his 35-hour work week as follows: $\frac{1}{5}$ of his time was spent in sorting mail; $\frac{1}{2}$ of his time in filing letters; and $\frac{1}{7}$ of his time in reception work. The rest of his time was devoted to messenger work. The percent of time spent on messenger work by the clerk during the week was most nearly

(A) 6%

(B) 10%

(C) 14%

(D) 16%

(E) 20%

15. In a school in which 40% of the enrolled students are boys, 80% of the boys are present on a certain day. If 1152 boys are present, the total school enrollment is

(A) 1440

(B) 2880

(C) 3600

(D) 5400

(E) 5760

16. Mrs. Morris receives a salary raise from $25,000 to $27,500. Find the percent of increase.

(A) 9

(B) 10

(C) 90

(D) 15

(E) $12\frac{1}{2}$

17. The population of Stormville has increased from 80,000 to 100,000 in the last 20 years. Find the percent of increase.

(A) 20

(B) 25

(C) 80

(D) 60

(E) 10

18. The value of Super Company Stock dropped from $25 a share to $21 a share. Find the percent of decrease.

(A) 4

(B) 8

(C) 12

(D) 16

(E) 20

19. The Rubins bought their home for $30,000 and sold it for $60,000. What was the percent of increase?

(A) 100

(B) 50

(C) 200

(D) 300

(E) 150

20. During the pre-holiday rush, Martin's Department Store increased its sales staff from 150 to 200 persons. By what percent must it now decrease its sales staff to return to the usual number of salespersons?

(A) 25

(B) $33\frac{1}{3}$

(C) 20

(D) 40

(E) 75

Percent Problems—Correct Answers

1.	**(B)**	6.	**(A)**	11.	**(A)**	16.	**(B)**
2.	**(A)**	7.	**(B)**	12.	**(C)**	17.	**(B)**
3.	**(D)**	8.	**(E)**	13.	**(D)**	18.	**(D)**
4.	**(B)**	9.	**(C)**	14.	**(D)**	19.	**(A)**
5.	**(E)**	10.	**(E)**	15.	**(C)**	20.	**(A)**

Problem Solutions—Percents

1. 10% = .10 = .1

    Answer: **(B)** 0.1

2. $5.37\% = .0537 = \dfrac{537}{10{,}000}$

    Answer: **(A)** $\dfrac{537}{10{,}000}$

3. Base (number following "of") $= \frac{5}{6}$
    Percentage (number following "is") $= \frac{3}{4}$

    Rate $= \dfrac{\text{Percentage}}{\text{Base}}$

    $\qquad$ = Percentage ÷ Base

    Rate $= \frac{3}{4} \div \frac{5}{6}$

    $\qquad = \frac{3}{4} \times \frac{6}{5}$

    $\qquad = \frac{9}{10}$

    $\frac{9}{10} = .9 = 90\%$

    Answer: **(D)** 90%

4. Base (number following "of") = 24
    Percentage (number following "is") = 14

    Rate = Percentage ÷ Base
    Rate = 14 ÷ 24
    $\qquad = .58\frac{1}{3}$
    $\qquad = 58\frac{1}{3}\%$

    Answer: **(B)** $58\frac{1}{3}\%$

5. 200% of 800 = 2.00 × 800
    $\qquad\qquad\qquad = 1600$

    Answer: **(E)** 1600

6. He must answer 80% of 35 correctly. There-
    fore, he may miss 20% of 35.
    20% of 35 = .20 × 35
    $\qquad\qquad = 7$

    Answer: **(A)** 7

7. Since $118.80 represents a 20% reduction,
    $118.80 = 80% of the regular price.

    Regular price $= \dfrac{\$118.80}{80\%}$

    $\qquad\qquad = \$118.80 \div .80$
    $\qquad\qquad = \$148.50$

    Answer: **(B)** $148.50

8. All the items in a circle graph total 100%.
    Add the figures given for housing, food,
    clothing, and taxes:

    $\qquad$ 26.2%
    $\qquad$ 28.4%
    $\qquad$ 12 %
    $\underline{+\ 12.7\%}$
    $\qquad$ 79.3%

    Subtract this total from 100% to find the
    percent for miscellaneous items:

    $\qquad$ 100.0%
    $\underline{-\ \ 79.3\%}$
    $\qquad$ 20.7%

    Answer: **(E)** 20.7%

9. Price of shuttlecocks = 24 × $.35 = $ 8.40
    Price of rackets $\quad$ = 4 × $2.75 = $11.00
    Total price $\qquad\quad$ = $\qquad\qquad$ $19.40

    Discount is 30%, and 100% − 30% = 70%

    Actual cost = 70% of 19.40
    $\qquad\qquad = .70 \times 19.40$
    $\qquad\qquad = 13.58$

    Answer: **(C)** $13.58

10. Subtract weight of wood after drying from
    original weight of wood to find amount of
    moisture in wood:

    $\qquad$ 10
    $\underline{-\ \ 8}$
    $\qquad$ 2 ounces of moisture in wood

    Moisture content $= \dfrac{2 \text{ ounces}}{10 \text{ ounces}} = .2 = 20\%$

    Answer: **(E)** 20%

11. Find the number of each kind of coin:

    10% of 800 $\ =\ $ .10 × 800 $\ =\ $ 80 dimes
    30% of 800 $\ =\ $ .30 × 800 $\ =\ $ 240 nickels
    60% of 800 $\ =\ $ .60 × 800 $\ =\ $ 480 quarters

    Find the value of the coins:

    $\quad$ 80 dimes $\ =\ $ 80 × .10 $\ =\ $ $ 8.00
    240 nickels $\ =\ $ 240 × .05 $\ =\ $ $\quad$ 12.00
    480 quarters $\ =\ $ 480 × .25 $\ =\ \underline{\quad 120.00}$
    $\qquad\qquad\qquad\qquad$ Total $\quad$ $140.00

    Answer: **(A)** less than $150

12. First solution contains 20% of 6 quarts of alcohol.

$$\text{Alcohol content} = .20 \times 6$$
$$= 1.2 \text{ quarts}$$

Second solution contains 60% of 4 quarts of alcohol.

$$\text{Alcohol content} = .60 \times 4$$
$$= 2.4 \text{ quarts}$$

Mixture contains: $1.2 + 2.4 = 3.6$ quarts alcohol

$6 + 4 = 10$ quarts liquid

Alcoholic strength of mixture $= \dfrac{3.6}{10} = 36\%$

Answer: **(C)** 36%

13. $2\frac{1}{2}\%$ of insured value = $348

$$\text{Insured value} = \frac{348}{2\frac{1}{2}\%}$$
$$= 348 \div .025$$
$$= \$13,920$$

$13,920 is 80% of total value

$$\text{Total value} = \frac{\$13,920}{80\%}$$
$$= \$13,920 \div .80$$
$$= \$17,400$$

Answer: **(D)** $17,400

14. $\frac{1}{5} \times 35 = 7$ hr sorting mail
$\frac{1}{2} \times 35 = 17\frac{1}{2}$ hr filing
$\frac{1}{7} \times 35 = \underline{5}$ hr reception
$ 29\frac{1}{2}$ hr accounted for

$35 - 29\frac{1}{2} = 5\frac{1}{2}$ hr left for messenger work

% spent on messenger work:

$$= \frac{5\frac{1}{2}}{35}$$
$$= 5\frac{1}{2} \div 35$$
$$= \frac{11}{2} \times \frac{1}{35}$$
$$= \frac{11}{70}$$
$$= .15\frac{5}{7}$$
$$= 15\frac{5}{7}\%$$

Answer: **(D)** most nearly 16%

15. 80% of the boys = 1152

$$\text{Number of boys} = \frac{1152}{80\%}$$
$$= 1152 \div .80$$
$$= 1440$$

40% of students = 1440

$$\text{Total number of students} = \frac{1440}{40\%}$$
$$= 1440 \div .40$$
$$= 3600$$

Answer: **(C)** 3600

16. Amount of increase = $2500

$$\text{Percent of increase} = \frac{\text{amount of increase}}{\text{original}}$$

$$\frac{2500}{25,000} = \frac{1}{10} = 10\%$$

Answer: **(B)** 10%

17. Amount of increase = 20,000

$$\text{Percent of increase} = \frac{20,000}{80,000} = \frac{1}{4} = 25\%$$

Answer: **(B)** 25%

18. Amount of decrease = $4

$$\text{Percent of decrease} = \frac{4}{25} = \frac{16}{100} = 16\%$$

Answer: **(D)** 16%

19. Amount of increase = $30,000

$$\text{Percent of increase} = \frac{30,000}{30,000} = 1 = 100\%$$

Answer: **(A)** 100%

20. Amount of decrease = 50

$$\text{Percent of decrease} = \frac{50}{200} = \frac{1}{4} = 25\%$$

Answer: **(A)** 25%

SHORTCUTS IN MULTIPLICATION AND DIVISION

There are several shortcuts for simplifying multiplication and division. Following the description of each shortcut, practice problems are provided.

Dropping Final Zeros

1. a. A zero in a whole number is considered a "final zero" if it appears in the units column or if all columns to its right are filled with zeros. A final zero may be omitted in certain kinds of problems.

   b. In decimal numbers, a zero appearing in the extreme right column may be dropped with no effect on the solution of a problem.

2. In multiplying whole numbers, the final zero(s) may be dropped during computation and simply transferred to the answer.

Examples:

```
    2310            129
  ×  150          × 210
    1155            129
    231             258
  346500          27090
```

```
    1760
  ×  205
    880
    352
  360800
```

Practice Problems

Solve the following multiplication problems, dropping the final zeros during computation.

1. 230
  × 12

2. 175
  × 130

3. 203
  × 14

4. 621
  × 140

5. 430
  × 360

6. 132
  × 310

7. 350
  × 24

8. 520
  × 410

9. 634
  × 120

10. 431
   × 230

Solutions to Practice Problems

1.
```
    230
  ×  12
    46
    23
   2760
```

2.
```
    175
  × 130
    525
    175
  22750
```

3.
```
    203
  ×  14
    812
    203
   2842
```
(no final zeros)

4.
```
    621
  × 140
   2484
    621
  86940
```

5.
```
    430
  × 360
    258
    129
  154800
```

6.
```
      132
    × 310
      132
      396
    40920
```

7.
```
      350
    ×  24
      140
       70
     8400
```

8.
```
      520
    × 410
       52
      208
    213200
```

9.
```
      634
    × 120
     1268
      634
    76080
```

10.
```
      431
    × 230
     1293
      862
    99130
```

Multiplying Whole Numbers by Decimals

3. In multiplying a whole number by a decimal number, if there are one or more final zeros in the multiplicand, move the decimal point in the multiplier to the right the same number of places as there are final zeros in the multiplicand. Then cross out the final zero(s) in the multiplicand.

Examples:

$$\begin{array}{r} 27500 \\ \times\ \ .15 \end{array} = \begin{array}{r} 275 \\ \times\ \ 15 \end{array}$$

$$\begin{array}{r} 1250 \\ \times\ .345 \end{array} = \begin{array}{r} 125 \\ \times\ 3.45 \end{array}$$

Practice Problems

Rewrite the following problems, dropping the final zeros and moving decimal points the appro-

priate number of spaces. Then compute the answers.

1.
```
     2400
    × .02
```

2.
```
      620
    × .04
```

3.
```
      800
    × .005
```

4.
```
      600
    × .002
```

5.
```
      340
    × .08
```

6.
```
      480
    ×  .4
```

7.
```
      400
    × .04
```

8.
```
     5300
    ×   .5
```

9.
```
      930
    ×  .3
```

10.
```
     9000
    × .001
```

Solutions to Practice Problems

The rewritten problems are shown, along with the answers.

1.
```
      24
    ×  2
      48
```

2. $\begin{array}{r} 62 \\ \times\ .4 \\ \hline 24.8 \end{array}$

3. $\begin{array}{r} 8 \\ \times\ .5 \\ \hline 4.0 \end{array}$

4. $\begin{array}{r} 6 \\ \times\ .2 \\ \hline 1.2 \end{array}$

5. $\begin{array}{r} 34 \\ \times\ .8 \\ \hline 27.2 \end{array}$

6. $\begin{array}{r} 48 \\ \times\ 4 \\ \hline 192 \end{array}$

7. $\begin{array}{r} 4 \\ \times\ 4 \\ \hline 16 \end{array}$

8. $\begin{array}{r} 530 \\ \times\ 5 \\ \hline 2650 \end{array}$

9. $\begin{array}{r} 93 \\ \times\ 3 \\ \hline 279 \end{array}$

10. $\begin{array}{r} 9 \\ \times\ 1 \\ \hline 9 \end{array}$

Dividing by Whole Numbers

4. a. When there are final zeros in the divisor but no final zeros in the dividend, move the decimal point in the dividend to the left as many places as there are final zeros in the divisor, then omit the final zeros.

Example: $2700. \overline{)\ 37523.} = 27. \overline{)\ 375.23}$

b. When there are fewer final zeros in the divisor than there are in the dividend, drop the same number of final zeros from the dividend as there are final zeros in the divisor.

Example: $250. \overline{)\ 45300.} = 25. \overline{)\ 4530.}$

c. When there are more final zeros in the divisor than there are in the dividend, move the decimal point in the dividend to the left as many places as there are final zeros in the divisor, then omit the final zeros.

Example: $2300. \overline{)\ 690.} = 23. \overline{)\ 6.9}$

d. When there are no final zeros in the divisor, no zeros can be dropped in the dividend.

Example: $23. \overline{)\ 690.} = 23. \overline{)\ 690.}$

Practice Problems

Rewrite the following problems, dropping the final zeros and moving the decimal points the appropriate number of places. Then compute the quotients.

1. $600. \overline{)\ 72.}$

2. $310. \overline{)\ 6200.}$

3. $7600 \overline{)\ 1520.}$

4. $46. \overline{)\ 920.}$

5. $11.0 \overline{)\ 220.}$

6. $700. \overline{)\ 84.}$

7. $90. \overline{)\ 8100.}$

8. $8100. \overline{)\ 1620.}$

9. $25. \overline{)\ 5250.}$

10. $41.0 \overline{)\ 820.}$

11. $800. \overline{)\ 96.}$

12. $650. \overline{)\ 1300.}$

13. $5500. \overline{)\ 110.}$

14. $36. \overline{)\ 720.}$

15. $87.0 \overline{)\ 1740.}$

Rewritten Practice Problems

1. 6.) .72

2. 31.) 620.

3. 76.) 15.2

4. 46.) 920.

5. 11.) 220.

6. 7.) .84

7. 9.) 810.

8. 81.) 16.2

9. 25.) 5250.

10. 41.) 820.

11. 8.) .96

12. 65.) 130.

13. 55.) 1.1

14. 36.) 720.

15. 87.) 1740.

Solutions to Practice Problems

```
         .12
1. 6. ) .72
```

```
         20
2. 31. ) 620.
        62
        ──
        00
```

```
          .2
3. 76. ) 15.2
        15 2
        ────
         0 0
```

```
         20
4. 46. ) 920.
        92
        ──
        00
```

```
         20
5. 11. ) 220.
        22
        ──
        00
```

```
         .12
6. 7. ) .84
```

```
         90
7. 9. ) 810.
       81
       ──
       00
```

```
          .2
8. 81. ) 16.2
        16 2
        ────
         0 0
```

```
         210
9. 25. ) 5250.
        50
        ──
        25
        25
        ──
        00
```

```
         20
10. 41. ) 820.
         82
         ──
         00
```

```
          .12
11. 8. ) .96
```

```
          2
12. 65. ) 130.
         130
         ───
         00
```

```
          .02
13. 55. ) 1.10
         1 10
         ────
          00
```

```
         20
14. 36. ) 720.
        72
        ──
        00
```

```
          20
15. 87. ) 1740.
         174
         ───
         00
```

Division by Multiplication

5. Instead of dividing by a particular number, the same answer is obtained by multiplying by the equivalent multiplier.

6. To find the equivalent multiplier of a given divisor, divide 1 by the divisor.

   Example: The equivalent multiplier of $12\frac{1}{2}$ is $1 \div 12\frac{1}{2}$ or .08. The division problem $100 \div 12\frac{1}{2}$ may be more easily solved as the multiplication problem $100 \times .08$. The answer will be the same. This can be helpful when you are estimating answers.

7. Common divisors and their equivalent multipliers are shown below:

Divisor	Equivalent Multiplier
$11\frac{1}{9}$	.09
$12\frac{1}{2}$	.08
$14\frac{2}{7}$	.07
$16\frac{2}{3}$	.06
20	.05
25	.04
$33\frac{1}{3}$	.03
50	.02

8. A divisor may be multiplied or divided by any power of 10, and the only change in its equivalent multiplier will be in the placement of the decimal point, as may be seen in the following table:

Divisor	Equivalent Multiplier
.025	40.
.25	4.
2.5	.4
25.	.04
250.	.004
2500.	.0004

Practice Problems

Rewrite and solve each of the following problems by using equivalent multipliers. Drop the final zeros where appropriate.

1. $100 \div 16\frac{2}{3} =$

2. $200 \div 25 =$

3. $300 \div 33\frac{1}{3} =$

4. $250 \div 50 =$

5. $80 \div 12\frac{1}{2} =$

6. $800 \div 14\frac{2}{7} =$

7. $620 \div 20 =$

8. $500 \div 11\frac{1}{9} =$

9. $420 \div 16\frac{2}{3} =$

10. $1200 \div 33\frac{1}{3} =$

11. $955 \div 50 =$

12. $900 \div 33\frac{1}{3} =$

13. $275 \div 12\frac{1}{2} =$

14. $625 \div 25 =$

15. $244 \div 20 =$

16. $350 \div 16\frac{2}{3} =$

17. $400 \div 33\frac{1}{3} =$

18. $375 \div 25 =$

19. $460 \div 20 =$

20. $250 \div 12\frac{1}{2} =$

Solutions to Practice Problems

The rewritten problems and their solutions appear below:

1. $100 \times .06 = 1 \times 6 = 6$

2. $200 \times .04 = 2 \times 4 = 8$

3. $300 \times .03 = 3 \times 3 = 9$

4. $250 \times .02 = 25 \times .2 = 5$

5. $80 \times .08 = 8 \times .8 = 6.4$

6. $800 \times .07 = 8 \times 7 = 56$

7. $620 \times .05 = 62 \times .5 = 31$

8. $500 \times .09 = 5 \times 9 = 45$

9. $420 \times .06 = 42 \times .6 = 25.2$

10. $1200 \times .03 = 12 \times 3 = 36$

11. $955 \times .02 = 19.1$

12. $900 \times .03 = 9 \times 3 = 27$

13. $275 \times .08 = 22$

14. $625 \times .04 = 25$

15. $244 \times .05 = 12.2$

16. $350 \times .06 = 35 \times .6 = 21$

17. $400 \times .03 = 4 \times 3 = 12$

18. $375 \times .04 = 15$

19. $460 \times .05 = 46 \times .5 = 23$

20. $250 \times .08 = 25 \times .8 = 20$

Multiplication by Division

9. Just as some division problems are made easier by changing them to equivalent multiplication problems, certain multiplication problems are made easier by changing them to equivalent division problems.

10. Instead of arriving at an answer by multiplying by a particular number, the same answer is obtained by dividing by the equivalent divisor.

11. To find the equivalent divisor of a given multiplier, divide 1 by the multiplier.

12. Common multipliers and their equivalent divisors are shown below:

Multiplier	Equivalent Divisor
$11\frac{1}{9}$	.09
$12\frac{1}{2}$	.08
$14\frac{2}{7}$	.07
$16\frac{2}{3}$	.06
20	.05
25	.04
$33\frac{1}{3}$	.03
50	.02

Notice that the multiplier-equivalent divisor pairs are the same as the divisor-equivalent multiplier pairs given earlier.

Practice Problems

Rewrite and solve each of the following problems by using division. Drop the final zeros where appropriate.

1. $77 \times 14\frac{2}{7} =$

2. $81 \times 11\frac{1}{9} =$

3. $475 \times 20 =$

4. $42 \times 50 =$

5. $36 \times 33\frac{1}{3} =$

6. $96 \times 12\frac{1}{2} =$

7. $126 \times 16\frac{2}{3} =$

8. $48 \times 25 =$

9. $33 \times 33\frac{1}{3} =$

10. $84 \times 14\frac{2}{7} =$

11. $99 \times 11\frac{1}{9} =$

12. $126 \times 33\frac{1}{3} =$

13. $168 \times 12\frac{1}{2} =$

14. $654 \times 16\frac{2}{3} =$

15. $154 \times 14\frac{2}{7} =$

16. $5250 \times 50 =$

17. $324 \times 25 =$

18. $625 \times 20 =$

19. $198 \times 11\frac{1}{9} =$

20. $224 \times 14\frac{2}{7} =$

Solutions to Practice Problems

The rewritten problems and their solutions appear below:

1. $.07 \overline{)\ 77.} = 7 \overline{)\ 7700.}^{\textstyle 1100.}$

2. $.09 \overline{)\ 81.} = 9 \overline{)\ 8100.}^{\textstyle 900.}$

3. $.05 \overline{)\ 475.} = 5 \overline{)\ 47500.}^{\textstyle 9500.}$

4. $.02 \overline{)\ 42.} = 2 \overline{)\ 4200.}^{\textstyle 2100.}$

5. $.03 \overline{)\ 36.} = 3 \overline{)\ 3600.}^{\textstyle 1200.}$

6. $.08 \overline{)\ 96.} = 8 \overline{)\ 9600.}^{\textstyle 1200.}$

7. $.06 \overline{)\ 126.} = 6 \overline{)\ 12600.}^{\textstyle 2100.}$

8. $.04 \overline{)\ 48.} = 4 \overline{)\ 4800.}^{\textstyle 1200.}$

9. $.03 \overline{)\ 33.} = 3 \overline{)\ 3300.}^{\textstyle 1100.}$

10. $.07 \overline{)\ 84.} = 7 \overline{)\ 8400.}^{\textstyle 1200.}$

11. $.09 \overline{)\ 99.} = 9 \overline{)\ 9900.}^{\textstyle 1100.}$

12. $.03 \overline{)\ 126.} = 3 \overline{)\ 12600.}^{\textstyle 4200.}$

13. $.08 \overline{)\ 168.} = 8 \overline{)\ 16800.}^{\textstyle 2100.}$

14. $.06 \overline{)\ 654.} = 6 \overline{)\ 65400.}^{\textstyle 10900.}$

15. $.07 \overline{)\ 154.} = 7 \overline{)\ 15400.}^{\textstyle 2200.}$

16. $.02 \overline{)\ 5250.} = 2 \overline{)\ 525000.}^{\textstyle 262500.}$

17. $.04 \overline{)\ 324.} = 4 \overline{)\ 32400.}^{\textstyle 8100.}$

18. $.05 \overline{)\ 625.} = 5 \overline{)\ 62500.}^{\textstyle 12500.}$

19. $.09 \overline{)\ 198.} = 9 \overline{)\ 19800.}^{\textstyle 2200.}$

20. $.07 \overline{)\ 224.} = 7 \overline{)\ 22400.}^{\textstyle 3200.}$

AVERAGES

1. a. The term average can technically refer to a variety of mathematical ideas, but on the test it refers to the **arithmetic mean.** It is found by adding the numbers given and then dividing this sum by the number of items being averaged.

Illustration: Find the arithmetic mean of 2, 8, 5, 9, 6, and 12.

SOLUTION: There are 6 numbers.

$$\text{Arithmetic mean} = \frac{2 + 8 + 5 + 9 + 6 + 12}{6}$$

$$= \frac{42}{6}$$

$$= 7$$

Answer: The arithmetic mean is 7.

b. If a problem calls for simply the average or the mean, it is referring to the arithmetic mean.

2. If a group of numbers is arranged in order, the middle number is called the **median.** If there is no single middle number (this occurs when there is an even number of items), the median is found by computing the arithmetic mean of the two middle numbers.

Example: The median of 6, 8, 10, 12, and 14 is 10.

Example: The median of 6, 8, 10, 12, 14, and 16 is the arithmetic mean of 10 and 12.

$$\frac{10 + 12}{2} = \frac{22}{2} = 11.$$

3. The **mode** of a group of numbers is the number that appears most often.

Example: The mode of 10, 5, 7, 9, 12, 5, 10, 5 and 9 is 5.

4. When some numbers among terms to be averaged occur more than once, they must be given the appropriate weight. For example, if a student received four grades of 80 and one of 90, his average would not be the average of 80 and 90, but rather the average of 80, 80, 80, 80, and 90.

To obtain the average of quantities that are weighted:

a. Set up a table listing the quantities, their respective weights, and their respective values.

b. Multiply the value of each quantity by its respective weight.

c. Add up these products.

d. Add up the weights.

e. Divide the sum of the products by the sum of the weights.

Illustration: Assume that the weights for the following subjects are: English 3, History 2, Mathematics 2, Foreign Languages 2, and Art 1. What would be the average of a student whose marks are: English 80, History 85, Algebra 84, Spanish 82, and Art 90?

SOLUTION:

Subject	Weight	Mark
English	3	80
History	2	85
Algebra	2	84
Spanish	2	82
Art	1	90

English	$3 \times 80 =$	240
History	$2 \times 85 =$	170
Algebra	$2 \times 84 =$	168
Spanish	$2 \times 82 =$	164
Art	$1 \times 90 =$	90
		832

Sum of the weights: $3 + 2 + 2 + 2 + 1 = 10$

$$832 \div 10 = 83.2$$

Answer: Average = 83.2

Note: On the test, you might go directly to a list of the weighted amounts, here totaling 832, and divide by the number of weights; or you might set up a single equation.

Illustration: Mr. Martin drove for 6 hours at an average rate of 50 miles per hour and for 2 hours at an average rate of 60 miles per hour. Find his average rate for the entire trip.

SOLUTION:

$$\frac{6(50) + 2(60)}{8} = \frac{300 + 120}{8} = \frac{420}{8} = 52\frac{1}{2}$$

Answer: $52\frac{1}{2}$

Since he drove many more hours at 50 miles per hour than at 60 miles per hour, his average rate should be closer to 50 than to 60, which it is. In general, average rate can always be found by dividing the total distance covered by the time spent traveling.

Practice Problems Involving Averages

1. The arithmetic mean of 73.8, 92.2, 64.7, 43.8, 56.5, and 46.4 is
   (A) 60.6
   (B) 62.9
   (C) 64.48
   (D) 75.48
   (E) 82.9

2. The median of the numbers 8, 5, 7, 5, 9, 9, 1, 8, 10, 5, and 10 is
   (A) 5
   (B) 7
   (C) 8
   (D) 9
   (E) 10

3. The mode of the numbers 16, 15, 17, 12, 15, 15, 18, 19, and 18 is
   (A) 15
   (B) 16
   (C) 17
   (D) 18
   (E) 19

4. A clerk filed 73 forms on Monday, 85 forms on Tuesday, 54 on Wednesday, 92 on Thursday, and 66 on Friday. What was the average number of forms filed per day?
   (A) 60
   (B) 72
   (C) 74
   (D) 92
   (E) 370

5. The grades received on a test by twenty students were: 100, 55, 75, 80, 65, 65, 85, 90, 80, 45, 40, 50, 85, 85, 85, 80, 80, 70, 65, and 60. The average of these grades is
   (A) 70
   (B) 72
   (C) 77
   (D) 80
   (E) 100

6. A buyer purchased 75 six-inch rulers costing 15¢ each, 100 one-foot rulers costing 30¢ each, and 50 one-yard rulers costing 72¢ each. What was the average price per ruler?
   (A) $26\frac{1}{8}$¢
   (B) $34\frac{1}{3}$¢
   (C) 39¢
   (D) 42¢
   (E) $77\frac{1}{4}$¢

7. What is the average of a student who received 90 in English, 84 in Algebra, 75 in French, and 76 in Music, if the subjects have the following weights: English 4, Algebra 3, French 3, and Music 1?
   (A) 81

(B) $81\frac{1}{2}$
(C) 82
(D) $82\frac{1}{2}$
(E) 83

Questions 8–10 refer to the following information.

A census shows that on a certain block the number of children in each family is 3, 4, 4, 0, 1, 2, 0, 2, and 2, respectively.

8. Find the average number of children per family.
   (A) 4
   (B) 3
   (C) $3\frac{1}{2}$
   (D) 2
   (E) $1\frac{1}{2}$

9. Find the median number of children.
   (A) 1
   (B) 2
   (C) 3
   (D) 4
   (E) 5

10. Find the mode of the number of children.
    (A) 0
    (B) 1
    (C) 2
    (D) 3
    (E) 4

Averages Problems—Correct Answers

1.	**(B)**	6.	**(B)**
2.	**(C)**	7.	**(E)**
3.	**(A)**	8.	**(D)**
4.	**(C)**	9.	**(B)**
5.	**(B)**	10.	**(C)**

Problem Solutions—Averages

1. Find the sum of the values:

   $73.8 + 92.2 + 64.7 + 43.8 + 56.5 + 46.4 = 377.4$

   There are 6 values.

   $$\text{Arithmetic mean} = \frac{377.4}{6} = 62.9$$

   Answer: **(B)** 62.9

2. Arrange the numbers in order:

   1, 5, 5, 5, 7, 8, 8, 9, 9, 10, 10

   The middle number, or median, is 8.

   Answer: **(C)** 8

3. The mode is that number appearing most frequently. The number 15 appears three times.

   Answer: **(A)** 15

4. Average $= \dfrac{73 + 85 + 54 + 92 + 66}{5}$

   $= \dfrac{370}{5}$

   $= 74$

   Answer: **(C)** 74

5. Sum of the grades $= 1440$.

   $$\frac{1440}{20} = 72$$

   Answer: **(B)** 72

6. $\begin{aligned} 75 \times 15¢ &= 1125¢ \\ 100 \times 30¢ &= 3000¢ \\ \underline{50} \times 72¢ &= \underline{3600¢} \\ 225 \quad\quad &\quad 7725¢ \end{aligned}$

   $$\frac{7725¢}{225} = 34\tfrac{1}{3}¢$$

   Answer: **(B)** $34\tfrac{1}{3}¢$

7.

Subject	Grade	Weight
English	90	4
Algebra	84	3
French	75	3
Music	76	1

   $(90 \times 4) + (84 \times 3) + (75 \times 3) + (76 \times 1)$
   $360 + 252 + 225 + 76 = 913$
   Weight $= 4 + 3 + 3 + 1 = 11$
   $913 \div 11 = 83$ average

   Answer: **(E)** 83

8. Average $= \dfrac{3 + 4 + 4 + 0 + 1 + 2 + 0 + 2 + 2}{9}$

   $= \dfrac{18}{9}$

   $= 2$

   Answer: **(D)** 2

9. Arrange the numbers in order:

   0, 0, 1, 2, 2, 2, 3, 4, 4

   Of the 9 numbers, the fifth (middle) number is 2.

   Answer: **(B)** 2

10. The number appearing most often is 2.

    Answer: **(C)** 2

RATIO AND PROPORTION

Ratio

1. A **ratio** expresses the relationship between two (or more) quantities in terms of numbers. The mark used to indicate ratio is the colon (:) and is read "to."

   Example: The ratio 2:3 is read "2 to 3."

2. A ratio also represents division. Therefore, any ratio of two terms may be written as a fraction, and any fraction may be written as a ratio.

   Example: $3:4 = \tfrac{3}{4}$
   $\tfrac{5}{6} = 5:6$

3. To simplify any complicated ratio of two terms containing fractions, decimals, or percents:

   a. Divide the first term by the second.

   b. Write as a fraction in lowest terms.

   c. Write the fraction as a ratio.

   Illustration: Simplify the ratio $\tfrac{5}{6} : \tfrac{7}{8}$

   SOLUTION: $\tfrac{5}{6} \div \tfrac{7}{8} = \tfrac{5}{6} \times \tfrac{8}{7} = \tfrac{20}{21}$
   $\tfrac{20}{21} = 20:21$

   Answer: 20:21

4. To solve problems in which the ratio is given:

   a. Add the terms in the ratio.

   b. Divide the total amount that is to be put into a ratio by this sum.

c. Multiply each term in the ratio by this quotient.

Illustration: The sum of $360 is to be divided among three people according to the ratio 3:4:5. How much does each one receive?

SOLUTION:
$$3 + 4 + 5 = 12$$
$$\$360 \div 12 = \$30$$
$$\$30 \times 3 = \$90$$
$$\$30 \times 4 = \$120$$
$$\$30 \times 5 = \$150$$

Answer: The money is divided thus: $90, $120, $150.

Proportion

5. a. A **proportion** indicates the equality of two ratios.

Example: 2:4 = 5:10 is a proportion. This is read "2 is to 4 as 5 is to 10."

b. In a proportion, the two outside terms are called the **extremes,** and the two inside terms are called the **means.**

Example: In the proportion 2:4 = 5:10, 2 and 10 are the extremes, and 4 and 5 are the means.

c. Proportions are often written in fractional form.

Example: The proportion 2:4 = 5:10 may be written $\frac{2}{4} = \frac{5}{10}$.

d. In any proportion, the product of the means equals the product of the extremes. If the proportion is a fractional form, the products may be found by cross-multiplication.

Example: In $\frac{2}{4} = \frac{5}{10}$, $4 \times 5 = 2 \times 10$.

e. The product of the extremes divided by one mean equals the other mean; the product of the means divided by one extreme equals the other extreme.

6. Many problems in which three terms are given and one term is unknown can be solved by using proportions. To solve such problems:

a. Formulate the proportion very carefully according to the facts given. (If any term is misplaced, the solution will be incorrect.) Any symbol may be written in place of the missing term.

b. Determine by inspection whether the means or the extremes are known. Multiply the pair that has both terms given.

c. Divide this product by the third term given to find the unknown term.

Illustration: The scale on a map shows that 2 cm represents 30 miles of actual length. What is the actual length of a road that is represented by 7 cm on the map?

SOLUTION: The map lengths and the actual lengths are in proportion—that is, they have equal ratios. If m stands for the unknown length, the proportion is:

$$\frac{2}{7} = \frac{30}{m}$$

As the proportion is written, m is an extreme and is equal to the product of the means, divided by the other extreme:

$$m = \frac{7 \times 30}{2}$$
$$m = \frac{210}{2}$$
$$m = 105$$

Answer: 7 cm on the map represents 105 miles.

Illustration: If a money bag containing 500 nickels weighs 6 pounds, how much will a money bag containing 1600 nickels weigh?

SOLUTION: The weights of the bags and the number of coins in them are proportional. Suppose w represents the unknown weight. Then

$$\frac{6}{w} = \frac{500}{1600}$$

The unknown is a mean and is equal to the product of the extremes, divided by the other mean:

$$w = \frac{6 \times 1600}{500}$$
$$w = 19.2$$

Answer: A bag containing 1600 nickels weighs 19.2 pounds.

Practice Problems Involving Ratio and Proportion

1. The ratio of 24 to 64 is
   (A) 1:64
   (B) 1:24
   (C) 20:100
   (D) 24:100
   (E) 3:8

2. The Baltimore Colts won 8 games and lost 3. The ratio of games won to games played is
   (A) 11:8
   (B) 8:3
   (C) 8:11
   (D) 3:8
   (E) 3:11

3. The ratio of $\frac{1}{4}$ to $\frac{3}{5}$ is
   (A) 1 to 3
   (B) 3 to 20
   (C) 5 to 12
   (D) 3 to 4
   (E) 5 to 4

4. If there are 16 boys and 12 girls in a class, the ratio of the number of girls to the number of children in the class is
   (A) 3 to 4
   (B) 3 to 7
   (C) 4 to 7
   (D) 4 to 3
   (E) 7 to 4

5. 259 is to 37 as
   (A) 5 is to 1
   (B) 63 is to 441
   (C) 84 is to 12
   (D) 130 is to 19
   (E) 25 is to 4

6. 2 dozen cans of dog food at the rate of 3 cans for $1.45 would cost
   (A) $10.05
   (B) $10.20
   (C) $11.20

(D) $11.60
(E) $11.75

7. A snapshot measures $2\frac{1}{2}$ inches by $1\frac{7}{8}$ inches. It is to be enlarged so that the longer dimension will be 4 inches. The length of the enlarged shorter dimension will be
   (A) $2\frac{1}{2}$ in
   (B) 3 in
   (C) $3\frac{3}{8}$ in
   (D) 4 in
   (E) 5 in

8. Men's white handkerchiefs cost $2.29 for 3. The cost per dozen handkerchiefs is
   (A) $27.48
   (B) $13.74
   (C) $9.16
   (D) $6.87
   (E) $4.58

9. A certain pole casts a shadow 24 feet long. At the same time another pole 3 feet high casts a shadow 4 feet long. How high is the first pole, given that the heights and shadows are in proportion?
   (A) 18 ft
   (B) 19 ft
   (C) 20 ft
   (D) 21 ft
   (E) 24 ft

10. The actual length represented by $3\frac{1}{2}$ inches on a drawing having a scale of $\frac{1}{8}$ inch to the foot is
    (A) 3.5 ft
    (B) 7 ft
    (C) 21 ft
    (D) 28 ft
    (E) 120 ft

11. Aluminum bronze consists of copper and aluminum, usually in the ratio of 10:1 by weight. If an object made of this alloy weighs 77 lb, how many pounds of aluminum does it contain?
    (A) 0.7
    (B) 7.0
    (C) 7.7
    (D) 70.7
    (E) 77.0

12. It costs 31 cents a square foot to lay vinyl flooring. To lay 180 square feet of flooring, it will cost
(A) $16.20
(B) $18.60
(C) $55.80
(D) $62.00
(E) $180.00

13. If a per diem worker earns $352 in 16 days, the amount that he will earn in 117 days is most nearly
(A) $3050
(B) $2575
(C) $2285
(D) $2080
(E) $1170

14. Assuming that on a blueprint $\frac{1}{8}$ inch equals 12 inches of actual length, the actual length in inches of a steel bar represented on the blueprint by a line $3\frac{3}{4}$ inches long is
(A) $3\frac{3}{4}$
(B) 30
(C) 36
(D) 360
(E) 450

15. A, B, and C invested $9,000, $7,000 and $6,000, respectively. Their profits were to be divided according to the ratio of their investment. If B uses his share of the firm's profit of $825 to pay a personal debt of $230, how much will he have left?
(A) $30.50
(B) $32.50
(C) $34.50
(D) $36.50
(E) $37.50

Ratio and Proportion Problems—Correct Answers

1. (E)	6. (D)	11. (B)
2. (C)	7. (B)	12. (C)
3. (C)	8. (C)	13. (B)
4. (B)	9. (A)	14. (D)
5. (C)	10. (D)	15. (B)

Problem Solutions—Ratio and Proportion

1. The ratio 24 to 64 may be written 24:64 or $\frac{24}{64}$. In fraction form, the ratio can be reduced:

$$\frac{24}{64} = \frac{3}{8} \text{ or } 3:8$$

Answer: (E) 3:8

2. The number of games played was $3 + 8 = 11$. The ratio of games won to games played is 8:11.

Answer: (C) 8:11

3. $\frac{1}{4} : \frac{3}{5} = \frac{1}{4} \div \frac{3}{5}$
$= \frac{1}{4} \times \frac{5}{3}$
$= \frac{5}{12}$
$= 5:12$

Answer: (C) 5 to 12

4. There are $16 + 12 = 28$ children in the class. The ratio of number of girls to number of children is 12:28.

$$\frac{12}{28} = \frac{3}{7}$$

Answer: (B) 3 to 7

5. The ratio $\frac{259}{37}$ reduces by 37 to $\frac{7}{1}$. The ratio $\frac{84}{12}$ also reduces to $\frac{7}{1}$. Therefore, $\frac{259}{37} = \frac{84}{12}$ is a proportion.

Answer: (C) 84 is to 12

6. The number of cans are proportional to the price. Let p represent the unknown price:
Then $\frac{3}{24} = \frac{1.45}{p}$

$p = \frac{1.45 \times 24}{3}$

$p = \frac{34.80}{3}$

$= 11.60

Answer: (D) $11.60

7. Let s represent the unknown shorter dimension:

$$\frac{2\frac{1}{2}}{4} = \frac{1\frac{7}{8}}{s}$$

$$s = \frac{4 \times 1\frac{7}{8}}{2\frac{1}{2}}$$

$$= \frac{\overset{1}{\cancel{4}} \times \frac{15}{8}}{2\frac{1}{2}}{}_2$$

$$= \frac{15}{2} \div 2\frac{1}{2}$$

$$= \frac{15}{2} \div \frac{5}{2}$$

$$= \frac{15}{2} \times \frac{2}{5}$$

$$= 3$$

Answer: (B) 3 in

8. If p is the cost per dozen (12):

$$\frac{3}{12} = \frac{2.29}{p}$$

$$p = \frac{\overset{4}{\cancel{12}} \times 2.29}{\underset{1}{\cancel{3}}}$$

$$= 9.16$$

Answer: (C) $9.16

9. If f is the height of the first pole, the proportion is:

$$\frac{f}{24} = \frac{3}{4}$$

$$f = \frac{\overset{6}{\cancel{24}} \times 3}{\underset{1}{\cancel{4}}}$$

$$= 18$$

Answer: (A) 18 ft

10. If y is the unknown length:

$$\frac{3\frac{1}{2}}{\frac{1}{8}} = \frac{y}{1}$$

$$y = \frac{3\frac{1}{2} \times 1}{\frac{1}{8}}$$

$$= 3\frac{1}{2} \div \frac{1}{8}$$

$$= \frac{7}{2} \times \frac{8}{1}$$

$$= 28$$

Answer: (D) 28 ft

11. Since only two parts of a proportion are known (77 is total weight), the problem must be solved by the ratio method. The ratio 10:1 means that if the alloy were separated into equal parts, 10 of those parts

would be copper and 1 would be aluminum, for a total of 10 + 1 = 11 parts.

$$77 \div 11 = 7 \text{ lb per part}$$

The alloy has 1 part aluminum.

$$7 \times 1 = 7 \text{ lb aluminum}$$

Answer: (B) 7.0

12. The cost (c) is proportional to the number of square feet.

$$\frac{\$.31}{c} = \frac{1}{180}$$

$$c = \frac{\$.31 \times 180}{1}$$

$$= \$55.80$$

Answer: (C) $55.80

13. The amount earned is proportional to the number of days worked. If a is the unknown amount:

$$\frac{\$352}{a} = \frac{16}{117}$$

$$a = \frac{\$352 \times 117}{16}$$

$$a = \$2574$$

Answer: (B) $2575

14. If n is the unknown length:

$$\frac{\frac{1}{8}}{3\frac{3}{4}} = \frac{12}{n}$$

$$n = \frac{12 \times 3\frac{3}{4}}{\frac{1}{8}}$$

$$= \frac{\overset{3}{\cancel{12}} \times \frac{15}{4}{}_1}{\frac{1}{8}}$$

$$= \frac{45}{\frac{1}{8}}$$

$$= 45 \div \frac{1}{8}$$

$$= 45 \times \frac{8}{1}$$

$$= 360$$

Answer: (D) 360

15. The ratio of investment is:

$$9,000:7,000:6,000 \quad \text{or} \quad 9:7:6$$

$$9 + 7 + 6 = 22$$

$825 \div 22 = $37.50 each share of profit

$7 \times $37.50 = $262.50 B's share of profit

$$\begin{array}{r} \$262.50 \\ - \ 230.00 \\ \hline \$ \ 32.50 \end{array} \text{ amount B has left}$$

Answer: (B) $32.50

POWERS AND ROOTS

1. The numbers that are multiplied to give a product are called the **factors** of the product.

   Example: In $2 \times 3 = 6$, 2 and 3 are factors.

2. If the factors are the same, an **exponent** may be used to indicate the number of times the factor appears.

   Example: In $3 \times 3 = 3^2$, the number 3 appears as a factor twice, as is indicated by the exponent 2.

3. When a product is written in exponential form, the number the exponent refers to is called the **base.** The product itself is called the **power.**

   Example: In 2^5, the number 2 is the base and 5 is the exponent.
   $2^5 = 2 \times 2 \times 2 \times 2 \times 2 = 32$, so 32 is the power.

4. a. If the exponent used is 2, we say that the base has been **squared,** or raised to the second power.

   Example: 6^2 is read "six squared" or "six to the second power."

   b. If the exponent used is 3, we say that the base has been **cubed,** or raised to the third power.

   Example: 5^3 is read "five cubed" or "five to the third power."

   c. If the exponent is 4, we say that the base has been raised to the fourth power. If the exponent is 5, we say the base has been raised to the fifth power, etc.

   Example: 2^8 is read "two to the eighth power."

5. A number that is the product of a whole number squared is called a **perfect square.**

   Example: 25 is a perfect square because $25 = 5^2$.

6. a. If a number has exactly two equal factors, each factor is called the **square root** of the number.

   Example: $9 = 3 \times 3$; therefore, 3 is the square root of 9.

   b. The symbol $\sqrt{}$ is used to indicate square root.

   Example: $\sqrt{9} = 3$ means that the square root of 9 is 3, or $3 \times 3 = 9$.

   c. In principle, all numbers have a square root. Although many square roots cannot be calculated exactly, they can be found to whatever degree of accuracy is needed (see item 8). Thus the square root of 10, $\sqrt{10}$, is *by definition* the number that equals 10 when it is squared—$\sqrt{10} \times \sqrt{10} = 10$.

   d. If a number has exactly three equal factors, each factor is called a **cube root.** The symbol $\sqrt[3]{}$ is used to indicate a cube root.

   Example: $8 = 2 \times 2 \times 2$; thus $2 = \sqrt[3]{8}$

   e. In general, the nth root is indicated as $\sqrt[n]{}$

7. The square root of the most common perfect squares may be found by using the following table, or by trial and error; that is, by finding the number that, when squared, yields the given perfect square.

Number	Perfect Square	Number	Perfect Square
1	1	10	100
2	4	11	121
3	9	12	144
4	16	13	169
5	25	14	196
6	36	15	225
7	49	20	400
8	64	25	625
9	81	30	900

   Example: To find $\sqrt{81}$, note that 81 is the perfect square of 9, or $9^2 = 81$. Therefore, $\sqrt{81} = 9$.

8. On the GRE you will only rarely have to find the square root of a number that is not a perfect square. The two most common square roots you will have to deal with are $\sqrt{2}$, which equals approximately 1.4, and $\sqrt{3}$, which equals approximately 1.7. Most times you will not have to convert these square roots to their equivalents since the answer choices will be in terms of the square roots, e.g., (A) $4\sqrt{3}$, etc.

The following method is the way to compute square roots of numbers that are not perfect squares. It is very effective, but it is long and you are unlikely to actually need it on the GRE.

a. Locate the decimal point.

b. Mark off the digits in groups of two in both directions beginning at the decimal point.

c. Mark the decimal point for the answer just above the decimal point of the number whose square root is to be taken.

d. Find the largest perfect square contained in the left-hand group of two.

e. Place its square root in the answer. Subtract the perfect square from the first digit or pair of digits.

f. Bring down the next pair.

g. Double the partial answer.

h. Add a trial digit to the right of the doubled partial answer. Multiply this new number by the trial digit. Place the correct new digit in the answer.

i. Subtract the product.

j. Repeat steps f-i as often as necessary.

You will notice that you get one digit in the answer for every group of two you marked off in the original number.

Illustration: Find the square root of 138,384.

$$SOLUTION: \qquad \begin{array}{r} 3 \\ \hline \sqrt{13'83'84.} \end{array}$$

$$3^2 = \quad \begin{array}{r} 9 \\ \hline 4\ 83 \end{array}$$

$$\begin{array}{r} 3\ \ 7\ \ 2. \\ \hline \sqrt{13'83'84.} \end{array}$$

$$3^2 = \quad \begin{array}{r} 9 \\ \hline 4\ 83 \end{array}$$

$$7 \times 67 = \quad \begin{array}{r} 4\ 69 \\ \hline 14\ 84 \end{array}$$

$$2 \times 742 = \quad \begin{array}{r} 14\ 84 \\ \hline \end{array}$$

The number must first be marked off in groups of two figures each, beginning at the decimal point, which, in the case of a whole number, is at the right. The number of figures in the root will be the same as the number of groups so obtained.

The largest square less than 13 is 9. $\sqrt{9} = 3$

Place its square root in the answer. Subtract the perfect square from the first digit or pair of digits. Bring down the next pair. To form our trial divisor, annex 0 to this root "3" (making 30) and multiply by 2.

483 ÷ 60 = 8. Multiplying the trial divisor 68 by 8, we obtain 544, which is too large. We then try multiplying 67 by 7. This is correct. Add the trial digit to the right of the doubled partial answer. Place the new digit in the answer. Subtract the product. Bring down the final group. Annex 0 to the new root 37 and multiply by 2 for the trial divisor:

$$2 \times 370 = 740$$
$$1484 ÷ 740 = 2$$

Place the 2 in the answer.

Answer: The square root of 138,384 is 372.

Illustration: Find the square root of 3 to the nearest hundredth.

SOLUTION:

$$\begin{array}{r} 1.\ 7\ \ 3\ \ 2 \\ \sqrt{3.00'00'00} \\ \end{array}$$

$$\begin{array}{r} 1^2 = 1 \\ 20 2\ 00 \\ 7 \times 27 = 1\ 89 \\ \hline 340 11\ 00 \\ 3 \times 343 = 10\ 29 \\ \hline 3460 71\ 00 \\ 2 \times 3462 = 69\ 24 \\ \hline \end{array}$$

Answer: The square root of 3 is 1.73 to the nearest hundredth.

9. When more complex items are raised to powers, the same basic rules apply.

a. To find the power of some multiplied item, find the power of each multiplicand and multiply those powers together.

Example: $(4x)^2 = (4x)(4x) = (4)(4)(x)(x) = (4)^2(x)^2 = 16x^2$

Example: $(2xy)^4 = (2)^4(x)^4(y)^4 = 16x^4y^4$

b. To find the power of some divided item or fraction, find the power of each part of the fraction and then divide in the manner of the original fraction.

Example: $\left(\dfrac{2}{x}\right)^2 = \left(\dfrac{2}{x}\right)\left(\dfrac{2}{x}\right) = \left(\dfrac{4}{x^2}\right)$

c. To find the result when two powers of the same base are multiplied together, *add* the exponents. You add the exponents because you are adding to the length of the string of the same base all being multiplied together.

Example: $(x^2)(x^3) = (x)(x) \cdot (x)(x)(x) = xxxxx = x^{(2+3)} = x^5$

Example: $2^a \cdot 2^b = 2^{(a+b)}$

d. To find the result when a power is raised to an exponent, *multiply* the exponents. You multiply the exponents together because you are multiplying the length of the string of the same base all being multiplied together.

Example: $(x^2)^3 = (x^2)(x^2)(x^2) = xxxxxx = x^{(2 \cdot 3)} = x^6$

e. When a power is divided by another power of the same base, the result is found by subtracting the exponent in the denominator (bottom) from the exponent in the numerator (top).

Example: $\dfrac{x^3}{x^2} = \dfrac{xxx}{xx} = x^{(3-2)} = x^1 = x$

Note: Any base to the first power, x^1, equals the base.

Example: $\dfrac{x^9}{x^6} = x^{(9-6)} = x^3$

Example: $\dfrac{x^2}{x^2} = \dfrac{xx}{xx} = x^{(2-2)} = x^0 = 1$

Note: Any base to the "zero-th" power, x^0, equals 1.

Example: $\dfrac{x^3}{x^4} = \dfrac{xxx}{xxxx} = \dfrac{1}{x} = x^{(3-4)} = x^{-1}$

f. A **negative exponent** is a reciprocal, as discussed in the earlier section on fractions.

Example: $z^{-3} = \left(\dfrac{z}{1}\right)^{-3} = \left(\dfrac{1}{z}\right)^{+3} = \dfrac{1^3}{z^3} = \dfrac{1}{z^3}$

Example: $(3p)^{-2} = \dfrac{1}{(3p)^{+2}} = \dfrac{1}{9p^2}$

Example: $(r^{-3})^{-6} = \dfrac{1}{(r^{-3})^{+6}} = \dfrac{1}{\left(\dfrac{1}{r^3}\right)^6} = \dfrac{1}{\dfrac{1}{r^{18}}}$

$= (1)\left(\dfrac{r^{18}}{1}\right) = r^{18}$

or $(r^{-3})^{-6} = r^{(-3)(-6)} = r^{+18}$

10. Some problems require that different powers be grouped together. Depending on the relationships, they can be grouped by doing the processes explained in #9 in the reverse direction.

Example: $9x^2 = 3^2 \cdot x^2 = (3x)^2$

Example: $\dfrac{81}{y^2} = \dfrac{9^2}{y^2} = \left(\dfrac{9}{y}\right)^2$

Example: $m^{12} = (m^5)(m^7)$ or $(m^{10})(m^2)$ etc.

Example: $z^{24} = (z^6)^4$ or $(x^8)^3$ etc.

11. The conditions under which radicals can be added or subtracted are much the same as the conditions for letters in an algebraic expression. The radicals act as a label, or unit, and must therefore be exactly the same. In adding or subtracting, we add or subtract the coefficients, or rational parts and carry the radical along as a label, which does not change.

Example: $\sqrt{2} + \sqrt{3}$ cannot be added
$\sqrt{2} + \sqrt[3]{2}$ cannot be added
$4\sqrt{2} + 5\sqrt{2} = 9\sqrt{2}$

Often, when radicals to be added or subtracted are not the same, simplification of one or more radicals will make them the same. To simplify a radical, we remove any perfect square factors from underneath the radical sign.

Example: $\sqrt{12} = \sqrt{4}\sqrt{3} = 2\sqrt{3}$
$\sqrt{27} = \sqrt{9}\sqrt{3} = 3\sqrt{3}$

If we wish to add $\sqrt{12} + \sqrt{27}$, we must first simplify each one. Adding the simplified radicals gives a sum of $5\sqrt{3}$.

Illustration: $\sqrt{125} + \sqrt{20} - \sqrt{500}$

SOLUTION:

$\sqrt{25}\,\sqrt{5} + \sqrt{4}\,\sqrt{5} - \sqrt{100}\,\sqrt{5} =$
$5\sqrt{5} + 2\sqrt{5} - 10\sqrt{5} =$
$-3\sqrt{5}$

Answer: $-3\sqrt{5}$

12. In multiplication and division we again treat the radicals as we would letters in an algebraic expression. They are factors and must be treated as such.

Example: $(\sqrt{2})\,(\sqrt{3}) = \sqrt{(2)(3)} = \sqrt{6}$

Example: $4\sqrt{2} \cdot 5\sqrt{3} = 20 \cdot \sqrt{6}$

Example: $(3\sqrt{2})^2 = 3\sqrt{2} \cdot 3\sqrt{2} = 9 \cdot 2 = 18$

Example: $\dfrac{\sqrt{8}}{\sqrt{2}} = \sqrt{4} = 2$

Example: $\dfrac{10\sqrt{20}}{\sqrt{4}} = \dfrac{\overset{5}{\cancel{10}}\sqrt{20}}{\cancel{2}} = 5\sqrt{20}$

Example: $\sqrt{2}\,(\sqrt{8} + \sqrt{18}) = \sqrt{16} + \sqrt{36}$
$= 4 + 6 = 10$

13. In simplifying radicals that contain several terms under the radical sign, we must combine terms before taking the square root.

Example: $\sqrt{16 + 9} = \sqrt{25} = 5$

Note: It is not true that $\sqrt{16 + 9} = \sqrt{16} + \sqrt{9}$, which would be $4 + 3$, or 7.

Example: $\sqrt{\dfrac{x^2}{16} - \dfrac{x^2}{25}} = \sqrt{\dfrac{25x^2 - 16x^2}{400}}$

$= \sqrt{\dfrac{9x^2}{400}} = \dfrac{3x}{20}$

Practice Problems Involving Roots

1. Combine $4\sqrt{27} - 2\sqrt{48} + \sqrt{147}$
   (A) $27\sqrt{3}$
   (B) $-3\sqrt{3}$
   (C) $9\sqrt{3}$
   (D) $10\sqrt{3}$
   (E) $11\sqrt{3}$

2. Combine $\sqrt{80} + \sqrt{45} - \sqrt{20}$
   (A) $9\sqrt{5}$
   (B) $5\sqrt{5}$
   (C) $-\sqrt{5}$
   (D) $3\sqrt{5}$
   (E) $-2\sqrt{5}$

3. Combine $6\sqrt{5} + 3\sqrt{2} - 4\sqrt{5} + \sqrt{2}$
   (A) 8
   (B) $2\sqrt{5} + 3\sqrt{2}$
   (C) $2\sqrt{5} + 4\sqrt{2}$
   (D) $5\sqrt{7}$
   (E) 5

4. Combine $\frac{1}{2}\sqrt{180} + \frac{1}{3}\sqrt{45} - \frac{2}{5}\sqrt{20}$
   (A) $3\sqrt{10} + \sqrt{15} + 2\sqrt{2}$
   (B) $\frac{16}{5}\sqrt{5}$
   (C) $\sqrt{97}$
   (D) $\frac{24}{5}\sqrt{5}$
   (E) none of these

5. Combine $5\sqrt{mn} - 3\sqrt{mn} - 2\sqrt{mn}$
   (A) 0
   (B) 1
   (C) $\sqrt{mn}$
   (D) mn
   (E) $-\sqrt{mn}$

6. Multiply and simplify: $2\sqrt{18} \cdot 6\sqrt{2}$
   (A) 72
   (B) 48
   (C) $12\sqrt{6}$
   (D) $8\sqrt{6}$
   (E) 36

7. Find $(3\sqrt{3})^3$
   (A) $27\sqrt{3}$
   (B) $81\sqrt{3}$
   (C) 81
   (D) $9\sqrt{3}$
   (E) 243

8. Multiply and simplify: $\frac{1}{2}\sqrt{2}\,(\sqrt{6} + \frac{1}{2}\sqrt{2})$
   (A) $\sqrt{3} + \frac{1}{2}$
   (B) $\frac{1}{2}\sqrt{3}$
   (C) $\sqrt{6} + 1$
   (D) $\sqrt{6} + \frac{1}{2}$
   (E) $\sqrt{6} + 2$

9. Divide and simplify: $\dfrac{\sqrt{32b^3}}{\sqrt{8b}}$

   (A) $2\sqrt{b}$
   (B) $\sqrt{2b}$
   (C) $2b$
   (D) $\sqrt{2b^2}$
   (E) $b\sqrt{2b}$

10. Divide and simplify: $\dfrac{15\sqrt{96}}{5\sqrt{2}}$

    (A) $7\sqrt{3}$
    (B) $7\sqrt{12}$
    (C) $11\sqrt{3}$
    (D) $12\sqrt{3}$
    (E) $40\sqrt{3}$

11. Simplify $\sqrt{\dfrac{x^2}{9} + \dfrac{x^2}{16}}$

    (A) $\dfrac{25x^2}{144}$

    (B) $\dfrac{5x}{12}$

    (C) $\dfrac{5x^2}{12}$

    (D) $\dfrac{x}{7}$

    (E) $\dfrac{7x}{12}$

12. Simplify $\sqrt{36y^2 + 64x^2}$
    (A) $6y + 8x$
    (B) $10xy$
    (C) $6y^2 + 8x^2$
    (D) $10x^2y^2$
    (E) cannot be simplified

13. Simplify $\sqrt{\dfrac{x^2}{64} - \dfrac{x^2}{100}}$

    (A) $\dfrac{x}{40}$

    (B) $-\dfrac{x}{2}$

    (C) $\dfrac{x}{2}$

    (D) $\dfrac{3x}{40}$

    (E) $\dfrac{3x}{80}$

14. Simplify $\sqrt{\dfrac{y^2}{2} - \dfrac{y^2}{18}}$

    (A) $\dfrac{2y}{3}$

    (B) $\dfrac{y\sqrt{5}}{3}$

    (C) $\dfrac{10y}{3}$

    (D) $\dfrac{y\sqrt{3}}{6}$

    (E) cannot be simplified

15. $\sqrt{a^2 + b^2}$ is equal to
    (A) $a + b$
    (B) $a - b$
    (C) $\sqrt{a^2} + \sqrt{b^2}$
    (D) $(a + b)(a - b)$
    (E) none of these

16. Which of the following square roots can be found exactly?
    (A) $\sqrt{.4}$
    (B) $\sqrt{.9}$
    (C) $\sqrt{.09}$
    (D) $\sqrt{.02}$
    (E) $\sqrt{.025}$

Root Problems—Correct Answers

1.	(E)	9.	(C)
2.	(B)	10.	(D)
3.	(C)	11.	(B)
4.	(B)	12.	(E)
5.	(A)	13.	(D)
6.	(A)	14.	(A)
7.	(B)	15.	(E)
8.	(A)	16.	(C)

Problem Solutions—Roots

1. $4\sqrt{27} = 4\sqrt{9}\sqrt{3} = 12\sqrt{3}$
   $2\sqrt{48} = 2\sqrt{16}\sqrt{3} = 8\sqrt{3}$
   $\sqrt{147} = \sqrt{49}\sqrt{3} = 7\sqrt{3}$
   $12\sqrt{3} - 8\sqrt{3} + 7\sqrt{3} = 11\sqrt{3}$

   Answer: (E) $11\sqrt{3}$

2. $\sqrt{80} = \sqrt{16}\sqrt{5} = 4\sqrt{5}$
   $\sqrt{45} = \sqrt{9}\sqrt{5} = 3\sqrt{5}$
   $\sqrt{20} = \sqrt{4}\sqrt{5} = 2\sqrt{5}$
   $4\sqrt{5} + 3\sqrt{5} - 2\sqrt{5} = 5\sqrt{5}$

   Answer: (B) $5\sqrt{5}$

3. Only terms with the same radical may be combined.
   $$6\sqrt{5} - 4\sqrt{5} = 2\sqrt{5}$$
   $$3\sqrt{2} + \sqrt{2} = 4\sqrt{2}$$

   Therefore we have $2\sqrt{5} + 4\sqrt{2}$

   Answer: (C) $2\sqrt{5} + 4\sqrt{2}$

4. $\frac{1}{4}\sqrt{180} = \frac{1}{4}\sqrt{36}\sqrt{5} = 3\sqrt{5}$
   $\frac{1}{3}\sqrt{45} = \frac{1}{3}\sqrt{9}\sqrt{5} = \sqrt{5}$
   $\frac{2}{3}\sqrt{20} = \frac{2}{3}\sqrt{4}\sqrt{5} = \frac{4}{3}\sqrt{5}$
   $3\sqrt{5} + \sqrt{5} - \frac{4}{3}\sqrt{5} = 4\sqrt{5} - \frac{4}{3}\sqrt{5} = 3\frac{1}{3}\sqrt{5} = \frac{16}{3}\sqrt{5}$

   Answer: (B) $\frac{16}{3}\sqrt{5}$

5. $5\sqrt{mn} - 5\sqrt{mn} = 0$

   Answer: (A) 0

6. $2\sqrt{18} \cdot 6\sqrt{2} = 12\sqrt{36} = 12 \cdot 6 = 72$

   Answer: (A) 72

7. $3\sqrt{3} \cdot 3\sqrt{3} \cdot 3\sqrt{3} = 27(3\sqrt{3}) = 81\sqrt{3}$

   Answer: (B) $81\sqrt{3}$

8. Using the distributive law, we have

   $$\tfrac{1}{2}\sqrt{12} + \tfrac{1}{4} \cdot 2 = \tfrac{1}{2}\sqrt{4}\sqrt{3} + \tfrac{1}{2} = \sqrt{3} + \tfrac{1}{2}$$

   Answer: (A) $\sqrt{3} + \tfrac{1}{2}$

9. Dividing the numbers in the radical sign, we have $\sqrt{4b^2} = 2b$

   Answer: (C) $2b$

10. $3\sqrt{48} = 3\sqrt{16}\sqrt{3} = 12\sqrt{3}$

    Answer: (D) $12\sqrt{3}$

11. $\sqrt{\dfrac{16x^2 + 9x^2}{144}} = \sqrt{\dfrac{25x^2}{144}} = \dfrac{5x}{12}$

    Answer: (B) $\dfrac{5x}{12}$

12. The terms cannot be combined and it is not possible to take the square root of separated terms.

    Answer: (E) cannot be simplified

13. $\sqrt{\dfrac{100x^2 - 64x^2}{6400}} = \sqrt{\dfrac{36x^2}{6400}} = \dfrac{6x}{80} = \dfrac{3x}{40}$

Answer: **(D)** $\dfrac{3x}{40}$

14. $\sqrt{\dfrac{18y^2 - 2y^2}{36}} = \sqrt{\dfrac{16y^2}{36}} = \dfrac{4y}{6} = \dfrac{2y}{3}$

Answer: **(A)** $\dfrac{2y}{3}$

15. It is not possible to find the square root of separate terms.

Answer: **(E)** none of these

16. In order to take the square root of a decimal, it must have an even number of decimal places so that its square root will have exactly half as many. In addition to this, the digits must form a perfect square ($\sqrt{.09} = .3$).

Answer: **(C)** $\sqrt{.09}$

ALGEBRAIC FRACTIONS

1. In reducing algebraic fractions, we must divide the numerator and denominator by the same factor, just as we do in arithmetic. We can never cancel terms, as this would be adding or subtracting the same number from the numerator and denominator, which changes the value of the fraction. When we reduce $\dfrac{6}{8}$ to $\dfrac{3}{4}$, we are really saying that $\dfrac{6}{8} = \dfrac{2 \cdot 3}{2 \cdot 4}$ and then dividing numerator and denominator by 2. We do not say $\dfrac{6}{8} = \dfrac{3+3}{3+5}$ and then say $\dfrac{6}{8} = \dfrac{3}{5}$. This is faulty reasoning in algebra as well. If we have $\dfrac{6t}{8t}$, we can divide numerator and denominator by 2t, giving $\dfrac{3}{4}$ as an answer. However, if we have $\dfrac{6+t}{8+t}$, we can do no more, as there is no factor that divides into the *entire* numerator as well as the *entire* denominator. Cancelling terms is one of the most frequent student errors. Don't get caught! Be careful!

Illustration: Reduce $\dfrac{3x^2 + 6x}{4x^3 + 8x^2}$ to its lowest terms.

SOLUTION: Factoring the numerator and denominator, we have $\dfrac{3x(x + 2)}{4x^2(x + 2)}$. The factors common to both numerator and denominator are x and (x + 2). Dividing these out, we arrive at $\dfrac{3}{4x}$.

Answer: $\dfrac{3}{4x}$

2. In adding or subtracting fractions, we must work with a common denominator and the same shortcuts we used in arithmetic.

Illustration: Find the sum of $\dfrac{1}{a}$ and $\dfrac{1}{b}$.

SOLUTION: Remember to add the two cross products and put the sum over the denominator product.

Answer: $\dfrac{b + a}{ab}$

Illustration: Add: $\dfrac{2n}{3} + \dfrac{3n}{2}$

SOLUTION: $\dfrac{4n + 9n}{6} = \dfrac{13n}{6}$

Answer: $\dfrac{13n}{6}$

3. In multiplying or dividing fractions, we may cancel a factor common to any numerator and any denominator. Always remember to invert the fraction following the division sign. Where exponents are involved, they are added in multiplication and subtracted in division.

Illustration: Find the product of $\dfrac{a^3}{b^2}$ and $\dfrac{b^3}{a^2}$.

SOLUTION: We divide a^2 into the first numerator and second denominator, giving $\dfrac{a}{b^2} \cdot \dfrac{b^3}{1}$. Then we divide b^2 into the first denominator and second numerator, giving $\dfrac{a}{1} \cdot \dfrac{b}{1}$. Finally, we multiply the resulting fractions, giving an answer of ab.

Answer: ab

Illustration: Divide $\dfrac{6x^2y}{5}$ by $2x^3$.

SOLUTION: $\dfrac{6x^2y}{5} \cdot \dfrac{1}{2x^3}$. Divide the first numerator and second denominator by $2x^2$, giving $\dfrac{3y}{5} \cdot \dfrac{1}{x}$. Multiplying the resulting fractions, we get $\dfrac{3y}{5x}$.

Answer: $\dfrac{3y}{5x}$

4. Complex algebraic fractions are simplified by the same methods used in arithmetic. Multiply *each term* of the complex fraction by the lowest quantity that will eliminate the fraction within the fraction.

Illustration: $\dfrac{\dfrac{1}{a} + \dfrac{1}{b}}{ab}$

SOLUTION: We must multiply *each term* by ab, giving $\dfrac{b + a}{a^2b^2}$ Since no reduction beyond this is possible, $\dfrac{b + a}{a^2b^2}$ is our final answer. Remember *never* to cancel terms unless they apply to the entire numerator or the entire denominator.

Answer: $\dfrac{b + a}{a^2b^2}$

Practice Problems Involving Algebraic Fractions

1. Find the sum of $\dfrac{n}{6} + \dfrac{2n}{5}$.
   (A) $\dfrac{13n}{30}$
   (B) $17n$
   (C) $\dfrac{3n}{30}$
   (D) $\dfrac{17n}{30}$
   (E) $\dfrac{3n}{11}$

2. Combine into a single fraction: $1 - \dfrac{x}{y}$
   (A) $\dfrac{1 - x}{y}$
   (B) $\dfrac{y - x}{y}$
   (C) $\dfrac{x - y}{y}$
   (D) $\dfrac{1 - x}{1 - y}$

   (E) $\dfrac{y - x}{xy}$

3. Divide $\dfrac{x - y}{x + y}$ by $\dfrac{y - x}{y + x}$.
   (A) 1
   (B) -1
   (C) $\dfrac{(x-y)^2}{(x+y)^2}$
   (D) $-\dfrac{(x-y)^2}{(x+y)^2}$
   (E) 0

4. Simplify: $\dfrac{1 + \dfrac{1}{x}}{\dfrac{y}{x}}$
   (A) $\dfrac{x + 1}{y}$
   (B) $\dfrac{x + 1}{x}$
   (C) $\dfrac{x + 1}{xy}$
   (D) $\dfrac{x^2 + 1}{xy}$
   (E) $\dfrac{y + 1}{y}$

5. Find an expression equivalent to $\left(\dfrac{2x^2}{y}\right)^3$.
   (A) $\dfrac{8x^5}{3y}$
   (B) $\dfrac{6x^6}{y^3}$
   (C) $\dfrac{6x^5}{y^3}$
   (D) $\dfrac{8x^5}{y^3}$
   (E) $\dfrac{8x^6}{y^3}$

6. Simplify: $\dfrac{\dfrac{1}{x} + \dfrac{1}{y}}{3}$
   (A) $\dfrac{3x + 3y}{xy}$
   (B) $\dfrac{3xy}{x + y}$
   (C) $\dfrac{xy}{3}$
   (D) $\dfrac{y + x}{3xy}$
   (E) $\dfrac{x + y}{3}$

7. $\dfrac{1}{a} + \dfrac{1}{b} = 7$ and $\dfrac{1}{a} - \dfrac{1}{b} = 3$.

   Find $\dfrac{1}{a^2} - \dfrac{1}{b^2}$.
   (A) 10
   (B) 7
   (C) 3
   (D) 21
   (E) 4

Algebraic Fractions—Correct Answers

1. **(D)**	5. **(E)**
2. **(B)**	6. **(D)**
3. **(B)**	7. **(D)**
4. **(A)**	

Solutions—Algebraic Fractions

1. $\dfrac{n}{6} + \dfrac{2n}{5} = \dfrac{5n + 12n}{30} = \dfrac{17n}{30}$

   Answer: **(D)** $\dfrac{17n}{30}$

2. $\dfrac{1}{1} - \dfrac{x}{y} = \dfrac{y - x}{y}$

   Answer: **(B)** $\dfrac{y - x}{y}$

3. $\dfrac{x - y}{x + y} \cdot \dfrac{y + x}{y - x}$

   Since addition is commutative, we may cancel $x + y$ with $y + x$, as they are the same quantity. However, subtraction is not commutative, so we may not cancel $x - y$ with $y - x$, as they are *not* the same quantity. We can change the form of $y - x$ by factoring out a $- 1$. Thus, $y - x = (-1)(x - y)$. In this form, we can cancel $x - y$, leaving an answer of $\dfrac{1}{-1}$, or -1.

   Answer: **(B)** -1

4. Multiply every term in the fraction by x, giving $\dfrac{x + 1}{y}$.

   Answer: **(A)** $\dfrac{x + 1}{y}$

5. $\dfrac{2x^2}{y} \cdot \dfrac{2x^2}{y} \cdot \dfrac{2x^2}{y} = \dfrac{8x^6}{y^3}$

   Answer: **(E)** $\dfrac{8x^6}{y^3}$

6. Multiply every term of the fraction by xy, giving $\dfrac{y + x}{3xy}$.

   Answer: **(D)** $\dfrac{y + x}{3xy}$

7. $\dfrac{1}{a^2} - \dfrac{1}{b^2}$ is equivalent to $\left(\dfrac{1}{a} + \dfrac{1}{b} \right) \left(\dfrac{1}{a} - \dfrac{1}{b} \right)$. We therefore multiply 7 by 3 for an answer of 21.

   Answer: **(D)** 21

PROBLEM-SOLVING IN ALGEBRA

1. In solving verbal problems, the most important technique is to read accurately. Be sure you understand clearly what you are asked to find. Then try to evaluate the problem in common-sense terms; use this to eliminate answer choices.

   Example: If two people are working together, their combined speed is greater than either one, but not more than twice as fast as the fastest one.

   Example: The total number of the correct answers cannot be greater than the total number of answers. Thus if x questions are asked and you are to determine from other information how many correct answers there were, they cannot come to 2x.

2. The next step, when common sense alone is not enough, is to translate the problem into algebra. Keep it as simple as possible.

   Example: 24 = what % of 12?

   Translation:
   $$24 = x\% \cdot 12$$
   $$\text{or } 24 = x\tfrac{1}{100} \cdot 12$$
   $$\text{or } 24 = \tfrac{x}{100} \cdot \tfrac{12}{1}$$

   Divide both sides by 12.
   $$2 = \tfrac{x}{100}$$

   Multiply both sides by 100.
   $$200 = x \text{ IN PERCENT}$$

3. Be alert for the "hidden equation." This is some necessary information so obvious in the stated situation that the question assumes that you know it.

   Example: Boys plus girls = total class

   Example: Imported wine plus domestic wine = all wine.

   Example: The wall and floor, or the shadow and the building, make a right angle (thus permitting use of the Pythagorean Theorem).

4. Always remember that a variable (letter) can have any value whatsoever within the terms of the problem. Keep the possibility of fractional and negative values constantly in mind.

5. **Manipulating Equations.** You can perform any mathematical function you think helpful to one side of the equation, *provided* you do precisely the same thing to the other side of the equation. You can also substitute one side of an equality for the other in another equation.

6. **Manipulating Inequalities.** You can add to or subtract from both sides of an inequality without changing the direction of the inequality.

   Example:
   $$8 > 5$$
   $$8 + 10 > 5 + 10$$
   $$18 > 15$$

   Example:
   $$3x > y + z$$
   $$3x + 5 > y + z + 5$$

   You can also multiply or divide both sides of the inequality by any POSITIVE number without changing the direction of the inequality.

   Example:
   $$12 > 4$$
   $$3(12) > 3(4)$$
   $$36 > 12$$

   Example:
   $$x > y$$
   $$3x > 3y$$

   If you multiply or divide an inequality by a NEGATIVE number, you REVERSE the direction of the inequality.

   Example:
   $$4 > 3$$
   $$(-2)(4) < (-2)(3)$$
   $$-8 < -6$$

   Example:
   $$x^2y > z^2x$$
   $$-3(x^2y) < -3(z^2x)$$

7. **Solving Equations.** The first step is to determine what quantity or letter you wish to isolate. Solving an equation for x means getting x on one side of the equals sign and everything else on the other.

   Example: $5x + 3 = y$
   Subtract 3.
   $$5x = y - 3$$
   Divide by 5.
   $$x = \frac{y - 3}{5}$$

   Aside from factoring, discussed later in this review, unwrapping an equation is a matter of performing three steps. These rules are stated in terms of *x*, but apply equally to all variables or variable expressions.

   Put all x on one side of the equation, if not already there. This can be done by adding, subtracting, dividing or multiplying. Sometimes other quantities come along.

   Example: $4x + 2 = 29 + bxy$
   Subtract bxy.
   $$4x + 2 - bxy = 29$$
   (continued below)

   Unpeel x by considering the structure of the whole side x is on as a single expression and perform the opposite operation. Addition and subtraction are opposites; multiplication and division are opposites; raising to powers and taking roots are opposites.

   Example: $14k + 8 = 22$
   Left is addition, so subtract 8.
   $$14k = 14$$
   Divide by 14.
   $$k = 1$$

   Continue step b until only terms with x in them are left.

   Example: (from above)
   $$4x + 2 - bxy = 29$$
   Subtract 2.
   $$4x - bxy = 29 - 2 = 27$$

   If only one x term is left, unravel to just x.

Example: $8x = 24$
              Divide by 8.
              $x = 3$

Example: $4x^2 = 36$
              Divide by 4.
              $x^2 = 9$
              Take square root. Note $\pm$.
              $x = \pm 3$

If more than one term with x in it is left, try to factor. While, in principle, many things are not factorable, on the GRE most polynomials will be factorable. (Factoring and polynomial multiplication are discussed in the next section of the math review.)

8. If there are two variables in an equation, it may be helpful to put all expressions containing one variable on one side and all the others on the other.

9. Expressing x in terms of y means having an equation with x alone on one side and some expression of y on the other, such as $x = 4y^2 + 3y + 4$.

10. We will review some of the frequently encountered types of algebra problems, although not every problem you may get will fall into one of these categories. However, thoroughly familiarizing yourself with the types of problems that follow will help you to translate and solve all kinds of verbal problems.

A. Coin Problems

In solving coin problems, it is best to change the value of all monies involved to cents before writing an equation. Thus, the number of nickels must be multiplied by 5 to give their value in cents; dimes must be multiplied by 10; quarters by 25; half-dollars by 50; and dollars by 100.

Illustration: Richard has $3.50 consisting of nickels and dimes. If he has 5 more dimes than nickels, how many dimes does he have?

SOLUTION:

$$\begin{aligned} \text{Let } x &= \text{the number of nickels} \\ x + 5 &= \text{the number of dimes} \\ 5x &= \text{the value of the nickels in cents} \\ 10x + 50 &= \text{the value of the dimes in cents} \\ 350 &= \text{the value of the money he has in cents} \\ 5x + 10x + 50 &= 350 \\ 15x &= 300 \\ x &= 20 \end{aligned}$$

Answer: He has 20 nickels and 25 dimes.

In a problem such as this, you can be sure that 20 would be among the multiple-choice answers. You must be sure to read carefully what you are asked to find and then continue until you have found the quantity sought.

B. Consecutive Integer Problems

Consecutive integers are one apart and can be represented by x, x+1, x+2, etc. Consecutive even or odd integers are two apart and can be represented by x, x+2, x+4, etc.

Illustration: Three consecutive odd integers have a sum of 33. Find the average of these integers.

SOLUTION: Represent the integers as x, x+2 and x+4. Write an equation indicating the sum is 33.

$$\begin{aligned} 3x + 6 &= 33 \\ 3x &= 27 \\ x &= 9 \end{aligned}$$

The integers are 9, 11, and 13. In the case of evenly spaced numbers such as these, the average is the middle number, 11. Since the sum of the three numbers was given originally, all we really had to do was to divide this sum by 3 to find the average, without ever knowing what the numbers were.

Answer: 11

C. Age Problems

Problems of this type usually involve a comparison of ages at the present time, several years from now, or several years ago. A person's age x years from now is found by adding x to his present age. A person's age x years ago is found by subtracting x from his present age.

Illustration: Michelle was 12 years old y years ago. Represent her age b years from now.

SOLUTION: Her present age is $12 + y$. In b years, her age will be $12 + y + b$.

Answer: $12 + y + b$

D. Interest Problems

The annual amount of interest paid on an investment is found by multiplying the amount of principal invested by the rate (percent) of interest paid.

$$\text{Principal} \cdot \text{Rate} = \text{Interest income}$$

Illustration: Mr. Strauss invests \$4,000, part at 6% and part at 7%. His income from these investments in one year is \$250. Find the amount invested at 7%.

SOLUTION: Represent each investment. Let x = the amount invested at 7%. Always try to let x represent what you are looking for.
$4000 - x$ = the amount invested at 6%
$.07x$ = the income from the 7% investment
$.06(4000 - x)$ = the income from the 6% investment
$.07x + .06(4000 - x) = 250$
$7x + 6(4000 - x) = 25000$
$7x + 24000 - 6x = 25000$
$x = 1000$

Answer: He invested \$1,000 at 7%.

E. Mixture

There are two kinds of mixture problems with which you could be familiar. These problems are rare, so this is best regarded as an extra-credit section and not given top priority. The first is sometimes referred to as dry mixture, in which we mix dry ingredients of different values, such as nuts or coffee.

Also solved by the same method are problems such as those dealing with tickets at different prices. In solving this type of problem, it is best to organize the data in a chart of three rows and three columns, labeled as illustrated in the following problem.

Illustration: A dealer wishes to mix 20 pounds of nuts selling for 45 cents per pound with some more expensive nuts selling for 60 cents per pound, to make a mixture that will sell for 50 cents per pound. How many pounds of the more expensive nuts should he use?

SOLUTION:

	No. of lbs.	Price/lb.	= Total Value
Original	20	.45	.45(20)
Added	x	.60	.60(x)
Mixture	20 + x	.50	.50(20+x)

The value of the original nuts plus the value of the added nuts must equal the value of the mixture. Almost all mixture problems require an equation that comes from adding the final column.

$$.45(20) + .60(x) = .50(20 + x)$$
Multiply by 100 to remove decimals.
$$45(20) + 60(x) = 50(20 + x)$$
$$900 + 60x = 1000 + 50x$$
$$10x = 100$$
$$x = 10$$

Answer: He should use 10 lbs. of 60-cent nuts.

In solving the second type, or chemical, mixture problem, we are dealing with percents rather than prices, and amounts instead of value.

Illustration: How much water must be added to 20 gallons of solution that is 30% alcohol to dilute it to a solution that is only 25% alcohol?

SOLUTION:

	No. of gals.	% alcohol	= Amt. alcohol
Original	20	.30	.30(20)
Added	x	0	0
New	20 + x	.25	.25(20 + x)

Note that the percent of alcohol in water is 0. Had we added pure alcohol to strengthen the solution, the percent would have been 100. The equation again comes from the last column. The amount of alcohol added (none in this case) plus the amount we had to start with must equal the amount of alcohol in the new solution.

$$.30(20) = .25(20 + x)$$
$$30(20) = 25(20 + x)$$
$$600 = 500 + 25x$$
$$100 = 25x$$
$$x = 4$$

Answer: 4 gallons.

F. Motion Problems

The fundamental relationship in all motion problems is that Rate · Time = Distance. The problems at the level of this examination usually derive their equation from a relationship concerning distance. Most problems fall into one of three types.

Motion in opposite directions. When two objects start at the same time and move in opposite directions, or when two objects start at points at a given distance apart and move toward each other until they meet, then the distance the second travels will equal one half the total distance covered.

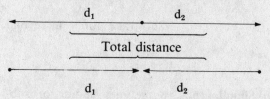

In either of the above cases, $d_1 + d_2$ = Total distance.

Motion in the same direction. This type of problem is sometimes called the "catch-up" problem. Two objects leave the same place at different times and different rates, but one "catches up" to the other. In such a case, the two distances must be equal.

Round trip. In this type of problem, the rate going is usually different from the rate returning. The times are also different. But if we go somewhere and then return to the starting point, the distances must be the same.

To solve any motion problem, it is helpful to organize the data in a box with columns for rate, time, and distance. A separate line should be used for each moving object. Remember that if the rate is given in *miles per hour*, the time must be in *hours* and the distance in *miles*.

Illustration: Two cars leave a restaurant at 1 P.M., with one car traveling east at 60 miles per hour and the other west at 40 miles per hour along a straight highway. At what time will they be 350 miles apart?

SOLUTION:

	Rate	Time	= Distance
Eastbound	60	x	60x
Westbound	40	x	40x

Notice that the time is unknown, since we must discover the number of hours traveled. However, since the cars start at the same time and stop when they are 350 miles apart, their times are the same.

$$60x + 40x = 350$$
$$100x = 350$$
$$x = 3\frac{1}{2}$$

Answer: In $3\frac{1}{2}$ hours, it will be 4:30 P.M.

Illustration: Gloria leaves home for school, riding her bicycle at a rate of 12 MPH. Twenty minutes after she leaves, her mother sees Gloria's English paper on her bed and leaves to bring it to her. If her mother drives at 36 MPH, how far must she drive before she reaches Gloria?

SOLUTION:

	Rate	Time	=	Distance
Gloria	12	x		12x
Mother	36	$x - \frac{1}{3}$		$36(x - \frac{1}{3})$

Notice that 20 minutes has been changed to $\frac{1}{3}$ of an hour. In this problem the times are not equal, but the distances are.

$$12x = 36(x - \frac{1}{3})$$
$$12x = 36x - 12$$
$$12 = 24x$$
$$x = \frac{1}{2}$$

Answer: If Gloria rode for $\frac{1}{2}$ hour at 12 MPH, the distance covered was 6 miles.

Illustration: Judy leaves home at 11 A.M. and rides to Mary's house to return her bicycle. She travels at 12 miles per hour and arrives at 11:30 A.M. She turns right around and walks home. How fast does she walk if she returns home at 1 P.M.?

SOLUTION:

	Rate	· Time	=	Distance
Going	12	$\frac{1}{2}$		6
Return	x	$1\frac{1}{2}$		$\frac{3}{2}x$

The distances are equal.
$$6 = \frac{3}{2}x$$
$$12 = 3x$$
$$x = 4$$

Answer: She walked at 4 MPH

G. Work Problems

In most work problems, a complete job is broken into several parts, each representing a fractional part of the entire job. For each fractional part, which represents the portion completed by one man, one machine, one pipe, etc., the numerator should represent the time actually spent working, while the denominator should represent the total time needed to do the entire job alone. The sum of all the individual fractions should be 1.

Illustration: John can wax his car in 3 hours. Jim can do the same job in 5 hours. How long will it take them if they work together?

SOLUTION: If multiple-choice answers are given, you should realize that the correct answer must be smaller than the shortest time given, for no matter how slow a helper may be, he does do part of the job and therefore it will be completed in less time.

	John	Jim
$\frac{\text{Time spent}}{\text{Total time needed to do job alone}}$	$\frac{x}{3}$ +	$\frac{x}{5}$ = 1

Multiply by 15 to eliminate fractions.

$$5x + 3x = 15$$
$$8x = 15$$
$$x = 1\frac{7}{8} \text{ hours}$$

11. In general, you need as many equations as you have unknowns in order to get a unique numerical solution.

12. The two methods for coping with two or more equations are called **substitution** and **simultaneous.** They overlap. You have used both many times.

Substitution. Whenever one unknown equals something, you can substitute that something for it.

Example: (1) $2x + 3y = 14$ } given
(2) $x = 2y$

Substitute 2y for x in first equation.
$$2(2y) + 3y = 14$$
$$4y + 3y = 14$$
Add up y's; divide by 7.
$$7y = 14$$
$$y = 2$$

Substitute for y in second equation.
$$x = 2(2)$$
$$x = 4$$

Simultaneous. Sometimes adding or subtracting whole equations is shorter.

Example: (1) $5x + 3y = 13$
(2) $2x + 3y = 7$
Subtract (2) from (1).
$$5x + 3y = 13$$
$$- [2x + 3y = 7]$$
$$[5x - 2x] + [3y - 3y] = [13 - 7]$$
$$3x = 6$$
Divide by 3.
$$x = 2$$
$$y = 1 \quad \text{by substitution}$$

Practice Problems—Algebra

1. Sue and Nancy wish to buy a gift for a friend. They combine their money and find they have $4.00, consisting of quarters, dimes, and nickels. If they have 35 coins and the number of quarters is half the number of nickels, how many quarters do they have?
   (A) 5
   (B) 10
   (C) 20
   (D) 3
   (E) 6

2. Three times the first of three consecutive odd integers is 3 more than twice the third. Find the third integer.
   (A) 9
   (B) 11
   (C) 13
   (D) 15
   (E) 7

3. Robert is 15 years older than his brother Stan. However, y years ago Robert was twice as old as Stan. If Stan is now b years old and $b > y$, find the value of $b - y$.
   (A) 13
   (B) 14
   (C) 15
   (D) 16
   (E) 17

4. How many ounces of pure acid must be added to 20 ounces of a solution that is 5% acid to strengthen it to a solution that is 24% acid?
   (A) $2\frac{1}{2}$
   (B) 5
   (C) 6
   (D) $7\frac{1}{2}$
   (E) 10

5. A dealer mixes a lbs. of nuts worth b cents per pound with c lbs. of nuts worth d cents per pound. At what price should he sell a pound of the mixture if he wishes to make a profit of 10 cents per pound?
   (A) $\dfrac{ab + cd}{a + c} + 10$

   (B) $\dfrac{ab + cd}{a + c} + .10$

   (C) $\dfrac{b + d}{a + c} + 10$

   (D) $\dfrac{b + d}{a + c} + .10$

   (E) $\dfrac{b + d + 10}{a + c}$

6. Barbara invests $2,400 in the Security National Bank at 5%. How much additional money must she invest at 8% so that the total annual income will be equal to 6% of her entire investment?
   (A) $2,400
   (B) $3,600
   (C) $1,000
   (D) $3,000
   (E) $1,200

7. Frank left Austin to drive to Boxville at 6:15 P.M. and arrived at 11:45 P.M. If he averaged 30 miles per hour and stopped one hour for dinner, how far is Boxville from Austin?
   (A) 120
   (B) 135
   (C) 180
   (D) 165
   (E) 150

8. A plane traveling 600 miles per hour is 30 miles from Kennedy Airport at 4:58 P.M. At what time will it arrive at the airport?
   (A) 5:00 P.M.
   (B) 5:01 P.M.
   (C) 5:02 P.M.
   (D) 5:20 P.M.
   (E) 5:03 P.M.

9. Mr. Bridges can wash his car in 15 minutes, while his son Dave takes twice as long to do the same job. If they work together, how many minutes will the job take them?
   (A) 5
   (B) $7\frac{1}{2}$
   (C) 10
   (D) $22\frac{1}{2}$
   (E) 30

10. The value of a fraction is $\frac{2}{5}$. If the numerator is decreased by 2 and the denominator increased by 1, the resulting fraction is equivalent to $\frac{1}{4}$. Find the numerator of the original fraction.

(A) 3
(B) 4
(C) 6
(D) 10
(E) 15

Algebra Problem-Solving— Correct Answers

1.	**(B)**	6.	**(E)**
2.	**(D)**	7.	**(B)**
3.	**(C)**	8.	**(B)**
4.	**(B)**	9.	**(C)**
5.	**(A)**	10.	**(C)**

Problem Solutions—Algebra Problem-Solving

1. Let x = number of quarters
    2x = number of nickels
    35 − 3x = number of dimes
    Write all money values in cents.
    $$25(x) + 5(2x) + 10(35 - 3x) = 400$$
    $$25x + 10x + 350 - 30x = 400$$
    $$5x = 50$$
    $$x = 10$$

    Answer: **(B)** 10

2. Let x = first integer
    x + 2 = second integer
    x + 4 = third integer
    $$3(x) = 3 + 2(x + 4)$$
    $$3x = 3 + 2x + 8$$
    $$x = + 11$$
    The third integer is 15.

    Answer: **(D)** 15

3. b = Stan's age now
    b + 15 = Robert's age now
    b − y = Stan's age y years ago
    b + 15 − y = Robert's age y years ago
    $$b + 15 - y = 2(b - y)$$
    $$b + 15 - y = 2b - 2y$$
    $$15 = b - y$$

    Answer: **(C)** 15

4.

	No. of oz.	% acid	= Amt. acid
Original	20	.05	1
Added	x	1.00	x
Mixture	20 + x	.24	.24(20 + x)

$1 + x = .24(20 + x)$ Multiply by 100 to eliminate decimal.
$$100 + 100x = 480 + 24x$$
$$76x = 380$$
$$x = 5$$

Answer: **(B)** 5

5. The a lbs. of nuts are worth a total of ab cents. The c lbs. of nuts are worth a total of cd cents. The value of the mixture is ab + cd cents. Since there are a + c pounds, each pound is worth $\frac{ab + cd}{a + c}$ cents.

    Since the dealer wants to add 10 cents to each pound for profit, and the value of each pound is in cents, we add 10 to the value of each pound.

    Answer: **(A)** $\frac{ab + cd}{a + c} + 10$

6. If Barbara invests x additional dollars at 8%, her total investment will amount to 2400 + x dollars.
    $$.05(2400) + .08(x) = .06(2400 + x)$$
    $$5(2400) + 8(x) = \mathbf{6(2400 + x)}$$
    $$12,000 + 8x = 14400 + 6x$$
    $$2x = 2400$$
    $$x = 1200$$

    Answer: **(E)** $1,200

7. Total time elapsed is $5\frac{1}{2}$ hours. However, one hour was used for dinner. Therefore, Frank drove at 30 m.p.h. for $4\frac{1}{2}$ hours, covering 135 miles.

    Answer: **(B)** 135

8. Time $= \dfrac{\text{Distance}}{\text{Rate}} = \dfrac{30}{600} = \dfrac{1}{20}$ hour, or 3 minutes.

   Answer: **(B)** 5:01 P.M.

9. Dave takes 30 minutes to wash the car alone.

   $$\frac{x}{15} + \frac{x}{30} = 1$$
   $$2x + x = 30$$
   $$3x = 30$$
   $$x = 10$$

   Answer: **(C)** 10

10. Let $2x =$ original numerator
    $5x =$ original denominator
    $$\frac{2x - 2}{5x + 1} = \frac{1}{4} \text{ Cross multiply}$$
    $$8x - 8 = 5x + 1$$
    $$3x = 9$$
    $$x = 3$$
    Original numerator is 2(3), or 6.

    Answer: **(C)** 6

POLYNOMIAL MULTIPLICATION AND FACTORING

1. A polynomial is any expression with two or more terms, such as $2x + y$ or $3z + 9m^2$.

2. A single term multiplied by another expression must multiply *every* term in the second expression.

   Example: $4(x + y + 2z) = 4x + 4y + 8z$

3. The same holds true for division.

   Example: $\dfrac{(a + b + 3c)}{3} = \dfrac{a}{3} + \dfrac{b}{3} + \dfrac{3c}{3}$
   $$= \frac{a}{3} + \frac{b}{3} + c$$

4. The FOIL method should be used when multiplying two binomials together.

Example: $(x + y)(x + y)$

First $\quad (x + y)(x + y) = x^2$

Outer $\quad (x + y)(x + y) = xy$

Inner $\quad (x + y)(x + y) = xy$

Last $\quad (x + y)(x + y) = y^2$

$$(x + y)(x + y) = x^2 + 2xy + y^2$$

5. You should know these three equivalencies by heart for the GRE.

   $(x + y)^2 = (x + y)(x + y) = x^2 + 2xy + y^2$
   $(x - y)^2 = (x - y)(x - y) = x^2 - 2xy + y^2$
   $(x + y)(x - y) = x^2 - y^2$

   Work all three out with the FOIL method. The x or y could stand for a letter, a number, or an expression.

   Example: $(m + 3)^2 = m^2 + 2 \cdot 3 \cdot m + 3^2$
   $$= m^2 + 6m + 9$$

   Example: $(2k - p)^2 = (2k)^2 - 2 \cdot 2k \cdot p + p^2$
   $$= 4k^2 - 4kp + p^2$$

6. You will not need much factoring on the exam. Most of what you do need was covered in the preceding points—if you just reverse the process of multiplication.

   Example: $3x + 6xy = 3x(1 + 2y)$

   Example: $2xyz + 4xy = 2xy(z + 2)$

7. One special situation (called a quadratic equation) occurs when an algebraic multiplication equals zero. Since zero can only be achieved in multiplication by multiplying by zero itself, one of the factors must be zero.

   Example: $(x + 1)(x + 2) = 0$
   Therefore, either $x + 1 = 0$, $x = -1$
   or $x + 2 = 0$, $x = -2$.

   In such a situation you simply have to live with two possible answers. This uncertainty may be important in Quantitative Comparison questions.

8. You may also need to factor to achieve a quadratic format.

Example: $x^2 + 2x + 1 = 0$
$(x + 1)(x + 1) = 0$

Thus, $x + 1 = 0$
$x = -1$ since both factors are the same.

GEOMETRY

Symbols

The most common symbols used in GRE geometry problems are listed below. The concepts behind the symbols will be explained in this section.

Angles
∠ or ⅄   angle (∠ C = angle C or ⅄ C = angle C)
     ∟   right angle (90°)

Lines
    ⊥   perpendicular, at right angles to
    ‖   parallel (line B ‖ line C)
    $\overline{BD}$ line or line segment BD

Circles
    ⊙   circle
    $\overset{\frown}{AC}$ arc AC

Angles

1. a. An **angle** is the figure formed by two lines meeting at a point.

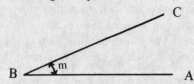

   b. The point B is the **vertex** of the angle and the lines BA and BC are the **sides** of the angle.

2. There are three common ways of naming an angle:

   a. By a small letter or figure written within the angle, as ⅄m.

   b. By a capital letter at its vertex, as ⅄ʙ.

   c. By three capital letters, the middle letter being the vertex letter, as ∠ABC.

3. a. When two straight lines intersect (cut each other), four angles are formed. If these four angles are equal, each angle is a **right angle** and contains 90°. The symbol ∟ is used to indicate a right angle.

Example:

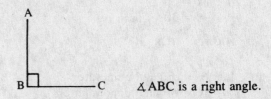

⅄ ABC is a right angle.

   b. An angle less than a right angle is an **acute angle.**

   c. If the two sides of an angle extend in opposite directions forming a straight line, the angle is a **straight angle** and contains 180°.

   d. An angle greater than a right angle (90°) and less than a straight angle (180°) is an **obtuse angle.**

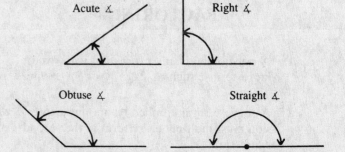

4. a. Two angles are **complementary** if their sum is 90°.

   b. To find the complement of an angle, subtract the given number of degrees from 90°.

Example: The complement of 60° is 90° − 60° = 30°.

5. a. Two angles are **supplementary** if their sum is 180°.

b. To find the supplement of an angle, subtract the given number of degrees from 180°.

Example: The supplement of 60° is 180° − 60° = 120°.

Lines

6. a. Two lines are **perpendicular** to each other if they meet to form a right angle. The symbol ⊥ is used to indicate that the lines are perpendicular.

   Example: ∠ABC is a right angle. Therefore, AB ⊥ BC.

   b. Lines that do not meet no matter how far they are extended are called **parallel lines.** Parallel lines are always the same perpendicular distance from each other. The symbol ∥ is used to indicate that two lines are parallel.

   Example: AB ∥ CD

Triangles

7. A **triangle** is a closed, three-sided figure. The figures below are all triangles.

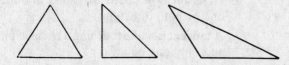

8. a. The sum of the three angles of a triangle is 180°.

   b. To find an angle of a triangle when you are given the other two angles, add the given angles and subtract their sum from 180°.

   Illustration: Two angles of a triangle are 60° and 40°. Find the third angle.

   SOLUTION: 60° + 40° = 100°
                  180° − 100° = 80°

   Answer: The third angle is 80°.

9. a. A triangle that has two equal sides is called an **isosceles triangle.**

   b. In an isosceles triangle, the angles opposite the equal sides are also equal.

10. a. A triangle that has all three sides equal is called an **equilateral triangle.**

    b. Each angle of an equilateral triangle is 60°.

11. a. A triangle that has a right angle is called a **right triangle.**

    b. In a right triangle, the two acute angles are complementary.

    c. In a right triangle, the side opposite the right angle is called the **hypotenuse** and is the longest side. The other two sides are called **legs.**

    Example: AC is the hypotenuse.
                  AB and BC are the legs.

12. The **Pythagorean Theorem** states that in a right triangle the square of the hypotenuse equals the sum of the squares of the legs. In the triangle above, this would be expressed as $\overline{AB}^2 + \overline{BC}^2 = \overline{AC}^2$. The simplest whole number example is $3^2 + 4^2 = 5^2$.

13. a. To find the hypotenuse of a right triangle when given the legs:

    a. Square each leg.

    b. Add the squares.

    c. Extract the square root of this sum.

    Illustration: In a right triangle the legs are 6 inches and 8 inches. Find the hypotenuse.

    SOLUTION: $6^2 = 36$ $8^2 = 64$
                      $36 + 64 = 100$
                          $\sqrt{100} = 10$

    Answer: The hypotenuse is 10 inches.

b. To find a leg when given the other leg and the hypotenuse of a right triangle:

a. Square the hypotenuse and the given leg.

b. Subtract the square of the leg from the square of the hypotenuse.

c. Extract the square root of this difference.

Illustration: One leg of a right triangle is 12 feet and the hypotenuse is 20 feet. Find the other leg.

SOLUTION: $12^2 = 144$ $\qquad 20^2 = 400$
$$400 - 144 = 256$$
$$\sqrt{256} = 16$$

Answer: The other leg is 16 feet.

14. Within a given triangle, the largest side is opposite the largest angle; the smallest side is opposite the smallest angle; and equal sides are opposite equal angles.

Quadrilaterals

15. a. A **quadrilateral** is a closed, four-sided figure in two dimensions. Common quadrilaterals are the **parallelogram, rectangle,** and **square.**

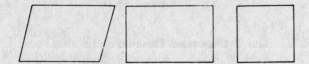

b. The sum of the four angles of a quadrilateral is 360°.

16. a. A **parallelogram** is a quadrilateral in which both pairs of opposite sides are parallel.

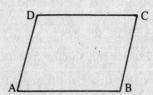

b. Opposite sides of a parallelogram are also equal.

c. Opposite angles of a parallelogram are equal.

17. A **rectangle** has all of the properties of a parallelogram. In addition, all four of its angles are right angles.

18. A **square** is a rectangle having the additional property that all four of its sides are equal.

Circles

19. A **circle** is a closed plane curve, all points of which are equidistant from a point within called the **center.**

20. a. A **complete circle** contains 360°.

b. A **semicircle** contains 180°.

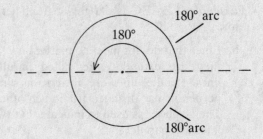

21. a. A **chord** is a line segment connecting any two points on the circle.

b. A **radius** of a circle is a line segment connecting the center with any point on the circle.

c. A **diameter** is a chord passing through the center of the circle.

d. A **secant** is a chord extended in either one or both directions.

e. A **tangent** is a line touching a circle at one and only one point.

f. The **circumference** is the curved line bounding the circle.

g. An **arc** of a circle is any part of the circumference.

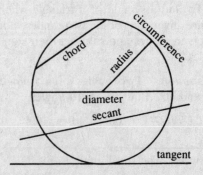

Note: The terms secant and chord are rarely used on the test.

22. a. A **central angle,** as ∠AOB in the figure below, is an angle whose vertex is the center of the circle and whose sides are radii. A central angle is equal to, or has the same number of degrees as, its intercepted arc.

    b. An **inscribed angle,** as ∠MNP, is an angle whose vertex is on the circle and whose sides are chords. An inscribed angle has half the number of degrees as its intercepted arc. ∠MNP intercepts arc MP and has half the degrees of arc MP.

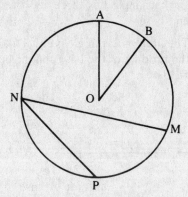

Perimeter

23. The **perimeter** of a two-dimensional figure is the distance around the figure.

Example: The perimeter of the figure above is 9 + 8 + 4 + 3 + 5 = 29.

24. a. The perimeter of a triangle is found by adding all of its sides.

    Example: If the sides of a triangle are 4, 5, and 7, its perimeter is 4 + 5 + 7 = 16.

    b. If the perimeter and two sides of a triangle are given, the third side is found by adding the two given sides and subtracting this sum from the perimeter.

Illustration: Two sides of a triangle are 12 and 15, and the perimeter is 37. Find the other side.

SOLUTION: 12 + 15 = 27
37 − 27 = 10

Answer: The third side is 10.

25. The perimeter of a rectangle equals twice the sum of the length and the width. The formula is P = 2(l + w).

Example: The perimeter of a rectangle whose length is 7 feet and width is 3 feet equals 2 × 10 = 20 feet.

26. The perimeter of a square equals one side multiplied by 4. The formula is P = 4s.

Example: The perimeter of a square, one side of which is 5 feet, is 4 × 5 feet = 20 feet.

27. a. The circumference of a circle is equal to the product of the diameter multiplied by π. The formula is C = πd.

    b. The number π (pi) is approximately equal to $\frac{22}{7}$, or 3.14 (3.1416 for greater accuracy). A problem will usually state which value to use; otherwise, express the answer in terms of "pi," π.

Example: The circumference of a circle whose diameter is 4 inches = 4π inches; or, if it is stated that $\pi = \frac{22}{7}$, the circumference is $4 \times \frac{22}{7} = \frac{88}{7} = 12\frac{4}{7}$ inches.

    c. Since the diameter is twice the radius, the circumference equals twice the radius multiplied by π. The formula is C = 2πr.

Example: If the radius of a circle is 3 inches, then the circumference = 6π inches.

    d. The diameter of a circle equals the circumference divided by π.

Example: If the circumference of a circle is 11 inches, then, assuming

$$\pi = \frac{22}{7},$$
$$\text{diameter} = 11 \div \frac{22}{7} \text{ inches}$$
$$= \overset{1}{\cancel{11}} \times \frac{7}{\underset{2}{\cancel{22}}} \text{ inches}$$
$$= \frac{7}{2} \text{ inches, or } 3\frac{1}{2} \text{ inches}$$

Area

28. a. In a figure of two dimensions, the total space within the figure is called the **area.**

    b. Area is expressed in square denominations, such as square inches, square centimeters, and square miles.

    c. In computing area, all dimensions must be expressed in the same denomination.

29. The area of a square is equal to the square of the length of any side. The formula is $A = s^2$.

    Example: The area of a square, one side of which is 6 inches, is $6 \times 6 = 36$ square inches.

30. a. The area of a rectangle equals the product of the length multiplied by the width. The length is any side; the width is the side next to the length. The formula is $A = l \times w$.

    Example: If the length of a rectangle is 6 feet and its width 4 feet, then the area is $6 \times 4 = 24$ square feet.

    b. If given the area of a rectangle and one dimension, divide the area by the given dimension to find the other dimension.

    Example: If the area of a rectangle is 48 square feet and one dimension is 4 feet, then the other dimension is $48 \div 4 = 12$ feet.

31. a. The altitude, or height, of a parallelogram is a line drawn from a vertex perpendicular to the opposite side, or base.

    Example: DE is the height.
    AB is the base.

    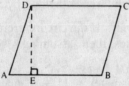

    b. The area of a parallelogram is equal to the product of its base and its height: $A = b \times h$.

Example: If the base of a parallelogram is 10 centimeters and its height is 5 centimeters, its area is $5 \times 10 = 50$ square centimeters.

    c. If given one of these dimensions and the area, divide the area by the given dimension to find the base or the height of a parallelogram.

Example: If the area of a parallelogram is 40 square inches and its height is 8 inches, its base is $40 \div 8 = 5$ inches.

32. a. The altitude, or height, of a triangle is a line drawn from a vertex perpendicular to the opposite side, called the base. Each triangle has three sets of altitudes and bases.

    b. The area of a triangle is equal to one-half the product of the base and the height: $A = \frac{1}{2}b \times h$.

    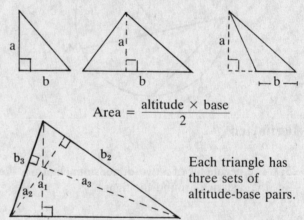

    $$\text{Area} = \frac{\text{altitude} \times \text{base}}{2}$$

    Each triangle has three sets of altitude-base pairs.

Example: The area of a triangle having a height of 5 inches and a base of 4 inches is $\frac{1}{2} \times 5 \times 4 = \frac{1}{2} \times 20 = 10$ square inches.

    c. In a right triangle, one leg may be considered the height and the other leg the base. Therefore, the area of a right triangle is equal to one-half the product of the legs.

Example: The legs of a right triangle are 3 and 4. Its area is $\frac{1}{2} \times 3 \times 4 = 6$ square units.

33. a. The area of a circle is equal to the radius squared, multiplied by π: $A = \pi r^2$.

Example: If the radius of a circle is 6 inches, then the area $= 36\pi$ square inches.

b. To find the radius of a circle given the area, divide the area by π and find the square root of the quotient.

Example: To find the radius of a circle of area 100π:

$$\frac{100\pi}{\pi} = 100$$
$$\sqrt{100} = 10 = \text{radius}.$$

34. Some figures are composed of several geometric shapes. To find the area of such a figure it is necessary to find the area of each of its parts.

Illustration: Find the area of the figure below:

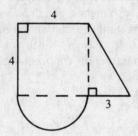

SOLUTION: The figure is composed of three parts: a square of side 4, a semi-circle of diameter 4 (the lower side of the square), and a right triangle with legs 3 and 4 (the right side of the square).

Area of square = 4^2 = 16
Area of triangle = $\frac{1}{2} \times 3 \times 4 = 6$
Area of semicircle is $\frac{1}{2}$ area of circle = $\frac{1}{2}\pi r^2$
Radius = $\frac{1}{2} \times 4 = 2$
Area = $\frac{1}{2}\pi r^2$
= $\frac{1}{2} \times \pi \times 2^2$
= 2π

Answer: Total area = $16 + 6 + 2\pi = 22 + 2\pi$.

Three-Dimensional Figures

35. a. In a three-dimensional figure, the total space contained within the figure is called the **volume;** it is expressed in **cubic denominations.**

b. The total outside surface is called the **surface area;** it is expressed in **square denominations.**

c. In computing volume and surface area, all dimensions must be expressed in the same denomination.

36. a. A **rectangular solid** is a figure of three dimensions having six rectangular faces meeting each other at right angles. The three dimensions are length, width and height.
    The figure below is a rectangular solid: "l" is the length, "w" is the width, and "h" is the height.

b. The volume of a rectangular solid is the product of the length, width, and height: $V = l \times w \times h$.

Example: The volume of a rectangular solid whose length is 6 feet, width 3 feet, and height 4 feet is $6 \times 3 \times 4 = 72$ cubic feet.

37. a. A **cube** is a rectangular solid whose edges are equal. The figure below is a cube; the length, width, and height are all equal to "e."

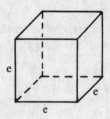

b. The volume of a cube is equal to the edge cubed: $V = e^3$.

Example: The volume of a cube whose height is 6 inches equals $6^3 = 6 \times 6 \times 6 = 216$ cubic inches.

c. The surface area of a cube is equal to the area of any side multiplied by 6.

Example: The surface area of a cube whose length is 5 inches = $5^2 \times 6 = 25 \times 6 = 150$ square inches.

38. The volume of a **circular cylinder** is equal to the product of π, the radius squared, and the height.

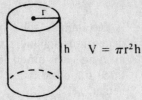

Example: A circular cylinder has a radius of 7 inches and a height of $\frac{1}{2}$ inch. Using $\pi = \frac{22}{7}$, its volume is

$$\tfrac{22}{7} \times 7 \times 7 \times \tfrac{1}{2} = 77 \text{ cubic inches}$$

39. The volume of a **sphere** is equal to $\frac{4}{3}$ the product of π and the radius cubed.

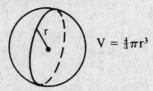

Example: If the radius of a sphere is 3 cm, its volume in terms of π is

$$\tfrac{4}{3} \times \pi \times 3 \text{ cm} \times 3 \text{ cm} \times 3 \text{ cm} = 36\pi \text{ cm}^3$$

Practice Problems Involving Geometry

1. If the perimeter of a rectangle is 68 yards and the width is 48 feet, the length is
   (A) 10 yd
   (B) 18 yd
   (C) 20 ft
   (D) 46 ft
   (E) 56 ft

2. The total length of fencing needed to enclose a rectangular area 46 feet by 34 feet is
   (A) 26 yd 1 ft
   (B) $26\tfrac{2}{3}$ yd
   (C) 48 yds
   (D) 52 yd 2 ft
   (E) $53\tfrac{1}{3}$ yd

3. An umbrella 50″ long can lie on the bottom of a trunk whose length and width are, respectively,
   (A) 26″, 30″
   (B) 39″, 36″
   (C) 31″, 31″
   (D) 40″, 21″
   (E) 40″, 30″

4. A road runs 1200 ft from A to B, and then makes a right angle going to C, a distance of 500 ft. A new road is being built directly from A to C. How much shorter will the new road be?
   (A) 400 ft
   (B) 609 ft
   (C) 850 ft
   (D) 1000 ft
   (E) 1300 ft

5. A certain triangle has sides that are, respectively, 6 inches, 8 inches, and 10 inches long. A rectangle equal in area to that of the triangle has a width of 3 inches. The perimeter of the rectangle, expressed in inches, is
   (A) 11
   (B) 16
   (C) 22
   (D) 24
   (E) 30

6. A ladder 65 feet long is leaning against the wall. Its lower end is 25 feet away from the wall. How much farther away will it be if the upper end is moved down 8 feet?
   (A) 60 ft
   (B) 52 ft
   (C) 14 ft
   (D) 10 ft
   (E) 8 ft

7. A rectangular bin 4 feet long, 3 feet wide, and 2 feet high is solidly packed with bricks whose dimensions are 8 inches, 4 inches, and 2 inches. The number of bricks in the bin is
   (A) 54
   (B) 320
   (C) 648
   (D) 848
   (E) none of these

8. If the cost of digging a trench is $2.12 a cubic yard, what would be the cost of digging a trench 2 yards by 5 yards by 4 yards?
   (A) $21.20
   (B) $40.00

(C) $64.00
(D) $84.80
(E) $104.80

9. A piece of wire is shaped to enclose a square, whose area is 121 square inches. It is then reshaped to enclose a rectangle whose length is 13 inches. The area of the rectangle, in square inches, is
(A) 64
(B) 96
(C) 117
(D) 144
(E) 234

10. The area of a 2-foot-wide walk around a garden that is 30 feet long and 20 feet wide is
(A) 104 sq ft
(B) 216 sq ft
(C) 680 sq ft
(D) 704 sq ft
(E) 1416 sq ft

11. The area of a circle is 49π. Find its circumference, in terms of π.
(A) 14π
(B) 28π
(C) 49π
(D) 98π
(E) 147π

12. In two hours, the minute hand of a clock rotates through an angle of
(A) 90°
(B) 180°
(C) 360°
(D) 720°
(E) 1080°

13. A box is 12 inches in width, 16 inches in length, and 6 inches in height. How many square inches of paper would be required to cover it on all sides?
(A) 192
(B) 360
(C) 720
(D) 900
(E) 1440

14. If the volume of a cube is 64 cubic inches, the sum of its edges is
(A) 48 in

(B) 32 in
(C) 24 in
(D) 16 in
(E) 12 in

Geometry Problems—Correct Answers

1.	**(B)**	6.	**(C)**	11.	**(A)**
2.	**(E)**	7.	**(C)**	12.	**(D)**
3.	**(E)**	8.	**(D)**	13.	**(C)**
4.	**(A)**	9.	**(C)**	14.	**(A)**
5.	**(C)**	10.	**(B)**		

Problem Solutions—Geometry

1.

48'   48'

Perimeter = 68 yards
Each width = 48 feet = 16 yards
Both widths = 16 yd + 16 yd = 32 yd
Perimeter = sum of all sides
Remaining two sides must total 68 − 32 = 36 yards.
Since the remaining two sides are equal, they are each 36 ÷ 2 = 18 yards.

Answer: **(B)** 18 yd

2. Perimeter = 2(46 + 34) feet
　　　　　 = 2 × 80 feet
　　　　　 = 160 feet
160 feet = 160 ÷ 3 yards = $53\frac{1}{3}$ yards

Answer: **(E)** $53\frac{1}{3}$ yd

3. The umbrella would be the hypotenuse of a right triangle whose legs are the dimensions of the trunk.

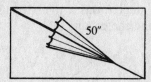

The Pythagorean Theorem states that in a right triangle, the square of the hypotenuse equals the sum of the squares of the legs. Therefore, the sum of the dimensions of the trunk squared must at least equal the length of the umbrella squared, which is 50^2 or 2500.

The only set of dimensions filling this condition is (E):

$$40^2 + 30^2 = 1600 + 900$$
$$= 2500$$

Answer: **(E)** 40", 30"

4. The new road is the hypotenuse of a right triangle, whose legs are the old road.

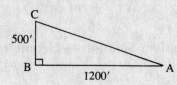

$$AC^2 = AB^2 + BC^2$$
$$AC = \sqrt{500^2 + 1200^2}$$
$$= \sqrt{250,000 + 1,440,000}$$
$$= \sqrt{1,690,000}$$
$$= 1300 \text{ feet}$$
$$\text{Old road} = 1200 + 500 \text{ feet}$$
$$= 1700 \text{ feet}$$
$$\text{New road} = 1300 \text{ feet}$$
$$\text{Difference} = 400 \text{ feet}$$

Answer: **(A)** 400 ft

5. Since $6^2 + 8^2 = 10^2$ (36 + 64 = 100), the triangle is a right triangle. The area of the triangle is $\frac{1}{2} \times 6 \times 8 = 24$ square inches. Therefore, the area of the rectangle is 24 square inches.

If the width of the rectangle is 3 inches, the length is $24 \div 3 = 8$ inches. Then the perimeter of the rectangle is $2(3 + 8) = 2 \times 11 = 22$ inches.

Answer: **(C)** 22

6. The ladder forms a right triangle with the wall and the ground.

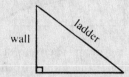

First, find the height that the ladder reaches when the lower end of the ladder is 25 feet from the wall:

$$65^2 = 4225$$
$$25^2 = 625$$
$$65^2 - 25^2 = 3600$$
$$\sqrt{3600} = 60$$

The ladder reaches 60 feet up the wall when its lower end is 25 feet from the wall.

If the upper end is moved down 8 feet, the ladder will reach a height of $60 - 8 = 52$ feet.

The new triangle formed has a hypotenuse of 65 feet and one leg of 52 feet. Find the other leg:

$$65^2 = 4225$$
$$52^2 = 2704$$
$$65^2 - 52^2 = 1521$$
$$\sqrt{1521} = 39$$

The lower end of the ladder is now 39 feet from the wall. This is $39 - 25 = 14$ feet farther than it was before.

Answer: **(C)** 14 ft

7. Convert the dimensions of the bin to inches:

$$4 \text{ feet} = 48 \text{ inches}$$
$$3 \text{ feet} = 36 \text{ inches}$$
$$2 \text{ feet} = 24 \text{ inches}$$
$$\text{Volume of bin} = 48 \times 36 \times 24 \text{ cubic inches}$$
$$= 41,472 \text{ cubic inches}$$
$$\begin{aligned}\text{Volume of} \\ \text{each brick}\end{aligned} = 8 \times 4 \times 2 \text{ cubic inches}$$
$$= 64 \text{ cubic inches}$$
$$41,472 \div 64 = 648 \text{ bricks}$$

Answer: **(C)** 648

8. The trench contains

$$2 \text{ yd} \times 5 \text{ yd} \times 4 \text{ yd} = 40 \text{ cubic yards}$$
$$40 \times \$2.12 = \$84.80$$

Answer: **(D)** \$84.80

9. Find the dimensions of the square: If the area of the square is 121 square inches, each side is $\sqrt{121} = 11$ inches, and the perimeter is $4 \times 11 = 44$ inches.

Next, find the dimensions of the rectangle: The perimeter of the rectangle is the same as the perimeter of the square, since the same length of wire is used to enclose either figure. Therefore, the perimeter of the rectangle is 44 inches. If the two lengths are each 13 inches, their total is 26 inches, and 44 − 26 inches, or 18 inches, remain for the two widths. Each width is equal to 18 ÷ 2 = 9 inches.

The area of a rectangle with length 13 in and width 9 in is 13 × 9 = 117 sq in.

Answer: **(C)** 117

10.

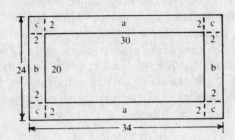

The walk consists of:

a. 2 rectangles of length 30 feet and width 2 feet.

Area of each rectangle = 2 × 30 = 60 sq ft.
Area of both rectangles = 120 sq ft

b. 2 rectangles of length 20 feet and width 2 feet.

Area of each = 2 × 20 = 40 sq ft
Area of both = 80 sq ft

c. 4 squares, each having sides measuring 2 feet.

Area of each square = 2^2 = 4 sq ft
Area of 4 squares = 16 sq ft

Total area of walk = 120 + 80 + 16
= 216 sq ft

Alternate solution:

Area of walk = Area of large rectangle
− area of small rectangle
= 34×24−30×20
= 816 − 600
= 216 sq ft

Answer: **(B)** 216 sq ft

11. If the area of a circle is 49π, its radius is $\sqrt{49}$

= 7. Then, the circumference is equal to 2 × 7 × π = 14π.

Answer: **(A)** 14π

12. In one hour, the minute hand rotates through 360°. In two hours, it rotates through 2 × 360° = 720°.

Answer: **(D)** 720°

13. Find the area of each surface:

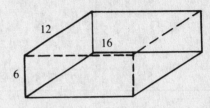

Area of top = 12 × 16 = 192 sq in
Area of bottom = 12 × 16 = 192 sq in
Area of front = 6 × 16 = 96 sq in
Area of back = 6 × 16 = 96 sq in
Area of right side = 6 × 12 = 72 sq in
Area of left side = 6 × 12 = + 72 sq in
Total surface area = 720 sq in

Answer: **(C)** 720

14. For a cube, V = e^3. If the volume is 64 cubic inches, each edge is $\sqrt[3]{64}$ = 4 inches.

A cube has 12 edges. If each edge is 4 inches, the sum of the edges is 4 × 12 = 48 inches.

Answer: **(A)** 48 in

COORDINATE GEOMETRY

Perhaps the easiest way to understand the coordinate axis system is as an analog to the points of the compass. If we take a plot of land, we can divide it into quadrants:

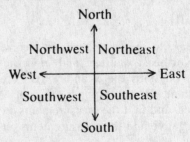

Now, if we add measuring units along each of the directional axes, we can actually describe any location on this piece of land by two numbers. For example, point P is located at 4 units East and 5 units North. Point Q is located at 4 units West and 5 units North. Point R is located at 4 units West and 2 units South. And Point T is located at 3 units East and 4 units South.

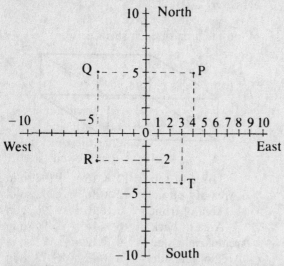

The coordinate system used in coordinate geometry differs from our map of a plot of land in two respects. First, it uses x and y axes divided into negative and positive regions.

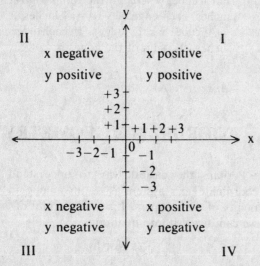

It is easy to see that Quadrant I corresponds to our Northeast quarter, and in it the measurements on both the x and y axes are positive. Quadrant II corresponds to our Northwest quarter, and in it the measurements on the x axis are negative and the measurements on the y axis

are positive. Quadrant III corresponds to the Southwest quarter, and in it both the x axis measurements and the y axis measurements are negative. Finally, Quadrant IV corresponds to our Southeast quarter, and there the x values are positive while the y values are negative.

Second, mathematicians adopt a convention called **ordered pairs** to eliminate the necessity of specifying each time whether one is referring to the x axis or the y axis. An ordered pair of coordinates has the general form (a, b). The first element always refers to the x value (distance left or right of the *origin*, or intersection, of the axes) while the second element gives the y value (distance up or down from the origin).

To make this a bit more concrete, let us *plot* some examples of ordered pairs, that is, find their locations in the system: Let us start with the point (3, 2). We begin by moving to the positive 3 value on the x axis. Then from there we move up two units on the y axis.

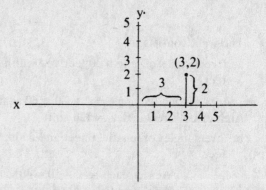

An alternative way of speaking about this is to say that the point (3, 2) is located at the intersection of a line drawn through the x value 3 parallel to the y axis and a line drawn through the y value 2 parallel to the x axis:

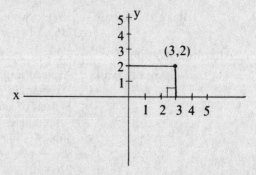

Both methods locate the same point. Let us now use the ordered pairs (−3, 2), (−2, −3) and (3, −2):

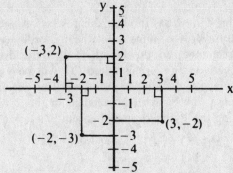

One important use of the coordinate axis system is that it can be used to draw a picture of an equation. For example, we know that the equation x = y has an infinite number of solutions:

x	1	2	3	5	0	−3	−5	etc.
y	1	2	3	5	0	−3	−5	

We can plot these pairs of x and y on the axis system:

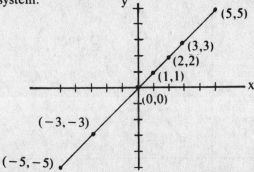

We can now see that a complete picture of the equation x = y is a straight line including all the real numbers such that x is equal to y.

Similarly, we might graph the equation y = 2x

x	−4	−2	−1	0	1	2	4
y	−8	−4	−2	0	2	4	8

After entering these points on the graph, we can complete the picture:

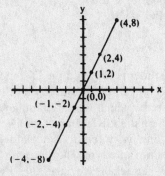

It too is a straight line, but it rises at a more rapid rate than does x = y.

A final use one might have for the coordinate system on the GRE is in graphing geometric figures:

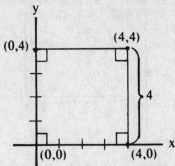

In this case we have a square whose vertices are (0, 0), (4, 0), (4, 4) and (0, 4). Each side of the square must be equal to 4 since each side is four units long (and parallel to either the x or y axis). Since all coordinates can be viewed as the perpendicular intersection of two lines, it is possible to measure distances in the system by using some simple theorems.

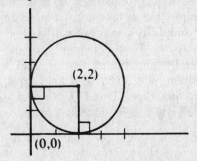

Illustration: What is the area of circle 0?

SOLUTION: In order to solve this problem, we need to know the radius of circle 0. The center of the circle is located at the intersection of x = 2 and y = 2, or the point (2, 2). So we know the radius is 2 units long and the area is 4π.

Answer: 4π

Illustration: What is the length of PQ?

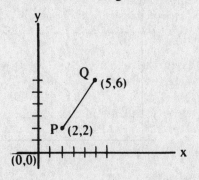

SOLUTION: We can find the length of PQ by constructing a triangle:

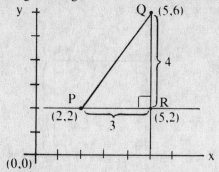

Now, we see that QR runs from (5, 6) to (5, 2) and so it must be 4 units long. We see that PR runs from (2, 2) to (5, 2) so it is 3 units long. We then use the Pythagorean Theorem to determine that PQ, which is the hypotenuse of our triangle, is 5 units long.

Answer: 5 units

It is actually possible to generalize on this example. Let us take any two points on the graph (for simplicity's sake we will confine the discussion to the First Quadrant, but the method is generally applicable, that is, will work in all quadrants and even with lines covering two or more quadrants) P and Q. Now let us assign the value (x_1, y_1) to P and (x_2, y_2) to Q.

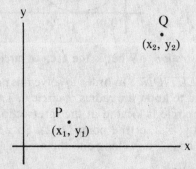

Then, following our method above, we construct a triangle so that we can use the Pythagorean Theorem:

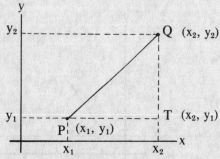

Point T now has the coordinates (x_2, y_1). Side PT will be $x_2 - x_1$ units long (the y coordinate does not change, so the length is only the distance moved on the x axis), and QT will be $y_2 - y_1$ (again, the distance is purely vertical, moving up from y_1 to y_2, with no change in the x value). Using the Pythagorean Theorem:

$$PQ^2 = PT^2 + QT^2$$
$$PQ^2 = (x_2 - x_1)^2 + (y_2 - y_1)^2$$
$$PQ = \sqrt{(x_2 - x_1)^2 + (y_2 - y_1)^2}$$

And we have just derived what is called the **Distance Formula.** We can find the length of any straight line segment drawn in a coordinate axis system (that is, the distance between two points in the system) using this formula.

Illustration: What is the distance between P and Q?

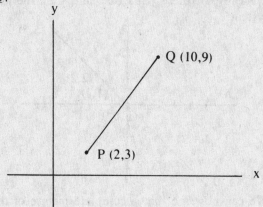

SOLUTION: Point P has the coordinates (2,3) and Q the coordinates (10,9). Using the formula:

$$PQ = \sqrt{(10 - 2)^2 + (9 - 3)^2}$$
$$PQ = \sqrt{8^2 + 6^2}$$
$$PQ = \sqrt{64 + 36}$$
$$PQ = \sqrt{100}$$
$$PQ = 10$$

Answer: 10

For those students who find the Distance Formula a bit too technical, be reassured that the Pythagorean Theorem (which is more familiar) will work just as well on the GRE. In fact, as a general rule, any time one is asked to calculate a distance which does not move parallel to one of the axes, the proper attack is to use the Pythagorean Theorem.

Practice Problems Involving Coordinate Geometry

1. AB is the diameter of a circle whose center is O. If the coordinates of A are (2,6) and the coordinates of B are (6,2), find the coordinates of O.
   (A) (4,4)
   (B) (4,−4)
   (C) (2,−2)
   (D) (0,0)
   (E) (2,2)

2. AB is the diameter of a circle whose center is O. If the coordinates of O are (2,1) and the coordinates of· B are (4,6) find the coordinates of A.
   (A) $(3,3\frac{1}{2})$
   (B) $(1,2\frac{1}{2})$
   (C) (0,−4)
   (D) $(2\frac{1}{2},1)$
   (E) $(-1,-2\frac{1}{2})$

3. Find the distance from the point whose coordinates are (4,3) to the point whose coordinates are (8,6).
   (A) 5
   (B) 25
   (C) $\sqrt{7}$
   (D) $\sqrt{67}$
   (E) 15

4. The vertices of a triangle are (2,1), (2,5), and (5,1). The area of the triangle is
   (A) 12
   (B) 10
   (C) 8
   (D) 6
   (E) 5

5. The area of a circle whose center is at (0,0) is 16π. The circle passes through each of the following points *except*
   (A) (4,4)
   (B) (0,4)
   (C) (4,0)
   (D) (−4,0)
   (E) (0,−4)

Coordinate Geometry Problems— Correct Answers

1. **(A)**
2. **(C)**
3. **(A)**
4. **(D)**
5. **(A)**

Problem Solutions— Coordinate Geometry

1. Find the midpoint of AB by averaging the x coordinates and averaging the y coordinates.
   $$\left(\frac{6+2}{2}, \frac{2+6}{2}\right) = (4, 4)$$
   Answer: **(A)** (4,4)

2. O is the midpoint of AB.
   $$\frac{x+4}{2} = 2 \qquad x + 4 = 4 \qquad x = 0$$
   $$\frac{y+6}{2} = 1 \qquad y + 6 = 2 \qquad y = -4$$
   A is the point (0,−4)
   Answer: **(C)** (0,−4)

3. $d = \sqrt{(8-4)^2 + (6-3)^2} = \sqrt{4^2 + 3^2} = \sqrt{16+9} = \sqrt{25} = 5$
   Answer: **(A)** 5

4. Sketch the triangle and you will see it is a right triangle with legs of 4 and 3.

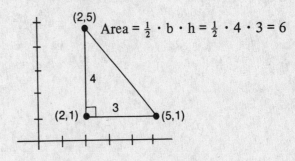

Area $= \frac{1}{2} \cdot b \cdot h = \frac{1}{2} \cdot 4 \cdot 3 = 6$

   Answer: **(D)** 6

5. Area of a circle $= \pi r^2$

$\pi r^2 = 16\pi \qquad r = 4$

Points B, C, D, and E are all 4 units from the origin. Point A is not.

Answer: **(A)** (4, 4)

Part Four

6 FULL-LENGTH PRACTICE EXAMINATIONS

ANSWER SHEET—PRACTICE EXAMINATION 1

Section I

1 Ⓐ Ⓑ Ⓒ Ⓓ Ⓔ	8 Ⓐ Ⓑ Ⓒ Ⓓ Ⓔ	15 Ⓐ Ⓑ Ⓒ Ⓓ Ⓔ	22 Ⓐ Ⓑ Ⓒ Ⓓ Ⓔ	29 Ⓐ Ⓑ Ⓒ Ⓓ Ⓔ	36 Ⓐ Ⓑ Ⓒ Ⓓ Ⓔ
2 Ⓐ Ⓑ Ⓒ Ⓓ Ⓔ	9 Ⓐ Ⓑ Ⓒ Ⓓ Ⓔ	16 Ⓐ Ⓑ Ⓒ Ⓓ Ⓔ	23 Ⓐ Ⓑ Ⓒ Ⓓ Ⓔ	30 Ⓐ Ⓑ Ⓒ Ⓓ Ⓔ	37 Ⓐ Ⓑ Ⓒ Ⓓ Ⓔ
3 Ⓐ Ⓑ Ⓒ Ⓓ Ⓔ	10 Ⓐ Ⓑ Ⓒ Ⓓ Ⓔ	17 Ⓐ Ⓑ Ⓒ Ⓓ Ⓔ	24 Ⓐ Ⓑ Ⓒ Ⓓ Ⓔ	31 Ⓐ Ⓑ Ⓒ Ⓓ Ⓔ	38 Ⓐ Ⓑ Ⓒ Ⓓ Ⓔ
4 Ⓐ Ⓑ Ⓒ Ⓓ Ⓔ	11 Ⓐ Ⓑ Ⓒ Ⓓ Ⓔ	18 Ⓐ Ⓑ Ⓒ Ⓓ Ⓔ	25 Ⓐ Ⓑ Ⓒ Ⓓ Ⓔ	32 Ⓐ Ⓑ Ⓒ Ⓓ Ⓔ	
5 Ⓐ Ⓑ Ⓒ Ⓓ Ⓔ	12 Ⓐ Ⓑ Ⓒ Ⓓ Ⓔ	19 Ⓐ Ⓑ Ⓒ Ⓓ Ⓔ	26 Ⓐ Ⓑ Ⓒ Ⓓ Ⓔ	33 Ⓐ Ⓑ Ⓒ Ⓓ Ⓔ	
6 Ⓐ Ⓑ Ⓒ Ⓓ Ⓔ	13 Ⓐ Ⓑ Ⓒ Ⓓ Ⓔ	20 Ⓐ Ⓑ Ⓒ Ⓓ Ⓔ	27 Ⓐ Ⓑ Ⓒ Ⓓ Ⓔ	34 Ⓐ Ⓑ Ⓒ Ⓓ Ⓔ	
7 Ⓐ Ⓑ Ⓒ Ⓓ Ⓔ	14 Ⓐ Ⓑ Ⓒ Ⓓ Ⓔ	21 Ⓐ Ⓑ Ⓒ Ⓓ Ⓔ	28 Ⓐ Ⓑ Ⓒ Ⓓ Ⓔ	35 Ⓐ Ⓑ Ⓒ Ⓓ Ⓔ	

Section II

1 Ⓐ Ⓑ Ⓒ Ⓓ Ⓔ	8 Ⓐ Ⓑ Ⓒ Ⓓ Ⓔ	15 Ⓐ Ⓑ Ⓒ Ⓓ Ⓔ	22 Ⓐ Ⓑ Ⓒ Ⓓ Ⓔ	29 Ⓐ Ⓑ Ⓒ Ⓓ Ⓔ	36 Ⓐ Ⓑ Ⓒ Ⓓ Ⓔ
2 Ⓐ Ⓑ Ⓒ Ⓓ Ⓔ	9 Ⓐ Ⓑ Ⓒ Ⓓ Ⓔ	16 Ⓐ Ⓑ Ⓒ Ⓓ Ⓔ	23 Ⓐ Ⓑ Ⓒ Ⓓ Ⓔ	30 Ⓐ Ⓑ Ⓒ Ⓓ Ⓔ	37 Ⓐ Ⓑ Ⓒ Ⓓ Ⓔ
3 Ⓐ Ⓑ Ⓒ Ⓓ Ⓔ	10 Ⓐ Ⓑ Ⓒ Ⓓ Ⓔ	17 Ⓐ Ⓑ Ⓒ Ⓓ Ⓔ	24 Ⓐ Ⓑ Ⓒ Ⓓ Ⓔ	31 Ⓐ Ⓑ Ⓒ Ⓓ Ⓔ	38 Ⓐ Ⓑ Ⓒ Ⓓ Ⓔ
4 Ⓐ Ⓑ Ⓒ Ⓓ Ⓔ	11 Ⓐ Ⓑ Ⓒ Ⓓ Ⓔ	18 Ⓐ Ⓑ Ⓒ Ⓓ Ⓔ	25 Ⓐ Ⓑ Ⓒ Ⓓ Ⓔ	32 Ⓐ Ⓑ Ⓒ Ⓓ Ⓔ	
5 Ⓐ Ⓑ Ⓒ Ⓓ Ⓔ	12 Ⓐ Ⓑ Ⓒ Ⓓ Ⓔ	19 Ⓐ Ⓑ Ⓒ Ⓓ Ⓔ	26 Ⓐ Ⓑ Ⓒ Ⓓ Ⓔ	33 Ⓐ Ⓑ Ⓒ Ⓓ Ⓔ	
6 Ⓐ Ⓑ Ⓒ Ⓓ Ⓔ	13 Ⓐ Ⓑ Ⓒ Ⓓ Ⓔ	20 Ⓐ Ⓑ Ⓒ Ⓓ Ⓔ	27 Ⓐ Ⓑ Ⓒ Ⓓ Ⓔ	34 Ⓐ Ⓑ Ⓒ Ⓓ Ⓔ	
7 Ⓐ Ⓑ Ⓒ Ⓓ Ⓔ	14 Ⓐ Ⓑ Ⓒ Ⓓ Ⓔ	21 Ⓐ Ⓑ Ⓒ Ⓓ Ⓔ	28 Ⓐ Ⓑ Ⓒ Ⓓ Ⓔ	35 Ⓐ Ⓑ Ⓒ Ⓓ Ⓔ	

Section III

1 Ⓐ Ⓑ Ⓒ Ⓓ	6 Ⓐ Ⓑ Ⓒ Ⓓ	11 Ⓐ Ⓑ Ⓒ Ⓓ	16 Ⓐ Ⓑ Ⓒ Ⓓ Ⓔ	21 Ⓐ Ⓑ Ⓒ Ⓓ Ⓔ	26 Ⓐ Ⓑ Ⓒ Ⓓ Ⓔ
2 Ⓐ Ⓑ Ⓒ Ⓓ	7 Ⓐ Ⓑ Ⓒ Ⓓ	12 Ⓐ Ⓑ Ⓒ Ⓓ	17 Ⓐ Ⓑ Ⓒ Ⓓ Ⓔ	22 Ⓐ Ⓑ Ⓒ Ⓓ Ⓔ	27 Ⓐ Ⓑ Ⓒ Ⓓ Ⓔ
3 Ⓐ Ⓑ Ⓒ Ⓓ	8 Ⓐ Ⓑ Ⓒ Ⓓ	13 Ⓐ Ⓑ Ⓒ Ⓓ	18 Ⓐ Ⓑ Ⓒ Ⓓ Ⓔ	23 Ⓐ Ⓑ Ⓒ Ⓓ Ⓔ	28 Ⓐ Ⓑ Ⓒ Ⓓ Ⓔ
4 Ⓐ Ⓑ Ⓒ Ⓓ	9 Ⓐ Ⓑ Ⓒ Ⓓ	14 Ⓐ Ⓑ Ⓒ Ⓓ	19 Ⓐ Ⓑ Ⓒ Ⓓ Ⓔ	24 Ⓐ Ⓑ Ⓒ Ⓓ Ⓔ	29 Ⓐ Ⓑ Ⓒ Ⓓ Ⓔ
5 Ⓐ Ⓑ Ⓒ Ⓓ	10 Ⓐ Ⓑ Ⓒ Ⓓ	15 Ⓐ Ⓑ Ⓒ Ⓓ	20 Ⓐ Ⓑ Ⓒ Ⓓ Ⓔ	25 Ⓐ Ⓑ Ⓒ Ⓓ Ⓔ	30 Ⓐ Ⓑ Ⓒ Ⓓ Ⓔ

Section IV

1 Ⓐ Ⓑ Ⓒ Ⓓ   6 Ⓐ Ⓑ Ⓒ Ⓓ   11 Ⓐ Ⓑ Ⓒ Ⓓ   16 Ⓐ Ⓑ Ⓒ Ⓓ Ⓔ   21 Ⓐ Ⓑ Ⓒ Ⓓ Ⓔ   26 Ⓐ Ⓑ Ⓒ Ⓓ Ⓔ

2 Ⓐ Ⓑ Ⓒ Ⓓ   7 Ⓐ Ⓑ Ⓒ Ⓓ   12 Ⓐ Ⓑ Ⓒ Ⓓ   17 Ⓐ Ⓑ Ⓒ Ⓓ Ⓔ   22 Ⓐ Ⓑ Ⓒ Ⓓ Ⓔ   27 Ⓐ Ⓑ Ⓒ Ⓓ Ⓔ

3 Ⓐ Ⓑ Ⓒ Ⓓ   8 Ⓐ Ⓑ Ⓒ Ⓓ   13 Ⓐ Ⓑ Ⓒ Ⓓ   18 Ⓐ Ⓑ Ⓒ Ⓓ Ⓔ   23 Ⓐ Ⓑ Ⓒ Ⓓ Ⓔ   28 Ⓐ Ⓑ Ⓒ Ⓓ Ⓔ

4 Ⓐ Ⓑ Ⓒ Ⓓ   9 Ⓐ Ⓑ Ⓒ Ⓓ   14 Ⓐ Ⓑ Ⓒ Ⓓ   19 Ⓐ Ⓑ Ⓒ Ⓓ Ⓔ   24 Ⓐ Ⓑ Ⓒ Ⓓ Ⓔ   29 Ⓐ Ⓑ Ⓒ Ⓓ Ⓔ

5 Ⓐ Ⓑ Ⓒ Ⓓ   10 Ⓐ Ⓑ Ⓒ Ⓓ   15 Ⓐ Ⓑ Ⓒ Ⓓ   20 Ⓐ Ⓑ Ⓒ Ⓓ Ⓔ   25 Ⓐ Ⓑ Ⓒ Ⓓ Ⓔ   30 Ⓐ Ⓑ Ⓒ Ⓓ Ⓔ

Section V

1 Ⓐ Ⓑ Ⓒ Ⓓ Ⓔ   6 Ⓐ Ⓑ Ⓒ Ⓓ Ⓔ   11 Ⓐ Ⓑ Ⓒ Ⓓ Ⓔ   16 Ⓐ Ⓑ Ⓒ Ⓓ Ⓔ   21 Ⓐ Ⓑ Ⓒ Ⓓ Ⓔ

2 Ⓐ Ⓑ Ⓒ Ⓓ Ⓔ   7 Ⓐ Ⓑ Ⓒ Ⓓ Ⓔ   12 Ⓐ Ⓑ Ⓒ Ⓓ Ⓔ   17 Ⓐ Ⓑ Ⓒ Ⓓ Ⓔ   22 Ⓐ Ⓑ Ⓒ Ⓓ Ⓔ

3 Ⓐ Ⓑ Ⓒ Ⓓ Ⓔ   8 Ⓐ Ⓑ Ⓒ Ⓓ Ⓔ   13 Ⓐ Ⓑ Ⓒ Ⓓ Ⓔ   18 Ⓐ Ⓑ Ⓒ Ⓓ Ⓔ   23 Ⓐ Ⓑ Ⓒ Ⓓ Ⓔ

4 Ⓐ Ⓑ Ⓒ Ⓓ Ⓔ   9 Ⓐ Ⓑ Ⓒ Ⓓ Ⓔ   14 Ⓐ Ⓑ Ⓒ Ⓓ Ⓔ   19 Ⓐ Ⓑ Ⓒ Ⓓ Ⓔ   24 Ⓐ Ⓑ Ⓒ Ⓓ Ⓔ

5 Ⓐ Ⓑ Ⓒ Ⓓ Ⓔ   10 Ⓐ Ⓑ Ⓒ Ⓓ Ⓔ   15 Ⓐ Ⓑ Ⓒ Ⓓ Ⓔ   20 Ⓐ Ⓑ Ⓒ Ⓓ Ⓔ   25 Ⓐ Ⓑ Ⓒ Ⓓ Ⓔ

Section VI

1 Ⓐ Ⓑ Ⓒ Ⓓ Ⓔ   6 Ⓐ Ⓑ Ⓒ Ⓓ Ⓔ   11 Ⓐ Ⓑ Ⓒ Ⓓ Ⓔ   16 Ⓐ Ⓑ Ⓒ Ⓓ Ⓔ   21 Ⓐ Ⓑ Ⓒ Ⓓ Ⓔ

2 Ⓐ Ⓑ Ⓒ Ⓓ Ⓔ   7 Ⓐ Ⓑ Ⓒ Ⓓ Ⓔ   12 Ⓐ Ⓑ Ⓒ Ⓓ Ⓔ   17 Ⓐ Ⓑ Ⓒ Ⓓ Ⓔ   22 Ⓐ Ⓑ Ⓒ Ⓓ Ⓔ

3 Ⓐ Ⓑ Ⓒ Ⓓ Ⓔ   8 Ⓐ Ⓑ Ⓒ Ⓓ Ⓔ   13 Ⓐ Ⓑ Ⓒ Ⓓ Ⓔ   18 Ⓐ Ⓑ Ⓒ Ⓓ Ⓔ   23 Ⓐ Ⓑ Ⓒ Ⓓ Ⓔ

4 Ⓐ Ⓑ Ⓒ Ⓓ Ⓔ   9 Ⓐ Ⓑ Ⓒ Ⓓ Ⓔ   14 Ⓐ Ⓑ Ⓒ Ⓓ Ⓔ   19 Ⓐ Ⓑ Ⓒ Ⓓ Ⓔ   24 Ⓐ Ⓑ Ⓒ Ⓓ Ⓔ

5 Ⓐ Ⓑ Ⓒ Ⓓ Ⓔ   10 Ⓐ Ⓑ Ⓒ Ⓓ Ⓔ   15 Ⓐ Ⓑ Ⓒ Ⓓ Ⓔ   20 Ⓐ Ⓑ Ⓒ Ⓓ Ⓔ   25 Ⓐ Ⓑ Ⓒ Ⓓ Ⓔ

PRACTICE EXAMINATION 1

SECTION I

30 minutes
38 questions

Directions: Each of the questions below contains one or more blank spaces, each blank indicating an omitted word. Each sentence is followed by five (5) lettered words or sets of words. Read and determine the general sense of each sentence. Then choose the word or set of words which, when inserted in the sentence, best fits the meaning of the sentence.

1. Even when his reputation was in _____, almost everyone was willing to admit that he had genius.
   (A) ascendancy
   (B) retaliation
   (C) eclipse
   (D) differentiation
   (E) rebuttal

2. How many of the books published each year in the United States make a(n) _____ contribution toward improving men's _____ with each other?
   (A) important—problems
   (B) standardized—customs
   (C) referential—rudeness
   (D) squalid—generalities
   (E) significant—relationships

3. No one can say for sure how _____ the awards have been.
   (A) determined
   (B) effective
   (C) reducible
   (D) effervescent
   (E) inborn

4. The medieval church condemned man's partaking in _____ pleasures.
   (A) educational
   (B) ascetic
   (C) ecclesiastical
   (D) sensual
   (E) hermetic

5. The fact that a business has _____ does not create an _____ for it to give away its wealth.
   (A) prospered—imperative
   (B) halted—impossibility
   (C) incorporated—impulse
   (D) supplemented—obligation
   (E) accumulated—aspect

6. When I watch drivers routinely slam their cars to a halt, _____ take corners on two wheels, and blunder wildly over construction potholes and railroad crossings, I consider it a _____ to automotive design that cars don't shake apart far sooner.
   (A) gradually—curiosity
   (B) sensibly—blessing
   (C) gracefully—misfortune
   (D) habitually—tribute
   (E) religiously—instruction

7. On the ground, liquid hydrogen must be stored in large stainless-steel tanks with double walls filled with _____ and evacuated to a high vacuum.
   (A) stones
   (B) air
   (C) insulation
   (D) aluminum
   (E) water

235

Directions: In each of the following questions, you are given a related pair of words or phrases in capital letters. Each capitalized pair is followed by five (5) lettered pairs of words or phrases. Choose the pair which best expresses a relationship similar to that expressed by the original pair.

8. PLUTOCRAT : WEALTH ::
    (A) autocrat : individual
    (B) theocrat : religion
    (C) oligarch : ruler
    (D) democrat : popularity
    (E) republican : conservation

9. HANDCUFFS : PRISONER ::
    (A) manacles : penitentiary
    (B) shoes : feet
    (C) leash : dog
    (D) tail : kite
    (E) ring : finger

10. JAVELIN : CANNONBALL ::
    (A) discus : sling
    (B) throw : catch
    (C) spear : bullet
    (D) arrow : shotput
    (E) Greek : Spanish

11. IMP : CHERUB ::
    (A) low : high
    (B) nettle : irk
    (C) bad : good
    (D) devil : angel
    (E) fork : arrow

12. RADIO : PHONOGRAPH ::
    (A) letter : book
    (B) picture : painting
    (C) television : show
    (D) movie : photograph
    (E) brush : canvas

13. IMMIGRATE : COUNTRY ::
    (A) alien : port
    (B) emigrate : ship
    (C) move : placement
    (D) patriot : flag
    (E) enlist : army

14. URGE : INSIST ::
    (A) pursue : hound
    (B) refuse : deny
    (C) expunge : purge
    (D) request : demand
    (E) impulse : push

15. GRAPNEL : ANCHOR ::
    (A) thong : pouch
    (B) hook : gaff
    (C) ship : steam
    (D) hold : cargo
    (E) single : serene

16. INDICTED : SENTENCED ::
    (A) impeached : removed
    (B) arraigned : tried
    (C) elected : served
    (D) guilty : punished
    (E) empaneled : closeted

Directions: Below each of the following passages, you will find questions or incomplete statements about the passage. Each statement or question is followed by lettered words or expressions. Select the word or expression that most satisfactorily completes each statement or answers each question in accordance with the meaning of the passage. After you have chosen the best answer, blacken the corresponding space on the answer sheet.

It has always been difficult for the philosopher or scientist to fit time into his view of the universe. Prior to Einsteinian physics, there was no truly adequate formulation of the relationship of time to the other forces in the universe, even though some empirical equations included time quantities. However, even the Einsteinian formulation is not perhaps totally adequate to the job of fitting time into the proper relationship with the other dimensions, as they are called, of space. The primary problem arises in relation to things which might be going faster than the speed of light, or have other strange properties.

Examination of the Lorentz-Fitzgerald formulas yields the interesting speculation that if something did actually exceed the speed of light it would have its mass expressed as an imaginary number and would seem to be going backwards in time. The barrier to exceeding the speed of light is the apparent need to have an infinite quantity of mass moved at exactly the speed of light. If this situation could be leaped over in a large quantum jump—which seems highly unlikely for masses that are large in normal circumstances—then the other side may be achievable.

The idea of going backwards in time is derived from the existence of a time vector that is negative, although just what this might mean to our senses in the unlikely circumstance of our experiencing this state cannot be conjectured.

There have been, in fact, some observations of particle chambers which have led some scientists to speculate that a particle called the tachyon may exist with the trans-light properties we have just discussed.

The difficulties of imagining and coping with these potential implications of our mathematical models points out the importance of studying alternative methods of notation for advanced physics. Professor Zuckerkandl, in his book *Sound and Symbol*, hypothesizes that it might be better to express the relationships found in quantum mechanics through the use of a notation derived from musical notations. To oversimplify greatly, he argues that music has always given time a special relationship to other factors or parameters or dimensions. Therefore, it might be a more useful language in which to express the relationships in physics where time again has a special role to play, and cannot be treated as just another dimension.

The point of this, or any other alternative to the current methods of describing basic physical processes, is that time does not appear—either by common experience or sophisticated scientific understanding—to be the same sort of dimension or parameter as physical dimensions, and is deserving of completely special treatment, in a system of notation designed to accomplish that goal.

One approach would be to consider time to be a field effect governed by the application of energy to mass—that is to say, by the interaction of different forms of energy, if you wish to keep in mind the equivalence of mass and energy. The movement of any normal sort of mass is bound to produce a field effect that we call positive time. An imaginary mass would produce a negative time field effect. This is not at variance with Einstein's theories, since the "faster" a given mass moves the more energy was applied to it and the greater would be the field effect. The time effects predicted by Einstein and confirmed by

experience are, it seems, consonant with this concept.

17. The "sound" of Professor Zuckerkandl's book title probably refers to
    (A) the music of the spheres
    (B) music in the abstract
    (C) musical notation
    (D) the seemingly musical sounds produced by tachyons
    (E) quantum mechanics

18. The passage supports the inference that
    (A) Einstein's theory of relativity is wrong
    (B) the Lorentz-Fitzgerald formulas contradict Einstein's theories
    (C) time travel is clearly possible
    (D) tachyons do not have the same sort of mass as any other particles
    (E) it is impossible to travel at precisely the speed of light

19. The tone of the passage is
    (A) critical but hopeful
    (B) hopeful but suspicious
    (C) suspicious but speculative
    (D) speculative but hopeful
    (E) impossible to characterize

20. The central idea of the passage can be best described as being which of the following?
    (A) Anomalies in theoretical physics notation permit intriguing hypotheses and indicate the need for refined notation of the time dimension.
    (B) New observations require the development of new theories and new methods of describing the new theories.
    (C) Einsteinian physics can be much improved on in its treatment of tachyons.
    (D) Zuckerkandl's theories of tachyon formation are preferable to Einstein's.
    (E) Time requires a more imaginative approach than tachyons.

21. According to the author, it is too soon to
    (A) call Beethoven a physicist
    (B) adopt proposals such as Zuckerkandl's
    (C) plan for time travel
    (D) study particle chambers for tachyon traces
    (E) attempt to improve current notation

22. It can be inferred that the author sees Zuckerkandl as believing that mathematics is a(n)
    (A) necessary evil
    (B) language
    (C) musical notation
    (D) great hindrance to full understanding of physics
    (E) difficult field of study

23. In the first sentence, the author refers to "philosopher" as well as to "scientist" because
    (A) this is part of a larger work
    (B) philosophers study all things
    (C) physicists get Doctor of Philosophy degrees
    (D) the study of the methods of any field is a philosophical question
    (E) the nature of time is a basic question in philosophy as well as physics

24. When the passage says the "particle called the tachyon may exist," the reader may infer that
    (A) scientists often speak in riddles
    (B) the tachyon was named before it existed
    (C) tachyons are imaginary in existence as well as mass
    (D) the tachyon was probably named when its existence was predicted by theory, but its existence was not yet known
    (E) many scientific ideas may not exist in fact

A legendary island in the Atlantic Ocean beyond the Pillars of Hercules was first mentioned by Plato in the *Timaeus*. Atlantis was a fabulously beautiful and prosperous land, the seat of an empire nine thousand years before Solon. Its inhabitants overran part of Europe and Africa, Athens alone being able to defy them. Because of the impiety of its people, the island was destroyed by an earthquake and inundation. The legend may have existed before Plato and may have sprung from the concept of Homer's Elysium. The possibility that such an island once existed has caused much speculation, resulting in a theory that pre-Columbian civilizations in America were established by colonists from the lost island.

25. The title below that best expresses the ideas of this passage is
    (A) A Persistent Myth
    (B) Geography According to Plato
    (C) The First Discoverers of America
    (D) Buried Civilizations
    (E) A Labor of Hercules

26. According to the passage, we may safely conclude that the inhabitants of Atlantis
    (A) were known personally to Homer
    (B) were ruled by Plato
    (C) were a religious and superstitious people
    (D) used the name Columbus for America
    (E) left no recorded evidence of their civilization

27. According to the legend, Atlantis was destroyed because the inhabitants
    (A) failed to obtain an adequate food supply
    (B) failed to conquer Greece
    (C) failed to respect their gods
    (D) believed in Homer's Elysium
    (E) had become too prosperous

Directions: Each of the following questions consists of a word printed in capital letters, followed by five (5) lettered words or phrases. Select the word or phrase which is most nearly *opposite* to the capitalized word in meaning.

28. RETALIATE:
    (A) maintain serenity
    (B) stand tall
    (C) turn the other cheek
    (D) improve relations with
    (E) entertain the views of

29. ANALYSIS:
    (A) dialysis
    (B) electrolysis
    (C) parenthesis
    (D) synthesis
    (E) emphasis

30. PEREMPTORY:
    (A) humble
    (B) resistant
    (C) weak

(D) spontaneous
(E) deferential

31. SALACIOUS:
    (A) expensive
    (B) wholesome
    (C) empty
    (D) religious
    (E) private

32. INSOLVENT:
    (A) physically pure
    (B) financially stable
    (C) metaphysically correct
    (D) chemically active
    (E) emotionally strong

33. HOMOGENEOUS:
    (A) parsimonious
    (B) consciousness
    (C) variegated
    (D) loquacious
    (E) differential

34. AMALGAMATE:
    (A) recriminate
    (B) procrastinate
    (C) scintillate

(D) segregate
(E) enjoin

35. TEMERITY:
    (A) imbroglio
    (B) diffidence
    (C) cognomen
    (D) effervescence
    (E) composure

36. MUTATION:
    (A) constancy
    (B) decency
    (C) adolescent
    (D) clangorous
    (E) unamended

37. SYBARITIC:
    (A) foolish
    (B) obdurate
    (C) consistent
    (D) austere
    (E) conservative

38. PROSAIC:
    (A) fulsome
    (B) mundane
    (C) extraordinary
    (D) certain
    (E) gregarious

STOP

END OF SECTION. IF YOU HAVE ANY TIME LEFT, GO
OVER YOUR WORK IN THIS SECTION ONLY. DO NOT
WORK IN ANY OTHER SECTION OF THE TEST.

SECTION II

30 minutes
38 questions

Directions: Each of the questions below contains one or more blank spaces, each blank indicating an omitted word. Each sentence is followed by five (5) lettered words or sets of words. Read and determine the general sense of each sentence. Then choose the word or set of words which, when inserted in the sentence, best fits the meaning of the sentence.

1. The professor _____ contemporary journalism for being too _____.
   - (A) berated—childish
   - (B) lauded—voyeuristic
   - (C) criticized—authentic
   - (D) requited—responsible
   - (E) attacked—important

2. Rattling his newspaper to show his _____, the husband made known his _____ of his wife's new breakfast table.
   - (A) calm—disposition
   - (B) irritation—approval
   - (C) duplicity—ingenuousness
   - (D) anger—disapproval
   - (E) opinion—character

3. His remarks were _____ and _____, indicative of his keen and incisive mind.
   - (A) unsentimental—deliberate
   - (B) ingenuous—noteworthy
   - (C) impartial—apolitical
   - (D) trenchant—penetrating
   - (E) apish—dramatic

4. The _____ of this poisonous algae has caused the _____ of many kinds of fish.
   - (A) proliferation—exodus
   - (B) genesis—genocide
   - (C) vagrancy—death
   - (D) affects—loss
   - (E) morality—decline

5. The new machine failed to _____ the garbage; as a result, the kitchen was filled to bursting with smelly leftovers.
   - (A) expand
   - (B) compact
   - (C) produce
   - (D) criticize
   - (E) procrastinate

6. According to legend, Daniel Webster made a _____ with Satan, but managed to talk his way out of it at the last moment.
   - (A) economy
   - (B) standard
   - (C) trawler
   - (D) van
   - (E) compact

7. When her purse fell overboard, Sally lost her _____, keys, wallet, and cigarettes.
   - (A) vehicle
   - (B) piano
   - (C) compact
   - (D) compost
   - (E) complexion

Directions: In each of the following questions, you are given a related pair of words or phrases in capital letters. Each capitalized pair is followed by five (5) lettered pairs of words or phrases. Choose the pair which best expresses a relationship similar to that expressed by the original pair.

8. MORALITY : LEGALITY ::
   - (A) home : court
   - (B) man : law
   - (C) mayoralty : gubernatorial
   - (D) priest : jury
   - (E) sin : crime

9. ELLIPSE : CURVE ::
   - (A) stutter : speech
   - (B) triangle : base
   - (C) revolution : distance
   - (D) square : polygon
   - (E) circumference : ball

10. SUGAR : SACCHARIN ::
   - (A) candy : cake

    (B) hog : lard
    (C) cane : sugar
    (D) spice : pepper
    (E) butter : margarine

11. REQUEST : ORDER ::
    (A) reply : respond
    (B) regard : reject
    (C) suggest : require
    (D) wish : crave
    (E) measure : ecstasy

12. WATER : FAUCET ::
    (A) fuel : throttle
    (B) liquid : solid
    (C) kitchen : sink
    (D) steam : pipe
    (E) leak : lumber

13. FLASK : BOTTLE ::
    (A) whiskey : milk
    (B) metal : glass
    (C) powder : liquid
    (D) quart : pint
    (E) brochure : tome

14. CALIBER : RIFLE ::
    (A) quality : shoot
    (B) compass : bore
    (C) army : navy
    (D) gauge : rails
    (E) cavalry : infantry

15. CHOP : MINCE ::
    (A) fry : bake
    (B) meat : cake
    (C) axe : mallet
    (D) cut : walk
    (E) stir : beat

16. PECCADILLO : CRIME ::
    (A) district attorney : criminal
    (B) hesitate : procrastinate
    (C) armadillo : shield
    (D) bushel : peck
    (E) sheriff : jail

Directions: Below each of the following passages, you will find questions or incomplete statements about the passage. Each statement or question is followed by lettered words or expressions. Select the word or expression that most satisfactorily completes each statement or answers each question in accordance with the meaning of the passage. After you have chosen the best answer, blacken the corresponding space on the answer sheet.

The vegetative forms of most bacteria are killed by drying in air, although the different species exhibit pronounced differences in their resistance. The tubercle bacillus is one of the more resistant, and vibrio cholera is one of the more sensitive to drying. In general, the encapsulated organisms are more resistant than the non-encapsulated forms. Spores are quite resistant to drying; the spores of the anthrax bacillus, for example, will germinate after remaining in a dry condition for ten years or more. The resistance of the pathogenic forms causing disease of the upper respiratory tract is of particular interest in connection with airborne infection, for the length of time that a droplet remains infective is a result, primarily, of the resistance of the particular microorganism to drying.

17. The passage uses the term "vegetative forms" to refer to
    (A) plants that infest human habitations
    (B) the growing stage of the bacteria as opposed to the dormant stage
    (C) the fact that bacteria are really vegetables
    (D) the similarities between some bacteria and most vegetables
    (E) the difficulty in classifying the types of bacteria

18. According to the passage, the risk of infection from airborne microorganisms would likely be greater during a(n)
    (A) heat wave
    (B) ice storm
    (C) windless period
    (D) time of high humidity
    (E) shortage of fuel oil

19. It may be inferred from the passage that
    (A) bacteria can be most easily killed by removal of moisture
    (B) drying out a house will eliminate the risk of airborne infection

    (C)   hot-air heating is better than steam heating because steam heating uses water

    (D)   spores are incapable of producing bacteria

    (E)   none of the above

20.   Tuberculosis is highly infectious because

    (A)   an airborne disease of the upper respiratory tract is easily spread to those coming in contact with a patient

    (B)   droplets of sputum remain infective for a long time due to the resistance of the organisms to drying

    (C)   spores are resistant to drying

    (D)   the causative organism is encapsulated

    (E)   none of these

Foods are overwhelmingly the most advertised group of all consumer products in the United States. Food products lead in expenditures for network and spot television advertisements, discount coupons, trading stamps, contests, and other forms of premium advertising. In other media—newspapers, magazines, newspaper supplements, billboards, and radio—food advertising expenditures rank near the top. Food manufacturers spend more on advertising than any other manufacturing group, and the nation's grocery stores rank first among all retailers.

Throughout the 1970's, highly processed foods have accounted for the bulk of total advertising. Almost all coupons, electronic advertising, national printed media advertising, consumer premiums (other than trading stamps) as well as most push promotion come from processed and packaged food products. In 1978, breakfast cereals, soft drinks, candy and other desserts, oils and salad dressings, coffee, and prepared foods accounted for only an estimated 20 percent of the consumer food dollar. Yet these items accounted for about one-half of all media advertising.

By contrast, highly perishable foods such as unprocessed meats, poultry, fish and eggs, fruits and vegetables, and dairy products accounted for over half of the consumer food-at-home dollar. Yet these products accounted for less than 8 percent of national media advertising in 1978, and virtually no discount coupons. These products tend to be most heavily advertised by the retail sector in local newspapers, where they account for an estimated 40 percent of retail grocery newspaper ads.

When measured against total food-at-home expenditures, total measured food advertising accounts for between 3 and 3.7 cents out of every dollar spent on food in the nation's grocery stores. A little less than one cent of this amount is accounted for by electronic advertising (mostly television) while incentives account for 0.6 cents. The printed media accounts for 0.5 cents and about one-third of one cent is comprised of discount coupon redemptions. The estimate for the cost of push promotion ranges from 0.7 to 1.4 cents. This range is necessary because of the difficulty in separating nonpromotional aspects of direct selling—transportation, technical, and other related services.

Against this gross consumer cost must be weighed the joint products or services provided by advertising. In the case of electronic advertising, the consumer who views commercial television receives entertainment, while readers of magazines and newspapers receive reduced prices on these publications. The consumer pays directly for some premiums, but also receives nonfood merchandise as an incentive to purchase the product. The "benefits" must, therefore, be subtracted from the gross cost to the consumer to fully assess the net cost of advertising.

Also significant are the impacts of advertising on food demand, nutrition, and competition among food manufacturers. The bulk of manufacturers' advertising is concentrated on a small portion of consumer food products. Has advertising changed the consumption of these highly processed products relative to more perishable foods such as meats, produce, and dairy products? Has the nutritional content of U.S. food consumption been influenced by food advertising? Has competition among manufacturers and retailers been enhanced or weakened by advertising? These are important questions and warrant continued research.

21.   The author's attitude toward advertising can be characterized as

    (A)   admiring

    (B)   condemning

    (C)   uncertain

    (D)   ambivalent

    (E)   inquisitive

22.   As used in the passage, the term "push promotion" means

    (A)   coupon redemption

(B) retail advertising
(C) advertising in trade journals
(D) direct selling
(E) none of the above

23. The author implies that advertising costs
   (A) are greater for restaurants than for at-home foods
   (B) should be discounted by the benefits of advertising to the consumer
   (C) are much higher in the United States than anywhere else in the world
   (D) for prepared foods are considerably higher than for natural foods for all media
   (E) cause highly processed foods to outsell unprocessed, fresh foods

24. The purpose of the article is to
   (A) warn about rising food advertising costs
   (B) let experts see how overextended food advertising has become
   (C) describe the costs of food advertising and the issues yet to be understood about its effects
   (D) congratulate the food industry on its effective advertising
   (E) calculate the final balance sheet for food advertising

25. All of the following are stated or implied to be important topics for further research EXCEPT
   (A) effects of advertising on food and nutrient consumption patterns
   (B) effects of advertising on food manufacturer competitive patterns
   (C) effects of advertising on meat consumption patterns
   (D) effects of advertising on out-of-home eating patterns
   (E) effects of advertising on "junk" food consumption patterns

26. According to the passage, all of the following are definitely false EXCEPT
   (A) more food is advertised in newspapers than on television
   (B) less money is spent advertising food than automobiles
   (C) more of the food advertising budget is

spent on push promotion than on television ads
   (D) less money is spent on food store advertising than on clothing store ads
   (E) food advertising is the leading group in radio advertising

27. If it were discovered that the nutritional content of the U.S. food supply were degraded by the advertising of highly processed foods and such advertising was totally banned, which of the following possible result of the ban could be inferred from the passage?
   (A) The subscription costs of publications might rise.
   (B) The cost of cable television might rise.
   (C) The cost of free television might rise.
   (D) Fewer consumers would watch certain television shows.
   (E) No possible effect can be forecast based on the passage.

Directions: Each of the following questions consists of a word printed in capital letters, followed by five (5) lettered words or phrases. Select the word or phrase that is most nearly *opposite* to the capitalized word in meaning.

28. INTRANSIGENT:
   (A) impassable
   (B) conciliatory
   (C) harsh
   (D) fly-by-night
   (E) corroborative

29. INGENUOUS:
   (A) granite-like
   (B) slow-witted
   (C) talented
   (D) devious
   (E) humanitarian

30. CANARD:
   (A) rebuttal
   (B) truth
   (C) image
   (D) flattery
   (E) blasphemy

31. DISINTERESTED:
   (A) opposed
   (B) avid

(C) superficial
(D) related
(E) partial

32. PROPITIATE:
    (A) anger
    (B) depart
    (C) hurt
    (D) applaud
    (E) promote

33. ABSOLVE:
    (A) muddy
    (B) blame
    (C) free
    (D) repent
    (E) recant

34. HEDONIST:
    (A) female
    (B) martinet
    (C) scientist
    (D) intellectual
    (E) puritan

35. CRETIN:
    (A) moron

(B) seer
(C) genius
(D) scholar
(E) talent

36. DECANT:
    (A) level off
    (B) upset greatly
    (C) tap
    (D) slosh out
    (E) cork firmly

37. ARRANT:
    (A) humble
    (B) deceptive
    (C) partial
    (D) wise
    (E) intrepid

38. WASTREL:
    (A) conservator
    (B) prodigal
    (C) lutist
    (D) noble
    (E) phantasm

STOP

END OF SECTION. IF YOU HAVE ANY TIME LEFT, GO
OVER YOUR WORK IN THIS SECTION ONLY. DO NOT
WORK IN ANY OTHER SECTION OF THE TEST.

SECTION III

30 minutes
30 questions

Directions: For each of the following questions two quantities are given, one in Column A and one in Column B. Compare the two quantities and mark your answer sheet with the correct lettered conclusion. These are your options:
   A: If the quantity in column A is the greater;
   B: if the quantity in Column B is the greater;
   C: if the two quantities are equal;
   D: if the relationship cannot be determined from the information given.
Common Information: In any question, information applying to both columns is centered between the columns and above the quantities in columns A and B. The common information applies to both columns. Any symbol that appears in both columns represents the same idea or quantity in both columns.

Numbers: All numbers used are real numbers.

Figures: Assume that the positions of points, angles, regions and so forth are in the order shown. Figures are assumed to lie in a plane unless otherwise indicated. Figures accompanying questions are intended to provide information you can use in answering the questions. However, unless a note states that a figure is drawn to scale, you should solve the problems by using your knowledge of mathematics and *not* by estimating sizes by sight or measurement.

Lines: Assume that lines shown as straight are indeed straight.

	COLUMN A	COLUMN B
1.	5% of 36	36% of 5
2.	$\sqrt{15}$	$\sqrt{5} + \sqrt{10}$

3.
$$(346 \times 23) + p = 34{,}731$$
$$(346 \times 23) + q = 35{,}124$$

	p	q

4.

$$x° < y°$$
PQRS is a rectangle

	PT	TQ

5.
$$x > 0$$

	x^2	$2x$

	COLUMN A	COLUMN B
6.	$\dfrac{4}{5} - \dfrac{3}{4}$	$\dfrac{1}{20}$
7.	the ratio 3:13	the ratio 13:51

8.
Let S_n be defined by the equation:
$$S_n = 3n + 2$$

	$S_5 + S_4$	$S_9 + S_8$

	COLUMN A	COLUMN B
9.	the cost of ten pounds of meat at $2.50 per pound.	the cost of five kilograms of meat at $5.00 per kilogram.
10.	$\dfrac{10}{10{,}000}$	$\dfrac{1000}{1{,}000{,}000}$

COLUMN A   COLUMN B

11.

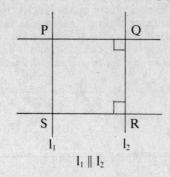

$$l_1 \parallel l_2$$

$$\overline{PQ} \qquad\qquad \overline{QR}$$

12. the number of pears in   the number of potatoes
     a cubical box with   in a cubical box with
     a side of 24 inches   a side of 36 inches

13. $4x^2 + 3x + 2x^2 + 2x = 3x^2 + 2x + 3x^2 + 2x + 3$

            x^2 9

14. $n \cdot 1 \cdot 1$ $n + 1 + 1$

15.

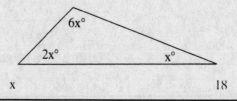

Directions: For each of the following questions, select the best of the answer choices and blacken the corresponding space on your answer sheet.

Numbers: All numbers used are real numbers.

Figures: The diagrams and figures that accompany these questions are for the purpose of providing information useful in answering the question. Unless it is stated that a specific figure is not drawn to scale, the diagrams and figures are drawn as accurately as possible. All figures are in a plane unless otherwise indicated.

16. From the time 6:15 P.M. to the time 7:45 P.M. of the same day, the minute hand of a standard clock describes an arc of
    (A)   30°
    (B)   90°
    (C)   180°

    (D)   540°
    (E)   910°

17. Which of the following fractions is the LEAST?
    (A) $\frac{7}{8}$
    (B) $\frac{7}{12}$
    (C) $\frac{8}{9}$
    (D) $\frac{1}{2}$
    (E) $\frac{6}{17}$

18. The length of each side of a square is $\frac{3x}{4} + 1$.
What is the perimeter of the square?
    (A) $x + 1$
    (B) $3x + 1$

(C) 3x + 4

(D) $\frac{9}{16}x^2 + \frac{3}{2}x + 1$

(E) It cannot be determined from the information given.

19. A truck departed from Newton at 11:53 A.M. and arrived in Far City, 240 miles away, at 4:41 P.M. on the same day. What was the approximate average speed of the truck on this trip?

(A) $\frac{5640}{5}$ MPH

(B) $\frac{16}{1200}$ MPH

(C) 50 MPH

(D) $\frac{240}{288}$ MPH

(E) $\frac{1494}{240}$ MPH

20. If m, n, o and p are real numbers, each of the following expressions equals m(nop) EXCEPT

(A) (op)(mn)
(B) ponm
(C) p(onm)
(D) (mp)(no)
(E) (mn)(mo)(mp)

Questions 21–25 are based on the following graphs:

US PLANE CRASHES

(Total passenger-miles in billions)

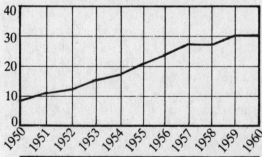

(Deaths per 100 million passenger-miles)

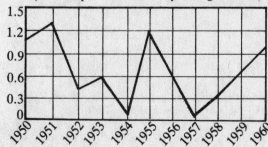

21. Which of the following conclusions may be inferred from the graphs?

   I.   The highest rate of passenger deaths per mile travelled during the period covered by the graphs occurred in 1951.
   II. The largest yearly increase in deaths per mile travelled occurred in the period 1954 to 1955.
   III. The rate of passenger deaths per mile travelled was approximately the same in both 1954 and 1957.

(A) I only
(B) II only
(C) I and II only
(D) III only
(E) I, II, and III

22. In which year did the longest uninterrupted period of increase in the rate of passenger deaths per mile travelled finally end?
(A) 1951
(B) 1953
(C) 1955
(D) 1957
(E) 1960

23. How many fatalities were reported in the year 1955?
(A) 240
(B) 2000
(C) 240,000
(D) 1.2 million
(E) 20 billion

24. The greatest number of fatalities were recorded in which year?
(A) 1960
(B) 1957
(C) 1955
(D) 1953
(E) 1951

25. In which year did the greatest number of passengers travel by air?
(A) 1960
(B) 1955
(C) 1953
(D) 1951
(E) Cannot be determined from the information given.

ABCD is a square

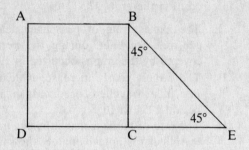

26. If the area of the triangle BCE is 8, what is the area of the square ABCD?
    (A) 16
    (B) 82
    (C) 8
    (D) 4
    (E) 22

27. The diagonal of the floor of a rectangular closet is $7\frac{1}{2}$ feet. The shorter side of the closet is $4\frac{1}{2}$ feet. What is the area of the closet in square feet?
    (A) 37
    (B) 27
    (C) $\frac{54}{4}$
    (D) $\frac{21}{4}$
    (E) 5

28. If the ratio of women to men in a meeting is 4 to 1, what percent of the persons in the meeting are men?
    (A) 20%
    (B) 25%
    (C) $33\frac{1}{3}\%$
    (D) 80%
    (E) 100%

29. Which of the following fractions expressed in the form $\frac{p}{q}$ is most nearly approximated by the decimal .PQ, where P is the tenths' digit and Q is the hundredths' digit?
    (A) $\frac{1}{8}$
    (B) $\frac{2}{9}$
    (C) $\frac{3}{4}$
    (D) $\frac{4}{5}$
    (E) $\frac{8}{9}$

30. If b books can be purchased for d dollars, how many books can be purchased for m dollars?
    (A) $\frac{bm}{d}$
    (B) bdm
    (C) $\frac{d}{bm}$
    (D) $\frac{b+m}{d}$
    (E) $\frac{b-m}{d}$

STOP

END OF SECTION. IF YOU HAVE ANY TIME LEFT, GO OVER YOUR WORK IN THIS SECTION ONLY. DO NOT WORK IN ANY OTHER SECTION OF THE TEST.

SECTION IV

30 minutes
30 questions

Directions: For each of the following questions two quantities are given, one in Column A and one in Column B. Compare the two quantities and mark your answer sheet with the correct lettered conclusion. These are your options:

A: If the quantity in Column A is the greater;
B: if the quantity in Column B is the greater;
C: if the two quantities are equal;
D: if the relationship cannot be determined from the information given.

Common Information: In any question, information applying to both columns is centered between the columns and above the quantities in columns A and B. The common information applies to both columns. Any symbol that appears in both columns represents the same idea or quantity in both columns.

Numbers: All numbers used are real numbers.

Figures: Assume that the position of points, angles, regions and so forth are in the order shown. Figures are assumed to lie in a plane unless otherwise indicated. Figures accompanying questions are intended to provide information you can use in answering the questions. However, unless a note states that a figure is drawn to scale, you should solve the problems by using your knowledge of mathematics and *not* by estimating sizes by sight or measurement.

Lines: Assume that lines shown as straight are indeed straight.

	COLUMN A	COLUMN B
1.	the number of hours in 7 days	the number of days in 24 weeks
2.	35% of 60	60% of 35

3.

PLAYER	AGE
Tom	30
Juanita	35
Brooke	28
Glenda	40
Marcia	22
Dwight	24

	COLUMN A	COLUMN B
	Tom's age	Average (arithmetic mean) age of the six players

4.
$$4 < m < 6$$
$$5 < n < 7$$

	COLUMN A	COLUMN B
	m	n

5.
A square region, P, and a rectangular region, Q, both have areas of 64.

	COLUMN A	COLUMN B
	length of a side of P	length of Q if its width is 4

6.
$$x > 0$$

	COLUMN A	COLUMN B
	$3x^3$	$(3x)^3$

7.
$$x \cdot y = 1$$
$$x \neq 0, y \neq 0$$

	COLUMN A	COLUMN B
	x	y

COLUMN A   COLUMN B

8.

the number of primes
of which 11 is an
integer multiple

the number of primes
of which 13 is an
integer multiple

9.

x, y, and z are consecutive positive
integers, not necessarily in that
order, and x and z are odd

xy   yz

10.

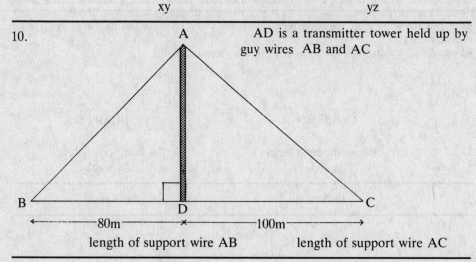

AD is a transmitter tower held up by
guy wires AB and AC

length of support wire AB   length of support wire AC

11.   2468 $8 + 6 \cdot 10 + 4 \cdot 10^2 + 2 \cdot 10^3$

12.

$$a^2 = b$$
$$a > 0$$

$\dfrac{2a}{b}$ $a \cdot a$

13.

l_1

$4x°$ $(x + 30)°$

l_2

x   10

14.

A family-size box of cereal contains
10 ounces more and costs 80¢ more
than the regular size box of cereal.

cost per ounce of the cereal
in the family-size box   8¢

COLUMN A   COLUMN B

15.   the number of different duos which can be formed from a group of 5 people   the number of different trios which can be formed from a group of 5 people

---

Directions: For each of the following questions, select the best of the answer choices and blacken the corresponding space on your answer sheet.

Numbers: All numbers used are real numbers.

Figures: The diagrams and figures that accompany these questions are for the purpose of providing information useful in answering the questions. Unless it is stated that a specific figure is not drawn to scale, the diagrams and figures are drawn as accurately as possible. All figures are in a plane unless otherwise indicated.

16. If $x = 3$ and $y = 2$, then $2x + 3y =$
    (A) 5
    (B) 10
    (C) 12
    (D) 14
    (E) 15

17. If the profit on an item is $4 and the sum of the cost and the profit is $20, what is the cost of the item?
    (A) $24
    (B) $20
    (C) $16
    (D) $12
    (E) Cannot be determined from the information given.

18. In 1950, the number of students enrolled at a college was 500. In 1970, the number of students enrolled at the college was $2\frac{1}{2}$ times as great as that in 1950. What was the number of students enrolled at the college in 1970?
    (A) 1250
    (B) 1000
    (C) 1750
    (D) 500
    (E) 250

19. If n is an integer between 0 and 100, then any of the following could be $3n + 3$ EXCEPT
    (A) 300
    (B) 297

(C) 208
(D) 63
(E) 6

20. A figure that can be folded over along a straight line so that the result is two equal halves which are then lying on top of one another with no overlap is said to have a line of symmetry. Which of the following figures has only one line of symmetry?
    (A) square
    (B) circle
    (C) equilateral triangle
    (D) isosceles triangle
    (E) rectangle

21. A laborer is paid $8 per hour for an 8-hour day and $1\frac{1}{2}$ times that rate for each hour in excess of 8 hours in a single day. If the laborer received $80 for a single day's work, how long did he work on that day?
    (A) 6 hr. 40 min.
    (B) 9 hr. 20 min.
    (C) 9 hr. 30 min.
    (D) 9 hr. 40 min.
    (E) 10 hr.

Questions 22–25 are based on the graphs on page 252.

22. According to the graphs, approximately how much money belonging to the investment portfolio was invested in high-risk stocks?
    (A) $95,000
    (B) $89,000
    (C) $50,000
    (D) $42,000
    (E) $36,000

23. Approximately how much money belonging to the investment portfolio was invested in state-issued bonds?
    (A) $260,000
    (B) $125,000
    (C) $34,000

INVESTMENT PORTFOLIO

Total Investment Profile

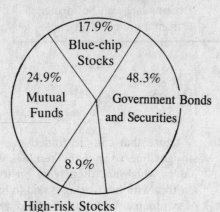

$1,080,192 = 100%

Government Bonds and Securities

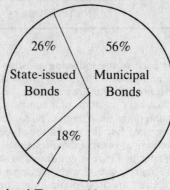

Municipal Bonds

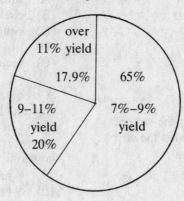

(D) $26,000
(E) $500

24. Which of the following was the greatest?
    (A) the amount of money invested in municipal bonds which yielded between 7% and 9%
    (B) the amount of money invested in municipal bonds which yielded over 9%
    (C) the amount of money invested in federal treasury notes
    (D) the amount of money invested in state-issued bonds
    (E) the amount of money invested in high-risk stocks

25. Which of the following earned the least amount of money for the investment portfolio?
    (A) municipal bonds
    (B) state-issued bonds

(C) government bonds and securities
(D) mutual funds
(E) Cannot be determined from the information given.

26. A vertex of square MNOP is located at the center of circle O. If arc NP is 4π units long, then the perimeter of the square MNOP is
    (A) 32
    (B) 32π
    (C) 64
    (D) 64π

(E) Cannot be determined from the information given.

27. How many minutes will it take to completely fill a water tank with a capacity of 3750 cubic feet if the water is being pumped into the tank at the rate of 800 cubic feet per minute and is being drained out of the tank at the rate of 300 cubic feet per minute?
   (A) 3 min. 36 sec
   (B) 6 minutes
   (C) 7 min. 30 sec.
   (D) 8 minutes
   (E) 1875 minutes

28. Paul is standing 180 yards due north of point P. Franny is standing 240 yards due west of point P. What is the shortest distance between Franny and Paul?
   (A) 60 yards
   (B) 300 yards
   (C) 420 yards
   (D) 900 yards
   (E) 9000 yards

29. If a rectangle has an area of $81x^2$ and a length of 27x, then what is its width?
   (A) 3x
   (B) 9x
   (C) $3x^2$
   (D) $9x^2$
   (E) $2128x^3$

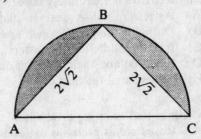

30. Triangle ABC is inscribed in a semicircle. What is the area of the shaded region above?
   (A) $2\pi - 2$
   (B) $2\pi - 4$
   (C) $4\pi - 4$
   (D) $8\pi - 4$
   (E) $8\pi - 8$

STOP

END OF SECTION. IF YOU HAVE ANY TIME LEFT, GO OVER YOUR WORK IN THIS SECTION ONLY. DO NOT WORK IN ANY OTHER SECTION OF THE TEST.

SECTION V

30 minutes
25 questions

Directions: Each of the following questions or groups of questions is based on a short passage or a set of propositions. In answering these questions it may sometimes be helpful to draw a simple picture or chart. When you have selected the best answer to each question, darken the corresponding circle on your answer sheet.

Questions 1–5

Asters are not as pretty as lilacs and don't smell as nice as either lilacs or daffodils.

Daffodils are prettier than lilacs, but don't smell as nice.

Irises are not as pretty as lilacs and don't smell as nice as daffodils or roses.

Lilacs are prettier than roses, but don't smell as nice.

1. Which of the following statements is neither definitely true nor definitely false?
   (A) Asters are not as pretty as lilacs.
   (B) Daffodils are prettier than asters.
   (C) Irises smell better than asters.
   (D) Lilacs do not smell as nice as daffodils.
   (E) Roses smell the best of all.

2. Which of the following is definitely true?
   (A) Roses are as pretty as daffodils.
   (B) Lilacs are as pretty as daffodils.
   (C) Irises are prettier than asters.
   (D) Daffodils do not smell as nice as irises.
   (E) Asters don't smell as nice as roses.

3. If irises are prettier than roses, then they are definitely prettier than which of the following?
   (A) asters only
   (B) daffodils only
   (C) lilacs only
   (D) asters and roses only
   (E) cannot be determined

4. Which of the following are both prettier and better smelling than asters?

   I. daffodils
   II. irises
   III. roses

   (A) I only
   (B) II only
   (C) III only
   (D) I and II only
   (E) I and III only

5. If dahlias are prettier than asters but do not smell as nice, then
   (A) dahlias might smell better than irises
   (B) dahlias might smell better than daffodils
   (C) dahlias might smell better than roses
   (D) dahlias cannot be prettier than lilacs
   (E) dahlias cannot be prettier than roses

Questions 6–8

PRO-ABORTION SPEAKER: Those who oppose abortion upon demand make the foundation of their arguments the sanctity of human life, but this seeming bedrock assumption is actually as weak as shifting sand. And it is not necessary to invoke the red herring that many anti-abortion speakers would allow that human life must sometimes be sacrificed for a greater good, as in the fighting of a just war. There are counter-examples to the principle of the sanctity of life which are even more embarrassing to pro-life advocates. It would be possible to reduce the annual number of traffic fatalities to virtually zero by passing federal legislation mandating a nationwide fifteen-mile-per-hour speed limit on *all* roads. You see, implicitly we have always been willing to trade off quantity of human life for quality.

ANTI-ABORTION SPEAKER: The analogy my opponent draws between abortion and traffic fatalities is weak. No one would propose such a speed limit. Imagine people trying to get to and from work under such a law, or imagine them trying to visit a friend or relatives outside their own neighborhoods, or taking in a sports event or a movie. Obviously such a law would be a disaster.

6. Which of the following best characterizes the anti-abortion speaker's response to the pro-abortion speaker?
   (A) His analysis of the traffic fatalities case actually supports the argument of the pro-abortion speaker.
   (B) His analysis of the traffic fatalities case is an effective rebuttal of the pro-abortion argument.
   (C) His response provides a strong affirmative statement of the anti-abortionist position.
   (D) His response is totally irrelevant to the issue raised by the pro-abortion speaker.
   (E) His counter-argument attacks the character of the pro-abortion speaker instead of the merits of his argument.

7. Which of the following represents the most logical continuation of the reasoning contained in the pro-abortion speaker's argument?
   (A) Therefore, we should not have any

laws on the books to protect human life.

(B) We can only conclude that the anti-abortionist is also in favor of strengthening enforcement of existing traffic regulations as a means of reducing the number of traffic fatalities each year.

(C) So the strongest attack on the anti-abortionist position is that he contradicts himself when he agrees that we should fight a just war even at the risk of considerable loss of human life.

(D) Even the laws against contraception are good examples of this tendency.

(E) The abortion question just makes explicit that which for long has remained hidden from view.

8. In his argument, the pro-abortionist makes which of the following assumptions?

  I. It is not a proper goal of a society to protect human life.
  II. The human fetus is not a human life.
  III. The trade-off between the number of human lives and the quality of those lives is appropriately decided by society.

(A) I only
(B) II only
(C) I and II only
(D) III only
(E) I, II, and III

Questions 9–12

The streets of Mainville are laid out regularly, with all roads and all drives parallel to each other. All the streets and all the avenues are also parallel to each other, and they are perpendicular to the roads and drives.

Magnolia Parkway runs from the intersection of Apple Street and Zinnia Drive to the intersection of Blueberry Avenue and Hyacinth Road.

Abbot Causeway is perpendicular to Magnolia Parkway.

9. Which of the following must be true?
(A) Magnolia Parkway is parallel to Maple Street.
(B) Magnolia Parkway is perpendicular to Maple Street.

(C) Magnolia Parkway intersects Maple Street.
(D) Magnolia Parkway does not intersect Maple Street.
(E) None of the above.

10. Which of the following must be false?
(A) Abbot Causeway is not parallel to Yellowstone Road.
(B) Abbot Causeway is not perpendicular to Oak Street.
(C) Melody Drive crosses Petunia Street.
(D) Melody Drive crosses Fanfare Road.
(E) Fanfare Road does not cross Petunia Street.

11. If all roads are laid out north to south and all of the streets are laid out east to west, which of the following is possible?

  I. Magnolia Parkway runs from northwest to southeast.
  II. Zinnia Drive runs east to west.
  III. Apple Street intersects Hyacinth Road.

(A) I only
(B) II only
(C) III only
(D) I and III only
(E) I, II, and III

12. If all of the blocks formed by roads, streets, avenues, and drives are one-quarter of a mile on a side, which of the following must be true?
(A) Magnolia Parkway is more than one-quarter of a mile in length.
(B) Apple Street is more than one-quarter of a mile in length.
(C) Hyacinth Road is less than one-quarter of a mile in length.
(D) All the streets and avenues are the same length.
(E) None of the roads and drives are the same length.

Questions 13–17

A construction company is building a pre-fabricated structure which requires specialized crane operators for five different parts of the job. Six operators are available: R, S, T, U, V, and W, and each phase will take one day and will be done by a single operator. Though an operator may do more than one phase of the job, no operator will work two days in a row.

Both R and S can handle any phase of the job.
T can work only on days immediately following days on which S has worked.
U can work only the days that T can.
V can only work on the third and fifth days of the job.
W can only work on the fourth day of the job.

13. Which of the following are true?

   I.   R could do up to three of the phases of the job.
   II.   S could do up to three of the phases of the job.
   III.   T could do no more than two of the phases of the job.

(A) I only
(B) II only
(C) III only
(D) II and III only
(E) I, II, and III

14. If S works the first day of the job, which of the following are true?

   I.   Only T or U can work the second day.
   II.   T, U, or R could work the second day.
   III.   R, S, or W could work the third day.

(A) I only
(B) II only
(C) III only
(D) I and III only
(E) I, II, and III

15. If R works the first day, which of the following are true?

   I.   S must work the second day.
   II.   S cannot work the third day.
   III.   Only T, U, or V can work on the third day.

(A) I only
(B) II only
(C) I and II only
(D) I and III only
(E) I, II, and III

16. If R works on both the first and third days, which of the following most accurately describes the possibilities on the fourth day?
(A) Only S is eligible to work.
(B) Only R, S, T, and W are eligible to work.
(C) Only S and W are eligible to work.
(D) Only R, S, and W are eligible to work.
(E) Only S, T, U and W are eligible to work.

17. R, S, and V do not work on the third day; therefore,
(A) R worked on the first day.
(B) Only S can work on the fourth day.
(C) Only R can work on the fourth day.
(D) Only W can work on the fourth day.
(E) Either T or U worked on the second day.

Questions 18–22

The parties to an important labor negotiation are two representatives of management, Morrison and Nelson; two representatives of labor, Richards and Smith; and the Federal Mediator, Jones. They are meeting at a round table with eight seats, and the order of seating has become a significant psychological part of the negotiations.

   I.   The two representatives of management always sit next to each other.
   II.   The two representatives of labor always sit with one seat between them.
   III.   Both sides like to make sure that they are as close to the mediator as the other side is, and no closer to the opposing side than necessary.
   IV.   The mediator prefers to have at least one seat between himself and any of the other negotiators.

18. If conditions I, II, and IV are met, which of the following is necessarily true?
(A) Jones sits next to one of the management representatives.
(B) Morrison sits next to one of the labor representatives.
(C) One of the labor representatives will sit next to either Morrison or Nelson.
(D) Either Richards or Smith sits next to Jones.
(E) None of the above is necessarily true.

19. If conditions I, II, and III are met, which of the following is NOT a possible seating arrangement of the negotiators, starting with Jones and going clockwise around the table?
    (A) Jones, Morrison, Nelson, empty, empty, Richards, empty, Smith
    (B) Jones, Nelson, Morrison, empty, empty, Smith, empty, Richards
    (C) Jones, Richards, empty, Smith, empty, empty, Nelson, Morrison
    (D) Jones, Smith, Richards, empty, empty, empty, Morrison, Nelson
    (E) All of the above are possible seating arrangements.

20. The Secretary of Labor joins the negotiations and sits across the table from the mediator. If all of the conditions are still met as much as possible, which of the following is true?

    I. A labor representative will sit next to the secretary.
    II. A management representative will sit next to the secretary.
    III. Both a labor representative and one from management will sit next to the mediator.

    (A) I only
    (B) II only
    (C) I and II only
    (D) I and III only
    (E) I, II, and III

21. If the two sides meet without the mediator and sit so that Morrison is seated directly opposite Smith, which of the following is possible?
    (A) Richards and Nelson will both be seated to Morrison's left and to Smith's right.
    (B) Richards will be as close to Morrison as he is to Smith.
    (C) Nelson will be separated from Richards by one seat.
    (D) Nelson will be separated from Smith by three seats.
    (E) Nelson and Richards will be seated directly across from each other.

22. If, under the original conditions, Morrison's aide joins the negotiations and sits next to Morrison, which of the following is not possible?
    (A) Richards sits directly opposite Morrison.
    (B) Richards sits directly opposite Morrison's aide.
    (C) Smith sits directly opposite Nelson.
    (D) Smith sits directly opposite Morrison's aide.
    (E) **Morrison's aide sits next to Jones.**

23. All high-powered racing engines have stochastic fuel injection. Stochastic fuel injection is not a feature which is normally included in the engines of production-line vehicles.

Passenger sedans are production-line vehicles.

Which of the following conclusions can be drawn from these statements?
    (A) Passenger sedans do not usually have stochastic fuel injection.
    (B) Stochastic fuel injection is found only in high-powered racing cars.
    (C) Car manufacturers do not include stochastic fuel injection in passenger cars because they fear accidents.
    (D) Purchasers of passenger cars do not normally purchase stochastic fuel injection because it is expensive.
    (E) Some passenger sedans are high-powered racing vehicles.

24. CLARENCE: Mary is one of the most important executives at the Trendy Cola Company.
    PETER: How can that be? I know for a fact that Mary drinks only Hobart Cola.

Peter's statement implies that he believes that
    (A) Hobart Cola is a subsidiary of Trendy Cola
    (B) Mary is an unimportant employee of Hobart Cola
    (C) all cola drinks taste pretty much alike
    (D) an executive uses only that company's products
    (E) Hobart is a better-tasting cola than Trendy

25. Current motion pictures give children a distorted view of the world. Animated features depict animals as loyal friends, compassionate creatures, and tender souls, while "spaghetti Westerns" portray men and women as deceitful and treacherous, cruel and wanton, hard and uncaring. Thus, children are taught to value animals more highly than other human beings.

Which of the following, if true, would weaken the author's conclusion?

I. Children are not allowed to watch "spaghetti Westerns."

II. The producers of animated features do not want children to regard animals as higher than human beings.

III. Ancient fables, such as *Androcles and the Lion*, tell stories of the cooperation between humans and animals, and they usually end with a moral about human virtue.

(A) I only
(B) II only
(C) I and II only
(D) III only
(E) I, II, and III

STOP

END OF SECTION. IF YOU HAVE ANY TIME LEFT, GO OVER YOUR WORK IN THIS SECTION ONLY. DO NOT WORK IN ANY OTHER SECTION OF THE TEST.

SECTION VI

30 minutes
25 questions

Directions: Each of the following questions or groups of questions is based on a short passage or a set of propositions. In answering these questions it may sometimes be helpful to draw a simple picture or chart. When you have selected the best answer to each question, darken the corresponding circle on your answer sheet.

Questions 1–4

The first three names in each set are names usually used for males.

The last two names in each set are names usually used for females.

Each name in a set begins with a different letter.

Each name in a set contains the same number of letters.

I.	Jack	Paul	Dave	June	Edna
II.	Pete	Mike	Henry	Emma	Mary
III.	Frank	James	Chuck	Nancy	Betty
IV.	Louis	Tommy	Greta	Linda	Annie
V.	Phil	Dick	Mona	Alma	Inga

1. Which name would correctly complete the following set?

Allen   Wally   _____   Eliza   Julia

(A) Ethel
(B) Mabel
(C) Waldo
(D) Harry
(E) Angus

2. All of the conditions established above are met by which of the sets?
   (A) I only
   (B) III only
   (C) I and V only
   (D) II and IV only
   (E) III and V only

3. Which set satisfies all of the conditions except the third?
   (A) I
   (B) II
   (C) III
   (D) IV
   (E) V

4. Which of the following substitutions would make its set meet the stated conditions?
   (A) "Mark" for "June" in set I
   (B) "Lila" for "Henry" in set II
   (C) "Boris" for "Frank" in set III
   (D) "Simon" for "Louis" in set IV
   (E) "Fred" for "Mona" in set V

Questions 5–6

A behavioral psychologist interested in animal behavior noticed that dogs who are never physically disciplined (e.g., with a blow from a rolled-up newspaper) never bark at strangers. He concluded that the best way to keep a dog from barking at strange visitors is to not punish the dog physically.

5. The psychologist's conclusion is based on which of the following assumptions?

   I. The dogs he studied never barked.
   II. Dogs should not be physically punished.
   III. There were no instances of an unpunished dog barking at a stranger which he had failed to observe.

   (A) I only
   (B) II only
   (C) III only
   (D) II and III only
   (E) I, II, and III

6. Suppose the psychologist decides to pursue his project further, and he studies twenty-five dogs which are known to bark at strangers. Which of the following possible findings would undermine his original conclusion?

   I. Some of the owners of the dogs studied did not physically punish the dog when it barked at a stranger.
   II. Some of the dogs studied were never physically punished.
   III. The owners of some of the dogs studied believe that a dog that barks at strangers is a good watchdog.

   (A) I only
   (B) II only
   (C) I and II only
   (D) II and III only
   (E) I, II, and III

7. Only White Bear gives you all-day deodorant protection and the unique White Bear scent.

   If this advertising claim is true, which of the following cannot also be true?

   I. Red Flag deodorant gives you all-day deodorant protection.
   II. Open Sea deodorant is a more popular deodorant than White Bear.
   III. White Bear after-shave lotion uses the White Bear scent.

   (A) I only
   (B) II only
   (C) I and III only
   (D) III only
   (E) All of the propositions could be true.

Questions 8–12

Paul, Quincy, Roger, and Sam are married to Tess, Ursula, Valerie, and Wilma, not necessarily in that order. Roger's wife is older than Ursula. Sam's wife is older than Wilma, who is Paul's sister. Tess is the youngest of the wives. Roger was the best man at Wilma's wedding.

8. If Quincy and his wife have a boy named Patrick, then
   (A) Tess will be Patrick's aunt
   (B) Valerie will be Patrick's aunt
   (C) Paul will be Patrick's cousin
   (D) Ursula will be Patrick's mother
   (E) none of the above

9. Which of the following is true?
   (A) Roger's wife is younger than Valerie.
   (B) Roger's wife is younger than Wilma.
   (C) Paul's wife is younger than Ursula.
   (D) Sam's wife is older than Valerie.
   (E) Quincy's wife is older than Ursula.

10. If each husband is exactly two years older than his wife, which of the following must be false?
    (A) Roger is older than Ursula.
    (B) Tess is younger than anyone.
    (C) Paul is younger than Sam.
    (D) Quincy is younger than Paul.
    (E) Valerie is younger than Paul.

11. If the wives were—from youngest to oldest—28, 30, 32, and 34 years old; and Paul, Quincy, Roger, and Sam were respectively 27, 29, 31, and 33 years old, which of the following must be false?
    (A) Tess is older than her husband.
    (B) Valerie is older than her husband.
    (C) Ursula is younger than Valerie's husband.
    (D) Wilma is younger than Ursula's husband.
    (E) Tess is younger than Wilma's husband.

12. If Tess and Valerie get divorced from their current husbands and marry each other's former husband, then
    (A) Sam's wife will be younger than Paul's wife
    (B) Sam's wife will be younger than Roger's wife
    (C) Roger's wife will be older than Quincy's wife
    (D) Roger's wife will be older than Paul's wife
    (E) Paul's wife will be younger than Quincy's wife

Questions 13–17

Six persons, J, K, L, M, N, and O, run a series of races with the following results.

O never finishes first or last.

L never finishes immediately behind either J or K.

L always finishes immediately ahead of M.

13. Which of the following, given in order from first to last, is an acceptable finishing sequence of the runners?
    (A) J, L, M, O, N, K
    (B) L, O, J, K, M, N
    (C) L, M, J, K, N, O
    (D) L, M, J, K, O, N
    (E) N, K, L, M, O, J

14. If, in an acceptable finishing sequence, J and K finish first and fifth respectively, which of the following must be true?
    (A) L finishes second.
    (B) O finishes third.
    (C) M finishes third.
    (D) N finishes third.
    (E) N finishes sixth.

15. If, in an acceptable finishing sequence, L finishes second, which of the following must be true?

    I. O must finish fourth.
    II. N must finish fifth.
    III. Either J or K must finish sixth.

    (A) I only
    (B) II only
    (C) III only
    (D) I and III only
    (E) I, II, and III

16. All of the following finishing sequences, given in order from 1 to 6, are acceptable EXCEPT
    (A) J, N, L, M, O, K
    (B) J, N, O, L, M, K
    (C) L, M, J, K, O, N
    (D) N, J, L, M, O, K
    (E) N, K, O, L, M, J

17. Only one acceptable finishing sequence is possible under which of the following conditions?

    I. Whenever J and K finish second and third respectively.
    II. Whenever J and K finish third and fourth respectively.
    III. Whenever J and K finish fourth and fifth respectively.

    (A) I only
    (B) II only
    (C) III only
    (D) I and II only
    (E) I, II, and III

Questions 18–22

Jack Caribe, the ocean explorer, is directing a study of the parrot fish, an important part of coral reef ecology. Each day he must schedule the diving teams. His crew consists of four professional scuba divers—Ken, Leon, Mabel, and Nina—and four marine biologists—Peter, Quentin, Rosemary, and Sue.

No one can dive more than twice a day and a professional diver must always be on the boat as the dive-master. Jack is not assigned, but can do any task he wishes, including dive-master.

Each dive team must have at least one professional diver and one biologist.

Mabel and Peter have fought, and Jack won't put them together for now. Mabel, a strong swimmer, works very badly with slow-paced Quentin.

Sue and Ken are recently married and always dive together.

18. If Nina is dive-master supervising three diving teams, which of the following is NOT a possible dive team?
    (A) Ken, Sue, and Peter
    (B) Ken, Sue, and Quentin
    (C) Leon, Peter, and Quentin
    (D) Leon, Peter, and Rosemary
    (E) Mabel and Rosemary

19. If Jack is the dive-master with four teams diving, how many different possible two-diver teams are there?
    (A) 6
    (B) 7
    (C) 8
    (D) 9
    (E) 10

20. If Mabel is the dive-master, which of the following is NOT a possible dive team?

    I. Peter, Quentin, and Rosemary
    II. Leon and Nina
    III. Ken, Sue, and Quentin
    IV. Ken, Peter, and Rosemary

    (A) I and II only
    (B) I, II, and III only
    (C) I, II, and IV only
    (D) III only
    (E) I, II, III, and IV

21. If biologist Olga joins the expedition and Leon is away getting supplies, which of the following is a possible schedule for the morning dive teams?
    (A) Ken, Sue, and Peter; Mabel, Olga, and Rosemary; Nina, Jack, and Quentin
    (B) Ken, Mabel, and Sue; Nina, Rosemary, Peter, and Olga
    (C) Ken, Olga, and Quentin; Rosemary, Sue, and Mabel
    (D) Olga, Rosemary, and Peter; Ken, and Sue; Nina and Mabel
    (E) Mabel, Olga, and Peter; Ken, Sue, and Quentin; Nina, Jack, and Rosemary

22. If Peter and Mabel become friends again and Leon is the dive-master, which of the following is a possible diving team?
    (A) Peter, Mabel, and Ken
    (B) Peter, Mabel, and Sue
    (C) Peter, Quentin, and Rosemary
    (D) Peter, Mabel, Ken, and Sue
    (E) Mabel, Sue, and Rosemary

23. During New York City's fiscal crisis of the late 1970's, governmental leaders debated whether to offer federal assistance to New York City. One economist who opposed the suggestion asked, "Are we supposed to help out New York City every time it gets into financial problems?"

    The economist's question can be criticized because it
    (A) uses ambiguous terms
    (B) assumes everyone else agrees New York City should be helped
    (C) appeals to emotions rather than using logic
    (D) relies upon second-hand reports rather than first-hand accounts
    (E) completely ignores the issue at hand

24. It is a well-documented fact that for all teen-aged couples who marry, the marriages of those who do not have children in the first year of their marriage survive more than twice as long as the marriages of those teenaged couples in which the wife does give birth within the first twelve months of marriage. Therefore, many divorces could be avoided if teenagers who marry were encouraged not to have children during the first year.

    The evidence regarding teenaged marriages supports the author's conclusion only if
    (A) in those couples in which a child was born within the first twelve months

there is not a significant number in which the wife was pregnant at the time of marriage

(B) the children born during the first year of marriage to those divorcing couples lived with the teenaged couple

(C) the child born into such a marriage did not die at birth

(D) society actually has an interest in determining whether or not people should get divorced if there are not children involved

(E) encouraging people to stay married when they do not plan to have any children is a good idea

25. There are no lower bus fares from Washington, D.C., to New York City than those of Flash Bus Line.

Which of the following is logically inconsistent with the above advertising claim?

I. Long Lines Airways has a Washington, D.C., to New York City fare which is only one-half that charged by Flash.

II. Rapid Transit Bus Company charges the same fare for a trip from Washington, D.C., to New York City as Flash charges.

III. Cherokee Bus Corporation has a lower fare from New York City to Boston than does Flash.

(A) I only
(B) II only
(C) I and II only
(D) I, II, and III
(E) None of the statements is inconsistent.

STOP

END OF SECTION. IF YOU HAVE ANY TIME LEFT, GO OVER YOUR WORK IN THIS SECTION ONLY. DO NOT WORK IN ANY OTHER SECTION OF THE TEST.

PRACTICE EXAMINATION 1—ANSWER KEY

Section I

1. C	5. A	9. C	13. E	17. B	21. C	25. A	29. D	33. C	37. D
2. E	6. D	10. C	14. D	18. E	22. B	26. E	30. E	34. D	38. C
3. B	7. C	11. D	15. B	19. D	23. E	27. C	31. B	35. B	
4. D	8. B	12. A	16. A	20. A	24. D	28. C	32. B	36. A	

Section II

1. A	5. B	9. D	13. E	17. B	21. E	25. D	29. D	33. B	37. C
2. D	6. E	10. E	14. D	18. D	22. D	26. C	30. B	34. E	38. A
3. D	7. C	11. C	15. E	19. E	23. B	27. A	31. E	35. C	
4. A	8. E	12. A	16. B	20. B	24. C	28. B	32. A	36. D	

Section III

1. C	4. A	7. B	10. C	13. C	16. D	19. C	22. E	25. E	28. A
2. B	5. D	8. B	11. D	14. B	17. E	20. E	23. A	26. A	29. E
3. B	6. C	9. C	12. D	15. A	18. C	21. E	24. A	27. B	30. A

Section IV

1. C	4. D	7. D	10. B	13. C	16. C	19. C	22. A	25. E	28. B
2. C	5. B	8. C	11. C	14. D	17. C	20. D	23. A	26. A	29. A
3. A	6. B	9. D	12. D	15. C	18. A	21. B	24. A	27. C	30. B

Section V

1. C	6. A	11. D	16. C	21. B
2. E	7. E	12. A	17. A	22. A
3. E	8. D	13. E	18. C	23. A
4. A	9. E	14. B	19. D	24. D
5. A	10. D	15. C	20. D	25. A

Section VI

1. D	6. B	11. C	16. D	21. B
2. B	7. E	12. A	17. E	22. D
3. A	8. A	13. D	18. D	23. E
4. E	9. C	14. E	19. A	24. A
5. C	10. D	15. C	20. C	25. E

EXPLANATORY ANSWERS

SECTION I

1. **(C)** Even indicates that there is some opposite meaning between the first part of the sentence, with the blank, and the second part, which says that he had genius. Since the second part is positive, the blank must be negative and must be something that properly describes a reputation. (A) and (C) are the only answers that properly describe a reputation, but (C) is negative, and thus correct.

2. **(E)** The second blank asks for something that can be improved between and among men. (A) and (C) fail since one does not seek to improve problems or rudeness, but rather to improve the habits, customs or relationships that lead to problems or rudeness—one doesn't want better problems, but reduced ones. Generalities is also not something which is improved. Between (B) and (E), the first word must describe the kind of contribution which might make an improvement. A significant improvement is more likely to do so than a standardized one; hence (E) is the best answer.

3. **(B)** All the answer choices are adjectives, but only (B) is the sort of thing that one would wonder about concerning an award. (A) is attractive, but it would be used in a sentence saying ". . . how the awards have been determined," rather than the given order. Thus, (B) is the best answer.

4. **(D)** This question requires a little thought about what pleasures the medieval church might be against. Education, while not very common, was certainly not forbidden. (B) and (C) describe the actual views of the church, since ascetic means being opposed to sensual pleasures, and ecclesiastical means being of the church. (D) and (E) present some difficulty since hermetic can mean of the occult as well as airtight. The church would probably be against the occult, but it would be occult practices that would be opposed, not occult pleasures alone. Sensual pleasures would definitely be opposed, so (D) is the best answer.

5. **(A)** The sentence structure shows that the first blank is the statement of having wealth the disposition of which is opposed in the second half of the sentence. Thus, only (A) is reasonable on the first blank since it is the only choice which describes a business that can give away wealth.

6. **(D)** The second part of the sentence is admiring of the ability of cars to last as long as they do under routine abuse, thus only (D) will fit with that spirit. In the first blank, we are carrying forward the idea of routine abuse. Gradually, sensibly, religiously and gracefully do not fit. Habitually does. Again, (D) is the best answer.

7. **(C)** There is a little peculiarity to this sentence in that it speaks of filling the walls with something and then of evacuating them to a high vacuum. It seems as if it were doing contradictory things to the same space. Therefore, we must ask what could be put into something that is then made into a vacuum. Clearly, air and water fail. The second idea in the sentence is that we are dealing with the storage of liquid hydrogen, which is very cold. Thus the idea of a vacuum bottle which is filled with insulation becomes reasonable. Hence, (C) is the best answer.

8. **(B)** A plutocrat is a ruler distinguished by his wealth. A theocrat is a ruler distinguished by religion. An oligarch and an autocrat are also rulers, and a democrat is a believer in the rule of the people or majority. However, wealth is a distinguishing characteristic, which (C) does not replicate. (A) is slightly more difficult to dismiss since an autocrat is an individual, ruling as such; but he is not selected or distinguished—prior to rule—by the characteristic of being an individual. All rulers are individuals. (E) is attempting to confuse the issue by claiming that a republican is interested in conservation. First of all, a republican with a lower-case *r* is someone who believes in government having the form of a republic. Conservation is the preserving of something, usually the natural world or environment.

9. **(C)** Handcuffs are used to control and restrict the movements of a prisoner. A leash does the same for a dog. (A) can be eliminated for the very reason that makes it appealing initially. The excellent relationship between handcuffs and manacles is absolutely not replicated between prisoner (a person) and penitentiary (an institution). All four of the other answer choices fit the probable first cut at a relationship—seeing that the handcuffs somehow go on the prisoner. (B), (C), and (E) all relate in the sense of the first word physically surrounding some part of the second

264

word. The last step can be taken either on the basis of the idea of restriction, as elaborated above, or on the basis of a dog being an independent entity, like a prisoner. Or the idea that shoes are helpful to the feet, while a leash is not helpful to the dog. The ring is decorative, while handcuffs and leashes are generally not.

10. **(C)** The javelin and the cannonball have a shape relationship of elongated and rod-shaped to spherical, which is duplicated in spear and bullet. In addition, the original pair are both weapons, one propelled by muscle power and one by gunpowder, which also fits (C). None of the others has such a balanced relationship. However, several have partial relationships. In (A), a discus and a javelin are both used in track and field; a sling is a weapon, but a discus really is not. Also, a sling is the delivery system and a cannonball is the missile. (B) has a good start since a javelin is certainly thrown, but not many people willingly catch cannonballs. (E) is easy to eliminate since even if one considers a javelin to be a Greek item, a cannonball is not particularly Spanish. (D) is the second-best answer since it shares the shape relationship described above with (C). The differences are that an arrow is a weapon, like a javelin and a spear, but it is a missile, being shot from a bow. A shotput is like a cannonball in composition and shape, but is not, as far as its being a shotput is concerned, either a weapon or something shot from a weapon. When shape is an issue, it is sometimes not the only issue.

11. **(D)** An imp is a junior-grade devil and a cherub is a junior-grade angel, roughly speaking. A devil and an angel have the same oppositeness. (A) and (C) have a feeling of oppositeness, but lack the specific structure of (D). (A) is merely opposite. (C) has the moral element, but is not about beings. The low and high is unlikely when there are specific moral referents available. The others are not even real opposites.

12. **(A)** A radio and a phonograph are both electronic appliances, but none of the answer choices are two related appliances. A radio and a phonograph both deal with the same type of information system—sound. All of the answer choices also exhibit this relationship to one degree or another. This tells us that we are at least on the right track. What are the further refinements we can make to the idea of similar media? A radio gives an impermanent sound, while a phonograph gives the possibility of being used again and again, and is designed to do that. (E) fails here, even if it survived the same media requirement. In (C), both are impermanent. In the other three answer choices, it appears at first that they are all permanent. (B) is difficult to deal with since both sides of the analogy are so similar, certainly much more similar than in the original pair. A movie

and a photograph and a letter and a book are the last two possibilities. The major difference between a movie and a photograph is that a movie moves. In the original pair, either both move or neither moves, depending on how you view it— the movement is to be interpreted in terms of the media, not the mechanism, since the media is the issue. In (A) there is somewhat less permanence in a letter than in a book, particularly in the intention. A book is intended to be around for a time, but a letter is usually, and typically, a transitory medium. This is not a perfect analogy, but with a little patience, it can be solved.

13. **(E)** To immigrate is to enter a country, and to enlist is to enter the army. Since the original pair are a verb and a noun, it is likely that the correct answer will either be the same or an adverb and an adjective. Thus (A) and (D) do not appeal. (B) looks good since immigrate is so close to emigrate—the exact opposite. But a ship is not the exact opposite of a country. Many analogies have little vertical relationships, but in evaluating an answer choice that does have a vertical relationship in one part of the pairs, you should demand that there be a relationship in the other side of the pairs as well. (C) is a verb and a noun and while immigrate is a kind of moving, the country is not the placement, but the place.

14. **(D)** Urge is a somewhat weaker form of insist, so the analogy relationship is one of degree. (B) and (C) have no degree idea and are eliminated. (E) has only a mild one and is weak. (A) and (D) are both quite good. In choosing between them, we must refer to the meanings of the words and go beyond the simple idea of degree. Urge and request are ideas that leave their object a choice, while insist and demand do not permit as much choice. (A) cannot show a similar affinity.

15. **(B)** A grapnel is a hook-like object that is used to hook over edges to hold a rope for climbing up walls or cliffs, etc. A gaff is a nautical type of hook, usually used to take fish aboard. Thus we have similar hooking types of objects, with one side of the pair being generally a land object and the other a nautical object. None of the other answer choices has any hook idea in them. Since this is an unusual idea, it is likely to be very powerful if it is present in all four parts of an analogy. None of the other choices has a strong synonym idea either.

16. **(A)** An indictment is an early part of a legal proceeding in which the nature of the charges is laid out. Similarly, an impeachment is the early part of another legal process in which the charges are laid out. The second part of each pair is the part of the process in which the punishment is meted out. (C) has some strength since it consists of a designation process and an end process, but it

has no secondary similarity as between the two processes described in the original pair and (A). In (B), the first word, arraigned, is similar to indicted, though not really the same in all respects, but tried is not the final outcome. (D) has the second part right, punished, but guilty is not the same as indicted, which precedes the finding of guilty, overlooking the difficulties that the answer presents us with different parts of speech.

17. **(B)** (A) and (D) are simply not related to the passage at all.

(B), (C), and (E) have some merit. (E) has the merit of being a topic in the book, but it is not clear that sound is a good reference to quantum mechanics. While quantum mechanics is mentioned by the book as a thing to be symbolized, the book also has to discuss the symbolization of music, and that seems to be much more related to sound than quantum mechanics.

Both (B) and (C) have the merit of referring to the music, but with a title that refers to "sound" AND "symbol," it seems likely that the sound part refers to music and the symbol part to the notational system, rather than the other way around.

18. **(E)** (A) becomes unlikely when the first paragraph calls Einsteinian physics a "truly adequate" system, even though it may not be totally correct. Other keys to not choosing this otherwise appealing answer choice are the reference to the Theory of Relativity, which is not specifically mentioned at all, and the last paragraph's reiteration of the correctness of Einstein.

(B) is referred to in the passage as a specification of the strangeness of Einsteinian physics, and thus is part of them rather than contradictory to them. (C) fails because of the several cautionary statements such as the "unlikely" event of our ever experiencing a reversed time flow.

(D) refers to the imaginary mass of tachyons, but the passage says only that the tachyon "may" exist, not that it does.

(E) has the flag word *precisely*, which tells you that the answer choice is not referring to going faster than light, but to attaining exactly the speed of light. The need to move an infinite quantity of mass to go exactly the speed of light is referred to as a barrier, and is intuitively unlikely.

19. **(D)** Speculative is certainly a fair characterization of the passage. (D) is preferable to (C) because the passage is hopeful that some of these speculative things may come to pass, rather than suspicious of anything. (E) is an unlikely choice for any question of this sort.

20. **(A)** As is usual with this sort of question, there are several good answers among which to choose. (D) is clearly wrong because Zuckerkandl is not stated to have any theories of tachyon formation.

(E) similarly fails for lack of reference to the passage. Its only appeal is its obscurity.

(A), (B), and (C) require closer inspection. (C) seems to find that Einsteinian physics cannot treat tachyons, but actually it is predicted by the formulas associated with Einsteinian physics that such strange things as reverse time flow might occur, so (C) is out. The primary difference between (A) and (B) is the question of whether it is the notation and theories on the one hand or the observations on the other which indicates the need for improved notation. (B), while a good abstract statement of the progress of science, does not "cover the waterfront" on this passage. The only observations cited in the passage support the theoretical speculations rather than disprove the theories. Hence, (A).

21. **(C)** It is certainly not too soon for (D), since that has happened. It seems likely that the time for (A) will never arrive, but it is not discussed in the passage. The author is clearly not satisfied with the current notational system, and thus (E) is definitely in order. While (B) has merit because the author does not endorse Zuckerkandl's ideas, (C) has more merit since (C) is definitely stated to be far from accomplishment, if indeed it is possible at all.

22. **(B)** In the author's admitted oversimplification of Zuckerkandl, he says that music might be a better language for physics. Better than what? Better than math, which is, thus, also seen as a language. (D) fails because of the word great, though even without that disqualifier it would be inferior to (B).

23. **(E)** Without attempting to probe the nature of philosophy, which is certainly not an issue on a test question, (E) best links the topic of the passage to philosophy. (A), (B), and (C) are flack and (D) should not seem very good. Perhaps the nature of any field is a philosophical question, but the methods must usually be just technical matters within the field.

24. **(D)** By citing the particular part of the passage, the question requires you to see what follows from that particular phraseology. The cited phrase has the interesting aspect that something is named by scientists which is not definitely in existence. The rest of the passage certainly spoke of the tachyon as being a theoretical object, so (D)'s statement about the timing of the naming of the tachyon is certainly a good bet. The tachyon is still not certainly known—in the passage's terms—but it does have a name. It is theoretically described and it therefore seems likely that no one would have named the object without some reason, though it was not yet actually discovered.

(A) is flack and should be dismissed quickly.

Such an answer choice is rarely correct unless it reflects a specific statement in the passage.

(C) may well be true, in a witty but somewhat paradoxical statement. However, even if it turns out there is no such thing as a tachyon, that is not what can be inferred from the cited passage.

Both (E) and (B) have some appeal. (B)'s dissolves on close inspection. The difference between (B) and (D) is the issue of whether the particle was named before it was known to exist or before it actually existed in the world. While it is possible that it is named and will only later come into existence, there is nothing in the passage about creating tachyons. Thus (D) is preferable to (B). (E) is a meritorious statement in that it is certainly true and we do know that it is true (definitely true that the ideas *may* not exist) but we have no information to support the qualifier many; so (E) fails.

25. **(A)** The passage stresses the endurance of the legend of Atlantis, an island first mentioned in Plato's *Timaeus*. Although (B) mentions Plato, geography is not relevant. Choice (C) also has some relation to the speculations about Atlantis, but only (A) covers the broadest possibilities.

26. **(E)** Since the main thrust of the passage indicates that Atlantis is a legendary island, no recorded evidence by its inhabitants could have been left. Thus, (E) is the only choice that could be derived.

27. **(C)** The passage states that the island was destroyed because of the "impiety of its people." There is no other cause mentioned.

28. **(C)** Retaliate means to return like for like, especially acting to revenge some wrong. To turn the other cheek means to not return like for like, but to return good for evil. As with many antonym problems, there seems little difficulty when the meaning of the word is read from the dictionary. In practice, you might have been attracted to (A) or (D) even if you had some idea of what retaliate meant. In order for (A) to be the correct opposite, retaliate would have to mean to lose serenity, or to become upset. While it is true that much retaliation is done while one is upset, the essence of retaliation is action, not merely the emotional state. (D)'s attraction stems from the understanding that retaliation will rarely improve relations with the object of the retaliation. Here, again, the failure of the wrong answer choice is not that it is without any merit, but that it is a different thing than the stem word, a result rather than an action. (E) suffers the same defect since it deals with broad-mindedness, while retaliation is not narrow-mindedness.

29. **(D)** Analysis is the breaking up of something into its parts. Synthesis is putting something together out of its parts. (C) might appeal to an over subtle thinker, since analysis is to some extent directed and productive thinking, while a parenthesis is an aside or tangent. However, a parenthesis is not necessarily unproductive, nor is analysis always to the point. Dialysis is a chemical process, such as kidney dialysis, which cleans the blood. Electrolysis is the use of electricity to change or, in the case of hair, to destroy something. Emphasis is the placing of stress or importance on something. Analysis has to do with structure, not importance.

30. **(E)** Peremptory means seizing the initiative and overriding other considerations. (B) and (D) are not very good, but (A) and (C) have some merit. Humble would be the opposite of arrogant, and a peremptory tone is often considered arrogant in the sense of taking over what should be the rights of others. However, peremptory specifically refers to the act of taking over control, and (E), deferential, refers specifically to the act of giving over control, which is even better. (C) has less merit than does (A), but reflects the understanding that it is an attempt of strength to preempt. It may be true that a weak person is not likely to be peremptory, but weak is a much broader term.

31. **(B)** Salacious means obscene; thus wholesome is the best opposite indicating a morally "good" quality in opposition to the morally "bad" quality of salacious. Also, wholesome has precisely the connotation of being sound of mind, while salacious implies the opposite. Religious is not a very good opposite since it refers to faithfulness to some system or religious beliefs, but does not imply any particular standard being followed. One man's religion may well be another's obscenity.

32. **(B)** Insolvent refers to the inability to raise so-called liquid assets such as cash, and thus to the condition of being unable to pay one's debts; hence (B). The other answer choices all echo other words unrelated in meaning to insolvent. (D), for instance, has some echo of the word solvent as a chemical, which is not the same as financially solvent. Insolvent refers only to financial matters.

33. **(C)** Homogeneous comes from the prefix *homo-*, meaning same and the root *gen*, meaning kind; thus the word means all of the same kind. Both (C) and (E) have merit. (C) refers to the state of being diversified, which is a precise opposite of the state of being all the same. (E)'s merit is primarily the inclusion of the word different within the word differential. (E) actually refers to the size or scope of a difference, which is related to the idea of there being a difference. This is not itself the estate of having differences, as (C) is. (A) means very thrifty, even stingy. (B) is the state of being conscious. (D) means talkative, from the root *loq-*, meaning talk or speech, as in eloquent.

34. **(D)** The root word amalgam is a combination of something. Thus combine is a very precise syno-

nym, leaving segregate, which means to separate, as a good opposite. (A) means to blame; (B), to delay; (C), to shine or glitter; and (E), to command or forbid.

35. **(B)** Temerity means boldness, even audacity. Diffidence, (B), is shyness or reluctance to advance or act. (A) is a difficult and embarrassing situation. (C) is a name, or nickname, from the root *nomen* meaning name, as in nomenclature; and *cog*, meaning known as, from the same root as cognition, thinking.

36. **(A)** Mutation means change. (A) is the noun form of constant. Mutation does not refer only to genetic mutation, but can mean any change from the original that is sudden and relatively permanent. (E) has some merit since it does at least refer to change. However, unamended means unchanged and would be a better opposite to mutated. Unamended does not refer to the thing or process itself.

37. **(D)** Sybaritic means loving luxury, or luxurious. (B), meaning stubborn, is no opposite. (D), the correct answer, means sparse and without luxury or ostentation. (E) has some association with being opposed to wild luxury, since a conservative in the original meaning of the word is someone who wishes to conserve things, and presumably not waste them. Similarly, a conservative party will not be sybaritic. However, conservative is much broader than austere or sybaritic, and is thus not as good an opposite as austere.

38. **(C)** Prosaic, meaning everyday or commonplace, derives from the word prose. Fulsome is so full that it is obnoxious. (B), mundane, is a synonym for prosaic, since it comes from the root *mundis*, meaning earth, and refers to typical earthly things, as opposed to glorious, heavenly things.

SECTION II

1. **(A)** Since the first word of each choice would acceptably complete the sentence up to "journalism," we cannot make any preliminary eliminations. As for the second word, it is logical to berate (chastise) for being childish. It is not logical to laud (praise) for being voyeuristic (unhealthily obsessed with sex), to criticize for being authentic (a positive expression), to requite (make amends) for being responsible, or to attack for being important.

2. **(D)** You can immediately eliminate (A), (C), and (E), because rattling a newspaper shows neither calm, duplicity, nor opinion. Looking more closely at (B), we now have: "Rattling his newspaper to show his irritation, the husband made known his approval of his wife's new breakfast table." Since showing irritation is certainly not a sign of approval, and since, according to (D), showing anger is a rational sign of disapproval, (D) is the only possible answer.

3. **(D)** You can eliminate (A), (B), (C), and (E) because in these cases either one or both of the words in each choice is an adjective describing qualities of remarks which are not necessarily indicative of a keen or incisive mind. Trenchant and penetrating, on the other hand, are synonyms; both are used specifically to describe keenness of mind.

4. **(A)** Choice (B) is unacceptable because genocide is used only in relation to people. Similarly, (C) and (E) are unacceptable because the terms vagrancy and morality are associated only with human beings. Choice (D) is unacceptable because it confuses affects (personal properties) with effects (results brought about). This leaves proliferation (growth and spreading out) of algae as the cause of the exodus (departure) of many kinds of fish.

5. **(B)** Because the new machine failed to make the garbage smaller, the garbage filled the kitchen. Compact is a transitive verb meaning make smaller.

6. **(E)** You can talk your way out of some sort of agreement, but not out of an economy, standard, trawler, or van. One of the lesser known meanings of compact is a brief agreement.

7. **(C)** What Sally lost were the contents of her purse. This would immediately preclude vehicle, piano, compost, or complexion. However, a compact is a small case containing powder, puff, and mirror, and is usually carried in a lady's purse.

8. **(E)** The original pair are two ways of judging the merit of actions. The two standards are based on different ideas. Both words in the original pair are abstractions, so it is likely that both of the parts of the correct answer will also be abstractions. (C) can be eliminated for not having any moral or legal play, while some of the others do. Both (D) and (E) have a first part that has some moral aspect and a second part that has some legal aspect. (A) has the first, perhaps, and (B) has the second, but neither has both. In choosing between (D) and (E), it is clear that sin and crime are both offenses against precisely the same standards, relatively, as in the original pair. The question then is how well (D) keeps the same relationship. A priest is concerned with morality, it is true, but he is also concerned with religion, which is not quite the same. A jury is concerned with legality, but actually is the trier of fact in most cases. Furthermore, the two are concrete and the origi-

nal pair are abstract. Since we have at least as good an abstract pair in (E), it is ahead on all counts.

9. **(D)** An ellipse is a kind of curve and a square is a kind of polygon. A polygon is a figure with many sides, each one of which is a straight line. None of the other answer choices have this relationship. (A) has a little appeal since a stutter is a kind of speech, but is in particular a defective kind of speech and an ellipse is not particularly defective. (E) has to do with geometry, as does (B), but in (E) we have a measurement and an object, which might have a shape related to the measurement. In (B) we have a potentially confusing relationship. A base is part of a triangle in the sense of being one of the constituent parts that go to make up a triangle. This is different from the idea of being part of a group, which is the relationship in the original pair.

10. **(E)** Sugar is the original substance and saccharin is the manufactured imitation. The same applies to butter and margarine. (B) and (C) have relationships of source to product or derivative. (D) is a general class and a member of the class. (A) is two types of the same thing. In (A) there is some appeal since both the stem words are sweeteners and both the words in (A) are sweet. However, since the stem pair are neither synonyms nor antonyms, there must be some other idea than merely general relationship.

11. **(C)** The relationship is one of strength and the freedom of the recipient to do as he wishes. (A) and (B) do not have the idea of degree at all. (C), (D), and (E) do have that idea, but (E) fails since (C) and (D) both have the additional concept of being words relating one person to another person or thing. (C) is superior in that it has not only the element of degree (require is stronger than suggest) but also the additional element of interaction between two people, an element not present in (D).

12. **(A)** Water and faucet relate in a few different ways. First of all a faucet carries a flow of water through it. But a more specific idea is that a faucet is a way of controlling the flow of water. The first idea would fit (D), but while steam and water both will flow, a pipe and a faucet should not jibe in your mind very well. A throttle, however, does control the flow of fuel just like a faucet controls the flow of water. (B) has only a rudimentary appeal since state of matter such as solid and liquid would most likely be something like water and ice, the liquid and solid forms of the same thing. (C)'s two parts relate to the original pair in a general way, but they do not relate to each other in any useful way. (E) has virtually no relationship in the choice at all.

13. **(E)** A flask is a small container; a bottle could be considered a larger one, perhaps. A brochure is a small type of publication, while a tome is definitely a larger one. This is not a perfect analogy and could be difficult since (A) presents a totally different idea. (C) and (D) do not relate to the original pair, except (D) might be backward. (B) is possible, but a flask need not be metal. (A) has the merit that one does think of whiskey being usually contained in a flask and milk in a bottle. However, that is a vertical relationship and (E) is a horizontal one, and the primary relationship is always preferred.

14. **(D)** Caliber is a way of measuring the size of rifles, since it refers to the size of the rifle barrel on the inside. Gauge is the way of measuring the width of the tracks or rails. The others have no measurement idea at all. Quality in (A) has some idea of connecting with caliber since one speaks of a high caliber as meaning high quality. Similarly (B)'s bore relates to rifle, but in each case the very strength of the secondary connection proves that there is no primary connection.

15. **(E)** This is a matter of degree. Mince is chopping very fine or very much. Beating is very vigorous stirring. Furthermore, both the original pair and (E) are cooking terms, which only (A) shares. (A) fails since there is no internal relationship.

16. **(B)** A peccadillo is a minor infraction; a crime is major. Hesitate is a small degree, while procrastinate is a high degree. Bushel and peck have some relationship of magnitude, but the verbs are preferable here since there is the idea of doing something very much.

17. **(B)** This answer can be approached two ways. The first that will occur to you is the elimination of answer choices. In an inference question, elimination must be done carefully until the proper answer appears. The second way is to go right to the issue of the usage of vegetative in the passage. This happens to reward a little "outside" knowledge of microbiology.

(A) is not mentioned anywhere, either in terms of plants or in terms of the disease possibilities of human habitations. (C) and (E) are also not mentioned. Any answer choice, like (C), that says something is a fact bears a heavy burden and must be examined carefully. Here it fails. (E) fails because the author does not seem to have any trouble classifying bacteria, since he throws around quite a few names. One point is to notice that bacillus is used to describe particular types of bacteria, as shown by the references in the first two sentences, which both discuss the same phenomenon, first as an aspect of bacteria and then in terms of bacillus characteristics exemplifying this process.

(D) has some merit, and in fact there are some similarities and the author is using that idea to describe the bacteria more concisely. However, the question stem is asking for the reason that the author is using the term as well as the significance of it—the burden of information it carries here. The vegetative stage is contrasted to the dormant stage such as with the anthrax bacillus, which will grow after being dry for ten years.

The direct way of approaching the answer is to see that the vegetative stage is a stage of vulnerability to the drying-out process, as contrasted to the spore stage, which is not as vulnerable. Since the spore stage is dormant, the vegetative phase is growth. The word germinate also helps, since a seed germinates and then grows into a plant.

18. **(D)** It is important to stick within the limits of the information that the passage gives you. The only item that is mentioned in this short passage in relation to the idea of increasing or decreasing the risk of infection is the susceptibility of various microorganisms to drying out. Therefore, the risk of infection will be great when the risk of drying out is least, that is, when it is humid. (B) will appeal to outside knowledge that getting chilled is supposed to increase the risk of infection. This may or may not be true, depending on which study you read, but it is definitely not in the passage.

19. **(E)** In order for a statement to be inferred, we must be convinced that there is a very good chance that the author will agree with the statement, given what he has already said.

(A) is not inferrable, because of the word most. It is stated in the passage that removing the moisture from a bacteria will kill it, but there is no comparison of methods made, and thus there can be no statement of relative merit or efficiency.

(B) cannot be inferred because the word eliminate is too strong. Certainly the passage permits the inference that drying out a house will reduce the chances of infection, but not that they will be eliminated entirely.

(C) is a little tricky since it plays on our idea that dry is good and wet is bad as far as infection is concerned. There are two objections to (C). First, it doesn't actually say anything about infection at all, which is a moderately serious objection since infection and bacteria are the sole topic of the passage. Second, and more important, steam heating does not mean that the air is any wetter than with any other form of heating. Steam heating is not the spraying of steam about the house, but the passage of steam through pipes, which become hot and radiate heat into the room. Although this requires a trifle of outside knowledge, the knowledge that steam heat does not mean steam in the air is within the reasonable bounds of common knowledge for GRE-takers.

20. **(B)** The passage makes it clear that infectiousness is a function of the resistance of the bacteria to drying, and also that the tubercle bacteria is one of the more resistant. There are two points to be made in addition to this citation to the passage. First, the tubercle bacillus' connection to tuberculosis is fair to ask about even though it is not common knowledge. The passage refers to tubercle and the question to tuberculosis. A knowledge of word parts might suffice to make the connection clear, but even if that failed, you should not choose (E) on the basis that the question is simply unrelated to the passage because the passage did not mention tuberculosis. That would indeed be unfair. Thus you can deduce the connection between tubercle and tuberculosis. Second, the question asks about infectiousness. All of the answers except (E) speak to aspects of the passage that might explain why something is infectious. However, the basic idea of the passage was the connection between drying out and dying on the part of microorganisms. Therefore, (B) and (C) are preferable in all likelihood, and a close examination of those two will likely lead you to the connection between the tubercle and tuberculosis as just described.

21. **(E)** The author is curious about the amount and effects of advertising, hence (E). No value judgments are made in the passage which could support (A), (B), or (D). (C) weakly reflects the author's desire to learn more about advertising.

22. **(D)** This term is not explicitly defined, but at the end of the fourth paragraph the range in costs of "push promotion" is explained by difficulties in separating out the elements of direct selling, hence (D). (A), (B), and (C) are unlikely from the second paragraph, which distinguishes them from "push promotion."

23. **(B)** (B) is stated in the next-to-last paragraph. (A) fails since restaurants are nowhere mentioned. (C), while true in the real world, is not stated in the passage. (D) has the difficulty that both prepared and natural are not in the passage and it is not entirely clear that these are identical to highly processed and highly perishable, respectively. Given the merit of (B), (D) can be eliminated. (E) is simply false, since highly processed foods are stated to account for only 20 percent of the food dollar.

24. **(C)** (C) describes the article perfectly. (A) and (D) fail for want of such value judgments in the passage. (E) is not done in any final way, though some discussion is given of the topic. (B) is not stated and may even go against the tenor of the passage since a statement that something is large does not imply that it is too large.

25. **(D)** (A), (B), and (C) are explicitly stated at the end of the last paragraph. (E) is implied because of the concern about highly processed versus less-processed foods. (D) is not there since no mention of restaurant versus home eating is made.

26. **(C)** This is a bit of a detail question, but general considerations can help. Food advertising is, overall, #1 in dollar volume, which eliminates (B) and (D), since we are looking for an exception to falseness. (E) speaks to radio ads only, and the first paragraph stated that, in radio, food is near the top.

    The other two discuss the breakdown of the food advertising dollar among the different media. The fourth paragraph states that television is less than 1 cent, incentives 0.6 cents, print 0.5 cents, and push promotion 0.7 to 1.4 cents. This shows that (A) is false, and also that (C) is indeterminate, which is to say not definitely false and, thus, the correct answer.

27. **(A)** (A) results from the author's attempt at a balance sheet, where he states that food ads subsidize publications. While it is true that free television is also subsidized by food ads, its cost will not rise since it is free. Cable television is not mentioned in the passage as having ads at all, so (B) is out, and the author does not claim that people watch programs for the ads, as (D) would have it. (E) fails when (A) succeeds.

28. **(B)** Intransigent means unwilling to compromise, while conciliatory means willing to compromise or reconcile when differences exist. (A) and (D) seem somewhat connected to the stem word because of the "trans" portion that is common to both intransigent and transportation. However, the real history of the word is that it comes from the same root as transact and means an unwillingness to have a transaction. This can serve as an example of being careful with word parts. The "trans" portion might have had some relation to (A) or (D), but the "sig" portion was not being taken into consideration, and thus an error could be made.

29. **(D)** One thing that you know about ingenuous is that it is NOT ingenious. Ingenuous means open and honest; thus devious is the best opposite.

30. **(B)** A canard is an untruth or a false report, hence (B). Canard is usually used to describe something that is unflattering as well as untrue ("a base canard"); thus (D) might appear to have some merit. Blasphemy is irreverence toward God or something sacred, which has some element of being (presumably) untrue, but it is a very specific word relating to sacred things, while canard is not limited in that way.

31. **(E)** DISinterested means not taking sides, being impartial—hence (E). UNinterested means having no desire to become involved in any way, which would be a good opposite to (B).

32. **(A)** Propitiate means to appease or make favorably inclined. Anger is a very good opposite to both shades of meaning. Hurt has some apparent merit, since hurting someone may well anger them, but it is the actual state of mind of being angry or unfavorably disposed which is the full opposite to propitiate. None of the other answers has any real opposite meaning to propitiate, though depart may seem acceptable if the stem word is unknown. The "pro" part of the stem word is not likely to be enough, by itself, to give a right answer.

33. **(B)** Absolve means to clear from blame, while blame means to assign guilt. Muddy might appeal if you thought that absolve meant simply to solve. While it is true that there are a few cases where the addition of a prefix changes the meaning very little, most words with prefixes have a significantly altered meaning. Repent also has to do with guilt, but it is a wish by the guilty person that he had not done his misdeeds. In some religious contexts, repentance may precede absolution, but they are not the same. Recant means to take back one's speech or change one's stated opinions, perhaps because of error. Free has no real connection to absolve.

34. **(E)** A hedonist is one who believes that pleasure or happiness is the highest good. This has often been used to mean specifically physical or sensual pleasure as being the highest good. A puritan is one who believes in a strict, even austere, religious life and frowns on physical pleasure. A martinet is a person who adheres strictly to the rules, but there is no connotation either for or against physical or sensual pleasures. As a person who appreciates the life of the mind and the value of ideas, an intellectual would be somewhat opposite to a hedonist, but need not be opposed to physical or sensual pleasure as is the puritan. A scientist may be seen as a subgroup of an intellectual in this problem.

35. **(C)** A cretin is a person of subnormal intellectual abilities. A genius has greater than normal intellectual capacity. A seer and a scholar are persons with intellectual achievements and wisdom, but these meanings are not referring to the capacity of the person so much as what has been done with that capacity. A talent need not be talented intellectually and thus is not necessarily an opposite of cretin. Moron is virtually a synonym for cretin.

36. **(D)** To decant means to pour off gently without disturbance. To slosh out would be to pour out roughly with great disturbance. Cork, meaning to seal in, also has some connection, but is not describing some movement of the liquid. The other answers have little connection as stated, though upset does oppose the gentleness of decant, and tap does refer to the process of opening up a barrel, as of beer. Level off appeals

because of the "cant" portion of decant, which originally meant to tilt, but now refers to pouring.

37. **(C)** Arrant means total or complete. Thus, partial is the best opposite. One of the most common usages is in the phrase arrant nonsense, meaning complete nonsense. This usage might lead to an association with foolishness and thus tempt you to choose wise. Arrant does NOT mean arrogant; thus, humble could be eliminated even if the exact meaning of arrant escaped you. Intrepid means brave and fearless, which is unconnected to arrant.

38. **(A)** A wastrel is a wasteful person, a spendthrift. A conservator is someone whose job, or nature, is to conserve or preserve things. A prodigal is very similar to a wastrel and thus not an opposite. A lutist plays a lute and a noble is highborn, of good breeding, but could be of whatever personality. A phantasm is a mirage or hallucination.

SECTION III

1. **(C)** "Of" in this case indicates multiplication. The product of 5 and 36 will be equal to the product of 36 and 5, and .05 and .36 will have the same number of decimal places; therefore, the two quantities must be equal. You do not need to actually do the multiplication in full.

2. **(B)** It is not possible to combine the two radicals of the right column. Although $\sqrt{5} \times \sqrt{10} = \sqrt{50}$, $\sqrt{5} + \sqrt{10} \neq \sqrt{15}$. The operation works only for multiplication. Since $\sqrt{15} < \sqrt{16}$, $\sqrt{15}$ must be less than 4. Since $\sqrt{5} > \sqrt{4}$, $\sqrt{5}$ must be greater than 2; and since $\sqrt{10}$ is greater than $\sqrt{9}$, $\sqrt{10}$ must be greater than 3. The two terms of the right column are slightly greater than 2 and 3 respectively, so their sum must be greater than 5. Column B is slightly greater than 5. Column A is less than 4.

3. **(B)** The (346×23) is only flack. It does not point to any difference between p and q. Since the first term of both equations is the same, we can assign it the constant value k. The given information can now be simplified:

$$k + p = 34{,}731$$
$$k + q = 35{,}124$$

Since 35,124 is greater than 34,731, q must be greater than p.

4. **(A)** Remember that the drawings in this subsection are not necessarily drawn to scale. Thus, you should not solve problems on the basis of a visual estimate of size or shape alone. However, manipulating the diagram in your mind—seeing what the possibilities are if some line is lengthened or shortened or some angle varied—can often help

you to see the answer to a quantitative comparison problem without computation, or at least will reduce your difficulties.

In this case, exploring what it means to say that $x° < y°$ can start with seeing what it would mean if $x° = y°$. As the first diagram shows, $x° = y°$ means that SRT has two equal legs, ST and TR. T will be in the middle of PQ, hence PT = QT. But as $y°$ gets larger, it will result in the line RT hitting the line PQ closer and closer to Q, thus making TQ smaller and PT larger. Therefore PT is always larger than TQ when $y° > x°$.

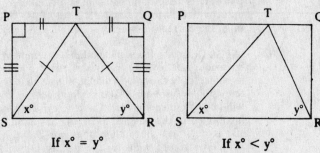

If $x° = y°$ If $x° < y°$

5. **(D)** Since x might be a fraction, it is not possible to determine which of the columns is greater. If x is $\frac{1}{2}$, then Column A is $\frac{1}{4}$ while Column B is 1, making Column B greater in that instance. But if x is 2, Column A is 4 and Column B is 4, making the two columns equal. Finally, if x is greater than 2, say 3, then Column A is 9 and Column B is 6, making A greater.

6. **(C)** Since the numbers here are relatively manageable, the easiest solution to this problem is to do the indicated arithmetic operation:

$$\frac{4}{5} - \frac{3}{4} = \frac{16 - 15}{20} = \frac{1}{20}$$

You might also notice that $\frac{4}{5} = 80\%$ and $\frac{3}{4} = 75\%$, with their difference being 5%, which is $\frac{1}{20}$.

7. **(B)** We can see that the fraction $\frac{3}{13} < \frac{3}{12}$, thus $\frac{3}{13} < \frac{1}{4}$; but $\frac{13}{51} > \frac{13}{52}$, thus $\frac{13}{51} > \frac{1}{4}$. Therefore, $\frac{3}{13} < \frac{1}{4} < \frac{13}{51}$, answer (B). We look for reference points. For example, the 52 cards in a deck are in four suits of 13 cards each.

8. **(B)** This problem uses the term S_n to indicate that whatever n may be, the S_n value will be found by multiplying n by 3 and adding 2 to the result. One way of solving this problem would be to do the actual work indicated for 5, 4, 9 and 8, finding that S_n for 5 is $S_5 = 3(5) + 2 = 17$ and $S_4 = 14$, $S_9 = 29$, $S_8 = 26$, with $17 + 14$ being smaller than $29 + 26$.

But there is really no reason to do the actual work. Since the QC issue is which column is bigger, we always pay attention to how things get bigger or smaller. S_n will get bigger as n gets bigger because it is just multiplying n by 3. Since Column A has two smaller numbers, the sum is smaller.

9. **(C)** The problem does *not* presuppose that the student is familiar with the metric system. The cost of the meat in Column A is: 10 lbs. × $2.50/lb. = $25.00. The cost of the meat in Column B is: 5 kilos × $5.00/kilo = $25.00.

10. **(C)** The problem is most easily solved by cancelling the zeros in each fraction:

$$\frac{1\cancel{0}}{10,00\cancel{0}} = \frac{1}{1000} \qquad \frac{1\cancel{000}}{1,000,\cancel{000}} = \frac{1}{1000}$$

So Column A and Column B are both $\frac{1}{1000}$ and equal.

11. **(D)** Do not try to solve a quantitative comparison by visually estimating lengths of lines. In this case, there is not sufficient information to deduce that PQRS is or is not a square—even though it is drawn as one. The following group of drawings will show that no conclusion regarding the relative lengths of PQ and QR is possible. PQ could be equal to QR, but it doesn't have to be.

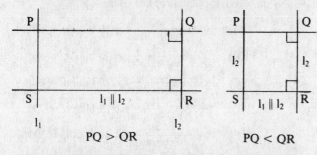

12. **(D)** The information supplied in the two columns is sufficient only to allow us to compute the *capacities* or *volumes* of the boxes described. We have no information regarding the size of pears or the size of potatoes, and we are not even told what part of each box's capacity is being used.

13. **(C)** The problem is most easily solved by grouping like terms and simplifying. We want the x terms on one side, pure numbers on the other.

$$4x^2 + 2x^2 + 3x + 2x = 3x^2 + 3x^2 + 2x + 2x + 3$$
$$6x^2 + 5x = 6x^2 + 4x + 3$$
$$x = 3$$

Since x = 3, x^2 must be 9 and the two columns are equal.

14. **(B)** The most natural approach here is to perform the indicated operations:

$$n \cdot 1 \cdot 1 = n \qquad n + 1 + 1 = n + 2$$

While the comparison n to n + 2 is simple, let us carry through the process completely to review comparing across the columns. It is possible to simplify across the comparison, that is, we subtract an n from both columns. (*Note:* It is permissible to add or subtract like terms from columns because such operations do not interfere

with the balance of an equality nor the direction of an inequality. It is also permissible to multiply or divide both columns by the same term, provided that the term is a positive one. One must not, however, multiply or divide both columns by a negative term, for such an operation would reverse the direction of an inequality; or by zero, for such an operation would destroy the equality.) So we are left with zero in Column A and 2 in Column B. B is greater.

15. **(A)** The figure is a triangle, so the sum of the interior angles must be 180°:

$$6x + 2x + x = 180°$$
$$9x = 180°$$
$$x = 20°$$

So Column A is greater than Column B.

16. **(D)** The minute hand will make one complete circle of the dial by 7:15. Then it will complete another half circle by 7:45. Since there are 360° in a circle, the arc travelled by the minute hand will be one full 360° plus half of another full 360° yielding 360° + 180° = 540°.

17. **(E)** One way of solving this problem would be to convert each of the fractions to a decimal or find a common denominator so that a direct comparison can be made. This is too time-consuming. Instead, anytime the GRE asks a question similar to this one, the student can be confident that there is very likely some shortcut available. Here the shortcut is to recognize that every answer choice, except for (E), is either equal to or greater than $\frac{1}{2}$. $\frac{7}{8}$ and $\frac{8}{9}$ are clearly much larger than $\frac{1}{2}$. $\frac{7}{12}$ must be greater than $\frac{1}{2}$ since $\frac{6}{12}$ is equal to $\frac{1}{2}$. But $\frac{8}{17}$ is less than $\frac{1}{2}$—$\frac{6}{12}$ would be $\frac{1}{2}$. So (E) is the smallest of the fractions. Even if the shortcut had eliminated only two or three answers, it would have been worthwhile.

18. **(C)** Even though it is not absolutely necessary to draw a figure to solve this problem, anyone finding the solution elusive will likely profit from a "return to basics":

$$\frac{3x}{4} + 1 \qquad \boxed{} \qquad \frac{3x}{4} + 1 \qquad P = 4\left(\frac{3x}{4} + 1\right)$$

Quickly sketching the figure may help you avoid the mistake of multiplying the side of the square by another side, giving the area, answer (D), not the perimeter. The perimeter will be 4s, not s^2: $4(\frac{3x}{4}+1) = \frac{12x}{4} + 4 = 3x + 4$.

19. **(C)** Average speed is nothing more than miles travelled over the time taken: rate (speed) =

$\dfrac{\text{distance}}{\text{time}}$ The elapsed time here is 4 hours and 48 minutes. 48 minutes is $\frac{4}{5}$ hours. Our formula then will be: $\dfrac{240 \text{ miles}}{4\frac{4}{5} \text{ hours}}$. We attack the problem by converting the denominator to a fraction: $4\frac{4}{5} = \frac{24}{5}$, and then we invert and multiply:

$$\frac{240 \text{ miles}}{4\frac{4}{5} \text{ hrs.}} = \frac{240}{\frac{24}{5}} = \frac{5}{24} \times 240 = 50 \text{ miles per hour.}$$

Notice that setting up the problem in this way avoids a lot of needless arithmetic. This is characteristic of the GRE. Most problems do not require a lengthy calculation. Usually the numbers used in constructing the questions are selected in a way that will allow for cancelling, factoring, or other shortcut devices. On the test, fractions are usually easier to work with than decimals.

20. **(E)** Multiplication is both associative and commutative. By associative, we mean that the grouping of the elements is not important—for example, $(5 \times 6) \times 7 = 5 \times (6 \times 7)$. By commutative we mean that the order of the elements is unimportant—for example, $5 \times 6 = 6 \times 5$. So (A), (B), (C), and (D) are all alternative forms for m(nop), but (E) is not: $(mn)(mo)(mp) = m^3nop$.

21. **(E)** Looking at the two charts, we see that the upper one, representing the total passenger miles, shows a smooth increase, generally speaking, while the lower one shows large changes. Since the lower one is deaths per passenger-mile, the sharp changes in the rate must be from sharp changes in the number of deaths.

　　Proposition I is inferable since the highest level reached by the line on the lower graph was approximately 1.3, in 1951. II is also inferable. The largest jump in the line on the lower graph, for a one-year period, occurred in the period 1954–1955. Finally, III is also inferable. The two low points on the line of the lower graph occurred in 1954 and 1957; both were approximately .1.

22. **(E)** The question stem asks about the *longest*, not the most severe or greatest increase. Although the *largest* increase ended in 1955, the *longest* increase lasted from 1956 until 1960. The word finally is also a clue.

23. **(A)** In 1955, total passenger-miles were 20 billion, and the fatality rate was 1.2 per 100 million miles. To compute the actual number of fatalities, we must multiply the total miles by the rate of fatalities (just as one multiplies 5 gallons by 25 miles per gallon to compute the total miles travelled as 125 miles): $20,000,000,000 \times \dfrac{1.2}{100,000,000} =$ (to make matters easier, we cancel zeros) $20,\cancel{000},\cancel{000},000 \times \dfrac{1.2}{100,\cancel{000},\cancel{000}} = 240$.

24. **(A)** Problem 23 shows us how the number of fatalities can be found. But it would be counterproductive to spend a lot of time computing the actual number of deaths for each of the five years mentioned. Instead, a rough estimate will suffice. At first glance, it appears that the only reasonable possibilities are 1951, 1955, and 1960, since the fatality rate (lower graph) is at least approximately equal in those years. Now, it is absolutely critical to realize that, though the fatality rate in 1951 was higher than the fatality rate in 1960 (1.3 compared with 1.0), there were three times as many miles travelled in 1960 than in 1951. Similarly, though the fatality rate was higher in 1955 than it was in 1960 (1.2 compared with 1.0), there were 50% more miles travelled in 1960 than in 1955. This reasoning shows that the largest numbers of fatalities occurred in 1960. Even though the fatality rate that year was not as high as those for 1955 and 1951, this was more than offset by the larger number of passenger-miles travelled. Of course, a longer method of attack is to actually do a rough calculation for each:

(A) 1951: $\dfrac{1.3}{100 \text{ million}} \times 10 \text{ billion} = 130$

(B) 1953: $\dfrac{.6}{100 \text{ million}} \times 15 \text{ billion} = 90$

(C) 1955: $\dfrac{1.2}{100 \text{ million}} \times 20 \text{ billion} = 240$

(D) 1957: $\dfrac{.1}{100 \text{ million}} \times 25 \text{ billion} = 25$

(E) 1960: $\dfrac{1}{100 \text{ million}} \times 30 \text{ billion} = 300$

25. **(E)** This problem is at once both easy and difficult. It is easily solved if the key word, passenger, is not overlooked. The lower graph records passenger miles travelled, but it tells us nothing about the number of different passengers who travelled those miles. The real-world likelihood that more passenger-miles *probably* means more passengers is only a probability and not a basis for a certain calculation.

26. **(A)** There is an easy and a more complicated way to handle this question. The more complex method is to begin with the formula for the area of a triangle: Area = $\frac{1}{2}$ (altitude)(base). Since angle CBE is equal to angle E, BC must be equal to CE, and it is possible to reduce the altitude to the base (or vice versa). So, Area = $\frac{1}{2}$ (side)^2. The area is 8, so $8 = \frac{1}{2}s^2$, and s = 4. Of course, s is also the side of the square, so the area of the square ABCD is s^2 or 16.

　　Now, an easier method of solving the problem is to recognize that BC and CE are equal to sides of the square ABCD, so the area of BCE is simply half that of the square. So the square must be double the triangle, or 16. A 45–45–90 right triangle is half of a square, and its hypotenuse is the diagonal of the square.

27. **(B)** Although some students will be able to solve this problem without the use of a diagram, for most drawing the floor plan of the closet is the logical starting point:

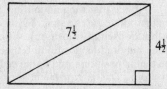

Now it becomes clear that the Pythagorean Theorem is the key to solving this problem. Once the dimensions are converted to fractions, the problem is simplified further: the triangle is a 3–4–5 right triangle $(\frac{9}{2}, \frac{12}{2}, \frac{15}{2})$. The two legs of the right triangle are simultaneously the width and length of the rectangle. So the area of the closet is: $\frac{9}{2} \times 6 = \frac{54}{2} = 27$.

28. **(A)** There are four times as many women as there are men, so if there are x men in the meeting, there are 4x women. This means that there is a total of 5x persons in the meeting (x + 4x). Since the men are x men out of a total of 5x, the men constitute one-fifth, or 20%. Choices (D) and (E) can be avoided by noting that there are more women than men in the room and men thus come to less than 50%.

29. **(E)** This is an unusual problem, one which requires careful reading rather than some clever mathematical insight. The question asks us to compare the fractions in the form $\frac{P}{Q}$ with the decimal .PQ. For example, we convert the fraction $\frac{1}{8}$ into the decimal .18 for purposes of comparison and ask how closely the second approximates the first. Since $\frac{1}{8}$ is .125, we see that the fit is not a very precise one. Similarly, with $\frac{2}{9}$, the corresponding decimal we are to compare is .29, but the actual decimal equivalent of $\frac{2}{9}$ is $.22\frac{2}{9}$. The equivalent for $\frac{3}{4}$ is .34, not even close to the actual decimal equivalent of .75. Similarly, for $\frac{4}{5}$, the artificially derived .45 is not very close to the actual decimal equivalent of .80; but for $\frac{8}{9}$ we use the decimal .89, and this is fairly close—the closest of all the fractions listed—to the actual decimal equivalent of $\frac{8}{9}$, which is .888.

If you have difficulties in finding the decimals for fractions, try to relate the fractions to percentages, which are in hundredths, or to other, more common decimal-fraction equivalencies. For example, one-third is probably known to you as approximately .33 or 33%. A ninth is one-third of a third; hence a ninth is approximately 33%/3 = 11% or .11. Eight-ninths is thus 8(11%) = 88%.

30. **(A)** If a problem seems a bit too abstract to handle using algebraic notation, a sometimes useful technique is to try to find a similar, more familiar situation. For example, virtually everyone could answer the following question: Books cost $5 each; how many books can be bought for $100? The calculation goes: $\frac{1 \text{ book}}{\$5} \times \$100 = 20$ books. So, too, here the number of books which can be purchased per d dollars must be multiplied by the number of dollars to be spent, m: $\frac{b}{d} \times m$, or $\frac{bm}{d}$.

Pursuing this line of attack, it might be worthwhile to point out that substitution of real numbers in problems like this is often an effective way of solving the problem. Since the variables and the formulas are general—that is, they do not depend upon any given number of books or dollars—the correct answer choice must work for all possible values. Suppose we assume, therefore, 2(b) books can be purchased for $5(d), and that the amount to be spent is $50(m). Most people can fall back onto common sense to calculate the number of books that can be purchased with $50: 20 books. But of the five formulas offered as answer choices, only (A) gives the number 20 when the values are substituted: For b = 2, d = 5 and m = 50, (A) = $\frac{(2)(50)}{5} = 20$, (B) = (2)(5)(50) = 500, (C) = $\frac{5}{(2)(50)} = \frac{1}{20}$, (D) = $\frac{2 + 50}{5} = \frac{52}{5}$, (E) = $\frac{2 - 50}{5} = \frac{-48}{5}$. Substitution will take longer than a direct algebraic approach, but it is much better than simply guessing, if you have the time and can't get the algebra to work right.

SECTION IV

1. **(C)** It would be a mistake to start multiplying before setting the two quantities up:

    24 hours/day $\times$ 7 days
    7 days/week $\times$ 24 weeks

    Both quantities are 24 $\times$ 7, and it is not necessary to multiply them out to see that they are equal.

2. **(C)** As in question 1, it is not necessary to actually carry out the indicated multiplication. Remembering that a % sign indicates that the number is the same as dividing by 100, each side becomes $\frac{(35)(60)}{100}$. Thus, (C). Always keep in mind that the % sign or a percentage is just a number like any other number. The % sign is equivalent to the fraction $\frac{1}{100}$.

3. **(A)** Although the most direct way to solve this problem is to add the column of ages and divide by 6 (average = 29.8), you may find it quicker to do a "running average." Assume that the average is 30 (Tom's age). If that is correct, then the sum of ages above 30 must balance exactly the sum of the ages below 30. Juanita makes the balance +5 (above 30). Brooks brings it down by 2, for a total

of +3. Glenda adds 10, for +13. Marcia brings it down by 8, for +5. Finally Dwight's age is 6 below 30, which brings the figure down to a –1. This shows that the average will be slightly below 30.

4. **(D)** Since m ranges between 4 and 6, and h ranges between 5 and 7, it is impossible to determine the relationship between m and n. For example, m and n might both be 5.5, or m might be 4.1 and n 6.9, or m might be 5.9 and n 5.1. Neither m nor n is restricted to integers.

5. **(B)** The side of the square must be 8, since $s^2 = 64$. The length of the rectangle Q must be 16, since $W \times L = 64$.

6. **(B)** The simplest way to solve this problem is first to perform the indicated operation for Column B: $(3x)^3 = 27x^3$. Now, since $x > 0$, x^3 must be positive, and it is permissible to divide both columns by x^3. The result is that Column A becomes 3 while column B becomes 9. $9 > 3$, so (B) is correct.

7. **(D)** Since it is not specified that x and y are equal to one another, the relationship is indeterminate. You can see this by visualizing x and y varying inversely with one another, e.g., when x is 2, y is $\frac{1}{2}$, when x is 3, y is $\frac{1}{3}$, etc. Also if you use substitution: if $x = 2$, then y must be $\frac{1}{2}$. On the other hand, x might be $\frac{1}{2}$, in which case y is 2.

8. **(C)** Since 11 is itself a prime number, it is factorable only by itself and 1, and that is one instance in which 11 is an integer multiple of a prime number. But it is also the only one. Any other number that is factorable by 11—say, 22—cannot, by definition, be a prime number (it would be factorable by 11 and some other number, as well as by itself and 1). Thirteen is also a prime number, which means that the only prime number of which it is an integer multiple is itself. So both 11 and 13 are each integer factors of only one prime number—themselves.

9. **(D).** Although we know that y is the even integer and that, of x and z, one is the next-largest and the other is the next-smallest integer from y, we do not know which is which. If x is the smaller and z the larger, then Column B may be greater, but if x is the larger and z the smaller, Column A may be greater. Consequently, the correct answer here must be (D).

10. **(B)** Of course, the problem is really about right triangles, not about transmitter towers, and the actual height of the tower is not important. The tower forms the common leg of two right triangles, so our triangles will have one leg of, say, length t. Then, the triangle on the left has a second leg which is shorter than the second leg of the triangle on the right (80 m vs. 100 m).

Consequently, the hypotenuse (the support wire) of the triangle on the left must be shorter than that of the triangle on the right.

11. **(C)** Notice that the number in Column A can be understood to be the sum of 2 times 1000 (the 2 is in the thousandths position), 4 times 100 (the 4 is in the hundredths position), 6 times 10 (the 6 is in the tenths position), and 8 (the eight is in the units position). This is equivalent to the expression in Column B. The only differences are that the ordering of the elements is reversed in Column B and the hundredths and thousandths are expressed in powers of ten.

12. **(D)** Since $a^2 = b$, we can substitute a^2 wherever b appears. Thus Column A can be rewritten as: $\frac{2a}{a^2}$, which is equal to $\frac{2}{a}$. Since a is positive, we can multiply both columns by a. Thus, Column A becomes 2, and Column B becomes (a)(a)(a), or a^3. Now it is easy to see that the relationship must be indeterminate. If a is a fraction, then Column A is greater. If a is a number like 2, then Column B is larger.

13. **(C)** Since vertical or opposite angles are equal, we know that $4x = x + 30$. Solving for x: $3x = 30$, $x = 10$; so the two columns are equal.

14. **(D)** To find the cost per ounce of the family-size box, we need to know both its size in ounces and its cost. While we know the relationship between the regular and family sizes for both of those items, we do not know the actual size or cost of the regular size and thus cannot use our knowledge of the relationship between the two sizes to any advantage. We wouldn't even know whether the family size or the regular size had the higher cost per ounce of cereal.

15. **(C)** One direct and simple way of solving this problem would be to count on your fingers the actual number of different duos and trios which could be formed from a group of five. The result is ten. A more elegant way of solving the problem is to recognize that $2 + 3 = 5$. In other words, each time a pair is selected to form a duo, three persons from the group have been left behind, and they form a trio. Or each time a different group of three is selected to form a trio, a pair of persons is left behind, and they constitute a duo. So even without calculating the actual number of different trios and duos that could be made, you can reach the conclusion that the number of possible combinations for each is the same.

16. **(C)** This problem simply requires finding the value of the expression $2x + 3y$, when $x = 3$ and $y = 2$: $2(3) + 3(2) = 12$.

17. **(C)** You do not need a course in business arithmetic to solve this problem, only the common-sense notion that profit is equal to gross revenue less cost. Expressed algebraically, we have P = GR − C; then, transposing the C term, we have C + P = GR, which is read: cost plus profit (or mark-up) is equal to gross revenue (or selling price). In this case, P = $4, GR = $20: C + 4 = 20, so C = 16.

18. **(A)** The information given says that the 1970 student population is $2\frac{1}{2}$ times as great as the 1950 student population. So: '70SP = '50SP × $2\frac{1}{2}$, or '70SP = 500 × $2\frac{1}{2}$ = 500 × $\frac{5}{2}$ = 1250.

19. **(C)** We must test each of the answer choices. The question asks for the one choice in which the answer is not equal to 3n + 3. In (A), for example, does 300 = 3n + 3? A quick manipulation will show that there is an integer, n, which solves the equation: 297 = 3n, so n = 99. For (C), however, no integral n exists: 3n + 3 = 208, 3n = 205, n = $68\frac{1}{3}$. So (C) is the answer we want. Another approach is to test each of the answer choices for being divisible by 3 since 3n + 3 is divisible by 3 when n is an integer. If the sum of all the single digits in a number add to a number divisible by 3, the number is itself divisible by 3; if not, not (208, for example: 2 + 0 + 8 = 10, is not divisible by 3). Being divisible by 3 does not mean an answer fits the conditions, but not being divisible by 3 means that it doesn't.

20. **(D)** The easiest approach to this problem is to draw the figures.

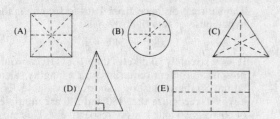

The dotted lines show possible lines of symmetry—that is, these are lines along which a paper cutout of the figure could be folded and the result will be that the two halves exactly match one another. (D) must be our answer, since it is the only figure with but one line of symmetry.

21. **(B)** This problem can, of course, be solved using an equation. We know that the laborer worked 8 hours @ $8 per hour, but what we need to know is how much overtime he worked. We let x be the number of overtime hours: (8 hrs. × $8/hr.) + (x hrs. × $12/hr) = $80. The $12/hr. is the laborer's overtime rate—that is, $8 × $1\frac{1}{2}$ = $12. Now it is a fairly simple matter to manipulate the equation:

$$64 + 12x = 80$$
$$12x = 16$$
$$x = \tfrac{16}{12}$$
$$x = 1\tfrac{1}{3}$$

Since $\frac{1}{3}$ of an hour is 20 minutes, the laborer worked 1 hour and 20 minutes of overtime, which, when added to the standard 8 hours, gives a total work day of 9 hours and 20 minutes.

Now, it is not absolutely necessary to use an equation. The equation is just a way of formalizing common sense reasoning, which might have gone like this: Well, I know he made $64 in a regular day. If he made $80 on a given day, $16 must have been overtime pay. His overtime rate is time-and-a-half, that is, $1\frac{1}{2}$ times $8/hr, or $12/hr. In the first hour of overtime he made $12, that leaves $4 more. Since $4 is one-third of $12, he has to work another one-third of an hour to make that, which is twenty minutes. So he works 8 hours at standard rates for $64, one full hour of overtime for another $12, and another $\frac{1}{3}$ of an overtime hour for $4. So $80 represents 9 hours and 20 minutes of work.

22. **(A)** This problem is both easy and difficult. Conceptually, the problem is easy to set up. High-risk stocks constitute 8.9% of the total investment of $1,080,192. To find the value of the high-risk stocks we just take 8.9% of $1,080,192. Then the problem becomes slightly difficult because it requires a tedious calculation—or at least it seems to. We say seems to because you do not actually have to do the arithmetic. The answer choices are spread fairly far apart; that is, they differ from one another by several thousands of dollars. Round 8.9% off to an even 9%, and $1,080,192 to 1,080,000. Then do the arithmetic in your head: 9% of one million is 90,000, then 9% of 80,000 is 7200, so you need an answer choice which is close to $97,000—slightly less since you rounded your percentage (8.9%) in an upward direction. With a bit of practice, you will find that this technique is more efficient than actually doing arithmetic.

23. **(B)** In this problem, the technique of rounding off and estimating is even more useful. The problem is easy enough to set up: Since state-issued bonds constituted 26% of all government bonds and securities, and since government bonds and securities constituted 48.3% of the total investment fund, state-issued bonds must constitute 26% of 48.3% of the total fund. To compute the dollar value of state-issued bonds, we need to find 26% of 48.3% of $1,080,192, but that will require substantial calculation. You can attack it in this way: 26% is close to one-fourth, and one-fourth of 48% would be 12%, so state-issued bonds are 12% of the total. Now, 10% of the total of $1,080,000 (rounded off), would be $108,000, and one-fifth of that (since 2% is one-fifth of 10%)

is approximately $20,000. So 12% must be approximately $128,000, answer (B).

24. **(A)** In this problem you can use the method of pairing. Make a rough comparison of answers (A) and (B). If you find that one of the two is clearly the larger, strike the smaller and proceed to compare answer (C) with the larger of (A) and (B). Again, this calculation will be a rough one, and if you find that one of the two is clearly larger, strike the smaller and proceed to compare the larger with (D). Follow this procedure until you have exhausted the list, and one answer remains as the largest. Now, if it turns out that any two answers are too close for a rough estimate to tell them apart, keep them both and compare them to the other answers before actually committing yourself to a detailed calculation, which is unlikely to be necessary. When there are two close answers, it is likely that a later one will supersede both of them.

In this problem we compare (A) and (B) first. Since both figures are shares of the same pie, we can compare their shares directly. Since the amount invested in municipal bonds with a 7–9% yield is 65%, (A) must be larger than (B) (the other two combined could account for only 35% of the pie), so we strike (B) and hold on to (A). Municipal bonds yielding 7–9% are 65% of all municipal bonds, and since municipal bonds account for 56% of all government bonds and securities, we can determine that the 7–9% yield municipal bonds account for roughly ⅔ of the 56% of all government bonds and securities, or slightly less than 40%. This shows that (B) must be larger than (C), since (C) accounts for only 18% of all government bonds and securities—nowhere near 40%. Similarly, we can eliminate (D) from consideration because state-issued bonds account for only 26% of all government bonds and securities—again, that is not even close to 40%. Finally, we compare (A) with (E). Since municipal bonds with a 7–9% yield constitute slightly less than 40% of all government bonds and securities, and since government bonds and securities account for approximately 48% of the entire investment fund, municipal bonds yielding 7–9% must account for 40% of that 48%, or approximately 19% of the total fund. High-risk stocks account for only 8.9% of the total fund, so (E) must be less than (A), and (A) is our answer.

25. **(E)** This question requires a careful reading of the stem. It asks which kind of investment *earned* the least amount of money, but this group of graphs shows the amount *invested* in types of investment. It cannot be assumed that each type of investment was equally profitable, so we have no way of determining which of the types of investment generated the most income.

26. **(A)** Since MNOP is a square, we know that angle O must be a right angle, that is, 90°. From that we

can conclude that arc NP is one-fourth of the entire circle. If arc NP is 4π units long, then the circumference of the circle must be 4 times that long, or 16π units. We are now in a position to find the length of the radius of circle O, and once we have the radius, we will also know the length of the sides of square MNOP, since ON and OP are both radii. The formula for the circumference of a circle is $C = 2\pi r$, so:

$$2\pi r = 16\pi$$
$$2\cancel{\pi}r = 16\cancel{\pi}$$
$$r = 8$$

So the side of the square MNOP must be 8, and its perimeter must be s + s + s + s or 4(8) = 32.

27. **(C)** The most direct way of solving this problem is first to compute the rate at which the water is filling the tank. Water is flowing into the tank at 800 cu. ft. per minute, but it is also draining out at the rate of 300 cu. ft. per minute. The net gain each minute, then, is 500 cu. ft. We then divide 3750 cu. ft. by 500 cu. ft./min., which equals 7.5 minutes. We convert the .5 minutes to 30 seconds, so our answer is 7 min. 30 sec.

28. **(B)** A quick sketch of the information provided in the problem shows that we need to employ the Pythagorean Theorem:

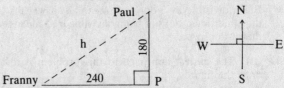

The shortest distance from Paul to Franny is the hypotenuse of this right triangle:

$$180^2 + 240^2 = h^2$$

It is extremely unlikely that the GRE would present a problem requiring such a lengthy calculation. So there must be a shortcut available. The key is to recognize that 180 and 240 are multiples of 60—3 × 60 and 4 × 60, respectively. This must be a 3,4,5 right triangle, so our hypotenuse must be 5 × 60 = 300.

29. **(A)** This problem requires a very simple insight: Area of rectangle = width × length. What makes it difficult is that many students—while they are able to compute the area of any rectangle in which the dimensions are given—"freak out" when dimensions are expressed in terms of a variable rather than real numbers. Those who keep a cool head will say, "Oh, the area is the width times the length." The area here is $81x^2$, the length is $27x$, therefore:

$$(W)(L) = Area$$
$$(W)(27x) = (81x^2)$$

Divide both sides by x:
$$(W)(27) = 81x$$
$$W = 3x$$

30. **(B)** To solve this problem, you must recognize that angle ABC is a right angle. That is because the triangle is *inscribed* in a semicircle (the vertex of the triangle is situated on the circumference of the circle), and an inscribed angle intercepts twice the arc. For example:

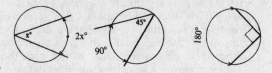

Once it is recognized that ABC is a right triangle, the shaded area can be computed by taking the area of the triangle from the area of the semicircle, or expressed in pictures:

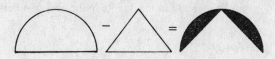

Line AC is the hypotenuse of ABC, so its length is:

$$AC^2 = (2\sqrt{2})^2 + (2\sqrt{2})^2$$
$$AC^2 = 8 + 8 = 16$$
$$AC = 4$$

AC is also the diameter of the circle, so the radius of the entire circle is 2 (radius is one-half diameter). We are now in a position to compute the area of the semicircle. Since the area of the entire circle would be πr^2, the area of the semicircle is $\dfrac{\pi r^2}{2}$: $\dfrac{\pi(2)^2}{2} = 2\pi$.

Then we compute the area of the triangle. The area of a triangle is $\frac{1}{2}ab$, and in any right triangle either of the two sides will serve as the altitude, the other serving as the base. For example:

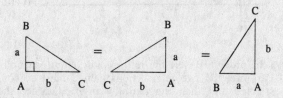

In this case, we have area = $\frac{1}{2}(2\sqrt{2})(2\sqrt{2}) = 4$. Referring to our pictorial representation of the problem:

$$\text{(semicircle)} - \text{(triangle)} = 2\pi - 4$$

SECTION V

Questions 1–5

Arranging the Information

This problem set concerns items arranged along two different and non-connected parameters: smell and prettiness. Since there is no connection between the two parameters (such as prettier flowers smell better, or whatever), the two can be analyzed separately:

```
              ←PRETTIER——less PRETTY→
A less pretty than L                L   A
D prettier than L             D     L   A
I less pretty than L          D     L   A
                                   ←I→
L prettier than R             D     L   A
                                   ←I→
                                   ←R→
```

```
Now for the smell    ←BETTER—SMELL—WORSE→
A not as nice as L or D              L   A
                                    ←D→
D not as nice as L                   L   D   A
I not as nice as D or R              L   D   A
                                   ←R×I→
L not as nice as R              R    L   D   A
                                   ← I→
```

Answering the Questions

1. **(C)** We are looking for indeterminancies, and, as the diagram shows, the smell relationship between irises and asters is unknown. (A), (B), and (E) are all definitely true, while (D) is false.

2. **(E)** (A), (B), and (D) are false, with (C) being possible, but unknown. (E) is definitely true since roses smell the best of all.

3. **(E)** The bottom of the prettiness scale has irises, roses, and asters all being in one group, whose interrelationships are not known. Even knowing how irises and roses relate does not solve the problem of how asters fit into the scheme of things. Thus, it is not determinable just what, if anything, irises are prettier than.

4. **(A)** The diagrams make it clear that only daffodils qualify. As discussed in problem 3, the relationship between the prettiness of roses, irises, and asters is not known.

5. **(A)** Be careful, when you enter this new item, not to conclude too much. Even though the diagram happens to list irises and asters next to each other in the smell scale, putting dahlias

below the asters does not make it below the irises. The new diagram is:

←BETTER—SMELL—WORSE→
L not as nice as R   R   L   D A←Dahlia→
                               ←I→

Thus, dahlias overlap irises and (A) is correct. The other choices are false.

6. **(A)** The anti-abortion speaker unwittingly plays right into the hands of the pro-abortion speaker. The "pro" speaker tries to show that there are many decisions regarding human life in which we allow that an increase in the quality of life justifies an increase in the danger to human life. All that the "anti" speaker does is to help prove this point. He says the quality of life would suffer if we lowered the speed limit to protect human life. Given this analysis, (B) must be incorrect, for the "anti" speaker's position is completely ineffective as a rebuttal. Moreover, (C) must be incorrect, for his response is not a strong statement of an anti-abortion position. (D) is incorrect, for while his response is of no value to the position he seeks to defend, it cannot be said that it is irrelevant. In fact, as we have just shown, his position is very relevant to that of the "pro" speaker's because it supports that position. Finally, (E) is not an appropriate characterization of the "anti" speaker's position, for he tries, however inartfully, to attack the merits of the "pro" speaker's position, not the character of that speaker.

7. **(E)** The "pro" speaker uses the example of traffic fatalities to show that society has always traded the quality of life for the quantity of life. Of course, he says, we do not always acknowledge that that is what we are doing; but if we were honest, we would have to admit that we were making a trade-off. Thus, (E) is the best conclusion of the passage. The author's defense of abortion amounts to the claim that abortion is just another case in which we trade off one life (the fetus) to make the lives of others (the survivors) better. The only difference is that the life being sacrificed is specifiable and highly visible in the case of abortion, whereas in the case of highway fatalities, no one knows in advance on whom the axe will fall. (A) certainly goes far beyond what the author is advocating. If anything, he probably recognizes that sometimes the trade-off will be drawn in favor of protecting lives, and thus we need some such laws. (B) must be wrong, first because the "anti" speaker claims this is not his position, and second because the "pro" speaker would prefer to show that the logical consequence of the "anti" speaker's response is an argument in favor of abortion. (C) is not an appropriate continuation because the author has already said this is a weak counter-example and that he has even stronger points to make. Finally, the author might be willing to accept contraception (D) as yet

another example of the trade-off, but his conclusion can be much stronger than that. The author wants to defend abortion, so the conclusion of his speech ought to be that abortion is an acceptable practice—not that contraception is an acceptable practice.

8. **(D)** This is a very difficult question. That III is an assumption the author makes requires careful reading. The author's attitude about the just war tips us off. He implies that this is an appropriate function of government and, further, that there are even clearer cases. Implicit in his defense of abortion is that a trade-off must be made and that it is appropriately a collective decision. I is not an assumption of the argument. Indeed, the author seems to assume, as we have just maintained, that the trade-off is an appropriate goal of society. Finally, the author does not assume II; if anything, he almost states that he accepts that the fetus is a life, but it may be traded off in exchange for an increase in the quality in the lives of others.

Questions 9–12

Arranging the Information

This is a map problem. The map can be constructed by first putting down one each of an unnamed street, avenue, road, and drive in accordance with the first part of the information.

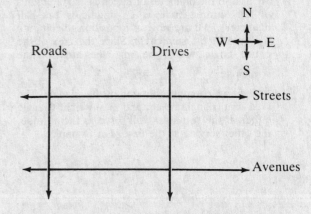

In order to insert the information about Magnolia Parkway, the two intersections named must be constructed and then the parkway inserted. Since the problem spends so much time describing angles between the various kinds of roadways, we can be sure that the angle between Magnolia Parkway and the other roadways will be of some interest. Since Magnolia Parkway is drawn between two points—the two intersections—its direction will depend on the relative placement of the points. There is nothing in the problem to prevent Hyacinth from being above or below, or for that matter even on the same level as, Zinnia. Therefore, Magnolia could have any angle whatsoever.

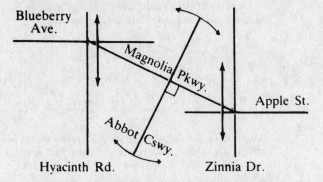

The last step is to put Abbot Causeway at right angles to Magnolia Parkway. Note that we do not know whether or not Magnolia Parkway and Abbot Causeway actually intersect, but only their relative angles. The floor in one room and the wall down the hall are perpendicular, but do not intersect.

Answering the Questions

9. **(E)** Since Magnolia Parkway could actually run in any direction at all, neither answer choice (A) nor (B) must be true, though they are both possible. Neither answer choice (C) nor (D) must be true, because there is no indication that Maple Street has anything to do with Magnolia Parkway, nor any that it doesn't. Hence, (E) is correct.

10. **(D)** Melody Drive and Fanfare Road are parallel, according to the given information, and therefore they cannot cross. If the question had used the word intersect, the answer would have still been the same, although some of the more subtle thinkers might have considered the possibility of the two running into each other end to end, as it were. This is not a subtle test and such refinements are out of place.

    (A) and (B) are not definitely false since Abbot's direction is determined by reference to Magnolia, and Magnolia can be any orientation at all, so these are both potentially true or false. (C) and (E) are also possibly true since a drive or road is perpendicular to a street.

11. **(D)** I is possible because Magnolia can be any direction. II is not possible because all drives are parallel to the roads and the roads are north/south. III is possible because streets are perpendicular to roads, so they might intersect. Hence, (D).

    This problem is noteworthy because the added

information was useful in evaluating only some of the statements and it turned out that the third statement was knowable and possible even though it did not have the same kinds of terms (direction versus intersection) as the information added in the question stem.

12. **(A)** Since both the distance between Zinnia and Hyacinth, and between Blueberry and Apple must be at least one-quarter of a mile, Magnolia must be at least as long as the diagonal of a square that is one-quarter mile on a side—that is, greater than one-quarter of a mile.

    (B) does not have to be true since it is possible for Apple Street to be just one block long. (C) is most reasonably interpreted as being false since a roadway would seem to have to be at least one block long. Though the real world does contain streets and alleys that are less than a regulation block long, this question stem specifically states that all of the blocks formed by these kinds of roadways are one-quarter mile long. Don't look for unfair tricks—they aren't there.

Questions 13–17

Arranging the Information

Since this is a flow or process situation where the interest is on who can go when, the information should be arranged to show that:
No two days in row
R, S anytime
T only after S (but not necessarily after S)
U = T
V = 3 or 5
W = 4

Answering the Questions

13. **(E)** All three statements are true.
    I and II are possible since both R and S could do the first, third, and fifth days of the job.
    III is possible, but only when S does the first and third days of the job, since T must follow S.

14. **(B)** Only II is possible. We wish to chart possibilities for the first three days, but we are especially interested in the ones which permit T and U to work on the second day, since that affects I and II. S on the first day makes T and U possible on the second day:

FIRST DAY	SECOND DAY	THIRD DAY
S	T or U	R, S, or V
OR S	R	S or V

Thus, we see that T, U, and R are possible on the

second day, which eliminites I. II is OK because it has no only.

III fails because W can work only on the fourth day.

15. **(C)** Only I and II are true. If R works the first day, only S can work the second day because T and U can only follow S and V and W can only work the third and fourth days, respectively. If S works the second day, he cannot work the third.

III is not true, because R could follow S and work the third day.

16. **(C)** As we saw in problem 15, if R works the first day, S must work the second day, but here R works the third day. U and T cannot follow R, eliminating answer choices (B) and (E). R cannot follow himself, which eliminates (B) (again) and (D). Since W can work the fourth day, (A) fails to cover all of the possibilities and (C) is correct.

Note that it is more accurate to say only that so and so can work and have that describe the only persons who can work than it is to include all who can work plus some who can't.

17. **(A)** (B), (C), and (D) focus on the fourth day's possibilities. (B) and (C) fail because they ignore W, who can also work on the fourth day. (D) fails because S could also work the fourth day.

Thus, we must consider the previous days as (A) and (E) and ask, if R, S, and V did not work the third day, who did? W couldn't, so it must have been either T or U, who worked the third day, not the second as (E) would have it. Thus, (E) is out and (A) in. If T or U worked the third day, then S must have worked the second day since those two can only follow S. Only R and S can work the first day and since they can't work two days in a row, R must have worked the first day.

Questions 18–22

Arranging the Information

Since all of the questions are "if" or conditional questions, we can expect that the original arrangement of information will not give a single, definite answer. Further, since question 18 uses only some of the information, we should start with that, adding the other conditions as we do the other problems.

Conditions I and II set up blocks which can then be moved. The management block is two seats and the labor three, with an empty one in the middle of the labor block. We do not know which of the two members of each side will occupy which of the seats in their block. IV sets up another block of three seats for the mediator, with him flanked by two empty seats.

Answering the Problems

18. **(C)** The three conditions used result in three blocks of 3, 3, and 2 seats, which add up to eight. Thus, we will have a definite arrangement:

We don't know who particularly is in the seats, only the grouping. (C) correctly notes that one labor person will sit next to one management person, whichever pair it might be.

(A) and (D) fail because IV specifically states that Jones will have empty seats on either side of him.

(B) fails only because we do not know which management representative will occupy the seat next to a labor representative.

(E) fails when (C) succeeds.

19. **(D)** In contrast to problem 18, IV is out and III is in. This means that the mediator will not have empty seats by him, but since III requires that the two parties be equally near the mediator, the nearer member of each side will be seated next to the mediator. Thus, the seating will be:

However, the labor and management parties could also switch sides to produce the following arrangement:

This is significant because the question asks specifically about the clockwise ordering of the negotiators. Since either labor negotiator could occupy either of the labor seats and either of the management negotiators could occupy either of the management seats, there are plenty of possibilities. The correct answer choice will be one which violates one of the basic rules I, II, or III.

(D) is correct because it has the two labor negotiators sitting next to each other in violation of condition II. All of the others satisfy the ideas of having management on one side of the mediator and labor on the other. management together. and labor seated with an empty seat between.

20. **(D)** The secretary sits opposite the mediator. and ALL the other conditions apply AS MUCH AS POSSIBLE. This means that some might be sacrificed. I and II say "always" while III and IV say "like" and "prefer." I and II take precedence. Here is the diagram with the secretary opposite the mediator and I and II satisfied:

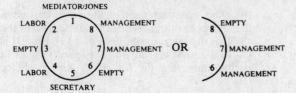

The diagram shows that conditions I and II could be met with the management negotiators either next to the mediator or next to the secretary. Condition III would have the management team sit next to the mediator. Condition IV cannot possibly be met without violating II. and since it is only a preference. it goes by the board. Thus. the final diagram is the preceding main one and the alternative listed on the right is eliminated by condition III.

Statements I and III in the problem are true. but II is false. as the diagram shows.

21. **(B)** Even though the mediator is absent. all of the applicable conditions are still in force. which are only I and II. III and IV do not apply since they refer to the mediator. who is not present. The only part of III that applies is keeping away from each other. Here is the diagram:

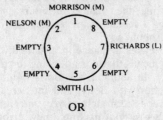

OR

These are the only two possibilities because they want to be as far away from each other as possible so Richard and Nelson would not sit next to each other. eliminating (A). (B) is not only possible so Richards and Nelson would not sit next to each other. eliminating (A). (B) is not only since these two sit in different relations to the two

negotiators who do sit opposite each other. (D) is unlikely in the first place. and amounts to sitting opposite Smith. which is where Morrison is.

22. **(A)** This problem puts us back to the situation with the mediator and all of the conditions operating. Since Morrison and Nelson always sit next to each other. the aide must be on the other side of Morrison making the management side a block of three seats in a row: Aide. Morrison. Nelson. But the aide and Nelson could flip-flop from one side of Morrison to the other. There are now six people. leaving only two empty chairs. Since one of those empty chairs must be between the two labor negotiators. there cannot be empty chairs on both sides of the mediator: thus. the mediator must be flanked by occupied seats. The middle management seat is Morrison. The diagram:

Since the two labor seats can also flip-flop between Smith and Richards. we must be careful.

(A) is not possible because the seat opposite Morrison must be empty. The aide and Nelson are opposite the two labor seats. so (B). (C). and (D) are possible. (E) is possible if that is where he happens to be.

23. **(A)** (C) and (D) are wrong because they extrapolate without sufficient information. (E) contradicts the last given statement and so cannot be a conclusion of it. That would be like trying to infer "all men are mortal" from the premise that "no men are mortal." (B) commits an error by moving from "all S are P" to "all P are S." Just because all racing engines have SFI does not mean that all SFI's are in racing engines. Some may be found in tractors and heavy-duty machinery.

24. **(D)** Peter's surprise is over the fact that an important executive of a company would use a competitor's product. hence (D). (B) is wrong because Peter's surprise is not due to Mary being unimportant; rather, he knows Mary is important, and that is the reason for his surprise. (E) is irrelevant to the exchange, for Peter imagines that, regardless of taste, Mary ought to consume the product she is responsible in part for producing. The same reasoning can be applied to (C). Finally, (A) is a distraction.

25. **(A)** The author's point depends upon the assumption that children see both animated features and "spaghetti Westerns." Obviously, if that assumption is untrue, he cannot claim that his conclusion follows. It may be true that children

get a distorted picture of the world from other causes, but the author has not claimed that. He claims only that it comes from their seeing animated features and "spaghetti Westerns." Presumably, the two different treatments cause the inversion of values. The intention of the producers in making the films is irrelevant since an action may have an effect not intended by the actor. Hence, II would not touch the author's point. Further, that there are other sources of information which present a proper view of the world does not prove that the problem cited by the author does not produce an inverted view of the world. So III would not weaken his point.

SECTION VI

Questions 1–4

Arranging the Information

This problem is one which presents a set of conditions and a group of situations to which the conditions are to be applied. The five sets do not necessarily meet all of the conditions. A preview of the question stems indicates that it is worthwhile to identify errors in the sets. It is probably more efficient to check all of them at once, condition by condition, since they are laid out so nicely.

In checking the first stated condition that the first three names in each set should be typically male names, you can just read down the columns of names. All of the names in columns one and two for all five sets are male names. In column three, however, you find that the last two, Greta and Mona from sets IV and V respectively, are female names and, thus, errors. You could circle or underline them to indicate the fact that they are errors.

Checking the second condition, that the names in the last two columns should be female names, produces no errors.

The requirement that each name in a set begin with a different letter does produce some errors. Remember that the duplication of first letters indicates that either of the two or more failing to meet the condition could be wrong. This sort of condition is somewhat different than the previous ones. With the first two conditions you could check each item individually and know for sure whether it was wrong. This condition is one of limitation where you cannot say whether it is Jack or June which is the problem in set I, Mike or Mary in II, or Louis or Linda in IV. Technically, it is not the names which are in error, but the sets.

A check of the last condition, that each of the names in a set be the same number of letters, shows Henry in II as the only problem. Again, technically it may not be Henry that is wrong, but the lack of agreement within the set. It could be that all four of the other names are wrong.

Answering the Questions

1. **(D)** The missing name must be a male name, in accordance with the first requirement, thus eliminating (A) and (B). The correct answer choice must also have a different first letter from any of the other names already in the set. Waldo (C) duplicates Wally, and Angus (E) duplicates Allen, which leaves only (D).

2. **(B)** Our general review of the conditions gives the answer to this problem. I is out because of the *J*'s. II is out because of the *M*'s and Henry. III is OK. IV and V are out for the female names in position three and the *L*'s in IV. Answer choice (B).

3. **(A)** The third condition is to have different first letters for all of the names. Set III satisfies all of the conditions without exception, so it cannot be the answer to this problem, which eliminates choice (C). Set I has only the error of the *J*'s, as described in the general discussion and in the discussion of problem 2; thus, choice (A) is correct. The other sets cited in answer choices (B), (D), and (E) have other forms of error, as previously described in the discussion of arranging the information.

4. **(E)** You have to be careful with a question like this, which seeks to correct some sort of error in the given information. Some of the suggested answers may correct one error only to make a new one. Answer choice (A), for example, corrects the problem of the *J*'s in set I, but puts a male name in the fourth position, which is a new error.

   (B) makes a similar error because, in the act of correcting the number-of-letters problem with Henry, a female name is placed where a male name should go.

   (C) makes a change in an already correct set, which means that it is not going to "make" set III correct. In addition, the Boris would duplicate a first letter with Betty, and thus create an error.

   (D) does accurately correct an error in set IV—the *L*'s—without making a new error, but this is not enough to make the set correct since it still has a female name in the third position.

   (E) is the correct answer because the substitution of Fred for Mona in set V solves the only problem that set had, without creating any new errors.

5. **(C)** III is an assumption of the psychologist. He observed the dogs for a certain period of time, and found that each time a stranger approached they kept silent. From those observed instances he concluded that the dogs never barked at strangers. Obviously his theory would be disproved (or at least it would have to be seriously qualified) if, when he was not watching, the dogs barked their

heads off at strangers. I is not assumed, however. The psychologist was concerned only with the dogs' reactions to strangers. As far as we know, he may have seen the dogs barking during a frolic in the park, or while they were being bathed, or at full moon. II is not an assumption the author makes. The author makes a factual claim: Dogs treated in this way do not bark at strangers. We have no basis for concluding that the author does or does not think that dogs ought or ought not to bark at strangers. In fact, it seems as likely that the author thinks a great way to train watch dogs is to hit them with rolled-up newspapers.

6. **(B)** II would undermine the psychologist's thesis that "only a beaten dog barks." It cites instances in which the dog was not beaten and still barked at strangers. This would force the psychologist to reconsider his conclusion about the connection between beating and barking. I is not like II. It does not state the dogs were never beaten; it states only that the dogs were not beaten when they barked at strangers. It is conceivable that they were beaten at other times. If they were, then even though they might bark at strangers (and not be beaten at that moment), they would not be counter-examples to the psychologist's theory. III is not an assumption of the psychologist, as we saw in the preceding question, so denying it does not affect the strength of his argument. The psychologist is concerned with the factual connection between beating a dog and its barking; information about the owners' feelings can hardly be relevant to that factual issue.

7. **(E)** Careful reading of the ad shows that all three propositions could be true even if the ad is correct. First, another deodorant might also give all-day protection. The ad claims that White Bear is the only deodorant which gives you *both* protection and scent—a vacuous enough claim since White Bear is probably the only deodorant with the White Bear scent. Of course, III is not affected by this point, since the White Bear Company may put its unique scent into many of its products. Finally, II is also not inconsistent with the ad—that another product is more popular does not say that it has the features the ad claims for the White Bear deodorant.

Questions 8–12

Arranging the Information

This is a situation with so few items in it that it looks likely to be completely determined once everything is fitted in. It is probably going to be helpful to keep track of the cross-references in a separate chart.

Entering the first item: Roger's wife is older than Ursula, and hence not Ursula.

PAUL	QUINCY	ROGER	SAM
		not U	
		older than U	
TESS	URSULA	VAL	WILMA
	not R		

	P	Q	R	S
T				
U		N		
V				
W				

"N" MEANS NOT SPOUSE OF
"Y" MEANS IS SPOUSE OF

Sam's wife is older than Wilma (and hence not Wilma), who is Paul's sister (and hence not Paul's wife).

Roger was best man at Wilma's wedding (and hence is not married to Wilma).

Wilma is not P's, R's, or S's wife, so must be Q's wife.

	P	Q	R	S
T	N			
U		N	N	
V		N		
W	N	Y	N	N

"N" MEANS NOT SPOUSE OF
"Y" MEANS IS SPOUSE OF

Tess is the youngest, and hence not S's or R's but P's wife.

	P	Q	R	S
T	Y	N	N	N
U	N	N	N	
V		N	N	
W	N	Y	N	N

"N" MEANS NOT SPOUSE OF
"Y" MEANS IS SPOUSE OF

This leads to the further deduction that U can only go with S, leaving R and V to go with each other.

	P	Q	R	S
T	Y	N	N	N
U	N	N	N	Y
V	N	N	Y	N
W	N	Y	N	N

"N" MEANS NOT SPOUSE OF
"Y" MEANS IS SPOUSE OF

We have the miscellaneous information that the ages of the wives are also in order. V, as R's wife, is older than Ursula, with T the youngest, and U is older than W, yielding, in age, V>U>W>T.

Paul is Wilma's sister.

We did not actually need the last item of information to find out the marriages.

Answering the Problems

8. **(A)** Quincy's wife's (Wilma) brother's (Paul) wife, Tess, will be Patrick's aunt, (A). You must look to Paul since that is the only brother/sister relationship, which is the only thing that could yield an aunt relationship.

9. **(C)** This is just a matter of checking on who is married to whom and using the age relationships,

previously developed. Paul's wife is Tess, who is youngest of all.

10. **(D)** The main idea here is to use the age relationships of the wives to help sort out the husbands. Since Wilma is older than Tess, their husbands Quincy and Paul must have the same relationship, thus, (D) is false.

(A) is true since Roger, older than the oldest wife, must be the oldest of the group, and (B) is true since Tess must be the youngest of all. The husbands are older than the wives and she is the youngest wife. (C) is true since the wives of these two have just that relationship.

(E) might or might not be true, but it is certainly not definitely false. The wives might be one day older than each other, or decades.

11. **(C)** Since the answer choices are all in terms of the marriages, let us arrange the information that way:

PAUL	27	QUINCY	29
TESS	28	WILMA	30
ROGER	31	SAM	33
VAL.	34	URS.	32

Note that since the husband's ages are generally younger, it is not surprising that in three of the couples the wife is older.

Reading from this chart we see that (C) is false.

12. **(A)** This goes back to the original information and does not use the information from the previous problem. We simply have to sort out who is married to whom, and use the age relationships developed previously.

The couples are P/V, Q/W, R/T, S/U and the ages are V>U>W>T. Sam's wife is still Ursula, and she is younger than only Valerie, who is now Paul's wife, choice (A), eliminating (B). (C) and (D) would be correct before the switch in spouses, when Valerie, the oldest wife, was married to Roger. Now, however, Tess, the youngest wife, is married to Roger, so they are false. (E) similarly would have been true before the divorces and remarriages, but not now.

Questions 13–17

This is a linear ordering set. We begin by summarizing the information for easy reference:

O ≠ 1st or 6th
L ≠ J ⎫ (We know that L > M, so this means
L ≠ K ⎬ L cannot be next to J or K in the line.)
L→M ⎭

13. **(D)** For this question, we simply check each choice against the initial conditions. On the

ground that O does not finish first or last, we eliminate (C). On the ground that L cannot be next in line to either J or K, we eliminate (A) and (E). Finally, since L must finish immediately ahead of M, we eliminate (B). Only (D) satisfies all of the restrictions.

14. **(E)** We begin by processing the additional information:

1	2	3	4	5	6
J				K	

This places the L-M combination in positions 3 and 4, respectively (to avoid the J-K conflict). And O must be in position 2, with N in position 6:

1	2	3	4	5	6
J	O	L	M	K	N

This shows that only (E) is true.

15. **(C)** We begin by processing the additional information:

1	2	3	4	5	6
N	L	M			

We put N in first because J, K, and O cannot be there. We know further that either J or K must be sixth, since O cannot finish last. But there are four possible arrangements using these restrictions:

1	2	3	4	5	6
N	L	M	O	J	K
N	L	M	O	K	J
N	L	M	K	O	J
N	L	M	J	O	K

Testing the statements, we see that I is merely possible but not necessary. II is definitely not possible. Finally, III is true under the assumptions given, so III alone is the correct choice.

16. **(D)** For this question, we test each arrangement against the initial conditions. We know that four of the five will be acceptable and that only one will not be acceptable. The exception is the correct choice. (D) is not acceptable since we have the impermissible arrangement of J in second place and L in third place.

17. **(E)** For this question, we must treat each statement as providing additional information. As for statement I, we get

1	2	3	4	5	6
N	J	K	O	L	M

With J and K in 2 and 3 respectively, we must put L in 5, and therefore M in 6. But O must then be in 4, with N in 1. So there is only one possible arrangement using this information. As for II, we have

1	2	3	4	5	6
L	M	J	K	O	N

With K in 4, we must put the L-M combination in 1 and 2. This means that N finishes last with O in position 5. So, again, the statement guarantees only one arrangement. Finally, III:

1	2	3	4	5	6
L	M	O	J	K	N

With J and K in 4 and 5, L and M must be in 1 and 2 or 2 and 3. But they cannot be in 2 and 3 for this would require O to be first or last. So L and M must be in 1 and 2; N must be in 6; and O must be in 3.

Questions 18–22

Arranging the Information

Previewing these problems and the information makes it clear that all we have is a partial description of what might be the diving arrangements. We can classify this either algebraically, by writing equations such as "M not P or Q," "K with S," or we can make a diagram showing the connections which are stated:

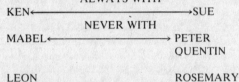

DIVERS   BIOLOGISTS

AT LEAST ONE PER TEAM OF EACH CATEGORY
                    ALWAYS WITH
    KEN◄————————————————►SUE
                    NEVER WITH
    MABEL◄———————————► PETER
                                QUENTIN

    LEON   ROSEMARY
    NINA
    DIVE-MASTER FROM
    THIS GROUP

Answering the Questions

18. **(D)** You must note the condition that there are three dive teams. Since there are seven people, not counting Jack or Nina, to be divided into 3 teams (one could stay aboard ship, but it doesn't matter), the teams must be 2, 2, and 2 or 3 persons. Ken and Sue are on one team. Mabel can't be with either Peter or Quentin so she must be with Rosemary; hence (D) is not possible, yielding (D) as the correct answer.

    That leaves Leon to be with either Peter or Quentin and the other of that pair to go with either Ken or Leon's team or stay on ship.

    If you wished to choose (A) or (B), you may have thought the newlyweds wouldn't dive with anyone, but all that was said was that they dive together. (C) and (E) are valid possibilities, as previously explained, which leaves (D).

19. **(A)** Ken and Sue are one team. Since Mabel won't dive with the two male biologists, she must

dive with Rosemary as a two-diver team. Nina and Leon on the one hand, and Peter and Quentin on the other, can trade freely and they can team up four ways (L & P, L & Q, N & P, and N & Q) for a grand total of six.

20. **(C)** Mabel's being the dive-master opens things up a little, but the basic restrictions still hold. I is not possible because they are all biologists. II is not possible because they are both professional divers with no biologist. III is possible in a way similar to that discussed in problem 18. IV is not possible because it involves splitting Ken and Sue. Hence, (C).

21. **(B)** (C) is out because it parts Ken and Sue. (D) has a team composed only of biologists or only of professional divers, and thus fails. (A) and (E) both fail to keep anyone on board as a dive-master. (B) is, thus, the answer. There is no limit to the size of the teams.

22. **(D)** (A), (B), and (E) all split Ken and Sue and thus are not possible. (C) fails for having only biologists. (D) is possible and the answer.

23. **(E)** This is a very sticky question, but it is similar to ones which have been on the GRE. The key here is to keep in mind that you are to pick the BEST answer, and sometimes you will not be very satisfied with any of them. Here (E) is correct by default of the others. (A) has some merit. After all, the real economist isn't very careful in his statement of his claim. But there is no particular again" when there is no evidence that we have ever been there before. But there is no particular term he uses which we could call ambiguous. (B) is wrong because although the economist assumes some people take that position (otherwise, against whom would he be arguing?), he does not imply that he alone thinks differently. (C) is like (A), a possible answer, but this interpretation requires additional information. You would have to have said to yourself, "Oh, I see that he is against it. He is probably saying this in an exasperated tone and in the context of a diatribe." If there were such additional information, you would be right, and (C) would be a good answer. But there isn't. (E) does not require this additional speculation and so is truer to the given information. (D) would also require speculation. (E) is not perfect, just BEST by comparison.

24. **(A)** The main point of the passage is that pregnancy and a child put strain on a young marriage, and that such marriages would have a higher survival rate without the strain of children. It would seem, then, that encouraging such couples not to have children would help them stay married; but that will be possible only if they have not already committed themselves, so to speak, to having a child. If the wife is already pregnant at

the time of marriage, the commitment has already been made, so the advice is too late. (B) and (C) are wrong for similar reasons. It is not only the continued presence of the child in the marriage which causes the stress, but the very pregnancy and birth. So (B) and (C) do not address themselves to the *birth* of the child, and that is the factor to which the author attributes the dissolution of the marriage. (D) is wide of the mark. Whether society does or does not have such an interest, the author has shown us a causal linkage, that is, a mere fact of the matter. He states: If this, then fewer divorces. He may or may not believe there should be fewer divorces. (E) is wrong for this reason also, and for the further reason that it says "do not *plan*" to have children. The author's concern is with children during the early part of the marriage. He does not suggest that couples should never have children.

25. **(E)** This question is primarily a matter of careful reading. The phrase "no lower bus fares" must not be read to mean that Flash uniquely has the lowest fare; it means only that no one else has a fare lower than that of Flash. It is conceivable that several companies share the lowest fare. So II is not inconsistent with the claim made in the advertisement. III is not inconsistent since it mentions the New York City to Boston route, and it is the Washington, D.C., to New York City route which is the subject of the ad's claim. Finally, I is not inconsistent since it speaks of an *air* fare and the ad's language carefully restricts the claim to *bus* fares.

ANSWER SHEET—PRACTICE EXAMINATION 2

Section I

1 Ⓐ Ⓑ Ⓒ Ⓓ Ⓔ   8 Ⓐ Ⓑ Ⓒ Ⓓ Ⓔ   15 Ⓐ Ⓑ Ⓒ Ⓓ Ⓔ   22 Ⓐ Ⓑ Ⓒ Ⓓ Ⓔ   29 Ⓐ Ⓑ Ⓒ Ⓓ Ⓔ   36 Ⓐ Ⓑ Ⓒ Ⓓ Ⓔ

2 Ⓐ Ⓑ Ⓒ Ⓓ Ⓔ   9 Ⓐ Ⓑ Ⓒ Ⓓ Ⓔ   16 Ⓐ Ⓑ Ⓒ Ⓓ Ⓔ   23 Ⓐ Ⓑ Ⓒ Ⓓ Ⓔ   30 Ⓐ Ⓑ Ⓒ Ⓓ Ⓔ   37 Ⓐ Ⓑ Ⓒ Ⓓ Ⓔ

3 Ⓐ Ⓑ Ⓒ Ⓓ Ⓔ   10 Ⓐ Ⓑ Ⓒ Ⓓ Ⓔ   17 Ⓐ Ⓑ Ⓒ Ⓓ Ⓔ   24 Ⓐ Ⓑ Ⓒ Ⓓ Ⓔ   31 Ⓐ Ⓑ Ⓒ Ⓓ Ⓔ   38 Ⓐ Ⓑ Ⓒ Ⓓ Ⓔ

4 Ⓐ Ⓑ Ⓒ Ⓓ Ⓔ   11 Ⓐ Ⓑ Ⓒ Ⓓ Ⓔ   18 Ⓐ Ⓑ Ⓒ Ⓓ Ⓔ   25 Ⓐ Ⓑ Ⓒ Ⓓ Ⓔ   32 Ⓐ Ⓑ Ⓒ Ⓓ Ⓔ

5 Ⓐ Ⓑ Ⓒ Ⓓ Ⓔ   12 Ⓐ Ⓑ Ⓒ Ⓓ Ⓔ   19 Ⓐ Ⓑ Ⓒ Ⓓ Ⓔ   26 Ⓐ Ⓑ Ⓒ Ⓓ Ⓔ   33 Ⓐ Ⓑ Ⓒ Ⓓ Ⓔ

6 Ⓐ Ⓑ Ⓒ Ⓓ Ⓔ   13 Ⓐ Ⓑ Ⓒ Ⓓ Ⓔ   20 Ⓐ Ⓑ Ⓒ Ⓓ Ⓔ   27 Ⓐ Ⓑ Ⓒ Ⓓ Ⓔ   34 Ⓐ Ⓑ Ⓒ Ⓓ Ⓔ

7 Ⓐ Ⓑ Ⓒ Ⓓ Ⓔ   14 Ⓐ Ⓑ Ⓒ Ⓓ Ⓔ   21 Ⓐ Ⓑ Ⓒ Ⓓ Ⓔ   28 Ⓐ Ⓑ Ⓒ Ⓓ Ⓔ   35 Ⓐ Ⓑ Ⓒ Ⓓ Ⓔ

Section II

1 Ⓐ Ⓑ Ⓒ Ⓓ Ⓔ   8 Ⓐ Ⓑ Ⓒ Ⓓ Ⓔ   15 Ⓐ Ⓑ Ⓒ Ⓓ Ⓔ   22 Ⓐ Ⓑ Ⓒ Ⓓ Ⓔ   29 Ⓐ Ⓑ Ⓒ Ⓓ Ⓔ   36 Ⓐ Ⓑ Ⓒ Ⓓ Ⓔ

2 Ⓐ Ⓑ Ⓒ Ⓓ Ⓔ   9 Ⓐ Ⓑ Ⓒ Ⓓ Ⓔ   16 Ⓐ Ⓑ Ⓒ Ⓓ Ⓔ   23 Ⓐ Ⓑ Ⓒ Ⓓ Ⓔ   30 Ⓐ Ⓑ Ⓒ Ⓓ Ⓔ   37 Ⓐ Ⓑ Ⓒ Ⓓ Ⓔ

3 Ⓐ Ⓑ Ⓒ Ⓓ Ⓔ   10 Ⓐ Ⓑ Ⓒ Ⓓ Ⓔ   17 Ⓐ Ⓑ Ⓒ Ⓓ Ⓔ   24 Ⓐ Ⓑ Ⓒ Ⓓ Ⓔ   31 Ⓐ Ⓑ Ⓒ Ⓓ Ⓔ   38 Ⓐ Ⓑ Ⓒ Ⓓ Ⓔ

4 Ⓐ Ⓑ Ⓒ Ⓓ Ⓔ   11 Ⓐ Ⓑ Ⓒ Ⓓ Ⓔ   18 Ⓐ Ⓑ Ⓒ Ⓓ Ⓔ   25 Ⓐ Ⓑ Ⓒ Ⓓ Ⓔ   32 Ⓐ Ⓑ Ⓒ Ⓓ Ⓔ

5 Ⓐ Ⓑ Ⓒ Ⓓ Ⓔ   12 Ⓐ Ⓑ Ⓒ Ⓓ Ⓔ   19 Ⓐ Ⓑ Ⓒ Ⓓ Ⓔ   26 Ⓐ Ⓑ Ⓒ Ⓓ Ⓔ   33 Ⓐ Ⓑ Ⓒ Ⓓ Ⓔ

6 Ⓐ Ⓑ Ⓒ Ⓓ Ⓔ   13 Ⓐ Ⓑ Ⓒ Ⓓ Ⓔ   20 Ⓐ Ⓑ Ⓒ Ⓓ Ⓔ   27 Ⓐ Ⓑ Ⓒ Ⓓ Ⓔ   34 Ⓐ Ⓑ Ⓒ Ⓓ Ⓔ

7 Ⓐ Ⓑ Ⓒ Ⓓ Ⓔ   14 Ⓐ Ⓑ Ⓒ Ⓓ Ⓔ   21 Ⓐ Ⓑ Ⓒ Ⓓ Ⓔ   28 Ⓐ Ⓑ Ⓒ Ⓓ Ⓔ   35 Ⓐ Ⓑ Ⓒ Ⓓ Ⓔ

Section III

1 Ⓐ Ⓑ Ⓒ Ⓓ   6 Ⓐ Ⓑ Ⓒ Ⓓ   11 Ⓐ Ⓑ Ⓒ Ⓓ   16 Ⓐ Ⓑ Ⓒ Ⓓ Ⓔ   21 Ⓐ Ⓑ Ⓒ Ⓓ Ⓔ   26 Ⓐ Ⓑ Ⓒ Ⓓ Ⓔ

2 Ⓐ Ⓑ Ⓒ Ⓓ   7 Ⓐ Ⓑ Ⓒ Ⓓ   12 Ⓐ Ⓑ Ⓒ Ⓓ   17 Ⓐ Ⓑ Ⓒ Ⓓ Ⓔ   22 Ⓐ Ⓑ Ⓒ Ⓓ Ⓔ   27 Ⓐ Ⓑ Ⓒ Ⓓ Ⓔ

3 Ⓐ Ⓑ Ⓒ Ⓓ   8 Ⓐ Ⓑ Ⓒ Ⓓ   13 Ⓐ Ⓑ Ⓒ Ⓓ   18 Ⓐ Ⓑ Ⓒ Ⓓ Ⓔ   23 Ⓐ Ⓑ Ⓒ Ⓓ Ⓔ   28 Ⓐ Ⓑ Ⓒ Ⓓ Ⓔ

4 Ⓐ Ⓑ Ⓒ Ⓓ   9 Ⓐ Ⓑ Ⓒ Ⓓ   14 Ⓐ Ⓑ Ⓒ Ⓓ   19 Ⓐ Ⓑ Ⓒ Ⓓ Ⓔ   24 Ⓐ Ⓑ Ⓒ Ⓓ Ⓔ   29 Ⓐ Ⓑ Ⓒ Ⓓ Ⓔ

5 Ⓐ Ⓑ Ⓒ Ⓓ   10 Ⓐ Ⓑ Ⓒ Ⓓ   15 Ⓐ Ⓑ Ⓒ Ⓓ   20 Ⓐ Ⓑ Ⓒ Ⓓ Ⓔ   25 Ⓐ Ⓑ Ⓒ Ⓓ Ⓔ   30 Ⓐ Ⓑ Ⓒ Ⓓ Ⓔ

Section IV

1 Ⓐ Ⓑ Ⓒ Ⓓ   6 Ⓐ Ⓑ Ⓒ Ⓓ   11 Ⓐ Ⓑ Ⓒ Ⓓ   16 Ⓐ Ⓑ Ⓒ Ⓓ Ⓔ   21 Ⓐ Ⓑ Ⓒ Ⓓ Ⓔ   26 Ⓐ Ⓑ Ⓒ Ⓓ Ⓔ

2 Ⓐ Ⓑ Ⓒ Ⓓ   7 Ⓐ Ⓑ Ⓒ Ⓓ   12 Ⓐ Ⓑ Ⓒ Ⓓ   17 Ⓐ Ⓑ Ⓒ Ⓓ Ⓔ   22 Ⓐ Ⓑ Ⓒ Ⓓ Ⓔ   27 Ⓐ Ⓑ Ⓒ Ⓓ Ⓔ

3 Ⓐ Ⓑ Ⓒ Ⓓ   8 Ⓐ Ⓑ Ⓒ Ⓓ   13 Ⓐ Ⓑ Ⓒ Ⓓ   18 Ⓐ Ⓑ Ⓒ Ⓓ Ⓔ   23 Ⓐ Ⓑ Ⓒ Ⓓ Ⓔ   28 Ⓐ Ⓑ Ⓒ Ⓓ Ⓔ

4 Ⓐ Ⓑ Ⓒ Ⓓ   9 Ⓐ Ⓑ Ⓒ Ⓓ   14 Ⓐ Ⓑ Ⓒ Ⓓ   19 Ⓐ Ⓑ Ⓒ Ⓓ Ⓔ   24 Ⓐ Ⓑ Ⓒ Ⓓ Ⓔ   29 Ⓐ Ⓑ Ⓒ Ⓓ Ⓔ

5 Ⓐ Ⓑ Ⓒ Ⓓ   10 Ⓐ Ⓑ Ⓒ Ⓓ   15 Ⓐ Ⓑ Ⓒ Ⓓ   20 Ⓐ Ⓑ Ⓒ Ⓓ Ⓔ   25 Ⓐ Ⓑ Ⓒ Ⓓ Ⓔ   30 Ⓐ Ⓑ Ⓒ Ⓓ Ⓔ

Section V

1 Ⓐ Ⓑ Ⓒ Ⓓ Ⓔ   6 Ⓐ Ⓑ Ⓒ Ⓓ Ⓔ   11 Ⓐ Ⓑ Ⓒ Ⓓ Ⓔ   16 Ⓐ Ⓑ Ⓒ Ⓓ Ⓔ   21 Ⓐ Ⓑ Ⓒ Ⓓ Ⓔ

2 Ⓐ Ⓑ Ⓒ Ⓓ Ⓔ   7 Ⓐ Ⓑ Ⓒ Ⓓ Ⓔ   12 Ⓐ Ⓑ Ⓒ Ⓓ Ⓔ   17 Ⓐ Ⓑ Ⓒ Ⓓ Ⓔ   22 Ⓐ Ⓑ Ⓒ Ⓓ Ⓔ

3 Ⓐ Ⓑ Ⓒ Ⓓ Ⓔ   8 Ⓐ Ⓑ Ⓒ Ⓓ Ⓔ   13 Ⓐ Ⓑ Ⓒ Ⓓ Ⓔ   18 Ⓐ Ⓑ Ⓒ Ⓓ Ⓔ   23 Ⓐ Ⓑ Ⓒ Ⓓ Ⓔ

4 Ⓐ Ⓑ Ⓒ Ⓓ Ⓔ   9 Ⓐ Ⓑ Ⓒ Ⓓ Ⓔ   14 Ⓐ Ⓑ Ⓒ Ⓓ Ⓔ   19 Ⓐ Ⓑ Ⓒ Ⓓ Ⓔ   24 Ⓐ Ⓑ Ⓒ Ⓓ Ⓔ

5 Ⓐ Ⓑ Ⓒ Ⓓ Ⓔ   10 Ⓐ Ⓑ Ⓒ Ⓓ Ⓔ   15 Ⓐ Ⓑ Ⓒ Ⓓ Ⓔ   20 Ⓐ Ⓑ Ⓒ Ⓓ Ⓔ   25 Ⓐ Ⓑ Ⓒ Ⓓ Ⓔ

Section VI

1 Ⓐ Ⓑ Ⓒ Ⓓ Ⓔ   6 Ⓐ Ⓑ Ⓒ Ⓓ Ⓔ   11 Ⓐ Ⓑ Ⓒ Ⓓ Ⓔ   16 Ⓐ Ⓑ Ⓒ Ⓓ Ⓔ   21 Ⓐ Ⓑ Ⓒ Ⓓ Ⓔ

2 Ⓐ Ⓑ Ⓒ Ⓓ Ⓔ   7 Ⓐ Ⓑ Ⓒ Ⓓ Ⓔ   12 Ⓐ Ⓑ Ⓒ Ⓓ Ⓔ   17 Ⓐ Ⓑ Ⓒ Ⓓ Ⓔ   22 Ⓐ Ⓑ Ⓒ Ⓓ Ⓔ

3 Ⓐ Ⓑ Ⓒ Ⓓ Ⓔ   8 Ⓐ Ⓑ Ⓒ Ⓓ Ⓔ   13 Ⓐ Ⓑ Ⓒ Ⓓ Ⓔ   18 Ⓐ Ⓑ Ⓒ Ⓓ Ⓔ   23 Ⓐ Ⓑ Ⓒ Ⓓ Ⓔ

4 Ⓐ Ⓑ Ⓒ Ⓓ Ⓔ   9 Ⓐ Ⓑ Ⓒ Ⓓ Ⓔ   14 Ⓐ Ⓑ Ⓒ Ⓓ Ⓔ   19 Ⓐ Ⓑ Ⓒ Ⓓ Ⓔ   24 Ⓐ Ⓑ Ⓒ Ⓓ Ⓔ

5 Ⓐ Ⓑ Ⓒ Ⓓ Ⓔ   10 Ⓐ Ⓑ Ⓒ Ⓓ Ⓔ   15 Ⓐ Ⓑ Ⓒ Ⓓ Ⓔ   20 Ⓐ Ⓑ Ⓒ Ⓓ Ⓔ   25 Ⓐ Ⓑ Ⓒ Ⓓ Ⓔ

PRACTICE EXAMINATION 2

SECTION I

30 minutes
38 questions

Directions: Each of the questions below contains one or more blank spaces, each blank indicating an omitted word. Each sentence is followed by five (5) lettered words or sets of words. Read and determine the general sense of each sentence. Then choose the word or set of words which, when inserted in the sentence, best fits the meaning of the sentence.

1. She was easily intimidated by her employer, who made a practice of _____ his authority over her.
   - (A) relinquishing
   - (B) compounding
   - (C) dismissing
   - (D) abusing
   - (E) denying

2. The children marveled at the strange foliage; it was their _____ to the tropics.
   - (A) voyage
   - (B) devotion
   - (C) introduction
   - (D) responsibility
   - (E) conduit

3. _____ and _____, she left many to mourn her generous heart when she died.
   - (A) Selfless—altruistic
   - (B) Thoughtful—rarefied
   - (C) Beloved—dogmatic
   - (D) Kind—ruthless
   - (E) Political—gentle

4. A wave of self-_____ convulsed her as she realized the _____ she had caused others.
   - (A) pity—suffering
   - (B) doubt—happiness
   - (C) contempt—pain
   - (D) esteem—service
   - (E) concern—inconvenience

5. The late-summer waters of the northern shore were _____ chilly for the vacationers who liked to swim.
   - (A) wonderfully
   - (B) disappointingly
   - (C) hopefully
   - (D) seasonally
   - (E) realistically

6. The innovations of the _____ Age have had _____ effects on people in all walks of life.
   - (A) Atomic—irrelevant
   - (B) Electronic—universal
   - (C) Bronze—pretentious
   - (D) Nuclear—profane
   - (E) Computer—marked

7. The _____ spectacle drew a(n) _____ shudder from the assembled guests.
   - (A) elaborate—credible
   - (B) grisly—horrified
   - (C) understated—appreciative
   - (D) glittering—approving
   - (E) grotesque—pleased

Directions: In each of the following questions, you are given a related pair of words or phrases in capital letters. Each capitalized pair is followed by five (5) lettered pairs of words or phrases. Choose the pair which best expresses a relationship similar to that expressed by the original pair.

291

8. ISLAND : OCEAN ::
   (A) hill : stream
   (B) forest : valley
   (C) oasis : desert
   (D) tree : field
   (E) peninsula : pier

9. MATHEMATICS : NUMEROLOGY ::
   (A) biology : botany
   (B) psychology : physiology
   (C) anatomy : medicine
   (D) astronomy : astrology
   (E) philosophy : science

10. DISLIKABLE : ABHORRENT ::
    (A) trustworthy : helpful
    (B) ominous : loving
    (C) silly : young
    (D) **tender : hard**
    (E) **difficult : arduous**

11. MINARET : MOSQUE ::
    (A) Christian : Moslem
    (B) steeple : church
    (C) dainty : grotesque
    (D) modern : classic
    (E) romantic : Gothic

12. WHEAT : CHAFF ::
    (A) wine : dregs
    (B) **bread : crumbs**
    (C) **laughter : raillery**
    (D) oat : oatmeal
    (E) crop : bird

13. DRAMA : DIRECTOR ::
    (A) class : principal
    (B) movie : scenario
    (C) actor : playwright
    (D) tragedy : Sophocles
    (E) magazine : editor

14. IMPLACABLE : GOAL ::
    (A) officious : procedure
    (B) zealous : method
    (C) infectious : disease
    (D) placid : mirror
    (E) inferable : conclusion

15. CARTOON : DRAWING ::
    (A) comic : painting
    (B) laughter : tears
    (C) crayon : brush
    (D) ditty : aria
    (E) caricature : portrait

16. INSOUCIANT : LIGHTHEARTED ::
    (A) merry : laughter
    (B) thieving : light-fingered
    (C) calm : unworried
    (D) grin : ecstatic
    (E) convalescent : illness

Directions: Below each of the following passages, you will find questions or incomplete statements about the passage. Each statement or question is followed by lettered words or expressions. Select the word or expression that most satisfactorily completes each statement or answers each question in accordance with the meaning of the passage. After you have chosen the best answer, blacken the corresponding space on the answer sheet.

However important we may regard school life to be, there is no gainsaying the fact that children spend more time at home than in the classroom. Therefore, the great influence of parents cannot be ignored or discounted by the teacher. They can become strong allies of the school personnel or they can consciously or unconsciously hinder and thwart curricular objectives.

Administrators have been aware of the need to keep parents apprised of the newer methods used in schools. Many principals have conducted workshops explaining such matters as the reading readiness program, manuscript writing, and developmental mathematics.

Moreover, the classroom teacher, with the permission of the supervisors, can also play an important role in enlightening parents. The many interviews carried on during the year as well as new ways of reporting pupils' progress, can significantly aid in achieving a harmonious interplay between school and home.

To illustrate, suppose that a father has been drilling Junior in arithmetic processes night after night. In a friendly interview, the teacher can help the parent sublimate his natural paternal interest into productive channels. He might be persuaded to let Junior participate in discussing the family budget, buying the food, using a yardstick or measuring cup at home, setting the clock, calculating mileage on a trip, and engaging in scores of other activities that have a mathematical basis.

If the father follows the advice, it is reasonable to assume that he will soon realize his son is making satisfactory progress in mathematics and, at the same time, enjoying the work.

Too often, however, teachers' conferences with parents are devoted to petty accounts of children's misdemeanors, complaints about laziness and poor work habits, and suggestions for penalties and rewards at home.

What is needed is a more creative approach in which the teacher, as a professional adviser, plants ideas in parents' minds for the best utilization of the many hours that the child spends out of the classroom.

In this way, the school and the home join forces in fostering the fullest development of youngsters' capacities.

17. The central idea conveyed in the above passage is that
(A) home training is more important than school training because a child spends so many hours with his parents
(B) teachers can and should help parents to understand and further the objectives of the school
(C) parents unwittingly have hindered and thwarted curricular objectives
(D) there are many ways in which the mathematics program can be implemented at home
(E) parents have a responsibility to help students to do their homework

18. The author directly discusses the fact that
(A) parents drill their children too much in arithmetic
(B) principals have explained the new art programs to parents
(C) a father can have his son help him construct articles at home
(D) a parent's misguided efforts can be redirected to proper channels
(E) there is not sufficient individual instruction in the classroom

19. It can reasonably be inferred that the author
(A) is satisfied with present relationships between home and school

(B) feels that the traditional program in mathematics is slightly superior to the developmental program
(C) believes that schools are lacking in guidance personnel
(D) feels that parent-teacher interviews can be made much more constructive than they are at present
(E) is of the opinion that teachers of this generation are inferior to those of the last generation

20. A method of parent-teacher communication NOT mentioned or referred to by the author is
(A) classes for parents
(B) new progress report forms
(C) parent-teacher interviews
(D) informal teas
(E) demonstration lesson

21. The author implies that
(A) participation in interesting activities relating to a school subject improves one's achievement in that area
(B) too many children are lazy and have poor work habits
(C) school principals do more than their share in interpreting the curriculum to the parents
(D) only a small part of the school day should be set apart for drilling in arithmetic
(E) teachers should occasionally make home visits to parents

22. The author's primary purpose in writing this passage is to
(A) tell parents to pay more attention to the guidance of teachers in the matter of educational activities in the home
(B) help ensure that every child's capacities are fully developed when he leaves school
(C) urge teachers and school administrators to make use of a much underused resource—the parent
(D) improve the teaching of mathematics
(E) brainwash parents into doing the best thing for their child's education

23. It is most reasonable to infer that the author is a(n)
    (A) elementary-school teacher
    (B) parent
    (C) student
    (D) college teacher
    (E) professor of education

24. The author would most approve of which of the following parental activities to assist in the learning of composition and writing skills?
    (A) one hour of supervised writing exercises nightly
    (B) encouraging the child to write letters to relatives
    (C) spelling words out loud with the child while washing the dishes
    (D) reviewing all the child's written schoolwork
    (E) giving the child money for good grades on written work

A philosophy of mutual deterrence is developing in CB warfare comparable to that in nuclear warfare. In fact, much of the literature on the subject repeats that the stalemate in the latter opens up the need for capability in the former. As an arms race, CBW does not present the spiraling costs of the ICBM–ABM systems, hence a movement to CB weapons (especially chemical) among some smaller nations. So far as the major powers are concerned, the elements in CBW which are in common with the nuclear arms race include the now accepted approach to that race. Thus in discussing control of CB warfare, an editorial in the British journal, *Nature*, concluded:

"The balance of terror between the great power blocs may not be to everybody's taste, but it is probably still the best way of avoiding war."

25. The writer in the British journal might feel that the research and development of CB systems should be
    (A) encouraged and expanded
    (B) conducted only by the major powers
    (C) immediately halted
    (D) maintained as it is now
    (E) considered necessary and desirable

26. The justification for the United States' participation in CB warfare programs is mainly due to the
    (A) need for undetectable weaponry
    (B) still untapped knowledge in the field
    (C) costliness of the nuclear programs
    (D) Soviet Union's having such a program
    (E) ability of modern research to develop them

27. The main purpose of this article is to
    (A) show the difficulties involved in stopping CB warfare programs
    (B) explain the cost of CB warfare
    (C) discuss alternatives to CB warfare
    (D) chronicle the history of CB warfare
    (E) make the reader aware of the dangers of CB warfare

Directions: Each of the following questions consists of a word printed in capital letters, followed by five (5) lettered words or phrases. Select the word or phrase which is most nearly *opposite* to the capitalized word in meaning.

28. MANSION:
    (A) hovel
    (B) hotel
    (C) motel
    (D) castle
    (E) house

29. ENDEMIC:
    (A) permanent
    (B) frustrating
    (C) terrorizing
    (D) democratic
    (E) pandemic

30. COMPENDIOUS:
    (A) profound
    (B) verbose
    (C) simple
    (D) ambiguous
    (E) miscellaneous

31. ASSUAGE:
    (A) cleanse
    (B) steady
    (C) aggravate
    (D) bless
    (E) advance

32. PRATE:
    (A) remark casually
    (B) laugh raucously
    (C) talk meaningfully
    (D) weep copiously
    (E) whisper fearfully

33. ARROGATE:
    (A) speak uncivilly
    (B) act rashly
    (C) play enthusiastically
    (D) take justifiedly
    (E) judge harshly

34. PROLIX:
    (A) terse
    (B) arid
    (C) speechless
    (D) upperclass
    (E) masterful

35. TYRO:
    (A) alert
    (B) democrat

    (C) fury
    (D) expert
    (E) collapse

36. SEDITION:
    (A) flotation
    (B) patriotism
    (C) conservation
    (D) merit
    (E) approval

37. TOUSLE:
    (A) shovel
    (B) groom
    (C) catch
    (D) caress
    (E) clean

38. TRANSIENT:
    (A) final
    (B) preserved
    (C) movable
    (D) agreeable
    (E) persistent

STOP

END OF SECTION. IF YOU HAVE ANY TIME LEFT, GO
OVER YOUR WORK IN THIS SECTION ONLY. DO NOT
WORK IN ANY OTHER SECTION OF THE TEST.

SECTION II

30 minutes
38 questions

Directions: Each of the questions below contains one or more blank spaces, each blank indicating an omitted word. Each sentence is followed by five (5) lettered words or sets of words. Read and determine the general sense of each sentence. Then choose the word or set of words which, when inserted in the sentence, best fits the meaning of the sentence.

1. Being more _____ to artistic activities, Miriam had difficulty _____ to secretarial work.
   (A) oriented—reacting

   (B) attuned—conforming
   (C) aligned—adapting
   (D) inured—turning
   (E) inclined—adjusting

2. Naturally _____ from birth, Arnold practiced hard to _____ his talents.
   (A) adept—perfect
   (B) handicapped—overcome
   (C) agile—supercede
   (D) gifted—limit
   (E) inept—develop

3. The teacher's pride was hurt when he discovered that half his class had _____ the exam.
   - (A) enjoyed
   - (B) reassessed
   - (C) flunked
   - (D) redeemed
   - (E) interpreted

4. The reporter's _____ probings finally brought results in the case.
   - (A) scattered
   - (B) severe
   - (C) obsessive
   - (D) relentless
   - (E) earnest

5. _____ mob began to form, full of angry men _____ incoherent threats.
   - (A) An excited—whispering
   - (B) A listless—shouting
   - (C) An ugly—gesturing
   - (D) A lynch—muttering
   - (E) A huge—waving

6. As a staunch _____ of our right to leisure time, Ken had few _____.
   - (A) proponent—friends
   - (B) advocate—defenders
   - (C) disciple—rivals
   - (D) defender—equals
   - (E) opponent—duties

7. In the _____ downpour, the girls managed to _____ us and disappear.
   - (A) ensuing—evade
   - (B) incessant—pervade
   - (C) uncouth—escape
   - (D) torrential—provoke
   - (E) insipid—avoid

Directions: In each of the following questions, you are given a related pair of words or phrases in capital letters. Each capitalized pair is followed by five (5) lettered pairs of words or phrases. Choose the pair which best expresses a relationship similar to that expressed by the original pair.

8. TELEPHONE : LETTER ::
   - (A) loudspeaker : microphone
   - (B) phonograph : manuscript
   - (C) telegraph : mail
   - (D) sound : sight
   - (E) brush : canvas

9. IMMIGRATION : ENTRANCE ::
   - (A) native : foreigner
   - (B) emigration : departure
   - (C) arrival : door
   - (D) travel : alien
   - (E) refuge : gate

10. HOTEL : SHELTER ::
    - (A) bed : pillow
    - (B) boat : transportation
    - (C) train : ride
    - (D) restaurant : drink
    - (E) home : recuperation

11. MOON : PLANET ::
    - (A) planet : star
    - (B) comet : asteroid
    - (C) Mercury : Jupiter
    - (D) star : nova
    - (E) crater : volcano

12. ASCETIC : LUXURY ::
    - (A) misogynist : women
    - (B) philosopher : knowledge
    - (C) capitalist : industry
    - (D) gourmet : hunger
    - (E) teacher : blackboard

13. SPASM : MUSCLE ::
    - (A) flash : light
    - (B) respite : thought
    - (C) tender : touch
    - (D) pinch : taste
    - (E) sound : noise

14. CORRUGATED : STRIPED ::
    - (A) cardboard : zebra
    - (B) dimpled : speckled
    - (C) rough : solid
    - (D) smooth : dotted
    - (E) bumpy : flashing

15. OXYGEN : GASEOUS ::
    - (A) feather : light
    - (B) mercury : fluid
    - (C) iron : heavy
    - (D) sand : grainy
    - (E) mountain : high

16. AGILE : ACROBAT ::
    (A) greasy : mechanic
    (B) peanuts : vendor
    (C) plant : fruit
    (D) eloquent : orator
    (E) fast : car

Directions: Below each of the following passages, you will find questions or incomplete statements about the passage. Each statement or question is followed by lettered words or expressions. Select the word or expression that most satisfactorily completes each statement or answers each question in accordance with the meaning of the passage. After you have chosen the best answer, blacken the corresponding space on the answer sheet.

Vacations were once the prerogative of the privileged few, even as late as the 19th century. Now they are considered the right of all, except for such unfortunate masses as, for example, the bulk of China's and India's population, for whom life, save for sleep and brief periods of rest, is uninterrupted toil.

Vacations are more necessary now than before because today the average life is less well-rounded and has become increasingly compartmentalized. I suppose the idea of vacations, as we conceive it, must be incomprehensible to primitive peoples. Rest of some kind has of course always been a part of the rhythm of human life, but earlier ages did not find it necessary to organize it in the way that modern man has done. Holidays and feast days were sufficient.

With modern man's increasing tensions, with the stultifying quality of so much of his work, this break in the year's routine became steadily more necessary. Vacations became mandatory for the purpose of renewal and repair. And so it came about that in the United States, the most self-indulgent of nations, the most tense and compartmentalized, vacations have come to take a predominant place in domestic conversation.

17. The title below that best expresses the ideas of this passage is:
    (A) Vacation Preferences
    (B) Vacations: The Topic of Conversation
    (C) Vacations in Perspective
    (D) The Well-Organized Vacation
    (E) Renewal, Refreshment and Repair

18. We need vacations now more than ever before because we have
    (A) a more carefree nature
    (B) much more free time
    (C) little diversity in our work
    (D) no emotional stability
    (E) a higher standard of living

19. It is implied in the passage that the lives of Americans are very
    (A) habitual
    (B) ennobling
    (C) patriotic
    (D) varied
    (E) independent

In my early childhood I received no formal religious education. I did, of course, receive the ethical and moral training that moral and conscientious parents give their children. When I was about ten years old, my parents decided that it would be good for me to receive some formal religious instruction and to study the Bible, if for no other reason than that a knowledge of both is essential to the understanding of literature and culture.

As lapsed Catholics, they sought a group which had as little doctrine and dogma as possible, but what they considered good moral and ethical values. After some searching, they joined the local Meeting of the Religious Society of Friends. Although my parents did not attend Meetings for Worship very often, I went to First Day School there regularly, eventually completing the course and receiving an inscribed Bible.

At the Quaker school, I learned about the concept of the "inner light" and it has stayed with me. I was, however, unable to accept the idea of Jesus Christ being any more divine than, say, Buddha. As a result, I became estranged from the Quakers who, though believing in substantially the same moral and ethical values as I do, and even the same religious concept of the inner light, had arrived at these conclusions from a premise which I could not accept. I admit that my religion is the poorer for having no revealed word and no supreme prophet, but my inherited aversion to dogmatism limits my faith to a Supreme Being and the goodness of man.

Later, at another Meeting for Worship, I found that some Quakers had similar though not so strong reservations about the Christian aspects of their belief. I made some attempt to rejoin a Meeting for Worship, but found that, though they remained far closer to me than any other organized religious group, I did not wish to become one again. I do attend Meeting for Worship on occasion, but it is for the help in deep contemplation which it brings rather than any lingering desire to rejoin the fold.

I do believe in a "Supreme Being" (or ground of our Being, as Tillich would call it). This Being is ineffable and not to be fully understood by humans. He is not cut off from the world and we can know him somewhat through the knowledge which we are limited to—the world. He is interested and concerned for humankind, but on man himself falls the burden of his own life. To me the message of the great prophets, especially Jesus, is that good is its own reward, and indeed the *only* possible rewards are intrinsic in the actions themselves. The relationship between each human and the Supreme Being is an entirely personal one.

It is my faith that each person has this unique relationship with the Supreme Being. To me that is the meaning of the inner light. The purpose of life, insofar as a human can grasp it, is to understand and increase this lifeline to the Supreme Being, this piece of divinity that *every* human has. Thus, the taking of any life by choice is the closing of some connection to God, and unconscionable. Killing anyone not only denies them their purpose, but corrupts the purpose of all men.

20. The author of the preceding passage is most probably writing in order to
    (A) persuade a friend to convert to Quakerism
    (B) **reassure a Friend that he has not become immoral**
    (C) explain the roots of his pacifism
    (D) analyze the meaning of the "inner light"
    (E) recall his parents' religious teachings

21. If offered a reward for doing a good deed, the author would
    (A) spurn the reward indignantly
    (B) accept it only as a token of the other person's feelings of gratitude

    (C) neither take nor refuse the reward
    (D) explain to the offerer that rewards are blasphemous
    (E) make any excuse at all to avoid taking the reward

22. According to the passage, the Quakers
    (A) are the group he wishes to become a member of again
    (B) have historically been pacifists
    (C) are Christians, but only in a weak sense
    (D) share basic religious thought with the author
    (E) are relatively dogmatic and doctrinaire

23. Which of the following would the author likely see as most divine?
    (A) Jesus Christ
    (B) Buddha
    (C) Mohammed
    (D) Moses
    (E) They would be seen as equally divine.

24. It can be inferred that
    (A) the author views the inner light as uniquely an attribute of Quakers
    (B) Quakers treat all men the same, whether they have inner light or not
    (C) the Catholics are not concerned with killing
    (D) the author's parents found Catholic religious views unsuitable or inadequate
    (E) Buddhist belief is as congenial to the author as Quaker belief

25. The author argues that
    (A) we must seek greater comprehension of our own inner lights
    (B) humans must always seek to increase the number of inner lights, hence, population increase is desirable
    (C) the unique relationship between each person and his inner light makes him more divine than those without an inner light
    (D) only a person without an inner light could kill
    (E) faith is essential to life, especially faith based on those most divine persons who are often called prophets

26. If the author were faced with a situation where the killing of another human would occur both by his action and his inaction, then
    (A) he could not act because it would kill someone
    (B) he could not fail to act because it would kill someone
    (C) he would have to kill himself to avoid the situation
    (D) he would have to abandon his beliefs
    (E) he would have to choose to act or not act on some basis other than whether a human would die

27. The author rejected which of the following aspects of religious thought?
    (A) the existence of God
    (B) the need to follow moral rules such as those in the Christian Bible
    (C) the divine nature of human beings
    (D) the revealed word of God
    (E) the value of sharing religious experiences

Directions: Each of the following questions consists of a word printed in captial letters, followed by five (5) lettered words or phrases. Select the word or phrase which is most nearly *opposite* to the capitalized word in meaning.

28. CONSONANT :
    (A) insuperable
    (B) incongruous
    (C) nonexistent
    (D) sounded
    (E) abundant

29. CONCISE :
    (A) wordy
    (B) mundane
    (C) ignorant
    (D) muddy
    (E) wrong

30. FECUND :
    (A) sinister
    (B) premier
    (C) young
    (D) barren
    (E) beneficial

31. FORTUITOUS :
    (A) unfortunate
    (B) unintelligent
    (C) discontent
    (D) fearful
    (E) pious

32. SATURNINE :
    (A) earthy
    (B) cheerful
    (C) complicated
    (D) maudlin
    (E) straight

33. FRANGIBLE :
    (A) argumentative
    (B) docile
    (C) insincere
    (D) sturdy
    (E) inedible

34. LETHARGY :
    (A) acidity
    (B) prodigy
    (C) rigidity
    (D) alertness
    (E) corpulence

35. CUPIDITY :
    (A) lovelessness
    (B) generosity
    (C) smartness
    (D) wastefulness
    (E) prodigality

36. PROTEAN :
    (A) depriving
    (B) flowering
    (C) uniform
    (D) universal
    (E) separate

37. COGENT :
    (A) repetitive
    (B) urgent
    (C) complicated
    (D) confined
    (E) fatuous

38. HIRSUTE :
    (A) naked
    (B) plain
    (C) melted
    (D) bald
    (E) clear

STOP

END OF SECTION. IF YOU HAVE ANY TIME LEFT, GO OVER YOUR WORK IN THIS SECTION ONLY. DO NOT WORK IN ANY OTHER SECTION OF THE TEST.

SECTION III

30 minutes
30 questions

Directions: For each of the following questions two quantities are given, one in Column A and one in Column B. Compare the two quantities and mark your answer sheet with the correct lettered conclusion. These are your options:

A: If the quantity in Column A is the greater;
B: if the quantity in Column B is the greater;
C: if the two quantities are equal;
D: if the relationship cannot be determined from the information given.

Common Information: In any question, information applying to both columns is centered between the columns and above the quantities in columns A and B. The common information applies to both columns. Any symbol that appears in both columns represents the same idea or quantity in both columns.

Numbers: All numbers used are real numbers.

Figures: Assume that the positions of points, angles, regions and so forth are in the order shown. Figures are assumed to lie in a plane unless otherwise indicated. Figures accompanying questions are intended to provide information you can use in answering the questions. However, unless a note states that a figure is drawn to scale, you should solve the problems by using your knowledge of mathematics and *not* by estimating sizes by sight or measurement.

Lines: Assume that lines shown as straight are indeed straight.

	COLUMN A	COLUMN B
1.	$x = -y$	
	x	y
2.	$\dfrac{1}{100}$	.01%
3.	The price of paper increased from $1.23 per ream to $1.48 per ream.	
	the percent increase in the price of paper	20%
4.	M is the average (arithmetic mean) of x and y.	
	$\dfrac{M + x + y}{3}$	$\dfrac{x + y}{2}$
5.	$(a + 2)(b + 3)$	$(a + 3)(b + 2)$

COLUMN A | COLUMN B

6. Q is the midpoint of line segment PR.

length of PQ | length of QR

7.
$$x - y \neq 0$$

$\dfrac{x^2 - y^2}{x - y}$ | $x + y$

8.

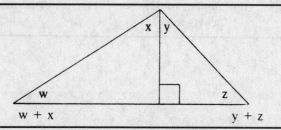

w + x | y + z

9. Planes X and Y are 300 miles apart and flying toward each other on a direct course and at constant speeds. X is flying at 150 miles per hour. After 40 minutes, they pass one another.

speed of plane Y | 150 miles per hour

10. 66.6% | $\dfrac{2}{3}$

11. the average (arithmetic mean) of the number of degrees in the angles of a pentagon | the average (arithmetic mean) of the number of degrees in the angles of a hexagon

12. A bookshelf contains 16 books written in French and 8 books written in Italian and no other books. 75% of the books written in French and 50% of the books written in Italian are removed from the bookshelf.

the proportion of the original number of books remaining on the shelf | $\dfrac{2}{3}$

13.

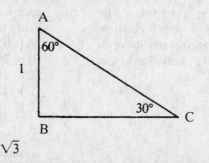

$\sqrt{3}$ | BC

	COLUMN A	COLUMN B

14.
$$x^2 - 1 = 0$$

x   1

___

15.   Tickets to a concert cost $25 and $13.
        An agent sells 11 tickets for a total
        price of $227.

        the number of $25-   the number of $13-
        tickets sold   tickets sold

___

Directions: For each of the following questions, select the best of the answer choices and blacken the corresponding space on your answer sheet.
Numbers: All numbers used are real numbers.
Figures: The diagrams and figures that accompany these questions are for the purpose of providing information useful in answering the questions. Unless it is stated that a specific figure is not drawn to scale, the diagrams and figures are drawn as accurately as possible. All figures are in a plane unless otherwise indicated.

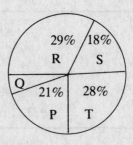

16. $\frac{3}{4} + \frac{4}{5} =$
    (A) $\frac{3}{5}$
    (B) $\frac{7}{20}$
    (C) $\frac{7}{9}$
    (D) $\frac{12}{9}$
    (E) $\frac{31}{20}$

17. If $x + 6 = 3$, then $x + 3 =$
    (A) -9
    (B) -3
    (C) 0
    (D) 3
    (E) 9

18. A person is standing on a staircase. He walks down 4 steps, up 3 steps, down 6 steps, up 2 steps, up 9 steps, and down 2 steps. Where is he standing in relation to the step on which he started?
    (A) 2 steps above
    (B) 1 step above
    (C) the same place
    (D) 1 step below
    (E) 2 steps below

19. What portion of the circle graph above belongs to sector Q?
    (A) 4%
    (B) 5%
    (C) 6%
    (D) 75%
    (E) 96%

20. $326(31) - 326(19)$ is
    (A) 3912
    (B) 704
    (C) 100
    (D) 32.6
    (E) 10

21. A professor begins his class at 1:21 PM and ends it at 3:36 PM the same afternoon. How many minutes long was the class?
    (A) 457
    (B) 215
    (C) 150
    (D) 135
    (E) 75

22. A sales representative will receive a 15% commission on a sale of $2800. If she has

already received an advance of $150 on that commission, how much more is she due on the commission?

(A) $120
(B) $270
(C) $320
(D) $420
(E) $570

23. If a circle has an area of $9\pi x^2$ units, what is its radius?

(A) 3
(B) 3x
(C) $3\pi x$
(D) 9x
(E) $81x^4$

24. Hans is taller than Gertrude, but he is shorter than Wilhelm. If Hans, Gertrude, and Wilhelm are heights x, y, and z, respectively, which of the following accurately expresses the relationships of their heights?

(A) x > y > z
(B) x < y < z
(C) y > x > z
(D) z < x < y
(E) z > x > y

25. For which of the following figures can the area of the figure be determined if the perimeter is known?

  I. a trapezoid
  II. a square
  III. an equilateral triangle
  IV. a parallelogram

(A) I only
(B) II only
(C) III only
(D) II and III only
(E) I, II, III, and IV

26. A child withdraws from his piggy bank 10% of the original sum in the bank. If he must add 90¢ to bring the amount in the bank back up to the original sum, what was the original sum in the bank?

(A) $1.00
(B) $1.90
(C) $8.10
(D) $9.00
(E) $9.90

27. If cylinder P has a height twice that of cylinder Q and a radius half that of cylinder Q, what is the ratio between the volume of cylinder P and the volume of cylinder Q?

(A) 1:8
(B) 1:4
(C) 1:2
(D) 1
(E) 2:1

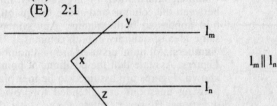

$l_m \parallel l_n$

28. In the figure above, which of the following is true?

(A) y + z = x
(B) y = 90°
(C) x + y + z = 180
(D) y = x + z
(E) z = x + y

29. If the width of a rectangle is increased by 25% while the length remains constant, the resulting area is what percent of the original area?

(A) 25%
(B) 75%
(C) 125%
(D) 225%
(E) Cannot be determined from the information given.

30. The sum of four consecutive odd positive integers is always

(A) an odd number
(B) divisible by 4
(C) a prime number
(D) a multiple of 3
(E) a multiple of 5

STOP

END OF SECTION. IF YOU HAVE ANY TIME LEFT, GO
OVER YOUR WORK IN THIS SECTION ONLY. DO NOT
WORK IN ANY OTHER SECTION OF THE TEST.

SECTION IV

30 minutes
30 questions

Directions: For each of the following questions two quantities are given, one in Column A and one in Column B. Compare the two quantities and mark your answer sheet with the correct lettered conclusion. These are your options:

A: If the quantity in Column A is the greater;
B: if the quantity in Column B is the greater;
C: if the two quantities are equal;
D: if the relationship cannot be determined from the information given.

Common Information: In any question, information applying to both columns is centered between the columns and above the quantities in columns A and B. The common information applies to both columns. Any symbol that appears in both columns represents the same idea or quantity in both columns.

Numbers: All numbers used are real numbers.

Figures: Assume that the positions of points, angles, regions and so forth are in the order shown. Figures are assumed to lie in a plane unless otherwise indicated. Figures accompanying questions are intended to provide information you can use in answering the questions. However, unless a note states that a figure is drawn to scale, you should solve the problems by using your knowledge of mathematics and *not* by estimating sizes by sight or measurement.

Lines: Assume that lines shown as straight are indeed straight.

COLUMN A	COLUMN B

1.

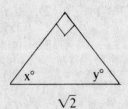

| x | y |

2.

$$x > 0$$
$$y > 0$$

| x% of y% of 100 | y% of x% of 100 |

3.

| 0.3 | $\sqrt{0.9}$ |

4.

| $(x + y)^2$ | $x(x + y) + y(x + y)$ |

5.

| $\dfrac{17}{8786}$ | $\dfrac{17}{8787}$ |

6.

| $-(3^6)$ | $(-3)^6$ |

7.

COLUMN A	COLUMN B

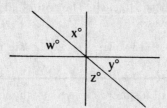

90 − (w + x)	90 − (y + z)

8.

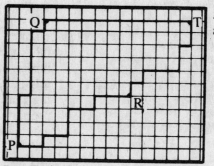

All angles
are right angles

distance from P to T via Q	distance from P to T via R

9.

the length of side of any equilat-eral polygon inscribed in circle O	the length of the diameter of circle O

10.

Peter's grade was higher than that of
Victor, and Victor's grade was less
than that of Georgette.

Georgette's grade	Peter's grade

11.

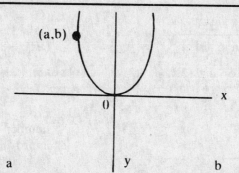

a	b

12.

3x + 5	2x + 3

13.

$$x < 0$$

$(x^3)^5$	$x^3 \cdot x^5$

14.

A man buys 16 shirts. Some of them
cost $13 each, while the remainder

COLUMN A   COLUMN B

cost $10 each. The cost of all 16 shirts
was $187.

| the number of $13 shirts
purchased | the number of $10 shirts
purchased |

15.   the volume of a sphere   the volume of a cube with
             with radius of 5   a side of 10

Directions: For each of the following questions, select the best of the answer choices and blacken the corresponding space on your answer sheet.
Numbers: All numbers used are real numbers.
Figures: The diagrams and figures that accompany these questions are for the purpose of providing information useful in answering the questions. Unless it is stated that a specific figure is not drawn to scale, the diagrams and figures are drawn as accurately as possible. All figures are in a plane unless otherwise indicated.

16.   If $(x-y)^2 = 12$ and $xy = 1$, then $x^2 + y^2 =$
     (A)   14
     (B)   13
     (C)   12
     (D)   11
     (E)   10

17.

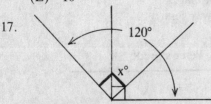

(*Note:* Figure not drawn to scale.)

What is the measure of angle x?
     (A)   30°
     (B)   45°
     (C)   60°
     (D)   90°
     (E)   240°

18.   If n is a positive integer and 95 and 135 are divided by n, and the remainders are 5 and 3 respectively, then n =
     (A)   6
     (B)   8
     (C)   10
     (D)   15
     (E)   21

19.   A student conducts an experiment in biology lab and discovers that the ratio of the number of insects in a given population having characteristic X to the number of insects in the population not having characteristic X is 5:3, and that $\frac{3}{8}$ of the insects having characteristic X are male insects. What proportion of the total insect population are male insects having the characteristic X?
     (A)   1
     (B) $\frac{5}{8}$
     (C) $\frac{6}{13}$
     (D) $\frac{15}{64}$
     (E) $\frac{1}{5}$

20.   If the following were arranged in order of magnitude, which term would be the middle number in the series?
     (A) $\frac{3^8}{3^6}$
     (B) $3^3 - 1$
     (C) 3^0
     (D) 3^{27}
     (E) $3(3^2)$

Questions 21–25 refer to the graph on the next page.

21.   From 1972 to 1977, inclusive, the total number of fares collected for subways was approximately how many million?
     (A)   1900
     (B)   1700
     (C)   1500
     (D)   1300
     (E)   1100

22.   From 1975 to 1977, the number of fares collected for subways dropped by approximately what percent?
     (A)   90

PUBLIC TRANSPORTATION IN METROPOLITAN AREA P

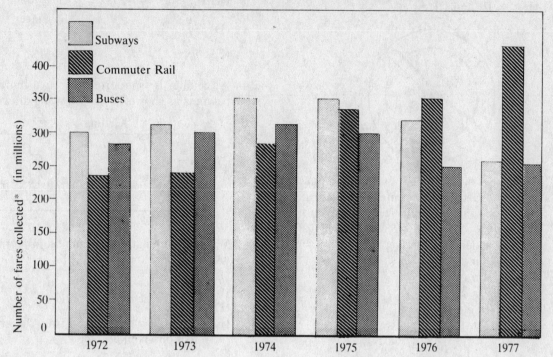

*One passenger paying one fare for one trip

(B) 33
(C) 25
(D) 15
(E) 9

23. If in 1974 the average subway fare collected was 50¢ and the average bus fare collected was 30¢, then the ratio of the total dollar amount of subway fares collected to the total dollar amount of bus fares was approximately
(A) $\frac{1}{4}$
(B) $\frac{1}{3}$
(C) $\frac{3}{5}$
(D) 1
(E) $\frac{7}{4}$

24. The number of commuter rail fares collected in 1977 accounted for approximately what percent of all fares collected on subways, buses, and commuter rail in that year?
(A) 200%
(B) 100%
(C) 50%
(D) 28%
(E) 12%

25. Approximately how many more commuter rail fares were collected in 1977 than were collected in 1972?
(A) 50 million
(B) 80 million
(C) 100 million
(D) 125 million
(E) 195 million

26. Lines l_m and l_n lie in the plane x and intersect one another on the perpendicular at point P. Which of the following statements must be true?

 I. A line which lies in plane x and intersects line l_m on the perpendicular at a point other than P does not intersect l_n.

 II. Line segment MN, which does not intersect l_m, does not intersect l_n.

 III. If line l_o lies in plane y and intersects l_m at point P, plane y is perpendicular to plane x.

(A) I only
(B) II only
(C) I and II only

(D) I and III only
(E) I, II, and III

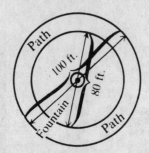

27. The fountain in the above illustration is located exactly at the center of the circular path. How many cubic feet of gravel are required to cover the circular garden path six inches deep with gravel?
(A) 5400π cu. ft.
(B) 4500π cu. ft.
(C) 1250π cu. ft.
(D) 450π cu. ft.
(E) 5π cu. ft.

28. A business firm reduces the number of hours its employees work from 40 hours per week to 36 hours per week while continuing to pay the same amount of money. If an employee earned x dollars per hour before the reduction in hours, how much does he earn per hour under the new system?

(A) $\dfrac{1}{10}$

(B) $\dfrac{x}{9}$

(C) $\dfrac{9x}{10}$

(D) $\dfrac{10x}{9}$

(E) $9x$

29. A ceiling is supported by two parallel columns as shown in the following drawing:

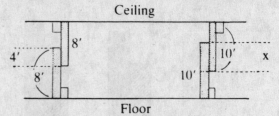

What is the length of segment x in feet?
(A) 10
(B) 8
(C) 6
(D) 4
(E) Cannot be determined from the information given.

30. A painter has painted one-third of a rectangular wall which is ten feet high. When she has painted another 75 square feet of wall, she will be three-quarters finished with the job. What is the length (the horizontal dimension) of the wall?
(A) 18 feet
(B) 12 feet
(C) 10 feet
(D) 9 feet
(E) 6 feet

STOP

END OF SECTION. IF YOU HAVE ANY TIME LEFT, GO
OVER YOUR WORK IN THIS SECTION ONLY. DO NOT
WORK IN ANY OTHER SECTION OF THE TEST.

SECTION V

30 minutes
25 questions

Directions: Each of the following questions or groups of questions is based on a short passage or a set of propositions. In answering these questions it may sometimes be helpful to draw a simple picture or chart. When you have selected the best answer to each question, darken the corresponding circle on your answer sheet.

Questions 1–4

P drank more at the Murchison's party than W and left later than V.

T drank more than P and less than V and left later than P and earlier than S.

U drank less than Q and more than V and left later than S.

W drank more than R and left earlier than V.

1. Which of the following left earliest?
   (A) P
   (B) S
   (C) T
   (D) U
   (E) W

2. Which of the following drank the least?
   (A) P
   (B) R
   (C) T
   (D) U
   (E) V

3. Based on the above information, which of the following is true?
   (A) V was the second to leave and drank the most.
   (B) U was the last to leave and drank the most.
   (C) T was the third-to-last to leave and drank more than at least three other partygoers.
   (D) S was the second-to-last to leave and drank the most.
   (E) None of the above is true.

4. If S drank more than W, which of the following drank more than S?
   (A) P and R

(B) P, Q, U, and V
(C) P, R, and Q
(D) everyone except R and W
(E) Cannot be determined from the information given.

Questions 5–6

During the 1970's the number of clandestine CIA agents posted to foreign countries increased 25 percent and the number of CIA employees not assigned to field work increased by 21 percent. In the same period, the number of FBI agents assigned to case investigation rose by 18 percent, but the number of non-case-working agents rose by only 3 percent.

5. The statistics best support which of the following claims?
   (A) More agents are needed to administer the CIA than are needed for the FBI.
   (B) The CIA needs more people to accomplish its mission than does the FBI.
   (C) The number of field agents tends to increase more rapidly than the number of non-field agents in both the CIA and the FBI.
   (D) The rate of change in the number of supervisory agents in an intelligence-gathering agency or a law-enforcement agency is proportional to the percentage change in the results produced by the agency.
   (E) At the end of the 1960's, the CIA was more efficiently administered than was the FBI.

6. In response to the allegation that it was more overstaffed with support and supervisory personnel than the FBI, the CIA could best argue:
   (A) The FBI is less useful than the CIA in gathering intelligence against foreign powers.
   (B) The rate of pay for a CIA non-field agent is less than the rate of pay for a non-investigating FBI agent.

(C) The number of FBI agents should not rise so rapidly as the number of CIA agents, given the longer tenure of an FBI agent.

(D) A CIA field agent working in a foreign country requires more back-up support than does an FBI investigator working domestically.

(E) The number of CIA agents is determined by the Congress each year when they appropriate funds for the agency, and the Congress is very sensitive to changes in the international political climate.

7. All effective administrators are concerned about the welfare of their employees, and all administrators who are concerned about the welfare of their employees are liberal in granting time off for personal needs; therefore, all administrators who are not liberal in granting time off for their employees' personal needs are not effective administrators.

If the argument above is valid, then it must be true that

(A) no ineffective administrators are liberal in granting time off for their employees' personal needs

(B) no ineffective administrators are concerned about the welfare of their employees

(C) some effective administrators are not liberal in granting time off for their employees' personal needs

(D) all effective administrators are liberal in granting time off for their employees' personal needs

(E) all time off for personal needs is granted by effective administrators

Questions 8–12

Lois wants to take four courses this semester. There are only seven courses in which she is interested and that do not conflict with her job: three science courses—biology, chemistry, and physics—and four humanities courses—English, French, music, and writing. To meet college requirements she must take two science courses this semester. There are some scheduling problems, however: English overlaps both chemistry and music, which are sequential; biology is given at the same time as French.

8. If Lois decides she will take English, what will her other three courses be?
(A) biology, physics, and chemistry
(B) biology, physics, and writing
(C) biology, physics, and French
(D) physics, chemistry, and writing
(E) physics, writing, and French

9. If the chemistry course is changed to a time which Lois cannot make, and she decides to take music, which of the following would be her schedule?
(A) biology, physics, English, and music
(B) biology, physics, French, and music
(C) biology, physics, writing, and music
(D) physics, English, French, and music
(E) physics, writing, English, and music

10. If Lois takes four courses this semester she cannot

I. take French and not take chemistry
II. take music and not take chemistry
III. take English and not take physics

(A) I only
(B) II only
(C) III only
(D) I and II only
(E) I and III only

11. Which of the following must always be true?

I. Lois must take physics if she takes music.
II. Lois must take chemistry if she takes French.
III. Lois must take French if she takes chemistry.

(A) I, II, and III
(B) II and III only
(C) I and II only
(D) III only
(E) II only

12. If the physics course is moved to the same time as English, and Lois takes physics, what further problem(s) does she face?
(A) She won't be able to take two science classes.
(B) She won't be able to take biology.
(C) She won't be able to take writing.

(D) She won't be able to take either biology or French.

(E) She won't be able to take four courses which interest her.

Questions 13–17

The coach of the Malibu University swimming team is planning his strategy for the rest of his team's meet with the State University swim team. Each event is scored on the basis of five points to the winner, three points for second place, and one point for third place. The score is currently tied, but the coach thinks his team can win because they have greater depth than the other team. The State University team has only enough good swimmers to just fill out their two entries for each of the last three events with one strong entry and one weak one. The last events are the individual medley, the medley relay, and the freestyle relay. Each relay team has four members. The coach considers these facts: State's top individual medley racer is sure to win, but their second entry can only manage a time of four minutes even.

13. What is the minimum number of points that Malibu has to score in the last three races in order to win the meet?
    (A) 14
    (B) 13
    (C) 12
    (D) 11
    (E) 10

14. If State's swimmers take first and third in the individual medley race, which of the following results for the last two races would still let Malibu win?
    (A) first place only in both races
    (B) first place in one race and second and third in the other
    (C) second and third in both races
    (D) first in one race and at least first and third in the other
    (E) There is no way for Malibu to win the meet.

15. Malibu swimmer George can only swim in one more race. He and Jim are the only Malibu swimmers who can beat four minutes in the individual medley. Under which of the following conditions would it be advanta-

geous for George NOT to swim in the individual medley race?
    (A) if adding George will move the medley relay team from fourth to third
    (B) if adding George to the freestyle relay team will move it from third to second
    (C) if adding George to one medley relay team allows shifting of swimmers so that they finish first and fourth instead of second and third
    (D) if adding George to the medley team allows shifting swimmers so that the results are a first and third in one race, and a second and third in the other rather than just two firsts
    (E) There are no conditions under which it is advantageous to hold George out of the individual medley race.

16. If Malibu places second and third in the individual medley race, at least how many of its entries must score points in order to guarantee that Malibu will win the meet?
    (A) 2
    (B) 3
    (C) 4
    (D) 5
    (E) Cannot be determined from the information given.

17. State's top individual medley swimmer is disqualified. If Malibu's two swimmers in that race finish in 3 minutes 57 seconds and 3 minutes 58 seconds respectively, which of the following is false?
    (A) If State places first and fourth in the other two races, they will still win the meet.
    (B) If Malibu places first and third in one relay, they do not even have to swim in the other in order to win the meet.
    (C) If three of Malibu's remaining swimmers score points, Malibu could still lose the meet.
    (D) If all four of State's relay teams score points, State could still lose the meet.
    (E) Even if only three of State's relay teams score points, State could still win the meet.

Questions 18–22

A collie, poodle, retriever, setter, and sheepdog live in separate houses on a five-house block with the Joneses, Kings, Lanes, Murrays, and Neffs—not necessarily in that order.

The sheepdog lives next door to the Lanes, as does the collie.

The Joneses have the heaviest dog and live next to the sheepdog.

The retriever weighs more than the setter or the poodle.

The Lanes live two houses away from the Joneses and from the Kings.

The Kings do not own the setter.

The sheepdog lives with the Murrays.

18. Which of the following is definitely false?
    (A) The poodle lives next to the collie.
    (B) The poodle does not live next to the sheepdog.
    (C) The sheepdog lives next to the collie.
    (D) The setter lives next to the sheepdog.
    (E) The retriever lives two houses from the setter.

19. Which of the following is definitely true?
    (A) The Joneses live next to the Neffs.
    (B) The Joneses live next to the collie.
    (C) The Joneses live at the opposite end of the block from the Lanes.
    (D) The Kings live next to the sheepdog.
    (E) The Kings live next to the collie.

20. If a cat named Kitzen goes to live with the second-heaviest dog, which of the following must be true?
    (A) Kitzen lives with the Kings.
    (B) Kitzen lives with the Lanes.
    (C) Kitzen lives with the Murrays.
    (D) Kitzen lives with the Neffs.
    (E) The answer cannot be determined from the information given.

21. If the Neffs and the Joneses trade houses, but the dogs living in the houses stay with the houses, which of the following now becomes true?
    (A) The poodle lives next to the Joneses.
    (B) The sheepdog lives next to the Joneses.
    (C) The setter lives next to the Neffs.
    (D) The collie lives with the Lanes.
    (E) The retriever lives with the Murrays.

22. If the Murrays move away and give their dog to the Lanes, which of the following would be true?
    (A) The sheepdog now lives with the collie.
    (B) The sheepdog does not now live with the poodle.
    (C) The sheepdog lives next to the Joneses.
    (D) The sheepdog lives next to the Kings.
    (E) The sheepdog lives next to the setter.

23. Clark must have known that his sister Janet and not the governess pulled the trigger, but he silently stood by while the jury convicted the governess. Any person of clear conscience would have felt terrible for not having come forward with the information about his sister, and Clark lived with that information until his death thirty years later. Since he was an extremely happy man, however, I conclude that he must have helped Janet commit the crime.

Which of the following assumptions must underlie the author's conclusion of the last sentence?
(A) Loyalty to members of one's family is conducive to contentment.
(B) **Servants are not to be treated with the same respect as members of the peerage.**
(C) Clark never had a bad conscience over his silence because he was also guilty of the crime.
(D) It is better to be a virtuous man than a happy one.
(E) It is actually better to be content in life than to behave morally towards one's fellow humans.

24. "Whom did you pass on the road?" the King went on, holding his hand out to the messenger for some hay.
    "Nobody," said the messenger.
    "Quite right," said the King. "This young lady saw him, too. So, of course, Nobody walks slower than you."

The King's response shows that he believes
(A) the messenger is a very good messenger

(B) "Nobody" is a person who might be seen

(C) the young lady's eyesight is better than the messenger's

(D) the messenger is not telling him the truth

(E) there was a person actually seen by the messenger on the road

25. New Evergreen Gum has twice as much flavor for your money as Spring Mint Gum, and we can prove it. You see, a stick of Evergreen Gum is twice as large as a stick of Spring Mint Gum, and the more gum, the more flavor.

Which of the following, if true, would undermine the persuasive appeal of the above advertisement?

I. A package of Spring Mint Gum contains twice as many sticks as a package of Evergreen Gum at the same price.

II. Spring Mint Gum has more concentrated flavor than Evergreen Gum.

III. Although a stick of Evergreen Gum is twice as large in volume as a stick of Spring Mint Gum, it weighs only 50% as much.

(A) I only

(B) II only

(C) I and II only

(D) II and III only

(E) I, II, and III

STOP

END OF SECTION. IF YOU HAVE ANY TIME LEFT, GO OVER YOUR WORK IN THIS SECTION ONLY. DO NOT WORK IN ANY OTHER SECTION OF THE TEST.

SECTION VI

30 minutes
25 questions

Directions: Each of the following questions or groups of questions is based on a short passage or a set of propositions. In answering these questions it may sometimes be helpful to draw a simple picture or chart. When you have selected the best answer to each question, darken the corresponding circle on your answer sheet.

Questions 1–5

The letters S, T, U, V, W, X, Y, and Z represent eight consecutive whole numbers, not necessarily in that order.

W is four more than Z and three less than X.

S is more than T and less than X.

U is the average of V and X.

1. If the lowest number of the series is 8, what is the value of W?
   (A) 10
   (B) 11
   (C) 12
   (D) 13
   (E) 14

2. Which of the following is (are) true?
   I. W is not the greatest number in the series.
   II. Z is not the greatest number in the series.
   III. X is not the greatest number in the series.

(A) I only
(B) II only
(C) I and II only
(D) I and III only
(E) I, II, and III

3. If V is less than W, which one of the following is a possible order of the numbers, starting with the highest number on the left?
   (A) X, S, U, W, V, T, Y, Z
   (B) X, S, T, W, V, U, Y, Z
   (C) Z, S, T, W, U, V, Y, X
   (D) X, T, S, V, W, U, Z, Y
   (E) X, U, S, T, W, V, Y, Z

4. If U did not have to be greater than V, which of the following is a new possibility?
   (A) X is one greater than U.
   (B) U is one greater than Z.
   (C) U is four less than W.
   (D) Z is two greater than U.
   (E) U is equal to W.

5. If Y is three greater than Z, which of the following is (are) true?

   I. W is greater than U.
   II. S is greater than W.
   III. Y is greater than V.
   IV. V is two less than Y.

   (A) I and II only
   (B) I and III only
   (C) I, II, and IV only
   (D) II, III, and IV only
   (E) none of the above

Questions 6–7

New Weight Loss Salons invites all of you who are dissatisfied with your present build to join our Exercise for Lunch Bunch. Instead of putting on even more weight by eating lunch, you actually cut down on your daily caloric intake by exercising rather than eating. Every single one of us has potential to be thin, so take the initiative and begin losing excess pounds today. Don't eat! Exercise! You'll lose weight and be healthier, happier, and more attractive.

6. Which of the following, if true, would weaken the logic of the argument made by the advertisement?

   I. Most people will experience increased desire for food as a result of the exercise and will lose little weight as a result of enrolling in the program.
   II. Nutritionists agree that skipping lunch is not a healthy practice.
   III. In our society, obesity is regarded as unattractive.
   IV. A person who is too thin is probably not in good health.

   (A) I only
   (B) I and II only
   (C) II and III only
   (D) III and IV only
   (E) I, II, and III

7. A person hearing this advertisement countered, "I know some people who are not overweight and are still unhappy and unattractive." The author of the advertisement could logically and consistently reply to this objection by pointing out that he never claimed that
   (A) being overweight is always caused by unhappiness
   (B) being overweight is the only cause of unhappiness and unattractiveness
   (C) unhappiness and unattractiveness can cause someone to be overweight
   (D) unhappiness necessarily leads to being overweight
   (E) unhappiness and unattractiveness are always found together

8. Clara prefers English Literature to Introductory Physics. She likes English Literature, however, less than she likes Basic Economics. She actually finds Basic Economics preferable to any other college course, and she dislikes Physical Education more than she dislikes Introductory Physics.

All of the following statements can be inferred from the information given above EXCEPT
   (A) Clara prefers Basic Economics to English Literature
   (B) Clara likes English Literature better than she likes Physical Education
   (C) Clara prefers Basic Economics to Advanced Calculus

(D) Clara likes World History better than she likes Introductory Physics

(E) Clara likes Physical Education less than she likes English Literature.

Questions 9–12

John is trying to figure out the best arrangement of spices in the spice rack of his small efficiency kitchen. The rack has two shelves with three spaces on each shelf. He decides that the six spices he uses most often, and thus wishes to put in the rack, are: basil, cumin, fennel, pepper, salt, and thyme. Since the thyme and the basil look similar and come in similar containers, the chances of confusion will be reduced if they are not placed next to each other either horizontally or vertically. Since the pepper and salt are usually both used at the same time, they should be next to each other on the same shelf.

9. Given the above information, which of the following arrangements is (are) unacceptable?

I. Thyme and basil can be on the same shelf.

II. Thyme and cumin can be on the same shelf.

III. Thyme and salt can be on the same shelf.

(A) Any of the above are acceptable.
(B) I only
(C) II only
(D) II and III only
(E) All cannot be true.

10. If the two left-hand spices on the upper shelf are thyme and cumin, respectively, which of the following is an acceptable arrangement of the lower shelf, reading from left to right?
(A) fennel, salt, basil
(B) fennel, pepper, basil
(C) basil, salt, pepper
(D) salt, pepper, basil
(E) salt, fennel, pepper

11. If the lower shelf has salt, pepper, and basil from left to right, how many possible arrangements are there for the upper shelf?
(A) 2
(B) 3

(C) 4
(D) 5
(E) 6

12. John buys a new brand of thyme and basil because it has more flavor. If the new containers are very similar to one another, and also are too tall to fit on the lower shelf, which of the following must be true?
(A) Either salt or pepper will be next to or below fennel.
(B) Salt will be below thyme.
(C) Pepper will be next to either fennel or cumin.
(D) Thyme will be above either salt or pepper.
(E) Basil will be above either salt or pepper.

Questions 13–17

Williams is the director of investments for a major pension fund. He believes that blue-chip common stocks and government securities will generally not do as well as corporate bonds in the coming year, but government regulations require that at least one-third of the fund's capital be in blue-chip common stocks and another third in government securities.

13. Under current regulations, what seems to be the best way for Williams to invest the pension fund?
(A) two-thirds government securities, one-third blue-chip stock
(B) two-thirds government securities, one-third corporate bonds
(C) one-third government securities, two-thirds corporate bonds
(D) one-third each government securities, blue-chip stocks, and corporate bonds
(E) half government securities and half blue-chip stocks

14. If the pension fund has $6 billion in assets, what is the maximum that Williams could invest in blue-chip stocks?
(A) $2 billion
(B) $3 billion
(C) $4 billion
(D) $5 billion
(E) $6 billion

15. If the government regulations are changed to require only one-quarter where one-third was previously required, Williams will probably
   (A) increase the fund's holdings of government securities
   (B) increase the fund's holdings of corporate bonds
   (C) increase the fund's holdings of blue-chip stock
   (D) hold less cash
   (E) hold more cash

16. If the return on government securities suddenly goes up five percentage points, Williams will probably
   (A) sell blue-chip stock to buy government securities.
   (B) sell corporate bonds to buy government securities
   (C) sell both corporate bonds and blue-chip stocks to buy government securities
   (D) keep the fund the way it was
   (E) His action cannot be predicted.

17. In the middle of the year, the fund is invested equally in corporate bonds, blue-chip stock, and government securities. The sudden merger of one of the main employers serviced by the fund results in the early retirement of thousands of workers, creating in turn a cash shortage for the fund. To generate the needed cash, Williams might do any one of the following EXCEPT
   (A) sell two times more corporate bonds than blue-chip stocks
   (B) sell two times more corporate bonds than government securities
   (C) sell only corporate bonds and blue-chip stocks
   (D) sell only government securities and blue-ship stock
   (E) sell only government securities and corporate bonds

Questions 18–22

Max is planning his sales calls for the next day. He is judged and paid by his company both on the basis of the number of calls he makes and the amount of sales he generates.

Acme Co. will take only one hour and will probably result in an order of 5 boxes.

Bell Corp. will take three hours and will either result in an order of 20 boxes or nothing.

Camera Shops, Inc., will take one hour and yield an order of 10 boxes.

Deland Bros. will take from one to three hours and probably result in an order of 10–30 boxes.

18. Under these conditions, what is the greatest number of boxes Max can reasonably hope to sell in a seven-hour working day?
   (A) 65
   (B) 60
   (C) 45
   (D) 40
   (E) 35

19. Under these conditions, what is the minimum number of boxes that Max can reasonably expect to sell in eight working hours?
   (A) none
   (B) 15
   (C) 20
   (D) 25
   (E) 35

20. If Max has sold 20 boxes to Deland Bros. and then his car breaks down and is not fixed until 2:00 P.M., what is the maximum sales figure for the day he can reasonably hope to achieve by 5:00 P.M.?
   (A) 20 boxes
   (B) 35 boxes
   (C) 40 boxes
   (D) 45 boxes
   (E) 55 boxes

21. If Max has an unbreakable thirty-minute luncheon appointment at 1:30 P.M., what is his best schedule for a 9:00 A.M. to 5:00 P.M. day?
   (A) Acme and Camera, then Bell and Deland
   (B) Bell and Acme, then Camera and, if time permits, Deland
   (C) Bell and Camera, then Deland and, if time permits, Acme
   (D) Camera and Bell, and Acme and Deland
   (E) Deland and Acme, then Camera and Bell

22. If Max is sick and has to carry all his calls over to the next day, when he must be at Edwards & Co. from 10:30 A.M. to 1:30

P.M., what would be his best schedule for the day from 9:00 A.M. to 5:00 P.M.?

(A) Deland, Edwards, Camera, and Bell
(B) Camera, Edwards, Deland and, if time permits, Acme
(C) Camera, Edwards, Acme and, if time permits, Deland
(D) Acme, Edwards, Deland and, if time permits, Camera
(E) Bell, Edwards, Deland and, if time permits, Camera

23. There is something irrational about our system of laws. The criminal law punishes a person more severely for having successfully committed a crime than it does a person who fails in his attempt to commit the same crime—even though the same evil intention is present in both cases. But under the civil law a person who attempts to defraud his victim but is unsuccessful is not required to pay damages.

Which of the following, if true, would most weaken the author's argument?

(A) Most persons who are imprisoned for crimes will commit another crime if they are ever released from prison.
(B) A person is morally culpable for his evil thoughts as well as for his evil deeds.
(C) There are more criminal laws on the books than there are civil laws on the books.
(D) A criminal trial is considerably more costly to the state than a civil trial.
(E) The goal of the criminal law is to punish the criminal, but the goal of the civil law is to compensate the victim.

24. An independent medical research team recently did a survey at a mountain retreat founded to help heavy smokers quit or cut down on their cigarette smoking. Eighty percent of those persons smoking three packs a day or more were able to cut down to one pack a day after they began to take End-Smoke with its patented desire suppressant. Try End-Smoke to help you cut down significantly on your smoking.

Which of the following could be offered as valid criticism of the above advertisement?

I. Heavy smokers may be physically as well as psychologically addicted to tobacco.
II. A medicine which is effective for very heavy smokers may not be effective for the population of smokers generally.
III. A survey conducted at a mountain retreat to aid smokers may yield different results than one would expect under other circumstances.

(A) I only
(B) II only
(C) III only
(D) II and III only
(E) I, II, and III

25. In his most recent speech, my opponent, Governor Smith, accused me of having distorted the facts, misrepresenting his position, suppressing information, and deliberately lying to the people.

Which of the following possible responses by this speaker would be LEAST relevant to his dispute with Governor Smith?

(A) Governor Smith would not have begun to smear me if he did not sense that his own campaign was in serious trouble.
(B) Governor Smith apparently misunderstood my characterization of his position, so I will attempt to state more clearly my understanding of it.
(C) At the time I made those remarks, certain key facts were not available, but new information uncovered by my staff does support the position I took at that time.
(D) I can only wish Governor Smith had specified those points he considered to be lies so that I could have responded to them now.
(E) With regard to the allegedly distorted facts, the source of my information is a Department of Transportation publication entitled "Safe Driving."

STOP

END OF SECTION. IF YOU HAVE ANY TIME LEFT, GO OVER YOUR WORK IN THIS SECTION ONLY. DO NOT WORK IN ANY OTHER SECTION OF THE TEST.

PRACTICE EXAMINATION 2—ANSWER KEY

Section I

1. D	5. B	9. D	13. E	17. B	21. A	25. B	29. E	33. D	37. B
2. C	6. E	10. E	14. A	18. D	22. C	26. D	30. B	34. A	38. E
3. A	7. B	11. B	15. E	19. D	23. E	27. A	31. C	35. D	
4. C	8. C	12. A	16. C	20. E	24. B	28. A	32. C	36. B	

Section II

1. E	5. D	9. B	13. A	17. C	21. B	25. A	29. A	33. D	37. E
2. A	6. D	10. B	14. B	18. C	22. D	26. E	30. D	34. D	38. D
3. C	7. A	11. A	15. B	19. A	23. E	27. D	31. A	35. B	
4. D	8. B	12. A	16. D	20. C	24. D	28. B	32. B	36. C	

Section III

1. D	4. C	7. C	10. B	13. C	16. E	19. A	22. B	25. D	28. A
2. A	5. D	8. C	11. B	14. D	17. C	20. A	23. B	26. D	29. C
3. A	6. C	9. A	12. B	15. A	18. A	21. D	24. E	27. C	30. B

Section IV

1. D	4. C	7. C	10. D	13. B	16. A	19. D	22. C	25. E	28. D
2. C	5. A	8. C	11. B	14. A	17. C	20. B	23. E	26. A	29. B
3. B	6. B	9. B	12. D	15. B	18. A	21. A	24. C	27. D	30. A

Section V

1. E	6. D	11. E	16. A	21. A
2. B	7. D	12. E	17. A	22. B
3. C	8. B	13. A	18. C	23. C
4. E	9. C	14. D	19. E	24. B
5. C	10. E	15. B	20. E	25. E

Section VI

1. C	6. B	11. C	16. E	21. C
2. C	7. B	12. A	17. D	22. B
3. A	8. D	13. D	18. A	23. E
4. B	9. A	14. C	19. D	24. D
5. E	10. D	15. B	20. C	25. A

EXPLANATORY ANSWERS

SECTION I

1. **(D)** One who intimidates his employees does so by improper use of his authority. Abusing is the obvious answer. The other choices clearly have no connection with use or abuse.

2. **(C)** If the foliage of the tropics seemed strange to the children, this would indicate that it was new or unusual to them. The missing space calls for an idea of newness or the first time. Only introduction conveys this sense.

3. **(A)** This question calls for a pair of synonyms descriptive of a "generous heart." Selfless ("never thinking of oneself") and altruistic ("thinking always of others first") fit this requirement. Of the other four choices, one is a pair of antonyms (kind and ruthless), and the remaining three are unrelated pairs.

4. **(C)** Choices (A), (D), and (E) are eliminated because neither self-pity nor self-esteem nor self-concern can convulse ("cause to writhe in suffering") anybody. Choice (B) is out because causing happiness to others rarely brings any self-doubt to a person.

5. **(B)** The shore is associated in the sentence with "vacationers who liked to swim." But "chilly" describes temperatures usually disliked by swimmers. Therefore, the chilliness of "late-summer waters" would cause the swimmers to become unhappy or displeased. Disappointed is a good synonym for displeased or unhappy; disappointingly is the best adverb to fill the gap. None of the other choices has anything to do with disappointment.

6. **(E)** Choice (A) is out because the Atomic Age has had relevant, not irrelevant, effects on people. Choice (B) is out because it would lead to a redundance (i.e., universal effects on people in all walks of life). Choices (C) and (D) are eliminated because pretentious and profane make no sense with effects. Only (E) makes sense.

7. **(B)** A "shudder" is never described as credible, appreciative, approving, or pleased. Therefore, (A), (C), (D), and (E) are eliminated. Only horrified makes good sense.

8. **(C)** An island can be thought of as a small spot of contrast in the ocean, as is the oasis in the desert. Another way of seeing the relationship is as an opposite one, but that is not as accurate or strong. (D) has some appeal since a single tree might stand in the middle of a field, but it is not part of the definition of tree for it to be alone in a field, while an island and an oasis are typically defined by their isolation.

9. **(D)** Mathematics is the serious and scientific approach to the relations between numbers, while numerology is a mystical and non-scientific approach to the same topic. Astronomy is similarly the scientific approach to relationships among the stars and planets, while astrology is the mystical and non-scientific approach to the same topic. All of the other pairs are either of various scientific disciplines, or of philosophy, which is not like the first part of the stem pair.

10. **(E)** The relationship is one of degree, with the first part of the pair being the lesser degree. (E) has this. Trustworthy and helpful may have some connection, but it is not one of degree. (D) is a relationship of opposites, and the others are more complex, if they are there at all.

11. **(B)** A minaret is the typical roofing design of a mosque, while a steeple is the typical roofing design of a church. This should be an easy question since the stem relates a part of a building to the whole building, and there is only one answer choice that duplicates this.

12. **(A)** Chaff is the waste or leftovers from sorting out wheat. Dregs are the same for wine. (C)'s only connection is that another meaning of chaff is to tease, and raillery is a type of joking. This is not enough. (D) and (E) are unconnected to the original ideas. (B) has some merit since crumbs are the leftovers of bread. However, chaff is a part of the wheat that never had any value, being the stems and such; similarly for dregs. Crumbs, however, were presumably the same as the bread and could have been eaten.

13. **(E)** The director is the person in charge of the content and presentation of a drama. Similarly, the editor is in charge of the content and presentation of a magazine. (D) does not work since there is no name in the original, and Sophocles was a playwright and a specific personage. Also, the first

part of (D) is an abstraction and the second isn't, which distinguishes it from the stem. (C) has two persons, which does not correlate with a person and an abstraction. (B) has a little merit since the scenario in some sense controls the movie, but we must look for a person who controls something, if possible. (A) is the second-best answer since the principal is certainly supposed to be in charge of the class, though teacher would be a better answer. However, the magazine and the drama are both artistic and creative endeavors, while the class is not, particularly for a principal.

14. **(A)** A goal is the object of someone who is implacable; an implacable person sticks to his goal, no matter what. An officious person is one who will stick to the rules and procedures, no matter what. (D) has the relationship that something which is placid, like a pond, might make a mirror. But this is a little farfetched for an analogy question and certainly is not the relationship of the stem pair. (C) is a situation of causation, since an infectious thing might cause a disease, but that is also wrong. (B) and (E) have some merit: A conclusion is a type of goal of a process of inference, or it is something that is presumably inferable. However, the goal is the object of a person who is implacable and a conclusion is not the object of a person who is inferable—if indeed a person can be inferable in the first place. (B) turns on the idea of a zealous person being strong on something, but it is not necessarily the method; but an officious person is definitely concerned with the procedures.

15. **(E)** A cartoon is a common and simplified type of drawing. A caricature is a simplified and, usually, common type of portrait. A ditty is a common or simplified sort of song, but it is stretching it a little to call it a simplified aria. (C) fails since a crayon need not be a common or vulgar type of implement relative to a brush. (A) and (B) try only to play with the humorous aspect of a cartoon.

16. **(C)** The relationship in the stem pair nearly is one of synonyms. Insouciant means literally carefree and is exactly lighthearted. A calm person is unworried. (A), (D), and (E) all have noun to adjective or adjective to noun relationships which are more difficult to fit into the original model of two adjectives. (B) and (C) fit that all right, and (B) could also be described as fitting the form that someone who is thieving is light-fingered, but it is no longer an emotion. Also, the stem pair are positive in tone.

17. **(B)** The number of hours at home is seen by the author as an opportunity to extend the work of the school, but not as being more important. The author says it is a great influence, but not that it is the greatest; thus, (A) fails. (C) and (D) are both

stated in the passage, but they are used as examples of (B)'s more general idea. (E) is, if anything, opposed, since the example of the parent helping with the homework was largely negative. If the more general mathematics usage ideas are considered helping with homework, then this is like (C) and (D): only an example of (B).

18. **(D)** (A) is incorrect since no generalization is made, only an example used. (B) and (E) are absent from the passage altogether. (C) is attractive, but not actually in the passage. It sounds like one of the things which might be done to help math, perhaps using the yardstick that is mentioned, but this is not, in fact, mentioned. (D) is the subject of the entire passage, and of the last several paragraphs in particular.

19. **(D)** (B), (C), and (E) are without foundation, and (A) is false. (D) is precisely what is urged by the author.

20. **(E)** This is a detail question. (E), a demonstration lesson, is not necessarily included in classes for parents since the classes for the parents would focus on what the parents should do at home, rather than reviewing, as such, what the children do at school. New progress report methods are mentioned, (B), as is (C).

21. **(A)** The passage made its point by giving an example in which interesting related activities led to improvement. Although the example was abstract to some extent, the author's use of it as a piece of evidence implies that he believes it to be true; thus, (A) is implied.

(D) picks up on the passage's negative evaluation of drill in the home and the types of non-drill reinforcements recommended by the author; however, since the focus of the passage is exclusively on home activities, only the weakest of inferences can be made about the author's views on activities at school. (D) is probably the second-best answer.

None of the other choices is much connected with the passage. (B) alleges laziness, but only inadequate support is seen as the student's problem in the passage. The only mention of a principal, (C), is in reference to his approval being sought for innovative or unusual teacher initiatives. (E) refers to visits by teachers to the parents at home, but the only parent-teacher communication urged in the passage is the reference to informal interviews, which need not be conducted at the parent's home.

22. **(C)** All of the answers touch upon the substance of the passage, and it is the differences among them which give the answer choice. The passage is aimed at teachers and specifies actions to be taken by teachers in order to influence the parents' future actions. Thus, (A) errs in claiming the passage speaks directly to the parent, as does (E).

(E) also suffers from the pejorative word brainwash, since the author believes that many parents are willing and eager to help their children and lack only proper guidance.

(D) takes the example of mathematics as the point, when all subjects are at issue.

(B) and (C) have the most merit. There can be no doubt that the author hopes to serve the purpose outlined in (B), to some small extent, by writing his passage, BUT the goal of having the child's capacities totally developed is most general and abstract, while the passage has a closer, clearer purpose as expressed by (C). (C) fits the passage much more closely than does (B), which could describe the ultimate purpose of hundreds of articles.

23. **(E)** Since the tone is one of instructing the teacher, (E) is very attractive, but the others must be eliminated. (B) and (C) fail because of the passage's instructions-to-the-teacher tone. (D) is not supported in the passage since no reference to college is needed nor present. (A) has the merit of focusing on the right sort of person since the passage refers to elementary school subjects such as arithmetic. However, while an elementary school teacher could be instructing his fellow teachers, it is precisely the job of the professor of education to do so; hence (E) is preferable.

24. **(B)** The passage states that mere drill work or rewarding schoolwork is not what the author has in mind; thus, (A), (C), and (E) are eliminated. (D) is not quite the same as the others, but it focuses on the parent working with the child rather than trying to incorporate learning experiences into the child's everyday life at home, which the author wishes to see done more. Thus (B), which encourages the child to write more outside of school, is precisely the sort of thing which the author has in mind.

25. **(B)** The quotation from the journal must be taken in the context of the entire passage. The passage states that the editorial was discussing the control of CB warfare, but that does not mean that the editorial approved of control. However, in speaking of a balance of terror as being a possible protection against war, the article is certainly not asking for more terror, but only that it be balanced. Thus (A) and (E) are weak. (C) fails since the editorial clearly feels that the balance is working. To be sure, one might have a balance of terror without CB warfare, but nothing in the quote from the editorial implies that the author of the editorial wishes to see CB warfare preparations stopped.

(B) and (D) both have merit. The editorial writer is plainly accepting, if not approving, of the way things are now. The major distinction to be drawn between the two answer choices is that (B) is restricted to the great powers and (D) is not. Since the quotation refers only to the great power blocs. (B) is the better answer because it stays within the scope of the quotation.

26. **(D)** Although the passage does not explicitly state the reasons for the United States' participation in CB warfare programs, there is evidence to support (D). The quotation from the editorial serves to point out how the same ideas have been taken from the nuclear arms situation and applied to the CB warfare situation. The key concept that has been borrowed is the balance of terror. A balance means that what one side has, the other must have. The only difficulty is the word mainly. The most important idea of the passage is the one stated in the first sentence and echoed in the final quotation—mutual deterrence and mutual balance of terror. Thus, the idea of mutuality and response to the other power bloc is paramount. This means that the major reason for one group having the weapons is that the other group has them or will have them. Thus, (D) is preferable because it fits in better with the major ideas of the passage.

27. **(A)** As discussed above, the major concept of the passage is to show the use of CB warfare as another element of the balance of terror and mutual deterrence. The passage does not *explain* the cost of CB warfare, though it refers to the cost as being low; thus, (B) fails. Nor are alternatives or history discussed, eliminating (C) and (D). (E) has a little merit in that the reader is made forcefully aware that CB warfare is regarded as powerful enough to take its place beside nuclear weapons as a part of the balance of terror in the world. Still, there is little discussion of the dangers of CB warfare as such. The inclusion of the CB warfare in the balance of terror, the very thing that preserves the precarious peace, is a strong indication that it will be difficult indeed to stop CB warfare programs.

It could be argued that this is not the main idea and that the first sentence is the main idea. However, of the answer choices available, (A) seems to serve best by the main idea and thrust of the passage.

28. **(A)** A mansion is a grand home, while a hovel is a very mean and poor one. Hotel and motel refer to transient accommodations that can be rented, but so could a mansion. A castle is grander than a mansion, while a house is a standard living accommodation. Hovel is the best opposite because it is poor, while the mansion is grand.

29. **(E)** This is a hard question because the word endemic is both uncommon and often misused. Endemic means peculiar to some locality or region, while pandemic means widespread, or among all peoples (*demos*). Both pandemic and endemic could be either permanent or temporary and might

well be frustrating or terrorizing, or the opposite, depending on the characteristic that was pandemic. Democratic merely shares the root word *demos.*

30. **(B)** Compendious means terse, briefly stated. It is an exposition which contains the whole matter in a brief way. Thus verbose, referring to the use of more words than necessary, is the best opposite. Ambiguous has some flavor of oppositeness. A compendious statement would be very clear and probably not ambiguous, but that is a byproduct of its including the entire subject in a brief statement. A subject that was ambiguous might, on the other hand, produce a compendious yet similarly ambiguous summary. Terse, however, does not mean simple.

31. **(C)** Assuage means to ease or make milder. Aggravate is a very precise opposite. None of the others has any real connection to the proper meaning of assuage.

32. **(C)** To prate is to talk foolishly or without meaning; hence (C) is the best opposite. Again, the other answers do not connect.

33. **(D)** Arrogate means to take without justification or right. (D) is a very precise opposite. This is mainly a matter of knowing the word, though the connection of arrogate with arrogant might lead you to guess the correct answer.

34. **(A)** This difficult word, prolix, means verbose or wordy. Terse means just the opposite. Speechless is not a good opposite. Since prolix means speaking in a particular way, the best opposite will be speaking in the opposite way. Upper class might look good at first, but the connection is to prole or proletarian, meaning working, or lower, class, which is incorrect. If you can pin down the basis for such an impulse and specify just what it is that draws you to an answer, you can often avoid an incorrect answer.

35. **(D)** A tyro is a rank beginner; thus, expert is the best opposite. Democrat appeals to tyrant, but that is a different word entirely. Alert, if it has any appeal at all, is reaching for the sound of tired.

36. **(B)** Sedition is working to undermine the established government or social order. Patriotism, while not a precise opposite, does speak to a love of the established country and political system. Flotation appeals to the echo of the word sediment, which does come from the same root as sedition, but means the material that is precipitated out of a liquid and settles on the bottom of the container, whereas sedition means the unsettling of the bottom, or roots, of a society. The other choices have only the appeal of being positive characteristics, while sedition would be generally viewed as negative.

37. **(B)** Tousle means to disarrange or roughen up, particularly hair. Groom is to arrange one's appearance and hair. Catch connects to toss, but you should avoid that since toss is not tousle. Caress is more of a synonym than an antonym, since tousling may often be a gesture of affection.

38. **(E)** Transient means something that lasts only for a short time. Thus persistent, meaning something that endures, is a very good opposite. Final also has real merit since the final decision is something that will not change and thus seems to endure in some sort of way. However, final is really opposite to preliminary, not transient. There is a tendency to think of passing things as leading up to some final, permanent resolution. Between final and persistent, the most salient difference is that a persistent thing will continue to exist, while many final things will pass away, such as final editions of a newspaper.

SECTION II

1. **(E)** Choice (D) is eliminated because being inured to one kind of activity has nothing to do with functioning in another kind of activity. According to the context of this sentence, adjusting to work is more accurate than adapting, conforming, or reacting. (A)'s, (B)'s, and (C)'s second words are inappropriate.

2. **(A)** Choices (B), (C), and (D) are eliminated immediately because nobody practices to overcome, supercede, or limit his talents. Choice (E) is out because a naturally inept person has no talents to develop. An adept person has talents that he can perfect.

3. **(C)** A teacher's pride is directly affected by his class's performance on an exam. Since the missing word must express that which will hurt the teacher's pride, we can fill in the gap with any suggestion of doing poorly or getting low grades on the exam. Flunked leaves no room for doubt, especially when the other four choices are relatively positive terms.

4. **(D)** A reporter's probings (investigations) will get results, provided that those probings are persistent. Choices (A), (B) and (C) have nothing to do with persistence. This leaves (D) and (E) as possibilities. However, finally implies that the probings were done over a long period of time without interruption. Relentless means without slowing down or stopping, and completes the thought perfectly. Earnest (serious) does not necessarily have anything to do with slowing down or stopping work in any way.

5. **(D)** In this item, the final two words are the key. It is impossible to shout, gesture, or wave incoherent threats. An excited mob wouldn't whisper.

6. **(D)** This sentence assumes that most people support having leisure time, ruling out (A) and (B). A staunch disciple is bad usage. That an opponent of leisure would have few duties is illogical.

7. **(A)** The first blank describes a downpour. (C), meaning ill-mannered, and (E), meaning without distinctive or attractive qualities, are not descriptive of a rainstorm and are thus incorrect. For the second blank we have a verb that is related to and immediately preceding the act of disappearing. (A), (C), and (E) do describe an action that might precede disappearance since the girls would need to get away from "us" first and then disappear, unless they could teleport. Thus, (B) and (D) are eliminated on the second blank, leaving (A) as the best answer. (D), provoke, is possible, but not as good as evade, since provoke is not particularly related to the disappearing.

8. **(B)** A telephone and a letter are both methods of communication. The difference between them is that a telephone is electronic and communicates through the medium of speech, while a letter is paper, or non-electronic, and communicates through the medium of writing. (A) is two electronic items, both of which work with sound, so that is not apt. (C) has the idea of electronic versus non-electronic, but both telegraph and mail involve writing. Sound and sight has some merit since speech relates to sound, and writing to sight, but there is no flavor of the relationship between types of appliances. (E) is two parts of the same medium. (B) has both analogous relationships and is best.

9. **(B)** Immigration is migration into, or entering, a place, while emigration is migration out of, or departing from, a place. (C) has real merit since immigration is an arrival of sorts and a door is an entrance of sorts; but notice the beginnings of an imbalance in the analogy if we use (C). The first part of the original pair uses the more specific term, but the second part of (C) uses the more specific term. In comparing with (B), we see that although (B) has an opposite idea—leaving—the relationship WITHIN the analogy pairs is the same. The first term in each pair is a type of migration, which is not true of (C). Thus, (B) is an example of a more specific relationship in the secondary, or vertical, way, but it is one that is carried through properly in the rest of the pair and thus is a strengthening idea. If we had emigration and the second part of the pair did not work as well as immigration/emigration, then the emigration answer choice would have been weak.

(A) is an antonym relationship, which is not the same as the original. (E) might have a little appeal since immigration is sometimes the search for a refuge and a gate can be an entrance, but this is weak and derivative and not nearly as strong as either (B) or (C).

10. **(B)** A hotel is a kind of shelter. A boat is a kind of transportation. (A) has the relationship of two things that are typically associated—the pillow is typically found on a bed. That does not work here. (D) and (E) have somewhat more appeal. A restaurant provides drink and a hotel provides shelter. Similarly, though with less force, a home provides recuperation. Note that (B) and (C) also fit this mold. The fact that the idea works for most of the answer choices tells us it is probably right, but needs refinement. The refinement here is how the provision takes place and how is the provision related to the institution or article in the front of the pair? The major purpose of a hotel is to provide shelter, and it is itself a form of shelter. This is not true of either (D) or (E). In distinguishing (B) from (C), we see that one difference is the difference between transportation and ride. Transportation is more general, and shelter is a very general idea and more like transportation than ride. A train is not really thought of as a type of ride, while a boat is defined as a type of transportation.

11. **(A)** A moon is associated with a planet in that it circles or orbits a planet. A planet similarly orbits a star. A planet is larger than a moon, and (C) has some idea of size difference, but so does (A). The additional idea of orbiting is very powerful because it is quite intrinsic to the idea of astronomy, from which field all of these terms come. Further, in (D) a nova is larger than a star, but is derived from a star, since a nova is an exploding star.

12. **(A)** An ascetic dislikes and avoids luxury, as a misogynist dislikes and avoids women. (B) fails since a philosopher seeks truth and likes it. (C) and (E) have internal relationships that are positive and typical; in each case the person is associated with the idea or object. (D) has some merit since a gourmet would certainly not like to be hungry. However, the idea of a gourmet is not that he eats to satisfy his hunger, but rather that he eats to satisfy his taste or palate. The stem *gyn*- in misogynist means woman, and *mis*- would mean against or opposed.

13. **(A)** A spasm is a brief, intense movement of a muscle, and by extension is any brief, intense action. A flash is a brief intense activity of light. (C) and (D) each contain half of a good analogy, pinch and touch, which, if combined as an answer choice, might be even better than flash and light. Respite is a restful break from something difficult—not the same at all. Sound and noise are nearly synonyms, but a spasm is not a muscle.

14. **(B)** Corrugated is having ridges, and striped is a two-dimensional equivalent. One might, for in-

stance, indicate in a painting that something was corrugated by making stripes. This idea of having the same shape but being two- and then three-dimensional is carried through very well by (B), dimpled and speckled. (A) is appealing, but the connection is a secondary one between corrugated and cardboard and between zebra and striped. (E) is the only other answer choice with any merit. Bumpy and flashing both have the idea of being intermittent, as do both of the original pair. However, (B) also has this idea as well as the further connection of the two- and three-dimensionality.

15. **(B)** Oxygen, under normal conditions, is gaseous; that is its typical state of matter. All of the answer choices have some of the idea that the adjective in the second position is a typical descriptor of the noun in the first position. This means that refinement is needed. One refinement would be to ask what sort of typical description is being given. All of the descriptions are physical, again confirming that we are on the right track. But gaseous describes a state of matter and only (B) has a similar adjective. (D)'s grainy is second best since it is a form idea, but grainy is a subdivision of solid, while fluid and gaseous are non-solids. It is a slight detraction from the merit of (B) that fluid is a term that includes gaseous, while there is no possibly similar link between oxygen and mercury.

16. **(D)** An acrobat must be agile as part of his trade. Similarly, an orator must be able to speak well or be eloquent, if he is to do his job right. (C)'s relationship is class to member of the class, which is incorrect. (B) does not describe a characteristic of the vendor, but rather what he sells. (E) describes a characteristic that a car might have, but it is not the only characteristic or even a necessary one for a car to have to be a good car. If the analogy had been speed : racecar, it would have been much stronger. (A) has some merit in that greasy is a typical characteristic of a mechanic. However, it is not something that helps him to do his job well, as agility and eloquence help, respectively, the acrobat and orator. Thus, (D) is best.

17. **(C)** The question is asking us for a summary statement of the passage to be the title of the passage. This must be correct in what it says and not make any mistakes. (A) fails because the passage is discussing the need for vacations, not the preferences for different kinds of vacations. (B) has the appeal of referring to the last sentence and the idea that vacations are a topic of conversation. However, the purpose of that statement is to show how important vacations are, not to say anything about conversational habits as such. (C) certainly has real merit since the effect of the passage is to give some context for and reasons

behind vacation practices. Thus, (C) has nothing particularly wrong with it, although it might have been even better if it had said something about the application of the author's ideas to the modern, industrialized world. (D) fails for similar reasons as (A): There is nothing in the passage about the content of the vacations, or their organization on an individual basis. There is some idea that the taking of vacations is well organized in the U.S. (E) has the merit of referring to the underlying need that vacations serve, but actually fails to mention the idea of vacations at all. Thus, (E) is inferior to (C), and (C) is the best answer. Note that a combination of several answers might have given an even stronger one. For instance, *Vacations in Perspective: The Increasing Need for Renewal, Refreshment, and Repair in the Industrialized World.* This is almost perfect, though much too long.

18. **(C)** This question asks for a specific piece of the author's argument. In this case the reason why "we" in the industrialized world need vacations more is the "stultifying" quality of our work, the need for a "break in the routine." Both these references should have indicated to you, when you read the passage, that the work is too unvaried day after day. Thus, (C) goes right to the heart of the matter. (A) and (D) are ideas not mentioned in the passage. (B) and (E) are also unmentioned and fall into that class of wrong answers that we might fall for from our general knowledge rather than from the passage. These answers might have great merit in the real world, but they are not based on the passage, so they are wrong on the test.

19. **(A)** This is really the same basic idea as the previous question, but in a different guise. We must, however, evaluate each answer choice. (A) is implied, as discussed above. (B) and (C) are simply nice things to say about ourselves that have no basis in the passage. (D) is the opposite of (A), and thus you could probably settle the both of them with the same line of reasoning. You might ask yourself whether there is anything in the passage to indicate that the lives of Americans are either varied or habitual. There might be nothing, but in this case there is and (D) is wrong and (A) is right. The only possible support for (D) in the passage is the fact that we do go on vacations, which are presumably somewhat varied, but the bulk of our lives is filled with habitual behavior. (E) fails since the whole tone of the passage is that people are not independent and do not have control over their lives, which is one of the reasons they need vacations.

20. **(C)** The form of this essay is to recount a number of formative historical aspects of the author's personal religious and moral development. The last paragraph states the author's current faith,

which has resulted from these influences. Thus, (C) is a good description of the passage's workings and purpose.

(A) catches the tone of the passage as being explanatory and directed, but the author does not consider himself a Quaker and thus it is improbable that (A) is correct. (B) has the word Friend with a capital letter, thus indicating that a Quaker is addressed. However, while the passage might serve the purpose stated in (B), it would only do so through the idea of (C), and, indeed, the significant differences which the author does find between himself and Quakers might upset (B)'s purpose.

(D) is only relevant to a very small portion of the passage and the analysis of the inner light that does occur primarily sets the stage for the pacifism of the last paragraph, which still leaves (C) preferable to (D). (E) is not really in the passage, since it is only the parents' attitudes toward religious dogmatism that are discussed, rather than any explicit teachings.

21. **(B)** Two types of reward are played with in this question and in the passage. In the passage, the idea of a good deed being its own reward refers to inner feelings generated by the knowledge of having done a good deed. In the question, the connotation is one of a financial or material reward. While these are different, there is no reason to believe that the author would refuse a financial reward—he has sworn no vow of poverty—but at the same time he would not want it to seem that the financial reward was the reason for the good deed.

(C) is impossible or unnecessarily complicated. You may have thought that this answer choice was a way of referring to the possibility of having the financial reward given to a charity or some such, but it does not say that and if you choose it you are reading too much into the answer choice.

(D) fails since there is no basis in the passage for having any idea as to what, if anything, the author might consider blasphemous. The financial reward does not necessarily obviate the spiritual one.

(A) and (E) both suppose that the author is totally opposed to receiving a financial reward, which is more than we know from the passage. We would only entertain an answer of this sort if all others were totally impossible—and even then you should be unhappy with so weak an answer.

In contrast to the other answer choices, (B) has the virtue of being considerate of the other person's feelings, which seems to be implied in the author's respect for the divinity of all other persons.

22. **(D)** The author states that the idea of "inner light" is basic to his views and he uses it in that way. He got this idea from the Quakers and restates that it is a shared thought.

(B) is something that some people may know to be true of many—though not all—Quakers in the real world. In this passage, however, the author makes absolutely no reference to the pacifism of the Quakers, and indeed only discusses his own pacifism after he has dissociated himself from the Quakers. If one were forced to choose between the Quakers being pacifists and preachers of holy crusades, the passage would support the former over the latter, but nothing is said about the historical nature of Quakerism in the passage.

(A) and (E) are specifically rejected in the passage and (C) is known to be true only of some Quakers at one Meeting for Worship.

23. **(E)** The author sees no reason for Jesus being more divine "than, say, Buddha." Thus, he likely sees all major religious leaders as being equally divine.

24. **(D)** The position taken by the author's parents can be inferred from the first sentence of the second paragraph, where the parents' dislike of doctrine and dogma is traced to their lapsed Catholicism, and thus a probable reason for the lapse.

(A) is false both because the author has an inner light and sees himself as a non-Quaker and because the last paragraph refers to "this piece of divinity that every human has."

(B) is false because the inner-light views of the author and the Quakers are stated to be the same, so the Quakers view all men as having an inner light.

(C) has no basis in the passage since the author's parents' dissatisfaction with Catholic views is not said to be in the matter of killing.

(E) is incorrect since the author states that he is closer to the Quakers than to any other organized religious group. While the organization of Buddhism is not the same as many Christian religions, it could not be called unorganized.

25. **(A)** (A) is stated in the last paragraph. (B) plays on the statement that we must "increase this lifeline" ("the inner light"). The increase is linked with understanding, and better refers to increased strength rather than numbers. (C) and (D) fail for the same reasons as 24 (A) and (B). (E) is either unsupported or, better, rejected in the passage since the author has a faith without help of prophets and which appears to be adequate for him, even though he says that it is poorer for lacking a prophet, etc. The extra divinity of prophets is also a questionable inference to base on this passage.

26. **(E)** This is a logical reasoning question. If both action and inaction will cause death, then death is no longer a difference between the options available and cannot be used to make the decision as to which option should be taken. (C) does not avoid the situation because it would simply be a method

of choosing inaction. (D) fails because beliefs should not be abandoned because of the existence of situations to which they do not apply. Note that when the author argues against "the taking of any life by choice," this does not mean only by action. Inaction is a choice, too.

27. **(D)** Choice (D) is explicitly rejected by the author when he says that his personal religion might be the poorer for having no revealed word. The difficulties in this problem stem more from the attractiveness of several of the other answer choices.

   (A) is explicitly agreed to by the author when he says that he limits his faith to a Supreme Being and the goodness of man. This statement of belief in the goodness of man is not the reason that the author can be said to believe in the divine nature of human beings. The concept of inner light is a piece of divinity in each man, according to the author, and will suffice to validate (C). (C) does not require that every piece of man be divine.

   (B) is agreeable to the author for two reasons. First, that is why his parents sent him to First Day School, and he is approving of their conduct. Second, and even more important, (B) is known from the author's approval of the general precepts of Jesus and from his own insistence on goodness for its own sake.

   (E) is deducible from the fact that the author found the entire experience of sharing religious experiences with the Quakers valuable as a child, and continues to find it valuable as an adult.

28. **(B)** Consonant means harmonious in sound and, by extension, harmonious and consistent in general. Incongruous means inconsistent, out of place, or inharmonious, and is a perfect opposite. An insuperable objection is one that cannot be overcome. Sounded has some relation to consonant, coming from the same *son* stem, meaning sound. However, that is not enough to create an antonym relationship.

29. **(A)** A concise piece of writing says a great deal in a few words. Both wordy and muddy have some opposite feeling, but the essential meaning of concise has to do with length, so wordy, meaning too long and with too many words, is a better opposite. Saying a great deal in a few words is likely to be clear, but that is a further association and not the main meaning. A concise statement might certainly be wrong, and even ignorant or mundane, which means commonplace or everyday.

30. **(D)** Fecund means very fertile and productive, which is precisely the opposite of barren. Premier is a play on the rhyme between fecund and second, which is, of course, misleading.

31. **(A)** A fortuitous event is both fortunate and unlooked for. Here, the only opposite available is

unfortunate, which, while not perfect, is the best. The *fortu-* stem might have been a hint to help you. Pious means full of piety for, or revering, God or some "superior" such as parents.

32. **(B)** A saturnine person has a gloomy disposition; thus, cheerful is a perfect opposite. Earthy has several meanings, the most common being coarse, unrefined, and unaffected. The fact that saturnine refers to the planet Saturn does not mean that earthy is at all opposite. Maudlin is tearfully or weakly sentimental, or even silly, when referring to a drunk.

33. **(D)** Frangible means breakable, even fragile. Sturdy is again the only opposite. Docile means easily managed or taught. Inedible appeals to some students, though the reasons are not clear. Perhaps frangible reminds them of some tropical fruit.

34. **(D)** Lethargy is a state of drowsy apathy, mental dullness, and lack of initiative. Alertness is pretty close to a perfect opposite. Acidity is the degree of acidness. A prodigy is someone with extraordinary gifts or talents in some field. Corpulence is fatness or fleshiness.

35. **(B)** Cupidity is greediness, wanting everything for oneself. Generosity is a willingness or desire to give things to others. While Cupid is the god of love, cupidity has come to mean unusually strong love of money. Lovelessness is not the opposite. Prodigality has some oppositeness to cupidity since prodigality means wanton wastefulness.

36. **(C)** Protean means changeable, particularly in shape or form. Uniform means to have one shape, or to be constant in some way. This is a nearly perfect opposite. Universal has some oppositeness in the sense of applying everywhere, and thus implying consistency or even constancy: A universal principle is uniformly applicable, perhaps. However, this is not as good an opposite as uniform, which directly addresses the issue of changeability of form and shape.

37. **(E)** A cogent argument is convincing and forceful. A fatuous statement is unreal, foolish, or illusory, and thus hardly convincing. This is not a perfect opposite. A cogent statement is often taken to be short and to the point, but it is only the "to the point" part which is correct. Cogency need not be related to length; thus (A) and (D) are inadequate. Similarly, cogent need not be simple, so there is no oppositeness in (C). Urgent connects to an idea of importance and time pressure, while cogency is about persuasiveness. One could be cogent about both urgent and non-urgent matters; thus (B) is not correct.

38. **(D)** Hirsute means hairy. Both naked and bald have direct merit, and plain and clear have a little

appeal, though no merit. Since hirsute means having hair, the perfect opposite would be not having hair, which is bald. Naked is not bad, but not as good as bald because it is a more general word, meaning without covering, while bald means without a covering of hair.

SECTION III

1. **(D)** Since no information is given directly about x or y, we cannot determine the relationship. Do not assume that since $x = -y$, y will be greater than $-y$ and thus greater than x. It is possible that y is a negative number, in which case x is a positive number and greater than y. Also, x and y could both be equal to zero.

2. **(A)** $\frac{1}{100}$ is equal to 1%, so Column A is greater. .01% expressed as a fraction is $\frac{1}{10,000}$.

3. **(A)** To compute a percentage increase, it is necessary to create a fraction: $\frac{\text{difference}}{\text{starting amount}}$. In this problem, the price of paper increased from \$1.23 to \$1.48, for a difference of \$0.25. Thus, our fraction is $\frac{.25}{1.23}$. If we actually needed to calculate the percentage increase, we would then divide 1.23 into .25 and multiply that quotient by 100 (to convert the decimal to a percent). For purposes of answering the quantitative comparison question, however, a rough estimate will be sufficient. The percentage increase in the price is more than $25 \div 125$, and that would be a $\frac{1}{5}$, or 20% increase. Thus Column A is slightly greater than 20%, so Column A must be greater.

4. **(C)** The intuitive way of solving this problem is to reason that $\frac{M + x + y}{3}$ is the *average* of M, x, and y, and that $\frac{x + y}{2}$ is the average of x and y. Since the average of any number and itself is *itself*—that is, the average of x and x is x—Column A must be equal to Column B. The same conclusion can be more rigorously demonstrated by substituting $\frac{x + y}{2}$ for M in column A:

$$\frac{\frac{x + y}{2} + x + y}{3} = \frac{\frac{x + y + 2(x + y)}{2}}{3} = \frac{3x + 3y}{6} = \frac{x + y}{2}$$

5. **(D)** The natural starting point for solving this problem is to perform the indicated operations—that is, to multiply the expressions:

$$(a + 2)(b + 3) \qquad (a + 3)(b + 2)$$
$$ab + 3a + 2b + 6 \qquad ab + 2a + 3b + 6$$

Of course, since ab and 6 are common to both expressions, those terms cannot make any difference in the comparison of the two columns.

After we strip away the ab terms and 6, we are left with $3a + 2b$ in Column A and $2a + 3b$ in Column B. Since no information is given about the relative magnitudes of a and b, the answer must be (D).

6. **(C)** The easiest way to get a handle on this question is to draw the line.

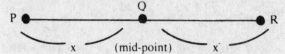

Since Q is the midpoint, we know that PQ is equal to QR.

7. **(C)** This problem requires that the expression in Column A be factored. From basic algebra you will recall that $(x + y)(x - y) = x^2 - y^2$. So the denominator of Column A can be factored into $(x + y)(x - y)$. Then the $x - y$ can be cancelled, leaving $x + y$ for both columns.

8. **(C)** To make the explanation easier to grasp, we add the following notation:

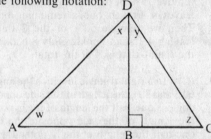

Since BD is perpendicular to AC, both triangle ABD and triangle CBD are right triangles. Consequently:

$$w + x + 90° = 180° \quad \text{and} \quad y + z + 90° = 180°$$
$$\text{so: } w + x = 90° \qquad \text{and } y + z = 90°$$

9. **(A)** The two planes converge on each other at the rate of 300 miles/40 minutes, or 300 miles/$\frac{2}{3}$ hr. That is a rate of 450 miles per hour—the *sum* of their speeds. Since plane X is flying at 150 MPH, plane Y must be flying at 300 MPH. Another way of solving the problem would be to reason that *if* plane Y were flying at 150 MPH, the two planes would be converging at the rate of 300 MPH and it would take a full hour, not 40 minutes, for them to pass. This shows that plane Y must be flying at a speed faster than 150 MPH.

10. **(B)** $\frac{2}{3} = 66.666\ldots\%$. That is a repeating decimal which never ends. But even though it cannot be expressed in regular decimal form, that decimal must be larger than 66.6%, which is 66.60%.

11. **(B)** The sum of the interior angles of a pentagon is 540°, and that of a hexagon is 720°. If you did not recall this, you could have computed the sum in the following way:

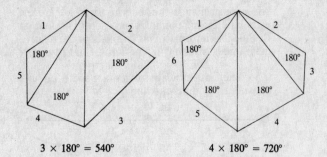

$$3 \times 180° = 540° \qquad\qquad 4 \times 180° = 720°$$

(Notice that the sum of the interior angles is unrelated to the relative lengths of the sides.)

The average size of the angles of the pentagon, then, is 540 divided by 5, or 108°. And the average size of the angles of the hexagon is 720° divided by 6, or 120°. The general rule is: The average size of the angle grows as the number of sides in the polygon increases.

12. **(B)** The shelf originally contains 24 books. We remove 75% of the 16 French books, or 12, which leaves 4 French books remaining on the shelf. Then we remove 50% of the 8 Italian books, leaving 4 Italian books. Only 8 books remain on the shelf—that is, $\frac{1}{3}$ of the total.

13. **(C)** In a right triangle in which the angles are 90°, 60°, and 30°, the length of the side opposite the 30° angle is one-half the length of the hypotenuse, and the length of the side opposite the 60° angle is one-half the length of the hypotenuse times $\sqrt{3}$. Since two of the angles of this triangle total 90°, and there are 180° in a triangle, angle B must equal 90°, and this is a right triangle. Side AB is opposite the 30° angle, and so must be one-half the hypotenuse. AB is 1; therefore, AC must be 2. BC, then, will be one-half the length of the hypotenuse times $\sqrt{3}$. So BC will be $\sqrt{3}$.

14. **(D)** There are several ways of solving this problem. One way is to manipulate the centered equation so that $x^2 = 1$. Then it should be clear that $x = \pm 1$, and so x might be +1 or −1. Similarly, one might factor $x^2 - 1$ to get $(x + 1)(x - 1) = 0$, showing that there are two values for x, only one of which is +1.

15. **(A)** This problem can be solved using simultaneous equations. Let x be the number of $13 tickets and y the number of $25 tickets.

THEN: $x + y = 11$
AND: $13x + 25y = 227$
By the first equation: $x = 11 - y$
Substituting in the second equation: $13(11 - y) + 25y = 227$
Then manipulating: $143 - 13y + 25y = 227$
  $12y = 84$
  $y = 7$

And if the number of $25 tickets is equal to 7, the number of $13 tickets is only 4, so Column A is greater. An easier and therefore a *better* way of solving the problem is to recognize that the *average* value of the tickets must be approximately $20. If an equal number of tickets had been sold (impossible, of course, since an odd number of tickets was sold), the average would have been midway between $13 and $25, or $19. Since the average is *above* $19, more of the expensive tickets must have been sold.

16. **(E)** A simple method for adding any two fractions is:

STEP A: Find the new denominator by multiplying the old ones.
STEP B: Multiply the numerator of the first fraction by the denominator of the second.
STEP C: Multiply the denominator of the first fraction by the numerator of the second.
STEP D: Add the results of B and C.
STEP E: Reduce, if necessary.

The process is more easily comprehended when presented in the following way:

$$\frac{a}{b} + \frac{c}{d} = \frac{ad + bc}{bd}$$

Here, we have:

$$\frac{3}{4} + \frac{4}{5} = \frac{15 + 16}{20} = \frac{31}{20}$$

17. **(C)** Since $x + 6 = 3$, $x = -3$. Then, substituting −3 for x in the second expression, $x + 3$ is $-3 + 3 = 0$.

18. **(A)** Probably the easiest way to solve this problem is just to count the steps on your fingers, but the same process can be expressed mathematically. Let those steps he walks down be assigned negative values, and those steps he walks up be positive. We then have: $-4 + 3 - 6 + 2 + 9 - 2 = +2$. So the person comes to rest two steps above where he started.

19. **(A)** In a circle graph such as this, the sectors must total 100%. The sectors P, R, S, and T account for 21%, 29%, 18%, and 28%, respectively, for a total of 96%. So Q must be 4%.

20. **(A)** The easiest way to solve this problem is to factor the 326 from both terms of the expression:

$$326(31 - 19) = 326(12) = 3912$$

Of course, you might actually do the arithmetic by multiplying first 326 by 31 and then 326 by 19 and then subtracting the smaller total from the larger. That takes quite a bit longer! But if you did not see the first way (factoring) and can manage the arithmetic in thirty or forty seconds, you should proceed with the *one* way you know to get the correct answer. However, the better approach by far is to find a way of avoiding the calculation.

21. **(D)** This is a problem which is most easily solved by literally counting on your fingers. From 1:21 to 2:21 is 60 minutes. From 2:21 to 3:21 is 60 minutes. So far we have a total of 120 minutes. Then, from 3:21 to 3:36 is 15 minutes, for a total of 135 minutes.

22. **(B)** First, we must compute the total commission that will be owed: 15% of $2800 = $420. Then we must take into account the fact that the sales representative has already received $150 of that sum. So she is now owed: $420 − $150 = $270.

23. **(B)** The area of a circle is pi times radius squared, or $A = \pi r^2$. Here the area is $9\pi x^2$. So we write: $9\pi x^2 = \pi r^2$. Notice that the π terms cancel out, leaving: $9x^2 = r^2$. Taking the square root of both sides of the equation: $\sqrt{9x^2} = \sqrt{r^2}$, so r = 3x.

24. **(E)** Since this problem deals with the heights of the individuals, a quite natural starting point would be to draw a picture:

Hans is taller than Gertrude:
H
G

Hans is shorter than Wilhelm:
W (z)
H (x)
G (y)

Given the picture, it is easily determined that W is taller than H who is taller than G, so z is greater than x is greater than y, or z > x > y.

25. **(D)** First, we can show that the area of the square and the area of the equilateral triangle are determinable from their respective perimeters. The square is more easily handled. Since the perimeter of the square is 4 times the length of one side, given the perimeter of the square it is possible to determine the side of the square. Then, once the side of the square is known, the area can be computed as side times side. The equilateral triangle is a bit trickier:

$$P = 3x \qquad A = \tfrac{1}{2}\left(\frac{\sqrt{3}\,x}{2}\right)\left(\frac{x}{2}\right)$$

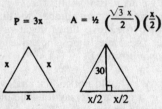

Given the perimeter, it is possible to determine the length of each leg of the triangle (leg = P/3, since each leg is equal). Now, since we know that an equilateral triangle has angles of 60°, and that a

perpendicular in this triangle drawn to the opposite base bisects the angle, we can set up a 90° − 30°—60° triangle. It will be possible to compute the length of each leg of such a triangle, given the length of the hypotenuse. Therefore, we can determine the altitude, and we know the base; so, given the perimeter, we can compute the area. Then, the easiest way to demonstrate that it is not possible to compute the area of a trapezoid or of a parallelogram on the basis of perimeter alone is to draw some pictures:

PARALLELOGRAM:

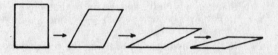

TRAPEZOID:

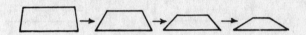

To prove this algebraically would require too much detailed work, but the student should be able to see intuitively that the area of the figures from left to right decreases, and that when the angles eventually become sharp enough, the area will be nearly zero.

26. **(D)** In simple English, the 90¢ the child must replace to bring the amount back up to its original amount is 10% of the original amount. Expressed in notation, that is:

$$90¢ = .10 \text{ of } x$$
$$\$9.00 = x$$

27. **(C)** Let us begin by assigning letters to the height and radius of each cylinder. Since most people find it easier to deal with whole numbers instead of fractions, let us say that cylinder Q has a radius of 2r, so that cylinder P can have a radius of r. Then, we assign cylinder Q a height of h so that P can have a height of 2h. Now, the formula for the volume of a cylinder is $\pi r^2 \times h$. So P and Q have volumes:

Volume $P = \pi(r)^2 \times 2h$ Volume $Q = (2\pi r)^2 \times h$
P = $2\pi r^2 h$ Q = $4\pi r^2 h$

Thus, the ratio of P:Q is $\dfrac{2\pi r^2 h}{4\pi r^2 h} = 2/4 = 1/2$.

28. **(A)** We begin by extending the lines to give this picture:

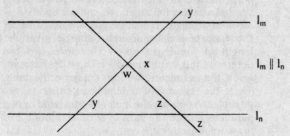

Then we add another angle y (lines l_m and l_n are parallel, so alternate interior angles are equal) and another z (opposite angles are equal). We know that $x + w = 180°$, and we know that $y + z + w = 180°$. So, $x + w = y + z + w$, and $x = y + z$.

29. **(C)** Let us begin by drawing the rectangle:

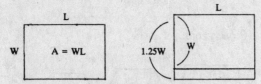

$$A = 1.25W \times L = 1.25WL$$

The original area is WL. The width of the new rectangle is $W + .25\,W$ or $1.25\,W$. So the new area is 1.25WL. It then follows that the new area is $\dfrac{1.25WL}{WL}$, or 125% of the old area.

30. **(B)** Let us take any odd integer, m. The next consecutive odd integer will be two more than m, or $m + 2$. The third integer in the series will be $m + 4$, and the fourth integer in the series will be $m + 6$. The sum of the four is: $(m) + (m + 2) + (m + 4) + (m + 6) = 4m + 12$. And when $(4m + 12)$ is divided by 4, the result is: $\dfrac{4m + 12}{4} = m + 3$. So the sum of the four consecutive odd integers is always evenly divisible by 4.

SECTION IV

1. **(D)** Although this is a right triangle, and though the hypotenuse has length $\sqrt{2}$, the triangle need not be a 45°–45°–90° triangle. The easiest way to show this is with a drawing:

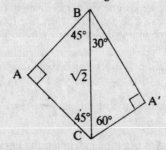

2. **(C)** Since it makes no difference in which order the elements are multiplied, Column A is equivalent to Column B.

3. **(B)** It is important to remember that the square root of a number between 0 and 1, whether expressed as a decimal or as a fraction, is *larger* than the number itself. For example, $\sqrt{\frac{1}{4}} = \frac{1}{2}$ but $\frac{1}{2} > \frac{1}{4}$. So, too, here $\sqrt{0.9}$ is actually greater than 0.9. Another method for solving the problem is to square both sides of the comparison. If the two quantities were originally equal, then squaring both sides will not upset the balance. Further, if either of the two quantities is greater than the other, squaring both sides will not interfere with the *direction* of the inequality. (It will interfere with the *magnitude* of the inequality, but the quantitative comparison question is a "yes or no" exercise: which is larger, *not* how much larger.) Squaring both sides:

$$(0.3)^2 \qquad (\sqrt{0.9})^2$$
$$.09 \qquad 0.9$$

Clearly, Column B is larger.

4. **(C)** Performing the multiplication in each column is the simplest approach to the question:

$$(x + y)^2 \qquad x(x + y) + y(x + y)$$
$$(x + y)(x + y) \qquad x^2 + xy + xy + y^2$$
$$x^2 + xy + xy + y^2 \qquad x^2 + 2xy + y^2$$
$$x^2 + 2xy + y^2$$

5. **(A)** One property of positive fractions is that, given the same denominator, the larger numerator makes the larger fraction and, conversely, given the same numerator, the larger denominator makes the *smaller* fraction. In this question, the numerators are equal. The fraction in Column B has the larger denominator, so it is actually smaller than the fraction in Column A.

6. **(B)** A quick glance at the two expressions shows that Column A must be negative and Column B positive. Whatever the absolute value of the number 3^6, in Column A it will be negative since it is prefixed with the minus sign. Column B, however, will be positive. The minus sign is enclosed within the parentheses. This indicates that we are raising *minus* three to the sixth power. Since six is an even number, the final result will be positive (negative times negative times negative times negative times negative times negative yields a positive).

7. **(C)** We should notice first that we are definitely not in a position to say that the magnitude of the unlabeled angles is 90°. But we need not make the assumption! We know that $w = y$ and $x = z$ because vertical angles are equal. Therefore, $w + x = y + z$. We can drop these expressions from both sides of our comparison. In effect, we are

subtracting equals from both sides of the comparison, a maneuver which, as we have already seen, will neither upset the balance of the original equality nor interfere with the direction of the inequality. This leaves us with 90 on both sides of the comparison, so we conclude that the original comparison must have been an equality.

8. **(C)** At first glance, the problem appears to be a difficult one. A closer look, however, shows that it is actually quite simple. Both paths cover the same vertical distance of 10 units and the same horizontal distance of 14 units. Since it makes no difference whether one moves vertically or horizontally first, the two paths are equal. Notice further that each path covers a distance of 24 units. That is equal to the sum of one width and one length of a rectangle with dimension 10 and 14 which could be constructed using P and T as vertices.

9. **(B)** Let us begin by inscribing an equilateral triangle in a circle:

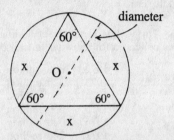

Since the longest chord of any circle is the chord drawn through the center of the circle (that is, the diameter of the circle), and since no side of the triangle can pass through the center, the side of the equilateral triangle must be shorter than the diameter of the circle in which it is inscribed. Having determined that, we then proceed to ask whether the length of the side of a square inscribed in the same circle is longer or shorter than that of the side of the equilateral triangle.

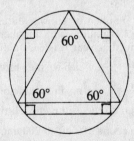

The side of the square is shorter, and we can see that the greater the number of sides, the shorter will be the length of those sides. From this we can conclude that for all equilateral polygons inscribed in circles, the side of the polygon will be shorter than the diameter of the circle.

10. **(D)** Using P, V, and G to represent Peter's, Victor's and Georgette's grades, respectively, the centered information tells us: $P > V$ and $G > V$. But we have no information regarding the relationship between P and G.

11. **(B)** The parabola drawn on the graph actually adds no information needed for solving the problem. Regardless of what figure is drawn through point (a,b), and there are of course an infinite number of different ones, point (a,b) is in the second quadrant—that is, the upper left-hand section of the coordinate system. In that quadrant all x-values are negative and all y-values are positive, so a must be negative and b must be positive. Therefore, b is greater than a.

12. **(D)** We simplify the comparison as much as possible. First we subtract 3 from both sides and then we subtract 2x from both sides. This reduces Column A to $x + 2$ and Column B to 0. We can now ask the simpler question: which is greater, $x + 2$ or 0? This is simpler because we can immediately see that the answer will depend on the value of x, information we lack.

13. **(B)** First, let us perform the indicated operations. In Column A we find a power raised to a power, and that calls for the multiplication of the two exponents: $(x^3)^5 = x^{3 \cdot 5} = x^{15}$. In Column B we find multiplication of like bases, so we add the exponents: $x^3 \cdot x^5 = x^{3+5} = x^8$. The centered information states that x is negative. Since a negative number raised to a power which is odd yields a negative number (negative times negative times negative . . . yields a negative number), Column A is negative. Column B, however, must be positive since it is raised to an even power. Consequently, whatever x might be, Column A is negative, Column B is positive; therefore, Column B must be greater than Column A.

14. **(A)** The problem can be worked out using simultaneous equations, but that is not the most efficient way of solving it. For that reason we will set up the equations (for the "afficionados"), but we will not actually solve for x and y. Let x be the number of shirts costing $13 and y the number costing $10:

$$x + y = 16$$
$$13x + 10y = 187$$

Final solution: $x = 9$ and $y = 7$.

We have omitted the detailed calculations because there is a simpler method. Let us assume, for the sake of argument, that the two columns are equal—that is, that the man bought equal numbers of both types of shirts. If we are correct in assuming that he bought eight $13 shirts and eight $10 shirts, then $(8 \times 13) + (8 \times 10)$ ought to equal $187. When we do the multiplication, we get the result $184. That tells us our original assumption of equal numbers was incorrect and, further, that the answer to the question is not (C). We should then make a second assumption, but should we assume that he bought more expensive shirts than we first guessed, or fewer? A moment of reflection will show that we should adjust our initial assumption to include a greater number of expensive shirts, for only by increasing that number will we add to the $184 which was the result of our original assumption. So we would next assume—again for the purposes of argument—that the man bought nine $13 shirts and only seven $10 shirts. But at this point we have already solved the problem! We do not need to know the precise ratio, e.g., whether 9:7, 10:6, 11:5, 12:4, 13:3, 14:2, or 15:1; we have already determined that the ratio is one of those listed, and so it must be the case that Column A is larger.

15. **(B)** This problem, too, can be solved with a little gimmick. It is not necessary to actually calculate the volumes in question. You need only recognize that the sphere will have a diameter of 10 and that this is equal to the side of the cube. This means that the sphere can be placed within the cube, so the cube must have a greater volume.

16. **(A)** We begin by multiplying $(x - y)^2$:

$$(x - y)(x - y) = x^2 - 2xy + y^2 = 12$$

Then we substitute 1 for xy:

$$x^2 - 2(1) + y^2 = 12$$
$$x^2 + y^2 = 14$$

17. **(C)** Let us begin by adding the following notation:

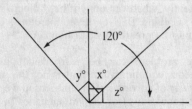

Since the entire angle is 120°, y + 90 = 120, so y = 30. Similarly, z + 90 = 120, so z = 30. Since x + y + z = 120, x + 30 + 30 = 120, so x = 60.

18. **(A)** Certainly the easiest and most direct way to solve this problem is to test each of the integers. There is no reason to try and find some fancy mathematical equation to describe the problem when a simple substitution of answer choices will do. When 95 is divided by 6, 10, and 15—answers (A), (C), and (D)—the remainder in each case is 5. And when 135 is divided by 10, the remainder is 5, not 3; and when 135 is divided by 15 there is a remainder of 0. When 135 is divided by 6, the

remainder is 3. So only 6 fits both the conditions for n.

19. **(D)** Since the ratio of insects with X to those without X is 5:3, we know that $\frac{5}{8}$ of the population has X. (There are 8 equal units—5 + 3—5 of which are insects with X.) Then, of those $\frac{5}{8}$, $\frac{3}{8}$ are male. So we take $\frac{3}{8}$ of the $\frac{5}{8}$ ($\frac{3}{8} \times \frac{5}{8}$), and that tells us that $\frac{15}{64}$ of the total population are male insects with X.

20. **(B)** We can order the elements by clarifying the exponents:

(A) $\frac{3^8}{3^6} = 3^{8-6} = 3^2 = 9$
(B) $3^3 - 1 = 27 - 1 = 26$
(C) $3^0 = 1$
(D) 3^{27} is too large to compute here, but is obviously the greatest quantity in the group.
(E) $3(3^2) = 3^3 = 27$

The order is (C), (A), (B), (E), (D); so (B) is the middle term.

21. **(A)** This is just a matter of adding up the total fares collected for subways in the six years:

1972:	300 million
1973:	325 million
1974:	350 million
1975:	350 million
1976:	320 million
1977:	260 million
	1905

22. **(C)** The number of fares collected in 1975 was 350 million, and the number of fares collected in 1977 was 260 million. The number of fares dropped by 90 million, but we are looking for the rate, or percentage, of decrease. So we set our fraction up, difference over starting amount, $\frac{90}{350}$, which is approximately 25%.

23. **(E)** The number of subway fares collected in 1974 was 350 million; the number of bus fares collected in that year was 315 million. Our ratio then is $\frac{50 \times 350}{30 \times 315}$, which we then reduce by a factor of 10, $\frac{5 \times 350}{3 \times 315}$, and again by a factor of 5, $\frac{5 \times 70}{3 \times 63}$; then we can do the arithmetic a little more easily: $\frac{350}{189}$. If we round 189 off to 200 and reduce again by a factor of 10, we get $\frac{35}{20}$, or $\frac{7}{4}$ as a good approximation of the ratio. Actually, we need not do all of this arithmetic. We can see at a glance that more subway fares were collected than bus fares; so, given that the subway fares are more

expensive, we can conclude that the revenues derived from subway fares were greater than those for bus fares, and that means our ratio must be greater than 1. Only (E) is possible.

24. **(C)** In 1977, the total number of fares collected was 260 (subways) + 425 (commuter rail) + 255 (bus) = 940 total. Of the 940 million fares collected, 425 were commuter rail fares, so the commuter rail fares accounted for about $\frac{1}{2}$, or 50%, of all the fares collected in that year.

25. **(E)** 425 million commuter rail fares were collected in 1977, and 230 million were collected in 1972. The difference is 195 million.

26. **(A)** Proposition I is necessarily true. Since lines l_m and l_n are perpendicular to one another, a line that intersects l_m on the perpendicular must be parallel to line l_n.

   Proposition II is not necessarily true. Line segment MN may fail to intersect l_m simply because it is too short—that is, if extended, for all we know MN will intersect l_n.

   Proposition III is not necessarily true. Line l_o may intersect l_m at point P without plane y's being perpendicular to plane x.

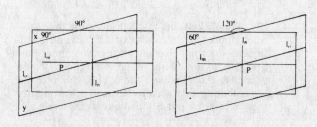

27. **(D)** The proper way to "visualize" this problem is to imagine that the gravel-covered walk will be a very squat-shaped cylinder with a donut hole removed (the circular region inside the walk). Expressed more abstractly, we need to compute the volume of a cylinder with a radius of 50 feet ($\frac{1}{2}$ of 100 = 50) and a height of 6 inches, or $\frac{1}{2}$ foot. Then we compute the volume of a cylinder with a radius of 40 feet ($\frac{1}{2}$ of 80 = 40) and a height of 6 inches, or $\frac{1}{2}$ foot. Then we subtract the second from the first and what is left is the volume we seek. Now, since both cylinders have the same height, it will be easier to compute the areas of the bases first and subtract before multiplying by $\frac{1}{2}$ foot.

   Area of larger circle: Area = $\pi r^2 = \pi(50)^2 = 2500\pi$.
   Area of smaller circle: Area = $\pi r^2 = \pi(40)^2 = 1600\pi$.

By subtracting 1600π from 2500π, we determine that the area of the garden path is 900π square

feet. To determine the volume of gravel we need, we then multiply that figure by $\frac{1}{2}$ foot (the depth of the gravel), and arrive at our answer 450π cu. ft.

28. **(D)** Let d stand for the hourly rate under the new system. Since the employee is to make the same amount per week under both systems, it must be the case that:

$$\frac{\$x}{\text{hr.}} \text{ times 40 hrs.} = \frac{\$d}{\text{hr.}} \text{ times 36 hrs.}$$

Now we must solve for d:

$$40x = 36d, \quad d = \frac{10x}{9}.$$

   The problem can also be solved in an intuitive way. Since the employee is working less time yet making the same weekly total, he must be earning slightly more per hour under the new system than under the old. Answer (A) is just the naked fraction $\frac{1}{10}$, without making reference to monetary units. Answer (B) implies that the employee is making $\frac{9}{10}$ as much per hour under the new system as under the old—that would be a decrease in the hourly rate. Similarly, (C) says that the employee is making only 90% of his old hourly rate and that, too, is a decrease. Finally, (E) says that the employee is making 9 *times* the hourly rate he made under the old system, a figure which is obviously out of line. The only reasonable choice is (D). The moral is: Even if you cannot set up the math in a technically correct way, use a little common sense.

29. **(B)** Since the columns are perpendicular to both ceiling and floor, we know that they are parallel. The left-hand column must be 12 feet long: If the two 8-foot pieces were laid end to end, they would total 16 feet, but there is a 4-foot overlap, so the length of the column is 16 feet minus 4 feet, or 12 feet. The right-hand column must also be 12 feet long. But the two 10-foot pieces, if laid end to end, would form a column 20 feet long. Therefore, the overlap, x, must be 8 feet (20 − x = 12).

30. **(A)** This problem must be solved in two stages. First, we need to calculate the total area of the wall. The information given in the problem states that $\frac{1}{3}$ of the job plus another 75 square feet equals $\frac{3}{4}$ of the job. In algebraic notation, this is:

$$\frac{1}{3}x + 75 = \frac{3}{4}x$$
$$75 = \frac{3}{4}x - \frac{1}{3}x$$
$$75 = \frac{5}{12}x$$
$$x = 180$$

So the entire wall is 180 square feet—that is, W × L = 180. We know that the height of the wall is 10 feet; so 10 × L = 180, and L = 18.

SECTION V

Questions 1–4

Arranging the Information

This set of questions presents two separate ideas for ordering the information. Previewing the question stems, especially numbers 1 and 2, indicates that at least a fair degree of certainty should be obtainable. Since the ideas of time of departure and relative amount drunk are separate, two diagrams must be constructed, one at a time. Starting with drinking:

←DRANK MORE——DRANK LESS→

P drank more than W				P	W
T drank more than P			T	P	W
T drank less than V		V	T	P	W
U drank less than Q can't do now					
U drank more than V	U	V	T	P	W
U drank less than Q OK now	Q	U	V	T	P	W
W drank more than R	Q	U	V	T	P	W	R

Now for departure times:

←LATER——EARLIER→

P later than V				P	V
T later than P			T	P	V
T earlier than S		S	T	P	V
U later than S	U	S	T	P	V
W earlier than V	U	S	T	P	V	W

Answering the Questions

With such complete diagrams, answering the questions is primarily a matter of reading the diagrams carefully. In this set of questions, there is no uncertainty at all.

1. **(E)** W left earlier than anyone else, so (E) must be the answer. Sometimes you may have a question where the very earliest (latest, greenest, whatever-est) is not listed as a possible answer choice and you have to check out the other answers more closely. It is usually a good idea to look for the most—earliest in this case—and see if that is an answer choice, because if it is available to be chosen, it must be the right answer.

2. **(B)** R drank less than anybody else, so (B) must be the answer. The same approach described for 1 would work here.

3. **(C)** The diagrams show that T was the third-to-last to leave and drank more than P, W, and R; hence, answer choice (C) is correct. Note that whenever you have such referential terms as most or third, they are to be interpreted within the context of the information given. Most, therefore, means "most—out of those about whom information was given or who were mentioned anyway."

   (A) fails because although the first part of it is true, U and Q both drank more than V. (B) is also partly true, but the answer we are looking for, and find in (C), must be completely true. U was "outdrunk" by Q. (D) also has the first part true and the last part false—or at least not known to be true. S's drinking was not characterized in any way in the information given. (E) fails because (C) succeeds.

4. **(E)** Simply knowing that S drank more than W—who drank the second-least of anyone mentioned—does not give any information about how S relates to any of the other partygoers. If you wanted to choose answer choice (D), you were not remembering that merely because S was greater than W did not put S into the first available slot above W.

5. **(C)** You should remember that there is a very important distinction to be drawn between numbers and percentages. For example, an increase from one murder per year to two murders per year can be described as a "whopping big 100% increase." The argument speaks only of percentages, so we would not want to conclude anything about the numbers underlying those percentages. Therefore, both (A) and (B) are incorrect. They speak of "more agents," and "more people," and those are numbers rather than percentages. Furthermore, if we would not want to draw a conclusion about numbers from data given in percentage terms, we surely would not want to base a conclusion about efficiency or work accomplished on percentages. Thus, (D) and (E) are incorrect. What makes (C) the best answer of the five is the possibility of making percentage comparisons *within* each agency. Within both agencies, the number of field agents increased by a greater *percentage* than the number of non-field agents.

6. **(D)** Keeping in mind our comments about (D) and (E) in the preceding question, (A) must be

wrong. We do not want to conclude from sheer number of employees anything about the actual work accomplished. (B) and (E) are incorrect for pretty much the same reason. The question stem asks us to give an argument defending the CIA against the claim that it is overstaffed. Neither rate of pay nor appropriations has anything to do with whether or not there are too many people on the payroll. (C) is the second-best answer, but it fails because it does not keep in mind the ratio of non-field to field agents. Our concern is not with the number of agents generally, but the number of support and supervisory workers (reread the question stem). (D) focuses on this nicely by explaining why the CIA should exprience a faster increase (which is to say, a greater percentage increase) in the number.

7. **(D)** Let us use letters to represent the categories. "All effective administrators" will be A. "Concerned about welfare" will be W. "Are liberal" will be L. The three propositions can now be represented as:

1. All A are W.
2. All W are L.
3. All non-L are not A.

Proposition 3 is equivalent to "all A are not non-L," and that is in turn equivalent to "all A are L." Thus, (D) follows fairly directly as a matter of logic. (A) is incorrect, for while we know that "all A are L," we would not want to conclude that "no L are A"—there might be some ineffective administrators who grant time off. They could be ineffective for other reasons. (B) is incorrect for the same reason. Even though all effective administrators are concerned about their employees' welfare, this does not mean that an ineffective administrator could not be concerned. He might be concerned, but ineffective for another reason. (C) is clearly false, given our propositions; we know that all effective administrators are liberal. Finally, (E) is not inferable. Just because all effective administrators grant time off does not mean that all the time off granted is granted by effective administrators.

Questions 8–12

Arranging the Information

In arranging this sort of information, where there are subgroups and the major conditions appear to be the cross connections between their members—as here with the two types of courses—the information may be arranged with an algebraic notation which here would give rise to the equations C NOT = E, B NOT = F, and E NOT = M, with the added notation that there must be two of B, C, or P chosen. To this must be added new deductions as they are made for each problem.

Another way of diagramming this information—which works well for situations of this particular sort, though it is not as general as the algebraic approach—is to list the two groups and connect different items with an annotated line indicating what sort of connection is being made: must go with, cannot go with, etc. Here this would look like this:

SCIENCES   OTHER COURSES

(must = 2)

            NOT WITH   NOT WITH
CHEMISTRY←————→ENGLISH←————————→MUSIC

            NOT WITH
BIOLOGY ←————————→FRENCH

PHYSICS   WRITING

Arrows are helpful in case the relationship is just a one-way situation, though that is not too common.

A further deduction would be that English and French cannot go together since either one of them forbids one of the sciences, and if they were both scheduled there would only be one science—which is not permitted.

Answering the Questions

8. **(B)** A step-by-step approach is the key. If Lois takes English, then chemistry and music are out. If chemistry is out, then physics and biology are the two sciences she must take. If biology is scheduled, then French is out. This leaves choice (B). The other answers all include some subject not possible. (A) is not wrong because it has three sciences. That is possible. (A) is wrong because chemistry can't be scheduled with English.

9. **(C)** If chemistry is out, then once again biology and physics are required. Biology precludes French and music displaces English, leaving answer choice (C).

    In any case, choices (A) and (E) are impossible because they have both English and music. Choice (B) is out because French cannot be with biology. Choice (D) also cannot be scheduled since it has both music and English which cannot be combined, as previously explained.

10. **(E)** I and III work by the same logic. In each case the taking of one of the non-science courses eliminates one of the science courses from consideration, thus requiring the other two science courses. II is trying to trap you into saying that since neither music nor chemistry can combine with English, they must combine with each other. This is not true. It is possible to have a curriculum of music, physics, biology, and writing.

11. **(E)** I here is trying the same trick as II in problem 10; it does not always have to be true. II must be true since French eliminates biology, and requires the other two sciences. III need not be true since a curriculum of chemistry, biology, writing, and music is but one counter-example.

12. **(E)** With Lois taking physics, now scheduled at the same time as English, she cannot take English, chemistry, or music because they overlap with the new physics time. Only French or biology may be taken, plus writing. This means that only three courses can be taken, (E), though two science courses can still be taken—eliminating (A). (B), (C), and (D) are eliminated by the schedule just discussed.

Questions 13–17

Arranging the Information

Previewing the questions indicates that the total points and the breakdown of points are the key issues. Nine points are awarded for each race (5 + 3 + 1), times three races yields 27 points at issue. Since the teams are tied now, 14 points in the last three races will win the meet. Since there are two entries from each team in each race, the most that a team could win in a single race is 8 points (5 + 3). For keeping track of the results for each alternative raised by the problems a simple chart will be enough:

	Ind Med	Med Relay	Free Relay
FIRST (5)			
SECOND (3)			
THIRD (1)			
TOTAL (9)			

Answering the Questions

13. **(A)** This was answered in the preceding discussion.

14. **(D)** You don't need to keep track of both teams' points once you know that 14 is the magic number. If State won first and third in the individual medley, then Malibu won second and three points. Therefore, Malibu needs eleven more points to win the meet. (D) provides exactly eleven (5 + 5 + 1). (A) yields only 10 (5 + 5). (B) only 9 (5 + 3 + 1), (C) only 8 (3 + 1 + 3 + 1). The incorrectness of (E) is proved by the validity of (D).

15. **(B)** The individual medley is set up with the idea that State's top swimmer is sure to win, with only second and third being at issue. If George swims, Malibu will get four points (3 + 1), but if George doesn't, then State's second swimmer will get the point for third place and Malibu will get only three points for second place. Thus, the loss to Malibu if George does not swim in the individual medley is one point.

There are two ways of computing the point value of the various coaching moves being contemplated. Both are correct and either one will work, but you have to use one or the other consistently. In this discussion, we are counting only the effect of the coaching move on Malibu's score. One could have said that taking George out of the individual medley will take away one point from Malibu AND give one to State, thus causing a difference of two points.

In order for it to be advantageous for Malibu for George to swim in another race, the net increase in the other race will have to be at least two points. If it is only one point, there is no advantage.

(A) will add only one point for third (1–0)—no advantage.

(B) will add two points (3–1), so it is an advantage.

(C) will add one point (5 −(3 + 1)), no advantage.

(D) will add nothing; Malibu scores ten points either way.

(E) is, of course, not true, given (B), but would not be an advantage anyway.

16. **(A)** This is a two-step problem. First, you must calculate how many points are needed; second, how many swimmers are needed to win those points. Fourteen is the magic number and Malibu has scored four in the individual medley, leaving ten. Two firsts will do the trick.

17. **(A)** The situation posited is that Malibu wins first and second in the individual medley, since State's other swimmer cannot beat four minutes even. This means that the score is 8 to 1 in favor of Malibu.

(A) is false because this would only earn State 10 more points for a total of 11 when 14 was needed.

(B) is true since that would add 8 more points to the Malibu total, making 16—enough for victory.

(C) is true because those three swimmers might be two thirds and a second, totalling only 5 points (3 + 1 + 1), which, when added to the 8 won in the individual medley, is only 13—not enough to guarantee victory.

(D) is possible since the minimum that four scoring teams could win is 8 points for second and third in each race. Eight plus the one point earned in the individual medley totals only nine.

(E) is possible since the three might be two firsts and a second, which would be 13 points to add to the one from the individual medley—yielding the magic total of 14.

Questions 18–22

Arranging the Information

There are three kinds of information—house order on the block, family name, and type of dog—and there are five items of each sort. Thus, we will have a grid that is 5 by 3.

HOUSE ORDER	1	2	3	4	5
DOG*					
FAMILY					

*Note that two of the dogs begin with the letter "s," so more than initials must be used.

Since the preview of the questions reveals no questions about subsets of the information set nor any questions about contradictions or redundancies, we can safely start with any statement and pick the third-from-last, which gives order of house information.

Setting up the preceding diagram is the most efficient way to approach the problem. Note that much of the other information does concern house order even though it does not directly number houses.

If the Lanes live two houses from both the other families, then the Lanes must live in the middle and the others at the ends. We will put the others in as 1 and 5, but remember that they might flip-flop.

HOUSE ORDER	1	2	3	4	5
DOG					
FAMILY	KINGS		LANES		JONESES

Now we can link in the next-to-last statement and the first statement's items.

HOUSE ORDER	1	2	3	4	5
DOG	NOT SETTER NOT SHEEP NOT COLLIE	SHEEP? COLLIE?	NOT SHEEP NOT COLLIE	SHEEP? COLLIE?	NOT SHEEP NOT COLLIE
FAMILY	KINGS		LANES		JONESES

Entering the second item, we find that the Kings can't have the sheepdog (since it is next to the Joneses) or any dog other than the poodle, and thus must have the poodle. Since the sheepdog lives next to the Joneses, it must be in position 4 (always remembering that the order could be left-to-right or right-to-left). This in turn means that the only slot available for the collie is at house 2.

HOUSE ORDER	1	2	3	4	5
DOG	POODLE	COLLIE	NOT SHEEP NOT COLLIE NOT POODLE	SHEEP	NOT SHEEP NOT COLLIE NOT POODLE HEAVIEST DOG
FAMILY	KINGS		LANES		JONESES

The next statement, that the retriever weighs more than the setter or poodle, means that the Joneses don't have either of the lighter dogs, which makes four dogs eliminated for them, and they must have the retriever. If the Joneses have the retriever then the only dog left for the Lanes is the setter.

HOUSE ORDER	1	2	3	4	5
DOG	POODLE	COLLIE	SETTER	SHEEPDOG	RETRIEVER
FAMILY	KINGS		LANES		JONESES

The last statement now fills in the last two families as being:

HOUSE ORDER	1	2	3	4	5
DOG	POODLE	COLLIE	SETTER	SHEEPDOG	RETRIEVER HEAVIEST DOG
FAMILY	KINGS	NEFFS	LANES	MURRAYS	JONESES

Answering the Questions

Almost all of these questions are largely a matter of reading from the diagram.

18. **(C)** The second statement also shows the falseness of (C) by itself.

19. **(E)** This can only be gotten quickly from the diagram.

20. **(E)** Although the heaviest dog is known (retriever), the rank-order of the other dogs by weight is not known, thus the answer to this question is not determinable.

21. **(A)** The Neffs now live with the collie and the Joneses with the retriever, in houses 2 and 5 respectively. When swapped, the Joneses in house 2 are next to the Kings and the poodle. Note that since we are looking for something which now becomes true, it must be something to do with the Joneses or the Neffs. Thus, (D) and (E) are improbable.

22. **(B)** The sheepdog will now be in house 3 with the Lanes and the setter; thus, (B) is correct and (A) false. (B) is the most general statement available, and thus deserving of a thorough review early in your work on the problem.

23. **(C)** Clark was unhappy if he had a clear conscience but knew, or Clark was happy if he knew but had an unclear conscience. It is not the case that Clark was unhappy, so he must have been happy. Since he knew, however, his happiness must stem from an unclear conscience. (A), (D), and (E) are incorrect because they make irrelevant value judgments. As was just shown, the author's point can be analyzed as a purely logical one. (B) is just distraction, playing on the connection between "governess" and "servant," which, of course, are not the same thing.

24. **(B)** The key here is that the word nobody is used in a cleverly ambiguous way—and, as many of you probably know, the "young lady" in the story is Lewis Carroll's Alice. This is fairly representative of his word play. (E) must be incorrect since it misses completely the little play on words: "I saw Nobody," encouraging a response such as "Oh, is he a handsome man?" (D) is beside the point, for the King is not interested in the messenger's veracity. He may be interested in his reliability (A); but, if anything, we should conclude the King finds the messenger unreliable since "nobody walks slower" than the messenger. (C) is wrong because the question is not a matter of eyesight. The King does not say, "If you had better eyes, you might have seen Nobody."

25. **(E)** The advertisement employs the term more in an ambiguous manner. In the context, one might expect the phrase more flavor to mean more highly concentrated flavor, that is, more flavor per unit weight. What the ad actually says, however, is that the sticks of Evergreen are *larger*, so if they are larger, there must be more *total* flavor. All three propositions, if they are true (as we are asked to assume they are), are good attacks on the ad. First, I, it is possible to beat the ad at its own game. If flavor is just a matter of chewing enough sticks, then Spring Mint is as good a deal because, flavor unit for flavor unit, it is no more expensive than Evergreen. Second, II would also undermine the ad by focusing on the ambiguity we have just discussed. Finally, III also uncovers another potential ambiguity. If the ad is comparing volume rather than weight, Spring Mint may be a better value. After all, who wants to buy a lot of air?

SECTION VI

Questions 1–5

Arranging the Information

The eight numbers are arranged, like all numbers, along a single line. The original information tells us that they are consecutive, so the diagram will be of eight slots, each right next to the other. Enter the information one item at a time.

This is the diagram:

$$\leftarrow \text{GREATER}\text{——}\text{SMALLER}\rightarrow$$

$$\underline{\quad}\ \underline{\quad}\ \underline{\quad}\ \underline{\quad}\ \underline{\quad}\ \underline{\quad}\ \underline{\quad}\ \underline{\quad}$$

W is four more than Z and three less than X—this defines the end points and W.

$$\leftarrow \text{GREATER}\text{——}\text{SMALLER}\rightarrow$$

$$\underline{X}\ \underline{\quad}\ \underline{\quad}\ \underline{W}\ \underline{\quad}\ \underline{\quad}\ \underline{\quad}\ \underline{Z}$$

S greater than T—cannot do now.

S less than X—redundant since X is largest, but these establish the relationship: $X > S > T$.

U is the average of V and X—this means that U is greater than V because the average is between two numbers and X is the largest number in the group. Furthermore, for every step that U is below X, V is the same number of steps below U. This establishes some possibilities:

$$\leftarrow \text{GREATER}\text{——}\text{SMALLER}\rightarrow$$

possibility #1 $\underline{X}\ \underline{U?}\ \underline{V?}\ \underline{W}\ \underline{\quad}\ \underline{\quad}\ \underline{\quad}\ \underline{Z}$

possibility #2 $\underline{X}\ \underline{\quad}\ \underline{U?}\ \underline{W}\ \underline{V?}\ \underline{\quad}\ \underline{\quad}\ \underline{Z}$

These are the only possibilities because U cannot take W's place, and if U is below W, then V will be below Z, which is not possible within the context of eight consecutive numbers. The final diagram shows the two possibilities and the notation that S is greater than T. Nothing is known about Y at all.

Answering the Questions

1. **(C)** Z is the lowest number in the series and W is four greater, and thus equal to $8 + 4 = 12$.

2. **(C)** I: As previously discussed, W cannot be the greatest number because it is less than X. As for II, Z cannot be the greatest number because it is less than W. Thus, I and II are true.

    III is false because X, being 7 greater than Z in a series of eight consecutive numbers, must be the greatest number.

3. **(A)** The question asks for a possible arrangement, so elimination of impossibilities is the proper approach. X is the greatest number, not Z, which eliminates answer choice (C). Z is the lowest number, which eliminates answer choices (C) (again) and (D). W is three less than X, and thus must be the fourth number from the left, which again eliminates answer choice (D) as well as (E). U, being the average of X and V, must lie exactly between them, which it does not in

answers (B), (C), (D), and (E). All of these considerations lead to the conclusion that only (A) is possible.

4. **(B)** Under the original conditions, U could not have been immediately above Z since there had to be room for V below U. With the removal of that requirement, (B) is now possible. (A) was a possibility anyway, so it is not the newly created possibility for which the problem asks. (C) is not possible because the eight numbers are consecutive numbers, and thus not equal to each other. (E) is wrong for the same reason. (D) violates the limitation that the numbers be a string of eight consecutive numbers. By placing U below Z, the difference between the highest and lowest numbers in the string becomes too great.

5. **(E)** If Y is three greater than Z, it goes just below W. This eliminates possibility 2, shown previously, and gives the following diagram. Once U and V and Y are tied down, so are S and T.

←GREATER——SMALLER→

X U V W Y S T Z

Inspection of the diagram indicates that none of the four statements is true, hence, answer choice (E) is correct.

6. **(B)** I would undermine the advertisement considerably. Since the point of the ad is that you will lose weight, any unforeseen effects which would make it impossible to lose weight would defeat the purposes of the program. II is less obvious, but it does weaken the ad somewhat. Although the ad does not specifically say you will be healthier for having enrolled in the program, surely the advantages of the program are less significant if you have to pay an additional, hidden cost, i.e., health. III, if anything, supports the advertisement. IV is irrelevant since the ad does not claim you will become too thin.

7. **(B)** This question is like one of those simple conversation questions: "X: All bats are mammals. Y: Not true, whales are mammals too." In this little exchange, B misunderstands A to have said that "All mammals are bats." In 7, the objection must be based on a misunderstanding. The objector must think that the ad has claimed that the only cause of unhappiness, etc., is being overweight, otherwise he would not have offered his counter-example. (A) is wrong because the ad never takes a stand on the *causes* of overweight conditions—only on a possible cure. This reasoning invalidates (C) and (D) as well. (E) makes a similar error, but about effects not about causes. The ad does not say everyone who is unhappy is unattractive, or vice versa.

8. **(D)** The easiest way to set this problem up is to draw a relational line:

PE   IP   EL   BE

Dislikes————————→Likes

We note that Clara likes Basic Economics better than anything else, which means she must like it better than Advanced Calculus. So even though Advanced Calculus does not appear on our line, since we know that Basic Economics is the maximum, Clara must like Advanced Calculus less than Basic Economics. So (C) can be inferred. But we do not know where World History ranks on the preference line, and since Introductory Physics is not a maximal or a minimal value, we can make no judgment regarding it and an unplaced course. Quick reference to the line will show that (A), (B), and (E) are inferrable.

Questions 9–12

Arranging the Information

Since three of the four questions are conditional questions introducing different variations or new information, you know that you will not get a definite result from the original set of information. This means that you should quickly sketch out the limitations and requirements in the original information, and spend most of your time in the answering of the questions.

In addition to the basic setup of there being two shelves with three spaces on each, there are only three relationships which are specified.

Thyme and basil are not next to each other.

Thyme and basil are not above or below each other.

Salt and pepper must be next to each other on the same shelf.

Answering the Questions

In answering the sort of question where there are many possibilities, it is often most efficient to focus on the limiting factors since there are fewer of them.

9. **(A)** All that the question asks is whether the three arrangements are unacceptable. Thus, all you have to do for each arrangement is to find one possibility of its being acceptable in order to eliminate the arrangement from consideration.

I. Thyme and basil on same shelf but not next to each other.   T ___ B

    Salt and pepper must be on the other shelf to be together.   T C B

Others fit in without problem. __S__ __P__ __F__
(This is only one possible arrangement.)

Thus, I is possible.

II is shown to be possibly acceptable by the same arrangement as given above for I. If you happened to have made a different arrangement for I, you would need to start with T and C on the same shelf, and see if you could fill it all in without violating any of the restrictions of the problem.

III: For T and S to be on the same shelf requires that one shelf be T, S, P (or any arrangement of the three which has S and P together). For example:

__T__   __S__   __P__

__C__   __F__   __B__

B can be added without being under T.
So III is acceptable also.

Since all of the arrangements are acceptable, the correct answer is (A).

10. **(D)** The wording of the problem means that your job is to find the four answer choices which are not acceptable. The correct answer choice is not necessarily the only way to meet the conditions, but merely a possibility.

One general rule is that salt and pepper have to be next to each other. Therefore, any shelf arrangement which does not have them next to each other is wrong. This eliminates (A), (B), and (E).

The difference between the remaining answer choices—(C) and (D)—is whether the basil is on the left or on the right. If the basil is on the left, it will be immediately below the thyme, which is forbidden. Hence, (D) is the only acceptable arrangement.

11. **(C)** The problem sets up this starting point:

__ __ __ __ __

__S__   __P__   __B__

This means that thyme cannot be in the upper right-hand slot; but there are no restrictions on cumin or fennel. The possibilities are these:

__T__	__C__	__F__	__T__	__F__	__C__
__S__	__P__	__B__	__S__	__P__	__B__
__C__	__T__	__F__	__F__	__T__	__C__
__S__	__P__	__B__	__S__	__P__	__B__

Since thyme is the limiting item, you should start your work with it. First place thyme in the left-hand slot and flip-flop the other two, then put

thyme in the middle slot and flip-flop the other two again = 4 ways.

12. **(A)** This is a problem where a condition is added. Even though new containers are bought, they are similar, and thus still must not be placed next to each other. The new condition is that they must both be in the top shelf. This means that the top shelf must have basil at one end and thyme at the other. Since salt and pepper still must be next to each other and there is only one empty space on the upper shelf, salt and pepper must be on the bottom shelf, though they can slide from side to side and could be placed with pepper on the left or on the right of the salt.

There are two ways of approaching this problem. Either you can focus on elimination of answer choices that are not acceptable by constructing counter-examples, or you can focus on trying to find an acceptable arrangement that meets the new conditions. Since it is a fairly loosely constrained situation, the former is more efficient, especially since it will at least provide the elimination of some answer choices.

If you try the elimination route, it is best to start with the simplest and most definite arrangements, since their unacceptability will likely be easier to demonstrate.

That (B), (C), and (D) are not necessarily true is shown by the acceptable arrangement:

__B__   __F/C__   __T__

__P__   __S__   __F/C__

(E) is shown to be false by interchanging B and T in the diagram. (A), however, must be true. In either position, F must be above or next to one of the pair S or P.

Questions 13–17

Arranging the Information

This is a problem where most of the action occurs in the questions rather than in the arranging of the given information. It is important, however, to get a grasp of what conditions there are.

There are three types of investments: corporate bonds, blue-chip common stocks, and government securities. That is all there is, unless something new is introduced in one of the questions. There is one regulation: one-third each in blue chips and government securities, which means that only the last third is discretionary for Williams. His other idea is that for the next year he would like bonds.

Answering the Questions

13. **(D)** Since Williams thinks that bonds are the best investment, but he can only put one-third of the fund's assets into them because of the regulations, one-third to each type of investment is the best he can do, choice (D).

    (B) and (C) violate the regulation. (A) and (E) violate Williams' sense of what is the best investment at this time.

14. **(C)** Although we noted in the previous problem that the best investment strategy, according to Williams' view of things, is one-third to each type of investment, he COULD invest two-thirds in blue-chip stocks. The regulation only says that there is to be a minimum of the two categories, not a maximum. Two-thirds of $6 billion is $4 billion.

15. **(B)** This is a matter of what his preferences are. He likes bonds, so if the opportunity presents itself, he will buy them. (D) and (E) are entirely outside the scope of the problem set.

16. **(E)** Although the increase in the return of government securities sounds very large, this is not a question that depends on how closely you follow the investment markets. Within the scope of government securities and blue-chip stocks. If he sells off, he must take care to maintain at least one-third of each of the required investments. Selling only government securities and blue-chip ments, which we simply do not know. If the rates were higher, he might well wish to change his investments. Hence, (D) is not adequate. (E) is the only possible answer.

17. **(D)** The key here is that he has invested one-third each in the three types of investments. This means that he has the minimum possible amount of government securities and blue chip stocks. If he sells off, he must take care to maintain at least one-third of each of the required investments. Selling only government securities and blue chip stocks will definitely lead him to an illegal situation, so (D) is not possible.

    The others are all acceptable since he can have more than one-third of the fund invested in a required security if he wants. Let us work (A) in detail as an example: Suppose he starts with 30 units of each type of investment:

    BONDS 30   STOCKS 30   GOV'T. SEC. 30

    If he sells twice as many bonds as stocks, say 20 and 10, he will still be legal since the stocks will still be one-third.

    BONDS 10   STOCKS 20   GOV'T. SEC. 30

Similar arguments apply to (B) and, in a more general way, to (C) and (E).

Questions 18–22

Arranging the Information

In a problem set of this sort, the major purpose of arranging the information in the beginning is to make it clear and easy to use. The points to note are that *both* calls and sales are used to judge Max's performance, so we cannot concentrate on just one of those factors. The statements that are phrased as "probably" should be construed as basically definite, especially in comparison to the even less certain other statements.

CUSTOMER	HOURS NEEDED	SALES IN BOXES
A	1	5
B	3	0 OR 20
C	1	10
D	1 TO 3	10 TO 30

Note that for Bell the sale will be either 0 or 20—not anything in between. Also, for Deland there is no connection between the number of hours he is there and the size of the order he lands. It will take as long as it takes, and he will make the sale that he makes.

Answering the Questions

18. **(A)** The reasonable maximum will be what happens if everything goes as well as it possibly can. If Deland takes two hours or less, Max can see all four customers. If he gets the maximum order from each, he will sell $5 + 20 + 10 + 30 = 65$ boxes.

19. **(D)** Again the word reasonably implies that nothing really unexpected will happen. (A), none, is not at all expected. There is no real question about what the minimum for each customer is from the preceding chart. The real question is whether he sees them all or not. The problem answers this by noting that he will work eight hours, which is long enough for him to see all four customers. The minimum is, thus, $5 + 0 + 10 + 10 = 25$ boxes.

20. **(C)** Max has 20 boxes sold, so the question is how many additional boxes can he sell from 2:00 P.M. to 5:00 P.M. If he sees Acme and Camera, he will probably sell 15 boxes, but if he spends those three hours at Bell, he might sell 20 boxes.

Thus, the maximum is 20 boxes to Deland and possibly 20 more to Bell, for a total of 40.

If you wanted to say (A), you probably were just saying how many he could sell in the afternoon, while the problem requested the "daily" sales figure.

21. **(C)** If Max schedules Deland after 2:00 P.M., that is improper. He could not know that he will have enough time since he must allow three hours for Deland if it happens to take that long. In addition, he would not want to omit Deland since they might give him his biggest order of the day and have the largest minimum order (tie with Camera).

For these reasons, (A), (B), and (D) are poor schedules.

(E) is defective because it schedules four hours of work starting at 2:00 P.M., which runs past the 5:00 P.M. deadline set by the problem.

Under schedule (C), Max will certainly see his best possibilities and still has a chance of seeing the fourth customer if things move quickly at Deland.

22. **(B)** In this situation, there is a 1½-hour slot before Edwards and 3½ hours afterward. (A) and (E) try to fit a three-hour customer into the 1½-hour slot, which is wrong. (C) claims to provide for seeing Deland if time permits, but the only flexibility is the Deland appointment itself, which cannot be forecast. Thus, (C) fails.

The difference between (D) and (B) is whether to be sure of Acme or Camera. Since Camera is a larger sale, it should get the guaranteed spot in the morning, eliminating (D).

A consideration not used much here, but of theoretical interest, is the choice between seeing Bell or Deland. He cannot see both of the three-hour customers. Deland is preferable to Bell for three reasons: (1) the minimum expected sale is higher, (2) the maximum expected sale is higher, and (3) there is the possibility of finishing early enough to also get to another customer.

23. **(E)** The point of the passage is that there is a seeming contradiction in our body of laws. Sometimes a person pays for his attempted misdeeds, and other times he does not pay for them. If there could be found a good reason for this difference, then the contradiction could be explained away. This is just what (E) does. It points out that the law treats the situations differently because it has different goals: Sometimes we drive fast because we are in a hurry, other times we drive slowly because we want to enjoy the scenery. (B) would not weaken the argument for it only intensifies the

contradiction. (D) makes an attempt to reconcile the seemingly conflicting positions by hinting at a possible goal of one action that is not a goal of the other. But, if anything, it intensifies the contradiction because one might infer that we should not try persons for attempted crimes because criminal trials are expensive, but we should allow compensation for attempted frauds because civil trials are less expensive. (C) and (A) are just distractions. Whether there are more of one kind of law than another on the books has nothing to do with the seeming contradiction. And whether persons are more likely to commit a second crime after they are released from prison does not speak to the issue of whether an unsuccessful attempt to commit a crime should be a crime in the first place.

24. **(D)** The ad is weak for two reasons. First, although it is addressed to smokers in general, the evidence it cites is restricted to heavy (three-packs-a-day) smokers. Second, the success achieved by the product was restricted to a highly specific and unusual location—the mountain retreat of a clinic with a population trying hard to quit smoking. Thus, II will undermine the appeal of the advertisement because it cites the first of the weaknesses. III also will tell against the ad since it mentions the second of these weaknesses. I, however, is irrelevant to the ad's appeal since the cause of a smoker's addiction plays no role in the claim of this ad to assist smokers in quitting or cutting down.

25. **(A)** The question stem asks us to focus on the "dispute" between the two opponents. What will be relevant to it will be those items which affect the merits of the issues, or perhaps those which affect the credibility of the parties. (C) and (E) both mention items—facts and their source—which would be relevant to the substantive issues. (B) and (D) are legitimate attempts to clarify the issues and so are relevant. (A) is not relevant to the issues nor is it relevant to the credibility (e.g., where did the facts come from) of the debaters. (A) is the least relevant because it is an *ad hominem* attack of the illegitimate sort.

ANSWER SHEET—PRACTICE EXAMINATION 3

Section I

1 Ⓐ Ⓑ Ⓒ Ⓓ Ⓔ   8 Ⓐ Ⓑ Ⓒ Ⓓ Ⓔ   15 Ⓐ Ⓑ Ⓒ Ⓓ Ⓔ   22 Ⓐ Ⓑ Ⓒ Ⓓ Ⓔ   29 Ⓐ Ⓑ Ⓒ Ⓓ Ⓔ   36 Ⓐ Ⓑ Ⓒ Ⓓ Ⓔ

2 Ⓐ Ⓑ Ⓒ Ⓓ Ⓔ   9 Ⓐ Ⓑ Ⓒ Ⓓ Ⓔ   16 Ⓐ Ⓑ Ⓒ Ⓓ Ⓔ   23 Ⓐ Ⓑ Ⓒ Ⓓ Ⓔ   30 Ⓐ Ⓑ Ⓒ Ⓓ Ⓔ   37 Ⓐ Ⓑ Ⓒ Ⓓ Ⓔ

3 Ⓐ Ⓑ Ⓒ Ⓓ Ⓔ   10 Ⓐ Ⓑ Ⓒ Ⓓ Ⓔ   17 Ⓐ Ⓑ Ⓒ Ⓓ Ⓔ   24 Ⓐ Ⓑ Ⓒ Ⓓ Ⓔ   31 Ⓐ Ⓑ Ⓒ Ⓓ Ⓔ   38 Ⓐ Ⓑ Ⓒ Ⓓ Ⓔ

4 Ⓐ Ⓑ Ⓒ Ⓓ Ⓔ   11 Ⓐ Ⓑ Ⓒ Ⓓ Ⓔ   18 Ⓐ Ⓑ Ⓒ Ⓓ Ⓔ   25 Ⓐ Ⓑ Ⓒ Ⓓ Ⓔ   32 Ⓐ Ⓑ Ⓒ Ⓓ Ⓔ

5 Ⓐ Ⓑ Ⓒ Ⓓ Ⓔ   12 Ⓐ Ⓑ Ⓒ Ⓓ Ⓔ   19 Ⓐ Ⓑ Ⓒ Ⓓ Ⓔ   26 Ⓐ Ⓑ Ⓒ Ⓓ Ⓔ   33 Ⓐ Ⓑ Ⓒ Ⓓ Ⓔ

6 Ⓐ Ⓑ Ⓒ Ⓓ Ⓔ   13 Ⓐ Ⓑ Ⓒ Ⓓ Ⓔ   20 Ⓐ Ⓑ Ⓒ Ⓓ Ⓔ   27 Ⓐ Ⓑ Ⓒ Ⓓ Ⓔ   34 Ⓐ Ⓑ Ⓒ Ⓓ Ⓔ

7 Ⓐ Ⓑ Ⓒ Ⓓ Ⓔ   14 Ⓐ Ⓑ Ⓒ Ⓓ Ⓔ   21 Ⓐ Ⓑ Ⓒ Ⓓ Ⓔ   28 Ⓐ Ⓑ Ⓒ Ⓓ Ⓔ   35 Ⓐ Ⓑ Ⓒ Ⓓ Ⓔ

Section II

1 Ⓐ Ⓑ Ⓒ Ⓓ Ⓔ   8 Ⓐ Ⓑ Ⓒ Ⓓ Ⓔ   15 Ⓐ Ⓑ Ⓒ Ⓓ Ⓔ   22 Ⓐ Ⓑ Ⓒ Ⓓ Ⓔ   29 Ⓐ Ⓑ Ⓒ Ⓓ Ⓔ   36 Ⓐ Ⓑ Ⓒ Ⓓ Ⓔ

2 Ⓐ Ⓑ Ⓒ Ⓓ Ⓔ   9 Ⓐ Ⓑ Ⓒ Ⓓ Ⓔ   16 Ⓐ Ⓑ Ⓒ Ⓓ Ⓔ   23 Ⓐ Ⓑ Ⓒ Ⓓ Ⓔ   30 Ⓐ Ⓑ Ⓒ Ⓓ Ⓔ   37 Ⓐ Ⓑ Ⓒ Ⓓ Ⓔ

3 Ⓐ Ⓑ Ⓒ Ⓓ Ⓔ   10 Ⓐ Ⓑ Ⓒ Ⓓ Ⓔ   17 Ⓐ Ⓑ Ⓒ Ⓓ Ⓔ   24 Ⓐ Ⓑ Ⓒ Ⓓ Ⓔ   31 Ⓐ Ⓑ Ⓒ Ⓓ Ⓔ   38 Ⓐ Ⓑ Ⓒ Ⓓ Ⓔ

4 Ⓐ Ⓑ Ⓒ Ⓓ Ⓔ   11 Ⓐ Ⓑ Ⓒ Ⓓ Ⓔ   18 Ⓐ Ⓑ Ⓒ Ⓓ Ⓔ   25 Ⓐ Ⓑ Ⓒ Ⓓ Ⓔ   32 Ⓐ Ⓑ Ⓒ Ⓓ Ⓔ

5 Ⓐ Ⓑ Ⓒ Ⓓ Ⓔ   12 Ⓐ Ⓑ Ⓒ Ⓓ Ⓔ   19 Ⓐ Ⓑ Ⓒ Ⓓ Ⓔ   26 Ⓐ Ⓑ Ⓒ Ⓓ Ⓔ   33 Ⓐ Ⓑ Ⓒ Ⓓ Ⓔ

6 Ⓐ Ⓑ Ⓒ Ⓓ Ⓔ   13 Ⓐ Ⓑ Ⓒ Ⓓ Ⓔ   20 Ⓐ Ⓑ Ⓒ Ⓓ Ⓔ   27 Ⓐ Ⓑ Ⓒ Ⓓ Ⓔ   34 Ⓐ Ⓑ Ⓒ Ⓓ Ⓔ

7 Ⓐ Ⓑ Ⓒ Ⓓ Ⓔ   14 Ⓐ Ⓑ Ⓒ Ⓓ Ⓔ   21 Ⓐ Ⓑ Ⓒ Ⓓ Ⓔ   28 Ⓐ Ⓑ Ⓒ Ⓓ Ⓔ   35 Ⓐ Ⓑ Ⓒ Ⓓ Ⓔ

Section III

1 Ⓐ Ⓑ Ⓒ Ⓓ   6 Ⓐ Ⓑ Ⓒ Ⓓ   11 Ⓐ Ⓑ Ⓒ Ⓓ   16 Ⓐ Ⓑ Ⓒ Ⓓ Ⓔ   21 Ⓐ Ⓑ Ⓒ Ⓓ Ⓔ   26 Ⓐ Ⓑ Ⓒ Ⓓ Ⓔ

2 Ⓐ Ⓑ Ⓒ Ⓓ   7 Ⓐ Ⓑ Ⓒ Ⓓ   12 Ⓐ Ⓑ Ⓒ Ⓓ   17 Ⓐ Ⓑ Ⓒ Ⓓ Ⓔ   22 Ⓐ Ⓑ Ⓒ Ⓓ Ⓔ   27 Ⓐ Ⓑ Ⓒ Ⓓ Ⓔ

3 Ⓐ Ⓑ Ⓒ Ⓓ   8 Ⓐ Ⓑ Ⓒ Ⓓ   13 Ⓐ Ⓑ Ⓒ Ⓓ   18 Ⓐ Ⓑ Ⓒ Ⓓ Ⓔ   23 Ⓐ Ⓑ Ⓒ Ⓓ Ⓔ   28 Ⓐ Ⓑ Ⓒ Ⓓ Ⓔ

4 Ⓐ Ⓑ Ⓒ Ⓓ   9 Ⓐ Ⓑ Ⓒ Ⓓ   14 Ⓐ Ⓑ Ⓒ Ⓓ   19 Ⓐ Ⓑ Ⓒ Ⓓ Ⓔ   24 Ⓐ Ⓑ Ⓒ Ⓓ Ⓔ   29 Ⓐ Ⓑ Ⓒ Ⓓ Ⓔ

5 Ⓐ Ⓑ Ⓒ Ⓓ   10 Ⓐ Ⓑ Ⓒ Ⓓ   15 Ⓐ Ⓑ Ⓒ Ⓓ   20 Ⓐ Ⓑ Ⓒ Ⓓ Ⓔ   25 Ⓐ Ⓑ Ⓒ Ⓓ Ⓔ   30 Ⓐ Ⓑ Ⓒ Ⓓ Ⓔ

Section IV

1 Ⓐ Ⓑ Ⓒ Ⓓ 6 Ⓐ Ⓑ Ⓒ Ⓓ 11 Ⓐ Ⓑ Ⓒ Ⓓ 16 Ⓐ Ⓑ Ⓒ Ⓓ Ⓔ 21 Ⓐ Ⓑ Ⓒ Ⓓ Ⓔ 26 Ⓐ Ⓑ Ⓒ Ⓓ Ⓔ

2 Ⓐ Ⓑ Ⓒ Ⓓ 7 Ⓐ Ⓑ Ⓒ Ⓓ 12 Ⓐ Ⓑ Ⓒ Ⓓ 17 Ⓐ Ⓑ Ⓒ Ⓓ Ⓔ 22 Ⓐ Ⓑ Ⓒ Ⓓ Ⓔ 27 Ⓐ Ⓑ Ⓒ Ⓓ Ⓔ

3 Ⓐ Ⓑ Ⓒ Ⓓ 8 Ⓐ Ⓑ Ⓒ Ⓓ 13 Ⓐ Ⓑ Ⓒ Ⓓ 18 Ⓐ Ⓑ Ⓒ Ⓓ Ⓔ 23 Ⓐ Ⓑ Ⓒ Ⓓ Ⓔ 28 Ⓐ Ⓑ Ⓒ Ⓓ Ⓔ

4 Ⓐ Ⓑ Ⓒ Ⓓ 9 Ⓐ Ⓑ Ⓒ Ⓓ 14 Ⓐ Ⓑ Ⓒ Ⓓ 19 Ⓐ Ⓑ Ⓒ Ⓓ Ⓔ 24 Ⓐ Ⓑ Ⓒ Ⓓ Ⓔ 29 Ⓐ Ⓑ Ⓒ Ⓓ Ⓔ

5 Ⓐ Ⓑ Ⓒ Ⓓ 10 Ⓐ Ⓑ Ⓒ Ⓓ 15 Ⓐ Ⓑ Ⓒ Ⓓ 20 Ⓐ Ⓑ Ⓒ Ⓓ Ⓔ 25 Ⓐ Ⓑ Ⓒ Ⓓ Ⓔ 30 Ⓐ Ⓑ Ⓒ Ⓓ Ⓔ

Section V

1 Ⓐ Ⓑ Ⓒ Ⓓ Ⓔ 6 Ⓐ Ⓑ Ⓒ Ⓓ Ⓔ 11 Ⓐ Ⓑ Ⓒ Ⓓ Ⓔ 16 Ⓐ Ⓑ Ⓒ Ⓓ Ⓔ 21 Ⓐ Ⓑ Ⓒ Ⓓ Ⓔ

2 Ⓐ Ⓑ Ⓒ Ⓓ Ⓔ 7 Ⓐ Ⓑ Ⓒ Ⓓ Ⓔ 12 Ⓐ Ⓑ Ⓒ Ⓓ Ⓔ 17 Ⓐ Ⓑ Ⓒ Ⓓ Ⓔ 22 Ⓐ Ⓑ Ⓒ Ⓓ Ⓔ

3 Ⓐ Ⓑ Ⓒ Ⓓ Ⓔ 8 Ⓐ Ⓑ Ⓒ Ⓓ Ⓔ 13 Ⓐ Ⓑ Ⓒ Ⓓ Ⓔ 18 Ⓐ Ⓑ Ⓒ Ⓓ Ⓔ 23 Ⓐ Ⓑ Ⓒ Ⓓ Ⓔ

4 Ⓐ Ⓑ Ⓒ Ⓓ Ⓔ 9 Ⓐ Ⓑ Ⓒ Ⓓ Ⓔ 14 Ⓐ Ⓑ Ⓒ Ⓓ Ⓔ 19 Ⓐ Ⓑ Ⓒ Ⓓ Ⓔ 24 Ⓐ Ⓑ Ⓒ Ⓓ Ⓔ

5 Ⓐ Ⓑ Ⓒ Ⓓ Ⓔ 10 Ⓐ Ⓑ Ⓒ Ⓓ Ⓔ 15 Ⓐ Ⓑ Ⓒ Ⓓ Ⓔ 20 Ⓐ Ⓑ Ⓒ Ⓓ Ⓔ 25 Ⓐ Ⓑ Ⓒ Ⓓ Ⓔ

Section VI

1 Ⓐ Ⓑ Ⓒ Ⓓ Ⓔ 6 Ⓐ Ⓑ Ⓒ Ⓓ Ⓔ 11 Ⓐ Ⓑ Ⓒ Ⓓ Ⓔ 16 Ⓐ Ⓑ Ⓒ Ⓓ Ⓔ 21 Ⓐ Ⓑ Ⓒ Ⓓ Ⓔ

2 Ⓐ Ⓑ Ⓒ Ⓓ Ⓔ 7 Ⓐ Ⓑ Ⓒ Ⓓ Ⓔ 12 Ⓐ Ⓑ Ⓒ Ⓓ Ⓔ 17 Ⓐ Ⓑ Ⓒ Ⓓ Ⓔ 22 Ⓐ Ⓑ Ⓒ Ⓓ Ⓔ

3 Ⓐ Ⓑ Ⓒ Ⓓ Ⓔ 8 Ⓐ Ⓑ Ⓒ Ⓓ Ⓔ 13 Ⓐ Ⓑ Ⓒ Ⓓ Ⓔ 18 Ⓐ Ⓑ Ⓒ Ⓓ Ⓔ 23 Ⓐ Ⓑ Ⓒ Ⓓ Ⓔ

4 Ⓐ Ⓑ Ⓒ Ⓓ Ⓔ 9 Ⓐ Ⓑ Ⓒ Ⓓ Ⓔ 14 Ⓐ Ⓑ Ⓒ Ⓓ Ⓔ 19 Ⓐ Ⓑ Ⓒ Ⓓ Ⓔ 24 Ⓐ Ⓑ Ⓒ Ⓓ Ⓔ

5 Ⓐ Ⓑ Ⓒ Ⓓ Ⓔ 10 Ⓐ Ⓑ Ⓒ Ⓓ Ⓔ 15 Ⓐ Ⓑ Ⓒ Ⓓ Ⓔ 20 Ⓐ Ⓑ Ⓒ Ⓓ Ⓔ 25 Ⓐ Ⓑ Ⓒ Ⓓ Ⓔ

PRACTICE EXAMINATION 3

SECTION I

30 minutes
38 questions

Directions: Each of the questions below contains one or more blank spaces, each blank indicating an omitted word. Each sentence is followed by five (5) lettered words or sets of words. Read and determine the general sense of each sentence. Then choose the word or set of words which, when inserted in the sentence, best fits the meaning of the sentence.

1. We should have _____ trouble ahead when the road _____ into a gravel path.
   (A) interrogated—shrank
   (B) anticipated—dwindled
   (C) expected—grew
   (D) enjoyed—transformed
   (E) seen—collapsed

2. The _____ of the waiter, fresh lobster, was all gone, so we _____ ourselves with crab.
   (A) suggestion—resolved
   (B) embarrassment—consoled
   (C) recommendation—contented
   (D) specialty—pelted
   (E) regrets—relieved

3. The _____ workroom had not been used in years.
   (A) derelict
   (B) bustling
   (C) bereft
   (D) bereaved
   (E) stricken

4. Tempers ran hot among the old-timers, who _____ the young mayor and his _____ city council.

   (A) despised—attractive
   (B) admired—elite
   (C) resented—reform
   (D) forgave—activist
   (E) feared—apathetic

5. With the discovery of _____ alternative fuel source, oil prices dropped significantly.
   (A) a potential
   (B) a feasible
   (C) a possible
   (D) a variant
   (E) an inexpensive

6. The masters of the world are the bacteria and viruses. They _____ all other life and all other life lives and reproduces merely to provide them with _____.
   (A) dominate—companionship
   (B) outnumber—room and board
   (C) infest—opportunity
   (D) serve—shelter
   (E) are symbiotic with—partners

7. He could understand that his prisoners would _____ him at first, but he had hoped that after all this time his fairness would inspire _____ rather than trepidation at his arrival.
   (A) misunderstand—love
   (B) escape—cordiality
   (C) abhor—loyalty
   (D) dislike—camaraderie
   (E) fear—trust

345

Directions: In each of the following questions, you are given a related pair of words or phrases in capital letters. Each capitalized pair is followed by five (5) lettered pairs of words or phrases. Choose the pair which best expresses a relationship similar to that expressed by the original pair.

8. CAT : MOUSE ::
   (A) bird : worm
   (B) dog : tail
   (C) trap : cheese
   (D) hide : seek
   (E) lion : snake

9. VANILLA : BEAN ::
   (A) tabasco : stem
   (B) chili : seed
   (C) mint : flower
   (D) ginger : root
   (E) sage : berry

10. ENERGY : DISSIPATE ::
    (A) battery : recharge
    (B) atom : split
    (C) food : eat
    (D) money : squander
    (E) gas : generate

11. NOSE : FACE ::
    (A) ring : finger
    (B) stem : root
    (C) knob : door
    (D) shoe : foot
    (E) vine : building

12. RIFLE : SOLDIER ::
    (A) bow : arrow
    (B) sword : knight
    (C) horse : cowboy
    (D) marine : tank
    (E) lock : robber

13. DEER : VENISON ::
    (A) pig : hog
    (B) sheep : mutton
    (C) lamb : veal
    (D) steer : steak
    (E) beef : stew

14. INEFFABLE : KNOWLEDGE ::
    (A) genial : interesting
    (B) puzzling : trick
    (C) frustrating : release
    (D) baffling : solution
    (E) controllable : rage

15. ICING : CAKE ::
    (A) veneer : table
    (B) ice : pond
    (C) pastry : bake
    (D) apple : pie
    (E) printing : page

16. CHALK : BLACKBOARD ::
    (A) door : handle
    (B) table : chair
    (C) ink : paper
    (D) pencil : writing
    (E) paint : wall

Directions: Below each of the following passages, you will find questions or incomplete statements about the passage. Each statement or question is followed by lettered words or expressions. Select the word or expression that most satisfactorily completes each statement or answers each question in accordance with the meaning of the passage. After you choose the best answer, blacken the corresponding space on the answer sheet.

There is a confused notion in the minds of many persons, that the gathering of the property of the poor into the hands of the rich does no ultimate harm, since in whosever hands it may be, it must be spent at last, and thus, they think, return to the poor again. This fallacy has been again and again exposed; but granting the plea true, the same apology may, of course, be made for blackmail, or any other form of robbery. It might be (though practically it never is) as advantageous for the nation that the robber should have the spending of the money he extorts, as that the person robbed should have spent it. But this is no excuse for the theft. If I were to put a turnpike on the road where it passes my own gate, and endeavor to exact a shilling from every passenger, the public would soon do away with my gate, without listening to any pleas on my part that it was as advantageous to them, in the end, that I should spend their shillings, as that they themselves should. But if, instead of outfacing them with a turnpike, I can only persuade them to come in and buy stones, or old iron, or any other useless thing, out of my ground, I may rob them to the same extent and, moreover, be thanked as a public benefactor and promoter of commercial prosperity. And this main question for the poor of England—for the poor of all countries—is wholly omitted in every treastise on the subject of wealth. Even by the laborers themselves, the operation of capital is regarded only in its effect on their immediate interests, never in the far more terrific power of its appointment of the kind and the object of labor. It matters little, ultimately, how much a laborer is paid for making anything; but it matters fearfully what the thing is which he is compelled to make. If his labor is so ordered as to produce food, fresh air, and fresh water, no matter that his wages are low; the food and the fresh air and water will be at last there, and he will at last get them. But if he is paid to destroy food and fresh air, or to produce iron bars instead of them, the food and air will finally *not* be there, and he will *not* get them, to his great and final inconvenience. So that, conclusively, in political as in household economy, the great question is, not so much what money you have in your pocket, as what you will buy with it and do with it.

17. We may infer that the author probably lived in the
    (A) 1960's in the United States
    (B) early days of British industrialization
    (C) 18th-century France
    (D) Golden Age of Greece
    (E) England of King Arthur

18. It can be inferred that the author probably favors
    (A) capitalism
    (B) totalitarianism
    (C) socialism
    (D) anarchism
    (E) theocracy

19. According to the passage, the individual should be particularly concerned with
    (A) how much wealth he can accumulate
    (B) the acquisition of land property rather than money
    (C) charging the customer a fair price
    (D) the quality of goods which he purchases with his funds
    (E) working as hard as possible

20. The passage implies that
    (A) "A stitch in time saves nine."
    (B) "It is better late than never."
    (C) "He who steals my purse steals trash."
    (D) "None but the brave deserve the fair."
    (E) "All's well that ends well."

21. It can be inferred that in regard to the accumulation of wealth the author
    (A) equates the rich with the thief
    (B) indicates that there are few honest businessmen
    (C) condones some dishonesty in business dealings
    (D) believes destruction of property is good because it creates consumer demand
    (E) says that the robber is a benefactor

22. What is the "main question for the poor" referred to by the author in the passages?
    (A) the use to which the laborer can put his money
    (B) the methods by which capital may be accumulated
    (C) the results of their work and their lack of authority to determine to what ends their work shall be put
    (D) whether full measure of recompense shall be accorded to the laboring person for the investment of his time in worthy work
    (E) the extent to which a man can call his life his own

23. According to the views expressed in the passage, people should be happiest doing which of the following?
    (A) mining ore for the manufacture of weapons
    (B) cleaning sewage ponds at a treatment plant
    (C) waiting tables for a rich man
    (D) helping a poor man do his job
    (E) studying economic theory

24. The author of the above passage would probably react to an energy shortage by
    (A) blaming the rich for the problem
    (B) urging that energy be used more efficiently and effectively
    (C) supporting the search for more oil,

coal, and other energy-producing mineral deposits

(D) denying that there is really any shortage at all

(E) fomenting revolution by the poor

Man, said Aristotle, is a social animal. This sociability requires peaceful congregation, and the history of mankind is mainly a movement through time of human collectivities that range from migrant tribal bands to large and complex civilizations. Survival has been due to the ability to create the means by which men in groups retain their unity and allegiance to one another.

Order was caused by the need and desire to survive the challenge of the environment. This orderly condition came to be called the "state," and the rules that maintained it, the "law." With time the partner to this tranquillity, man marched across the centuries of his evolution to the brink of exploring the boundaries of his own galaxy. Of all living organisms, only man has the capacity to interpret his own evolution as progress. As social life changed, the worth and rights of each member in the larger group, of which he was a part, increased. As the groups grew from clans to civilizations, the value of the individual did not diminish, but became instead a guide to the rules that govern all men.

25. The best expression of the main idea of this article is
   (A) oppression and society
   (B) the evolution of man
   (C) man's animal instincts
   (D) the basis for social order
   (E) a history of violence and strife

26. The author would expect the greatest attention to individual rights and values to be found in
   (A) farming communities
   (B) small villages
   (C) prehistoric families
   (D) nomadic tribes
   (E) modern cities

27. According to the article, man's uniqueness is attributed to the fact that he is
   (A) evolving from a simpler to a more complex being

(B) a social animal
(C) capable of noting his own progress
(D) capable of inflicting injury and causing violence
(E) able to survive by forming groups with allegiance to one another

Directions: Each of the following questions consists of a word printed in capital letters, followed by five (5) lettered words or phrases. Select the word or phrase which is most nearly *opposite* to the capitalized word in meaning.

28. REFRACTORY:
   (A) refreshing
   (B) burdensome
   (C) privileged
   (D) manageable
   (E) upright

29. ADROIT:
   (A) deterred
   (B) skillful
   (C) foolish
   (D) sinister
   (E) awkward

30. PALLIATE:
   (A) apologize
   (B) hesitate
   (C) wait impatiently
   (D) decide finally
   (E) worsen

31. VILIFY:
   (A) sing the praises of
   (B) show satisfaction with
   (C) regard with distrust
   (D) welcome with glee
   (E) accept halfheartedly

32. IRASCIBLE:
   (A) placid
   (B) fortuitous
   (C) shameless
   (D) entrancing
   (E) yielding

33. GELID:
   (A) chilly

(B) solid
(C) mature
(D) pallid
(E) boiling

34. CONDIGN:
(A) unavoidable
(B) unsatisfactory
(C) unguarded
(D) undeserved
(E) uninitiated

35. PUNCTILIOUS:
(A) tardy
(B) correct
(C) careless
(D) apathetic
(E) repulsive

36. FECKLESS:
(A) spotted
(B) fatuous
(C) fawning
(D) strong
(E) calm

37. INSOLENT:
(A) sullen
(B) rich
(C) determined
(D) kind
(E) affable

38. SERENDIPITOUS:
(A) calm
(B) planned
(C) flat
(D) evil
(E) regulated

STOP

END OF SECTION. IF YOU HAVE ANY TIME LEFT, GO
OVER YOUR WORK IN THIS SECTION ONLY. DO NOT
WORK IN ANY OTHER SECTION OF THE TEST.

SECTION II

30 minutes
38 questions

Directions: Each of the questions below contains one or more blank spaces, each blank indicating an omitted word. Each sentence is followed by five (5) lettered words or sets of words. Read and determine the general sense of the sentence. Then choose the word or set of words which, when inserted in the sentence, best fits the meaning of the sentence.

1. The product of a _____ religious home, he often found _____ in prayer.
   (A) zealously—distraction
   (B) devoutly—solace
   (C) vigorously—comfort
   (D) fanatically—misgivings
   (E) pious—answers

2. Our _____ objections finally got us thrown out of the stadium.
   (A) hurled
   (B) modest
   (C) wary
   (D) vocal
   (E) pliant

3. Only a single wall still stood in mute _____ to Nature's force.
   (A) evidence

(B) tribute
(C) remainder
(D) memory
(E) testimony

4. After completing her usual morning chores,
    Linda found herself _____ tired.
    (A) surprisingly
    (B) erratically
    (C) buoyantly
    (D) forcibly
    (E) unceasingly

5. The current spirit of _____ among
    the various departments of the university
    has led to a number of _____
    publications which might not otherwise
    have been written.
    (A) competition—angry
    (B) futility—significant
    (C) cooperation—interdisciplinary
    (D) patriotism—American
    (E) machoism—pugilistic

6. Human senses are designed to ____ specific
    stimuli, and after a focus is achieved, other
    sensory data is _____.
    (A) look for—heightened
    (B) respond to—insulated
    (C) concentrate on—discounted
    (D) favor—added up
    (E) create—born

7. Immigrants arriving in a new country have
    the special problem of _____ their
    established behaviors and learning new hab-
    its whose results are _____.
    (A) abandoning—uncertain
    (B) strengthening—different
    (C) controlling—guaranteed
    (D) loosening—definite
    (E) maintaining—simpler

Directions: In each of the following questions, you are
given a related pair of words or phrases in capital
letters. Each capitalized pair is followed by five (5)
lettered pairs of words or phrases. Choose the pair
which best expresses a relationship similar to that
expressed by the original pair.

8. MONEY : EMBEZZLEMENT ::
    (A) bank : cashier
    (B) writing : plagiarism
    (C) remarks : insult
    (D) radiation : bomb
    (E) death : murder

9. FOIL : FENCE ::
    (A) pencil : mark
    (B) road : run
    (C) gloves : box
    (D) train : travel
    (E) bow : bend

10. CLIMB : TREE ::
    (A) row : canoe
    (B) ascend : cliff
    (C) throw : balloon
    (D) file : nail
    (E) float : loan

11. LION : CUB ::
    (A) duck : drake
    (B) rooster : chicken
    (C) human : child
    (D) mother : daughter
    (E) fox : vixen

12. ROOM : HOUSE ::
    (A) refrigerator : kitchen
    (B) chair : room
    (C) cabin : ship
    (D) wheel : car
    (E) cockpit : plane

13. ACORN : OAK ::
    (A) fig : bush
    (B) flower : stalk
    (C) nut : plant
    (D) bulb : tulip
    (E) branch : leaf

14. SORROW : DEATH ::
    (A) laugh : cry
    (B) plum : peach
    (C) happiness : birth
    (D) fear : hate
    (E) confusion : anger

15. EXPLOSION : DEBRIS ::
    (A) fire : ashes
    (B) flood : water
    (C) famine : war
    (D) disease : germ
    (E) heat : burn

16. SOLECISM : GRAMMAR ::
    (A) divorce : marriage
    (B) foul : rules
    (C) incest : family
    (D) stumble : running
    (E) apostasy : dogma

Directions: Below each of the following passages, you will find questions or incomplete statements about the passage. Each statement or question is followed by lettered words or expressions. Select the word or expression that most satisfactorily completes each statement, or answers each question in accordance with the meaning of the passage. After you have chosen the best answer, blacken the corresponding space on the answer sheet.

The deliberate violation of constituted law (civil disobedience) is never morally justified if the law being violated is not the prime target or focal point of the protest. While our government maintains the principle of the Constitution by providing methods for and protection of those engaged in individual or group dissent, the violation of law simply as a technique of demonstration constitutes rebellion.

Civil disobedience is by definition a violation of the law. The theory of civil disobedience recognizes that its actions, regardless of their justification, must be punished. However, disobedience of laws not the subject of dissent, but merely used to dramatize dissent, is regarded as morally as well as legally unacceptable. It is only with respect to those laws which offend the fundamental values of human life that moral defense of civil disobedience can be rationally supported.

For a just society to exist, the principle of tolerance must be accepted, both by the government in regard to properly expressed individual dissent and by the individual toward legally established majority verdicts. No individual has a monopoly on freedom and all must tolerate opposition. Dissenters must accept dissent from their dissent, giving it all the respect they claim for themselves. To disregard this principle is to

make civil disobedience not only legally wrong but morally unjustifiable.

17. The author's attitude toward civil disobedience is one of
    (A) indifference
    (B) admiration
    (C) hostility
    (D) respect
    (E) contempt

18. What would the author most likely feel about a demonstration against apartheid which resulted in the disruption of businesses not associated with the problem in any way?
    (A) profound antipathy toward the goal of the demonstration
    (B) severe condemnation of the location of the businesses
    (C) tolerant acceptance of the demonstration's results
    (D) amused indifference toward the demonstrator's goals
    (E) regretful disapproval of the methods of protest

19. It can be inferred from the passage that
    (A) a just society cannot accept illegal civil disobedience
    (B) a just society cannot accept immoral actions of any sort
    (C) dissenters who use civil disobedience cannot use it merely to dramatize their cause
    (D) civil disobedience is sometimes the right thing to do
    (E) many authorities respect dissent as necessary to the functioning of a free society

The Planning Commission asserts that the needed reduction in acute care hospital beds can best be accomplished by closing the smaller hospitals, mainly voluntary and proprietary. This strategy follows from the argument that closing entire institutions saves more money than closing the equivalent number of beds scattered throughout the health system.

The issue is not that simple. Larger hospitals generally are designed to provide more complex care. Routine care at large hospitals costs more than the same care given at smaller hospitals. Therefore, closure of all the small hospitals would commit the city to paying considerably more for inpatient care delivered at acute care hospitals than would be the case with a mixture of large and small institutions. Since reimbursement rates at the large hospitals are now based on total costs, paying the large institutions a lower rate for routine care would simply raise the rates for complex care by a comparable amount. Such a reimbursement rate adjustment might make the charges for each individual case more accurately reflect the actual costs, but there would be no reduction in total costs.

There is some evidence that giant hospitals are not the most efficient. Service organizations—and medical care remains largely a service industry—frequently find that savings of scale have an upper limit. Similarly, the quality of routine care in the very largest hospitals appears to be less than optimum. Also, the concentration of all hospital beds in a few locations may affect the access to care.

Thus, simply closing the smaller hospitals will not necessarily save money or improve the quality of care.

Since the fact remains that there are too many acute care hospital beds in the city, the problem is to devise a proper strategy for selecting and urging the closure of the excess beds, however many it may turn out to be.

The closing of whole buildings within large medical centers has many of the cost advantages of closing the whole of smaller institutions, because the fixed costs can also be reduced in such cases. Unfortunately, many of the separate buildings at medical centers are special use facilities, the relocation of which is extremely costly. Still, a search should be made for such opportunities.

The current lack of adequate ambulatory care facilities raises another possibility. Some floors or other large compact areas of hospitals could be transferred from inpatient to ambulatory uses. Reimbursement of ambulatory services is chaotic, but the problem is being addressed. The overhead associated with the entire hospital should not be charged even *pro rata* to the ambulatory facilities. Even if it were, the total cost would probably be less than that of building a new facility. Many other issues would also need study, especially the potential overcentralization of ambulatory services.

The Planning Commission language seems to imply that one reason for closing smaller hospitals is that they are "mainly voluntary and proprietary," thus, preserving the public hospital system by making the rest of the hospital system absorb the needed cuts. It is important to preserve the public hospital system for many reasons, but the issue should be faced directly and **not hidden behind arguments about hospital size. If indeed that was the meaning.**

20. The best title for the passage would be
    (A) Maintaining Adequate Hospital Facilities
    (B) Defending the Public Hospitals
    (C) **Methods of Selecting Hospital Beds to Be Closed**
    (D) Protecting the Proprietary and Voluntary Hospitals
    (E) Economic Efficiency in Hospital Bed Closings

21. The Planning Commission is accused by the author of being
    (A) unfair
    (B) racist
    (C) foolish
    (D) shortsighted
    (E) ignorant

22. On the subject of the number of hospital beds the author
    (A) is in complete agreement with the Planning Commission
    (B) wishes to see large numbers of beds closed
    (C) wishes to forestall the closing of any more hospital beds
    (D) is unsure of the number of excess beds there really are
    (E) wishes to avoid exchanging quantity for quality

23. **All of the following are reasons the author opposes the Planning Commission's recommendation EXCEPT**
    (A) service industries have an upper limit for savings of scale
    (B) single buildings of large centers may be closable instead of smaller hospitals

(C) public hospitals have a unique contribution to make and should not be closed

(D) the smaller hospitals recommended for closure provide services more cheaply than larger hospitals

(E) hospitals are service organizations

24. With which of the following would the author probably NOT agree?

(A) Large medical centers provide better and more complex care than do smaller hospitals.

(B) Reimbursement rates do not necessarily reflect the actual costs of providing medical care to a given patient.

(C) Patients needing only routine medical care can often be distinguished from those requiring complex care prior to hospitalization.

(D) Too much centralization of ambulatory care is possible.

(E) Access to medical care is an important issue.

25. The author's purpose in discussing ambulatory care is to

(A) discuss alternatives to closing hospital beds

(B) present a method of reducing the fiscal disadvantages of closing only parts of larger hospitals

(C) show another opportunity for saving money

(D) help preserve the public hospital system

(E) attack the inefficient use of space in larger hospitals

26. With which of the following is the author LEAST likely to agree?

(A) a proposal to save costs in a prison system by building only very large prison complexes

(B) a plan to stop the closing of any beds whatsoever in the city, until the costs of various alternatives can be fully considered

(C) an order by the Planning Commission mandating that no public hospitals be closed

(D) a proposal by an architecture firm that

new hospital buildings have centralized record systems

(E) a mayoral commission being formed to study the plight of the elderly

27. How does the author feel that his suggestions for closing inpatient beds could impact on the ambulatory care system?

(A) Ambulatory care costs will probably be reduced.

(B) A reduction of hospital beds will increase the demand for ambulatory services.

(C) Smaller hospitals will have to cut back ambulatory services to stay fiscally viable.

(D) The Planning Commission would order the opening of new ambulatory services.

(E) The use as ambulatory facilities of the space made available in large hospitals by bed closings might result in having too many ambulatory services based in large hospitals.

Directions: Each of the following questions consists of a word printed in capital letters, followed by five (5) lettered words or phrases. Select the word or phrase which is most nearly *opposite* to the capitalized word in meaning.

28. FETID:

(A) in an embryonic state

(B) easily enraged

(C) acclaimed by peers

(D) reduced to skin and bones

(E) having a pleasant odor

29. ILLUSORY:

(A) nimble

(B) realistic

(C) powerful

(D) underrated

(E) remarkable

30. DOUR:

(A) gay

(B) sweet

(C) wealthy

(D) responsive
(E) noiseless

31. MENDACIOUS:
   (A) broken
   (B) efficacious
   (C) truthful
   (D) destructive
   (E) brilliant

32. ENERVATE:
   (A) debilitate
   (B) fortify
   (C) introduce
   (D) conclude
   (E) escalate

33. DISCRETE:
   (A) loud
   (B) combined
   (C) loose
   (D) circle
   (E) major

34. PRIMITIVE:
   (A) polite
   (B) naive
   (C) weak
   (D) sophisticated
   (E) knowledgeable

35. PARTITION:
   (A) solidify
   (B) unify
   (C) parse
   (D) enjoin
   (E) maintain

36. CLANDESTINE:
   (A) aboveground
   (B) public
   (C) outside
   (D) burnt out
   (E) physical

37. PHLEGMATIC:
   (A) hoarse
   (B) voluntary
   (C) oral
   (D) effusive
   (E) impulsive

38. MANUMIT:
   (A) throw
   (B) lock
   (C) promise
   (D) uncountable
   (E) enslave

STOP

END OF SECTION. IF YOU HAVE ANY TIME LEFT, GO
OVER YOUR WORK IN THIS SECTION ONLY. DO NOT
WORK IN ANY OTHER SECTION OF THE TEST.

SECTION III

30 minutes
30 questions

Directions: For each of the following questions two quantities are given, one in Column A
and one in Column B. Compare the two quantities and mark your answer sheet with the
correct lettered conclusion. These are your options:
   A: If the quantity in Column A is the greater:

B: if the quantity in Column B is the greater:
C: if the two quantities are equal:
D: if the relationship cannot be determined from the information given.

Common Information: In any question, information applying to both columns is centered between the columns and above the quantities in columns A and B. The common information applies to both columns. Any symbol that appears in both columns represents the same idea or quantity in both columns.

Numbers: All numbers used are real numbers.

Figures: Assume that the positions of points, angles, regions and so forth are in the order shown. Figures are assumed to lie in a plane unless otherwise indicated. Figures accompanying questions are intended to provide information you can use in answering the questions. However, unless a note states that a figure is drawn to scale, you should solve the problems by using your knowledge of mathematics and *not* by estimating sizes by sight or measurement.

Lines: Assume that lines shown as straight are indeed straight.

	COLUMN A	COLUMN B
1.	the distance travelled by a car with an average speed of 30 miles per hour	the distance travelled by a car with an average speed of 40 miles per hour
2.	The number of tens in 46	The number of thousands in 3612
3.	7.6351123	7.636

4.

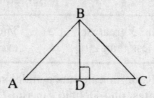

	AD	DC
5.	$\dfrac{12}{10-8}$	$\dfrac{12}{10-6}$

6.

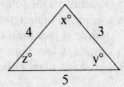

	$z° + y°$	$x°$
7.	the area of a square with side 30 inches	the area of a square with side two feet six inches

	COLUMN A	COLUMN B

8.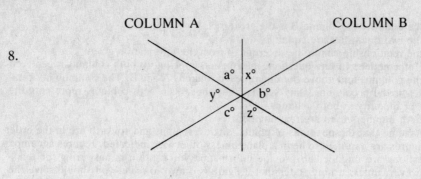

	x + y + z	a + b + c

Questions 9 and 10 refer to the following figure:

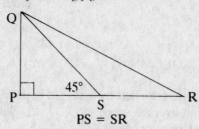

PS = SR

9.	PS	QP

10.	the area of PQS	the area of SQR

11.	The fraction of a day represented by 16 hours	The fraction of an hour represented by 45 minutes

12.	The sum of the 3 greatest odd integers less than 20	The sum of the 3 greatest even integers less than 20

13. Roberta can run a mile in 7.2 minutes, and Debbie can run 7.2 miles in an hour.

Roberta's average rate per hour	Debbie's average rate per hour

14. The relationships among the grades of 5 students are as follows:
    A's grade is higher than that of B.
    E's grade is less than that of D.
    D's grade is less than that of C.
    B's grade is higher than that of C.

E's grade	A's grade

15.
$$x = \frac{1}{4}\left(3x + \frac{8}{x^2}\right)$$

x	2

Directions: For each of the following questions, select the best of the answer choices and blacken the corresponding space on your answer sheet.

Numbers: All numbers used are real numbers.

Figures: The diagrams and figures that accompany these questions are for the purpose of providing information useful in answering the questions. Unless it is stated that a specific figure is not drawn to scale, the diagrams and figures are drawn as accurately as possible. All figures are in a plane unless otherwise indicated.

16. Of the following which is LEAST?
    (A) $\frac{3}{5}$
    (B) $\frac{2}{3}$
    (C) $\frac{17}{29}$
    (D) $\frac{2}{7}$
    (E) $\frac{4}{5}$

17. If a square MNOP has an area of 16, then its perimeter is
    (A) 4
    (B) 8
    (C) 16
    (D) 32
    (E) 64

18. John has more money than Mary but less than Bill. If the amounts held by John, Mary and Bill are x, y, and z, respectively, which of the following is true?
    (A) $z < x < y$
    (B) $x < z < y$
    (C) $y < x < z$
    (D) $y < z < x$
    (E) $x < y < z$

19. If $x = 3$ and $(x - y)^2 = 4$, then y could be
    (A) -5
    (B) -1
    (C) 0
    (D) 5
    (E) 9

20. 10% of 360 is how much more than 5% of 360?
    (A) 5
    (B) 9
    (C) 18
    (D) 36
    (E) 48

21. If $x^2 + 3x + 10 = 1 + x^2$, then $x^2 =$
    (A) 0
    (B) 1
    (C) 4
    (D) 7
    (E) 9

Questions 22–25 refer to the information in the graph on page 358.

22. In the year 1971, approximately how many vehicles that were purchased were imported?
    (A) 2.25 million
    (B) 6 million
    (C) 8.25 million
    (D) 14.25 million
    (E) 21 million

23. The percent increase in the average purchase price of a vehicle from 1950 to 1970 was approximately
    (A) 75%
    (B) 150%
    (C) 225%
    (D) 275%
    (E) 340%

24. In which of the following time periods was there the greatest increase in the total number of family-owned vehicles purchased?
    (A) 1950–1951
    (B) 1959–1960
    (C) 1960–1962
    (D) 1964–1966
    (E) 1971–1974

25. Between 1950 and 1974, the average number of vehicles owned per household increased by approximately what percent?
    (A) 1.1%
    (B) 2.2%
    (C) 50%
    (D) 100%
    (E) 220%

26. Which of the following must be true?

    I. Any two lines which are parallel to a third line are also parallel to each other.

PURCHASES OF FAMILY-OWNED VEHICLES IN COUNTRY X
(in millions of units)

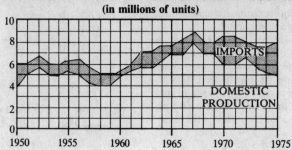

FINANCIAL FACTORS OF
FAMILY-OWNED VEHICLE PURCHASE

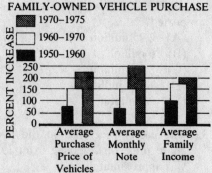

AVERAGE NUMBER OF VEHICLES
OWNED PER HOUSEHOLD

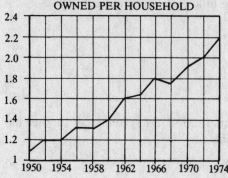

II. Any two planes which are parallel to a third plane are parallel to each other.

III. Any two lines which are parallel to the same plane are parallel to each other.

(A) I only
(B) II only
(C) I and II only
(D) II and III only
(E) I, II, and III

27. An item costs 90% of its original price. If 90¢ is added to the discount price, the cost of the item will be equal to its original price. What is the original price of the item?
(A) $.09
(B) $.90
(C) $9.00
(D) $9.90
(E) $9.99

28. In the figure below, the coordinates of the vertices A and B are (2,0) and (0,2), respectively. What is the area of the square ABCD?
(A) 2
(B) 4
(C) $4\sqrt{2}$
(D) 8
(E) $8\sqrt{2}$

29.

$\dfrac{n}{m} =$

(A) 12
(B) 12mn
(C) 12m + 12y
(D) 0
(E) mx + ny

30. In circle O shown to the right, MN > NO.
All of the following must be true EXCEPT
(A) MN < 2MO
(B) x > y
(C) z = y
(D) x = y + z
(E) x > 60°

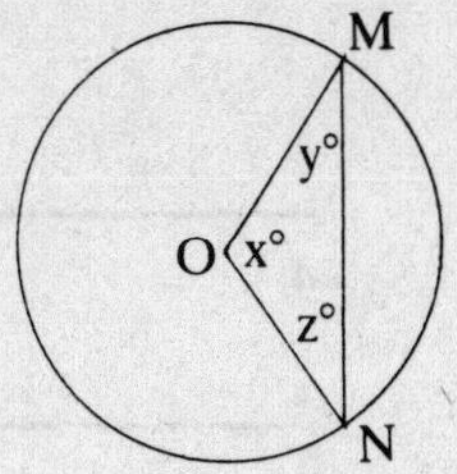

STOP

END OF SECTION. IF YOU HAVE ANY TIME LEFT, GO
OVER YOUR WORK IN THIS SECTION ONLY. DO NOT
WORK IN ANY OTHER SECTION OF THE TEST.

SECTION IV

30 minutes
30 questions

Directions: For each of the following questions two quantities are given, one in Column A and one in Column B. Compare the two quantities and mark your answer sheet with the correct lettered conclusion. These are your options:
  A: If the quantity in Column A is the greater;
  B: if the quantity in Column B is the greater;
  C: if the two quantities are equal;
  D: if the relationship cannot be determined from the information given.
Common Information: In any question, information applying to both columns is centered between the columns and above the quantities in columns A and B. The common information applies to both columns. Any symbol that appears in both columns represents the same idea or quantity in both columns.
Numbers: All numbers used are real numbers.
Figures: Assume that the positions of points, angles, regions and so forth are in the order shown. Figures are assumed to lie in a plane unless otherwise indicated. Figures accompanying questions are intended to provide information you can use in answering the questions. However, unless a note states that a figure is drawn to scale, you should solve the problems by using your knowledge of mathematics and *not* by estimating sizes by sight or measurement.
Lines: Assume that lines shown as straight are indeed straight.

COLUMN A	COLUMN B

1. $\qquad$ 10 $\qquad$ $\dfrac{1}{0.1} + \dfrac{0.1}{10}$

2. $l_1 \parallel l_2$

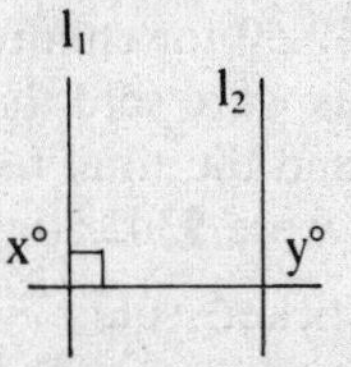

x $\qquad$ y

	COLUMN A	COLUMN B

3. $3 \times \frac{1}{3} \times 6 \times \frac{1}{6}$ $4 \times \frac{1}{4} \times 7 \times \frac{1}{7}$

---

4. $3x + 2 = 11$

x   2

---

5. $x > 0$ and $y > 0$

5% of x   5% of y

6.

5.1

x°   y° + z°

---

7. $\frac{x}{3} - 16 = 32$

$\frac{y}{4} + 12 = 24$

x   y

---

8. $x > 0$

$x(x + 3) + 2(x + 3)$ $(x + 3)^2$

---

9.   AB and CD are diameters of the same circle.

AC   BD

---

10. $1^{x - y} = 1$

x   y

11.

PQ   RP

---

12.   Tickets to a concert cost $5 for adults and $2.50 for children. 29 more adult tickets were sold than children's tickets, and the total receipts from ticket sales were $302.50.

the number of adult tickets sold   50

COLUMN A COLUMN B

13. the number of integer multiples the number of integer multiples
of 4 between 281 and 301 of 5 between 2401 and 2419

14.

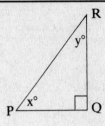

$$\frac{x°}{y°} = \frac{2}{1}$$

$\dfrac{PQ}{PR}$ $\qquad$ $\dfrac{1}{2}$

15.

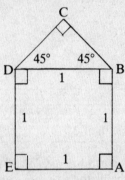

the area enclosed by polygon ABCDE $\qquad$ 1.25

Directions: For each of the following questions, select the best of the answer choices and blacken the corresponding space on your answer sheet.

Numbers: All numbers used are real numbers.

Figures: The diagrams and figures that accompany these questions are for the purpose of providing information useful in answering the questions. Unless it is stated that a specific figure is not drawn to scale, the diagrams and figures are drawn as accurately as possible. All figures are in a plane unless otherwise indicated.

16. $\frac{1}{5} - \frac{3}{4} =$
   (A) $-\frac{7}{9}$
   (B) $-\frac{3}{5}$
   (C) $-\frac{1}{20}$
   (D) $\frac{1}{20}$
   (E) $\frac{3}{5}$

17. Into how many line segments, each 2 inches long, can a line segment one and one-half yards long be divided?
   (A) 9
   (B) 18
   (C) 27
   (D) 36
   (E) 48

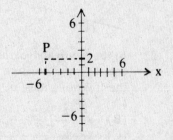

18. In the figure on the preceding page, the coordinates of point P are
    (A) (−5,−2)
    (B) (−5,2)
    (C) (−2,5)
    (D) (2,−5)
    (E) (5,2)

19. If circle O has a radius of 4, and if P and Q are points on circle O, then the maximum length of arc which could separate P and Q is
    (A) 8π
    (B) 4π
    (C) 4
    (D) 2π
    (E) 2

20. All of the following are prime numbers EXCEPT
    (A) 13
    (B) 17
    (C) 41
    (D) 79
    (E) 91

21. A girl at point X walks 1 mile east, then 2 miles north, then 1 mile east, then 1 mile north, than 1 mile east, then 1 mile north to arrive at point Y. From point Y, what is the shortest distance to point X?
    (A) 7 miles
    (B) 6 miles
    (C) 5 miles
    (D) 2.5 miles
    (E) 1 mile

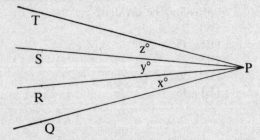

22. In the figure above, the measure of ∠QPS is equal to the measure of ∠TPR. Which of the following must be true?
    (A) x = y
    (B) y = z
    (C) x = z

(D) x = y = z
(E) none of the above

Questions 23–27 refer to the following graph:

QUARTERLY ANNUAL PROFIT RATES* FOR DEPARTMENT STORE X

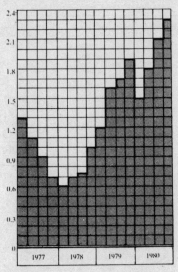

Millions of Dollars

*ANNUAL PROFIT RATE = 4× THE ACTUAL PROFITS MADE IN THAT QUARTER

23. Approximately what was the actual profit made by Department Store X in the second quarter of 1979?
    (A) $6.4 million
    (B) $1.6 million
    (C) $1.2 million
    (D) $0.4 million
    (E) $0.3 million

24. For the time period shown on the graph, in which of the following quarters did Department Store X make the least amount of profits?
    (A) third quarter of 1980
    (B) second quarter of 1979
    (C) first quarter of 1979
    (D) third quarter of 1978
    (E) second quarter of 1977

25. During the period 1978–1980, inclusive, how many quarters exceeded an annual profit rate of $1.5 million?
    (A) 6
    (B) 5

(C) 4
(D) 3
(E) 2

26. In the year 1980, total profit made by Department Store X was approximately
    (A) $30.2 million
    (B) $7.6 million
    (C) $1.9 million
    (D) $1.2 million
    (E) $.75 million

27. The total annual profit made by Department Store X increased by approximately what percent from 1977 to 1980 inclusive?
    (A) 40%
    (B) 50%
    (C) 90%
    (D) 120%
    (E) 150%

28. $4 - 3(2 + 1(3 - (2 + 3) + 2) + 2) + 4 =$
    (A) -4
    (B) 0
    (C) 2
    (D) 8
    (E) 12

29. Newtown is due north of Oscarville. Highway L runs 31° south of east from Newtown and Highway M runs 44° north of east from Oscarville. If L and M are straight, what is the measure of the acute angle they form at their intersection?
    (A) 105°
    (B) 89°
    (C) 75°
    (D) 59°
    (E) 46°

30. If a sum of money is divided equally among n children, each child will receive $60. If another child is added to the group, then when the sum is divided equally among all the children, each child will receive a $50 share. What is the sum of money?
    (A) $3000
    (B) $300
    (C) $110
    (D) $10
    (E) Cannot be determined from the information given.

STOP

END OF SECTION. IF YOU HAVE ANY TIME LEFT, GO
OVER YOUR WORK IN THIS SECTION ONLY. DO NOT
WORK IN ANY OTHER SECTION OF THE TEST.

SECTION V

30 minutes
25 questions

Directions: Each of the following questions or groups of questions is based on a short passage or a set of propositions. In answering these questions it may sometimes be helpful to draw a simple picture or chart. When you have selected the best answer to each question, darken the corresponding circle on your answer sheet.

Questions 1–4

To apply for a Dark Days Fellowship, a student must see the Dean of Students, fill out a financial statement, and obtain a thesis approval from either Professor Fansler or Professor Cross.

A student must see the Dean of Students before filling out the financial statement in order to make sure that it is filled out correctly.

The Dean of Students has office hours for students only on Thursday and Friday mornings, and Monday and Tuesday afternoons.

The Financial Aid Office, where the financial statement has to be filed in person, is open only Monday and Tuesday mornings, Wednesday afternoons, and Friday mornings.

Professor Fansler is in her office only on Monday and Tuesday mornings.

Professor Cross is in his office only on Tuesday and Friday mornings.

1. A student has already seen the Dean of Students and wishes to complete the rest of the application process in one day. If he must obtain his approval from Professor Fansler, when should he come to the campus?
   (A) Monday morning only
   (B) Tuesday morning only
   (C) Friday morning only
   (D) either Monday or Tuesday morning
   (E) either Monday, Tuesday, or Friday morning

2. If a student completed her application process in one visit, which of the following must be false?

   I. She got her thesis approved by Professor Cross.
   II. She got her thesis approved by Professor Fansler.
   III. She completed everything in the afternoon.

   (A) I only
   (B) II only
   (C) III only
   (D) I and III only
   (E) II and III only

3. If a student wanting to apply for a Dark Days Fellowship has classes only on Tuesdays and Thursdays and doesn't want to make an extra trip to the campus, which of the following is true?

   I. The thesis approval must be obtained from Professor Fansler.

II. The thesis approval must be obtained from Professor Cross.
III. The entire application process can be completed in one day.
IV. The entire application process can be completed within the same school week.

   (A) I and II only
   (B) II and III only
   (C) I, II, and III only
   (D) None of the statements is true.
   (E) All of the statements are true.

4. A student has already obtained thesis approval from Professor Fansler. She wishes to complete the application process in only one more visit. When can she do this?
   (A) Monday or Tuesday only
   (B) Monday, Tuesday, or Friday only
   (C) Friday morning only
   (D) any morning except Wednesday
   (E) any morning except Wednesday or Thursday

5. PROFESSOR: Under the rule of primogeniture, the first male child born to a man's first wife is always first in line to inherit the family estate.

   STUDENT: That can't be true; the Duchess of Warburton was her father's only surviving child by his only wife and she inherited his entire estate.

   The student has misinterpreted the professor's remark to mean which of the following
   (A) Only men can father male children.
   (B) A daughter cannot be a first-born child.
   (C) Only sons can inherit the family estate.
   (D) Illegitimate children cannot inherit their fathers' property.
   (E) A woman cannot inherit her mother's property.

6. As dietician for this 300-person school I am concerned about the sudden shortage of beef. It seems that we will have to begin to serve fish as our main source of protein. Even though beef costs more per pound

than fish, I expect that the cost I pay for protein will rise if I continue to serve the same amount of protein using fish as I did with beef.

The speaker makes which of the following assumptions?
(A) Fish is more expensive per pound than beef.
(B) Students will soon be paying more for their meals.
(C) Cattle ranchers make greater profits than fishermen.
(D) Per measure of protein, fish is more expensive than beef.
(E) Cattle are more costly to raise than fish.

Questions 7–9

The detective is following a subject who goes into a new seven-story office building. The detective doesn't want to risk sharing the elevator with the subject. Fortunately the building has a modern elevator panel which shows the location of the elevator and exactly to which up and down calls it is responding.

The subject got on the elevator with two other persons.

Each floor of the building has only one office, and it is not possible to use the stairway to go from floor to floor.

The elevator stopped on the third, fourth, fifth, and seventh floors. There were no calls for the elevator at those floors.

The elevator returned directly to the lobby from the seventh floor and was empty when it arrived.

7. If the detective assumes that the subject did not push more than one floor button or do anything suspicious in front of any witnesses, which of the following is the detective's safest conclusion?
(A) The subject got off at either the fifth or the seventh floor.
(B) The subject got off at the fourth, fifth, or seventh floor.
(C) The subject got off at the fifth floor.
(D) The subject got off at the fourth or fifth floor.
(E) The subject got off at the third or fourth floor.

8. If, on the next trip, the elevator stops at the second, third, and seventh floors going up, and the sixth floor coming down, on how many different floors must the detective consider checking for the subject?
(A) 6
(B) 5
(C) 4
(D) 3
(E) 2

9. The detective learns that one of the persons riding the elevator with the subject got out on the fourth floor, and someone else got in on that floor. On which floor(s) is(are) the subject(s) most likely to have gotten out?

  I.   the third floor
  II. the fourth floor
  III. the fifth floor
  IV. the seventh floor

(A) I and II only
(B) I, II, and III only
(C) I, II, and IV only
(D) III and IV only
(E) I, II, III, and IV

Questions 10–11

  I.   All wheeled conveyances which travel on the highway are polluters.
  II. Bicycles are not polluters.
  III. Whenever I drive my car on the highway, it rains.
  IV. It is raining.

10. If the above statements are all true, which of the following statements must also be true?
(A) Bicycles do not travel on the highway.
(B) Bicycles travel on the highway only if it is raining.
(C) If my car is not polluting, then it is not raining.
(D) I am now driving my car on the highway.
(E) My car is not a polluter.

11. The conclusion "my car is not polluting" could be logically deduced from statements I–IV if statement
(A) II were changed to: "Bicycles are polluters."

(B) II were changed to: "My car is a polluter."

(C) III were changed to: "If bicycles were polluters, I would be driving my car on the highway."

(D) IV were changed to: "Rainwater is polluted."

(E) IV were changed to: "It is not raining."

Questions 12–16

I. Some Z are not Y.
II. Some Y are not X.
III. Some X are not Z.
IV. All X are not Y.

12. Which of the following can be deduced from conditions I, II, and III?
    (A) There are no X that are both Y and Z.
    (B) Some X are not Y.
    (C) Some Z are not X.
    (D) Some Y are not Z.
    (E) None of the above.

13. Which of the following must be false, given conditions I, II, III, and IV?
    (A) There are no X that are neither Y nor Z.
    (B) There are no Z that are not X.
    (C) There are no X that are Z.
    (D) There are no Y that are Z.
    (E) None of the above.

14. Given the above conditions, which of the following conditions adds no new information?

    I. No Z are both X and Y.
    II. Some X are neither Z nor Y.
    III. Some Y are neither X nor Z.

    (A) I only
    (B) II only
    (C) III only
    (D) I and II only
    (E) I and III only

15. Which of the following is inconsistent with the given information?
    (A) Some Z are not X.
    (B) Some Y are not Z.
    (C) No X are not Z.

(D) No Y are not Z.

(E) All of the above are inconsistent with the given information.

16. If no Z are Y and no X are Z, which of the following must be false?
    (A) Some Z are neither X nor Y.
    (B) Some Y are neither X nor Z.
    (C) Some X are neither Y nor Z.
    (D) No Z are never X.
    (E) No Z are never non-Y.

Questions 17–22

The National Zoo has a very active panda bear colony. One day six of the pandas broke out of their compound and visited the seals. After they were returned to their compound, they were examined by the Panda-keeper. The following facts were recorded.

Bin-bin is fatter than Ging-ging and drier than Eena.
Col-col is slimmer than Fan-fan and wetter than Ging-ging.
Dan-dan is fatter than Bin-bin and wetter than Ging-ging.
Eena is slimmer than Ging-ging and drier than Col-col.
Fan-fan is slimmer than Eena and drier than Bin-bin.
Ging-ging is fatter than Fan-fan and wetter than Bin-bin.

17. Which of the pandas is (are) fatter than Eena and drier than Ging-ging?
    (A) Dan-dan only
    (B) Fan-fan only
    (C) Bin-bin only
    (D) both Fan-fan and Col-col
    (E) both Dan-dan and Bin-bin

18. Which of the pandas is both slimmer and wetter than Eena?
    (A) Ging-ging
    (B) Fan-fan
    (C) Dan-dan
    (D) Col-col
    (E) Bin-bin

19. Which of the following is (are) both fatter and wetter than Ging-ging?
    (A) Fan-fan

(B) Dan-dan
(C) Col-col
(D) Fan-fan and Col-col
(E) Eena and Dan-dan

20. Which of the following is the driest?
 (A) Col-col
 (B) Dan-dan
 (C) Eena
 (D) Fan-fan
 (E) Ging-ging

21. Which of the following statements must be false?

 I. Dan-dan is drier than Col-col.
 II. Fan-fan is wetter than Dan-dan.
 III. Dan-dan is three inches fatter than Ging-ging.

 (A) I only
 (B) II only
 (C) III only
 (D) I and II only
 (E) II and III only

22. A new panda, Yin-yin, is purchased from the Peking Zoo. If dominance in panda bears is determined by fatness, then what will Yin-yin's rank be if he is fatter than Fan-fan and slimmer than Bin-bin?
 (A) second from the top
 (B) third from the top
 (C) fourth from the top
 (D) next to the bottom
 (E) Cannot be determined from the information given.

23. In *The Adventure of the Bruce-Partington Plans,* Sherlock Holmes explained to Dr. Watson that the body had been placed on top of the train while the train paused at a signal.

 "It seems most improbable," remarked Watson.

 "We must fall back upon the old axiom," continued Holmes, "that when all other contingencies fail, whatever remains, however improbable, must be the truth."

 Which of the following is the most effective criticism of the logic contained in Holmes' response to Watson?

(A) You will never be able to obtain a conviction in a court of law.
(B) You can never be sure you have accounted for all other contingencies.
(C) You will need further evidence to satisfy the police.
(D) The very idea of putting a dead body on top of a train seems preposterous.
(E) You still have to find the person responsible for putting the body on top of the train.

24. Rousseau assumed that human beings in the state of nature are characterized by a feeling of sympathy toward their fellow humans and other living creatures. In order to explain the existence of social ills, such as the exploitation of man by man, Rousseau maintained that our natural feelings are crushed under the weight of unsympathetic social institutions.

Rousseau's argument described above would be most strengthened if it could be explained how
(A) creatures naturally characterized by feelings of sympathy for all living creatures could create unsympathetic social institutions
(B) we can restructure our social institutions so that they will foster our natural sympathies for one another
(C) modern reformers might lead the way to a life which is not inconsistent with the ideals of the state of nature
(D) non-exploitative conduct could arise in conditions of the state of nature
(E) a return to the state of nature from modern society might be accomplished

25. Judging by the architecture, I would say that the chapel dates from the early eighteenth century. Furthermore, the marble threshold to the refectory is worn to a depth of one and three-eighths inches at the middle. Since the facilities were designed to accommodate approximately forty monks, I estimate that the monastery was occupied for approximately seventy-five years before it was abandoned, and that date would coincide with the violent civil and religious wars of the first decade of the 1800's.

Which of the following is NOT an assumption made by the author in describing the dates of the buildings?

(A)   The marble threshold he studied is the same one originally included in the building.

(B)   Architectural features can be associated with certain historical periods.

(C)   The monastery he is investigating was nearly fully occupied during the time span in question.

(D)   There is a correlation between usage and wear of marble flooring.

(E)   Religious organizations have often abandoned outlying monasteries during times of political strife.

STOP

END OF SECTION. IF YOU HAVE ANY TIME LEFT, GO OVER YOUR WORK IN THIS SECTION ONLY. DO NOT WORK IN ANY OTHER SECTION OF THE TEST.

SECTION VI

30 minutes
25 questions

Directions: Each of the following questions or groups of questions is based on a short passage or a set of propositions. In answering these questions it may sometimes be helpful to draw a simple picture or chart. When you have selected the best answer to each question, darken the corresponding circle on your answer sheet.

Questions 1–3:

Five cats, F, G, H, J, and K, are being tested for three parts in a cat-food commercial. The on-camera cats must eat heartily and avoid fighting with each other. F is the best eater, but the most likely to fight. G and H eat best only when they are together, but fight with K.

1.   If J is sick and cannot perform, which of the following can be inferred about an attempt to film the commercial?

   I.   F, G, and H will do the commercial.
  II.   G and H will fight with each other.
 III.   The cats will likely fight during the filming.

(A)   I only
(B)   II only

(C)   III only
(D)   I and III only
(E)   I, II, and III

2.   If G and J go home, how many additional peaceful cats will be needed to fill out the cast?

(A)   0
(B)   1
(C)   2
(D)   3
(E)   The commercial cannot be successfully filmed.

3.   If F calms down and will no longer fight, how many different casts of cats are available?

(A)   1
(B)   2
(C)   3
(D)   4
(E)   5

4.   Which of the following activities would depend upon an assumption which is inconsistent with the judgment that you cannot argue with taste?

(A)   a special exhibition at a museum

(B) a beauty contest
(C) a system of garbage collection and disposal
(D) a cookbook filled with old New England recipes
(E) a movie festival

Questions 5–6

Stock market analysts always attribute a sudden drop in the market to some domestic or international political crisis. I maintain, however, that these declines are attributable to the phases of the moon, which also cause periodic political upheavals and increases in tension in world affairs.

5. Which of the following best describes the author's method of questioning the claim of market analysts?
   (A) He presents a counter-example.
   (B) He presents statistical evidence.
   (C) He suggests an alternative causal linkage.
   (D) He appeals to generally accepted beliefs.
   (E) He demonstrates that market analysts' reports are unreliable.

6. It can be inferred that the author is critical of the stock analysts because he
   (A) believes that they have oversimplified the connection between political crisis and fluctuations of the market
   (B) knows that the stock market generally shows more gains than losses
   (C) suspects that stock analysts have a vested interest in the stock market, and are therefore likely to distort their explanations
   (D) anticipates making large profits in the market himself
   (E) is worried that if the connection between political events and stock market prices becomes well known, unscrupulous investors will take advantage of the information

Questions 7–11

Farmer Brown has a large square field divided into nine smaller squares, all equal, arranged in three rows of three fields each. One side of the field runs exactly east-west.

The middle square must be planted with rice because it is wet.
The wheat and barley should be contiguous so that they can be harvested all at once by the mechanical harvester.
Two of the fields should be planted with soybeans.
The northwesternmost field should be planted with peanuts, and the southern third of the field is suitable only for vegetables.

Questions 7–9 refer to the following squares:
(A) the square immediately north of the rice
(B) the square immediately east of the rice
(C) the square immediately west of the rice
(D) the square immediately east of the peanuts
(E) the square immediately northeast of the rice

7. Which square cannot be planted with soybeans?

8. Which square cannot be planted with wheat?

9. If Farmer Brown decides to plant the wheat next to the peanuts, in which square will the barley be?

10. If the three southern squares are planted, from west to east, with squash, tomatoes, and potatoes, which vegetables could be planted next to soybeans?

   I. Squash
   II. Tomatoes
   III. Potatoes

   (A) I only
   (B) II only
   (C) III only
   (D) I and III only
   (E) I, II, and III

11. If Farmer Brown decides not to plant any peanuts or wheat, what is the maximum number of fields of vegetables that he could plant?
   (A) 3

(B) 5
(C) 6
(D) 7
(E) 8

Questions 12–15

  I. L, M, Z, and P are all possible.
 II. All M are L.
III. All L are Z.
IV. No M are Z.
 V. Some Z are L.
VI. No P are both M and L but not Z.

12. Which of the above statements contradicts previous ones?
(A) III
(B) IV
(C) V
(D) VI
(E) None of the statements contradicts previous statements.

13. If statements II and III are true, which of the other statements must also be true?
(A) IV only
(B) V only
(C) VI only
(D) IV and V only
(E) V and VI only

14. If X is an L, it must also be a(n)
(A) M only
(B) P only
(C) Z only
(D) L and Z only
(E) L, P, and Z

15. Given the above statements, which of the following must be false?
(A) There are some L's.
(B) Some Z are not L.
(C) There are some P's which are Z's but not M or L.
(D) There cannot be any Z's that are not L or M.
(E) None of the above are necessarily false.

Questions 16–22

Captain Mulhouse is choosing the last part of his crew for the sailboat *Fearsome*, with which he hopes to earn the right to defend the America's Cup. He needs four more crew members, of whom at least two must be grinders for the winches, with the others being sail trimmers.

The candidates for grinder are David, Erica, and Francis.
The candidates for trimmer are Larry, Mary, Nancy, and Paul.
Nancy will not crew with Paul.
Erica will not crew with Larry.
David will not crew with Nancy.

16. If Nancy is chosen, which of the following must be other members of the crew?
(A) David, Erica, and Mary
(B) Erica, Francis, and Larry
(C) Erica, Francis, and Mary
(D) Erica, Francis, and Paul
(E) Francis, Larry, and Mary

17. If Paul is chosen, which candidates will NOT be chosen to be on the crew?
(A) David, Erica, and Francis
(B) David, Erica, and Mary
(C) David, Francis, and Larry
(D) David, Francis, and Mary
(E) Erica, Francis, and Larry

18. Given the above statements about the relationships among the potential crew members, which of the following must be true?

  I. If David is rejected, then Mary must be chosen.
 II. If David is rejected, then Francis must be chosen.
III. If David is chosen, then Paul must also be chosen.

(A) II only
(B) III only
(C) I and II only
(D) I and III only
(E) II and III only

19. If Larry is chosen as a trimmer, which of the following could be the other members of crew?

  I. David, Francis, and Mary
 II. David, Francis, and Nancy
III. David, Francis, and Paul

(A) I only
(B) II only
(C) III only
(D) I and II only
(E) I and III only

20. Which of the following statements must be true?

   I. If Captain Mulhouse chooses Larry, then Francis must also be chosen.
   II. If Captain Mulhouse chooses Mary, then Nancy must also be chosen.
   III. If Larry is chosen, Nancy cannot be chosen.

   (A) I only
   (B) I and II only
   (C) I and III only
   (D) II and III only
   (E) I, II, and III

21. If Paul is chosen to be part of the *Fearsome*'s crew and David is not, who must be the other members of the crew?
   (A) Erica, Francis, and Larry
   (B) Erica, Francis, and Mary
   (C) Erica, Francis, and Nancy
   (D) Erica, Mary, and Nancy
   (E) Francis, Larry, and Mary

22. If Erica makes the crew and Francis does not, which of the following statements must be true?

   I. Paul will be a member of the crew.
   II. Mary will be a member of the crew.

   (A) both I and II
   (B) neither I nor II
   (C) I only
   (D) II only
   (E) either I or II, but not both

23. Since Ronnie's range is so narrow, he will never be an outstanding vocalist.

   The statement above is based on which of the following assumptions?

   I. A person's range is an important indicator of his probable success or failure as a professional musician.

   II. Vocalizing requires a range of at least two and one-half octaves.
   III. Physical characteristics can affect how well one sings.

   (A) I only
   (B) II only
   (C) I and III
   (D) III only
   (E) I, II, and III

24. MARY: All of the graduates from Midland High School go to State College.
    ANN: I don't know. Some of the students at State College come from North Hills High School.

   Ann's response shows that she has interpreted Mary's remark to mean that
   (A) most of the students from North Hills High School attend State College
   (B) none of the students at State College are from Midland High School
   (C) only students from Midland High School attend State College
   (D) Midland High School is a better school than North Hills High School
   (E) some Midland High School graduates do not attend college

25. All Burrahobbits are Trollbeaters, and some Burrahobbits are Greeblegrabbers.

   If these statements are true, which of the following must also be true?

   I. If something is neither a Trollbeater nor a Greeblegrabber, it cannot be a Burrahobbit.
   II. It is not possible to be a Trollbeater without being a Greeblegrabber.
   III. An elf must be either a Trollbeater or a Greeblegrabber.

   (A) I only
   (B) II only
   (C) I and II only
   (D) III only
   (E) I, II, and III

STOP
END OF SECTION. IF YOU HAVE ANY TIME LEFT, GO OVER YOUR WORK IN THIS SECTION ONLY. DO NOT WORK IN ANY OTHER SECTION OF THE TEST.

PRACTICE EXAMINATION 3—ANSWER KEY

Section I

1.	B	10.	D	19.	D	28.	D	37.	E
2.	C	11.	C	20.	E	29.	E	38.	B
3.	A	12.	B	21.	A	30.	E		
4.	C	13.	B	22.	C	31.	A		
5.	E	14.	D	23.	B	32.	A		
6.	B	15.	A	24.	B	33.	E		
7.	E	16.	C	25.	D	34.	D		
8.	A	17.	B	26.	E	35.	C		
9.	D	18.	C	27.	C	36.	D		

Section II

1.	B	10.	B	19.	D	28.	E	37.	D
2.	D	11.	C	20.	E	29.	B	38.	E
3.	E	12.	C	21.	D	30.	A		
4.	A	13.	D	22.	D	31.	C		
5.	C	14.	C	23.	C	32.	B		
6.	C	15.	A	24.	A	33.	B		
7.	A	16.	B	25.	B	34.	D		
8.	B	17.	D	26.	A	35.	B		
9.	C	18.	E	27.	E	36.	B		

Section III

1.	D	7.	C	13.	A	19.	D	25.	D
2.	A	8.	C	14.	B	20.	C	26.	C
3.	B	9.	C	15.	C	21.	E	27.	C
4.	D	10.	C	16.	D	22.	A	28.	D
5.	A	11.	B	17.	C	23.	E	29.	A
6.	C	12.	A	18.	C	24.	C	30.	D

Section IV

1.	B	7.	A	13.	A	19.	B	25.	A
2.	C	8.	B	14.	C	20.	E	26.	C
3.	C	9.	C	15.	C	21.	C	27.	C
4.	A	10.	D	16.	D	22.	C	28.	A
5.	D	11.	A	17.	C	23.	D	29.	C
6.	A	12.	C	18.	B	24.	D	30.	B

372

Section V

1.	D	6.	D	11.	E	16.	D	21.	B
2.	E	7.	B	12.	E	17.	C	22.	E
3.	D	8.	B	13.	A	18.	D	23.	B
4.	C	9.	E	14.	D	19.	B	24.	A
5.	C	10.	A	15.	C	20.	D	25.	E

Section VI

1.	C	6.	A	11.	B	16.	C	21.	B
2.	C	7.	E	12.	B	17.	E	22.	A
3.	C	8.	C	13.	C	18.	C	23.	D
4.	B	9.	E	14.	D	19.	E	24.	C
5.	C	10.	D	15.	D	20.	C	25.	A

EXPLANATORY ANSWERS

SECTION I

1. **(B)** As most people do not enjoy trouble, and as you can't interrogate it, we may logically conclude that they foresaw, or anticipated, trouble. A road doesn't grow into a path, nor does it collapse into one.

2. **(C)** The word waiter makes it clear that it is a dining situation that is being described. Thus, the crab will not be used to pelt, throw at, or resolve ourselves. This eliminates (A) and (D). (E) would also be a rather peculiar usage and should be eliminated. Between (B) and (C), the decision can be made by noting the structure of the sentence. The lobster is clearly the result of some act of the waiter. It is possible that the lobster is the embarrassment of the waiter, but more reasonable that it was his recommendation, especially since its being gone resulted in the eating of crab. Thus, (C) is the best choice.

3. **(A)** Derelict in this sense means empty, abandoned. Only people are bereaved or bereft. Bustling means busy and is thus incompatible with disuse.

4. **(C)** This sentence implies discord between the old-timers and the young mayor. Old-timers are likely to resent those officials who are trying to change, or reform, things.

5. **(E)** There may be many possible alternative fuel sources, but unless they are inexpensive, they won't affect the price of gas.

6. **(B)** Since the burden of the sentence is that the bacteria and viruses are the masters, (D) and (E) do not work because they do not describe a situation of virus mastery in the first blank. For the second blank, the idea that viruses and bacteria live off all other life, (B) is a good carrying through of the idea of mastery. (A) fails since companionship is not required by bacteria or provided them by humans or birds. (C) is second-best, but opportunity is rather general, and (B) describes just which opportunity is being offered and taken, thus (B) is the best answer choice.

7. **(E)** Since the author of the sentence is clearly a guard or something like that of the prisoners, he would expect some negative reaction from them. The word trepidation after the second blank is a contrast to the second blank and also describes the kind of feeling which was expected at first, but which the author finds disappointing now. Trepidation is alarm, or mild fear or unease; thus (E), fear, is best for the first blank. The second blank can be approached as either being the opposite of trepidation, which could be trust, again (E), or by asking what would best describe the result of a guard treating his prisoners with fairness. It is unlikely that a prisoner would ever love his guard or be loyal to him, though (B), (D), and (E) are all acceptable.

8. **(A)** The relationship between cat and mouse is predator to prey. (A) shows this same relationship between bird and worm. A dog may chase its tail, but not as a predator. A lion may on occasion kill a snake, but it is not its typical prey. (D) has the merit of evoking the idea of a cat-and-mouse game being hide and seek. Of course, it is the mouse (second element) which hides and the cat which seeks. A purely verbal relationship such as would be needed to justify choice (D) is absent from the GRE. Trap and cheese has no merit aside from the alleged fact that mice like cheese.

9. **(D)** A vanilla bean is the source of the flavoring vanilla. We thus have a product and a source, or original form. Ginger is a root. None of the other choices correctly state the source or form of the flavoring cited. Tabasco comes from peppers, as does chili. Mint and sage are leaves.

10. **(D)** Energy is something that is dissipated. Money is squandered. The linkage is strengthened by noting that dissipated has the idea that there was no beneficial result from the expenditure of energy. The same holds true for squander. (A) has no merit since recharging a battery is just the opposite of dissipating energy: it is collecting it and making it useful. (B) has some merit in that the result of splitting an atom is certainly the release and dissipation of a great deal of energy, but it is a process of splitting, which itself is not dissipating. (C) has a little real merit since eating food certainly results in the food being broken down and changed, but it is not intrinsically wasteful or lacking in purpose. (E)'s only merit is that a gas will likely dissipate after it is generated. This is totally inadequate.

11. **(C)** A nose is a part of a face that sticks out. A knob is a part of a door that also sticks out. The first guess at an analogy might say that a nose goes

374

on the face. This would fit all five of the answer choices and thus be good, but would need refinement. The next thing would be to look at the answer choices and see the different ways that the first item goes onto the second item. (A) and (D) have the first item go over and around the second item. (B) merely has the first item as an extension of the second. (E) has the first item as something that is on the surface of the second item, but does not particularly stick out, but rather clings closely to the surface. (C) is the relationship that relates to the original pair in the best way.

12. **(B)** A rifle is the typical weapon of a soldier, at least as a soldier would be understood today. A sword is a typical weapon of a knight. In approaching this problem it is clear that weapons are an issue, or at least tools. (E) is not a tool of the robber, but rather a tool against him, so that's out. (A) has a weapon in the first slot, but instead of the user of the weapon in the second slot, we find another weapon. This fails. (C) has a tool of the cowboy, but it is not the same as a rifle. It may be true that a horse is the cowboy's best friend and the rifle is the soldier's best friend, but that is no basis for an analogy question on the GRE. Marine and tank in (D) would be very nice, except that it is backward. This does not happen often, but it happens.

13. **(B)** Venison is the name for meat from a deer. Mutton is the name for meat from a sheep. (C) is simply wrong since veal is meat from a young cow, not a lamb, which is a young sheep. (E) is very weak since a stew can be made with any meat. (A) fails because both of the words are names for the same group of animals and not the name for the meat from those animals, which is pork. (D) is the second-best answer, since when you order a steak in a restaurant, you will get the meat of a steer. However, that is not the name of the meat of a steer, but of a particular cut of meat. Steer meat also comes in many other cuts. Thus, steak is not the name of a type of meat from a particular animal, and (B) is correct.

14. **(D)** Something that is ineffable cannot be known. Something that is baffling cannot be solved. (C) has some merit since one might say of a certain situation that it is frustrating because there is no release from it, but that is an awkward way of putting it and not really what frustrating means. In (B), one finds that a trick is puzzling, but that is positive in its connection, while the original analogy is negative. (E) has no real connection since the essence of a rage is not whether or not it is controllable. Similarly for genial and interesting. Thus, (D) is the answer.

15. **(A)** The first idea of the analogy between icing and cake would be either that the icing goes on the cake or that it is a part of the cake. All of the answer choices meet one of these criteria or both. (C) and (D) do not have any special merit because they are baking terms. On the contrary, if they were to work, they would have to be even tighter than some other, non-overlapping answer choice. (C) fails because baking is the process of making pastry, and cake is not a process here. Ice might cake up on some exposed part of a house or plane or something, but what is meant here is plain old icing on the cake. (D) fails because the apple is only in the pie and not on it. (E) would fail with the additional idea that the icing is a significant layer on top of the cake and the thickness of the print on the page is not something that is significant enough to come to our attention. No other answer choice but (A) has the idea of decoration and beauty that is implicit in the stem pair. One speaks of the icing on the cake as the last touch to making something just right. A veneer is a thin layer of beautiful wood that is laid over another material to make a beautiful finish or outside appearance. Unlike the ice in the pond, it is applied by people for a particular purpose. Thus, (A) is the best answer.

16. **(C)** Chalk is used to make marks on a blackboard. They are associated through the process of writing. (A) can be eliminated since a door and a handle are separate parts of the same operation or mechanism, but there is nothing that has one of them making a mark on the other. (C), (D), and (E) do have that marking idea. (B), like (A), is only a physical relationship and no process is invoked. (D) can be eliminated since its second item is the name of the process rather than the thing that is written upon. In contrasting (C) and (E), the major difference is the typical use of ink and paper for writing. While it is true that paper and ink are used for things other than writing, and paint can be used to write on a wall, these are not the typical uses which first come to mind. Thus, (C) is better than (E). One slight difficulty is that chalk is solid and thus is both the material deposited on the surface and the implement that is held. Pen and brush might do as well as ink and paint.

17. **(B)** The passage makes only one geographic reference, and that is to England, with the use of "this is the question" for England. Thus, (A), (C), and (D) are out. Since the author is doing a fairly modern analysis of the problems of distributing wealth, it is not likely that he lived in King Arthur's time. Hence, (B) rather than (E).

18. **(C)** (B), (D), and (E) are eliminated on the simple grounds that there is nothing in the passage on which to base them. The preference for (C) over (A) is not great, but can be arrived at by considering that what the author is advocating is paying less attention to the wages and the money part of the economy and more towards its ultimate ends. The denial of the virtue of money and the

implication that the rich are robbers (by analogy) also tend away from capitalism at least, if not toward socialism.

19. **(D)** (D) is included in the concluding sentence of the passage. (A) and (E) are specifically disputed in the passage, since it is the entire process that matters and not merely the pay rate or effort. (C) is not disputed, but is not emphasized either, while (B) is simply absent.

20. **(E)** The passage emphasizes that it is the ends of the productive process that are critical, thus giving some support to (E). (C) has some appeal since money as such is not too important to the author, but its uses are important. (A), (B), and (D) derive any attractiveness they may have solely from the relative obscurity of (E).

21. **(A)** While the author stops short of outright accusation of the rich as robbers, they are treated in much the same manner in the passage, which creates the analogy desired.

(E) is untrue. The author says that one might as well say the robber is a benefactor, or at least does no harm, but this is a way of disputing a statement, not agreeing with it.

(D) fails since the passage is generally opposed to waste, while (B) and (C) are incorrect because only dishonesty is mentioned in relation to business.

22. **(C)** The choice is between (A) and (C). (B) is of no interest to the author, while (D) is only acceptable for the last three words. (E) is relevant but far too general.

(A) refers to the last sentence and (C) refers to the sentences immediately after the posing of the great question. The distinction here is that (A) describes the great question for ALL members of society, while (C) describes the plight of the poor specifically.

23. **(B)** (B) is preferable because it is something that helps to provide the necessities of life—clean air and water, etc. (D) fails since it does not specify the job. (A) is not strong since weapons are generally destructive, though this is not impossible. (C) is less attractive than (B) since it has no stated positive value. The dislike of the rich would also enter into it. (E) is attractive since it is clear that this is something of which the author has done a great deal. It is clearly the second-best choice, but is not as good as (B) since there is no clear message in the passage as to the value of studying theory. If (D) specifically were the arousal of the laborer to his best interests, that might be even better than (B) since it would mean all would do good work and not just the one.

24. **(B)** (A) is attractive since the author certainly is not in favor of the rich or most of their works. However, his main point—the "main question for the poor"—is the use to which the resources of society are to be put. He will definitely see that it is waste and poor use of resources which lead to such problems as an energy shortage, since he has claimed that there will be enough of the good things if only everyone would work at the right things in the right way.

While (C) has the advantage of being a very simple and direct response to an energy shortage, we are looking for something in the passage to link to our answer, and there is really nothing to support the idea that the author wishes to see more mineral exploitation. On the contrary, he denigrates such activities.

(D) has no basis in the passage, but might appear to have the connection that the author does believe that there are enough resources to go around. Thus it might be mistakenly inferred that he would deny the shortage altogether. This is mistaken because the author says in the passage that all sorts of shortages and a despoiling of the environment are perfectly possible—even likely—if nothing is changed.

(E), like (A), is something the author might well like to do on general principles, but there is no immediate link to the question, especially not in preference to (B).

25. **(D)** Choices (A) and (E) are incorrect because neither oppression nor violence are mentioned or implied in the passage. Choices (B) and (C) are also incorrect; evolution and instinct are mentioned in the passage, but as supporting ideas rather than as the central theme. We are left with choice (D), which does relate the main idea—the concept of social order—which is mentioned or at least implied in almost every sentence.

26. **(E)** The author states in the second paragraph that "as social life changed, the worth and rights of each member in the larger group, of which he was a part, increased." Since the social groups grew from clans to civilizations, the largest social group mentioned in the choices was "modern cities." It can therefore be assumed that the greatest attention to rights and values will be found there.

27. **(C)** It is stated very clearly that "of all living creatures, only man has the capacity to interpret his own evolution as progress." Choices (A), (B), (D), and (E) are all characteristics of many living organisms and therefore would not be unique to man.

28. **(D)** Refractory means stubborn or unmanageable. (D) is a perfect opposite to that meaning of refractory. None of the other answer choices connects to this meaning.

29. **(E)** Adroit means expert in something, particularly manual or mental tasks. Awkward is a good

opposite to the manual dexterity meaning of adroit. Skillful is close to being a synonym. Sinister comes from the Latin root meaning left, and although adroit comes from the Latin root meaning right, they are not opposites in English.

30. **(E)** Palliate means to make less severe or bad. Worsen is a perfect opposite.

31. **(A)** Vilify means to heap insults on. (A), (B), and (D) all have some merit. (A) is better since insult and praise are perfect opposites. The use of the word sing might be somewhat confusing since it is an idiomatic usage and one would not sing insults, but one does sing praises. Presumably one would not do (B) or (D) if one was vilifying someone, but they are not direct opposites. (E) would be opposite something that meant accept totally, not vilify.

32. **(A)** Irascible means irritable, and sounds like it, too. Placid is a very good opposite since a placid **person is not easily disturbed. Fortuitous means fortunate; entrancing means able to put one into a** trance, presumably a trance of delight. Shameless is the only word, other than placid, which is a personality characteristic, but it is not the same sort of thing at all.

33. **(E)** Gelid means frozen. Boiling is a good opposite since these are the two normal extremes of water. Chilly means mildly cold and has a connection to gelid, but a good antonym will be the same thing in an opposite way and mildly cold (chilly) is not as good an opposite to very cold (gelid) as is very hot (boiling).

34. **(D)** Condign means deserved or fitting, particularly of a punishment. Undeserved is a rather precise opposite. Unguarded might echo the use of condign with punishments, but it is not correct.

35. **(C)** A punctilious person takes extreme care over all aspects of his duties. Careless is taking no care or even extremely poor care. Tardy, meaning late, tries to reach for the word punctual, but that means on the dot (punct-) in terms of time, while punctilious means up to the dot or mark in terms of care and completeness. Correct has no merit since it describes something that is done conscienciously or scrupulously, and thus is not opposite at all.

36. **(D)** Feckless means weak, ineffective, feeble, or worthless. Strong is opposite to one of the meanings (feeble). Fatuous means foolish and ineffective; fawning is to seek favor by servile behavior. Calm might have some appeal, but the connection is to the word reckless, not feckless.

37. **(E)** Insolent means boldly rude. Affable means polite. This is a good opposite, though a word meaning extremely polite would be even better. Sullen is more of a synonym than an antonym. Kind is a positive personality trait and insolence is a negative one, but that is never enough for an antonym. More precision is required.

38. **(B)** A serendipitous discovery is a desirable but unsought result. The degree of desirability is not the issue so much as the unplanned nature of the discovery. Thus, planned is an acceptable opposite, while evil is not. There is no moral connotation to serendipity. Regulated is probably the second-best answer choice and has real merit. However, regulated applies more to control than specifically to planning, and thus is not quite to the point.

SECTION II

1. **(B)** To say a pious religious home is redundant. Only (B) completes the thought and intent of the sentence.

2. **(D)** The objections mentioned must have been vocal to get them thrown out.

3. **(E)** A single wall implies that, formerly, there were other walls. That only one wall still stood is testimony, not tribute, to Nature's power. Evidence to is poor diction.

4. **(A)** Assuming that routine activity is not exhausting, it would be surprising to find yourself exhausted by it one day.

5. **(C)** (E) fails since pugilistic, in the second blank, is not the way to describe articles unless they are about boxing. (D) is also poor since we have no particular indication that the university is in the United States or the Americas. In considering the first blank, we might discount (B) on the grounds that among is hinting at a relationship between the various departments and futility is not a relationship word, while cooperation and competition are precisely that. In choosing between (A) and (C), we would have to ask whether competition would be more likely to breed angry articles or if cooperation would lead to interdisciplinary ones. Since we are talking about the departments of a university, interdisciplinary is very apt, while competition in a university need not yield angry articles. Thus, (C) is the best answer choice.

6. **(C)** The first blank is something that leads up to having a focus on specific stimuli. (E) is rather a poor lead-in to focus, but the others are all possible. For the second blank, (B) and (D) are inadequate since the other data would not be insulated without some statement of what they were insulated from, if indeed sensory data being

insulated makes any sense at all. Isolated would have worked, perhaps, but that is not present. Added up is also inadequate, though added might have been acceptable. In choosing between (A) and (C), we have to take the workings of the pair of words into account. In (A) the situation would be that the focus starts in one place and then other things are somehow increased by the focus being in one place. This is a little strange, but (C) is a perfectly reasonable situation. If the senses are designed for specific stimuli, then it would be most reasonable that other stimuli would fade. Hence, (C) is the best answer.

7. **(A)** If new behaviors are learned, then the likelihood is that the old behaviors are changed. Also, the situation of being in a new country would mean changes are needed. Thus, (A) and (D) are the best ways of filling in the first blank. The difference between (A) and (D) for the second blank could not be sharper. (A) says uncertain and (D) says definite. If one is learning new habits in a new country, it is more reasonable to speak of uncertainties presenting a problem than of definite results presenting a problem. Thus, (A) is the better answer choice.

8. **(B)** Embezzlement is the unlawful taking of money. Plagiarism is the unlawful taking of a writing. The idea of lawful and unlawful uses of things can create a number of special words, which make interesting analogy problems. (E) is the only other choice to have an unlawful idea, and murder is certainly unlawful death, but it is the giving of death, if you will, rather than the taking of it and thus does not conform to the original pair as well as (B). (A) links only to the idea of money and does not replicate any relationship from the original. (C) and (D) have no idea of unlawfulness. Thus, (B) is the best answer.

9. **(C)** A foil is a type of sword used in fencing. Gloves are a type of equipment used in boxing. (A) has merit since a pencil is used to mark, but (C) is just as good on that level and also carries the idea of sporting equipment. Likewise, (B) and (D) have some idea of the first word being a way of performing the second, but it is not as good as (C). (E) does have an idea of sporting equipment, but the activity referred to in the second word, bending, is done to the bow and not with it and is not the sport itself.

10. **(B)** Climb is what one does to a tree in order to get to the top of it. Ascend is the word that is used to describe the climbing of a cliff. Scale could also be used, but it isn't here. The other answer choices, except (C), are also fairly typical actions performed with or to the objects mentioned in the second position. However, they lack the additional idea of being a way of getting to the top of

the item mentioned. (C) lacks even that and hence fails totally. Thus, (B) is the best answer.

11. **(C)** Cub is the name given to a young lion. Child is the name given to a young human. A drake is a male duck, and a vixen is a female fox. Rooster is a male chicken. Mother and daughter are only different in age, but have the similarity of belonging to the same family, which a lion and cub do not necessarily do.

12. **(C)** A room is a part of a house and in particular it is usually a living unit of the house. A cabin is a living unit of a ship. (A), (B), and (D) all have the idea of the first item being in the second one, but they are not constituent parts in the way a house is made up of a number of rooms. (C) and (E) both have the idea of the first item's being spaces inside the second item. However, a cabin is a living space and a cockpit is not; thus, (C) is the best answer.

13. **(D)** "Great oaks from little acorns grow," and tulips grow from bulbs. (A) and (C), while relationships between living things, are not the seed to the final plant. (B) and (E) also lack the idea of the seed, though they do have the merit of having the leaf or flower grow out of the stalk or branch. (B) and (E) would make a reasonable analogy with each other, but not with the given stem pair. Thus, (D) is the best answer.

14. **(C)** Sorrow is the appropriate and typical feeling accompanying a death. Happiness is the appropriate and typical feeling accompanying birth. In each case the feeling is felt by others than the dead or new-born person, of course. None of the other answer choices has a feeling and an event appropriate to the feeling. Indeed, none of the others has any event at all.

15. **(A)** The leftovers after an explosion is debris. The leftovers after a fire are ashes. As a first approximation, one might have tried the idea of the first item leading to or causing the second item. (C) does not fit this concept and is eliminated. (D) does but is backward. The leftovers from a flood, (B), are more properly the flotsam and jetsam deposited about the landscape rather than the water itself, which *is* the flood. In distinguishing (A) from (E), the decisive issue is that in the original pair and in (A), the second item is a waste product, while in (E) the burn is a resulting hurt. One would throw out debris and ashes, but one would not throw out the burn.

16. **(B)** A solecism is a violation of the rules of good speech, including the rules of grammar. A foul is a violation of the rules of a game. (A) refers to the end of a marriage, not a mistake or a violation of the rules, and so is not adequate. In (E), apostasy is the total desertion of some dogma, but not an error under the rules of the dogma; or if it is an

error, it is so severe as to be in a different class than solecism. In (C), incest is certainly a violation of the normal rules of how a family should operate, but the word family does not refer to the *rules* of family life. Mores might have worked, but it is not present. (B) and (D) are both clearly errors. However, the difference between them is that the stumble is an error in doing the act of running, while a foul is an error in following the rules of something. Since a solecism can be an error in following the rules of grammar, (B) is the better answer.

17. **(D)** As the author states that the principle of tolerance must be accepted by both parties, his attitude toward civil disobedience is not one of hostility or contempt. Answers (C) and (E), then, are wrong. Choice (A) is also incorrect, as is choice (B), since the author does not totally admire civil disobedience. (D) is the best answer.

18. **(E)** The use of the word apartheid, which refers to the principles of racial separation practiced in South Africa, is not particularly relevant to answering the question. The focus of the passage is that civil disobedience is only proper when the laws broken are themselves the main focus of dissent. The incidental breaking of laws is not proper since there could be actions that spill over from the dissent into other areas of improper action. While the situation posed in the question stem does not specifically relate to the breaking of a law, the procedural concerns of the author are the ones that must be carried forward into the new situation. Therefore (E), which projects that the author would disapprove of the harm to innocent bystanders, is quite in accord with the focus in the passage on making sure that the actions of dissent are sharply focused on their object.

(A) and (D) are certainly not correct since the author has not indicated anything which would indicate to us his views about the issue at hand. Indeed, the issue being protested is not relevant to the author. It is true that he believes that only affronts to fundamental human values are the proper subject of civil disobedience, but we are not being asked to make such judgments, only to judge the procedural issues raised in the passage. Thus, (A) and (D) fail.

(B) is wrong since there is no basis on which to say that the author has or would have any opinion about the location of any business. On the contrary, the businesses are portrayed as the innocent bystanders (if the question says they are innocent bystanders, then they are innocent bystanders).

(C) is the converse of (E) and fails for all the reasons that (E) succeeds. The only merit of (C) is that it uses the word tolerant, which is certainly dear to the heart of the author. But the mere appearance of a word is not enough to make an answer correct.

19. **(D)** On structural grounds, (D) should be the answer choice to which you give first attention, quite apart from any matter of content. All four of the other answer choices are very strong statements with cannot or necessary. (D), on the other hand, only says "sometimes," which is much weaker.

(A) fails on grounds of meaning, since all civil disobedience is, by definition, illegal, and yet it is sometimes acceptable when it is done for the proper purposes and in the proper way.

(C) fails on careful reading since it is stating that the dissenters cannot use civil disobedience in a particular way, and the fact of the matter is that they can use it in any way they wish, but the author disapproves of their using it in this way.

(B) and (E) are the sort of statements that are hard to quarrel with, but they are not particularly relevant to this passage. The only requirement that the author imposes on the just society is that it be tolerant. This may not mean that it does or can accept immoral actions, whatever accept might amount to, but it certainly does not mean that the just society cannot accept these actions. (E) has problems with the idea of many authorities, since this is unclear from the passage, and, even more importantly, has the word free. There is absolutely nothing of any kind in the passage about a free society, but only about a just one. There may be a connection between the two ideas, but it is not made in the passage and thus we should not make it unless it is inescapable, which it isn't.

20. **(E)** (D) is of no interest to the author. (A), (B), and (C) are topics mentioned in the passage, but only as serving the general analysis of the Planning Commission's proposal. Thus, (E) is more descriptive of the actual passage.

21. **(D)** The author's argument essentially states that the commission may be right as far as it goes, but it is not that simple. This implies that the commission has been shortsighted. It is true that because of the shortsightedness, the author views the plan as foolish, and perhaps somewhat ignorant, but these derive from the shortsightedness, and the tone is respectful rather than condemnatory. (A) and (B) have no basis.

22. **(D)** (A) is attractive, but the word complete kills it. The author is clearly unsure of the number of beds that should be closed and sees that as a future issue. (B) and (C) fail for the same reason. (E) sounds good, but is not really mentioned.

23. **(C)** All of the statements are agreeable to the author, but (C) is specifically stated by the passage not to be properly addressed in the context of the commission's proposal. Because of (A) and (E), large hospitals may not be more efficient. (B) and (D) are both reasons why small hospitals should not be closed.

24. **(A)** (A) is only half agreeable. The author states the larger centers provide more complex care, and if the larger hospitals do not provide the most efficient care—as the author claims they don't— then it is certainly probable that they do not definitely provide the better care than smaller hospitals of the sort that can be received at both kinds of facilities.

    (B) is inferable from the statement that only overall costs are used to set rates. (C) is inferable from the author's support of the existence of institutions that can only provide that sort of care, while also supporting quality. (D) is stated to be a possible problem. (E) is inferable from the concern shown for greater or lesser access in the third and fifth paragraphs.

25. **(B)** The author knows that he cannot simply say to the commission that they shouldn't close the smaller hospitals. He must present evidence that it is not the best approach to the agreed-upon goal of saving money and closing unneeded beds— hence, (B). (A) is false since closing beds is agreed to by the author. (C) is true, but not as precise as (B); also the word another is troublesome since it is actually an alternative which is proposed. (D) is not currently at issue. (E) is appealing, but the inefficiencies of larger hospitals are not stated to be in the use of space.

26. **(A)** Prisons are, in a manner of speaking, service organizations (like hospitals), and thus very large ones may not be more efficient, according to the author; thus, (A). (B) is probably just what the author wants, since he is unsure of the number of beds that should be closed anyway. (C) is stated to be agreeable to the author in the last paragraph. (D) and (E) are indeterminable. There is no basis for agreement or disagreement given in the passage.

27. **(E)** The concern about possible *over*-centralization of ambulatory services is raised in the context of the proposal to close portions of the larger hospitals rather than the entirety of smaller hospitals. This juxtaposition of the two means that the author believes that closing parts of the larger hospitals might have the poor result of turning over so much space in those locations to ambulatory care that a disproportionate part of the ambulatory care system would reside at the larger hospitals. His use of the prefix over- indicates disapproval.

    The only references to the costs of ambulatory care are to its chaos and to some needs to keep it down. This implies a concern by the author that ambulatory care costs might increase, not that they might be decreased. Hence, (A) fails.

    (B) and (C) refer to connections that are not in the passage. The author refers to increasing the facilities for ambulatory services, but not to increasing the demand, which he seems to think is there already. If you answered (C), you are answering from current events and not from the passage.

    (D) has the appeal of being something that the author would probably like to have happen, but it is not implicit in the passage that the Planning Commission has the power to bring it about, and he certainly does not ask it. Rather, the force of the argument about the use of the space left by the closed portions of larger medical centers is that this space would certainly not go to waste.

28. **(E)** Fetid means having a bad or offensive odor; thus, (E) is a very good opposite. Embryonic means not yet born or fully developed.

29. **(B)** Illusory means based on an illusion, thus not realistic. Nimble means agile and physically well coordinated.

30. **(A)** Dour means gloomy or sullen, and gay is an excellent opposite. Sweet plays on the idea of sour, which does have some real merit since a dour disposition can also be referred to as sour. However, since we are speaking of personalities, gay is a better opposite to dour/sour than is sweet, since a sweet disposition is not so much cheerful as amiable or gracious. They are fairly close, however.

31. **(C)** Mendacious means lying and untruthful, so (C) is a perfect opposite. Broken plays on the mend- part of the word, as does destructive. Efficacious means efficient and effective.

32. **(B)** Enervate means to weaken significantly. Fortify means to strengthen. Debilitate means to weaken and is essentially a synonym, rare on the GRE as an answer choice.

33. **(B)** Discrete means separate, as in three discrete parts. One thing that you know about the word is that it is NOT discreet, which means tactful and quiet, thus (A) and (C) are incorrect. Combined is a good opposite, if not perfect.

34. **(D)** Primitive means basic, undeveloped, but not necessarily strong: thus, (C) is incorrect. Similarly, (A) is not connected. The other three answer choices are all referring to various levels of development of different ideas. The contrast between the answer choices shows that naive is a low level of development of understanding of the way things work, and is thus more of a synonym than an opposite. Sophisticated has to do with a highly developed understanding of something, while knowledgeable has to do with having a great deal of knowledge about something. Thus, sophisticated has the connotation of great development, which corresponds to the sense of primitive as having very little development.

35. **(B)** Partition means to divide into parts. Both (A) and (B) have some meaning of joining together, which is opposite to partition. In distinguishing solidify from unify, you might ask what the opposite of solid is. Since the opposite of solid is liquid, and partition refers to dividing into parts rather than liquefying, solidify is not correct. Parse means to separate into parts grammatically and is thus either the same as the stem word, or unrelated. Maintain is also unrelated. Enjoin is a word that has a superficial appeal since joining is what is wanted in an answer. However, enjoin means to legally forbid something from happening.

36. **(B)** Clandestine means secret, private, or concealed, usually on purpose. (A), (B), and (C) all have some merit. Outside, by itself, is not the opposite of hidden. Aboveground and public are therefore the two best answers, and both have a real oppositeness to clandestine. In choosing between them, the key factor is the very specific way in which aboveground works versus the more general meaning of public. The perfect opposite to aboveground is underground, which certainly means hidden, but public specifically means that it is revealed. Underground/aboveground refers more to the legitimacy of the activity—can it stand the light of day?—than to whether it is hidden or not. While it is true that clandestine activities by certain groups have, in recent years, been characterized as illicit, that is not part of the original meaning of the word clandestine. The shady flavor comes from the idea that a clandestine activity may be kept hidden by deception.

37. **(D)** Phlegmatic means cooly self-possessed and undemonstrative. Effusive means to make a great demonstration of feeling. Hoarse connects to the idea of phlegm in the throat, which might make one hoarse, but that is not helpful here.

38. **(E)** Manumit means to free a slave; hence enslave is a perfect opposite.

SECTION III

1. **(D)** Since we do not know for how long either car travelled, we cannot draw any conclusion about how far the cars travelled. For example, if both travelled for an equal amount of time, then car B will have travelled farther. But if car B travelled for one hour while car A travelled for two hours, then car A would have travelled farther (60 miles versus 40 miles).

2. **(A)** The number 46 is equal to 4(10) plus 6. The number 3612 is equal to 3(1000) plus 6(100) plus 1(10) plus 2. So there are four tens in 46, and there are three thousands in 3612, so our answer must be (A).

3. **(B)** Since 7.636 is greater than 7.635, the numbers following the third-place digit (5) are irrelevant to the comparison. No matter how far the decimal on the left is extended, it will never reach 7.636.

4. **(D)** Although BD is perpendicular to AC, we should not conclude that it bisects AC:

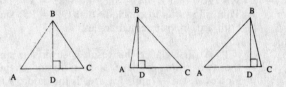

These configurations are consistent with the information given in the problem and show that no conclusion about AD and DC is possible.

5. **(A)** Probably the easiest way to solve this problem is to perform the indicated operations:

$$\frac{12}{2} = 6 \qquad \frac{12}{4} = 3$$

So Column A is greater than Column B.

6. **(C)** Since the dimensions of this triangle are 3, 4, and 5, it must be a right triangle: $5^2 = 4^2 + 3^2$. The converse of the Pythagorean Theorem (the square of the hypotenuse of a right triangle is equal to the sum of the squares of the two other sides) is that any triangle in which the square of the longest side is equal to the sum of the squares of the two remaining sides is a right triangle. Since this is a right triangle and 5 is the longest side, 5 must be opposite a 90° angle. The two remaining angles must total 90° since there are 180° in any triangle. Since x is 90° and z + y = 90°, the two columns are equal.

7. **(C)** Rather than actually doing the calculation (that is, multiplying 30 by 30 and then converting the measurements in Column B to inches and multiplying them), the problem is more easily solved by recognizing that the sides of the two squares are equal in length. 2 feet 6 inches is equal to 30 inches. Since both have equal sides, and since the area of a square is solely a function of the length of its side (s × s = area), our two squares must be equal in area.

8. **(C)** Since vertical angles are equal, we know that a = z, b = y, and c = x. Therefore, a + b + c must be equal to x + y + z.

9. **(C)** The proper way of approaching this question is to fill in the blanks in the figure:

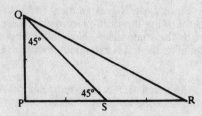

We know that x = 45°, since 90° + 45° + x = 180°. That allows us to conclude that QP = PS, since both are opposite equal angles.

10. **(C)** At first glance this result is surprising since the two triangles have such different shapes. However, the formula for area is the guide. Area is equal to height times base divided by 2. If the height and base are equal, then the area will be equal. PS = SR, so the bases are equal. The heights are equal since the line PQ is a measure of the height of both triangles since it is the perpendicular distance from Q to the base of both triangles.

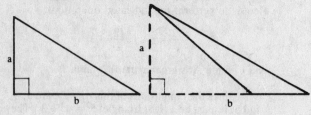

Since the triangles have bases *and* altitudes of equal length, their areas too must be equal—despite the fact that they have different shapes.

11. **(B)** Since there are 24 hours in a day, 16 hours represents $\frac{16}{24}$ of a day, or $\frac{2}{3}$. Then, since there are 60 minutes in an hour, 45 minutes represents $\frac{45}{60}$ of an hour, or $\frac{3}{4}$. Since $\frac{3}{4}$ is larger than $\frac{2}{3}$, our answer choice is (B).

12. **(A)** The three greatest odd integers less than 20 are 19, 17, 15; the even ones less than 20 are 18, 16, 14. You could add them up to get 51 in Column A and 48 in Column B. But why bother? 19 > 18, 17 > 16, and 15 > 14, so the odds have it.

13. **(A)** We already know Debbie's average rate per hour; that is given in the centered information as 7.2 miles/hour. How, then, are we to compute the rate for Roberta? One way, among many others, of doing this is to set up a direct proportion:

$$\frac{1 \text{ mile}}{7.2 \text{ minutes}} = \frac{x \text{ miles}}{60 \text{ minutes}}$$

This is the mathematical way of writing "If Roberta runs 1 mile every 7.2 minutes, then she can run x miles in 60 minutes." Arithmetically, we then cross-multiply to solve for x:

$$7.2x = 60$$
$$x = 8.33$$

So Roberta's speed is greater than Debbie's, and (A) must be the answer.

14. **(B)** The best approach to this problem may be to set up a number line.

A's grade is higher than that of B.

B's grade is higher than that of C.

D's grade is less than that of C.

E's grade is less than that of D.

This shows us that A's grade is the greatest and E's is the least. So Column B must be greater than Column A.

15. **(C)** This is a rather difficult problem. But the difficulty is not in the starting—it lies between the starting and the finishing. There is really only one starting point, and that is to manipulate the centered equation to find x, since x is what we are asked about:

$$x = \frac{1}{4}\left(3x + \frac{8}{x^2}\right)$$

Multiplying by 4: $4x = 3x + \frac{8}{x^2}$

Subtracting 3x: $x = \frac{8}{x^2}$

Multiplying by x^2: $x^3 = 8$
So: $x = 2$

Since x = 2, the two columns must be equal. There is yet another note to be made. Since this was a difficult problem, it might have been wise to skip it in order to get on to the remaining fifteen problems in the section. It would have been a mistake to spend 4 or 5 minutes trying to solve this item, when the questions which follow are much easier.

16. **(D)** Of course, one sure method for comparing the fractions is to convert each to its decimal equivalent and then to compare the equivalents directly. That process, however, will surely be too time-consuming, and is, in any event, totally unnecessary. The "test-wise" approach to a problem of this sort is to find a benchmark by which each of the fractions can be measured. In this case, it appears that $\frac{1}{2}$ will do nicely. We can then see that $\frac{3}{5}$, $\frac{2}{3}$, $\frac{17}{29}$, and $\frac{4}{5}$ are all greater than $\frac{1}{2}$, while $\frac{3}{7}$ is less than $\frac{1}{2}$. So $\frac{3}{7}$ must be the smallest of the group.

17. **(C)** The formula for the area of a square is *side times side*. Since the square has an area of 16, we know s × s = 16, s² = 16, so side = 4. Then we compute the perimeter of the square as the sum of the lengths of its four sides: 4 + 4 + 4 + 4 = 16.

18. **(C)** Since John has more money than Mary, we note that x is greater than y. Then, John has less money than Bill has, so x is less than z. This gives us x > y or y < x and x < z. Thus (C), y < x < z.

19. **(D)** One way to attack this question is to multiply the expression $(x - y)^2$ and then substitute the value 3 for x. $(x - y)^2 = 4$, so $x^2 - 2xy + y^2 = 4$. Then, if x = 3, we have $(3)^2 - 2(3)y + y^2 = 4$, or $9 - 6y + y^2 = 4$. Now we rewrite that in standard form (grouping like terms and arranging terms in descending order of exponents): $y^2 - 6y + 5 = 0$. At this juncture, the mathematicians will factor the expression on the left: $(y - 5)(y - 1) = 0$. Thus, the two roots of the equation are 5 and 1. So, 5 is a possible value.

Of course, a non-mathematical attack is also possible. We know that one of the five answers must be correct. So, we can simply try each one until we find one that will fit in the equation. For this we begin by putting 3 in for x: $(3 - y)^2 = 4$. We then test (A): $(3 - -5)^2 = (8)^2 = 64$ and 64 ≠ 4, so we know that −5 is not a possible value for y. On the other hand, if we try (D): $(3 - 5)^2 = (-2)^2 = 4$, and 4 does equal 4. We have taken a shortcut here by not working each of the answer choices.

20. **(C)** There are several ways of running the calculation for this problem. One way is to reason: 10% of 360 is 36. Since 5% is one half of 10%, 5% of 360 is one half of 36, or 18. Since 10% of 360 is 36, and since 5% of 360 is 18, the difference between the two is 36 − 18 = 18.

21. **(E)** Again, perhaps the most natural starting point for a solution is working on the expression, rearranging by grouping like terms. $x^2 + 3x + 10 = 1 + x^2$. By transposing (subtracting from both sides) the x^2 term, we see that the x^2 is eliminated:

$$3x + 10 = 1, \text{ so } 3x = -9, \text{ and } x = -3$$

Although the x^2 term was eliminated from our initial expression, we know the value of x. It is now a simple matter to substitute −3 for x in the expression x^2, and we learn $x^2 = 9$.

22. **(A)** The question tests whether you understand how to read the chart. This chart is cumulative. By that we mean that the number of imports is added to the number of domestic vehicles. In 1971, 6 million domestic vehicles were purchased. Then, the number of imports is the *difference* between 6 million (the top of the domestic-production part of the chart) and 8.25 million (the top of the import-production part of the chart). 8.25 − 6 = 2.25 million. The number 8.25 million is the *combined total* of import and domestic cars.

23. **(E)** For the information necessary to answer this question, we consult the Financial Factors graph. The left-hand grouping of bars shows us the *Percent Increase* in the average purchase price. From 1950 to 1960, the average purchase price rose by 75%. Then, from 1960 to 1970, it rose by another 150%. Given this, we can compute the total percent increase. Now, it would be an error simply to add these two numbers together. The 150% increase starts from a larger *base* than does the 75% increase. Suppose that the average purchase price in 1950 is x (or, for the non-mathematicians, we might just assume a nice round number such as $100). Then, from 1950 to 1960, that number increased by 75%. Since 75% of x is .75x, the increase was .75x (or 75% of $100 or $75), bringing the average price up to 1.75x (or $100 + $75 = $175). Then we have another 150% increase on top of the 1.75x. 150% of 1.75x is 2.625x (or $262.50), which must then be added to the 1.75x (or $175). This brings the average price to approximately 4.40x (or $440). We started with an average purchase price of x ($100); we ended with an average purchase price of 4.40x ($440). So we can now compute the percentage increase. Percentage increase is found by taking the difference between the two values and forming a fraction, placing the difference over the earlier total: $\frac{4.40x - x}{x} = \frac{3.40x}{x} = 3.40$. Then the 3.40 is converted from a decimal to a percentage by multiplying by 100, so the total percentage increase is 340%.

24. **(C)** For this question we use the method of compare and eliminate. From 1950 to 1951, purchases increase by slightly less than 1 million. Then, from 1959 to 1960, purchases also grew by slightly less than 1 million. But instead of trying to refine our comparison at this point, let us place both (A) and (B) on the back burner, and then we can check the remaining choices to see whether one of them is larger than both (A) and (B). We move to (C), and the increase in vehicles purchased was about 1½ million. So we can eliminate both (A) and (B), and we did that without trying to be very precise about the value for (A) and (B). Then we move to (D). From 1964 to 1966 purchases appear to have risen by just about one million, so we eliminate (D) from consideration, preserving (C) as our best choice thus far. Finally, we check (E). From 1971 to 1974 the total actually declined, so (C) must be our answer.

25. **(D)** We explained the method for computing percentage increase when we examined question 23 of this series. We create a fraction using the

difference between the two totals as the numerator and the earlier total as the denominator. Here the average number of vehicles owned increases from about 1.1 in 1950—notice the chart does not begin at zero—to 2.2 in 1974. The difference between 2.2 and 1.1. is 1.1, and the earlier total is 1.1, so our fraction is $\frac{1.1}{1.1} = 1$. Then we multiply that decimal number by 100 to convert to a percentage: $1 \times 100 = 100\%$.

26. **(C)** Proposition I is true. It is the geometry theorem that two lines parallel to a third must be parallel to each other.

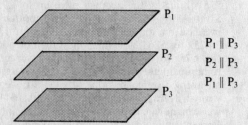

$l_1 \parallel l_2$
$l_3 \parallel l_2$
$\therefore l_1 \parallel l_3$

Proposition II is also necessarily true. Just as with lines, if two planes are parallel to a third plane, they must likewise be parallel to each other.

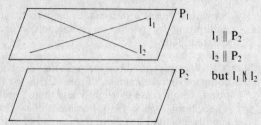

P_1
P_2
P_3

$P_1 \parallel P_3$
$P_2 \parallel P_3$
$P_1 \parallel P_3$

Proposition III, however, is not necessarily true. Two lines might be drawn in a plane parallel to another plane and yet intersect with one another:

P_1
l_1
l_2
P_2

$l_1 \parallel P_2$
$l_2 \parallel P_2$
but $l_1 \nparallel l_2$

27. **(C)** We all know the simple formula that price minus discount equals discounted price—that much is just common-sense arithmetic. What we sometimes overlook, however, is the fact that the discounted price can be expressed either in monetary terms, e.g., $5.00 or 37¢, or in percentage terms, e.g., 50% of the original price. In this case, the discount is given as a percentage of the original price. So we have, original price − 90¢ = 90% of original price; or, using x for the original price: $x − \$.90 = .9x$. This is an equation with only one variable, so we proceed to solve for x: $.1x = \$.90$, so $x = \$9.00$.

28. **(D)** We begin by computing the length of the side of the square ABCD. Since the x and y axes meet on the perpendicular, we have a right triangle formed by the origin (the point of intersection of x and y) and points A and B. Since point A has the coordinates (2,0), we know that OA is two units long—the x coordinate is 2. Similarly, point B is two units removed from O, so OB is also two units long. Thus, the two legs of our right triangle are 2 and 2. Using the Pythagorean Theorem:

$$2^2 + 2^2 = s^2, \text{ so } s = \sqrt{8} = 2\sqrt{2}$$

Now that we have the length of the side, we compute the area of ABCD by side × side: $(2\sqrt{2})(2\sqrt{2}) = 8$.

29. **(A)** This problem is particularly elusive since there is no really clear starting point. One way of getting a handle on it is to manipulate the expression $\frac{x}{y} + \frac{n}{m}$. If we add the two terms together using the common denominator of my, we have $\frac{mx + ny}{my}$. We can see that this bears a striking similarity to the first equation given in the problem: mx + ny = 12 my. If we manipulate that equation by dividing both sides by my, we have $\frac{mx + ny}{my} = 12$. But since $\frac{x}{y} + \frac{n}{m}$ is equivalent to $\frac{mx + ny}{my}$, we are entitled to conclude that $\frac{x}{y} + \frac{n}{m}$ is also equal to 12.

30. **(D)** This problem, too, is fairly difficult. The difficulty stems from the fact that its solution requires several different formulas. For example, we can conclude that (A) is necessarily true. MN is not a diameter. We know this since a diameter passes through the center of the circle. So whatever the length of MN, it is less than that of the diameter (the diameter is the longest chord which can be drawn in a circle). Since 2MO would be equal to a diameter (twice the radius is the diameter), and since MN is less than a diameter, we can conclude that MN is less than 2MO. We also know that z = y. Since MO and NO are both radii of circle O, they must be equal. So we know that in triangle MNO, MO = NO; and since angles opposite equal sides are equal, we conclude that z = y. (B) requires still another line of reasoning. Since MN is greater than NO, the angle opposite MN, which is x, must be greater than the angle opposite NO, which is y. So x is greater than y. Finally, (E) requires yet another line of reasoning. If MN were equal to NO, it would also be equal to MO, since MO and NO are both radii. In that case, we would have an equilateral triangle and all angles would be 60°. Since MN is greater than MO and NO, the angle opposite MN, which is x, must be greater than 60°. So (D) must be the correct answer. A moment's reflection will show that it is not necessarily true that x = y + z. This would be true only in the event that MNO is a right triangle, but there is no information given in the problem from which we are entitled to conclude that x° = 90°.

SECTION IV

1. **(B)** One sure approach to this problem is to perform the addition indicated in the right-hand column: $\frac{1}{0.1} + \frac{0.1}{10} = \frac{100 + .1}{10} = \frac{100.1}{10} = 10.01$. This shows that Column B is larger. A quicker way of finding the correct answer is to divide .1 into 1, which yields 10. Then, no matter what the second term of Column B turns out to be, when it is added to the first term, the sum must be greater than 10.

2. **(C)** Since l_1 and l_2 are parallel, the third line creates a whole set of angle relationships, e.g., alternate interior angles are equal, and so on. For this problem, all we really need to see is that x and y must be equal since the transverse cuts the parallel lines on the perpendicular (all angles created must be equal to 90°). Because x and y are both 90°, our answer must be (C).

3. **(C)** The first line of attack on a problem like this is to cancel, thereby simplifying the comparison:

$$\frac{\cancel{3}}{\cancel{4}} \times \frac{\cancel{1}}{\cancel{3}} \times \frac{\cancel{6}}{\cancel{7}} \times \frac{\cancel{1}}{\cancel{6}} = 1$$
$$\frac{\cancel{4}}{\cancel{1}} \times \frac{\cancel{1}}{\cancel{4}} \times \frac{\cancel{7}}{\cancel{1}} \times \frac{\cancel{1}}{\cancel{7}} = 1$$

It is clear that 1 is equal to 1, so our answer must be (C).

4. **(A)** Since we are asked about x, the first line of attack here must be to solve for x in the centered equation:

$$3x + 2 = 11$$
$$3x = 9$$
$$x = 3$$

Since x is 3, and 3 is greater than 2, our answer must be (A). Merely substituting 2 for x would only eliminate (C).

5. **(D)** One approach is to recognize that no comparison of 5% of an unspecified number and 5% of a different unspecified number is possible. For those who had any difficulty with this insight, however, a good attack on the problem would be to divide both sides of the comparison by 5%. This effectively removes the 5%, reducing the comparison to x versus y. Now it is even easier to see that the answer must be (D) since no information is provided about x and y except the fact that each is greater than zero.

6. **(A)** This is a relatively difficult problem. To solve it, the student needs to recognize that if the triangle had dimensions of 3, 4, and 5 it would be a right triangle: $3^2 + 4^2 = 5^2$. That is to say, all triangles which have dimensions that satisfy the Pythagorean Theorem must have a 90° angle. If we knew that x was 90°, we would know that the remaining two angles would have to total to 90° because there are 180° in a triangle. But this is not a case of a 3–4–5 triangle, and 3, 4, and 5.1 will not satisfy the Pythagorean Theorem, so this is *not* a right triangle. Given that it is not a right triangle, then, we need to ask in what way does it differ from a right triangle. The answer is that the side 5.1 is slightly larger than 5, which would have given us a right triangle. So, too, angle x must be slightly larger than 90°. Now if x is slightly larger than 90°, the sum of the remaining two angles must be slightly less than 90° because, again, there are only 180° in a triangle. So x° must be greater than y° + z°.

7. **(A)** We begin our attack on this problem by solving for x and y in the equations given:

$$\frac{x}{3} - 16 = 32 \qquad \frac{y}{4} + 12 = 24$$
$$\frac{x}{3} = 48 \qquad \frac{y}{4} = 12$$
$$x = 144 \qquad y = 48$$

Since x is larger than y, our answer must be (A).

Another method would be to see that $\frac{x}{3}$ with 16 subtracted is larger than $\frac{y}{4}$ with 12 added. Thus $\frac{x}{3}$ is much larger, relatively speaking, than $\frac{y}{4}$ and, even though the 4 versus 3 in the denominator is a reason for $\frac{y}{4}$ to be smaller than $\frac{x}{3}$, it might seem clear that x must be larger. There is no problem with negative numbers since both $\frac{x}{3}$ and $\frac{y}{4}$ are positive, which means that both x and y are positive.

8. **(B)** Performing the indicated operations:

Column A	Column B
x(x + 3) + 2(x + 3)	$(x + 3)^2$
$x^2 + 3x + 2x + 6$	(x + 3)(x + 3)
$x^2 + 5x + 6$	$x^2 + 6x + 9$

Subtracting x^2, 5x, and 6 from both columns:

0	x + 3

Since x > 0, Column B is greater than 3, and therefore larger than Column A.

9. **(C)** Let us first draw the picture:

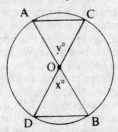

Now, most students will intuitively see that AC must be equal to BD no matter what the magnitudes of x and y are. (Note: We mean by 'intuitively' not measurement or reliance on eye-estimation, but merely the sort of thing where one says, "I can't prove it, but I know it must be correct ") A simple proof can also be given. Since x and y are equal (vertical angles are equal), they intercept ~qual arcs (cut off equal parts of the circle). The chords (AC and BD) subtend (join) equal . of the same circle and so must be equal.

Another way of proving that AC = BD is to point out that AO and CO are radii and are equal to DO and BO, which are also radii. Then we know that x and y are equal, so AOC and DOB are congruent triangles. Consequently, the third sides lmust also be equal.

10. **(D)** At first glance, it might appear that x and y must be equal. After all, any number raised to the zero power is equal to 1. And this reasoning would be sound if the base were anything except 1. For 1 raised to any power is equal to 1:

$$1^{7-1} = 1^6 = 1$$
$$1^{7-5} = 1^2 = 1$$

So the values of x and y are not important: 1 raised to any power is still just 1.

11. **(A)** We begin by filling in more details:

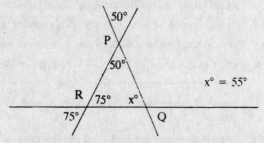

This is because vertical angles are equal. Then we can compute the remaining angle as 55° (50° + 75° + x = 180°, x = 55°). Now, in any given triangle, the larger the angle the longer the side. Since PQ is opposite a 75° angle while RP is opposite a 55° angle, PQ must be larger than RP.

12. **(C)** It is possible to solve this comparison using simultaneous equations or substitution: Let x be the number of adult tickets, and let y be the number of children's tickets. Then x − y = 29, and 5x + 2.5y = 302.50. But there is an easier way. Let us assume, for the purposes of analysis, that the number of adult tickets sold was exactly 50. On that assumption, the receipts derived from adult tickets was $250. We know further, on that assumption, that 21 tickets were sold for $2.50, and total receipts from children's tickets would be $52.50. Combining our two totals, we come up with gross sales of $302.50. And since that is the total receipts specified in the centered information, we have proved that the number of adult tickets is 50.

If the resulting total dollars had not equalled what the problem told us it should, then (C) would be eliminated as a possible answer choice. If the total based on the assumption of the columns being equal was high, then fewer tickets were sold than assumed.

13. **(A)** This problem is solved by merely counting on one's fingers. The first multiple of 4 greater than 281 is 284 (284 divided by 4 = 71), the second is 288, the third is 292, the fourth is 296, and the fifth is 300. So there are five multiples of 4 between 281 and 301. The first multiple of 5 greater than 2401 is 2405, the second is 2410, the third is 2415 and that is the last one that is less than 2419. So there are only three multiples of 5 between 2401 and 2419. Since 5 is greater than 3, our answer choice must be (A).

Another method would be to notice that there are more numbers from 281 to 301 than from 2401 to 2419 and that you cover more ground with a multiple of 5 than a multiple of 4, so Column A would be a longer distance on the number line in smaller pieces, while Column B would be a smaller distance and larger pieces. The specification of multiples might work against that since we are not addressing the length, but the number of multiples, but Column A starts with a multiple of 4 while Column B starts just after a multiple of 5.

14. **(C)** This is a fairly difficult problem. The first thing to realize is that x = 60° and y = 30°. We learn this by a calculation. Since x is twice as large as y, we know that x = 2y. Then we also know that x + y = 90. By substitution, we have y + 2y = 90, so y = 30 and x = 60. We can now see that we have the special case of the right, or 30:60:90, triangle. In such a triangle, the side opposite the 30° angle is equal to one-half the hypotenuse, and the side opposite the 60° angle is equal to one-half the hypotenuse times the square root of three:

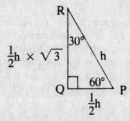

Since PR is the hypotenuse, PQ is the side opposite the 30°angle, and PQ = ½PR. So we can substitute ½PR for PQ in the right column: $\frac{\frac{1}{2}PR}{PR} = \frac{1}{2}$; so our two columns are equal.

15. **(C)** It is possible to go through an entire computation here. By the Pythagorean Theorem, DC and CB must be:

$$s^2 + s^2 = 1^2$$
$$2s^2 = 1$$
$$s = \sqrt{\tfrac{1}{2}}$$
$$s = \frac{1}{\sqrt{2}} = \frac{\sqrt{2}}{2}$$

Then DC and CB can function as altitude and base of DCB, and we use the formula for the area of a triangle: $\frac{1}{2}ab = \frac{1}{2}(\sqrt{2}/2)(\sqrt{2}/2) = \frac{1}{4}$. The area of the square is easily gotten as $1 \times 1 = 1$. So the area of the entire figure is $1 + \frac{1}{4}$ or 1.25. But there is an easier way to solve the problem:

We can see intuitively that DCB is $\frac{1}{4}$ the area of the square. Since the area of the square is 1, the area of DCB must be $\frac{1}{4}$, and the combined areas are 1.25, the area of the entire polygon ABCDE.

16. **(D)** This is a relatively easy problem. It can be solved by doing the subtraction: $\frac{4}{5} - \frac{3}{4} = \frac{16 - 15}{20} = \frac{1}{20}$. In this case, a substitution of percentages for fractions might be useful if you are knowledgeable about the equivalencies: $\frac{4}{5} = 80\%$ and $\frac{3}{4} = 75\%$. $80\% - 75\% = 5\% = \frac{1}{20}$.

17. **(C)** First we must convert one and one-half yards into inches. There are 36 inches in a yard, so one and one-half yards must contain $36 + 18$ or 54 inches. Now, to determine how many two-inch segments there are in 54 inches, we just divide 54 by 2, which equals 27. So there must be 27 two-inch segments in a segment which is one and one-half yards long.

18. **(B)** It is important to remember that the positive x values are to the right of the origin (the intersection between the x and y axes), and that the negative values on the x axis are to the left of the origin. Also, the positive y values are above the origin, while the negative y values are below the x axis.

```
                y
        (−,+)  |  (+,+)
         II    |    I
    ───────────┼───────────  x
         III   |    IV
        (−,−)  |  (+,−)
```

When reading an ordered pair such as (x,y) (called ordered because the first place is always the x-coordinate and the second place is always the y-coordinate), we know the first element is the movement on the horizontal or x axis, while the second element of the pair gives us the vertical distance. In this case, we are five units to the left of the origin, so that gives us an x value of negative 5. We are 2 units above the horizontal axis, so that gives us the second value (y) of +2. Thus our ordered pair is (−5,2), answer (B).

19. **(B)** The formula for computing the circumference of a circle is $2\pi r$. In this case our radius is 4, so the circumference of the circle is 8π. Now, P and Q will be as far apart as they can possibly be when they are directly opposite one another:

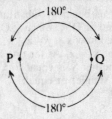

Or a half circle away from each other. So the maximum distance by which P and Q could be separated—measured by the circumference of the circle and not as the crow flies—is one-half the circumference, or 4π.

20. **(E)** Remember that a prime number is an integer which has only itself and 1 as integral factors. Thus, 13, 17, 41, and 79 are all prime numbers because their only factors are 13 and 1, 17 and 1, 41 and 1, and 79 and 1, respectively. 91, however, is not a prime number since it can be factored by 7 and 13 as well as by 1 and 91.

21. **(C)** The natural starting point here would be to draw the picture:

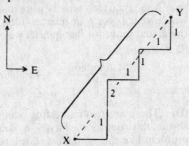

Since directions are perpendicular, we can perform the needed calculation with the Pythagorean Theorem. To simplify things, we can show that the above picture is equivalent to this:

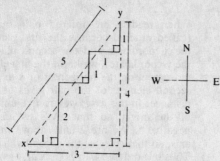

Now we can solve for the distance between X and Y with one use of the Pythagorean Theorem. Since the two legs of the right triangle are 3 and 4, we know that the hypotenuse must be 5. (Remember that 3, 4, and 5, or any multiples thereof such as 6, 8, and 10, always make a right triangle.)

22. **(C)** Let us begin by substituting x, y, and z for ∠QPS and ∠TPR. Since ∠QPS and ∠TPR are equal, we know x + y = z + y, and since y = y, we know that x = z. As for (A) and (B), we do not know whether y is equal to x and z; it could be larger or smaller or equal:

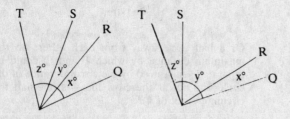

We can also eliminate (D) since we have no information that would lead us to conclude that all three are of equal measure.

23. **(D)** The footnote at the bottom of the chart tells us that the annual rate, that is shown in the table, is computed by taking the actual profits made in the quarter and multiplying by 4. An annual rate for a quarter shows how the store would do in a year if the quarter's activity were maintained for a whole year (over four quarters). So, to compute the actual profit for that quarter we need to divide by 4:

$$\frac{\$1.6 \text{ million}}{4} = \$.4 \text{ million}$$

24. **(D)** There are two interesting points to be made about this question. First, in dealing with a problem like this, you must start from the answer choices. In essence, the question asks "of the following five choices . . . ." It is often a waste of time to go first to the chart to find the quarter in which profits were actually the lowest for all quarters shown on the chart. That is, in fact, the first quarter of 1978, but that does not appear as

an answer choice. Second, although the number recorded by the graph is actually four times that of actual profits (see question 23 above), there is no need to divide each of these by four. Obviously, the greater the annual profit rate, the larger the actual profit made in the quarter. In this case, the smallest annual rate of the five listed in the problem occurred in the third quarter of 1978, about $0.75 million, so the actual profits must have been smallest in that quarter.

25. **(A)** This is a fairly simple problem. We need only consult the graph for that period to see that in six quarters, the annual profit rate exceeded $1.5 million: 2nd quarter of 1979 ($1.6 million), 3rd quarter of 1979 ($1.7 million), 4th quarter of 1979 ($1.9 million), 2nd quarter of 1980 ($1.8 million), 3rd quarter of 1980 ($2.1 million), and 4th quarter of 1980 ($2.3 million).

26. **(C)** Remember that the amount reported on the graph is four times the actual profits made in the quarter. So, if we take the annual profit rate for each quarter and divide it by four, we will have the actual profits for each quarter. We can then add those numbers up to get the annual profits (actual). It is a bit simpler, however, just to add the four annual rates and then divide the whole thing by 4:

1st	1.5 million
2nd	1.8 million
3rd	2.1 million
4th	2.3 million
Total	7.7 million

$7.7 million divided by four = $1.925 million. So the actual profit in that year was about $1.9 million.

In practice, however, an estimate rather than a complete calculation will suffice since the answer choices are fairly far apart, though (C) and (D) are somewhat similar. The four quarters of 1980 go up, with the balance point or average somewhere around 1.8. Since that was the annualized figure, (C) would be good choice. (D) and (E) are impossible since each of the four quarters had rates above those choices, while (A) and (B) are figures beyond the highest reach of the chart.

27. **(C)** Again, we can simply use annual rates. There is no reason to divide everything by 4 for each quarter. The annual rates for 1977 are:

1st	1.3 million
2nd	1.1 million
3rd	0.9 million
4th	0.7 million
Total	4.0 million

We can retrieve the total for 1980 from question 26 above, and work the percentage change formula: $\frac{7.7 - 4.0}{4.0} = \frac{3.7}{4.0} = $ about $\frac{8}{10}$ which is 90%. Again, estimation can save work. The four quarters of 1977 are in orderly progression, with the midpoint being 0.9. As noted for problem 26, the 1980 profits can be estimated at 1.8 or slightly less (1st quarter is farther below 1.8 than other quarters are above 1.8). An increase from 0.9 to 1.8 would be a 100% increase, which is closest to (C).

28. **(A)** This problem is rather tedious, though it is not conceptually difficult. Let us start working in the interior:

$$4 - 3(2 + 1(3 - (2 + 3) + 2) + 2) + 4$$
$$4 - 3(2 + 1(3 - \quad 5 \quad + 2) + 2) + 4$$
$$4 - 3(2 + 1(\quad\quad 0 \quad) + 2) + 4$$
$$4 - 3(2 + \quad\quad 0 \quad + 2) + 4$$
$$4 - 3(\quad\quad\quad 4 \quad) + 4$$
$$4 \quad -12 \quad\quad\quad + 4$$
$$- 4$$

29. **(C)** By this juncture the drill should be well known. We must begin by drawing a picture:

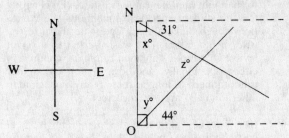

Now, since the angles at N and O are 90°, we can compute the magnitude of x and y: $x = 90° - 31° = 59°$, and $y = 90° - 44° = 46°$. Then, since x, y, and z are the interior angles of a triangle, we know $x + y + z = 180°$. Substituting for x and y, we have $59° + 46° + z = 180°$, and we solve for z: $z = 75°$. Since z is the acute angle of intersection between the two highways, our answer must be (C).

30. **(B)** Let us use x to represent the sum of money. Then we know that when x is divided equally by n, the result is $60; or, expressed in formal notation: $\frac{x}{n} = 60$. We then know that when x is divided by n + 1 (that is the original number plus another child), the result is $50, or $\frac{x}{n + 1} = 50$. Now, let us manipulate these equations so that we isolate n:

$$\frac{x}{n} = 60 \qquad \frac{x}{n + 1} = 50$$
$$\frac{x}{60} = n \qquad \frac{x}{50} = n + 1$$
$$\frac{x}{60} = n \qquad \left(\frac{x}{50}\right) - 1 = n$$

Since n = n, we know that $x/60 = x/50 - 1$, and we have an equation with only one variable: $x/60 - x/50 = -1$, so:

$$\frac{5x - 6x}{300} = -1$$
AND: $\quad -x = -300$
SO: $\quad\quad x = 300$

The sum of money is $300 and our answer is (B). (Note that you could also solve for n; in this case n = 5, and 5 × $60 = $300.)

SECTION V

Questions 1–4

Arranging the Information

This problem has two aspects, the order in which items have to be done and the times during the week when the various offices and individuals are available. Note that although the first statement in the information set does seem to give some feeling that thesis approval by the professors must come after the filling out of the application, this would be reading too much into the problem. In fact, the additional statements about the required order of events indicate, by silence about the timing of thesis approval, that the approval can come after the visit to the dean. Question 4 supports this by putting the approval process ahead of the other items. The filing at the Financial Aid Office must be last.

Since the information is given to us in terms of mornings and afternoons, that is the way to arrange it. There are no immediate interactions between the items of information (such as might have been the case if Professor Fansler's office hours were always three days after Professor Cross's, or if the Dean's hours were described in terms of those of the Financial Aid Office). Therefore, a straight listing of the information on hours is all that is required.

	MON.	TUES.	WED.	THUR.	FRI.
AM	Fin. Aid	Fin. Aid		Dean	Dean
	Fansler	Fansler			Fin. Aid
		Cross			Cross
PM	Dean	Dean			
			Fin. Aid		

DEAN MUST PRECEDE FIN. AID; FIN. AID LAST; PROF'S PRE/POST DEAN.

Answering the Questions

1. **(D)** Since the thesis must be approved by Fansler only and not by Cross, only Monday and Tuesday mornings are possibilities, which eliminates (C) and (E). The student also has to go to the Financial Aid Office after seeing the professor.

Since the Financial Aid Office is open on both Monday and Tuesday mornings, both of those times are good; hence, (D) rather than (A) or (B).

2. **(E)** This problem is, of course, separate from the preceding one, so we must consider that the student is starting out fresh and needs to see the Dean, a professor, and the Financial Aid Office. They are asking for what must be false, so we seek elimination by seeing possibilities.

I is not necessarily false, because it is possible to have thesis approval from Professor Cross and complete the job in one day. On Friday morning all three of the required parties are open for business and, ignoring waiting time (which you do because if they didn't bring it up, you shouldn't), there would be no problem. This eliminates answer choices (A) and (D).

II is false because Professor Fansler's approval can only be obtained on Monday or Tuesday morning. While it is true that both the Financial Aid Office and the Dean are open on Mondays and Tuesdays, the order is wrong. By the time the Dean is open for business the Financial Aid Office is closed, so the application cannot be filed that day. This eliminates answer (C).

III is also false because neither of the professors is available in the afternoon. Hence, (B) is out and (E) is correct.

3. **(D)** This problem does not require that the process be completed in any particular time, but only that all the action take place on Tuesdays and Thursdays. Since both professors have office hours on Tuesdays, statements I and II are not necessarily true. As it happens, this is enough to give you the answer since all of the answer choices except (D) allege that either I or II or both are true.

III is false because on Thursdays only the Dean is open, and because on Tuesdays the Financial Aid Office closes before the Dean opens, as was previously discussed.

IV requires you to interpret what a school week might be. If a mere seven-day period was intended (start on Thursday and complete on the following Tuesday), that would not be called a "school" week. A school week is Monday through Friday, and the application cannot be done on a consecutive Tuesday and Thursday. Thus, all four of the statements are false.

4. **(C)** On Wednesday and Thursday only one of the proper offices is open, so they are not possible one-visit days, but this only eliminates (D). Friday morning is a possible one-visit time, which eliminates answer choice (A). Monday and Tuesday mornings, while blessed with open offices for the professors and the Financial Aid Office, do not have the Dean, so (E) is eliminated (as is (D) for the second time).

Monday and Tuesday have the problem of

order of office openings previously referred to, and thus are not one-visit days—which eliminates (B), leaving (C) as the answer.

5. **(C)** Notice that the student responds to the professor's comment by saying, "That can't be true," and then uses the Duchess of Warburton as a counter-example. The Duchess would only be a counter-example to the professor's statement had the professor said that women cannot inherit the estates of their families. Thus, (C) must capture the student's misinterpretation of the professor's statement. What has misled the student is that he has attributed too much to the professor. The professor has cited the general rule of primogeniture—the eldest male child inherits—but he has not discussed the special problems which arise when no male child is born. In those cases, presumably a non-male child will have to inherit. (E) incorrectly refers to inheriting from a mother, but the student is discussing a case in which the woman inherited her father's estate. (D) is wrong for the student specifically mentions the conditions which make a child legitimate: born to the wife of her father. (A) was inserted as a bit of levity: Of course, only men can *father* children of either sex. Finally, first-born or not, a daughter cannot inherit as long as there is any male child to inherit, so (B) must be incorrect.

6. **(D)** The key phrase in this paragraph is "beef costs more per pound than fish." A careful reading would show that (A) is in direct contradiction to the explicit wording of the passage. (B) cannot be inferred since the dietician merely says, "I pay." Perhaps he intends to keep the price of a meal stable by cutting back in other areas. In any event, this is an example of not going beyond a mere factual analysis to generate policy recommendations, unless the question stem specifically invites such an extension, e.g., which of the following courses of action would the author recommend? (C) makes an unwarranted inference. From the fact that beef is more costly one would not want to conclude that it is more profitable. (E) is wrong for this reason also. (D) is correct because it focuses upon the per measure cost of protein, which explains why a fish meal will cost the dietician more than a beef meal, even though fish is less expensive per pound.

Questions 7–9

Arranging the Information

The question stems and the original information indicate that the items of interest will be what projections can be made on the basis of the given information. This means that there will be less time spent on arranging and more spent on working out the problems.

The starting information boils down to the conclusion that the subject got off at the third, fourth, fifth, or seventh floor. Since there were only three people on the elevator, this should immediately raise in your mind the possibility of subterfuge.

Answering the Questions

7. **(B)** The question stem adds a condition that builds on the fact that someone obviously pressed buttons for more than one floor, since the elevator carrying only three people, stopped four times and no one got on the elevator. There is no reason to assume on the test that either of the other two riders pushed two buttons, though in real life it is certainly a possibility. Rather, the limitation is that the subject, who is the likeliest to have pressed two buttons, would not have pressed two buttons so long as there were others in the elevator. Therefore, the second button pressed by the subject must have been after the other two riders got off the elevator. The earliest stop at which both could have gotten off the elevator is the third floor.

If we assume, as we must for the problem, that at most three buttons were pressed when the elevator started (one for each rider), then the subject could have pressed the extra button either after the third floor (if both other riders got off there) or after the fourth floor (if one rider got off at each of the third and fourth floors). Therefore, the subject did not get off at the third floor but may have gotten off at any one of the other floors. Thus, answer choice (E) is eliminated for saying that the subject may have gotten off at the third floor. Each of the other answers is possible, but we are looking for the safest conclusion, which is the one which has the least chance of being wrong. (B) is the safest conclusion because it is definitely correct within the parameters of the question. (A) omits the possibility that the subject got off at the fourth floor, (C) the fourth and seventh, and (D) the seventh.

8. **(B)** The preceding discussion in 7 indicates that there are only three possible floors on the way up the building. However, that deduction is based on the detective's assumption as stated in the question stem. This assumption does NOT carry over into the problem. If we do not have the limitation on the actions of the subject posited in 7, then the first upward ride of the elevator yields four possible floors on which the subject may have left the elevator. The downward empty return from seven limits nothing.

The second up-and-down trip described in this question stem mentions two additional floors, two and six, but only six is a possible location of the subject. The elevator stopped at two on the way up, and therefore could not have brought the subject to two. The stairs are closed. If the subject got off on seven the first trip, then he may have gone down to six on the second trip, thus three, four, five, six, and seven are all possibilities, hence, answer (B).

9. **(E)** This seems a peculiar result, but we must be certain that we do not assume more than the problem gives us. The problem does not tell us that the subject was on the elevator when it reached the fourth floor. He may have exited on the third floor. Also, he may have exited on the fourth floor since we only know what is explicitly stated. The detective might have learned this piece of information indirectly, rather than from the people getting on and off the elevator. In any case, he knows only what they say.

The original reason for putting the subject on the top two floors was the fact that there were more stops than people, but this proves to be false for this problem. Thus, the person getting on at four may have been going to the fifth or seventh floor, leaving the other as well as three and four as possible exits for the subject. Thus, (E).

10. **(A)** Statements I and II combine to give us (A). If all wheeled conveyances which travel on the highway are polluters, and a bicycle does not travel on the highway, then a bicycle cannot be a polluter. If (A) is correct, (B) must be incorrect because bicycles do not travel on the highways at all. (C) and (D) make the same mistake. III must be read to say "if I am driving, it is raining," not "if it is raining, I am driving." (E) is clearly false since my car is driven on the highway. Don't make the problem harder than it is.

11. **(E)** Picking up on our discussion of (C) and (D) in the previous question, III must read "if I am driving, then it is raining." Let that be: "If P, then Q." If we then had not-Q, we could deduce not-P. (E) gives us not-Q by changing IV to "it is not raining." Changing I or II or even both is not going to do the trick, for they don't touch the relationship between my driving my car and rain—they deal only with pollution and we need the car to be connected. Similarly, if we change III to make it deal with pollution, we have not adjusted the connection between my driving and rain, so (C) must be wrong. (D) is the worst of all the answers. Whether rainwater is polluted or not has nothing to do with the connection between my driving and rain. Granted, there is the unstated assumption that my car only pollutes when I drive it, but this is O.K.

Questions 12–16

Arranging the Information

If we indicate the idea of "some" by putting the number of the proposition with a question mark over the two areas of a Venn diagram, we will get the following for propositions I, II, and III:

Diagram 1:

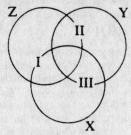

Adding the information from proposition IV, we get:

Diagram 2

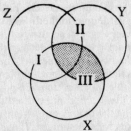

Answering the Questions

12. **(E)** Refer to Diagram 1. The three statements we are dealing with here are simply indications as to where some things are and say nothing about where things aren't. Thus, (A) cannot be known to be true from I, II, and III, and is eliminated.

  The same general argument eliminates answer choices (B), (C), and (D). Since the "some" statements covered areas divided into two parts in the diagram, we cannot know which of the two areas is the actual inhabited location, or perhaps both are. The areas pointed to in the three answer choices are indicated here:

Diagram 3:

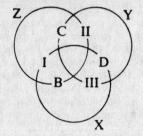

13. **(A)** Referring to Diagram 2, we see that one of the areas at first thought to be possibly inhabited in accordance with statement III is rendered impossible by statement IV's obliteration of the overlap between X and Y. This, in turn, means that only the area of X has something in it. Hence, (A) is impossible and the answer sought.

  (B) and (C) refer to the two areas governed by statement I, and we do not know whether one or both of these has members. Similar reasoning applies to answer choice (D).

14. **(D)** I is already known since statement IV of the original information forbids X to be also Y. II is known for the same reasons that (A) in 13 is false. III is uncertain since I of the original information says only that there is either some member of Y + Z, or both. Hence, (D).

15. **(C)** (A) is possibly true since the Z-things which are not also Y-things might not have characteristic X. (B) is possibly true since the pure Y region is left open (logically possible). For the same reason (D) is possible: the open pure Y region does not assert there are pure Y-things—only that they are possible. (E) is incorrect since (A), (B), and (D) are possibly true. (C), however, is equivalent to "All X are Z" and that is inconsistent with the diagram.

16. **(D)** Coding in the additional information gives us this diagram:

Diagram 4:

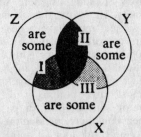

  From this diagram we see that there are some individual items which are only X, others only Y, and others only Z. No overlap of any sort is permitted. (D) falsely states that Z must be X. (E) states that you cannot find a Z except for those Z that are not Y, which is correct.

Questions 17–22

Arranging the Information

Previewing the question stems for this set of questions shows that there is only one conditional question and it is based on a new individual. This leads you to suppose that you should be able to completely describe this situation. In addition, a preview of the general information at the start of the problem set indicates that there are only two ways in which the pandas are to be related to each other and that the two ways—wet/dry and fat/slim—are both separate.

Let us first arrange the information into a usable format, starting with the fat/slim idea. Each piece of information must fit in with some previously arranged piece of information in order to create a complete and valid arrangement. Since each panda's name begins with a different letter, we can use single letters to indicate each panda.

←FATTER————SLIMMER→

B fatter
than G

  B   G

C slimmer than F—
can't do now

D fatter than B	D	B	G	
E slimmer than G	D	B	G	E
F slimmer than E	D	B	G	E	F

C slimmer than F—
can do now

	D	B	G	E	F	C

G fatter than F—
redundant

Now we can do the dry/wet idea.

←DRIER————WETTER→

B drier than E	B	E	

C wetter than G—
can't do now

D wetter than G—
can't do now

E drier than C	B	E	C

C wetter than G—
can do now

	B	E	C
		← G	

D wetter than G—
can do now

	B	E	C
	←————G	D→	

F drier than B	F	B	E	C
		←————G	D→	

G wetter than B	F	B	E	C
		←————G	D→	

Answering the Questions

17. **(C)** Only B is on the fatter (left) side of E and also on the drier (left) side of G.

18. **(D)** Only C is both slimmer (right) and wetter (right) than E.

19. **(B)** Only D is both fatter (left) and wetter (right) than G. Even though the exact wetness position of D is not known, it is wetter than G.

20. **(D)** F is the driest (left-most) in the final diagram.

21. **(B)** I is not false for sure because the exact wetness relationship between D and C is not known. D might be wetter or drier than C. II is definitely false since F is drier than D. III is not knowable from the given information since the exact amounts by which the various pandas are fatter or slimmer is not stated. D is fatter than G, but not necessarily by three inches. However, the statement is not false because it might be true. Thus, only II is definitely false.

22. **(E)** The exact rank cannot be determined because the new panda Y's being slimmer than B and fatter than F leaves unclear the relationship between Y and pandas G and E.

23. **(B)** We have seen examples of the form of argument Holmes has in mind before: "P or Q; not-P; therefore, Q." Here, however, the first premise of Holmes' argument is more complex: "P or Q or R . . . S," with as many possibilities as he can conceive. He eliminates them one by one until no single possibility is left. The logic of the argument is perfect, but the weakness in the form is that it is impossible to guarantee that all contingencies have been taken into account. Maybe one was overlooked. Thus, (B) is the correct answer. (A), (C), and (E) are wrong for the same reason. Holmes' method is designed to answer a particular question—in this case, "Where did the body come from?" Perhaps the next step is to apply the method to the question of the identity of the murderer as (E) suggests, but at this juncture he is concerned with the preliminary matter of how the murder was committed. In any event, it would be wrong to assail the logic of Holmes' deduction by complaining that it does not prove enough. Since (A) and (C) are even more removed from the particular question raised, they, too, must be wrong. Finally, (D) is nothing more than a reiteration of Watson's original comment, and Holmes has already responded to it.

24. **(A)** Although we do not want to argue theology, perhaps a point taken from that discipline will make this question more accessible: "If God is only good, from where does evil come?" Rousseau, at least as far as his argument is characterized here, faces a similar problem. If man is by his very nature sympathetic, what is the source of his non-sympathetic social institutions? (A) poses this critical question. The remaining choices each commit the same fundamental error. Rousseau *describes* a situation. The paragraph never suggests that he proposed a *solution*. Perhaps Rousseau considered the problem of modern society irremediable.

25. **(E)** Here we are looking for the unstated or hidden assumptions of the author. (A) is one because the author dates the building by measuring the wear and tear on the threshold, but if that were a replacement threshold installed, say, 50 years after the building was first built, the author's calculations would be thrown off completely. So, to reach the conclusion he does, he must have assumed that he was dealing with the original threshold. (C) is very similar. The calculations work—based as they are on the estimated capacity of the monastery—only if the author is right about the number of people walking across the door sill. So it also follows that (D) is something he assumes. After all, if marble tended

to wear out spontaneously instead of under use—if sometimes it just evaporates—then the whole process of calculating time as a function of wear would be ill-founded. (E) is correct. The author uses the wars he cites to help him date *this particular group* of buildings. He never suggests that this has occurred often.

SECTION VI

Questions 1–3:

Arranging the Information

Previewing the questions indicates that the complex issue is the fighting. Thus, the diagram must keep track of combinations.

$$F \leftarrow\text{not with any}\rightarrow \underset{\underset{\downarrow}{\overset{\text{not}}{\overset{\text{with}}{|}}}}{\underbrace{G \text{ with } H}} \; J$$
$$K$$

Answering the Questions

1. **(C)** I is not inferable since there is no reason to prefer F to K as an addition to G and H. We are not given any reason to prefer eating to non-fighting and thus cannot judge the relative problems with F and K. II is not inferable since there is nothing that tells us that G and H will fight with each other, only with K. III is inferable since the only combinations available have to include fighters. If F is included, there is likely to be fighting. If F is not included, then G, H, and K will fight.

2. **(C)** If G and J go home, then only H, K, and F are left. All of these cats will fight with each other for reasons similar to those outlined for question 1. Therefore, two new cats are needed to combine with either H or K.

3. **(C)** Since the purposes of a cat cast are established in the situation description, we know that an available cast means one that will have a good chance of succeeding. With F calmed down, the only remaining problem is the fighting between G, H, and K. However, G and H should be together since we are told that they eat well together, and that is the goal of the commercial filming. Thus, we have G and H, who can be with J or with F, and we have F with K and J. Although we do not know how well K and J eat, they will at least not

fight and that is sufficient for them to qualify as available. Thus, there are three possible casts available.

4. **(B)** The proposition that you cannot argue with taste says that taste is relative. Since we are looking for an answer choice inconsistent with that proposition, we seek an answer choice that argues that taste, or aesthetic value, is absolute, or at least not relative—that there are standards of taste. (B) is precisely that.

   (C) and (D) are just distractions, playing on the notion of taste in the physical sense and the further idea of the distasteful; but these superficial connections are not strong enough.

   (A), (B), and (E) are all activities in which there is some element of aesthetic judgment or appreciation. In (A), the holding of an exhibition, while implying some selection principle and, thus, some idea of a standard of taste, does not purport to truly judge aesthetics in the way that (B), precisely a beauty *contest,* does. The exhibition may be of historical or biographical interest, for example. (E) also stresses more of the exhibition aspect than the judging aspect. You should not infer that all movie festivals are contests, since the word festival does not require this interpretation and, in fact, there are festivals at which the judging aspect is minimal or non-existent. The Cannes Film Festival, while perhaps the best-known, is not the only type of movie festival there is. The questions are not tests of your knowledge of the movie industry.

5. **(C)** Take careful note of the exact position the author ascribes to the analysts: They *always* attribute a sudden drop to a crisis. The author then attacks this simple causal explanation by explaining that, though a crisis is followed by a market drop, the reason is not that the crisis causes the drop but that both are the effects of some common cause, the changing of the moon. Of course, the argument seems implausible, but our task is not to grade the argument, only to describe its structure. (A) is not a proper characterization of that structure since the author never provides a specific example. (B), too, is inapplicable since no statistics are produced. (D) can be rejected since the author is attacking generally accepted beliefs rather than appealing to them to support his position. Finally, though the author concedes the reliability of the reports, (E), in question, he wants to draw a different conclusion from the data.

6. **(A)** Given the implausibility of the author's alternative explanation, he is probably speaking tongue-in-cheek, that is, he is ridiculing the analysts for *always* attributing a drop in the market to a political crisis. But whether you took the argument in this way or as a serious attempt to explain the fluctuations of the stock market, (A)

will be the correct answer. (E) surely goes beyond the mere factual description at which the author is aiming, as does (D) as well. The author is concerned with the *causes* of fluctuations; nothing suggests that he or anyone else is in a position to exploit those fluctuations. (C) finds no support in the paragraph, for nothing suggests that he wishes to attack the credibility of the source rather than the argument itself. Finally, (B) is inappropriate to the main point of the passage. Whether the market ultimately evens itself out has nothing to do with the causes of the fluctuations.

Questions 7–11

Arranging the Information

This problem set describes a layout or map situation. One clue is its being a set of regular shapes and the other is the use of compass directions. You have to distinguish between conditions which lead to definite squares being definite crops and ones which simply describe relationships between crops.

If two sides of the field run east-west, the other sides run north-south, and the field is aligned with the compass.

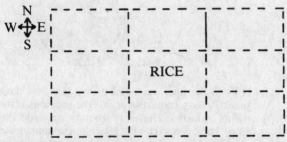

The information about wheat and barley cannot be coded into the diagram now, nor can the information about the soybeans, but peanuts can.

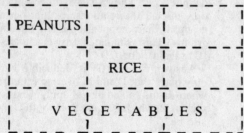

Answering the Questions

Questions 7, 8, and 9 refer to five squares. Let us locate them on the map:

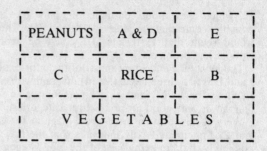

If the four unallocated fields are to be planted with one field of wheat, one of barley, and two of soybeans, the wheat and barley have to be two of the upper right-hand fields in order to be next to each other.

7. **(E)** If field (E) is planted with soybeans, then the wheat and barley cannot be next to each other.

8. **(C)** If (C) is planted with wheat, the barley cannot be next to it.

9. **(E)** Although there are two fields next to the peanuts, we have already eliminated (C) from consideration as a wheat field. Thus, the wheat must be in the field just north of the rice (A)/(D), and the barley must be in field (E) to be next to the wheat.

10. **(D)** The rice is in the middle, so the tomatoes cannot be next to the soybeans, eliminating II— AND answer choices (B) and (E). Either of the fields to the east or west of the rice field could be planted with the soybeans, as previously discussed; thus, I and III are possible, and (D) is correct.

    Note that the squash actually must be next to the soybeans, but that also means it is possible.

11. **(B)** It is a fair assumption that the other crops mentioned are to be planted and only the ones specifically omitted are not planted (to do otherwise would be mere nitpicking). This means that there will be one field of rice and barley, and two of soybeans—leaving five for vegetables.

Questions 12–15

Arranging the Information

This is a problem in which the main issue is the overlapping of different sets of groups, which means that Venn diagrams are a good method of arranging the information. This type of problem usually requires that the majority of your time be spent in arranging the information and somewhat less in answering the questions. However, a preview of the questions indicates that some of the statements might contradict some of the other statements. Question 13 indicates that statements I, II, and III are to be taken as true, and question

12, which asks about contradiction, only asks about possible contradiction after I, II, and III. Thus, it would seem that I, II, and III could be arranged without any problems.

The most efficient arrangement of the information of I and II is in a three-circle (Venn) diagram with circles standing for L, M, and Z. Remember that a Venn diagram is only good for up to three categories.

We will now draw a three-circle diagram for L, M, and Z. Statement I only indicates that there is some possibility of there being each of the four categories. It does not mean, for instance, that there will be an L by itself that is not any of the others, etc. This does not affect the diagram.

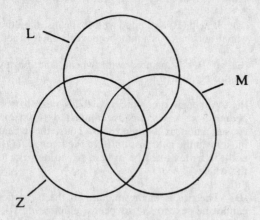

Statement II is coded into the diagram by marking out the parts of the diagram where M is not L.

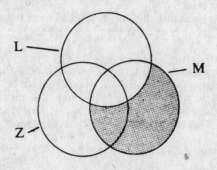

Statement III is coded into the diagram by eliminating the parts of the diagram where L is not Z, leaving us with this:

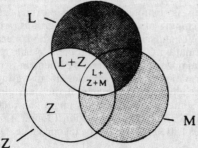

Thus, what remains possible is L with Z, L with M and Z, and Z by itself.

Answering the Questions

12. **(B)** Statement III was successfully integrated with the previous statements without encountering any problem, so answer choice (A) is eliminated. Statement IV, however, does present a problem. If no M are Z, this means that there can be no M found inside the Z circle. However, the only place where M can be found, after coding the first three statements, is inside the Z circle. The elimination of the possibility of having L, M, and Z together will eliminate the possibility of having M altogether, which is forbidden by statement I. Thus, answer choice (B) is correct. Note that one must proceed in order in this particular problem because the question asks about contradictions with all previous statements, which means that the first one with a contradiction must be the answer sought. Both statements V and VI are fully compatible with the following diagrams:

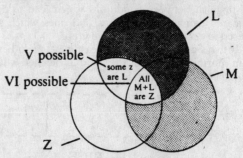

13. **(C)** In the previous question we saw that statement IV was contradictory to the previous statements, which excludes it from being deducible from statements II and III, eliminating answer choices (A) and (D). Statement V is not deducible from the others because it states that there are actually some Z. The existence of any Z is definitely not known since statements II and III only discuss the relationships that pertain to the groups if there happen to be any members of the groups. This eliminates answer choices (B) and (D) (again), and (E).

Answer choice (C) is deducible because the only place that L and M overlap is in the location where L and M and also Z apply. Thus, anything, such as P, which is going to be both L and M must also be Z.

14. **(D)** From the diagram we can see that there are two possible locations within the L area. One location is the LMZ area and the other is the LZ area. Thus, all L are Z, as statement III has said. The only reason that you would use the diagram instead of just relying on the original statement is

to make sure that there was no further limitation that had snuck in, as happened with M, all of which are also Z (ignoring the contradiction problem). You cannot make any statement about the overlap between P and X because statement VI only states where P will not be found and makes no promises that there are P's that actually are M and L, etc.

15. **(D)** The diagram shows that there is a definite possible area of Z which does not overlap any part of the L or M areas; therefore, it is still possible for Z to be by itself. It would be wrong to say that there definitely was some Z by itself, but it is also wrong to say that there cannot be any Z by itself.

(A) is not false since statement I states that L is possible. (B) is not known to be true or false. The statement that some Z are L does not make it false or true to say some Z are not L. As discussed in the previous problem, the actual occurrence of P's other than under M and L is still an open question, and (C) is, thus, not false. (E) is eliminated with the discovery that (D) is false.

Questions 16–22

Arranging the Information

Previewing the questions shows that most of them are conditional questions, and the setup of the situation is of that nature, too. This means that most of the work will be in answering the questions rather than in determining the arrangement of the information.

At least 2 of D E F

Either 1 or 2 from L M N P

Total of 4

N not=P

E not=L

D not=N, thus, if N, neither P nor D

Answering the Questions

16. **(C)** If Nancy is chosen, then both David and Paul are out. Since at least two out of the trio of David, Erica, and Francis must be chosen, the elimination of David results in the forced selection of Erica and Francis, which eliminates answer choices (A) and (E). Since Nancy will not work with Paul, he cannot be a member of the crew, and answer choice (D) is eliminated. Since Erica is selected, as previously noted, and Erica will not work with Larry, answer choice (B) is eliminated, and we find that the crew will be Francis, Erica, Mary, and Nancy.

17. **(E)** If Paul is chosen, the only direct restriction is that Nancy is eliminated from the crew. This leaves only the restriction of the grinders versus the sail trimmers. If you wanted to select answer choice (A) because you thought there could only be two grinders, you missed the fact that the only restriction on the number of grinders versus sail trimmers was that AT LEAST two of the crew additions had to be grinders, which leaves open the possibility of all three of the grinder candidates being accepted. Thus, answer choice (A) is possible.

Answer choice (E), however, is not possible because Erica will not work with Larry as the answer choice requires. The other answer choices, (B), (C), and (D), do not violate any of the restrictions laid down by the problem.

18. **(C)** I must be true because if David is rejected, then the only two remaining grinder candidates—Erica and Francis—must be chosen. The selection of Erica means the elimination of Larry, leaving Mary, Nancy, and Paul. However, since Nancy will not work with Paul, only one of those two may be chosen, which gives Mary a definite berth on the boat.

II follows from the first sentence of the discussion of I.

III does not have to be true. The selection of David permits the selection of a crew such as David, Francis, Mary, and Paul or the selection of a crew without Paul—such as David, Francis, Mary, and Larry.

Thus, the answer is that I and II must be true and III is a maybe.

19. **(E)** As hinted at by the structure of the three Roman-numeral propositions, the acceptance of Larry as a crew member eliminates Erica from consideration, and thus requires the selection of David and Francis. The selection of David means that Nancy cannot be chosen, which leaves either Mary or Paul as acceptable candidates to fill the last sail trimmer slot with Larry. I and III are, thus, possible and II is not.

20. **(C)** I must be true since the choice of Larry eliminates Erica and requires the choice of David and Francis, as noted in question 19.

II is not necessarily true since the choice of Mary imposes no further restrictions on the choice of crew, so Mary and Nancy may or may not crew together.

III is also necessarily true. If Larry is chosen, Erica cannot be chosen; and this means David and Francis must be picked to meet the minimum number of two grinders. With David on the crew, Nancy cannot be on the crew.

21. **(B)** The choice of Paul eliminates Nancy, and, thus, answer choices (C) and (D). The omission of David forces the choice of Erica and Francis, which in turn eliminates Larry, and, thus, answer choices (A) and (E), leaving only Mary to fill out the crew, as stated in answer choice (B).

22. **(A)** If Erica makes the crew and Francis does not, this leaves David to fill in the second grinder slot. Erica's presence eliminates Larry, and David's eliminates Nancy, leaving a crew of David, Erica, Mary, and Paul. Thus, both I and II must be true.

23. **(D)** It is important not to attribute more to an author than he actually says or implies. Here the author states only that Ronnie's range is narrow so he will not be an outstanding vocalist. Vocalizing is only one kind of music career, so I, which speaks of professional musicians, takes us far beyond the claim the author actually makes. II also goes beyond what the author says. He never specifies what range an outstanding vocalist needs, much less what range is required to vocalize without being outstanding. Finally, III is an assumption since the author moves from a physical characteristic to a conclusion regarding ability.

24. **(C)** Ann's response would be appropriate only if Mary had said, "All of the students at State College come from Midland High." That is why (C) is correct. (D) is wrong because they are talking about the background of the students, not the reputations of the schools. (E) is wrong, for the question is from where the students at State College come. (B) is superficially relevant to the exchange, but it, too, is incorrect. Ann would not reply to this statement, had Mary made it, in the way she did reply. Rather, she would have said, "No, there are some Midland students at State College." Finally, Ann would correctly have said (A) only if Mary had said, "None of the students from North Hills attends State College," or, "Most of the students from North Hills do not attend State College." But Ann makes neither of these responses, so we know that (A) cannot have been what she thought she heard Mary say.

25. **(A)** Perhaps a small diagram is the easiest way to show this problem.

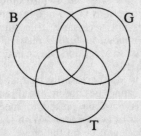

We will show that "all B are T" by eliminating that portion of the diagram where some area of B is not also inside T:

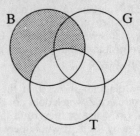

Now, let us put an x to show the existence of those B's which are G's:

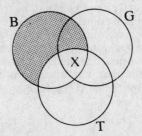

The diagram shows us that I is true. Since the only areas left for B's are within the T circle, the G condition is unimportant. II is not inferable. Although there is some overlap of the G and T circles, there is also some non-overlap. This shows that it may be possible to be a T without also being a G. III is not inferable since our diagrams are restricted to the three categories B, G, and T and say nothing about things outside of those categories.

ANSWER SHEET—PRACTICE EXAMINATION 4

Section I

1 Ⓐ Ⓑ Ⓒ Ⓓ Ⓔ 8 Ⓐ Ⓑ Ⓒ Ⓓ Ⓔ 15 Ⓐ Ⓑ Ⓒ Ⓓ Ⓔ 22 Ⓐ Ⓑ Ⓒ Ⓓ Ⓔ 29 Ⓐ Ⓑ Ⓒ Ⓓ Ⓔ 36 Ⓐ Ⓑ Ⓒ Ⓓ Ⓔ
2 Ⓐ Ⓑ Ⓒ Ⓓ Ⓔ 9 Ⓐ Ⓑ Ⓒ Ⓓ Ⓔ 16 Ⓐ Ⓑ Ⓒ Ⓓ Ⓔ 23 Ⓐ Ⓑ Ⓒ Ⓓ Ⓔ 30 Ⓐ Ⓑ Ⓒ Ⓓ Ⓔ 37 Ⓐ Ⓑ Ⓒ Ⓓ Ⓔ
3 Ⓐ Ⓑ Ⓒ Ⓓ Ⓔ 10 Ⓐ Ⓑ Ⓒ Ⓓ Ⓔ 17 Ⓐ Ⓑ Ⓒ Ⓓ Ⓔ 24 Ⓐ Ⓑ Ⓒ Ⓓ Ⓔ 31 Ⓐ Ⓑ Ⓒ Ⓓ Ⓔ 38 Ⓐ Ⓑ Ⓒ Ⓓ Ⓔ
4 Ⓐ Ⓑ Ⓒ Ⓓ Ⓔ 11 Ⓐ Ⓑ Ⓒ Ⓓ Ⓔ 18 Ⓐ Ⓑ Ⓒ Ⓓ Ⓔ 25 Ⓐ Ⓑ Ⓒ Ⓓ Ⓔ 32 Ⓐ Ⓑ Ⓒ Ⓓ Ⓔ
5 Ⓐ Ⓑ Ⓒ Ⓓ Ⓔ 12 Ⓐ Ⓑ Ⓒ Ⓓ Ⓔ 19 Ⓐ Ⓑ Ⓒ Ⓓ Ⓔ 26 Ⓐ Ⓑ Ⓒ Ⓓ Ⓔ 33 Ⓐ Ⓑ Ⓒ Ⓓ Ⓔ
6 Ⓐ Ⓑ Ⓒ Ⓓ Ⓔ 13 Ⓐ Ⓑ Ⓒ Ⓓ Ⓔ 20 Ⓐ Ⓑ Ⓒ Ⓓ Ⓔ 27 Ⓐ Ⓑ Ⓒ Ⓓ Ⓔ 34 Ⓐ Ⓑ Ⓒ Ⓓ Ⓔ
7 Ⓐ Ⓑ Ⓒ Ⓓ Ⓔ 14 Ⓐ Ⓑ Ⓒ Ⓓ Ⓔ 21 Ⓐ Ⓑ Ⓒ Ⓓ Ⓔ 28 Ⓐ Ⓑ Ⓒ Ⓓ Ⓔ 35 Ⓐ Ⓑ Ⓒ Ⓓ Ⓔ

Section II

1 Ⓐ Ⓑ Ⓒ Ⓓ Ⓔ 8 Ⓐ Ⓑ Ⓒ Ⓓ Ⓔ 15 Ⓐ Ⓑ Ⓒ Ⓓ Ⓔ 22 Ⓐ Ⓑ Ⓒ Ⓓ Ⓔ 29 Ⓐ Ⓑ Ⓒ Ⓓ Ⓔ 36 Ⓐ Ⓑ Ⓒ Ⓓ Ⓔ
2 Ⓐ Ⓑ Ⓒ Ⓓ Ⓔ 9 Ⓐ Ⓑ Ⓒ Ⓓ Ⓔ 16 Ⓐ Ⓑ Ⓒ Ⓓ Ⓔ 23 Ⓐ Ⓑ Ⓒ Ⓓ Ⓔ 30 Ⓐ Ⓑ Ⓒ Ⓓ Ⓔ 37 Ⓐ Ⓑ Ⓒ Ⓓ Ⓔ
3 Ⓐ Ⓑ Ⓒ Ⓓ Ⓔ 10 Ⓐ Ⓑ Ⓒ Ⓓ Ⓔ 17 Ⓐ Ⓑ Ⓒ Ⓓ Ⓔ 24 Ⓐ Ⓑ Ⓒ Ⓓ Ⓔ 31 Ⓐ Ⓑ Ⓒ Ⓓ Ⓔ 38 Ⓐ Ⓑ Ⓒ Ⓓ Ⓔ
4 Ⓐ Ⓑ Ⓒ Ⓓ Ⓔ 11 Ⓐ Ⓑ Ⓒ Ⓓ Ⓔ 18 Ⓐ Ⓑ Ⓒ Ⓓ Ⓔ 25 Ⓐ Ⓑ Ⓒ Ⓓ Ⓔ 32 Ⓐ Ⓑ Ⓒ Ⓓ Ⓔ
5 Ⓐ Ⓑ Ⓒ Ⓓ Ⓔ 12 Ⓐ Ⓑ Ⓒ Ⓓ Ⓔ 19 Ⓐ Ⓑ Ⓒ Ⓓ Ⓔ 26 Ⓐ Ⓑ Ⓒ Ⓓ Ⓔ 33 Ⓐ Ⓑ Ⓒ Ⓓ Ⓔ
6 Ⓐ Ⓑ Ⓒ Ⓓ Ⓔ 13 Ⓐ Ⓑ Ⓒ Ⓓ Ⓔ 20 Ⓐ Ⓑ Ⓒ Ⓓ Ⓔ 27 Ⓐ Ⓑ Ⓒ Ⓓ Ⓔ 34 Ⓐ Ⓑ Ⓒ Ⓓ Ⓔ
7 Ⓐ Ⓑ Ⓒ Ⓓ Ⓔ 14 Ⓐ Ⓑ Ⓒ Ⓓ Ⓔ 21 Ⓐ Ⓑ Ⓒ Ⓓ Ⓔ 28 Ⓐ Ⓑ Ⓒ Ⓓ Ⓔ 35 Ⓐ Ⓑ Ⓒ Ⓓ Ⓔ

Section III

1 Ⓐ Ⓑ Ⓒ Ⓓ 6 Ⓐ Ⓑ Ⓒ Ⓓ 11 Ⓐ Ⓑ Ⓒ Ⓓ 16 Ⓐ Ⓑ Ⓒ Ⓓ Ⓔ 21 Ⓐ Ⓑ Ⓒ Ⓓ Ⓔ 26 Ⓐ Ⓑ Ⓒ Ⓓ Ⓔ
2 Ⓐ Ⓑ Ⓒ Ⓓ 7 Ⓐ Ⓑ Ⓒ Ⓓ 12 Ⓐ Ⓑ Ⓒ Ⓓ 17 Ⓐ Ⓑ Ⓒ Ⓓ Ⓔ 22 Ⓐ Ⓑ Ⓒ Ⓓ Ⓔ 27 Ⓐ Ⓑ Ⓒ Ⓓ Ⓔ
3 Ⓐ Ⓑ Ⓒ Ⓓ 8 Ⓐ Ⓑ Ⓒ Ⓓ 13 Ⓐ Ⓑ Ⓒ Ⓓ 18 Ⓐ Ⓑ Ⓒ Ⓓ Ⓔ 23 Ⓐ Ⓑ Ⓒ Ⓓ Ⓔ 28 Ⓐ Ⓑ Ⓒ Ⓓ Ⓔ
4 Ⓐ Ⓑ Ⓒ Ⓓ 9 Ⓐ Ⓑ Ⓒ Ⓓ 14 Ⓐ Ⓑ Ⓒ Ⓓ 19 Ⓐ Ⓑ Ⓒ Ⓓ Ⓔ 24 Ⓐ Ⓑ Ⓒ Ⓓ Ⓔ 29 Ⓐ Ⓑ Ⓒ Ⓓ Ⓔ
5 Ⓐ Ⓑ Ⓒ Ⓓ 10 Ⓐ Ⓑ Ⓒ Ⓓ 15 Ⓐ Ⓑ Ⓒ Ⓓ 20 Ⓐ Ⓑ Ⓒ Ⓓ Ⓔ 25 Ⓐ Ⓑ Ⓒ Ⓓ Ⓔ 30 Ⓐ Ⓑ Ⓒ Ⓓ Ⓔ

Section IV

1 Ⓐ Ⓑ Ⓒ Ⓓ 6 Ⓐ Ⓑ Ⓒ Ⓓ 11 Ⓐ Ⓑ Ⓒ Ⓓ 16 Ⓐ Ⓑ Ⓒ Ⓓ Ⓔ 21 Ⓐ Ⓑ Ⓒ Ⓓ Ⓔ 26 Ⓐ Ⓑ Ⓒ Ⓓ Ⓔ

2 Ⓐ Ⓑ Ⓒ Ⓓ 7 Ⓐ Ⓑ Ⓒ Ⓓ 12 Ⓐ Ⓑ Ⓒ Ⓓ 17 Ⓐ Ⓑ Ⓒ Ⓓ Ⓔ 22 Ⓐ Ⓑ Ⓒ Ⓓ Ⓔ 27 Ⓐ Ⓑ Ⓒ Ⓓ Ⓔ

3 Ⓐ Ⓑ Ⓒ Ⓓ 8 Ⓐ Ⓑ Ⓒ Ⓓ 13 Ⓐ Ⓑ Ⓒ Ⓓ 18 Ⓐ Ⓑ Ⓒ Ⓓ Ⓔ 23 Ⓐ Ⓑ Ⓒ Ⓓ Ⓔ 28 Ⓐ Ⓑ Ⓒ Ⓓ Ⓔ

4 Ⓐ Ⓑ Ⓒ Ⓓ 9 Ⓐ Ⓑ Ⓒ Ⓓ 14 Ⓐ Ⓑ Ⓒ Ⓓ 19 Ⓐ Ⓑ Ⓒ Ⓓ Ⓔ 24 Ⓐ Ⓑ Ⓒ Ⓓ Ⓔ 29 Ⓐ Ⓑ Ⓒ Ⓓ Ⓔ

5 Ⓐ Ⓑ Ⓒ Ⓓ 10 Ⓐ Ⓑ Ⓒ Ⓓ 15 Ⓐ Ⓑ Ⓒ Ⓓ 20 Ⓐ Ⓑ Ⓒ Ⓓ Ⓔ 25 Ⓐ Ⓑ Ⓒ Ⓓ Ⓔ 30 Ⓐ Ⓑ Ⓒ Ⓓ Ⓔ

Section V

1 Ⓐ Ⓑ Ⓒ Ⓓ Ⓔ 6 Ⓐ Ⓑ Ⓒ Ⓓ Ⓔ 11 Ⓐ Ⓑ Ⓒ Ⓓ Ⓔ 16 Ⓐ Ⓑ Ⓒ Ⓓ Ⓔ 21 Ⓐ Ⓑ Ⓒ Ⓓ Ⓔ

2 Ⓐ Ⓑ Ⓒ Ⓓ Ⓔ 7 Ⓐ Ⓑ Ⓒ Ⓓ Ⓔ 12 Ⓐ Ⓑ Ⓒ Ⓓ Ⓔ 17 Ⓐ Ⓑ Ⓒ Ⓓ Ⓔ 22 Ⓐ Ⓑ Ⓒ Ⓓ Ⓔ

3 Ⓐ Ⓑ Ⓒ Ⓓ Ⓔ 8 Ⓐ Ⓑ Ⓒ Ⓓ Ⓔ 13 Ⓐ Ⓑ Ⓒ Ⓓ Ⓔ 18 Ⓐ Ⓑ Ⓒ Ⓓ Ⓔ 23 Ⓐ Ⓑ Ⓒ Ⓓ Ⓔ

4 Ⓐ Ⓑ Ⓒ Ⓓ Ⓔ 9 Ⓐ Ⓑ Ⓒ Ⓓ Ⓔ 14 Ⓐ Ⓑ Ⓒ Ⓓ Ⓔ 19 Ⓐ Ⓑ Ⓒ Ⓓ Ⓔ 24 Ⓐ Ⓑ Ⓒ Ⓓ Ⓔ

5 Ⓐ Ⓑ Ⓒ Ⓓ Ⓔ 10 Ⓐ Ⓑ Ⓒ Ⓓ Ⓔ 15 Ⓐ Ⓑ Ⓒ Ⓓ Ⓔ 20 Ⓐ Ⓑ Ⓒ Ⓓ Ⓔ 25 Ⓐ Ⓑ Ⓒ Ⓓ Ⓔ

Section VI

1 Ⓐ Ⓑ Ⓒ Ⓓ Ⓔ 6 Ⓐ Ⓑ Ⓒ Ⓓ Ⓔ 11 Ⓐ Ⓑ Ⓒ Ⓓ Ⓔ 16 Ⓐ Ⓑ Ⓒ Ⓓ Ⓔ 21 Ⓐ Ⓑ Ⓒ Ⓓ Ⓔ

2 Ⓐ Ⓑ Ⓒ Ⓓ Ⓔ 7 Ⓐ Ⓑ Ⓒ Ⓓ Ⓔ 12 Ⓐ Ⓑ Ⓒ Ⓓ Ⓔ 17 Ⓐ Ⓑ Ⓒ Ⓓ Ⓔ 22 Ⓐ Ⓑ Ⓒ Ⓓ Ⓔ

3 Ⓐ Ⓑ Ⓒ Ⓓ Ⓔ 8 Ⓐ Ⓑ Ⓒ Ⓓ Ⓔ 13 Ⓐ Ⓑ Ⓒ Ⓓ Ⓔ 18 Ⓐ Ⓑ Ⓒ Ⓓ Ⓔ 23 Ⓐ Ⓑ Ⓒ Ⓓ Ⓔ

4 Ⓐ Ⓑ Ⓒ Ⓓ Ⓔ 9 Ⓐ Ⓑ Ⓒ Ⓓ Ⓔ 14 Ⓐ Ⓑ Ⓒ Ⓓ Ⓔ 19 Ⓐ Ⓑ Ⓒ Ⓓ Ⓔ 24 Ⓐ Ⓑ Ⓒ Ⓓ Ⓔ

5 Ⓐ Ⓑ Ⓒ Ⓓ Ⓔ 10 Ⓐ Ⓑ Ⓒ Ⓓ Ⓔ 15 Ⓐ Ⓑ Ⓒ Ⓓ Ⓔ 20 Ⓐ Ⓑ Ⓒ Ⓓ Ⓔ 25 Ⓐ Ⓑ Ⓒ Ⓓ Ⓔ

PRACTICE EXAMINATION 4

SECTION I

30 minutes
38 questions

Directions: Each of the questions below contains one or more blank spaces, each blank indicating an omitted word. Each sentence is followed by five (5) lettered words or sets of words. Read and determine the general sense of each sentence. Then choose the word or set of words which, when inserted in the sentence, best fits the meaning of the sentence.

1. Over the _____ of the sirens, you could still hear the hoarse _____ of his voice.
   (A) babble—roar
   (B) drone—power
   (C) gibbering—cries
   (D) wail—sound
   (E) groaning—whisper

2. Working _____ under the pressure of time, Edmond didn't notice his _____ mistake.
   (A) leisurely—stupid
   (B) frantically—inevitable
   (C) rapidly—careless
   (D) sporadically—simple
   (E) continually—redundant

3. Held up only by a _____ steel cable, the chairlift was _____ to carry only two people.
   (A) slender—instructed
   (B) single—intended
   (C) sturdy—obliged
   (D) massive—designed
   (E) narrow—appointed

4. Since he is a teacher of English, we would not expect him to be guilty of a _____.

   (A) solecism
   (B) schism
   (C) misdemeanor
   (D) crime
   (E) strike

5. The servant's attitude was so _____ that it would have been _____ to anyone with an appreciation of sincerity.
   (A) natal—clear
   (B) hybrid—available
   (C) sycophantic—obnoxious
   (D) doleful—responsible
   (E) refulgent—candid

6. The theory of our justice system seems to be that incarcerating _____ in the company of their fellows will somehow teach them ethical standards, but experience shows that people tend to become _____ those with whom they most closely associate.
   (A) felons—angry with
   (B) malefactors—interested in
   (C) unfortunates—friendly with
   (D) defendants—marked by
   (E) criminals—more like

7. The trial was conducted in _____ manner, full of _____.
   (A) an incredible—proper procedures
   (B) a negligent—sworn testimony
   (C) a judicial—spectacular denouements
   (D) a theatrical—extravagant histrionics
   (E) an outrageous—erudite citations

Directions: In each of the following questions, you are given a related pair of words or phrases in capital letters. Each capitalized pair is followed by five (5) lettered pairs of words or phrases. Choose the pair which best expresses a relationship similar to that expressed by the original pair.

8. BLOW : HORN ::
   (A) switch : tracks
   (B) light : lamp
   (C) go over : map
   (D) accelerate : engine
   (E) tune : radio

9. FEATHERS : PLUCK ::
   (A) goose : down
   (B) garment : weave
   (C) car : drive
   (D) wool : shear
   (E) leg : pull

10. MODESTY : ARROGANCE ::
    (A) debility : strength
    (B) cause : purpose
    (C) passion : emotion
    (D) finance : pauper
    (E) practice : perfection

11. BAY : OCEAN ::
    (A) mountain : valley
    (B) plain : forest
    (C) peninsula : continent
    (D) cape : reef
    (E) island : sound

12. SPINDLE : SPOOL ::
    (A) thread : needle
    (B) rod : reel
    (C) straight : curved
    (D) spoke : rim
    (E) axle : wheel

13. SETTING : GEM ::
    (A) stage : play
    (B) socket : bulb
    (C) hole : plug
    (D) margin : text
    (E) frame : painting

14. FRANGIBLE : BROKEN ::
    (A) smelly : offensive
    (B) candid : unwelcome
    (C) brittle : destroyed
    (D) fluid : liquefied
    (E) pliable : bent

15. INTERRUPT : HECKLE ::
    (A) disrupt : intrude
    (B) tease : hector
    (C) maintain : uphold
    (D) condemn : implore
    (E) speech : performance

16. MERCHANDISE : SHOPLIFTER ::
    (A) men : kidnapper
    (B) pride : insult
    (C) bank : peculator
    (D) cattle : rustler
    (E) mansion : burglar

Directions: Below each of the following passages, you will find questions or incomplete statements about the passage. Each statement or question is followed by lettered words or expressions. Select the word or expression that most satisfactorily completes each statement, or answers each question in accordance with the meaning of the passage. After you have chosen the best answer, blacken the corresponding space on the answer sheet.

The enemy, also, reaped some benefit of his eagerness for honor. For when Ptolemy, after he had entered Pelusium, in his rage and spite against the Egyptians, designed to put them to the sword, Antony withstood him, and hindered the execution. In all the great and frequent skirmishes and battles, he gave continual proofs of his personal valor and military conduct; and once in particular, by wheeling about and attacking the rear of the enemy, he gave the victory to the assailants in the front, and received for this service signal marks of distinction. Nor was his humanity towards the deceased Archelaus less taken notice of. He had been formerly his guest and acquaintance, and, as he was now compelled, he fought him bravely while alive, but, on his death, sought out his body and buried it with royal honors. The consequence was that he left behind him a great name among the Alexandrians, and all who were serving in the Roman army looked upon him as a most gallant soldier.

17. According to this passage, Antony graciously provided Archelaus with
    (A) friendship
    (B) statesmanship
    (C) burial
    (D) hospitality
    (E) military prowess

18. Which of the following can be inferred from the passage?
    (A) There was great friendship between Romans and Egyptians.
    (B) Antony was a great ally of Ptolemy's.
    (C) Archelaus was the greatest general of the Egyptians
    (D) Antony was a great soldier.
    (E) Archelaus and Antony were great friends.

19. The author's attitude toward Antony is best described as
    (A) adulatory
    (B) appraising
    (C) admiring
    (D) inquisitive
    (E) intelligent

Every profession or trade, every art, and every science has its technical vocabulary, the function of which is partly to designate things or processes which have no names in ordinary English, and partly to secure greater exactness in nomenclature. Such special dialects, or jargons, are necessary in technical discussion of any kind. Being universally understood by the devotees of the particular science or art, they have the precision of a mathematical formula. Besides, they save time, for it is much more economical to name a process than to describe it. Thousands of these technical terms are very properly included in every large dictionary, yet, as a whole, they are rather on the outskirts of the English language than actually within its borders.

Different occupations, however, differ widely in the character of their special vocabularies. In trades and handicrafts and other vocations, such as farming and fishing, that have occupied great numbers of men from remote times, the technical vocabulary is very old. It consists largely of native words, or of borrowed words that have worked themselves into the very fiber of our language. Hence, though highly technical in many particu-lars, these vocabularies are more familiar in sound, and more generally understood, than most other technicalities. The special dialects of law, medicine, divinity, and philosophy have also, in their older strata, become pretty familiar to cultivated persons, and have contributed much to the popular vocabulary. Yet, every vocation still possesses a large body of technical terms that remain essentially foreign, even to educated speech. And the proportion has been much increased in the last fifty years, particularly in the various departments of natural and political science and in the mechanic arts. Here new terms are coined with the greatest freedom, and abandoned with indifference when they have served their turn. Most of the new coinages are confined to special discussions and seldom get into general literature or conversation. Yet, no profession is nowadays, as all professions once were, a closed guild. The lawyer, the physician, the man of science, and the cleric associates freely with his fellow creatures, and does not meet them in a merely professional way. Furthermore, what is called popular science makes everybody acquainted with modern views and recent discoveries. Any important experiment, though made in a remote or provincial laboratory, is at once reported in the newspapers, and everybody is soon talking about it—as in the case of the Roentgen rays and wireless telegraphy. Thus, our common speech is always taking up new technical terms and making them commonplace.

20. Which of the following words is least likely to have started its life as jargon?
    (A) sun
    (B) calf
    (C) plow
    (D) loom
    (E) hammer

21. The author's main purpose in the passage is to
    (A) describe a phenomenon
    (B) argue a belief
    (C) propose a solution
    (D) stimulate action
    (E) be entertaining

22. When the author refers to professions as no longer being "closed guilds," he means that
    (A) it is much easier to become a professional today than it was in the past

(B) there is more social intercourse between professionals and others

(C) popular science has told their secrets to the world

(D) anyone can now understand anything in a profession

(E) apprenticeships are no longer required

23. If the author of the passage wished to study a new field, he would probably
    (A) call in a dictionary expert
    (B) become easily discouraged
    (C) look to the histories of the words in the new field
    (D) pay careful attention to the new field's technical vocabulary
    (E) learn how to coin new jargon in the field

24. The writer of this article was probably a(n)
    (A) linguist
    (B) attorney
    (C) scientist
    (D) politician
    (E) physician

25. The author of the passage probably lived in
    (A) 1904 in India
    (B) 1914 in the United States
    (C) 1944 in Russia
    (D) 1964 in England
    (E) 1974 in France

26. It seems that the passage implies
    (A) the English language is always becoming larger and larger
    (B) the words of the English language are always changing
    (C) one can never be sure of what a word means without consulting an expert
    (D) technical terms in most non-scientific fields have little chance of becoming part of the main body of the language in these scientific days
    (E) such old-time farming words as harrow and farrow are not really technical terms at all.

27. Which of the following is (are) NOT an advantage of jargon?

    I. Jargon permits experts to make short explanations of technical matters to other experts.

    II. Jargon saves money.
    III. Jargon is mathematical.
    IV. Jargon is more precise than ordinary language for describing special topics.

    (A) I only
    (B) II and III only
    (C) I and IV only
    (D) I, III, and IV only
    (E) I, II, III, and IV

Directions: Each of the following questions ...sts of a word printed in capital letters, followed by five (5) lettered words or phrases. Select the word or phrase which is most nearly *opposite* to the capitalized word in the meaning.

28. PIQUANT:
    (A) factitious
    (B) vain
    (C) insipid
    (D) slow
    (E) colorful

29. OPPORTUNE:
    (A) suprisingly agreeable
    (B) closely berthed
    (C) sharply edged
    (D) badly shaped
    (E) poorly timed

30. PETULANT:
    (A) pliable
    (B) equable
    (C) uncouth
    (D) abnormal
    (E) untouchable

31. SAVORY:
    (A) sad
    (B) hidden
    (C) lost
    (D) unpalatable
    (E) light

32. FULFILLED:
    (A) satirical
    (B) dry
    (C) gorgeous
    (D) delectable
    (E) needy

33. RECLUSIVE:
    (A) joined
    (B) obscure
    (C) gregarious
    (D) urban
    (E) repetitive

34. COURTEOUS:
    (A) flaccid
    (B) emollient
    (C) insolent
    (D) scrupulous
    (E) flinching

35. USURP:
    (A) rise rapidly
    (B) use fully
    (C) produce quickly
    (D) hold carefully
    (E) own rightfully

36. ACRIMONIOUS:
    (A) legal
    (B) severe
    (C) cursive
    (D) harmonious
    (E) flippant

37. SKEPTIC:
    (A) cryptic
    (B) believer
    (C) support
    (D) eminent
    (E) caricature

38. INDUBITABLE:
    (A) wavering
    (B) aesthetic
    (C) unmitigated
    (D) questionable
    (E) belabored

STOP

END OF SECTION. IF YOU HAVE ANY TIME LEFT, GO
OVER YOUR WORK IN THIS SECTION ONLY. DO NOT
WORK IN ANY OTHER SECTION OF THE TEST.

SECTION II

30 minutes
38 questions

Directions: Each of the questions below contains one or more blank spaces, each blank indicating an omitted word. Each sentence is followed by five (5) lettered words or sets of words. Read and determine the general sense of each sentence. Then choose the word or set of words which, when inserted in the sentence, best fits the meaning of the sentence.

1. The _____ of the early morning light _____ the room, making it larger and cozier at once.
    (A) brilliance—shattered
    (B) softness—transformed
    (C) harshness—transfigured
    (D) warmth—disfigured
    (E) glare—annihilated

2. As _____ of the original team, Mickey had free _____ to all their games.
    (A) a survivor—advice
    (B) a scholar—passage
    (C) an institution—admission
    (D) an organizer—submission
    (E) a member—entrance

3. The presence of armed guards _____ us from doing anything disruptive.
    (A) defeated

(B) excited
(C) irritated
(D) prevented
(E) encouraged

4. A careful _____ of the house re-
    vealed no clues.
    (A) dissemination
    (B) incineration
    (C) autopsy
    (D) dereliction
    (E) examination

5. For his diligent work in astronomy, Profes-
    sor Wilson was _____ at the banquet
    as _____ of the Year.
    (A) taunted—Teacher
    (B) praised—Lobotomist
    (C) lauded—Scientist
    (D) honored—Astrologer
    (E) welcomed—Administrator

6. The attorney is _____ debater; he
    _____ the cross-questioning of the
    Supreme Court Judge.
    (A) a forceful—anticipates
    (B) an intelligent—enjoys
    (C) an inept—dreads
    (D) a fatigued—ignores
    (E) a foolish—interrupts

7. Although there have been _____
    delightful tunes, recent popular music can
    hardly be called _____.
    (A) successful—aesthetic
    (B) individually—significant
    (C) some—new
    (D) increasingly—strong
    (E) many—debased

Directions: In each of the following questions, you are
given a related pair of words or phrases in capital
letters. Each capitalized pair is followed by five (5)
lettered pairs or words or phrases. Choose the pair
which best expresses a relationship similar to that
expressed by the original pair.

8. TEPID : HOT ::
    (A) pat : slap

(B) winter : summer
(C) topple : tumble
(D) cool : gel
(E) rain : storm

9. RIB : UMBRELLA ::
    (A) column : ceiling
    (B) hub : wheel
    (C) crank : engine
    (D) trunk : tree
    (E) rafter : roof

10. TADPOLE : FROG ::
    (A) gander : goose
    (B) caterpillar : butterfly
    (C) cub : lioness
    (D) frog : fish
    (E) chick : hen

11. WOOL : SHEEP ::
    (A) quill : porcupine
    (B) mohair : goat
    (C) scale : fish
    (D) shell : lobster
    (E) feather : bird

12. CAT : FELINE ::
    (A) horse : equine
    (B) tiger : carnivorous
    (C) bird : vulpine
    (D) chair : furniture
    (E) sit : recline

13. RUSTICITY : URBANITY ::
    (A) silk : wool
    (B) rust : steel
    (C) caution : daring
    (D) private : public
    (E) verbose : windy

14. CLOTHES : CLOSET ::
    (A) feet : rug
    (B) actor : script
    (C) ink : pen
    (D) beetle : insect
    (E) book : literature

15. PEPPER : BERRY ::
    (A) nutmeg : mace
    (B) persimmon : fruit
    (C) fennel : vegetable
    (D) basil : leaf
    (E) salt : rock

16. TOURNIQUET : BLEEDING ::
    (A) mint : breath
    (B) phenol : digestion
    (C) metronome : time
    (D) pressure : release
    (E) anodyne : pain

Directions: Below each of the following passages, you will find questions or incomplete statements about the passage. Each statement or question is followed by lettered words or expressions. Select the word or expression that most satisfactorily completes each statement, or answers each question in accordance with the meaning of the passage. After you have chosen the best answer, blacken the corresponding space on the answer sheet.

Whenever two or more unusual traits or situations are found in the same place, it is tempting to look for more than a coincidental relationship between them. The high Himalayas and the Tibetan plateau certainly have extraordinary physical characteristics, and the cultures which are found there are also unusual, though not unique. However, there is no intention of adopting Montesquieu's view of climate and soil as cultural determinants. The ecology of a region merely poses some of the problems faced by the inhabitants of the region, and while the problems facing a culture are important to its development, they do not determine it.

The appearance of the Himalayas during the late Tertiary Period and the accompanying further raising of the previously established ranges had a marked effect on the climate of the region. Primarily, of course, it blocked the Indian monsoon from reaching Central Asia at all. Secondarily, air and moisture from other directions were also reduced.

Prior to the raising of the Himalayas, the land now forming the Tibetan uplands had a dry continental climate with vegetation and animal life similar to that of much of the rest of the region on the same parallel, but somewhat different than that of the areas farther north,

which were already drier. With the coming of the Himalayas and the relatively sudden drying out of the region, there was a severe thinning out of the animal and plant populations. The ensuing incomplete Pleistocene glaciation had a further thinning effect, but significantly did not wipe out life in the area. Thus, after the end of the glaciation there were only a few varieties of life extant from the original continental species. Isolated by the Kunlun range from the Tarim basin and Turfan depression, species which had already adapted to the dry steppe climate, and would otherwise have been expected to flourish in Tibet, the remaining native fauna and flora multiplied. Armand describes the Tibetan fauna as not having great variety, but being "striking" in the abundance of the particular species that are present. The plant life is similarly limited in variety, with some observers finding no more than seventy varieties of plants in even the relatively fertile Eastern Tibetan valleys, with fewer than ten food crops. Tibetan "tea" is a major staple, perhaps replacing the unavailable vegetables.

The difficulties of living in an environment at once dry and cold, and populated with species more usually found in more hospitable climes, are great. These difficulties may well have influenced the unusual polyandrous societies typical of the region. Lattimore sees the maintenance of multiple-husband households as being preserved from earlier forms by the harsh conditions of the Tibetan uplands, which permitted no experimentation and "froze" the cultures which came there. Kawakita, on the other hand, sees the polyandry as a way of easily permitting the best householder to become the head husband regardless of age. His detailed studies of the Bhotea village of Tsumje do seem to support this idea of polyandry as a method of talent mobility in a situation where even the best talent is barely enough for survival.

In sum, though arguments can be made that a pre-existing polyandrous system was strengthened and preserved (insofar as it has been) by the rigors of the land, it would certainly be an overstatement to lay causative factors of any stronger nature to the ecological influences in this case.

17. What are the "unusual situations and traits" referred to in the first sentence?

I. patterns of animal and plant growth
II. food and food preparation patterns of the upland Tibetans
III. social and familial organization of typical Tibetan society

(A) I only
(B) II only
(C) III only
(D) I and III only
(E) I, II, and III

18. What was the significance of the fact that the Pleistocene glaciation did not wipe out life entirely in the area?
(A) Without life, man could not flourish either.
(B) The drying out was too sudden for most plants to adapt to the climate.
(C) If the region had been devoid of life, some of the other species from nearby arid areas might possibly have taken over the area.
(D) The variety of Tibetan life was decreased.
(E) None of the above.

19. Which of the following most likely best describes Tibetan "tea"?
(A) a pale brown, clear, broth-like drink
(B) a dark brown tea drink, carefully strained
(C) a nutritious mixture of tea leaves and rancid yak butter
(D) a high caffeine drink
(E) a green tinted drink similar to Chinese basket-fried green tea

20. The purpose of the passage is to
(A) describe Tibetan fauna and flora
(B) describe the social organization of typical Tibetan villages
(C) analyze the causes of Tibet's unusual animal and plant populations
(D) analyze the possible causal links between Tibetan ecology and society
(E) probe the mysteries of the sudden appearance of the Himalayas

21. The author's knowledge of Tibet is probably
(A) based on firsthand experience
(B) the result of lifelong study

(C) derived only from books
(D) derived from Chinese sources
(E) limited to geological history

22. In which ways are the ideas of Lattimore and Kawakita totally opposed?
(A) Lattimore forbids change and Kawakita requires it.
(B) Kawakita opposes change and Lattimore favors it.
(C) Lattimore sees polyandry as primitive and Kawakita views it as modern.
(D) Lattimore criticizes polyandry as inefficient, but Kawakita finds it highly efficient.
(E) Their ideas are not totally opposed on any point.

23. According to the passage, which of the following would probably be the most agreeable to Montesquieu?
(A) All regions have different soils and, thus, different cultures.
(B) Some regions with similar climates will have similar cultures.
(C) Cultures in the same area, sharing soil and climate, will be essentially identical.
(D) European cultures are liberated to some degree from determinism.
(E) The plants of a country, by being the food of its people, cause the people to have similar views to one another.

24. The species of fauna and flora remaining in Tibet after the Pleistocene glaciation can properly be called continental because they
(A) are originally found in continental climates
(B) are the only life forms in Tibet, which is as big as a continent
(C) have been found in other parts of the Asian continent
(D) are found in a land mass that used to be a separate continent
(E) cannot be found on islands

The modern biographer's task is often seen as one of presenting the "dynamics" of the personality he is studying rather than giving the reader documents from which to deduce the personality. The biographer hopes to achieve a reasonable likeness so that the unearthing of more material will not alter the picture he has drawn. He hopes that new revelations will add dimension to his study but not change its lineaments appreciably. After all, he usually has had enough material to permit him to reach conclusions and to paint his portrait. With this abundance of material he can select moments of high drama and find episodes to illustrate character and make for vividness. In any event, biographers, I think, must recognize that the writing of a life may not be as "scientific" or as "definitive" as we have pretended. Biography partakes of a large part of the subjective side of man, and we must remember that those who walked abroad in our time may have one appearance for us—but will seem quite different to posterity.

25. The title below that best expresses the ideas of this passage is
    (A) The Dynamic Personality
    (B) The Growing Popularity of Biography
    (C) The Scientific Biography
    (D) A Verdict of Posterity
    (E) An Approach to Biography

26. According to the author, which is the real task of the modern biographer?
    (A) Interpreting the character revealed to him by the study of the presently available data.
    (B) Viewing the life of the subject in the biographer's own image.
    (C) Leaving to the reader the task of interpreting the character from contradictory evidence.
    (D) Collecting facts and setting them down in chronological order.
    (E) Being willing to wait until all the facts on the subject have been uncovered.

27. Which of the following would be the strongest criticism of the work of modern biographers as defined by the above passage?
    (A) Writing about modern figures will often fail to properly appreciate their place in history because insufficient time has passed for accurate historical judgment.
    (B) By presenting only, or primarily, his

conclusions about the character of his subject rather than the evidence upon which those conclusions are based, the modern biographer reduces the reader's ability to judge the worth of those judgments.
    (C) Illustrating a life with vivid pictures detracts from the reader's understanding of the prose itself.
    (D) By changing the style and content of biographies to suit modern tastes, it becomes impossible to compare old and modern biographical information.
    (E) Many authorities find that scientific judgments of character are impossible and, thus, only pretentious nonsense to attempt.

Directions: Each of the following questions consists of a word printed in capital letters, followed by five (5) lettered words or phrases. Select the word or phrase which is most nearly *opposite* to the capitalized word in meaning.

28. DELETERIOUS:
    (A) impulsive
    (B) salubrious
    (C) pathetic
    (D) inclusive
    (E) antipathetic

29. PUISSANCE:
    (A) ignorance
    (B) approbation
    (C) impotence
    (D) repudiation
    (E) malaise

30. SYCOPHANCY:
    (A) speak harmoniously
    (B) shout harshly
    (C) push forcefully
    (D) advise candidly
    (E) grasp greedily

31. ABERRATION:
    (A) typical behavior
    (B) correct manners
    (C) straight aim
    (D) full truthfulness
    (E) major improvement

32. ANOMALOUS:
   (A) capacious
   (B) vicious
   (C) connected
   (D) meaningful
   (E) usual

33. COGNIZANCE:
   (A) idiom
   (B) ignorance
   (C) abeyance
   (D) anecdote
   (E) fetish

34. QUIESCENT:
   (A) restless
   (B) exempt
   (C) malignant
   (D) mendicant
   (E) farcical

35. ESCHEW:
   (A) traduce
   (B) invite

   (C) use
   (D) emanate
   (E) strengthen

36. TACITURN:
   (A) dubious
   (B) garrulous
   (C) strategic
   (D) pleasant
   (E) gullible

37. RECONDITE:
   (A) miniature
   (B) philosopher
   (C) arable
   (D) peasant
   (E) obvious

38. REDUNDANT:
   (A) dilatory
   (B) apocryphal
   (C) astute
   (D) necessary
   (E) bare

STOP

END OF SECTION. IF YOU HAVE ANY TIME LEFT, GO
OVER YOUR WORK IN THIS SECTION ONLY. DO NOT
WORK IN ANY OTHER SECTION OF THE TEST.

SECTION III

30 minutes
30 questions

Directions: For each of the following questions two quantities are given, one in Column A and one in Column B. Compare the two quantities and mark your answer sheet with the correct lettered conclusion. These are your options:
   A: If the quantity in Column A is the greater;
   B: if the quantity in Column B is the greater;
   C: if the two quantities are equal;
   D: if the relationship cannot be determined from the information given.
Common Information: In any question, information applying to both columns is centered between the columns and above the quantities in columns A and B. The common information applies to both columns. Any symbol that appears in both columns represents the same idea or quantity in both columns.
Numbers: All numbers used are real numbers.

Figures: Assume that the positions of points, angles, regions, and so forth are in the order shown. Figures are assumed to lie in a plane unless otherwise indicated. Figures accompanying questions are intended to provide information you can use in answering the questions. However, unless a note states that a figure is drawn to scale, you should solve the problems by using your knowledge of mathematics and *not* by estimating sizes by sight or measurement.

Lines: Assume that lines shown as straight are indeed straight.

	COLUMN A	COLUMN B
1.	$\sqrt{9}$	$\sqrt{5} + \sqrt{4}$
2.	$\frac{1}{6}$	16%

3.
$$x^2 - 4 = 0$$

	COLUMN A	COLUMN B
	x	2
4.	the cost of three pounds of grapes	the cost of four pounds of bananas
5.	$0.17 + 6.01 + 5.27832$	12

6.

	COLUMN A	COLUMN B
	$\dfrac{\text{area of sector P}}{\text{area of sector Q}}$	$\dfrac{\text{area of sector R}}{\text{area of sector S}}$

7.

	COLUMN A	COLUMN B
	x	30

8.
$$x > 0 \text{ and } y < 0$$

	COLUMN A	COLUMN B
	$x^2 + y^2$	$(x + y)^2$

9.
x is 150% of y and y > 0

	COLUMN A	COLUMN B
	x	y

	COLUMN A	COLUMN B

10.

| The number the minute hand points to after turning 480° clockwise. | The number the minute hand points to after turning 720° clockwise. |

11.

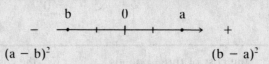

| $(a - b)^2$ | $(b - a)^2$ |

12.

$$2^m = 64$$
$$3^n = 81$$

| m | n |

13.

Room P

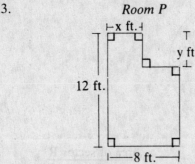

Room Q

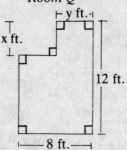

| perimeter of room P | perimeter of room Q |

14.

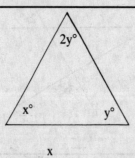

| x | 2y |

15.

| Total weight of x cartons each weighing y pounds | Total weight of y cartons each weighing x pounds |

Directions: For each of the following questions, select the best of the answer choices and blacken the corresponding space on your answer sheet.
Numbers: All numbers used are real numbers.
Figures: The diagrams and figures that accompany these questions are for the purpose of providing information useful in answering the questions. Unless it is stated that a specific figure is not drawn to scale, the diagrams and figures are drawn as accurately as possible. All figures are in a plane unless otherwise indicated.

16. If w, x, y, and z are real numbers, each of the following equals w(x + y + z) EXCEPT
    (A) wx + wy + wz
    (B) (x + y + z)w
    (C) wx + w(y + z)
    (D) 3w + x + y + z
    (E) w(x + y) + wz

17. .1% of 10 =
    (A) 1
    (B) .1
    (C) .01
    (D) .001
    (E) .0001

18. If x = +4, then (x − 7)(x + 2) =
    (A) −66
    (B) −18
    (C) 0
    (D) 3
    (E) 17

19. If 2x + y = 7 and x − y = 2, then x + y =
    (A) 6
    (B) 4
    (C) $\frac{3}{2}$
    (D) 0
    (E) −5

20. A girl rode her bicycle from home to school, a distance of 15 miles, at an average speed of 15 miles per hour. She returned home from school by walking at an average speed of 5 miles per hour. What was her average speed for the round trip if she took the same route in both directions?
    (A) 7.5 miles per hour
    (B) 10 miles per hour
    (C) 12.5 miles per hour
    (D) 13 miles per hour
    (E) 25 miles per hour

21. In the square below with side 4, the ratio $\frac{\text{area of shaded region}}{\text{area of unshaded region}} =$
    (A) $\frac{2 + x}{4}$
    (B) $\frac{4 - x}{8}$
    (C) 2
    (D) $\frac{4 + x}{4 - x}$
    (E) 2x

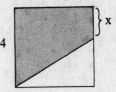

22. Ned is two years older than Mike, who is twice as old as Linda. If the ages of the three total 27 years, how old is Mike?
    (A) 5 years
    (B) 8 years
    (C) 9 years
    (D) 10 years
    (E) 12 years

23. A taxicab charges $1.00 for the first one-fifth mile of a trip and 20¢ for each following one-fifth mile or part thereof. If a trip is $2\frac{1}{2}$ miles long, what will be the fare?
    (A) $2.60
    (B) $3.10
    (C) $3.20
    (D) $3.40
    (E) $3.60

24. What is the side of a square if its area is $36x^2$?
    (A) 9
    (B) 9x
    (C) $6x^2$
    (D) 6
    (E) 6x

25. If Susan has $5 more than Tom, and if Tom has $2 more than Ed, which of the following exchanges will ensure that each of the three has an equal amount of money?
    (A) Susan must give Ed $3 and Tom $1.
    (B) Tom must give Susan $4 and Susan must give Ed $5.
    (C) Ed must give Susan $1 and Susan must give Tom $1.
    (D) Susan must give Ed $4 and Tom must give Ed $5.
    (E) Either Susan or Ed must give Tom $7.

26. A perfect number is one which is equal to the sum of all its positive factors that are less than the number itself. Which of the following is a perfect number?
    (A) 1
    (B) 4
    (C) 6
    (D) 8
    (E) 10

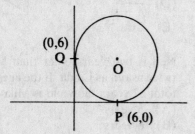

27.

In the figure above, the coordinates of points P and Q are (6,0) and (0,6), respectively. What is the area of the circle O?
    (A) 36π
    (B) 12π
    (C) 9π
    (D) 6π
    (E) 3π

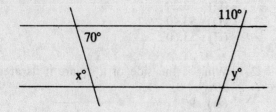

28. In the figure shown (bottom left), x + y =
    (A) 50
    (B) 140
    (C) 180
    (D) 220
    (E) 240

29. A cylinder has a radius of 2 ft. and a height of 5 ft. If it is already 40% filled with a liquid, how many more cubic feet of liquid must be added to fill it to capacity?
    (A) 6π
    (B) 8π
    (C) 10π
    (D) 12π
    (E) 16π

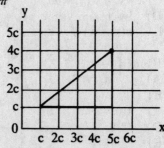

30. In the figure above, a triangle is superimposed on a grid in which all angles are right angles. If the area of the above triangle is 54, then c =
    (A) 3
    (B) 6
    (C) 10
    (D) 12
    (E) Cannot be determined from the information given.

STOP

END OF SECTION. IF YOU HAVE ANY TIME LEFT, GO
OVER YOUR WORK IN THIS SECTION ONLY. DO NOT
WORK IN ANY OTHER SECTION OF THE TEST.

SECTION IV

30 minutes
30 questions

Directions: For each of the following questions two quantities are given, one in Column A and one in Column B. Compare the two quantities and mark your answer sheet with the correct lettered conclusion. These are your options:

  A: If the quantity in Column A is the greater:
  B: if the quantity in Column B is the greater:
  C: if the two quantities are equal;
  D: if the relationship cannot be determined from the information given.

Common Information: In any question, information applying to both columns is centered between the columns and above the quantities in columns A and B. The common information applies to both columns. Any symbol that appears in both columns represents the same idea or quantity in both columns.

Numbers: All numbers used are real numbers.

Figures: Assume that the positions of points, angles, regions, and so forth are in the order shown. Figures are assumed to lie in a plane unless otherwise indicated. Figures accompanying questions are intended to provide information you can use in answering the questions. However, unless a note states that a figure is drawn to scale, you should solve the problems by using your knowledge of mathematics and *not* by estimating sizes by sight or measurement.

Lines: Assume that lines shown as straight are indeed straight.

	COLUMN A	COLUMN B
1.	$343 - \dfrac{343}{2}$	$\dfrac{343}{2}$

2.
$$6x = 6$$

	COLUMN A	COLUMN B
	$\dfrac{x}{6}$	$\dfrac{6}{x}$

3. On the real number line, n is between p and m and $m < n$.

	COLUMN A	COLUMN B
	n	p
4.	$\dfrac{1}{63} - \dfrac{1}{69}$	$\dfrac{1}{65} - \dfrac{1}{67}$
5.	.06% of 1.34	1.34% of .06
6.	$3x^2 + 5$	$2x^2 + 4$

7. The digit 2 in the numeral 423,978 indicates $2 \cdot 10^b$.

	COLUMN A	COLUMN B
	b	5

COLUMN A	COLUMN B

8.

$$x = -3$$
$$y = -5$$

$(x - y)^2$	$(x + y)^2$

9.

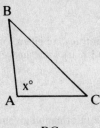 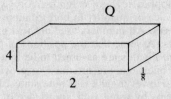

$$x° < y°$$

BC	QR

10.

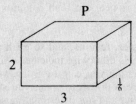

The volume of rectangular solid P	The volume of rectangular solid Q

11.

The greatest prime factor of 208	13

12.

$$x + 2.3 = 2y + 1.6$$

x	y

13.

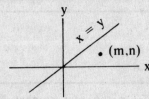

m	n

14.

$$x*y = \frac{x + y}{xy} \text{ for all real numbers such}$$
that $xy \neq 0$.

$1*2$	$2*1$

15.

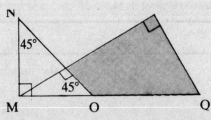

Area of triangle MNO	Area of shaded portion

Directions: For each of the following questions, select the best of the answer choices and blacken the corresponding space on your answer sheet.

Numbers: All numbers used are real numbers.

Figures: The diagrams and figures that accompany these questions are for the purpose of providing information useful in answering the questions. Unless it is stated that a specific figure is not drawn to scale, the diagrams and figures are drawn as accurately as possible. All figures are in a plane unless otherwise indicated.

16. $(1.50)(2) =$
    (A) $\frac{1}{2}$
    (B) 1
    (C) $\frac{3}{2}$
    (D) $\frac{5}{2}$
    (E) 3

17. If $x = -2$, then $(x - 5)(x + 5) =$
    (A) -49
    (B) -21
    (C) 0
    (D) 9
    (E) 35

18. If an item which ordinarily costs $90 is discounted by 25%, what is the new selling price?
    (A) $22.50
    (B) $25.00
    (C) $45.00
    (D) $67.50
    (E) $112.50

19. During the time period covered by the chart, in how many years was the attrition rate for Sophomores greater than that for Freshmen?
    (A) 6
    (B) 10
    (C) 18
    (D) 21
    (E) 24

20. Between 1965 and 1970, the attrition rate for Juniors
    (A) increased by 100%
    (B) increased by 50%
    (C) increased by 20%
    (D) remained virtually unchanged
    (E) declined by 5%

21. In 1970 the ratio of the number of Freshmen who left College X to the number of Juniors who left College X was
    (A) 3:1
    (B) 3:2
    (C) 1
    (D) 2:3
    (E) Cannot be determined from the information given.

22. Which of the following propositions can be inferred from the graph?

    I. Between 1970 and 1975, the number of Freshmen leaving College X dropped by 20%.

Questions 19–23 refer to the following graph.

ATTRITION RATE AT COLLEGE X*

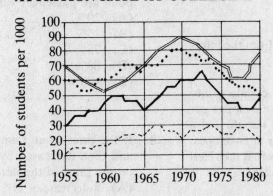

*Includes all students who voluntarily dropped out, took a leave of absence, were expelled for academic or disciplinary reasons, or left college for any other reasons

——————— Freshmen   ·········· Sophomores   ——————— Juniors   – – – – Seniors

DISTRIBUTION	NUMBER IN POPULATION
Having X Having Y	25
Having X Lacking Y	10
Lacking X Having Y	25
Lacking X Lacking Y	40

II. In 1970, twenty more Juniors left College X than left College X in 1965.
III. During the period 1966 to 1969, only the rate of attrition for Seniors was decreasing.

(A) I only
(B) II only
(C) I and II only
(D) III only
(E) I, II, and III

23. For which of the four classes was the attrition rate in 1980 approximately 25% less than it had been in 1970?

I. Freshmen
II. Sophomore
III. Juniors
IV. Seniors

(A) I only
(B) I and II only
(C) III only
(D) II and III only
(E) I, II, III, and IV

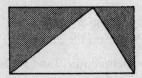

24. In the rectangle above, what is the ratio of
$$\frac{\text{area of shaded region}}{\text{area of unshaded region}}?$$
(A) $\frac{1}{4}$
(B) $\frac{1}{2}$
(C) 1
(D) $\frac{2}{1}$
(E) Cannot be determined from the information given.

25. Earl can stuff advertising circulars into envelopes at the rate of 45 envelopes per minute and Ellen requires a minute and a half to stuff the same number of envelopes. Working together, how long will it take Earl and Ellen to stuff 300 envelopes?
(A) 15 minutes
(B) 4 minutes
(C) 3 minutes 30 seconds
(D) 3 minutes 20 seconds
(E) 2 minutes

26. The table above gives the distribution of two genetic characteristics, X and Y, in a population of 100 subjects. What is the ratio of
$$\frac{\text{number of subjects having X}}{\text{number of subjects having Y}}?$$
(A) $\frac{7}{5}$
(B) 1
(C) $\frac{5}{7}$
(D) $\frac{7}{10}$
(E) $\frac{1}{4}$

27. If the ratio of the number of passenger vehicles to all other vehicles passing a checkpoint on a highway is 4 to 1, what percent of the vehicles passing the checkpoint are passenger vehicles?
(A) 20%
(B) 25%
(C) 75%
(D) 80%
(E) 400%

28. If the price of an item is increased by 10% and then decreased by 10%, the net effect on the price of the item is
(A) a decrease of 11%
(B) a decrease of 1%
(C) no change
(D) an increase of 1%
(E) an increase of 99%

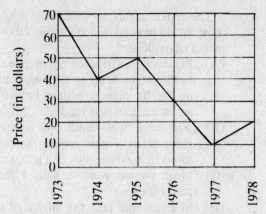

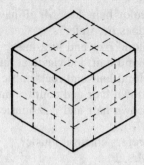

29. The graph above shows the yearly prices (in dollars) for a certain commodity. For which one-year period was the percentage decrease in price the greatest?
    (A) 1973–1974
    (B) 1974–1975
    (C) 1975–1976
    (D) 1976–1977
    (E) 1977–1978

30. The figure above represents a wooden block 3 inches on an edge, all of whose faces are painted black. If the block is cut up along the dotted lines, 27 blocks result, each 1 cubic inch in volume. Of these, how many will have no painted faces?
    (A) 1
    (B) 3
    (C) 4
    (D) 5
    (E) 7

STOP

END OF SECTION. IF YOU HAVE ANY TIME LEFT, GO OVER YOUR WORK IN THIS SECTION ONLY. DO NOT WORK IN ANY OTHER SECTION OF THE TEST.

SECTION V

30 minutes
25 questions

Directions: Each of the following questions or groups of questions is based on a short passage or a set of propositions. In answering these questions it may sometimes be helpful to draw a simple picture or chart. When you have selected the best answer to each question, darken the corresponding circle on your answer sheet.

Questions 1–3

Mr. and Mrs. N and Mr. and Mrs. P each have different tastes in music. One prefers classical, one jazz, one rock, and the last country music. Of the four, only two have blond hair and one of these likes jazz best. The wife with blond hair likes country music and her husband likes classical music best. Mrs. P has brown hair.

1. What is Mrs. P's preferred music?
   (A) classical
   (B) jazz
   (C) rock
   (D) country
   (E) Cannot be determined from the information given.

2. What color hair does Mr. P have and what music does he prefer?
   (A) blond hair and jazz music
   (B) blond hair and classical music
   (C) blond hair and rock music
   (D) brown hair and country music
   (E) brown hair and jazz music

3. Who prefers classical music?
   (A) Mrs. P
   (B) Mr. P
   (C) Mrs. N
   (D) Mr. N
   (E) Cannot be determined from the information given.

4. When this proposal to reduce welfare benefits is brought up for debate, we are sure to hear claims by the liberal congressmen that the bill will be detrimental to poor people. These politicians fail to understand, however, that budget reductions are accompanied by tax cuts—so everyone will have more money to spend, not less.

   Which of the following, if true, would undermine the author's position?

   I. Poor people tend to vote for liberal congressmen who promise to raise welfare benefits.
   II. Poor people pay little or no taxes so that a tax cut would be of little advantage to them.
   III. Any tax advantage which the poor will receive will be more than offset by cuts in the government services they now receive.

   (A) I only
   (B) II only
   (C) II and III only
   (D) III only
   (E) I, II, and III

5. Many people ask, "How effective is Painaway?" So, to find out we have been checking the medicine cabinets of the apartments in this typical building. As it turns out, eight out of ten contain a bottle of Painaway. Doesn't it stand to reason that you, too, should have the most effective pain-reliever on the market?

The appeal of this advertisement would be most weakened by which of the following pieces of evidence?
   (A) Painaway distributed complimentary bottles of medicine to most apartments in the building two days before the advertisement was made.
   (B) The actor who made the advertisement takes a pain-reliever manufactured by a competitor of Painaway.
   (C) Most people want a fast, effective pain-reliever.
   (D) Many people take the advice of their neighborhood druggists about pain-relievers.
   (E) A government survey shows that many people take a pain-reliever before it is really needed.

6. CLYDE: You shouldn't drink so much wine. Alcohol really isn't good for you.

   GERRY: You're wrong about that. I have been drinking the same amount of wine for fifteen years, and I never get drunk.

   Which of the following responses would best strengthen and explain Clyde's argument?
   (A) Many people who drink as much white wine as Gerry does get very drunk.
   (B) Alcohol does not always make a person drunk.
   (C) Getting drunk is not the only reason alcohol is not good for a person.
   (D) If you keep drinking white wine, you may find in the future that you are drinking more and more.
   (E) White wine is not the only drink that contains alcohol.

Questions 7–12

Six compounds are being tested for possible use in a new ant poison, "Sweet 'N' Deadly."

   I. U is sweeter than V and more deadly than Z.
   II. V is sweeter than Y and less deadly than Z.
   III. W is less sweet than X and less deadly than U.

IV. X is less sweet and more deadly than Y.

V. Y is less sweet and more deadly than U.

VI. Z is sweeter than U and less deadly than W.

7. Which of the following is the sweetest?
   (A) V
   (B) W
   (C) X
   (D) Y
   (E) Z

8. Which of the following is (are) both sweeter and more deadly than V?
   (A) U only
   (B) W only
   (C) Z only
   (D) U and Z only
   (E) U and W only

9. Which of the following adds no new information about sweetness to the statements which preceeded it?
   (A) II
   (B) III
   (C) IV
   (D) V
   (E) VI

10. Which of the following is (are) sweeter than Y and more deadly than W?
    (A) U only
    (B) V only
    (C) Z only
    (D) U and V only
    (E) Z and V only

11. Which of the following is the least deadly?
    (A) U
    (B) V
    (C) W
    (D) Y
    (E) Z

12. Which of the following is the most deadly?
    (A) Z
    (B) W
    (C) U
    (D) Y
    (E) X

Questions 13–17

I. There are five pieces of lost luggage lined up in a row by themselves for customs inspection; the items weigh variously 5, 10, 15, 20, and 25 pounds. The items to be identified are a trunk, a box, a crate, a suitcase, and a hatbox; and the nationalities of the owners are American, Belgian, German, Swedish, and Turkish, not necessarily in that order.

II. The fifth item weighs 10 pounds.

III. The Swedish traveller's luggage has luggage on both sides of it.

IV. The Turkish traveller owns the item weighing 15 pounds.

V. The traveller who owns the 5-pound second item has lost a box.

VI. The American owns the item in the middle, which weighs 20 pounds.

VII. The German does not own the hatbox, which weighs less than all but one of the other items.

VIII. The item on the left is the heaviest and is a trunk.

13. Which of the following can be derived from statements I, III, and VI?
    (A) The Swede owns the first or second item.
    (B) The Swede owns the first or fourth item.
    (C) The Swede owns the second or fourth item.
    (D) The Swede owns the third or fourth item.
    (E) The Swede owns a 10-pound box.

14. What does the German own?
    (A) a 25-pound trunk
    (B) a 25-pound box
    (C) a 25-pound crate
    (D) a 10-pound hatbox
    (E) a 5-pound hatbox

15. Which of the following statements is false?
    (A) The Turk's missing luggage is heavier than the Belgian's.
    (B) The 5-pound item plus the American's item weigh the same as the German's item.
    (C) The Turk's missing luggage weighs more than the Swede's.

(D) The American's missing luggage weighs more than the German's.
(E) The crate is not next to the 25-pound item.

16. Which of the following is true?
(A) The first item is owned by the Swede.
(B) The 10-pound item is owned by the Belgian.
(C) The suitcase is owned by the Turk.
(D) The crate is owned by the American.
(E) The box is owned by the German.

17. Which of the following additional pieces of information would, if true, allow the determination of the types of luggage that weigh 15 and 20 pounds?

  I. The crate weighs more than the suitcase.
  II. The crate is twice as heavy as the hatbox.
  III. The combined weight of the box and hatbox equals the weight of the suitcase.

(A) I only
(B) I and II only
(C) I and III only
(D) II and III only
(E) I, II, and III

Questions 18–22

There are four grades of milk cows in the Bellman herd: AA, AAA, AAAA, and AAAAA. These are sometimes called 2A, 3A, 4A and 5A. These classifications are based on the amount and quality of the milk produced by a cow, or in the case of a bull, the qualities of the bull's mother. AA cows produce less milk of lesser quality and AAAAA cows produce the greatest quantity and the highest quality. The Bellmans have an extensive breeding program. The primary goal of the breeding program is to produce better grades of cattle, but sometimes other factors such as resistance to disease, fertility, and even temperament are considered in making the breeding decisions.

The milk-producing abilities of a cow are inherited primarily from its mother; but if the father is two or more grades different from the

mother, then the offspring's grade will be one grade different from the mother's grade in the direction of the father's grade.

18. If a calf is grade 3A, which of the following pairs could have been its parents?
(A) A father who was grade AAAAA and a mother who was grade AA.
(B) A father who was grade AA and a mother who was grade AAAAA.
(C) A father who was grade AAA and a mother was was grade AA.
(D) A father who was grade AAAA and a mother who was grade AAAAA.
(E) A father who was grade AAAAA and a mother who was grade AAAA.

19. If it is found that resistance to hoof and mouth disease is associated with having had grade 2A or 3A fathers, which of the following grades of cows will probably be least resistant?
(A) AA
(B) AAA
(C) AAAA
(D) AAAAA
(E) All grades will have the same resistance.

20. If the Bellmans notice that the offspring of grade 4A cattle are the gentlest and easiest to handle, which of the following is the best method of quickly introducing the trait of gentleness into the largest part of the heard while getting the best milk results?
(A) Breeding AAAA bulls to all the cows.
(B) Breeding AAAA bulls to the AAAAA cows and AAAA cows to all the other bulls.
(C) Breeding AAAA cows to all the bulls.
(D) Breeding AAAAA cows to all the bulls.
(E) Instituting a random breeding program.

21. Which of the following must be true?

  I. AA and AAAAA cannot be interbred.
  II. A 2A bull and a 4A cow produce a higher-grade calf than a 4A bull and a 3A cow.

III. The father of a 4A bull must have been grade 3A, 4A, or 5A.

(A) None of the statements must be true.
(B) I only
(C) II only
(D) I and III only
(E) II and III only

22. A certain hide color is found to breed true; that is, if either parent has the hide color, the calf will have the hide color. If the hide color is first noticed in grade AA cattle, at least how many generations, not including the first 2A cow or bull with the hide color, will it take to have a grade AAAAA cow with the hide color?
(A) two
(B) three
(C) four
(D) five
(E) six

23. We must do something about the rising cost of our state prisons. It now costs an average of $132 per day to maintain a prisoner in a double-occupancy cell in a state prison. Yet, in the most expensive cities in the world, one can find rooms in the finest hotels which rent for less than $125 per night.

The argument above might be criticized in all of the following ways EXCEPT
(A) it introduces an inappropriate analogy
(B) it relies on an unwarranted appeal to authority
(C) it fails to take account of costs which prisons have but hotels do not have
(D) it misuses numerical data
(E) it draws a faulty comparison

24. Doctors, in seeking a cure for *aphroditis melancholias*, are guided by their research into the causes of *metaeritocas polymanias* because the symptoms of the two diseases occur in populations of similar ages, manifesting symptoms in both cases of high fever, swollen glands, and lack of appetite. Moreover, the incubation period of both diseases is virtually identical, so these medical researchers are convinced that the virus responsible for *aphroditis melancholias* is very similar to that responsible for *metaeritocas polymanias*.

The conclusion of the author rests on the presupposition that
(A) *metaeritocas polymanias* is a more serious public health hazard than *aphroditis melancholias*
(B) for every disease, modern medical science will eventually find a cure
(C) saving human life is the single most important goal of modern technology
(D) *aphroditis melancholias* is a disease which occurs only in human beings
(E) diseases with similar symptoms will have similar causes

25. I. Everyone who has not read the report either has no opinion in the matter or holds a wrong opinion about it.
II. Everyone who holds no opinion in the matter has not read the report.

Which of the following best describes the relationship between the two above propositions?
(A) If II is true, I may be either false or true.
(B) If II is true, I must also be true.
(C) If II is true, I is likely to be true.
(D) If I is true, II must also be true.
(E) If II is fale, I must also be false.

STOP

END OF SECTION. IF YOU HAVE ANY TIME LEFT, GO
OVER YOUR WORK IN THIS SECTION ONLY. DO NOT
WORK IN ANY OTHER SECTION OF THE TEST.

SECTION VI

30 minutes
25 questions

Directions: Each of the following questions or groups of questions is based on a short passage or a set of propositions. In answering these questions it may sometimes be helpful to draw a simple picture or chart. When you have selected the best answer to each question, darken the corresponding circle on your answer sheet.

Questions 1–4

Seven children, J, K, L, M, N, O, and P, are students at a certain grammar school with grades 1 through 7.

One of these children is in each of the seven grades.

N is in the first grade, and P is in the seventh grade.

L is in a higher grade than K.

J is in a higher grade than M.

O is in a grade somewhere between K and M.

1. If there are exactly two grades between J and O, which of the following must be true?
   (A) K is in the second grade.
   (B) J is in the sixth grade.
   (C) M is in a higher grade than K.
   (D) L is in a grade between M and O.
   (E) K and L are separated by exactly one grade.

2. If J is in the third grade, which of the following must be true?
   (A) K is in grade 4 and L is in grade 5.
   (B) K is in grade 5 and L is in grade 6.
   (C) L is in grade 4 and M is in grade 6.
   (D) M is in grade 2 and K is in grade 4.
   (E) O is in grade 4 and L is in grade 5.

3. If K is in the second grade, in which of the following grades, respectively, could M and J be?

   I. 3 and 4
   II. 4 and 5
   III. 4 and 6

   (A) I, but not II and not III
   (B) II, but not I and not III
   (C) I or III, but not II

   (D) II or III, but not I
   (E) I, II, or III

4. If J and N are separated by exactly two grades, which of the following must be true?
   (A) M is in grade 2.
   (B) L is in grade 3.
   (C) K is in a lower grade than J.
   (D) K is in a lower grade than O.
   (E) O is in a grade between J and N.

5. JOCKEY: Horses are the most noble of all animals. They are both loyal and brave. I knew of a farm horse which died of a broken heart shortly after its owner died.

   VETERINARIAN: You're wrong. Dogs can be just as loyal and brave. I had a dog who would wait every day on the front steps for me to come home, and if I did not arrive until midnight, he would still be there.

   All of the following are true of the claims of the jockey and the veterinarian EXCEPT:
   (A) Both claims assume that loyalty and bravery are characteristics that are desirable in animals.
   (B) Both claims are, in principle, untestable, so neither can be empirically confirmed or denied.
   (C) Both claims assume that human qualities can be attributed to animals.
   (D) Both claims are supported by only a single example of animal behavior.
   (E) Neither claim is supported by evidence other than the opinion and observations of the speakers.

6. If George graduated from the University after 1974, he was required to take Introductory World History.

   The statement above can be logically deduced from which of the following?
   (A) Before 1974, Introductory World His-

tory was not a required course in the University.

(B) Every student who took Introductory World History at the University graduated after 1974.

(C) No student who graduated from the University before 1974 took Introductory World History.

(D) All students graduating from the University after 1974 were required to take Introductory World History.

(E) Before 1974, no student was not permitted to graduate from the University without having taken Introductory World History.

7. Children in the first three grades who attend private schools spend time each day working with a computerized reading program. Public schools have very few such programs. Tests prove, however, that public-school children are much weaker in reading skills when compared to their private-school counterparts. We conclude, therefore, that public-school children can be good readers only if they participate in a computerized reading program.

The author's initial statements logically support his conclusion only if which of the following is also true?

(A) All children can learn to be good readers if they are taught by a computerized reading program.

(B) All children can learn to read at the same rate if they participate in a computerized reading program.

(C) Better reading skills produce better students.

(D) Computerized reading programs are the critical factor in the better reading skills of private-school students.

(E) Public-school children can be taught better math skills.

Questions 8–12

In Dullsville, streets and roads run east–west and alternate with each other at $\frac{1}{4}$-mile intervals.

Easy Street is 1 mile north of Main Street.

Main Street is $\frac{3}{4}$ mile south of Abbey Road.

Tobacco Road is $\frac{3}{4}$ mile south of Main Street.

Mean Street is $\frac{1}{2}$ mile south of Main Street.

8. Which of these roads or streets is farthest from Main Street?

(A) Easy Street

(B) Tobacco Road

(C) Abbey Road

(D) Tobacco Road and Abbey Road are equally far.

(E) Tobacco Road and Easy Street are equally far.

9. An additional road, Royal, could be in any of the following locations except:

(A) $\frac{1}{4}$ mile north of Easy Street

(B) $\frac{1}{4}$ mile north of Mean Street

(C) $\frac{1}{2}$ mile south of Abbey Road

(D) 1 mile north of Mean Street

(E) 1 mile north of Tobacco Road

10. What is the distance between Abbey Road and Mean Street?

(A) $\frac{3}{4}$ mile

(B) 1 mile

(C) $1\frac{1}{4}$ miles

(D) $1\frac{1}{2}$ miles

(E) 2 miles

11. Sunrise Strip runs directly North-South across Dullsville's streets and roads. If a car starts going down Sunrise Strip at Abbey Road, then makes a U-turn at Tobacco Road and goes back to Main Street, about how far does it travel?

(A) $3\frac{1}{4}$ miles

(B) 3 miles

(C) $2\frac{1}{2}$ miles

(D) $2\frac{1}{4}$ miles

(E) 2 miles

12. What is the greatest distance between any two of the roadways named?

(A) 1 mile

(B) $1\frac{1}{2}$ miles

(C) $1\frac{3}{4}$ miles

(D) 2 miles

(E) $2\frac{1}{4}$ miles

Questions 13–17

City College is selecting a four-person debate team. There are seven candidates of equal ability: X, Y, and Z, who attend the West campus, and L, M, N, and P, who attend the East campus. The team must have two members from each campus. Also, the members must be able to work well with all the other members of the team.

Debaters Y and L, Z and N, and L and M are incompatible pairs.

13. If debater Y is rejected and M is selected, the team will consist of
    (A) L, M, X, and Z
    (B) M, N, X, and Z
    (C) M, N, P, and X
    (D) M, N, P, and Z
    (E) M, P, X, and Z

14. If debater L is on the team, what other debaters must be on the team as well?
    (A) M, X, and Z
    (B) N, X, and Z
    (C) P, N, and Z
    (D) P, X, and Y
    (E) P, X, and Z

15. If both Y and Z are selected, which of the other debaters are thereby assured of a place on the team?
    (A) both L and M
    (B) both M and P
    (C) only N
    (D) both N and P
    (E) only P

16. Which of the following must be false?

    I. Debaters M and Z cannot be selected together.
    II. Debaters N and Y cannot be selected together.
    III. Debaters P and Z cannot be selected together.

    (A) I only
    (B) II only
    (C) III only
    (D) I and III
    (E) I, II, and III

17. Which of the following statements is true of debater X?

    I. Debater X must be selected as one of the West campus members of the team.
    II. Debater X must be selected if debater N is selected.
    III. Debater X cannot be selected if both L and N are rejected.

(A) I only
(B) II only
(C) III only
(D) I and II
(E) I, II, and III

Questions 18–22

Jon is decorating his apartment and is trying to arrange his six Pop Art paintings on the east and west walls of his living room. The paintings are each multicolor representations of one of the letters of the alphabet: E, H, M, O, R, T.

Jon does not want the three letters on each wall to make any common English words. Also, the colors of the O and E do not look good next to each other, nor do the T and O go together well.

18. If Jon puts the M, O, and T on the west wall, which of the following is true?

    I. O will be on one end of the west wall.
    II. H and R will not be, respectively, the left and right paintings on the east wall.
    III. E cannot be in the middle of the east wall.

    (A) I only
    (B) II only
    (C) I and II only
    (D) I and III only
    (E) I, II, and III

19. If Jon puts the E, H, and M on the east wall, which of the following must be true?
    (A) The E cannot be in the center of the east wall.
    (B) The O cannot be in the center of the west wall.
    (C) The R and M cannot face each other.
    (D) The T and M cannot face each other.
    (E) The H and R cannot face each other.

20. If Jon's mother is coming to visit and Jon decides to celebrate the visit by having his paintings spell "mother" starting with the leftmost painting on the east wall and going on around the room, which of the following must be false?
    (A) T is next to O.
    (B) H is next to E.
    (C) O is opposite E.

(D) T is opposite R.
(E) None of the above is false.

21. Which of the following is not possible?
(A) H, M, and R to be on the same wall
(B) T, H, and E to be on the same wall
(C) T and O to be opposite each other
(D) M and O to be opposite each other
(E) E and O to be opposite each other

22. If Jon trades his M painting for another O painting just like the one he has now, which of the following must be false?
(A) Either R or H will be next to either T or E.
(B) Either R or H will be next to an O.
(C) The O's can be on opposite walls in the middle.
(D) The T will be opposite either O or E.
(E) All of the above are possible.

23. The new car to buy this year is the Goblin. We had 100 randomly selected motorists drive the Goblin and the other two leading sub-compact cars. Seventy-five drivers ranked the Goblin first in handling. Sixty-nine rated the Goblin first in styling. From the responses of these 100 drivers, we can show you that they ranked Goblin first overall in our composite category of style, performance, comfort, and drivability.

The persuasive appeal of the advertisement's claim is most weakened by its use of the undefined word
(A) randomly
(B) handling
(C) first

(D) responses
(E) composite

24. I maintain that the best way to solve our company's present financial crisis is to bring out a new line of goods. I challenge anyone who disagrees with this proposed course of action to show that it will not work.

A flaw in the preceding argument is that it
(A) employs group classifications without regard to individuals
(B) introduces an analogy that is weak
(C) attempts to shift the burden of proof to those who would object to the plan
(D) fails to provide statistical evidence to show that the plan will actually succeed
(E) relies upon a discredited economic theory

25. I. No student who commutes from home to university dates a student who resides at a university.
     II. Every student who lives at home commutes to his university, and no commuter student ever dates a resident student.

Which of the following best describes the relationship between the two sentences above?
(A) If II is true, I must also be true.
(B) If II is true, I must be false.
(C) If II is true, I may be either true or false.
(D) If I is true, II is unlikely to be false.
(E) If II is false, I must also be false.

STOP

PRACTICE EXAMINATION 4—ANSWER KEY

Section I

1.	D	10.	A	19.	C	28.	C	37.	B
2.	C	11.	C	20.	A	29.	E	38.	D
3.	B	12.	E	21.	A	30.	B		
4.	A	13.	E	22.	B	31.	D		
5.	C	14.	E	23.	D	32.	E		
6.	E	15.	B	24.	A	33.	C		
7.	D	16.	D	25.	B	34.	C		
8.	B	17.	C	26.	B	35.	E		
9.	D	18.	D	27.	C	36.	D		

Section II

1.	B	10.	B	19.	C	28.	B	37.	E
2.	E	11.	B	20.	D	29.	C	38.	D
3.	D	12.	A	21.	C	30.	D		
4.	E	13.	C	22.	E	31.	A		
5.	C	14.	C	23.	C	32.	E		
6.	C	15.	D	24.	A	33.	B		
7.	B	16.	E	25.	E	34.	A		
8.	A	17.	E	26.	A	35.	C		
9.	E	18.	C	27.	B	36.	B		

Section III

1.	B	7.	C	13.	C	19.	B	25.	A
2.	A	8.	A	14.	B	20.	A	26.	C
3.	D	9.	A	15.	C	21.	D	27.	A
4.	D	10.	A	16.	D	22.	D	28.	B
5.	B	11.	C	17.	C	23.	D	29.	D
6.	A	12.	A	18.	B	24.	E	30.	A

Section IV

1.	C	7.	B	13.	A	19.	A	25.	B
2.	B	8.	B	14.	C	20.	B	26.	D
3.	B	9.	D	15.	D	21.	E	27.	D
4.	A	10.	C	16.	E	22.	D	28.	B
5.	C	11.	C	17.	B	23.	C	29.	D
6.	A	12.	D	18.	D	24.	C	30.	A

Section V

1.	C	6.	C	11.	B	16.	B	21.	A
2.	A	7.	E	12.	E	17.	E	22.	A
3.	D	8.	D	13.	C	18.	A	23.	B
4.	C	9.	D	14.	A	19.	D	24.	E
5.	A	10.	A	15.	D	20.	B	25.	A

Section VI

1.	B	6.	D	11.	D	16.	E	21.	A
2.	B	7.	D	12.	C	17.	B	22.	C
3.	D	8.	A	13.	E	18.	C	23.	E
4.	A	9.	D	14.	E	19.	B	24.	C
5.	B	10.	C	15.	B	20.	D	25.	A

EXPLANATORY ANSWERS

SECTION I

1. **(D)** Sirens may drone or wail, but they don't babble, gibber, or groan. Hoarse sound is a better choice than hoarse power.

2. **(C)** "The pressure of time" indicates a need to work quickly. Assuming that mistakes are not inevitable or redundant, answer (C) is the only logical choice. The first blank is best filled by either frantically or rapidly.

3. **(B)** This sentence is concerned with the design of the lift. As it says "held up only by," we may assume that the cable is not large, which eliminates (C) and (D). Of the three remaining options, only intended (B) completes the sentence logically.

4. **(A)** The only thing known about the person described is that he is an English teacher. A solecism is a mistake in grammar and thus is a violation of the type of expertise expected of an English teacher. A schism, meaning a split of some sort, is as likely in English teachers as in anyone else, presumably. Similar comments can be made about the other answer choices.

5. **(C)** The word sincerity gives us a reference point from which to work. Thus, the second blank describes the reaction of someone valuing sincerity to an action described in the first blank. Therefore, the first blank must have something to do with sincerity. Only (C) does that, and a sycophant who is insincere would be obnoxious to someone who valued sincerity. Natal means of birth, hybrid is a mixed breed, doleful is sad, and refulgent is shining.

6. **(E)** Let us read the sentence closely. It speaks of incarcerating, which means jailing, some type of person with his fellows, that is, with others like him. Further, this companionship is theoretically supposed to teach ethical standards, BUT (the author disagrees with the theory) somehow experience shows that the theory does not work.

First of all, since the theory described is one of teaching ethics, the objects of the teaching will not be defendants, who are not yet judged guilty, nor probably unfortunates who are simply unlucky. A much better answer is criminals deserving of jailing. When we eliminate (C) and (D), we see that one sort of criminal or another. (A), (B), or (E), is thrown in with other criminals and that this does not improve his ethical standards because of the second blank.

(B) fails for the second blank since being interested in one's fellow criminals does not explain the failure to learn ethical standards. One might be interested in them and see how terrible they were. (A) is a little better since anger might be opposed to learning ethical standards, but (E)'s "more like" explains the whole problem. Putting someone in with criminals will make them more criminal, not less. Thus (E) is the best answer.

7. **(D)** The second blank is the evidence justifying the characterization stated in the first blank. (A) fails since proper procedures are not incredible, that is, difficult to believe. (B) fails since being full of sworn testimony is not negligent for a trial. (C) fails since a judicial manner means a measured and reasonable manner, which does not match with spectacular revelations. (E) fails since erudite citations are learned and knowledgeable, and that would not be outrageous in a trial. (D) fits well since histrionics refers to dramatics and theatricality.

8. **(B)** Blow is the verb that describes the activation of a horn. Light is the verb that describes the activation of a lamp. The other answer choices are all verbs that are typical actions to do with the nouns that are the second parts of the pair. However, none of them activate the noun. (D), accelerate, has some connotation of activating an engine, but it is really only the speeding up, not the starting that is at issue. Thus, it is not the same.

9. **(D)** Pluck is the particular verb that is used to indicate the removal of feathers. Shear is the particular word that is used to indicate the removal of hair in general and wool in particular. (A) connects only in the sense that down is feathers. However there is no similarity in the relationship within the respective pairs. All the other answer choices do have words that relate the first item as a noun to which the second item, a verb, can be done. However, only (D) has the idea of removal. Thus (D) is the best answer.

10. **(A)** Modesty and arrogance are personality traits and antonyms. The only answer choice which concerns anything like a personality trait is (C), but these two terms are synonyms, so (C) is

incorrect. Of the other answer choices, only (A) has any sort of specific oppositeness since debility means weakness; thus, it is the best answer. In (D), finance is the field and does not denote a rich person.

11. **(C)** A bay is a somewhat cut-off arm of the ocean. A peninsula is a somewhat cut-off arm of the land. (A) fails since the relationship is an opposition. (B) has some idea of opposition as well since a plain is basically treeless. (E) straddles the fence, as it were, but the relationship is between two small parts of larger ideas, which is not the relationship in the original pair. (D) has a similar weakness since both a cape and a reef are pieces of land partly and totally in the sea. This is an interesting relationship, but not the same as the original pair. This leaves (C) as the best answer.

12. **(E)** A spindle is the axle on which a spool turns. Wheel and axle have the same relationship. (A) has the idea of the first term going through the second, but lacks the special concept of an axle or spindle. (C) has some merit, but straight versus round would have been much stronger. (E) contains the idea of shape plus the idea of function and would be better. (D) has a straight item and a round item, but the straight item is part of the round item rather than the thing about which the round item revolves, as in the original and in (E). (B) is the second-best answer, but fails since a rod is not necessarily the thing about which the reel revolves. In addition, the idiomatic connection of a rod and reel is a fishing rod and reel. The reel is attached to the rod and does not revolve around it at all, but revolves on its own spindle. Thus, (E) is the best answer choice.

13. **(E)** A setting surrounds a gem and is designed to show the gem off to the best advantage. A frame is supposed to do the same thing for a painting. (B) and (C) both have the idea of the second term being in the first term, but have no additional idea of setting it off or enhancing it. (D) has a little idea, particularly if one were thinking of an illustrated margin, but that is not really mentioned here. (A) is the second-best answer since a stage is where the play occurs. However, it is the stage setting which is designed to show the play off to best advantage, not the stage as such. Thus, (E) is the best answer.

14. **(E)** Frangible means breakable, thus the original pair have the relationship of a potentiality and the realization of that potentiality. Pliable is bendable, and the realization of the potentiality is to be bent. (A), (B), and (C) do not have the idea of a realization of the specific potential of the first word. To be smelly is not specifically to have the potential of offending, but rather to have the potential of being smelled. In (D), a fluid can be either a liquid or a gas, and thus the potentiality for being liquefied is not really inherent in the fact

that something is a fluid any more than in something being any other state of matter. Thus, (E) is the only answer choice to show a potentiality and the strict achievement of that specific potentiality.

15. **(B)** Heckling is forceful and unpleasant interrupting. Hectoring is forceful and unpleasant teasing, though teasing has a playful feel to it which is entirely absent from hectoring. (D) has no similarity between the two elements and is eliminated. (A) has only a very slight similarity and the first item is more intense than the second, so it is in the wrong order and fails. (C) has a similarity, but not a great deal of difference in degree or intensity. (E) presents a situation which could possibly be construed as having some difference of intensity in that a performance might not be merely a speech but a complete performance. However, since a performance is a much more general term than a speech, this answer also fails and leaves (B) as the best answer choice.

16. **(D)** A shoplifter is a stealer of merchandise, specifically items that are for sale. A rustler is specifically a stealer of cattle. (B) fails since there is no illegality in it. (C) and (E) show the site of the crime, but not the item taken. (A) is the second best answer choice since a kidnapper could be thought of as a stealer of men. However, if someone said that a person was a thief, you would be surprised to find that the person was actually a kidnapper since that is a different sort of crime. We normally distinguish crimes against property from crimes against persons. Thus, (A) is a different sort of crime, as we normally classify these things, and (D) is the best answer.

17. **(C)** The only thing that Antony did for Archelaus was to make sure that he received a proper burial. This was out of Antony's own sense of honor, since the author states in the first sentence that Antony was eager for honor. (A) fails since there is no statement that the two were friends, but only acquaintances. (D) likewise fails since it states in the passage that Antony was Archelaus' guest, not the other way around. (E) and (B) both are qualities that Antony possessed, but they were not extended to Archelaus graciously since the two were on opposing sides. Thus, (C) is the best answer.

18. **(D)** All of the answer choices use the word great. When a word is repeated like this, which occasionally occurs for three or four answers, your attention is naturally directed to that word. Great is an extreme word and we must therefore look for something which was great. (A) certainly fails since the two countries were at war. We know this because Ptolemy is against the Egyptians, Antony is on Ptolemy's side, and the Roman army admires Antony, which is a fair implication that it was the Romans and Egyptians who were fighting.

(B) has some merit, but, at the same time, Antony does oppose some of Ptolemy's policies. (C) is not clear. Although Archelaus was definitely a soldier, since Antony fought him bravely, we do not know for sure that he was a general, much less how he might rank compared to the other Egyptian officers. (E) is not true since the passage is careful to say that they were merely acquaintances. (D) is certainly true since his military prowess is much in evidence and admired by all. Thus (D) is preferable to (B) since (D) is certain, while (B) is only possible.

19. **(C)** The author clearly approves of Antony, but he is not adulatory since he does point out how some of Antony's actions were of benefit to the enemy. Furthermore, the phrase "eagerness for honor" has a less than blindly approving tone. Admiring is a better choice than adulatory. Inquisitive and appraising both have some merit since the author is definitely looking into what Antony has done. However, appraising has the connotation of being somewhat skeptical, trying to find the true worth, as opposed to the apparent worth. There is no distinction of this sort being made, and thus admiring remains the best. Inquisitive is not really an attitude toward a person unless you are merely curious. Similarly, it is not clear that one's attitude toward a person would be intelligent. Remember that the question stem asked for the author's attitude toward Antony, not his evaluation of what characteristics Antony had.

20. **(A)** Jargon is stated to be a technical term, though the passage notes that in farming and other old and widespread occupations, the words will often be generally familiar. (A), sun, is not a technical term in any field, while the other four are technical terms for, respectively, husbandry, farming, weaving, and carpentry.

21. **(A)** None of the answer choices has any statement of the topic of the passage, but only a general form. The passage is descriptive only; hence (A). (C) and (D) are not done. (E) seems unlikely in this rather dry passage. (B) has the slight merit of the fact that the description given is a sort of argument that the phenomenon described does exist, but that is not so well described as a belief. Hence (A), not (B).

22. **(B)** It is important not to let outside knowledge interfere with understanding how THIS author is using a term. Although guilds in the Middle Ages were hard to get into, (A), and often required apprenticeships, (E), this is not in the passage since it is modern times that are under discussion.

(D) is too strong and (C)'s references to secrets is a little strange since it is only the reports not the secrets that are broadcast; but the strength of (B) is that it is one of the two specific statements following the phrase at issue. (C), the second-best answer, is not precisely what is stated about popular science in the passage.

23. **(D)** Since the author chose vocabulary to write an article about, he most likely studied it since it reflects the best way to discuss things in the field, as the passage states. (A), (B), and (E) have little to do with the passage. (D) is preferable to (C) because (D) includes (C) and also refers to actually learning knowledge in the new field.

24. **(A)** Since the passage primarily concerns words and their use, meanings, and history, (A) is the best answer. There is no specific support for any of the other answers.

25. **(B)** The last two sentences give us our best evidence for time and place. Roentgen rays and wireless telegraphy are key terms. They are obsolete terms for X-rays and radio, respectively, and certainly have an old-fashioned feel about them. The sentence with provincial in it tells us that the country of the author probably has knowledge of advanced science and many newspapers. The omission of radio and television from the list of media is also significant. (D) and (E) fail because of the date, since television and radio would surely be mentioned in those years. (A) fails since India was not a science center (nor a media center) in 1904. (B) is preferable to (C) since 1944 had radio and 1914 didn't.

26. **(B)** Since technical words come and go, (B) is very strong. (A) would only be true if words never left the language, which the passage does not say and common sense forbids. (C) fails since it refers to all words. (D) is shown to be false by the last sentence, if not the whole passage. (E) overlooks the author's position that such words as these are still technical words, even though common.

27. **(C)** These issues are discussed in the early part of the passage. The correct analysis of these four propositions depends largely on being sensitive to some restricted meanings of the words used in the passage. II is not true even though the passage says that the use of jargon is "economical," the commodity saved is time, not money. III fails for a similar reason. While the use of jargon permits "the precision of a mathematical formula," that does not mean that the jargon need be mathematical.

I is an advantage of jargon that is directly stated and is the real point of the comment on the economical nature of jargon. IV is also stated in the passage, deriving from the mathematically precise nature of jargon that that passage lauds. The qualifying phrase "for describing special topics" makes this proposition much easier to support since ordinary language can be perfectly precise for ordinary topics.

Your everyday perception that much jargon may not work as wonderfully as this author believes is, of course, irrelevant.

28. **(C)** Piquant means spicy or sharp, particularly in flavor, though one might speak of a piquant memory or other sensation. It usually is a positive idea. It comes from the same root as pique (as in to pique one's interest). Insipid means exactly to be without sufficient flavor or taste to be interesting. Factitious means false or artificial.

If they do not know what insipid means, some students might choose slow on the grounds that to pique interest is to sharpen or quicken interest, but that is a special use of the word quicken and is not opposite to slow. Furthermore, a vague opposite of a word only related to the stem word is not more than a stab at an answer and one should not be surprised if it is wrong.

29. **(E)** Opportune means something that is well timed, such as the arrival of a hero to rescue the heroine from the railroad tracks just as the train is about to crush her.

30. **(B)** A petulant person is given to showing sudden irritation over small things. An equable person is even-tempered and always behaves calmly and reasonably. Pliable means flexible or easy to shape or control. Uncouth means rude and vulgar. The others are unconnected to temperament.

31. **(D)** Savory means tasty, delicious. Unpalatable literally means that something is not pleasing to the palate. The other answers have nothing to do with taste.

32. **(E)** Fulfilled means to have been completed. A fulfilled person is one who has completed or done what he needed to do for his own happiness, in contrast to a fulfilled order, which is merely completed or done satisfactorily. The latter is perhaps the major meaning of the word, but there is no answer choice to connect to it. Thus, needy, while not a perfect opposite, is the best answer available. Dry plays on the idea of filling, but this is too far removed to work. Fulfilled does come from some idea of being filled fully, but now has only the metaphorical usage of completion of a task or duty or need and not the original physical meaning.

33. **(C)** A reclusive person is one who does not like to meet other people and keeps to himself as much as possible. Gregarious describes a person who seeks out companionship and likes it. This is essentially a perfect opposite. Joined has some feeling of oppositeness since a reclusive person is separate from other persons, but gregarious is more precise. Similarly, urban has a trace of oppositeness since a reclusive person might be thought to be someone who is out in a faraway place, but actually a word such as anchorite or hermit would fit better for that sort of meaning. Obscure also has some feeling of being unusual and difficult to find and not quite in the midst of other things, but this is not nearly so good as gregarious.

34. **(C)** Courteous means observing good manners and being very polite. Being insolent is just the opposite—rude and insulting. The others have little connection to modes of behavior. Flaccid means limp; an emollient softens up things, especially living tissues; and scrupulous is conscientious and taking great care.

35. **(E)** To usurp something is to take and possess it when you have no right to it. Own rightfully is a good opposite. Use fully tries to play on the *usu-* in usurp. Hold carefully has the idea of holding or possessing something, but has no connotation as to the rightfulness of the possession.

36. **(D)** Acrimonious means to be sharp-tongued, and an acrimonious argument is bitter and hurtful. Harmonious discussion is when all the parties are in harmony. Severe is more of a synonym than an antonym, meaning extreme or harsh. Flippant has some oppositeness in that a flippant comment is a lighthearted one, certainly not meant to hurt; however, harmonious is better since it is positive in just the way that acrimonious is negative. Cursive is a style of handwriting or refers to something that runs together.

37. **(B)** A skeptic is one who is questioning and probing, usually about some belief. A believer is one who believes. The phrase true believer would be a better opposite since it means accepting a belief without question. But believer is the best available answer. Cryptic means encoded or difficult to decipher. Eminent is well known or highly regarded in some field. A caricature is a portrait of someone which grossly distorts and emphasizes one or two features of the subject.

38. **(D)** Indubitable means doubtless or undoubtable, or the connection is clear. A questionable item is precisely something about which one has doubts. Aesthetic refers to the appreciation of beauty. Unmitigated means without any redeeming features; and a belabored point in an argument is one which is worked over at great and excessive length.

SECTION II

1. **(B)** For the light to make the room cozier, it must be soft, not harsh. This implies that the light enhanced the room, rather than disfigured it.

2. **(E)** A person may be an institution, but not an institution of a team. It is more likely that a member of the original team, rather than a scholar, would have a free pass.

3. **(D)** Armed guards are intended to prevent any kind of disruption. Answer (D) is the only logical and grammatical choice.

4. **(E)** The sentence implies that the house was being searched, and since you don't perform an autopsy on a house, (E) is the best choice.

5. **(C)** An astronomer would not be honored as an astrologer, much less as an administrator. An astronomer is a scientist and banquets are honors.

6. **(C)** The first blank gives a characteristic of the debater that leads to his taking the action described in the second blank. (A) and (B) fail since the fact that someone is a forceful debater would not mean that they anticipate questions. Being an intelligent debater would not necessarily indicate enjoyment. An intelligent debater might anticipate, but that combination is not available. An inept debater would certainly dread questioning. A fatiqued debater might miss, or fail to hear, the questions, but he would not ignore them by choice, which is what ignore implies. An attorney who interrupts a judge is probably foolish as an attorney, but his debating skills would not be described as foolish, which is not a good way of describing skills in any case. Thus, (C) is the best answer.

7. **(B)** The although tells you that there is some contrast between the first part of the sentence and the second. (A) fails since the fact that there have been successful, delightful tunes does not contrast to the idea of the music's being aesthetic or relating to beauty. Aesthetic is not very well used here in any case; aesthetically pleasing would be better. (B) does have a contrast between individual tunes, which have been delightful, and the whole of the music production, which has not been significant. (C) has some appeal, but there is not much contrast between delightful and new, making it a weaker sentence. (D) is the second best answer, though strong is a rather unspecific term and is only somewhat contrasted to increasingly delightful. (E) fails since the existence of many delightful tunes does not contrast with the idea of debased, or lowered in standards.

8. **(A)** Tepid is a mild or moderate temperature and hot is an extreme of the same sort of thing. A pat is a mild touching and a slap is an extreme one of the same sort. (B) fails since it has antonyms. (C) and (E) fail since they essentially have synonyms with no clear difference in the intensity of the words cited. (D) appeals since cool is slightly on the cool side, while tepid is slightly on the warm side. However, the very strength of this relation-

ship means that if (D) is to be the correct answer, there must be a similar strength between the second parts of the original and the answer choice. Gel does not mean icy. Gelid has that meaning. Gel merely means something that is gelatinous, like Jello. Thus, (A) is the best answer choice.

9. **(E)** At first, there might seem no relationship between rib and umbrella, but the little spokes that run from the center of the umbrella outwards and hold the umbrella up are called ribs. A rafter performs a similar function for a roof. (B), (C), and (D) all contain first items that are at the center of the second items and which, in (B) and (C), do not hold anything up. The trunk of the tree is more like a column, but (A) is preferable.

   (A) and (E) are the two best choices. The difference between them is that a rafter is part of the roof that it supports, while the column is not part of the ceiling that it supports. This is also shown by the fact that a rafter runs parallel to the roof, while a column is perpendicular to the ceiling.

10. **(B)** A good first cut at this problem would be to see that a tadpole is a young frog. (A) and (D) are eliminated by this idea and the fact that the other three agree indicates that we are probably on the right track. A gander is a male goose, not a young one. What difference is there between the three remaining answer choices? Well, (B) is about an insect, (C), a mammal, and (E), a bird. None of those help much since the original is about an amphibian. Using the idea of refinement, we might ask ourselves what is the relationship between this sort of young and this sort of adult. At this point we might see that a tadpole undergoes drastic changes before it becomes a frog, as does a caterpillar before it becomes a butterfly. The other two have no similar developmental changes. Thus, (B) is the best answer. It is a slight weakness of (B) that only some caterpillars become butterflies and others become moths.

11. **(B)** Wool is the special name of the shorn hair of the sheep when it is used in making cloth. Mohair is the special name for the shorn hair of the goat when used in making cloth. All of the answer choices concern the outer coverings of a particular animal. However, only wool and mohair are hairs.

12. **(A)** Feline means catlike; thus the correct answer will have an animal and an adjective derived from that animal. Equine means horselike, and thus (A) is the best answer. Vulpine in (C) means wolflike. (D) and (E) are not serious contenders once (A)'s merits are disclosed. (B) has some appeal since it is certainly true that a tiger is carnivorous. However, this is a characteristic of tigers rather than an adjective meaning tigerlike.

13. **(C)** The stem pair are opposites. Rusticity means

being like the country, or rural and unsophisticated, while urbanity means being sophisticated. The stem pair are thus both personality characteristics. If there is an answer choice that uses personality characteristics, I will certainly give it a good look. (C) does, and the characteristics are clearly opposite to each other. (E) has characteristics, but they are synonyms. (D) has two adjectives that are opposites, but they are not personality characteristics and there is no special connection that they have to the stem pair that might make us choose (D) over (C). (A) and (B) are not even clear opposites.

14. **(C)** That clothes go in a closet will likely be the first relationship that comes to mind. Only (C) continues that idea with ink going into a pen. In addition, both clothes and ink are stored in the appointed place until they are used. In (A), feet might be in a rug, but that is not a typical place and feet are certainly not stored in a rug.

15. **(D)** There is some knowledge required for this problem. It helps to know that pepper comes from berries that are dried. Peppercorns are dried berries. Basil is (usually) a dried leaf. All of the answer choices have as the first element a spice or flavoring of some sort, except for (B), which merely has a fruit. Salt is not a rock, nor does nutmeg come from mace, though both are from the same plant. (C) is, perhaps, the second-best answer choice since fennel is a vegetable. There are two ways of going beyond that to distinguish (C) and (D). First, fennel is not actually the seasoning, but fennel seeds are. Secondly, a berry and a leaf are parts of a plant, while vegetable is a type of plant.

16. **(E)** A tourniquet is a specific mechanism for the purpose of stopping bleeding. This suggests (C) since a metronome is a mechanism. However, the metronome does not do to time what a tourniquet does to bleeding, so the analogy fails. The only workable answer choice is (E). An anodyne is a painkiller and thus acts to stop pain. A phenol is a chemical, but has nothing in particular to do with digestion. Mint stops bad breath, but not breath.

17. **(E)** I and III are clearly indicated by the phrase physical characteristics and cultures. II is a combination of the two. Food is a physical characteristic in terms of what is available, and the preparation is a cultural aspect. Hence, all three are referred to in the passage. (E).

18. **(C)** (B) is the result primarily of the Himalayas' sudden appearance, rather than the glaciation, and (D) is of both. What we need is the idea of what would have been different if the existing plants had been entirely wiped out. (A) and (C) both speak to that, and (A) has some merit, though it is weakened by the word flourish, which

seems extreme. Though the use of life without any adjective seems odd, this is done in both (A) and (C). In (A), however, there is no sense of development or implication. (C) tells us what would have been different to the concern of the passage at that point—the diversity and type of fauna and flora. Note that the word possibly in (C) protects it from the criticism that the Kunlun range cut off other life from coming in, as does the non-specific reference to nearby arid areas. (E) would only be chosen if all of the others were definitely bad.

19. **(C)** We know only two things about the Tibetan tea. First, it is in written quotes, which means it is not just regular tea. Second, it is a possible replacement for vegetables. These both fit (C) better than any of the other answer choices. If you were reluctant to choose (C) because it sounded unlikely, you are wrong for two reasons. First, and the most important, it is almost exclusively the relationship to the passage that matters. Second, that is what Tibetan tea really is.

20. **(D)** (A), (B), and (C) are all in the passage, but they serve the purpose stated in (D). (E) is not mentioned as mysterious.

21. **(C)** The passage is full of references to the findings of others, which supports (B) and (C). (A) is unsupported by the few statements made in the passage without references. None of the statements refers to any firsthand experience by the author, eliminating (A). There is no special emphasis on China to support (D), and there is much in the passage other than geology, (E). Between (B) and (C), one must choose between the strong items in each choice—"lifelong" and "only." While the passage displays some erudition, it is not clear that a lifelong study is indicated, but all of the information can come from books and almost all of it certainly does, hence, (C).

22. **(E)** Although Lattimore and Kawakita have different emphases as to the source of the polyandry, it is not stated nor required that polyandry must be either preserved from earlier forms or an efficient way of selecting the householder. The other answers reflect differences which are not required.

23. **(C)** Montesquieu is stated to believe that climate and soil are cultural determinants, that is, they determine what the culture of the inhabitants of an area will be. (D) is unrelated to this idea, and (E) focuses on the food, not the soil and climate as such. (A) and (B) mention only one of the two factors said to be important to Montesquieu. (C) clearly states the idea of soil and climate being determinative of culture.

24. **(A)** The term continental climate is used in the passage with only a partial explication of what it might mean. However, the passage stresses the fact that the fauna and flora which were found in pre-glacial Tibet were typical of the entire region, though reduced in variety. Thus, the continental species are those found in a continental climate, the details of which you do not need to know.

(B) and (D) refer to events which are totally outside the scope of the passage and are therefore highly unlikely to be correct. (E) has the merit of referring to the location of the species and the idea that species are restricted to certain locations because of the environmental attributes of the locations. However, there is no mention of islands in the passage and, even more importantly, the fact that some species are not found on islands is not enough to classify it as continental in the way that term is used in the passage. Also, the idea of never being on any island of any sort is a little bizarre since there are doubtless islands in Tibet which have some of the species found in Tibet.

(C) has the merit of referring to the species' location in Asia, but it is not enough to just say "other parts" of Asia; Asia is very big. Also, the answer choice is not limited in any way and really means that these species are found all over Asia, which the passage makes clear is not the case.

25. **(E)** In a simple sense, (E) is the best answer because the other answers do not relate to the passage. (A) fails because the reference to "dynamic" in the passage is to the dynamics of personality and not as a characterization of a particular personality. (B) is simply not mentioned. (C) is not presented except to say that scientific biography may not be as easy as had been thought, but the modern biographer, not the scientific one, is the topic, and it is not even clear from the passage that these two types of biographers are the same, though they may overlap. (D) connects to the last sentence, in which the author allows that the future ideas about a biography subject are likely to be different than ours. But that is not the main idea. The last idea is often important, but need not be the most important. (E) is correct because the point of the passage is to describe and discuss the approach to biography that the author calls modern biography. And that is just what it does.

26. **(A)** The qualifying word in (A) is presently, and that is just fine with the author. Even though he knows that the future may come to a different conclusion, the modern biographer must do what he can with the materials available. (B) is inadequate since the author makes no such claim. It may be true that there are limitations of this sort, but it is not the modern biographer's real task. (C) is precisely what the modern biographer does not do, so it is wrong. (D), like (C), ignores the whole thrust of the passage that the modern biographer

interprets rather than merely setting down the facts in chronological order. (E) is clearly opposite to the thrust of the last sentence, which indicates that one must do the best one can even though there will be reinterpretations later. Thus, (A) is the best answer.

27. **(B)** The question asks us to do two things. First, we must be clear as to the definition of modern biographers that is given in the passage, and, second, we must see what criticisms are presented and how they agree with the passage. It is most likely that the answer choice is a criticism implied by the very definition of the modern biographer that is given in the passage. (B) meets that criterion since the passage specifically states that the original documents are not presented, except for a few illustrations, and thus the reader does not have the opportunity to make his own judgments. This clearly is a deficit and it is necessary to the kinds of biography that the author is describing.

(A) is certainly a criticism, but it is not as strong as (B) for two reasons. If this criticism were to be accepted, then no contemporary biography could ever be done and the author does not seem to be that critical. Also, the last sentence does not actually say that the views of future historians will be more accurate than those of current historians, only that they will be different. Secondly, this is an idea that is fully discussed in the passage and thus less likely to be the proper answer for a question that is clearly seeking something a little outside the scope of the passage as presented.

(C) fails since it uses the other meaning of illustration—a picture or drawing—rather than the actual meaning given in the text, of an example. In addition, it just doesn't make much sense. (D) is certainly an interesting criticism, but there is nothing in the passage that either supports the allegation that this change in technique was done to suit modern tastes or that it is therefore difficult to compare information. If there is any difficulty in comparing information, it will be because of the lack of direct documentation as described in (B). (E) is much too strong and there is no citation for "many" authorities. Equally important, the passage merely says that making a scientific judgment in these matters may not be as easy as was imagined, not that it is impossible.

28. **(B)** Deleterious means harmful, particularly to health or welfare. Salubrious means healthful, which makes it nearly a perfect opposite to one of the meanings of deleterious.

Inclusive tries to play on the root *delete-* in the word deleterious. However, delete comes from a Latin root and deleterious from a similar-looking Greek root. The other words have no real connection either. Pathetic means deserving of pity, but antipathetic means having a negative feeling towards something.

29. **(C)** Puissance means power, and impotence means lack of power. Approbation is strong approval; repudiation means disavowal. Malaise is sickness, particularly a general weakness without apparent cause.

30. **(D)** Sycophancy is servile, self-serving flattery and a sycophant is a "yes-man." The answer choices are all verbs, which is somewhat unusual, and you should have noticed the difficulty. However, since ALL of the answer choices are verbs, the part of speech does not tell you which answer choice to choose. Advising candidly is precisely the opposite of what a sycophant would do since a sycophant always agrees.

31. **(A)** An aberration is untypical behavior, particularly untypical bad behavior. Typical behavior is thus a perfect opposite. Major improvement has some oppositeness in that an aberration is likely a worse action than is typical, but there is nothing in (E) that connects to the "typical" portion of the meaning of aberration. (D) and (B) have some of the same difficulty except that they do not connect to any part of aberration as well as (E) does.

32. **(E)** Anomalous means something unusual, irregular, or abnormal. Usual is a perfect opposite since it includes the idea of relating to the general run of events. Anomalous things are often difficult to explain, but that is a derived meaning. Meaningful has some merit in the sense that abnormal items might lack meaning in the usual ways, but it is a bare echo of the real meaning of the word. Similarly, connected might appeal in the sense that an anomalous event is not connected to the usual rules or circumstances. Vicious would appeal only if one thought of the stem word as referring to animalistic. Capacious, meaning having a large capacity, usually in a physical way, is simply unrelated.

33. **(B)** Cognizance means the range or scope of knowledge, from a Latin root meaning to come to know. Ignorance is not, perhaps, a perfect opposite, but is clearly better than any of the others since it refers to the scope of lack of knowledge and none of the others refer to knowledge or learning in any way.

34. **(A)** Quiescent means being at rest or quiet. Restless refers to not being at rest, having a need for unceasing movement, such as the restless sea. This is not a perfect opposite, but the other answer choices have nothing to do with the idea of being quiet. Malignant means evil or harmful; a mendicant is a beggar; and farcical means being farcelike, a sham.

35. **(C)** To eschew means to avoid something in the sense of abstaining from it. One would eschew coarse language by not using it. Use is then a bit of a single partial opposite. Invite has some opposite flavor since it means to ask something into your area, but contrasted with use, it is the action in relation to the thing that is the issue. Traduce means to slander or falsely speak ill of someone. Emanate means to radiate out from, such as heat or light emanating from a source.

36. **(B)** Taciturn describes someone who speaks very little. This relates to the word tacit, which means unspoken, as in a tacit understanding. Garrulous, meaning talkative, is a good opposite, though it does have the additional flavor of talking about unimportant things. Dubious, meaning doubtful, and gullible, meaning one too easily deceived, are not connected to taciturn. Pleasant has some feeling of oppositeness because a silent person may be thought of as unpleasant, even sullen, but it is an associated meaning and not a definition of taciturn.

37. **(E)** Recondite means obscure, especially referring to a little-known item of knowledge. There is some flavor of recondite knowledge being profound as well. Obvious, a good opposite to the idea of obscure, means easy to see, while recondite refers somewhat more to the number of people who know the item rather than the ease with which it can be learned or found out. Philosopher and peasant are nouns that play on the -ite ending, which sometimes signifies a noun rather than an adjective, though such nouns as anchorite derive from adjectival roots. Arable means useful for farming, and miniature means very small.

38. **(D)** Redundant means excess, surplus, and duplicative. Necessary is a good opposite to the idea of surplus. None of the other words relate to this idea. Dilatory means late or tardy; an apocryphal story is one that is probably not true; astute means clever or smart. Bare, in the sense of the cupboard being bare or empty, has some trace of oppositeness but is not right because it has no connotation of non-redundancy, only that it has no redundant contents.

SECTION III

1. **(B)** In treating radicals (square roots), it is important to keep in mind that the numbers under the radicals may be combined only when the two radicals are being multiplied, not when the radicals are being added. Thus $\sqrt{5}\sqrt{4}$ is the standard notation for $\sqrt{5} \times \sqrt{4}$; the symbol for multiplication is omitted just as it is in algebraic notation (e.g., a times b is written ab). In this problem, the indicated operation is addition, not multiplication. While $\sqrt{5}\sqrt{4} = \sqrt{20}$, $\sqrt{5} + \sqrt{4} \neq \sqrt{9}$. Having established that, the problem is now easily solved. We know that $\sqrt{9} = 3$. (Note: $\sqrt{9} = 3$ not $\sqrt{9} =$

+ or − 3.) The printed radical is by convention a *non-negative* number. Only when we have $x^2 = 9$, do we have $x = \pm 3$, and that is because we are taking the square root of both sides of the equation:

$$x^2 = 9$$
$$x = \pm \sqrt{9}$$
$$x = \pm 3$$

Notice that the $\pm$ symbol was inserted in front of the radical *before* taking the square root of 9.

As for Column B, $\sqrt{4} = 2$. And we also know that $\sqrt{5} > \sqrt{4}$, so $\sqrt{5} > 2$. This means that Column B is 2 plus something greater than 2, and thus totals something greater than 4, so B must be greater than A.

2. **(A)** Knowing the common fraction-percent equivalents would make this problem a cinch: $\frac{1}{6} = 16\frac{2}{3}\%$. But even if one does not remember that, the problem is easily solved by dividing 6 into 1: $6\overline{)1.00}^{.16\frac{2}{3}}$. So, Column A is greater than Column B.

3. **(D)** Here we can use the information about positive and negative roots discussed in question 1 above. The direct attack here is to solve for x:

$$x^2 - 4 = 0$$
$$x^2 = 4$$
$$x = \pm \sqrt{4}$$
$$x = \pm 2$$

This shows that x might be either + or −2. To be sure, if $x = +2$, Column A is equal to Column B; but if $x = -2$, Column B is greater. This shows that our answer must be (D).

4. **(D)** Without knowing how much fruit costs per pound, we have no way of determining which costs more, three pounds of grapes or four pounds of bananas. We cannot assume that B is greater just because the bananas weigh more.

5. **(B)** You can solve this problem by performing the addition in Column A, but we have seen some problems in previous exercises in which the arithmetic would be too time-consuming. This problem borders on being one of those. If your first reaction was to add, and you then added the three numbers in less than 20 seconds, your're on firm ground. However, if you took 30 to 45 seconds to complete the addition, you should look for a shortcut. In this case, it is easy to see that the second and third terms are roughly 6 and 5. That will add up to 11. It remains only to ask whether the additional decimals in all three terms will total 1 ($11 + 1 = 12$). A quick glance shows that they do not add up to as much as 1, so Column B must be greater than Column A.

6. **(A)** Q and S are approximately equal, while P is much larger than R, thus making Column A larger. Since this is a chart, it is likely that the scale is true. Even if you calculated S as 20%, you would then be left with the comparison $\frac{45\%}{15\%}$ to $\frac{15\%}{20\%}$, which need not be computed since the fractions can be compared on the basis of the denominators (bottoms) being equal and the numerators (tops) being different. The computation would show Column A as $\frac{9}{4}$ and Column B as $\frac{3}{4}$.

7. **(C)** We get started by filling in missing details. We are looking to connect our x's with a known shape.

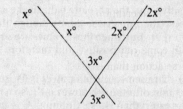

We complete the interior of the triangle using the principle that opposite angles are equal. Then, we know that the sum of the interior angles of a triangle is 180°, so:

$$x + 2x + 3x = 180°$$
$$6x = 180°$$
$$x = 30°$$

This shows that Column A and Column B are equal.

8. **(A)** Since the left expression is not factorable, the best way to begin is to multiply the right-hand expression and then strip everything from the comparison which will not make a difference: $(x + y)^2 = (x + y)(x + y) = x^2 + 2xy + y^2$. Now we see that we have an x^2 and a y^2 term on both sides of the comparison, so we strip them away (by subtracting x^2 and y^2 from both sides). This leaves 0 in Column A and $+2xy$ in Column B. But the centered information states that x is positive and y is negative. So $2xy$ must be *negative*, which makes it less than 0. Column B is less than Column A so the answer is (A).

9. **(A)** This is one of those cases where the algebraic statement is probably easier to grasp than the English equivalent: "x is 150% of y" means $x = 1.5y$. We can see from this that since $y > 0$, $1.5y$ must be larger than y.

10. **(A)** A complete revolution of the minute hand will cover 360° (there are 360° around the center of a circle). So if the minute hand covers 480°, it will make one full turn coming back to the 3, then it will continue for another 120°, which is a third of the circle. Since there are 12 numbers on the face

of the clock, one-third of that is four numbers, so we add four numbers to the 3, arriving at 7. As for Column B, 720° is just two full turns, so the minute hand will go around twice, coming to rest again on the 3. So Column A is 7 while Column B is only 3.

11. **(C)** There are a couple of ways of approaching this problem. One is to do the indicated multiplication. The result in each case will be $a^2 - 2ab + b^2$, which shows that no matter what the values for a and b are, the expressions must be equal. Another approach is to notice that $a - b$ and $b - a$ both measure the distance from a to b. One of them does so by moving from positive to negative, the other does so by moving from negative to positive, but the absolute value is the same in both cases (the numerical value) though the signs are different. But when these values are squared, they both come out positive and therefore equal.

12. **(A)** 2 raised to the 6th power is 64, so m must be 6. 3 raised to the 4th power is 81, so n must be 4. 6 is greater than 4, so Column A is greater than Column B.

13. **(C)** We are looking to compare the perimeters, or the length of the walls, of the rooms. First we note that we are given information that all the angles are right angles. This is one point of similarity. Another point of similarity is that the two rooms are both 12 ft. by 8 ft. with a notch taken out. Since all the walls are at right angles, we know that the length of the right to left walls in each room must total 8 feet, plus the other two, which total 8 feet also, even though we do not know what x and y are. The two cross segments in room P, for instance, are x and $8 - x$ feet respectively. For Room Q they are y and $8 - y$ feet.

Similarly, the walls in the 12-foot direction must be 12 feet on each side of the room, even though broken up. Thus the total perimeter will be the same for both rooms. It is exactly 40 feet in both instances, though you do not need to compute it. For P it would be $12 + y + (12 - y) + x + (8 - x) + 8 = 40$, and similarly for Q. Note that you cannot make a comparison of the areas.

14. **(B)** Since x is an angle of an equilateral triangle $(6 = 6 = 6)$, we know that $x° = 60°$. Substituting 60° for x in the left-hand figure, we see that $60° + y° + 2y° = 180°$. So $3y = 120°$, and $y = 40°$. Now we know that $x = 60°$ and that $2y = 80°$, so Column B is greater than Column A.

15. **(C)** To compute the weight of the left-hand column, we must multiply x cartons by y pounds/cartons and get xy pounds. To compute the weight of the right-hand column we multiply y cartons by x pounds/carton and get yx pounds. But since $xy = yx$, the columns must be equal.

16. **(D)** By multiplying out the given expression, we learn $w(x + y + z) = wx + wy + wz$, which shows that (A) is an equivalent expression. Second, given that it does not matter in multiplication in which order the elements are listed (i.e., $2 \times 3 = 3 \times 2$), we can see that (B) is also an equivalent expression. From $wx + wy + wz$, we can factor the w's out of the first two terms: $w(x + y) + wz$, which shows that (E) is an equivalent expression. Finally, we could also factor the w's from the last two terms: $wx + w(y + z)$, which shows that (C) is an equivalent expression. (D) is not, however, equivalent: $w + w + w + x + y + z$. The 3 would make you suspicious of (D).

17. **(C)** The answers tell you that the issue is the decimal point. The percent sign signifies that the number has been multiplied by 100. To convert a percentage to a decimal, we divide by 100 and drop the percent sign, and this is equivalent to moving the decimal point two places to the left and dropping the percent sign. Thus, $.1\% = .001$. Then when we multiply by ten, we move the decimal point one place to the right: $.001 \times 10 = .01$. So our answer is (C).

18. **(B)** The most direct solution to this problem is to substitute the value +4 for x: $(+4 - 7)(+4 + 2) = (-3)(6) = -18$. Substitute before multiplying to keep it simple.

19. **(B)** Here we need to solve the simultaneous equations. Though there are different methods, one way to find the values of x and y is first to redefine y in terms of x. Since $x - y = 2$, $x = 2 + y$. We can now use $2 + y$ as the equivalent of x and substitute $2 + y$ for x in the other equation:

$$2(2 + y) + y = 7$$
$$4 + 2y + y = 7$$
$$3y = 3$$
$$y = 1$$

Once we have a value of y, we substitute that value into either of the equations. Since the second is a bit simpler, we may prefer to use it: $x - 1 = 2$, so $x = 3$. Now we can determine that $x + y$ is $3 + 1$, or 4.

Another approach would be to add the two equations together so that the y term will cancel itself out:

$$2x + y = 7$$
$$+ (\ x - y = 2)$$
$$3x = 9, \text{ thus } x = 3.$$

20. **(A)** Average speed requires total distance divided by total time. Therefore it is incorrect to average the two speeds together for, after all, the girl moved at the slower rate for three times as long as she moved at the faster rate, so they cannot be weighted equally. The correct way to solve the problem is to reason that the girl covered

the 15 miles by bicycle in 1 hour. She covered the 15 miles by walking in 3 hours. Therefore, she travelled a total of 30 miles in a total of 4 hours. 30 miles/4 hours = 7.5 miles per hour.

21. **(D)** While we know by inspection that the shaded area is larger—the diagonal of a rectangle divides the rectangle in half—the answer choices tell us more is needed though (C) is eliminated. We begin by noting that the area which is left unshaded is a triangle with a 90° angle. This means that we have an altitude and a base at our disposal. Then we note that the shaded area is the area of the square minus the area of the triangle. So we are in a position to compute the area of the square, the triangle, and the shaded part of the figure. In the first place, the base of the triangle—which is the unshaded area of the figure—is equal to the side of the square, 4. The altitude of that triangle is four units long less the unknown distance x, or $4 - x$. So the area of the triangle, $\frac{1}{2}ab$, is $\frac{1}{2}(4 - x)(4)$. The area of the square is 4×4, or 16, so the shaded area is 16 minus the triangle, which we have just determined is $\frac{1}{2}(4 - x)(4)$. Let us first pursue the area of the triangle:

$$\tfrac{1}{2}(4 - x)(4) = (4 - x)(2) = 8 - 2x$$

Substituting in the shaded portion:

$$16 - (8 - 2x) = 8 + 2x$$

Now we complete the ratio. $8 + 2x$ goes on the top, since that is the shaded area, and $8 - 2x$ goes on the bottom, since that is the unshaded area: $\dfrac{8 + 2x}{8 - 2x}$. And we reduce by 2 to yield $\dfrac{4 + x}{4 - x}$.

22. **(D)** Since Linda is the youngest and the other ages are derived from hers, let us assign the value x for Linda's age. In that case Mike will be 2x years old, since he is twice as old as Linda. Finally, Ned will be $2x + 2$ since he is two years older than Mike. Our three ages are: Linda, x; Mike, 2x; and Ned, $2x + 2$. We know that these three ages total 27. Hence, $x + 2x + 2x + 2 = 27$. And now we solve for x:

$$5x + 2 = 27$$
$$5x = 25$$
$$x = 5$$

So Linda is 5 years old. Then, if Linda is 5, Mike must be 10 years old.

23. **(D)** Since our rates are by fifths of a mile, let us begin the solution by figuring out how many fifths of a mile (or parts thereof) there are in this trip. In $2\frac{2}{5}$ miles there are 12 fifths. Then we add another fifth for the additional bit of distance between $2\frac{2}{5}$ and $2\frac{1}{2}$ miles. So the whole trip can be broken down into 13 segments of one-fifth (or part of one-fifth). For the first, the charge is $1.00. That leaves 12 more segments, the charge for each of which is 20¢, giving a total charge for those 12

segments of $2.40. Now, the total charge for the trip is $1.00 for the first one-fifth of a mile and $2.40 for the remaining segments, or $3.40.

24. **(E)** We know that the formula for the area of a square is $s^2 = $ area. So $s^2 = 36x^2$, and, taking the square root of both sides we learn $s = 6x$. (Note: there is no question here of a negative solution since geometrical distances are always positive.)

25. **(A)** Since we do not know how much money Ed has, we must assign that amount the value of x. We now establish that Tom has $x + 2$ since he has $2 more than Ed; and we know that Susan has $(x + 2) + 5$, which is $x + 7$, since she has $5 more than Tom. We want to divide this money equally. The natural thing to do, then, is to add up all the money and divide it by 3. The total held by all three individuals is: $x + x + 2 + x + 2 + 5 = 3x + 9$. Dividing that by 3, we want everyone to have $x + 3$. Ed has x so he needs to receive 3. Tom has $x + 2$ so he needs to receive 1. Susan has $x + 7$ so she needs to rid herself of 4. Susan gets rid of this 4 by giving 1 to Tom and 3 to Ed, giving us answer choice (A).

Some shortcutting is possible by considering that Susan has the most money, and then Tom and then Ed. Therefore, any answer which has Ed give up money cannot result in equal shares, eliminating (C) and (E). Furthermore, since Susan has the most, she must give up the most. In (D) Tom gives more than Susan, so this is eliminated. In (B), Susan gives out more than Tom, but she also receives from Tom, so her net giving out is only $1, compared to Tom's $4, so this is also wrong, which leaves (A).

26. **(C)** Do not let the term perfect number throw you. Accept the definition of any such oddball term and apply it to the problem. Since the factors of 6 less than 6 itself are 1, 2, and 3, 6 is the perfect number $(1 + 2 + 3 = 6)$. 1 is not a perfect number since there are no factors of 1 less than itself. 4 is not a perfect number since the factors of 4 less than 4 are 1 and 2 and $1 + 2 \neq 4$. Nor is 8 a perfect number since the factors of 8 which are less than 8 itself are 1, 2, and 4, and those total 7, not 8. Finally, 10 is not a perfect number since the key factors here are 1, 2, and 5, which total 8, not 10.

27. **(A)** By connecting Q and O or P and O, it can be seen that the radius of circle O is 6 units. (Remember, when a circle is named after a point, that point is the center of the circle.) The formula for the area of a circle is πr^2, so the area of circle O is: $\pi(6)^2 = 36\pi$.

28. **(B)** We are given information about angles in the top of the figure and asked about angles in the bottom. The task, then, is to connect these items. We do not know that the horizontal lines are parallel, nor can we prove it. We do, however,

have a quadrilateral figure and several straight lines to work with. Considering the figure with a, b, and c as the three angles of the quadrilateral other than the 70°, we see:

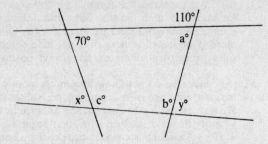

Angle a is on a straight line with 110° and thus equals 70°. We are looking only for x + y, so we need not have each individually. Working our way down through the quadrilateral, we see that the total degrees in the quadrilateral, as for all such figures, is 360°. Thus, b + c + 70° + 70° = 360° and b + c = 220°. Now, at last, we are on the right line. Again using the fact that a straight line totals 180° we see:

$$\begin{array}{rl} x + c & = 180 \\ y + b & = 180 \\ \hline x + y + b + c & = 360 \end{array}$$

Since we know b + c = 220, we can solve by substituting to get x + y + 220 = 360; thus x + y = 140.

29. **(D)** We begin by computing the capacity of the cylinder, which is πr^2 times height. Since the radius is 2 and the height is 5, the capacity of this cylinder is $\pi(2)^2 \times 5 = 20\pi$ cu. ft. It is already 40% full, which means that 60% of the capacity is left. 60% of 20π cu. ft. $= 12\pi$ cu. ft., and that is the answer we seek.

30. **(A)** We are seeking c, but the given information is about the area of the triangle, while c is a distance. However, the formula for the area of triangles connects distance to area, so we should compute the area in terms of c. We know that we have a right angle in the lower right-hand corner of the figure. So, this gives us an altitude and a base. The altitude is 3c units long and the base is 4c units long. So, the area is $\frac{1}{2}ab$ or $\frac{1}{2}(3c)(4c) = \frac{1}{2}(12c^2) = 6c^2$. And this is equal to 54: $6c^2 = 54$; so $c^2 = 9$ and c = 3.

SECTION IV

1. **(C)** Of course, it is possible to perform the subtraction indicated in Column A, and to do so probably would not require more than 30 seconds: $343 - \frac{343}{2} = \frac{686 - 343}{2} = \frac{343}{2}$. A better way of solving the problem, however, is to reason: 343/2 is one-half of 343. To take any number and subtract half of that number leaves half of the number. So the two quantities must be equal. Since this is early in the subsection, look for a shortcut.

2. **(B)** First, simplify the centered information: 6x = 6; therefore x = 1. Once you know x = 1, then substitute 1 for x in each column. Column A becomes $\frac{1}{6}$ and Column B becomes $\frac{6}{1}$. Since $\frac{1}{6}$ is less than $\frac{6}{1}$, our answer choice must be (B).

3. **(B)** Since n is between p and m, we have either m < n < p or p > n > m. Since m < n, the former must be true and, thus, n must be less than p, so Column B is larger and (B) is the correct answer.

4. **(A)** It would probably take too long to actually do the indicated calculations. Therefore, we should look for a shorter method. In each column we have the same process—subtraction. We can observe that $\frac{1}{63}$ is the largest of the four fractions in the problem and that $\frac{1}{69}$ is the smallest of the four. In turn, $\frac{1}{65}$ is the second-largest, while $\frac{1}{67}$ is the second-smallest. Thus, the smallest fraction is taken away from the largest while the second-smallest is taken away from the second-largest. Therefore, Column A must be larger (just as, for example, 9 − 3 is larger than 7 − 5).

5. **(C)** This problem is typical of the GRE. The two quantities must be equal. The order of multiplication is irrelevant and the number of decimal places is equal in both columns:

$$.0006 \times 1.34 = .0134 \times .06$$

Or the % sign can be taken as the fraction $\frac{1}{100}$, yielding:

$$(.06)(\tfrac{1}{100})(1.34) = (1.34)(\tfrac{1}{100})(.06)$$

6. **(A)** Although there are no restrictions on the values of x, we know that it is permissible to subtract equal quantities from both columns (that will not interfere with the comparison). Here we subtract $2x^2$ from both columns. The result is

$$x^2 + 5 \qquad 4$$

Then, just to make things as simple as possible, we subtract 4 from both columns and the result is:

$$x^2 + 1 \qquad 0$$

We must now ask what values x might have. Since there is no restriction on the values x might assume, x can range over the entire set of real numbers. But no matter what x is, so long as x ≠ 0, x^2 will be positive. Even if x is 0, $x^2 + 1$ will be greater than 0 (0 + 1 > 0), and if x has a value greater than 0, that will just make x^2 even larger. So Column A is always greater than Column B.
    Another, shorter way of approaching this prob-

lem would be to note that we have the same process in both columns—addition. The 5 in Column A is bigger than the 4 in Column B, so if the $3x^2$ is also bigger than $2x^2$, A will be larger. Since x^2 must be positive, more often it will yield a larger number.

7. **(B)** If you were schooled in the "new math," you may find this problem easy; otherwise, it takes a bit longer to work out. The key to the problem is that the number 423,978 is equal to 400,000 plus 20,000 plus 3,000 plus 900 plus 70 plus 8. Now each of these terms can be expressed using powers of ten: $4 \times 10^5, 2 \times 10^4, 3 \times 10^3, 9 \times 10^2, 70 \times 10^1$, and 8. The digit 2 then is used in the slot for 10^4; therefore, b must be 4. 5 is greater than 4, so Column B is greater.

8. **(B)** One sure way of solving the problem is to substitute the values -3 and -5 for x and y, respectively. Before we do that, however, the following word of warning is in order for the students well versed in math: in this case the fact that x and y are negative means that the absolute value of x − y will be *less* than the absolute value of x + y. Consequently, when we square x − y and x + y, both will be positive, but Column B will be greater. Now, with that note to the mathematicians, we can solve the problem by substituting—a direct, simple, and sure way of getting a right answer:

$$(-3 - -5)^2 \qquad (-3 + -5)^2$$
$$2^2 \qquad\qquad -8^2$$
$$4 \qquad\qquad +64$$

9. **(D)** This problem teaches a very important lesson: It is better to rely on your intuitive knowledge of geometry than to try to memorize formulas. In this case, many students will pick answer (B). Their justification will be the well-known principle that "the larger the angle of a triangle, the larger the opposite side." The rule is absolutely correct, but it is incompletely stated and really applies only within a given triangle. Since the angles belong to *different* triangles it doesn't apply here. Studying principles of math is a good idea, but knowing when to apply the principles is absolutely essential. The following group of drawings should make it clear that no comparison is possible:

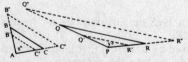

10. **(C)** The formula for computing the volume of a rectangular solid such as a box is width times length times height. For Column A, this is $2 \times 3 \times \frac{1}{6} = 1$. For Column B this is $4 \times 2 \times \frac{1}{8} = 1$. So the two volumes are equal.

11. **(C)** We begin our solution by dividing 13 into 208, with 16 the result. Now we know that either 13 is the largest prime factor of 208 or that the largest prime factor of 208 is paired as a multiple with some number between 1 and 208. The following consideration leads us to this conclusion. First, neither 14 nor 15 are factors of 208 (and in any event are not prime numbers). This lets us know that 13 and 16 are the pair of factors which are most nearly equal. Any other pair of factors will be spread farther apart. Importantly, however, when we find that 208 is factorable by 104, for example, we know that the other element of that pair will be a number between 1 and 13. So, though 104 and 2 are factors, we can quickly isolate all pairs of factors by working our way up from 1 to 13. They are 1 and 208, 2 and 104, 4 and 52, 8 and 26, and 13 and 16. Although 208 has some factors that are larger than 13, e.g., 208, none of these are prime. So the largest prime factor is 13, and the two columns are equal.

Another way of approaching this problem would be to use the important principle of doing what you know how to do. Since 208 is even, we could simply divide it by 2, getting 104. Dividing by 2 again gives us 52. Doing it again yields 26, and once again leaves 13, which is a familiar prime, and equal to Column B.

12. **(D)** In this equation, we have no powers, roots, radicals, or the like. But the equation is not just letters; we also have a number in the equation so the numbers could be consolidated all on one side or the other, such as x + .7 = 2y. Since there are two variables and only one equation, we do not have a definite solution to the situation as it stands. If it had been that x plus a number equalled just y with no multiplier, then we would know for sure how x and y relate. What you are most concerned about is whether this relationship is definite, whether one of the variables is ALWAYS greater, less than, or equal to the other. It should be fairly clear to you that this equation permits x and y to be different, so you might ask yourself if they could be the same, and the answer here is "yes," since if both were equal to .7, the equation would work. Since x and y could be different and they could be the same, the relationship cannot be tied down.

Alternatively, you could substitute some simple positive and negative numbers and compute that x is sometimes greater than y and sometimes smaller. It's better if you can just see it quickly.

For the mathematicians, there is yet another possible solution (among many others) which we can show. First, it should be clear that the .7 makes no difference to the comparison—we could as easily use 1 or even 0. The only difference will be the precise point at which x and y are equal. Having simplified the problem, say, to x + 1 = 2y, which is $y = \frac{1}{2}x + \frac{1}{2}$ (the numbers are easier), one can sketch the line roughly on a graph:

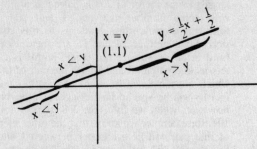

In the second quandrant, x is negative and y is positive, so x is less than y. In the first quadrant, though, both x and y are positive; since the slope of the line is $\frac{1}{2}$, the values for x climb more rapidly than do the values for y.

13. **(A)** In the last problem we mentioned the coordinate axis for the mathematicians. Here, everyone will need to understand the use of the axis. In this case, we have the graph of the equation x = y, which is a straight line passing through the origin (0,0). Since (m,n) is in the first quadrant, both m and n must be positive. Then, since (m,n) is below the line x = y, the x coordinate must be greater than the y coordinate. Had they been equal, the point (m,n) would have fallen on the line. Since it fails to fall on the line, it is as though one went over x units on the x axis, but did not go up quite as far in the vertical direction, so the point fell short. Thus, x must be greater than y, and so, too, m must be greater than n.

14. **(C)** In problems involving some defined operations, such as ∗, the best attack is usually to substitute the values suggested. In the case of Column A, we use 1 for x and 2 for y. Looking at the centered information, we substitute: $\frac{1 + 2}{(1)(2)} = \frac{3}{2}$. For Column B, we reverse x and y: $\frac{2 + 1}{(2)(1)} = \frac{3}{2}$. So the two columns are equal.

It might happen to strike you that Columns A and B are simply swapping the x and y in the input to the ∗ function. If we look at the operations that ∗ is calling for, we see that one is addition and the other multiplication. In both of those operations, order doesn't matter: xy = yx and x + y = y + x. (We say that both addition and multiplication are "commutative"—order is not important.) Therefore, the answers would be the same for both columns. If something like that strikes you, it is worth a little following up. However, if what you think is a shortcut doesn't seem to be getting you anywhere, drop it!

15. **(D)** The easiest way to solve this problem is to try to redraw the figure in a way that preserves the specified relationships but also shows that a definite answer cannot be reached:

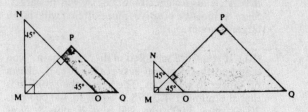

Both configurations are permissible. We still have the right angles preserved, and we still have the 45° angles preserved. This shows that the given information is not sufficient to allow us to reach a conclusion about the relationship between the sizes of the regions.

16. **(E)** This is a very easy problem. One need only do the indicated operation. Multiply 1.50 by 2: $(1.50)(2) = 3.00 = 3$.

17. **(B)** Again, we have a relatively easy problem. We must substitute −2 for x, and then multiply: $(-2 - 5)(-2 + 5)$. $(-2 - 5) = -7$, and $(-2 + 5) = 3$. Then, $(-7)(3) = -21$, since a negative number times a positive number gives a negative number. Thus, answer (B) is correct.

18. **(D)** While it is possible to set up a formula for this problem: Original Price − Discount = Discounted Price, a little common sense is a better attack. The discount is 25% of the original price, and 25% of $90 is $22.50. If the item originally cost $90, and we are getting a discount of $22.50, the new price will be $67.50.

19. **(A)** This is a fairly straightforward chart question. We need only count the number of years in which the dotted line ("Sophomores") exceeded (was above) the double line ("Freshmen"). This first occurred in 1959 and continued in 1960, 1961, 1962, 1963, and 1964 (when "Sophomores" was barely larger than "Freshmen"). It came to an end in 1965, when the two were equal. "Sophomores" remains well below "Freshmen" until 1977 when it almost reached the level of "Freshmen," but not quite. So, in only six years did the attrition rate for Sophomores exceed that of Freshmen.

20. **(B)** In 1965 the attrition rate for Juniors was 40 per 1000. In 1970, it was 60 per 1000. So, it increased by 20 during that time. To compute that increase, we take the difference, 20, and divide by the original, or starting, quantity, which is 40. $\frac{20}{40} = \frac{1}{2}$, or a 50% increase, answer choice (B).

21. **(E)** Reading the chart carefully is an important part of the exercise. In this case, the chart gives

the attrition rate, that is, the number of students per 1000 who left the college. The chart does not provide any information about the actual number of students leaving. For example, in 1970 the attrition rate for freshmen was 90 students per every 1000, but that does not say how many freshmen actually left. If there were 1000 freshmen, we could conclude 90 left. If there were 2000, we would know that 180 left, and so on. But without the additional information regarding the size of the classes, we cannot conclude anything about the numbers of students who left. And without that information, we cannot compute a ratio between the number of freshmen leaving and the number of juniors leaving.

22. **(D)** The reasoning of our explanation to question 21 provides the key to this question and an important reminder of the importance of attending carefully to the title, margins, and footnotes of the chart as a source of information. Neither I nor II can be inferred since we have no information about the *numbers* involved. We have the attrition *rate*—that is, the number per 1000 who left. But without additional information we can conclude nothing about the actual numbers involved. III is, however, inferable from the graph. During that period, only the dashed line ("Seniors") declined on the graph.

23. **(C)** We are looking for those categories, if there are any, where the drop from 1970 to 1980 was $\frac{1}{4}$ of the 1970 total, for that will indicate a decrease of 25%. (After a 25% decrease, the new total will be 25% less than the old total.) For freshmen the drop was from 90 to 75, a difference of 15 over a starting value of 90; $\frac{15}{90}$ is much less than $\frac{1}{4}$. For sophomores, the value drops from 80 to 50, a difference of 30 over a starting value of 80; $\frac{30}{80}$ is greater than 25%. For juniors, the drop was from 60 to 45, a difference of 15 over a starting value of 60, $\frac{15}{60}$—the 25% decrease we seek. Finally, the senior attrition rate dropped from 23 to 20, such a small percentage change that eyeballing the line would be enough. Only the juniors' rate decreased by 25% from 1970 to 1980—III only.

24. **(C)** Let us begin our solution by dropping a perpendicular from the upper vertex of the triangle:

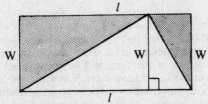

This divides the rectangle into two other rectangles, each with a diagonal running across it:

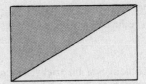

It should be intuitively clear that the diagonal of a rectangle divides the rectangle in half since all sides and angles are equal. Therefore, the left shaded area is equal to the left unshaded area and the right shaded area is equal to the right unshaded area, which means the total shaded area is equal to the total unshaded area. Thus, the triangle has half the area of the rectangle. This is actually the proof of the formula you use to find the area of a triangle—$A = (\text{height})(\text{base})\frac{1}{2}$. Remember this situation since it could easily come up in one problem or another.

25. **(B)** Since Earl and Ellen will be working together we add their work rates:

$$\frac{\text{Number of tasks}}{\text{Time}} + \frac{\text{Number of tasks}}{\text{Time}}$$
$$= \frac{\text{Number of tasks together}}{\text{Time}}$$

In this case:

$$\frac{45 \text{ envelopes}}{60 \text{ seconds}} + \frac{45 \text{ envelopes}}{90 \text{ seconds}} = \frac{300 \text{ envelopes}}{x \text{ seconds}}$$

Or: $\frac{45}{60} + \frac{45}{90} = \frac{300}{x}$
To make the arithmetic simpler, we reduce fractions:
$$\frac{3}{4} + \frac{1}{2} = \frac{300}{x}.$$
Then we add: $\frac{10}{8} = \frac{300}{x}$.
And solve for x: $x = 300(\frac{8}{10}) = 240$ seconds.
Since 240 seconds is equal to 4 minutes, our answer is (B).
If you are not comfortable with fractions, you could have kept to minutes.

Another way to approach this problem would be to try to get the rate of each worker in envelopes per minute. Earl is already known to work at 45 envelopes per minute. Ellen takes $1\frac{1}{2}$ minutes for the same work. Thus, 45 envelopes are done in three half-minutes. 45 divides by 3 nicely, as we often find on the GRE, so Ellen does 15 envelopes in $\frac{1}{2}$ minute or 30 envelopes per minute. 45 per minute + 30 per minute = 75 per minute, which means $\frac{300}{75} = 4$ minutes.

26. **(D)** First, let us count the number of subjects having characteristic X. The first two categories are those subjects having X (25 also have Y, 10 do not have Y but do have X), which is a total of 35. Then those subjects having Y are entered in the first and third categories (25 also have X, 25 have

Y but lack X), for a total of 50. Our ration is 35/50, which, when reduced by a factor of 5, is equal to 7/10.

27. **(D)** This problem is a bit tricky, but not really difficult. When dealing with a ratio, say 4 to 1, it is important to remember that the number of parts is the sum of these two numbers. So we might say we have five parts—four parts are passenger vehicles, one part is all other vehicles—and that is how we get a ratio of 4 to 1. But this means that 4 parts out of the total of 5 parts are passenger vehicles, and 4 out of 5 is $\frac{4}{5}$, or 80%. Answer (E) makes the mistake of forgetting that although there are four times as many passenger cars as all other vehicles, the passenger vehicles constitute only $\frac{4}{5}$ of the total number.

28. **(B)** Let us logically approach this problem before even trying to calculate it. Although we have a 10% increase and then a 10% decrease, we must always ask ourselves "10% of what?" The increase was 10% of the original price, but the decrease was 10% of the higher price and consequently the decrease is bigger than the increase and the result at the end is less than the starting price, which eliminates answer choices (C), (D), and (E). Similarly, on logical grounds, it is hard to see how a 10% decrease from a 10% higher price could be equal to an 11% decrease from the starting price; that seems too much, which leaves (B) as the answer.

If we wish to compute the answer, let us start by saying that the original price of the item is x. A 10% increase in that price will be one-tenth of x, or .1x. When we add the increase to the original price, we find our increased price is 1.1x. We must then take away ten percent of that. Ten percent of 1.1x is .11x, and subtracting .11x from 1.1x, we get .99x. We started with x; we ended with .99x, so we lost .01x, which is 1%.

29. **(D)** First, we must note that the question asks for *percentage* decrease, not simply decrease in price. And percentage change is a function of the absolute change or difference over the starting value. We begin our solution by noting that both (B) and (E) mention periods in which the price increased, so we know that neither of them could be correct. Then we run a quick calculation of percentage decrease for the remaining three:

(A) $\dfrac{70 - 40}{70} = \dfrac{30}{70}$, for slightly less than 50% decrease.

(C) $\dfrac{50 - 30}{50} = \dfrac{20}{50}$, for slightly less than 50% decrease.

(D) $\dfrac{30 - 10}{30} = \dfrac{20}{30}$, for a $66\frac{2}{3}$% decrease.

So (D) is greater than both (A) and (C).

30. **(A)** This is an interesting problem in that no formula is going to solve it. Instead, it requires the use of some good old common sense. Perhaps the solution is more easily visualized if we explode the cube.

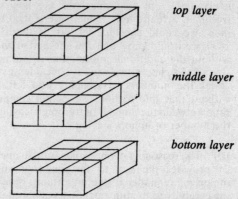

top layer

middle layer

bottom layer

All of the small cubes on the top and the bottom layers will have at least one side painted. In the middle layer, the outer eight smaller cubes encircle the center cube, which is protected on top by the top layer, on the bottom by the bottom layer, and on the remaining four sides by the outside of the sandwich layer:

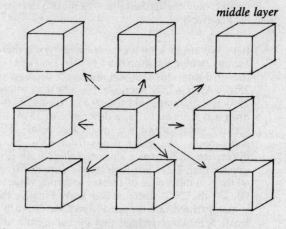

middle layer

SECTION V

Questions 1–3

ARRANGING THE INFORMATION

The three question stems are all "what is it" questions, so we know that the situation is one in which the arrangement is stable or fixed, and a large proportion of the time will be spent in arranging the information. We have a setup in which there are three items of information to be sorted out about the four people: names, musical preference, and hair color. There is an auxiliary relationship in that there are two couples.

Since the situation is a fixed one, with relatively few parameters, we will do it in one chart:

NAME	Mrs. N.	Mr. N	Mrs. P	Mr. P
MUSIC				
HAIR				

Since the situation is fixed and we are using a single chart, and there are not that many pieces of information, we might consider whether there are any pieces of information which would be most helpful to enter out of order because they are fixed. The very last piece of information, that Mrs. P. has brown hair, can be the rock on which our diagram is founded.

NAME	Mrs. N.	Mr. N	Mrs. P	Mr. P
MUSIC				
HAIR			Brown	

We might now look for something which links to that information. If nothing did, we would just enter information, but there is an item which links: the wife with blond hair likes country. This must be Mrs. N. since we have determined that Mrs. P has brown hair. We thus learn both the hair color and musical preference of Mrs. N. This gives us the following diagram:

NAME	Mrs. N.	Mr. N	Mrs. P	Mr. P
MUSIC	Country			
HAIR	Blond		Brown	

The same sentence contains another piece of information we can now link up: the blond wife's husband (Mr. N) likes classical music. This yields:

NAME	Mrs. N	Mr. N	Mrs. P	Mr. P
MUSIC	Country	Classical		
HAIR	Blond		Brown	

We can now consider the last pieces of information—there are only two blonds and one of them likes jazz. We have previously determined that one of the blonds likes country, so we must now determine who the other blond might be. It cannot be Mr. N, for he likes classical music, nor can it be Mrs. P, since she has brown hair. Therefore, Mr. P must have blond hair and like jazz.

NAME	Mrs. N	Mr. N	Mrs. P	Mr. P
MUSIC	Country	Classical		Jazz
HAIR	Blond		Brown	Blond

We can now make the inference that Mrs. P. likes rock music since that is the only possibility left. We do not know what color hair Mr. N has except that it is not blond since the two blonds have been accounted for. So our final diagram looks like this:

NAME	Mrs. N	Mr. N	Mrs. P	Mr. P
MUSIC	Country	Classical	Rock	Jazz
HAIR	Blond	Not blond	Brown	Blond

Answering the Questions

All the answers can be read from the diagram.

1. **(C)** Music tastes are fully determined.

2. **(A)** Mr. P has blond hair and likes jazz.

3. **(D)** Mr. N likes classical music.

4. **(C)** The author is arguing that the budget cuts will not ultimately be detrimental to the poor since the adverse effects will be more than offset by beneficial ones. II and III attack both elements of this reasoning. II points out that there will be no beneficial effects to offset the harmful ones, and III notes that the harmful effects will be so harmful that they will outweigh any beneficial ones that might result. I, however, is not relevant to the author's point. The author is arguing a point of economics. How the congressmen get themselves elected has no bearing on that point.

5. **(A)** The author reasons from the premise "there are bottles of this product in the apartments" to the conclusion "therefore, these people believe the product is effective." The ad obviously wants the hearer to infer that the residents of the apartments decided themselves to purchase the product because they believed it to be effective. (A) directly attacks this linkage. If it were true that the company gave away bottles of the product, this would sever that link. (B) does weaken the ad, but only marginally. To be sure, we might say to ourselves, "Well, a person who touts a product and does not use it himself is not fully to be trusted." But (B) does not aim at the very structure of the argument as (A) does. (C) can hardly weaken the argument since it appears to be a premise on which the argument itself is built. (C) therefore actually strengthens the appeal of the advertisement. It also does not link to Painaway's effectiveness. (D) seems to be irrelevant to the appeal of the ad. The ad is designed to change the hearer's mind, so the fact that he does not now accept the conclusion of the ad is not an argument against the ability of the ad to accomplish its stated objective. Finally, (E) is irrelevant to the purpose of the ad for reasons very similar to those cited for (D).

6. **(C)** The weakness in Gerry's argument is that he assumes, incorrectly, that getting drunk is the only harm Clyde has in mind. Clyde could respond very effectively by pointing to some other harms of alcohol. (A) would not be a good response for Clyde since he is concerned with Gerry's welfare. The fact that other people get drunk when Gerry does not is hardly a reason for Gerry to stop drinking. (B) is also incorrect. That other people do or do not get drunk is not going to strengthen Clyde's argument against Gerry. He needs an argument that will impress Clyde, who apparently does not get drunk. (D) is perhaps the second-best answer, but the explicit wording of the paragraph makes it unacceptable. Gerry has been drinking the same quantity for fifteen years. Now, admittedly it is possible he will begin to drink more

heavily, but that *possibility* would not be nearly so strong a point in Clyde's favor as the *present* existence of harm (other than inebriation). Finally, (E) is irrelevant, since it is white wine which Gerry does drink.

Questions 7–12

Arranging the Information

We have two separate dimensions here: sweetness and deadliness. Sweetness is presumably a surrogate for attractiveness to ants. The preview of the question stems reinforces the conclusion that these two are the basic ideas and also tells us that we have a question about redundancy, at least insofar as information about sweetness goes. Let us arrange the information about sweetness.

	←LESS—SWEET—MORE→
I. U sweeter than V	V U
II. V sweeter than Y	Y V U
III. W less sweet than X— cannot enter yet	
IV. X less sweet than Y	X Y V U
Now enter III:	W X Y V U
V. Y less sweet than U— ALREADY KNOWN (Q # 9)	
VI. Z sweeter than U	W X Y V U Z

Now let us do deadliness:

	←LESS—DEADLY—MORE→
I. U deadlier than Z	Z U
II. V less deadly than Z	V Z U
III. W less deadly than U	V Z U ←——W→
IV. X deadlier than Y— cannot enter yet	
V. Y deadlier than U	V Z U Y ←——W→
Now Enter IV:	V Z U Y X ←——W→
VI. Z less deadly than W	V Z W U Y X

Answering the Questions

7. **(E)** Z is the sweetest of the compounds.

8. **(D)** U and Z are sweeter than V, and both of the compounds are also deadlier than V.

9. **(D)** As noted during the arrangement phase of the problem, V added no new information to the sweetness classification.

10. **(A)** V, U, and Z are sweeter than Y, and U, Y, and X are deadlier than W. Thus, only U meets both criteria.

11. **(B)** V is the least deadly.

12. **(E)** X is the most deadly.

Questions 13–17

Arranging the Information

There are four things to know about each piece of luggage: position, type, weight, and owner. Five pieces times four kinds of information about each piece is a grid of $5 \times 4 = 20$ boxes.

Question 13 should be done first since it uses only part of the information, but since none of the questions asks about contradiction or redundancy, the order in which the particular information statements are done after question 13 is answered will not make any difference. Questions 14, 15, and 16 indicate that pretty much the entire story is known about the luggage, but question 17 indicates that at least two parts of the grid will not be definitely completed.

The grid outline from statement I:

POSITION	1	2	3	4	5
TYPE					
WEIGHT					
OWNER					

Entering item II:

POSITION	1	2	3	4	5
TYPE					
WEIGHT					10 lbs
OWNER					

Entering item III:

POSITION	1	2	3	4	5
TYPE					
WEIGHT					10 lbs
OWNER	not Sw	Sw?	Sw?	Sw?	not Sw

Entering item VI:

POSITION	1	2	3	4	5
TYPE					
WEIGHT			20 lbs		10 lbs
OWNER	not Sw	Sw?	Amer	Sw?	not Sw
	not Amer	not Amer		not Amer	not Amer

At this point Question 13 is answerable, as shown in the following "Answering the Problems" section.

Now we enter the other items of information. IV can only be partially entered since there is only the negative inference to be made that anything not 15 pounds cannot be the Turk's, which needs to be kept in mind in entering each further piece of information. V can be entered now:

POSITION	1	2	3	4	5
TYPE		box			
WEIGHT		5 lbs	20 lbs		10 lbs
OWNER	not Sw	Sw?	Amer	Sw?	not Sw
	not Amer	not Amer		not Amer	not Amer
		not Turk			not Turk

Now enter VII, since VI has already been entered. VII tells us that the hatbox weighs 10 pounds (second-from-lightest), and thus is the fifth item, and it is not owned by the German.

POSITION	1	2	3	4	5
TYPE		box			hatbox
WEIGHT		5 lbs	20 lbs		10 lbs
OWNER	not Sw	Sw?	Amer	Sw?	not Sw
	not Amer	not Amer		not Amer	not Amer
		not Turk			not Turk
					not Germ

Notice that we can now do some more with the owner line: Since 5 cannot be any of the other four, it must be Belgian.

OWNER	not Sw	Sw?	Amer	Sw?	Belg
	not Amer	not Amer		not Amer	
	not Belg	not Belg		not Belg	
		not Turk			

Now we enter VIII. Since this is the last item, we expect to have many interactions and to all but complete the remaining blanks at this point. Here is what it looks like after filling in only the direct information in VIII:

POSITION	1	2	3	4	5
TYPE	trunk	box			hatbox
WEIGHT	25 lbs	5 lbs	20 lbs		10 lbs
OWNER	not Sw	Sw?	Amer	Sw?	Belg
	not Amer	not Amer		not Amer	
	not Belg	not Belg		not Belg	

Our further deductions are these:
—Since the Turk has a 15-pound item, his cannot be in position 1, which makes position one not American or Swedish or Belgian or Turkish, and thus must be German.
—Since the weights are known for positions 1, 2, 3, and 5, position 4 must be the last possibility: 15 pounds and position 4 must, therefore, also be the Turk's item.
—Since the ownership of item 1 is German, 3 American, 4 Turkish, and 5 Belgian, 2 must be Swedish.
—The crate and the suitcase might be in either position 3 or 4. Note that question 17, which indicated that there was some uncertainty in the final grid, would not directly name the uncertain portions of the grid, but refers to them through the weights, which are certain. This is typical.

Thus, the final grid looks like this:

POSITION	1	2	3	4	5
TYPE	trunk	box	crate / suitcase	suitcase / crate	hatbox
WEIGHT	25 lbs	5 lbs	20 lbs	15 lbs	10 lbs
OWNER	Germ	Sw	Amer	Turk	Belg

Answering the Problems

13. **(C)** As can be seen from the preceding third diagram, these statements tell us that the Swede owns the second or fourth item since his luggage is surrounded by other luggage and had to be either 2, 3, or 4, and the American is 3. Choices (A) and (B) incorrectly allege position 1 is possible. (D) errs in saying that position 3 is possible when that is the American. (E) refers to the 10-pound box, which is position 5 and not surrounded by other luggage.

14. **(A)** This is answered from the grid. The German owns a 25-pound trunk, not a 25-pound box or crate. VIII by itself rules out answers (B) and (C). V by itself rules out items (B) and (E).

15. **(D)** The American's luggage is 20 pounds and the German's 25. Thus, (D) is false and the answer sought. (A) is true since Turk = 15 pounds and Belgian = 10. (B) is true since American = 20, German = 25, and 20 + 5 = 25. (C) is true since Turk = 15 and Swede = 5. (E) is true even though the exact location of the crate is unknown; it is position 3 or 4, while the trunk is position 1—thus, not next to it.

16. **(B)** The 10-pound hatbox is owned by the Belgian. (C) and (D) cannot be known since those items' positions are not certain. (A) and (E) are simply false.

17. **(E)** Each of the statements is sufficient. Anything which will distinguish the crate from the suitcase or tie down either one of them will do the trick. One of them is 20 pounds and owned by the American, the other is 15 pounds and owned by the Turk.

   I. works since it tells us the crate must be the 20-pound item.
  II. works since it tells us that the crate is the 20-pound item.
 III. works since it tells us that the suitcase is the 15-pound item.

Questions 18–22

Arranging the Information

The whole first paragraph is mostly background. The real meat of the setup is in the second paragraph, where the method of determining the grade of a calf from the grades of its parents is laid out.

If father = mother or +/− 1 grade, child = mother.
If father +2 or 3 from mother, child = mother +1.
If father −2 or 3 from mother, child = mother −1.
Permissible grades 2A, 3A, 4A, and 5A.

Since the question stems are largely conditional, this small amount of information in the arranging end of the job is to be expected. Most of the work will be in the questions.

Answering the Questions

18. **(A)** A 2A mother's calf will be raised one grade if the father is either 4A or 5A; hence, answer choice (A) yields a 3A child.

    Since the calf's grade must always be within one grade of its mother's grade, a 3A calf could not have had a 5A mother. This eliminates answer choices (B) and (D). Count the A's carefully.

    (C) fails because although the father is higher than the 2A mother, he is only one grade higher, and thus cannot lift the calf to 3A. (E)'s breeding will produce a 4A calf, which, while preferable from the Bellmans' perspective perhaps, is not a preferable answer choice when you are trying to explain a 3A result.

19. **(D)** The least resistant grades will be those that could not possibly have had 2A or 3A fathers, if any. 5A offspring can only be the result of 5A mothers and 5A or 4A fathers. Any other father would be sufficiently below the 5A mother to lower the offspring to 4A. By the same sort of reasoning, the 2A offspring would be the most resistant since they must have had a 2A or 3A father. The others would be in-between since it is likely that some of them did have 2A or 3A fathers. As the discussion shows, it is not true that all of the grades will have the same resistance; thus, (E) fails.

20. **(B)** Answer choices (A), (B), and (C) all have some merit since they will each result in all of the next generation of cattle having at least one 4A parent, and thus presumably be more gentle. Though (D) does improve the milk-producing qualities of the herd, it will do nothing to enhance gentleness. Thus, (D) is eliminated. (E) could not be correct since a random breeding program would leave some non-gentle offspring, which (B) avoids.

    Since (A), (B), and (C) all have good results on gentleness, you must tell them apart and choose the best answer on the basis of their effect on milk quality and quantity. (A) will upgrade the 2A cows' offspring, but the other cows will have the same grade calves as they are themselves. (C), on the other hand, will eliminate 5A grades from the herd altogether.

    (B) is preferable to either (A) or (C) because it will preserve 5A grades, unlike (C), and it will improve the herd more than (C)—since it is using higher-grade cows rather than higher-grade bulls, and the cows will pull up the grades more than the bulls, according to the given information.

21. **(A)** Statement I has no basis whatever in the problem set, so it cannot be known to be true. II is not true because a 2A bull and a 4A cow produce a 3A offspring, and so does the breeding of a 4A bull to a 3A cow. III is also false since a 2A bull and a 5A cow will produce a 4A calf. Thus, all three statements are false.

22. **(A)** The key to this problem is the phrase at least, which permits you to assume the most favorable permissible conditions without worrying about what might actually happen down on the dairy farm. Since we want to raise the grade rapidly, and a high-grade mother will raise grade more rapidly than a high-grade father, we will assume that we start with a 2A hide color bull which is bred to a 5A cow, producing a 4A bull offspring. That is the first generation. This 4A hide color bull is then bred to another 5A cow to produce a 5A hide color offspring in the second generation after the first hide color animal.

23. **(B)** The chief failing of the argument is that it draws a false analogy. Since prisons are required to feed and maintain as well as house prisoners (not to mention the necessity for security), the analogy to a hotel room is weak at best. (C) focuses on this specific shortcoming. Remember, in evaluating the strength of an argument from analogy it is important to look for dissimilarities which might make the analogy inappropriate. Thus, (A) and (E) are also good criticisms of the argument. They voice the general objection of which (C) is the specification. (D) is also a specific objection—the argument compares two numbers which are not at all similar, but that does not apply here. (B) is not a way in which the argument can be criticized, for the author never cites any authority.

24. **(E)** The author cites a series of similarities between the two diseases, and then, in his last sentence, he writes, "So . . . ," indicating that his conclusion that the causes of the two diseases are similar rests upon the other similarities he has listed. Answer (E) correctly describes the basis of the argument. (A) is incorrect, for nothing in the passage indicates that either disease is a public health hazard, much less that one disease is a greater hazard than the other. (B) is unwarranted for the author states only that the scientists are looking for a cure for *aphroditis melancholias*. He does not state that they will be successful; and even if there is a hint of that in the argument, we surely would not want to conclude on that basis that scientists will eventually find a cure for *every* disease. (C), like (A), is unrelated to the conclu-

sion the author seeks to establish. All he wants to maintain is that similarities in the symptoms suggest that scientists should look for similarities in the causes of these diseases. He offers no opinion of the ultimate goal of modern technology, nor does he need to do so. His argument is complete without any such addition. (D) is probably the second-best answer, but it is still completely wrong. The author's argument, based on the assumption that similarity of effect depends upon similarity of cause, would neither gain nor lose persuasive force if (D) were true. After all, many diseases occur in both man and other animals, but at least (D) has the merit—which (A), (B), and (C) all lack—of trying to say something about the connection between the causes and effects of disease.

25. **(A)** The form of the argument can be represented using letters as:

   I. All R are either O or W. (All non-Readers are non-Opinionholders or Wrong.)

   II. All O are R.

If II is true, I might be either false or true, since it is possible that there are some who have not read the report who hold right opinions. That is, even if II is true and all O are R, that does not tell us anything about all the R's, only about the O's. The rest of the R's might be W's (wrong opinionholders) or something else altogether (right opinionholders). By this reasoning we see that we cannot conclude that I is definitely true, so (B) must be wrong. Moreover, we have no ground for believing I to be more or less likely true, so (C) can be rejected. As for (D), even if we assume that all the R's are *either* O or W, we are not entitled to conclude that all O's are R's. There may be someone without an opinion who has read the report. Finally, (E), if it is false that all the O's (non-opinionholders) are R's, that tells us nothing about all R's and their distribution among O and W.

SECTION VI

Questions 1–4

Here we have a linear ordering problem, a type now very familiar. We begin by summarizing the information:

   N = 1 and P = 7
   L > K
   J > M
   K > O > M or K < O < M

1. **(B)** We begin by processing the additional information. For J and O to be separated by exactly two grades, it must mean that they are in grades 2 and 5 or grades 3 and 6, though not necessarily in that order:

1	2	3	4	5	6	7
N	J			O		P
N	O			J		P
N		O			J	P
N		J			O	P

We can eliminate all but the third possibility. The first arrangement is not possible because we cannot honor the requirement J > M. The second is not possible because we cannot place O between K and M. The fourth is not possible for the same reason. Using only the third possibility, we know further:

	1	2	3	4	5	6	7
	N	K	O	M	L	J	P
OR:	N	K	O	L	M	J	P
OR:	N	M	O	K	L	J	P

This proves (B) is necessarily true. The diagram further shows that (A), (C), (D), and (E) are only possibly, though not necessarily, true.

2. **(B)** We begin by processing the additional information:

1	2	3	4	5	6	7
N	M	J	O	K	L	P

With J in grade 3, M must be in grade 2. And we know that L must be a higher grade than K and, further, that O must go between K and M. This means that O, K, and L must be in grades 4, 5, and 6, respectively. The diagram shows that (B) is necessarily true, and that each of the remaining choices is necessarily false.

3. **(D)** The proper means of attack on this question is to test each of the three statements. Since there are only three, this can be done in a reasonable amount of time. As for statement I:

1	2	3	4	5	6	7
N	K	M	J			P

We see there is no place for O between K and M. So this is not possible. As for statement II:

1	2	3	4	5	6	7
N	K		M	J		P

This will allow us to place O between K and M, and placing L in grade 6 ensures that L is in a grade higher than K. So statement II is possible. As for statement III:

1	2	3	4	5	6	7
N	K		M		J	P

This allows us to place O in grade 3, and therefore between K and M. And we can place L in grade 5, which respects all other conditions. So statement III is also possible. Our correct answer must therefore be (D), II and III are possible, though I is not possible.

4. **(A)** We begin by processing the additional information:

$$1 \quad 2 \quad 3 \quad 4 \quad 5 \quad 6 \quad 7$$
$$N \quad M \quad J \quad O \quad K \quad L \quad P$$

We separate J from M by one grade by placing J in grade 3, which means that M, to be in a lower grade, must be in grade 2. Next, we reason that for L to be in a grade higher than K, and yet allowing that O must be between K and M, we have O, K, and L in grades 4 through 6, respectively. The diagram, therefore, proves that (A) is correct while each of the other choices is necessarily false.

5. **(B)** Notice that there is much common ground between the jockey and the veterinarian. The question stem asks you to uncover the areas on which they are in agreement by asking which of the answer choices is NOT a shared assumption. Note that the exception can be an area neither has as well as an area only one has. Examine the dialogue. Both apparently assume that human emotions can be attributed to animals since they talk about them being loyal and brave (C), and both take those characteristics as being noble—that is, admirable (A). Neither speaker offers scientific evidence but rests content with an anecdote (E) and (D). As for (B), it would seem that some kind of study of animal behavior might resolve the issue. We could find out how horses and dogs would react in emergency circumstances—do they show concern for human beings, or do they watch out for themselves? Importantly, it may be wrong to attribute such emotions to animals, but whatever behavior is taken by the speakers to be evidence of those emotions can be tested. So their claims—animals behave in such a way—are, in principle, testable.

6. **(D)** Note the question stem very carefully: We are to find the answer choice *from which* we can deduce the sample argument. You must pay very careful attention to the question stem in every problem. (D) works very nicely as it gives us the argument structure: "All post-1974 students are required. . . . George is a post-1974 student. Therefore, George is required. . . ." Actually, the middle premise is phrased in the conditional (with an "if"), but our explanation is close enough, even if it is a bit oversimplified. (A) will not suffice, for while it describes the situation before 1974, it just does not address itself to the post-1974 situation. And George is a post-1974 student. (B) also fails. We cannot conclude from the fact that all of those who took the course graduated after 1974 that George was one of them (anymore than we can conclude from the proposition that all airline flight attendants lived after 1900 and that Richard Nixon, who lived after 1900, was therefore one of them). (C) fails for the same reason that (A) fails. (E) is a bit tricky because of the double negative. It makes the sentence awkward. The easiest way to handle such a sentence is to treat the double negative as an affirmative. The negative cancels the negative, just as in arithmetic a negative number times a negative number yields a positive number. So (E) actually says that before 1974 the course was not required. That is equivalent to (A) and must be wrong for the same reason.

7. **(D)** The author's recommendation that public schools should have computerized reading programs depends upon the correctness of his explanation of the present deficiency in reading skills in the public schools. His contrast with private-school students shows that he thinks the deficiency can be attributed to the lack of such a program in the public schools. So, one of the author's assumptions, and that is what the question stem is asking about, is that the differential in reading skills is a result of the availability of a computerized program in the private-school system and the lack thereof in the public-school system. (E) is, of course, irrelevant to the question of reading skills. (C) tries to force the author to assume a greater burden than he has undertaken. He claims that the reading skills of public-school children could be improved by a computerized reading program. He is not concerned to argue the merits of having good reading skills. (A) and (B) are wrong for the same reason. The author's claim must be interpreted to mean "of children who are able to learn, all would benefit from a computerized reading program." When the author claims that "public-school children can be good readers," he is not implying that all children can learn to be good readers nor that all can learn to read equally well.

Questions 8–12

Arranging the Information

At first, this looks like it is going to be a map problem, but reading the question stems and the given information shows that there is really only one direction that is at issue: north–south. Furthermore, there is a numerical aspect in that the streets are laid out regularly with a regular distance between them. Thus, the real situation is similar to a ladder or musical scale and we have only to worry about one direction. Perhaps a good first step is to lay out a series of slots which symbolically will all be a quarter of a mile from each other, and which will alternate roads and streets.

←SOUTH————NORTH→

	St	Rd	St	Rd	St	Rd	St	Rd	St	Rd
Easy—1 mile north of Main St.	__	__	__	__	Main	__	__	__	Easy	__
Main—$\frac{3}{4}$ mile south of Abbey Rd.	__	__	__	__	Main	__	Abbey	Easy	__	
Tobacco Rd—$\frac{3}{4}$ mile south of Main St.	__	Tob	__	__	Main	__	Abbey	Easy	__	
Mean St—$\frac{1}{2}$ mile south of Main St.	__	Tob	Mean	__	Main	__	Abbey	Easy	__	

Answering the Questions

8. **(A)** As the diagram shows, Easy Street is farthest.

9. **(D)** The diagram shows that all of the cited locations are as yet unnamed thoroughfares, but the reason that (D) is correct is that this location cannot be a road. This is why the diagram should be drawn to include all of the information at your disposal, which in this case includes the idea that roads and streets alternate.

10. **(C)** Abbey Road is five steps of the ladder from Mean Street, with each step being a quarter of a mile for a total distance of $1\frac{1}{4}$ miles.

11. **(D)** Although we have a north–south thoroughfare being named in the problem, it is only being used as a surrogate for distance and the problem is essentially no different than problem 10. Just count the steps and figure out the distance. It is six steps to Tobacco Road and three more back to Main Street. Nine steps equals $2\frac{1}{4}$ miles.

12. **(C)** Easy Street is the northernmost street and Tobacco Road is the southernmost. They are seven steps away, which equals $1\frac{3}{4}$ miles. If you don't want to do any work with fractions, just count up $\frac{1}{4}$, $\frac{1}{2}$, $\frac{3}{4}$ . . . .

Questions 13–17

Arranging the Information

The major issue is who can and can't be on the team with particular other candidates.

WEST CAMPUS   EAST CAMPUS

(TWO FROM EACH CAMPUS)

XYZ   LMNP

Y←NOT WITH→L←NOT WITH→M

Z←NOT WITH→N

Answering the Questions

13. **(E)** The rejection of Y requires the selection of X and Z. The selection of Z forbids N. The selection of M bars L, leaving only M, P, X, and Z, choice (E).

   (C) and (D) fail for lack of two West campus members. (A) puts L and M together, which is wrong, and (B) puts Z and N together, which is forbidden.

14. **(E)** L's inclusion bars Y and M; Y's omission requires the inclusion of X and Z to have two West campus members, leaving only (E).

   (A) and (D) wrongly put L with M and Y, respectively. (B) has Z and N, which is not permitted, while (C) has only one West campus member.

15. **(B)** The selection of Y and Z excludes L and N, respectively, thus assuring the selection of P and M, choice (B).

   (A), (C), and (D) wrongly claim the selection of excluded members, and (E) omits the necessity of having M.

16. **(E)** The answer to problem 15 gives an example of M, P, and Z being on the same team, thus falsifying statements I and III. N, P, Y, and X is a possible team which shows the error of II, hence, (E).

17. **(B)** I is not true since we can select team Y, Z, P, and M. II is true since N's selection eliminates Z, requiring the selection of both X and Y to ensure that there are two West campus members. III is false since the rejection of L and N, while not requiring the selection of X, still permits it: M, P, X, and Z.

Questions 18–22

Arranging the Information

O will not go next to T or E. The condition of not forming a common three-letter word cannot be usefully listed out. A simple alertness to the words formed is sufficient. English words are formed only left to right, however.

Answering the Questions

18. **(C)** I is true because if O is in the middle, it will be next to T, which is forbidden. II is a little more complicated. If M, O, and T are on one wall, then H, E, and R are the paintings on the other wall.

These will form the word her if H and R are the left and right paintings on the east wall.

III, however, is not required since the east wall could be REH, which is not a common English word.

19. **(B)** O cannot be the center painting since it would then be between R and T, placing it next to T, which is forbidden. Also, both ROT and TOR are words, though TOR is not so common.

(A) is not correct since MEH is possible. (C) is possible with:

T	R	O
E	M	H

(D) is possible with:

M	H	E
T	R	O

(E) is possible with:

M	H	E
T	R	O

20. **(D)** The diagram is this:

M	O	T
R	E	H

Since the word runs from left to right as you turn around in the middle of the room, (A), (B), and (C) are true, while (D) is false. (E) fails when (D) succeeds.

21. **(A)** If H, M, and R are on the one wall, this leaves only E, O, and T for the other wall, which is incorrect since O would have to be next to at least one forbidden partner.

(B) is possible if the wall is arranged E H T, so no word is formed. (C) is possible:

H	T	E
M	O	R

(D) is also possible:

T	M	E
R	O	H

E is possible too:

E	R	T
O	M	H

22. **(C)** After the trade Jon has O, O, T, H, E, and R. Note that the new O painting is the same color as the original, and thus also cannot go next to T or E.

(C) is impossible since to have the O's in the middle of both walls would guarantee that they would be next to the T and the E, which is not permitted. The diagram looks like this:

O	O	
		R/H
T	E	

However, the order on each side could be different.

The O's cannot be on the same side as the T or E. Answers (A) and (B) both turn on the same idea that either the R or the H will be on one side or the other.

(D) can be false, but is not necessarily false, and thus is not the answer sought.

23. **(E)** Now, it must be admitted that a liar can abuse just about any word in the English language, and so it is true that each of the five answer choices is *conceivably* correct. But it is important to keep in mind that you are looking for the BEST answer, which will be the one word which, more than all the others, is likely to be abused. As for (A), while there may be different ways of doing a random selection, we should be able to decide whether a sample was, in fact, selected fairly. Although the ad may be lying about the selection of participants in the study, we should be able to determine whether they are lying. In other words, though they may not have selected the sample randomly, they cannot escape by saying, "Oh, by *random* we meant anyone who liked the Goblin." The same is true of (C), "first." That is a fairly clear term. You add up the answers you got, and one will be at the top of the list. The same is true of (D)—a "response" is an answer. Now, (B) is open to manipulation. By asking our question correctly, that is, by finagling a bit with what we mean by handling, we can influence the answers we get. For example, compare: "Did you find the Goblin handled well?" "Did you find the Goblin had a nice steering wheel?" "Did you find the wheel was easy to turn?" We could keep it up until we found a question that worked out to give a set of "responses" from "randomly" selected drivers who would rank the Goblin "first." Now, if the one category itself is susceptible to manipulation, imagine how much easier it will be to manipulate a "composite" category. We have only to take those individual categories in which the Goblin scored well, construct from them a "composite" category, and announce the Goblin "first" in the overall category. There is also the question of how the composite was constructed, weighted, added, averaged, etc.

24. **(C)** The problem with this argument is that it contains no argument at all. Nothing is more frustrating than trying to discuss an issue with someone who will not even make an attempt to prove his case, whose only constructive argument is: "Well, that is my position. If I am wrong, you prove I am wrong." This is an illegitimate attempt to shift the burden of proof. The person who advances the argument naturally has the burden of giving some argument for it. (C) points out this problem. (A) is incorrect because the author uses no group classifications. (B) is incorrect because the author does not introduce any analogy. (D) is

a weak version of (C). It is true the author does not provide statistical evidence to prove his claim, but neither does he provide any kind of argument at all to prove his claim. So if (D) is a legitimate objection to the paragraph (and it is), then (C) must be an even stronger objection. So any argument for answer (D)'s being the correct choice ultimately supports (C) even more strongly. The statement contained in (E) may or may not be correct, but the information in the passage is not sufficient to allow us to isolate the theory upon which the speaker is operating. Therefore, we cannot conclude that it is or is not discredited.

25. **(A)** If II is true, then both independent clauses of II must be true. This is because a sentence which has the form "P and Q" (Eddie is tall and John is short) can be true only if both sub-parts are true. If either is false (Eddie is not tall or John is not short) or if both are false, then the entire sentence makes a false claim. If the second clause of II is true, then I must also be true, for I is actually equivalent to the second clause in II. That is, if "P and Q" is true, then Q must itself be true. On this basis, (B) and (C) can be seen to be incorrect. (D) is wrong, for we can actually define the interrelationship of I and II as a matter of logic: We do not have to have recourse to a probabilistic statement. (E) is incorrect since a statement of the form "P and Q" might be false and Q could still be true—if P is false "P and Q" is false even though Q is true.

ANSWER SHEET—PRACTICE EXAMINATION 5

Section I

1 Ⓐ Ⓑ Ⓒ Ⓓ Ⓔ   8 Ⓐ Ⓑ Ⓒ Ⓓ Ⓔ   15 Ⓐ Ⓑ Ⓒ Ⓓ Ⓔ   22 Ⓐ Ⓑ Ⓒ Ⓓ Ⓔ   29 Ⓐ Ⓑ Ⓒ Ⓓ Ⓔ   36 Ⓐ Ⓑ Ⓒ Ⓓ Ⓔ

2 Ⓐ Ⓑ Ⓒ Ⓓ Ⓔ   9 Ⓐ Ⓑ Ⓒ Ⓓ Ⓔ   16 Ⓐ Ⓑ Ⓒ Ⓓ Ⓔ   23 Ⓐ Ⓑ Ⓒ Ⓓ Ⓔ   30 Ⓐ Ⓑ Ⓒ Ⓓ Ⓔ   37 Ⓐ Ⓑ Ⓒ Ⓓ Ⓔ

3 Ⓐ Ⓑ Ⓒ Ⓓ Ⓔ   10 Ⓐ Ⓑ Ⓒ Ⓓ Ⓔ   17 Ⓐ Ⓑ Ⓒ Ⓓ Ⓔ   24 Ⓐ Ⓑ Ⓒ Ⓓ Ⓔ   31 Ⓐ Ⓑ Ⓒ Ⓓ Ⓔ   38 Ⓐ Ⓑ Ⓒ Ⓓ Ⓔ

4 Ⓐ Ⓑ Ⓒ Ⓓ Ⓔ   11 Ⓐ Ⓑ Ⓒ Ⓓ Ⓔ   18 Ⓐ Ⓑ Ⓒ Ⓓ Ⓔ   25 Ⓐ Ⓑ Ⓒ Ⓓ Ⓔ   32 Ⓐ Ⓑ Ⓒ Ⓓ Ⓔ

5 Ⓐ Ⓑ Ⓒ Ⓓ Ⓔ   12 Ⓐ Ⓑ Ⓒ Ⓓ Ⓔ   19 Ⓐ Ⓑ Ⓒ Ⓓ Ⓔ   26 Ⓐ Ⓑ Ⓒ Ⓓ Ⓔ   33 Ⓐ Ⓑ Ⓒ Ⓓ Ⓔ

6 Ⓐ Ⓑ Ⓒ Ⓓ Ⓔ   13 Ⓐ Ⓑ Ⓒ Ⓓ Ⓔ   20 Ⓐ Ⓑ Ⓒ Ⓓ Ⓔ   27 Ⓐ Ⓑ Ⓒ Ⓓ Ⓔ   34 Ⓐ Ⓑ Ⓒ Ⓓ Ⓔ

7 Ⓐ Ⓑ Ⓒ Ⓓ Ⓔ   14 Ⓐ Ⓑ Ⓒ Ⓓ Ⓔ   21 Ⓐ Ⓑ Ⓒ Ⓓ Ⓔ   28 Ⓐ Ⓑ Ⓒ Ⓓ Ⓔ   35 Ⓐ Ⓑ Ⓒ Ⓓ Ⓔ

Section II

1 Ⓐ Ⓑ Ⓒ Ⓓ Ⓔ   8 Ⓐ Ⓑ Ⓒ Ⓓ Ⓔ   15 Ⓐ Ⓑ Ⓒ Ⓓ Ⓔ   22 Ⓐ Ⓑ Ⓒ Ⓓ Ⓔ   29 Ⓐ Ⓑ Ⓒ Ⓓ Ⓔ   36 Ⓐ Ⓑ Ⓒ Ⓓ Ⓔ

2 Ⓐ Ⓑ Ⓒ Ⓓ Ⓔ   9 Ⓐ Ⓑ Ⓒ Ⓓ Ⓔ   16 Ⓐ Ⓑ Ⓒ Ⓓ Ⓔ   23 Ⓐ Ⓑ Ⓒ Ⓓ Ⓔ   30 Ⓐ Ⓑ Ⓒ Ⓓ Ⓔ   37 Ⓐ Ⓑ Ⓒ Ⓓ Ⓔ

3 Ⓐ Ⓑ Ⓒ Ⓓ Ⓔ   10 Ⓐ Ⓑ Ⓒ Ⓓ Ⓔ   17 Ⓐ Ⓑ Ⓒ Ⓓ Ⓔ   24 Ⓐ Ⓑ Ⓒ Ⓓ Ⓔ   31 Ⓐ Ⓑ Ⓒ Ⓓ Ⓔ   38 Ⓐ Ⓑ Ⓒ Ⓓ Ⓔ

4 Ⓐ Ⓑ Ⓒ Ⓓ Ⓔ   11 Ⓐ Ⓑ Ⓒ Ⓓ Ⓔ   18 Ⓐ Ⓑ Ⓒ Ⓓ Ⓔ   25 Ⓐ Ⓑ Ⓒ Ⓓ Ⓔ   32 Ⓐ Ⓑ Ⓒ Ⓓ Ⓔ

5 Ⓐ Ⓑ Ⓒ Ⓓ Ⓔ   12 Ⓐ Ⓑ Ⓒ Ⓓ Ⓔ   19 Ⓐ Ⓑ Ⓒ Ⓓ Ⓔ   26 Ⓐ Ⓑ Ⓒ Ⓓ Ⓔ   33 Ⓐ Ⓑ Ⓒ Ⓓ Ⓔ

6 Ⓐ Ⓑ Ⓒ Ⓓ Ⓔ   13 Ⓐ Ⓑ Ⓒ Ⓓ Ⓔ   20 Ⓐ Ⓑ Ⓒ Ⓓ Ⓔ   27 Ⓐ Ⓑ Ⓒ Ⓓ Ⓔ   34 Ⓐ Ⓑ Ⓒ Ⓓ Ⓔ

7 Ⓐ Ⓑ Ⓒ Ⓓ Ⓔ   14 Ⓐ Ⓑ Ⓒ Ⓓ Ⓔ   21 Ⓐ Ⓑ Ⓒ Ⓓ Ⓔ   28 Ⓐ Ⓑ Ⓒ Ⓓ Ⓔ   35 Ⓐ Ⓑ Ⓒ Ⓓ Ⓔ

Section III

1 Ⓐ Ⓑ Ⓒ Ⓓ   6 Ⓐ Ⓑ Ⓒ Ⓓ   11 Ⓐ Ⓑ Ⓒ Ⓓ   16 Ⓐ Ⓑ Ⓒ Ⓓ Ⓔ   21 Ⓐ Ⓑ Ⓒ Ⓓ Ⓔ   26 Ⓐ Ⓑ Ⓒ Ⓓ Ⓔ

2 Ⓐ Ⓑ Ⓒ Ⓓ   7 Ⓐ Ⓑ Ⓒ Ⓓ   12 Ⓐ Ⓑ Ⓒ Ⓓ   17 Ⓐ Ⓑ Ⓒ Ⓓ Ⓔ   22 Ⓐ Ⓑ Ⓒ Ⓓ Ⓔ   27 Ⓐ Ⓑ Ⓒ Ⓓ Ⓔ

3 Ⓐ Ⓑ Ⓒ Ⓓ   8 Ⓐ Ⓑ Ⓒ Ⓓ   13 Ⓐ Ⓑ Ⓒ Ⓓ   18 Ⓐ Ⓑ Ⓒ Ⓓ Ⓔ   23 Ⓐ Ⓑ Ⓒ Ⓓ Ⓔ   28 Ⓐ Ⓑ Ⓒ Ⓓ Ⓔ

4 Ⓐ Ⓑ Ⓒ Ⓓ   9 Ⓐ Ⓑ Ⓒ Ⓓ   14 Ⓐ Ⓑ Ⓒ Ⓓ   19 Ⓐ Ⓑ Ⓒ Ⓓ Ⓔ   24 Ⓐ Ⓑ Ⓒ Ⓓ Ⓔ   29 Ⓐ Ⓑ Ⓒ Ⓓ Ⓔ

5 Ⓐ Ⓑ Ⓒ Ⓓ   10 Ⓐ Ⓑ Ⓒ Ⓓ   15 Ⓐ Ⓑ Ⓒ Ⓓ   20 Ⓐ Ⓑ Ⓒ Ⓓ Ⓔ   25 Ⓐ Ⓑ Ⓒ Ⓓ Ⓔ   30 Ⓐ Ⓑ Ⓒ Ⓓ Ⓔ

Section IV

1 Ⓐ Ⓑ Ⓒ Ⓓ   6 Ⓐ Ⓑ Ⓒ Ⓓ   11 Ⓐ Ⓑ Ⓒ Ⓓ   16 Ⓐ Ⓑ Ⓒ Ⓓ Ⓔ   21 Ⓐ Ⓑ Ⓒ Ⓓ Ⓔ   26 Ⓐ Ⓑ Ⓒ Ⓓ Ⓔ

2 Ⓐ Ⓑ Ⓒ Ⓓ   7 Ⓐ Ⓑ Ⓒ Ⓓ   12 Ⓐ Ⓑ Ⓒ Ⓓ   17 Ⓐ Ⓑ Ⓒ Ⓓ Ⓔ   22 Ⓐ Ⓑ Ⓒ Ⓓ Ⓔ   27 Ⓐ Ⓑ Ⓒ Ⓓ Ⓔ

3 Ⓐ Ⓑ Ⓒ Ⓓ   8 Ⓐ Ⓑ Ⓒ Ⓓ   13 Ⓐ Ⓑ Ⓒ Ⓓ   18 Ⓐ Ⓑ Ⓒ Ⓓ Ⓔ   23 Ⓐ Ⓑ Ⓒ Ⓓ Ⓔ   28 Ⓐ Ⓑ Ⓒ Ⓓ Ⓔ

4 Ⓐ Ⓑ Ⓒ Ⓓ   9 Ⓐ Ⓑ Ⓒ Ⓓ   14 Ⓐ Ⓑ Ⓒ Ⓓ   19 Ⓐ Ⓑ Ⓒ Ⓓ Ⓔ   24 Ⓐ Ⓑ Ⓒ Ⓓ Ⓔ   29 Ⓐ Ⓑ Ⓒ Ⓓ Ⓔ

5 Ⓐ Ⓑ Ⓒ Ⓓ   10 Ⓐ Ⓑ Ⓒ Ⓓ   15 Ⓐ Ⓑ Ⓒ Ⓓ   20 Ⓐ Ⓑ Ⓒ Ⓓ Ⓔ   25 Ⓐ Ⓑ Ⓒ Ⓓ Ⓔ   30 Ⓐ Ⓑ Ⓒ Ⓓ Ⓔ

Section V

1 Ⓐ Ⓑ Ⓒ Ⓓ Ⓔ   6 Ⓐ Ⓑ Ⓒ Ⓓ Ⓔ   11 Ⓐ Ⓑ Ⓒ Ⓓ Ⓔ   16 Ⓐ Ⓑ Ⓒ Ⓓ Ⓔ   21 Ⓐ Ⓑ Ⓒ Ⓓ Ⓔ

2 Ⓐ Ⓑ Ⓒ Ⓓ Ⓔ   7 Ⓐ Ⓑ Ⓒ Ⓓ Ⓔ   12 Ⓐ Ⓑ Ⓒ Ⓓ Ⓔ   17 Ⓐ Ⓑ Ⓒ Ⓓ Ⓔ   22 Ⓐ Ⓑ Ⓒ Ⓓ Ⓔ

3 Ⓐ Ⓑ Ⓒ Ⓓ Ⓔ   8 Ⓐ Ⓑ Ⓒ Ⓓ Ⓔ   13 Ⓐ Ⓑ Ⓒ Ⓓ Ⓔ   18 Ⓐ Ⓑ Ⓒ Ⓓ Ⓔ   23 Ⓐ Ⓑ Ⓒ Ⓓ Ⓔ

4 Ⓐ Ⓑ Ⓒ Ⓓ Ⓔ   9 Ⓐ Ⓑ Ⓒ Ⓓ Ⓔ   14 Ⓐ Ⓑ Ⓒ Ⓓ Ⓔ   19 Ⓐ Ⓑ Ⓒ Ⓓ Ⓔ   24 Ⓐ Ⓑ Ⓒ Ⓓ Ⓔ

5 Ⓐ Ⓑ Ⓒ Ⓓ Ⓔ   10 Ⓐ Ⓑ Ⓒ Ⓓ Ⓔ   15 Ⓐ Ⓑ Ⓒ Ⓓ Ⓔ   20 Ⓐ Ⓑ Ⓒ Ⓓ Ⓔ   25 Ⓐ Ⓑ Ⓒ Ⓓ Ⓔ

Section VI

1 Ⓐ Ⓑ Ⓒ Ⓓ Ⓔ   6 Ⓐ Ⓑ Ⓒ Ⓓ Ⓔ   11 Ⓐ Ⓑ Ⓒ Ⓓ Ⓔ   16 Ⓐ Ⓑ Ⓒ Ⓓ Ⓔ   21 Ⓐ Ⓑ Ⓒ Ⓓ Ⓔ

2 Ⓐ Ⓑ Ⓒ Ⓓ Ⓔ   7 Ⓐ Ⓑ Ⓒ Ⓓ Ⓔ   12 Ⓐ Ⓑ Ⓒ Ⓓ Ⓔ   17 Ⓐ Ⓑ Ⓒ Ⓓ Ⓔ   22 Ⓐ Ⓑ Ⓒ Ⓓ Ⓔ

3 Ⓐ Ⓑ Ⓒ Ⓓ Ⓔ   8 Ⓐ Ⓑ Ⓒ Ⓓ Ⓔ   13 Ⓐ Ⓑ Ⓒ Ⓓ Ⓔ   18 Ⓐ Ⓑ Ⓒ Ⓓ Ⓔ   23 Ⓐ Ⓑ Ⓒ Ⓓ Ⓔ

4 Ⓐ Ⓑ Ⓒ Ⓓ Ⓔ   9 Ⓐ Ⓑ Ⓒ Ⓓ Ⓔ   14 Ⓐ Ⓑ Ⓒ Ⓓ Ⓔ   19 Ⓐ Ⓑ Ⓒ Ⓓ Ⓔ   24 Ⓐ Ⓑ Ⓒ Ⓓ Ⓔ

5 Ⓐ Ⓑ Ⓒ Ⓓ Ⓔ   10 Ⓐ Ⓑ Ⓒ Ⓓ Ⓔ   15 Ⓐ Ⓑ Ⓒ Ⓓ Ⓔ   20 Ⓐ Ⓑ Ⓒ Ⓓ Ⓔ   25 Ⓐ Ⓑ Ⓒ Ⓓ Ⓔ

PRACTICE EXAMINATION 5

SECTION I

30 minutes
38 questions

Directions: Each of the questions below contains one or more blank spaces, each blank indicating an omitted word. Each sentence is followed by five (5) lettered words or sets of words. Read and determine the general sense of each sentence. Then choose the word or set of words which, when inserted in the sentence, best fits the meaning of the sentence.

1. Politics, because of its overemphasis on expediency, often places candidates in the _____ position of supporting candidates they attacked only months before.
   - (A) anomalous
   - (B) piquant
   - (C) succulent
   - (D) strategic
   - (E) embarrassing

2. Often criticism may be more effectively made by _____ than by direct censure.
   - (A) writing
   - (B) malignity
   - (C) innuendo
   - (D) illusion
   - (E) collusion

3. In the face of an uncooperative Congress, the Chief Executive may find himself _____ to accomplish the political program to which he is committed.
   - (A) impotent
   - (B) permitted
   - (C) neutral
   - (D) contingent
   - (E) equipped

4. Because of his _____ sense of his own importance, Larry often tried to _____ our activities.
   - (A) exaggerated—monopolize
   - (B) inflated—autonomize
   - (C) insecure—violate
   - (D) modest—dominate
   - (E) egotistic—diffuse

5. After such _____ meal, we were all quick to _____ Arlene for her delicious cooking.
   - (A) a fearful—congratulate
   - (B) an enormous—console
   - (C) a delightful—avoid
   - (D) a heavy—thank
   - (E) a wonderful—applaud

6. The use of color to express feeling is so _____ in Van Gogh's paintings that the canvas seems to fairly _____ the museum-goer.
   - (A) ingenious—fall
   - (B) emphatic—insult
   - (C) subtle—echo in
   - (D) sensitive—seduce
   - (E) successful—cry out to

7. The monopoly capitalists of the early 1900's saw both the factories and the workers as _____ without rights or feelings, whose only useful purpose was to _____ profits.
   - (A) animals—assist
   - (B) machinery—increase
   - (C) beings—garner
   - (D) resources—guarantee
   - (E) objects—allow

Directions: In each of the following questions, you are given a related pair of words or phrases in capital letters. Each capitalized pair is followed by five (5) lettered pairs of words or phrases. Choose the pair which best expresses a relationship similar to that expressed by the original pair.

8. MOUTH : ORIFICE ::
   (A) eye : sight
   (B) nose : odor
   (C) ear : projection
   (D) touch : felt
   (E) taste : tongue

9. WORKER : BONUS ::
   (A) capitalist : dividends
   (B) banker : interest
   (C) sports : winning
   (D) horse : spur
   (E) actor : applause

10. RIGID : FLEXIBLE ::
    (A) hard : brittle
    (B) stubborn : yielding
    (C) steel : rubbery
    (D) hostile : honest
    (E) muscle : tone

11. EATING : GOBBLE ::
    (A) speaking : jabber
    (B) drinking : guzzle
    (C) running : sprint
    (D) seeing : believing
    (E) shoving : pushing

12. SIN : FORGIVE ::
    (A) error : mistake
    (B) reign : authority
    (C) debt : release
    (D) wrong : code
    (E) accident : intentional

13. SENSATION : ANESTHETIC ::
    (A) breathe : lung
    (B) reaction : drug
    (C) sound : muffler
    (D) poison : detoxicant
    (E) disease : vaccine

14. GUN : HOLSTER ::
    (A) foot : shoe
    (B) ink : pen
    (C) books : shelf
    (D) sword : scabbard
    (E) shot : cannon

15. MIST : RAIN ::
    (A) fog : cloud
    (B) shadow : sun
    (C) snow : hail
    (D) breeze : gale
    (E) foam : sea

16. PHARMACIST : DRUGS ::
    (A) psychiatrist : ideas
    (B) mentor : drills
    (C) mechanic : troubles
    (D) chef : foods
    (E) nurse : diseases

Directions: Below each of the following passages, you will find questions or incomplete statements about the passage. Each statement or question is followed by five lettered words or expressions. Select the word or expression that most satisfactorily completes each statement or answers each question in accordance with the meaning of the passage. After you choose the best answer, blacken the corresponding space on the answer sheet.

Shams and delusions are esteemed for soundest truths, while reality is fabulous. If men would steadily observe realities only, and not allow themselves to be deluded, life, to compare it with such things as we know, would be like a fairy tale and the Arabian Nights' entertainments. If we respect only what is inevitable and has a right to be, music and poetry would resound along the streets. When we are unhurried and wise, we perceive that only great and worthy things have any permanent and absolute existence—that petty fears and petty pleasures are but the shadow of the reality. This is always exhilarating and sublime. By closing the eyes and slumbering, and consenting to be deceived by shows, men establish and confirm their daily life of routine and habit everywhere, which still is built on purely illusory foundations. Children, who play life, discern its true law and relations more clearly than men, who fail to live it worthily, but who think that they are wiser by experience: that is, by failure.

I have read in a Hindu book that there was a

king's son who, being expelled in infancy from his native city, was brought up by a forester, and, growing up to maturity in that state, imagined himself to belong to the barbarous race with which he lived. One of his father's ministers, having discovered him, revealed to him what he was, and the misconception of his character was removed, and he knew himself to be a prince. "So soul," continues the Hindu philosopher, "from the circumstances in which it is placed, mistakes its own character, until the truth is revealed to it by some holy teacher, and then it knows itself to be *Brahme*."

We think that that *is* which *appears* to be. If a man should give us an account of the realities he beheld, we should not recognize the place in his description. Look at a meeting-house, or a court-house, or a jail, or a shop, or a dwelling-house, and say what that thing really is before a true gaze, and they would all go to pieces in your account of them. Men esteem truth remote, in the outskirts of the system, behind the farthest star, before Adam and after the last man. In eternity there is indeed something true and sublime. But all these times and places and occasions are now and here. God himself culminates in the present moment, and will never be more divine in the lapse of all ages. And we are enabled to apprehend at all what is sublime and noble only by the perpetual instilling and drenching of the reality that surrounds us. The universe constantly and obediently answers to our conceptions; whether we travel fast or slow, the track is laid for us. Let us spend our lives in conceiving, then. The poet or the artist never yet had so fair and noble a design but some of his posterity at least could accomplish it.

17. The writer's attitude toward the arts is one of
    (A) indifference
    (B) suspicion
    (C) admiration
    (D) repulsion
    (E) reluctant respect

18. The author believes that children are often more acute than adults in their appreciation of life's relations because
    (A) children know more than adults
    (B) children can use their experience better

(C) children's eyes are unclouded by failure
(D) experience is the best teacher
(E) the child is father to the man

19. The passage implies that human beings
    (A) cannot distinguish the true from the untrue
    (B) are immoral if they are lazy
    (C) should be bold and fearless
    (D) believe in fairy tales
    (E) have progressed culturally throughout history

20. The word fabulous in the second line means
    (A) wonderful
    (B) delicious
    (C) birdlike
    (D) incomprehensible
    (E) illusion

21. The author is primarily concerned with urging the reader to
    (A) meditate on the meaninglessness of the present
    (B) look to the future for enlightenment
    (C) appraise the present for its true value
    (D) honor the wisdom of past ages
    (E) spend more time in leisure activities

22. The passage is primarily concerned with problems of
    (A) history and economics
    (B) society and population
    (C) biology and physics
    (D) theology and philosophy
    (E) music and art

23. Which of the following best describes the author's idea of the relationship between man and the universe?
    (A) Each person's mind can control the galaxies.
    (B) What you see is what you get.
    (C) Our lives are predetermined.
    (D) We may choose to live quickly or slowly.
    (E) Poets cannot conceive of their posterity.

A glance at five leading causes of death in 1900, 1910, and 1945, years representing in some measure the early and late practice of physicians of that time, shows a significant trend. In 1900 these causes were (1) tuberculosis, (2) pneumonia, (3) enteritis, typhoid fever, and other acute intestinal diseases, (4) heart diseases, and (5) cerebral hemorrhage and thrombosis. Ten years later the only change was that heart disease had moved from fourth to fifth place, tuberculosis now being second, and pneumonia third.

In 1945, however, the list had changed profoundly. Heart diseases were far out in front; cancer, which had come up from eighth place, was second; and cerebral hemorrhage and thrombosis, third. Fatal accidents, which had been well down the list, were now fourth, and nephritis was fifth. All of these are, of course, composites rather than single diseases, and it is significant that, except for accidents, they are characteristic of the advanced rather than the early or middle years of life.

24. On the basis of the passage, which of the following statements is most tenable?
    (A) A cure for cancer will be found within this decade.
    (B) Many of the medical problems of today are problems of the gerontologist (specialist in medical problems of old age).
    (C) Older persons are more accident-prone than are younger persons.
    (D) Tuberculosis has been all but eliminated.
    (E) Heart disease will be conquered within this decade.

25. Which one of the following trends is *least* indicated in the passage?
    (A) As one grows older, one is more subject to debilitating disease.
    (B) Pneumonia has become less common.
    (C) Relative to mortality rates for acute intestinal diseases, the mortality rate for cancer has increased.
    (D) The incidence of heart disease has increased.
    (E) Cancer has become more prevalent.

26. Which one of the following statements is most nearly correct?
    (A) Such mortality trends are caused by decreased infant mortality.

(B) The changes in the data reported are a function of improved diagnosis and reporting.
(C) The mortality data are based on the records of physicians who practiced continuously from 1900 to 1945.
(D) There appears to be a greater change in the mortality patterns from 1910 to 1945 than in the decade ending in 1910.
(E) none of the above

27. It can be inferred from reading this passage that
    (A) longevity increased between 1900 and 1910
    (B) longevity increased steadily between 1910 and 1945
    (C) longevity increased significantly between 1900 and 1945
    (D) longevity was not a factor in these findings
    (E) the causes of death listed did not effect any increase in longevity

Directions: Each of the following questions consists of a word printed in capital letters, followed by five (5) lettered words or phrases. Select the word or phrase which is most nearly *opposite* to the capitalized word in meaning.

28. RESTITUTION:
    (A) inflation
    (B) cataclysm
    (C) deprivation
    (D) constitution
    (E) anonymity

29. PARSIMONY:
    (A) closely held
    (B) free spending
    (C) acting apishly
    (D) poorly expressed
    (E) modish frugality

30. PERSPICUITY:
    (A) homelike ambiance
    (B) precise meaning
    (C) vague memory
    (D) partial fulfillment
    (E) mental dullness

31. PREPOSTEROUS:
    (A) complaisant
    (B) conceited
    (C) apologetic
    (D) credible
    (E) sincere

32. SANCTIMONIOUS:
    (A) proud
    (B) stubborn
    (C) wealthy
    (D) devout
    (E) impervious

33. EXTIRPATE:
    (A) preserve
    (B) inseminate
    (C) ingratiate
    (D) enter
    (E) daub

34. CAPRICIOUS:
    (A) redoubtable
    (B) constant
    (C) phlegmatic
    (D) solitary
    (E) ignominious

35. CASUISTRY:
    (A) resultant
    (B) interior
    (C) sediment
    (D) verity
    (E) beauty

36. CONTUMELY:
    (A) willingness
    (B) sporadically
    (C) praise
    (D) augmented
    (E) tractability

37. SEDULOUS:
    (A) vociferous
    (B) derelict
    (C) concomitant
    (D) itinerant
    (E) onerous

38. IMPERTURBABLE:
    (A) militant
    (B) cynical
    (C) conical
    (D) agitated
    (E) flattering

STOP

END OF SECTION. IF YOU HAVE ANY TIME LEFT, GO
OVER YOUR WORK IN THIS SECTION ONLY. DO NOT
WORK IN ANY OTHER SECTION OF THE TEST.

SECTION II

30 minutes
38 questions

Directions: Each of the questions below contains one or more blank spaces, each blank indicating an omitted word. Each sentence is followed by five (5) lettered words or sets of words. Read and determine the general sense of each sentence. Then choose the word or set of words which, when inserted in the sentence, best fits the meaning of the sentence.

1. With _____ a thought for his own safety, Gene _____ dashed back across the courtyard.
    (A) even—quickly
    (B) scarcely—courageously
    (C) barely—cautiously

    (D) seldom—swiftly
    (E) hardly—randomly

2. The _____ of the *Titanic* could have been avoided if more safety _____ had been taken.
    (A) tragedy—precautions
    (B) embargo—preservers
    (C) disaster—reservations
    (D) crew—measures
    (E) fiasco—inspectors

3. We are _____ going to have to face the reality that the resources of Earth are _____.
    (A) finally—worthless
    (B) gradually—limitless
    (C) eventually—finite
    (D) quickly—unavailable
    (E) seldom—vanished

4. Though many thought him a tedious old man, he had a _____ spirit that delighted his friends.
    (A) perverse
    (B) juvenile
    (C) meek
    (D) leaden
    (E) youthful

5. _____, the factories had not closed, and those who needed work most were given a chance to survive during the economic disaster.
    (A) Unintentionally
    (B) Mercifully
    (C) Blithely
    (D) Importunately
    (E) Tragically

6. There was a _____ all about the estate, and the _____ concerned the guards.
    (A) pall—shroud
    (B) focus—scrutiny
    (C) hush—quiet
    (D) coolness—temper
    (E) talent—genius

7. Some works of literature hold one's interest to the very last page, but others serve only as a _____, to be kept handily at a bedside table.
    (A) resource
    (B) reference
    (C) soporific
    (D) pleasure
    (E) reminder

Directions: In each of the following questions, you are given a related pair of words or phrases in capital letters. Each capitalized pair is followed by five (5) lettered pairs of words or phrases. Choose the pair which best expresses a relationship similar to that expressed by the original pair.

8. KARATE : FOOT ::
    (A) judo : chop
    (B) bridge : hand
    (C) fencing : foil
    (D) boxing : ring
    (E) baseball : bat

9. INCISOR : MOLAR ::
    (A) canine : bicuspid
    (B) scissor : file
    (C) upper : lower
    (D) sharp : foolish
    (E) knife : hammer

10. GOURMAND : GOURMET ::
    (A) wisdom : epicureanism
    (B) spaghetti : chopped liver
    (C) atrophy : empathy
    (D) good : plenty
    (E) indiscriminate : selective

11. TRESS : HAIR ::
    (A) pat : butter
    (B) slice : lox
    (C) bevy : beauties
    (D) land : cotton
    (E) skein : wool

12. LIBEL : SLANDER ::
    (A) telephone : telegraph
    (B) copier : plagiarist
    (C) intentional : unintentional
    (D) written : oral
    (E) printed : handwritten

13. WATER : COLANDER ::
    (A) dust : broom
    (B) chaff : sifter
    (C) sand : dune
    (D) fluid : pipette
    (E) shale : flat

14. DECIBEL : SOUND ::
    (A) calorie : weight
    (B) volt : electricity
    (C) temperature : weather
    (D) color : light
    (E) area : distance

15. ASTUTE : STUPID ::
    (A) scholar : idiotic
    (B) agile : clumsy
    (C) lonely : clown
    (D) dunce : ignorant
    (E) intelligent : smart

16. QUEUE : PEOPLE ::
    (A) gaggle : geese
    (B) pile : sand
    (C) stack : books
    (D) string : pearls
    (E) file : letters

Directions: Below each of the following passages, you will find questions or incomplete statements about the passage. Each statement or question is followed by lettered words or expressions. Select the word or expression that most satisfactorily completes each statement or answers each question in accordance with the meaning of the passage. After you have chosen the best answer, blacken the corresponding space on the answer sheet.

When an animal is presented with food he will salivate. If a bell is repeatedly presented shortly before the food is administered, the animal will begin to salivate soon after the sound of the bell, even if the food is not offered. With repeated trials of the bell followed by the food (conditioning trials), the latency of the response (that is, the time interval between the advent of the bell and the beginning of salivation) decreases. This process is called conditioning, and salivation to the sound of the bell is termed the conditioned response. The conditioned response may be unlearned or extinguished if the bell is presented a number of times without being followed by food (extinction trials).

Under such conditions, the latency of the conditioned response gradually increases until it does not take place at all. One theory holds that after each conditioning trial a finite amount of excitation is left which facilitates the occurrence of the conditioned response, and also that a finite amount of inhibition is left which inhibits the occurrence of the conditioned response.

17. If the conditioned response, salivation, is extinguished
    (A) its latency decreases
    (B) the food was presented without the bell
    (C) the amount of inhibition is greater than the amount of excitation
    (D) the animal is no longer hungry
    (E) none of these

18. According to the theory advanced at the end of the passage, which of the following is NOT possible?
    (A) Continued training will have no effect whatever.
    (B) A response can get so well established that it will never fail.
    (C) Responses other than salivation will not necessarily differ in the amount of training required to achieve a response.
    (D) No matter how many times an extinction trial is run, retraining is still possible.
    (E) The measurement of residual excitation and inhibition can be measured in all cases, though some measurements might be indirect.

19. As used in the passage, the term "latency" most nearly means
    (A) unfulfilled potential
    (B) delayed excitation
    (C) tendency for an action to not occur
    (D) improvements in response time
    (E) experimental deviations from the norm

Suppose you go into a fruiterer's shop, wanting an apple—you take up one, and on biting it you find it is sour; you look at it, and see that it is hard and green. You take up another one, and that, too, is hard, green, and sour. The shopman offers you a third; but, before biting it, you examine it, and find that it is hard and green, and you immediately say that you will not have it, as it must be sour, like those that you have already tried.

Nothing can be more simple than that, you think; but if you will take the trouble to analyse and trace out into its logical elements what has been done by the mind, you will be greatly surprised. In the first place you have performed the operation of induction. You find that, in two experiences, hardness and greenness in apples went together with sourness. It was so in the first case, and it was confirmed by the second. True, it is a very small basis, but still it is enough from which to make an induction; you generalize the facts, and you expect to find sourness in apples where you get hardness and greenness. You found upon that a general law, that all hard and green apples are sour; and that, so far as it goes, is a perfect induction. Well, having got your natural law in this way, when you are offered another apple which you find is hard and green, you say, "All hard and green apples are sour; this apple is hard and green; therefore, this apple is sour." That train of reasoning is what logicians call a syllogism, and has all its various parts and terms—its major premises, its minor premises, and its conclusion. And, by the help of further reasoning, which, if drawn out, would have to be exhibited in two or three other syllogisms, you arrive at your final determination. "I will not have that apple." So that, you see, you have, in the first place, established a law by induction, and upon that you have founded a deduction, and reasoned out the special particular case.

Well now, suppose, having got your conclusion of the law, that at some times afterwards, you are discussing the qualities of apple with a friend; you will say to him, "It is a very curious thing, but I find that all hard and green apples are sour!" Your friend says to you, "But how do you know that?" You at once reply, "Oh, because I have tried them over and over again, and have always found them to be so." Well, if we were talking science instead of common sense, we should call that an experimental verification. And, if still opposed, you go further, and say, "I have heard from the people in Somersetshire and Devonshire, where a large number of apples are grown, and in London, where many apples are sold and eaten, that they have observed the same thing. It is also found to be the case in Normandy, and in North America. In short, I find it to be the universal experience of mankind wherever attention has been directed to the subject." Whereupon, your friend, unless he is a very unreasonable man, agrees with you, and is convinced that you are quite right in the conclusion you have drawn. He believes, although perhaps he does not know he believes it, that the more extensive verifications have been made, and results of the same kind arrived at—that the more varied the conditions under which the same results are attained, the more certain is the ultimate conclusion, and he disputes the question no further. He sees that the experiment has been tried under all sorts of conditions, as to time, place, and people, with the same result; and he says with you, therefore, that the law you have laid down must be a good one, and he must believe it.

20. The writer is probably
    (A) French
    (B) English
    (C) American
    (D) Italian
    (E) none of the above

21. "All giraffes are beautiful and graceful.
    Twiga is a giraffe.
    Twiga is beautiful and graceful."

    According to the passage, the above reasoning is a(n)
    (A) empirical verification
    (B) induction from cases
    (C) syllogism
    (D) experimental conclusion
    (E) developmental sequence

22. Apples are used
    (A) in order to convince the reader that fruit has no intellect
    (B) to illustrate the subject of the passage
    (C) to give color to the story
    (D) to show how foolish logic is
    (E) to compare various types of persons

23. The author has the approach of a(n)
    (A) scientist
    (B) artist
    (C) novelist

(D) economist
(E) businessman

24. The term "natural law" as it appears in the text refers to
(A) common sense
(B) the "honor system"
(C) the result of an induction
(D) the order of nature
(E) a scientific discovery

25. Which of the following would be the best title for the passage?
(A) Discovering the Natural Laws of Apples
(B) The Uses of Induction
(C) Syllogistic Reasoning in Common Circumstances
(D) Experimental Verification As an Adjunct to Reasoning
(E) The Logic of Everyday Reasoning

26. If you find a hard and green apple that is not sour, you should
(A) try more apples to see if the natural law has changed
(B) eat the rest of the apple at once
(C) reject the law stating that hard and green apples are usually sour
(D) conduct further investigations and make adjustments to the law of apples as necessary
(E) all of the above

27. According to the above passage, the significance of "extensive verification" of a general law is that

I. general laws are difficult to disprove
II. the more extensively a law is tested, the truer it is
III. if a law holds up in a variety of situations, then it is more than likely based on some general characteristic of the world

(A) I only
(B) II only
(C) III only
(D) II and III only
(E) I, II, and III

Directions: Each of the following questions consists of a word printed in capital letters, followed by five (5) lettered words or phrases. Select the word or phrase which is most nearly *opposite* to the capitalized word in meaning.

28. PROFUSION:
(A) travesty
(B) validity
(C) scarcity
(D) retraction
(E) antidote

29. TEMPERATE:
(A) aged
(B) unlimited
(C) truncated
(D) productive
(E) inebriated

30. MITIGATION:
(A) aggravation
(B) verdancy
(C) obscenity
(D) restriction
(E) imposition

31. INIQUITY:
(A) fairness
(B) rectitude
(C) peace
(D) apostasy
(E) calmness

32. PROTUBERANCE:
(A) cadence
(B) habitation
(C) indentation
(D) attachment
(E) recession

33. EFFULGENCE:
(A) murky
(B) harshness
(C) mercenary
(D) quiet
(E) mundane

34. AMELIORATE:
(A) increase
(B) worsen
(C) clasp
(D) dissemble
(E) curl

35. BENIGN:
    (A) sick
    (B) poor
    (C) damaged
    (D) evil
    (E) morose

36. SALUTARY:
    (A) noxious
    (B) objectionable
    (C) moderate
    (D) farewell
    (E) antiseptic

37. ALIENATE:
    (A) go native
    (B) say clearly
    (C) make friends
    (D) give freely
    (E) promise solemnly

38. DROLLERY:
    (A) firm warning
    (B) serious statement
    (C) incredible threat
    (D) witty aside
    (E) frank admission

STOP

END OF SECTION. IF YOU HAVE ANY TIME LEFT, GO
OVER YOUR WORK IN THIS SECTION ONLY. DO NOT
WORK IN ANY OTHER SECTION OF THE TEST.

SECTION III

30 minutes
30 questions

Directions: For each of the following questions two quantities are given, one in Column A and one in Column B. Compare the two quantities and mark your answer sheet with the correct lettered conclusion. These are your options:
   A: If the quantity in Column A is the greater;
   B: if the quantity in Column B is the greater;
   C: if the two quantities are equal;
   D: if the relationship cannot be determined from the information given.

Common Information: In any question, information applying to both columns is centered between the columns and above the quantities in columns A and B. The common information applies to both columns. Any symbol that appears in both columns represents the same idea or quantity in both columns.

Numbers: All numbers used are real numbers.

Figures: Assume that the positions of points, angles, regions and so forth are in the order shown. Figures are assumed to lie in a plane unless otherwise indicated. Figures accompanying questions are intended to provide information you can use in answering the questions. However, unless a note states that a figure is drawn to scale, you should solve the problems by using your knowledge of mathematics and *not* by estimating sizes by sight and measurement.

Lines: Assume that lines shown as straight are indeed straight.

COLUMN A	COLUMN B

1. Value of 4 coins — Value of 5 coins

2.
$$x + 7 = 8$$
$$x + y = 6$$

x	y

3. $\sqrt{9}$ — 3

4.
Jack is taller than Kate.
Kate is taller than Linda.
Linda is taller than Mike.

$\dfrac{\text{Jack's height}}{\text{Mike's height}}$ — 4

5. $n > 1$

$n + n + 1 + n + 2 + n + 3$ — $n(n + 1)(n + 2)(n + 3)$

6. The area of a circle with a diameter of 2 yards — The area of a circle with a radius of 3 feet

7. The negative of -4 — -4

8. The weight of a pound of feathers — The weight of a pound of lead

9. x is the greatest integer less than -10

x^2 — 100

10. $\left(\frac{34}{68}\right)^2$ — $\frac{1}{2}$

11. $x = \left(\frac{1}{2}\right)\left(\frac{2}{3}\right)\left(\frac{3}{4}\right)\left(\frac{4}{5}\right)$

x — $\frac{1}{5}$

12.

PQRS is a rectangle

Perimeter of shaded area — Perimeter of PQRS

13. $-2(-x - 2)$ — $-4 + 2x$

14.
$$x > 1$$
$$y > 1$$

xy — $x + y$

COLUMN A   COLUMN B

15.

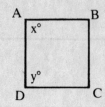

AB = BC = CD = DA

x   y

_____

Directions: For each of the following questions, select the best of the answer choices and blacken the corresponding space on your answer sheet.
Numbers: All numbers used are real numbers.
Figures: The diagrams and figures that accompany these questions are for the purpose of providing information useful in answering the questions. Unless it is stated that a specific figure is not drawn to scale, the diagrams and figures are drawn as accurately as possible. All figures are in a plane unless otherwise indicated.

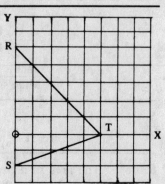

16. There are just two ways in which 5 may be expressed as the sum of two different positive (nonzero) integers, namely, $5 = 4 + 1 = 3 + 2$. In how many ways may 9 be expressed as the sum of two different positive (nonzero) integers?
    (A) 3
    (B) 4
    (C) 5
    (D) 6
    (E) 7

17. A board 7 feet 9 inches long is divided into three equal parts. What is the length of each part?
    (A) 2 ft. 7 in.
    (B) 2 ft. $6\frac{1}{3}$ in.
    (C) 2 ft. $8\frac{1}{3}$ in.
    (D) 2 ft. 8 in.
    (E) 2 ft. 9 in.

18. What is the smallest possible integer $K > 1$ such that $R^2 = S^3 = K$, for some integers R and S?
    (A) 4
    (B) 8
    (C) 27
    (D) 64
    (E) 81

19. Triangle RST is superimposed on a coordinate system in which all angles are right angles. The number of square units in the area of triangle RST is
    (A) 10
    (B) 12.5
    (C) 15.5
    (D) 17.5
    (E) 20

20. Which of the following has the same value as $\frac{P}{Q}$?
    (A) $\frac{P - 2}{Q - 2}$
    (B) $\frac{1 + P}{1 + Q}$
    (C) $\frac{P^2}{Q^2}$
    (D) $\frac{3P}{3Q}$
    (E) $\frac{P + 3}{Q + 3}$

21. In the accompanying figure, ACB is a straight angle and DC is perpendicular to CE. If the number of degrees in angle ACD is represented by x, the number of degrees in angle BCE is represented by
    (A) $90 - x$
    (B) $x - 90$

(C) 90 + x
(D) 180 − x
(E) 45 + x

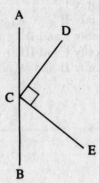

22. The diagonal of a rectangle is 5. The area of the rectangle
(A) must be 12
(B) must be 24
(C) must be 25
(D) must be 50
(E) Cannot be determined from the information given.

Questions 23–24 refer to the accompanying circle graph, which shows how a certain family distributes its expenditures.

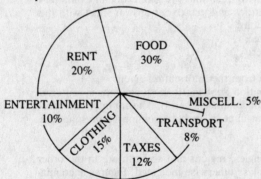

23. If the family spends a total of $650 per month, how much are its monthly taxes?
(A) $78.00
(B) $72.22
(C) $66.30
(D) $48.00
(E) $12.00

24. How many degrees should there be in the central angle showing clothing, taxes, and transportation combined?
(A) 100
(B) 110
(C) 120

(D) 126
(E) 130

25. A boy takes a 25-question test and answers all questions. His score is obtained by giving him 4 points for each correct answer, and then subtracting 1 point for each wrong answer. If he obtains a score of 70, how many questions did he answer correctly?
(A) 17
(B) 18
(C) 19
(D) 20
(E) 21

26. A man travels a certain distance at 60 miles per hour and returns over the same road at 40 miles per hour. What is his average rate for the round trip in miles per hour?
(A) 42
(B) 44
(C) 46
(D) 48
(E) 50

27. Six tractors can plow a field in 8 hours if they all work together. How many hours will it take 4 tractors to do the job?
(A) 9
(B) 10
(C) 11
(D) 12
(E) 14

28. Which of the following numbers is the smallest?
(A) $\frac{1}{5}$
(B) $\sqrt{5}$
(C) $\frac{1}{\sqrt{5}}$
(D) $\frac{\sqrt{5}}{5}$
(E) $\frac{1}{5\sqrt{5}}$

29. The cost of 30 melons is d dollars. At this rate, how many melons can you buy for 80 cents?
(A) $\frac{24}{d}$
(B) $\frac{240}{d}$

(C) 24d

(D) $\dfrac{3d}{8}$

(E) $\dfrac{8d}{3}$

30. The sum of three consecutive odd numbers is always divisible by I. 2, II. 3, III. 5, IV. 6
    (A) only I
    (B) only II
    (C) only I and II
    (D) only I and III
    (E) only II and IV

STOP

END OF SECTION. IF YOU HAVE ANY TIME LEFT, GO OVER YOUR WORK IN THIS SECTION ONLY. DO NOT WORK IN ANY OTHER SECTION OF THE TEST.

SECTION IV

30 minutes
30 questions

Directions: For each of the following questions two quantities are given, one in Column A and one in Column B. Compare the two quantities and mark your answer sheet with the correct lettered conclusion. These are your options:
  A: If the quantity in Column A is the greater;
  B: if the quantity in Column B is the greater;
  C: if the two quantities are equal;
  D: if the relationship cannot be determined from the information given.

Common Information: In any question, information applying to both columns is centered between the columns and above the quantities in columns A and B. The common information applies to both columns. Any symbol that appears in both columns represents the same idea or quantity in both columns.

Numbers: All numbers used are real numbers.

Figures: Assume that the positions of points, angles, regions and so forth are in the order shown. Figures are assumed to lie in a plane unless otherwise indicated. Figures accompanying questions are intended to provide information you can use in answering the questions. However, unless a note states that a figure is drawn to scale, you should solve the problems by using your knowledge of mathematics and *not* by estimating sizes by sight and measurement.

Lines: Assume that lines shown as straight are indeed straight.

COLUMN A	COLUMN B
1.	$x = -1$
$x^3 + x^2 - x + 1$	$x^3 - x^2 + x - 1$
2. The edge of a cube whose volume is 27	The edge of a cube whose total surface area is 54

COLUMN A	COLUMN B

3. $\dfrac{\frac{1}{2}+\frac{1}{3}}{\frac{2}{3}}$ $\dfrac{\frac{2}{3}}{\frac{1}{2}+\frac{1}{3}}$

4.   .02 $\sqrt{.02}$

5.

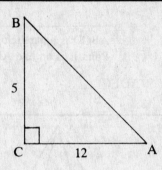

$(AB)^2$ $(AC)^2 + 5CB$

6.   Area of circle   Area of a square
with radius 7   with side 7

7.

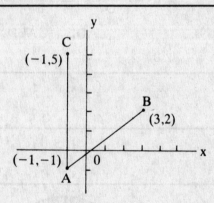

The length of AB   The length of AC

8.

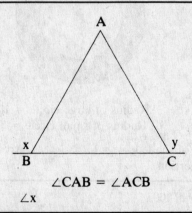

$\angle CAB = \angle ACB$

$\angle x$ $\angle y$

COLUMN A   COLUMN B

9.

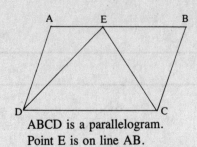

ABCD is a parallelogram.
Point E is on line AB.

area of △DEC   area of △AED
                         + Area △EBC

10.

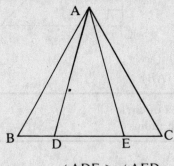

∠ADE > ∠AED

∠B   ∠C

11.   a < 0 < b

a^2 $\dfrac{b}{2}$

12.   rt > 0

r   t

13.

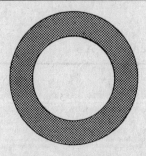

Radius of large circle = 10
Radius of small circle = 7

Area of shaded   Area of small circle
portion

14.   4% of .003   3% of .004

COLUMN A   P   COLUMN B

15.

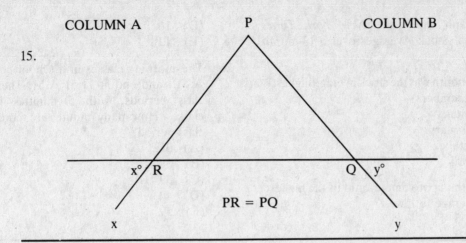

PR = PQ

x   y

Directions: For each of the following questions, select the best of the answer choices and blacken the corresponding space on your answer sheet.

Numbers: All numbers used are real numbers.

Figures: The diagrams and figures that accompany these questions are for the purpose of providing information useful in answering the questions. Unless it is stated that a specific figure is not drawn to scale, the diagrams and figures are drawn as accurately as possible. All figures are in a plane unless otherwise indicated.

16. In the figure, a rectangular piece of cardboard 18 inches by 24 inches is made into an open box by cutting a 5-inch square from each corner and building up the sides. What is the volume of the box in cubic inches?
    (A) 560
    (B) 1,233
    (C) 1,560
    (D) 2,160
    (E) 4,320

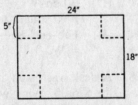

17. The figure below represents the back of a house. Find, in feet, the length of one of the equal rafters PQ or QR, if each extends 12 inches beyond the eaves.
    (A) 19
    (B) 21
    (C) 23
    (D) 25
    (E) 43

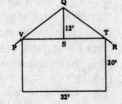

18. The scale of a certain map is $\frac{3}{4}$ inch = 9 miles. Find, in square miles, the actual area of a park represented on the map by a square whose side is $\frac{7}{8}$ inch.
    (A) $10\frac{1}{2}$
    (B) 21
    (C) $110\frac{1}{4}$
    (D) 121
    (E) $125\frac{2}{3}$

19. If t represents the tens digit and u the units digit of a two-digit number, then the number is represented by
    (A) t + u
    (B) tu
    (C) 10u + t
    (D) 10t + u
    (E) ut

Answer Questions 20–22 with reference to the graph below.

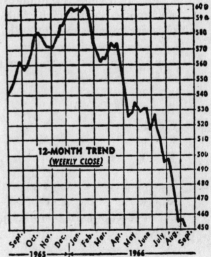

The graph shows the *New York Times* Industrial Stock Averages over a 12-month period.

20. In what month was the stock average highest?
    (A) December
    (B) January
    (C) February
    (D) October
    (E) April

21. What is the approximate ratio of the highest stock average to lowest?
    (A) 4 : 3
    (B) 5 : 3
    (C) 2 : 1
    (D) 3 : 2
    (E) 5 : 2

22. During what 3-month period did the stock market experience the greatest decline?
    (A) Sept.–Nov.
    (B) Nov.–Jan.
    (C) Feb.–April
    (D) May–July
    (E) July–Sept. '66

23. The pages of a typewritten report are numbered from 1 to 100 by hand. How many times will it be necessary to write the number 5?
    (A) 10
    (B) 11
    (C) 12
    (D) 19
    (E) 20

24. A clock that gains two minutes each hour is synchronized at midnight with a clock that loses one minute an hour. What will be the difference, in minutes, between the times shown on the two clocks when a third clock correctly shows noon?
    (A) 36
    (B) 24
    (C) 14
    (D) 12
    (E) 0

25. The number 6 is called a perfect number because it is the sum of all its integral divisors except itself. Another perfect number is
    (A) 36
    (B) 28
    (C) 24

    (D) 16
    (E) 12

26. The morning classes in a school begin at 9 A.M., and end at 11:51 A.M. There are 4 class periods, with 5 minutes between classes. How many minutes are there in each class period?
    (A) $37\frac{3}{4}$
    (B) $38\frac{1}{2}$
    (C) 39
    (D) 40
    (E) 59

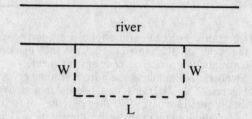

river

W | | W

L

27. A man plans to build a fenced-in enclosure along a riverbank, as shown in the figure. He has 90 feet of fencing available for the three sides of the rectangular enclosure. All of the following statements are true EXCEPT
    (A) L + 2W = 90
    (B) The area of the enclosure is LW.
    (C) The area of the enclosure is 90W − 2W².
    (D) When W = 20, the enclosed area is 1000 square feet.
    (E) The enclosed area is greatest when L = W.

28. A desk was listed at $90.00 and was bought for $75.00. What was the rate of discount?
    (A) 15%
    (B) $16\frac{2}{3}$%
    (C) 18%
    (D) 20%
    (E) 24%

29. In the figure below, a running track goes around a football field in the shape of a rectangle with semicircles at each end, with dimensions as indicated on the figure. The distance around the track in yards is
    (A) $100 + 60\pi$
    (B) $200 + 30\pi$
    (C) 320
    (D) $200 + 60\pi$
    (E) $100 + 30\pi$

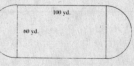

30. In the figure below, if angle P may take on values between 90° and 180°, exclusive, which inequality best expresses the possible values of the base x?

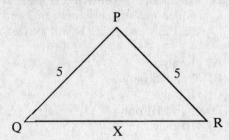

(A) $5 < x < 10$
(B) $5\sqrt{3} < x < 10$
(C) $7 < x < 10$
(D) $5\sqrt{2} < x < 10$
(E) $5\sqrt{2} < x < 5\sqrt{3}$

STOP

END OF SECTION. IF YOU HAVE ANY TIME LEFT, GO OVER YOUR WORK IN THIS SECTION ONLY. DO NOT WORK IN ANY OTHER SECTION OF THE TEST.

SECTION V

30 minutes
25 questions

Directions: Each of the following questions or groups of questions is based on a short passage or a set of propositions. In answering these questions it may sometimes be helpful to draw a simple picture or chart. When you have selected the best answer to each question, darken the corresponding circle on your answer sheet.

Questions 1–3

A slot player may possess only one token at a time.

A blue token in slot 19 produces a prize and one yellow token.

A blue token is obtained by putting a yellow or green token in slot 10, or a pink token in slot 15.

Pink tokens are obtained by putting a white token in slot 8.

A white token can be obtained from the cashier only by exchanging another token other than a yellow one for it.

1. The procedure fails to specify how to get which of the following?
   (A) a prize without first getting a yellow token
   (B) as many prizes as one wants
   (C) a green token
   (D) a prize without first getting a green token
   (E) a yellow token

2. Once a player has won a prize, which of the following is possible as the player's next play?
   (A) obtaining a white token from cashier
   (B) playing slot 10
   (C) playing slot 15
   (D) playing slot 19
   (E) playing slot 8

3. If you have a green token, what other colors of token can you get?
   (A) blue only
   (B) pink, blue, or yellow only
   (C) green, blue, or yellow only

(D) blue or yellow only

(E) all the other colors

4. Why pay outrageously high prices for imported sparkling water when there is now an inexpensive water carbonated and bottled here in the United States at its source—Cold Springs, Vermont. Neither you nor your guests will taste the difference, but if you would be embarrassed if it were learned that you were serving a domestic sparkling water, then serve Cold Springs Water—but serve it in a leaded crystal decanter.

The advertisement rests on which of the following assumptions?

I. It is difficult if not impossible to distinguish Cold Springs Water from imported competitors on the basis of taste.

II. Most sparkling waters are not bottled at the source.

III. Some people may purchase an imported sparkling water over a domestic one as a status symbol.

(A) I only

(B) II only

(C) III only

(D) I and II only

(E) I and III only

5. In our investigation of this murder, we are guided by our previous experience with the Eastend Killer. You will recall that in that case the victims were also carrying a great deal of money when they were killed, but the money was not taken. As in this case, the murder weapon was a pistol. Finally, in that case the murders were also committed between six in the evening and twelve midnight. So we are probably after someone who looks very much like the Eastend Killer who was finally tried, convicted, and executed: 5′11″ tall, a mustache, short brown hair, walks with a slight limp.

The author makes which of the following assumptions?

I. Crimes similar in detail are likely to be committed by perpetrators who are similar in physical appearance.

II. The Eastend Killer has apparently escaped from prison and has resumed his criminal activities.

III. The man first convicted as the Eastend Killer was actually innocent, and the real Eastend Killer is still loose.

(A) I only

(B) I and II only

(C) II only

(D) I and III only

(E) III only

6. The main ingredient in this bottle of Dr. John's Milk of Magnesia is used by nine out of ten hospitals across the country as an antacid and laxative.

If this advertising claim is true, which of the following statements must also be true?

I. Nine out of ten hospitals across the country use Dr. John's Milk of Magnesia for some ailments.

II. Only one out of ten hospitals in the country does not treat acid indigestion and constipation.

III. Only one out of ten hospitals across the country does not recommend Dr. John's Milk of Magnesia for patients who need a milk of magnesia.

(A) I only

(B) II only

(C) I and III

(D) I, II, and III

(E) None of the statements is necessarily true.

Questions 7–11

The tribe of Ater is divided into three clans—first, second, and third.

Only men and women of the same clan may marry.

On maturity, sons of couples in the first and second clans move down one rank, while sons of the third clan join the first.

On maturity, daughters of the second and third clans move up a rank and daughters of the first clan join the third.

Only mature Ater may marry.

7. Is it ever possible for an Ater woman born of the first clan to marry her nephew?
   (A) Yes, but only the son of her brother.
   (B) Yes, but only the son of her sister.
   (C) Yes, but only the daughter of her brother.
   (D) Yes, but only the daughter of her sister.
   (E) No.

8. Into what clans were the parents of an adult second clan male born?
   (A) father first clan, mother first clan
   (B) father first clan, mother third clan
   (C) father second clan, mother third clan
   (D) father second clan, mother first clan
   (E) father third clan, mother second clan

9. If a baby is born into the third clan, its mother's mother's mother could have been born to adult parents of what clan(s)?
   (A) first, second, or third
   (B) first and second only
   (C) first and third only
   (D) second only
   (E) third only

10. An Ater man has a granddaughter who is married to a man in the second clan. In what clan(s) could he be?
    (A) first only
    (B) second only
    (C) third only
    (D) first or second
    (E) second or third

11. Which of the statements about the Ater may be inferred from the information given?
    I. A sister and brother may not marry.
    II. A man may not marry his mother.
    III. A woman may not marry her grandson.
    (A) I only
    (B) II only
    (C) I and II only
    (D) I and III
    (E) I, II, and III

Questions 12–16

J, K, L, M, N, P, and Q get on an empty express bus at 10th Street. The bus only stops every ten blocks. No one else gets on the bus, and no one leaves and gets back on. Nobody gets off at 30th Street or at 60th Street. When the bus pulls away from 80th Street, there are three people left on the bus.

Both P and Q get off before 80th Street, with P getting off at an earlier stop than Q.

12. If J gets off the bus on the second stop after M does, at which street(s) could J have gotten off?
    (A) 20th and 40th
    (B) 20th, 40th, and 70th
    (C) 40th and 70th
    (D) 50th, 70th, and 80th
    (E) 70th and 80th

13. If L, M, and N are on the bus after 80th Street, which of the following is true?
    I. Each of the other passengers could have gotten off at separate stops.
    II. There was at least one stop at which no one got off.
    III. No one got off at 80th Street.
    (A) I only
    (B) I and II only
    (C) I and III only
    (D) II and III only
    (E) I, II, and III

14. If K and L get off at separate stops before 80th Street, which of the following must be false?
    (A) J did not get off the bus.
    (B) M did not get off the bus.
    (C) N did not get off the bus.
    (D) Q did not get off the bus.
    (E) None of the above.

15. If P left the bus after M did, and no one got off at 70th Street, then
    (A) everyone who left the bus left at a different stop
    (B) Q left at either 50th or 80th Streets
    (C) P left at either 50th or 80th Streets
    (D) M left after J
    (E) Q left after J

16. If X, Y, and Z got on the bus at 20th, 30th, and 40th Streets, respectively, and stayed on

the bus for 3, 4, and 5 stops, respectively, how many persons were on the bus when it arrived at 90th Street?

(A) 1
(B) 2
(C) 3
(D) 4
(E) Cannot be determined from the information given.

Questions 17–23

A philosophical foundation presents six once-a-month lecture series, with no dates conflicting:

Metaphysics—August through January

Epistemology—April through October

Ethics—January through September

Esthetics—March through June

Political Philosophy—October through April

Philosophy of Science—October through December

17. During which month are the fewest lectures given?
(A) January
(B) February
(C) June
(D) August
(E) September

18. What is the largest number of lectures that can be attended in a single month?
(A) 7
(B) 6
(C) 5
(D) 4
(E) 3

19. What two series taken together fill the year without overlap?
(A) Metaphysics and Esthetics
(B) Political Philosophy and Epistemology
(C) Epistemology and Metaphysics
(D) Political Philosophy and Ethics
(E) Ethics and Philosophy of Science

20. During how many months of the year must a student attend to hear all the lectures on Metaphysics, Epistemology, and Esthetics?
(A) 11

(B) 10
(C) 9
(D) 8
(E) 7

21. How many lecture series last more than 6 months?
(A) 1
(B) 2
(C) 3
(D) 4
(E) 5

22. How many different lecture series can be attended in September, October, and November?
(A) 2
(B) 3
(C) 4
(D) 5
(E) 6

23. How many different lectures can be attended in January, February, and March?
(A) 12
(B) 10
(C) 8
(D) 6
(E) 4

24. Is your company going to continue to discriminate against women in its hiring and promotion policies?

The above question might be considered unfair for which of the following reasons?

I. Its construction seeks a "yes" or "no" answer where both might be inappropriate.
II. It is internally inconsistent.
III. It contains a hidden presupposition which the responder might wish to contest.

(A) I only
(B) II only
(C) I and II only
(D) I and III only
(E) I, II, and III

Ms. Evangeline Rose argued that money and time invested in acquiring a professional degree are totally wasted. As evidence supporting her argument, she offered the case of a man who, at considerable expense of money and time, completed his law degree and then married and lived as a house-husband taking care of their children, and worked part time at a day care center so his wife could pursue her career.

25. Ms. Rose makes the unsupported assumption that

(A) an education in the law is useful only in pursuing law-related activities
(B) what was not acceptable twenty-five years ago may very well be acceptable today
(C) wealth is more important than learning
(D) professional success is a function of the quality of one's education
(E) only the study of law can be considered professional study

STOP

END OF SECTION. IF YOU HAVE ANY TIME LEFT, GO OVER YOUR WORK IN THIS SECTION ONLY. DO NOT WORK IN ANY OTHER SECTION OF THE TEST.

SECTION VI

30 minutes
25 questions

Directions: Each of the following questions or groups of questions is based on a short passage or a set of propositions. In answering these questions it may sometimes be helpful to draw a simple picture or chart. When you have selected the best answer to each question, darken the corresponding circle on your answer sheet.

Questions 1–3

3 masters, L, M, and N, and 3 experts, O, P, and Q, compete in a special tournament.

All the competitors play all the other players once.

1 point is gained for defeating an expert.

2 points are gained for defeating a master.

Masters lose 2 points for each game lost.

Experts lose 1 point for each game lost.

1. What is the highest score that a master can obtain if he loses 2 games?
   (A) 0

(B) 1
(C) 2
(D) 3
(E) 4

2. How many games does an expert have to win to be sure of coming in ahead of a master who lost to the other masters?
   (A) 1
   (B) 2
   (C) 3
   (D) 4
   (E) 5

3. If P wins all his games except the one against L, and did not lose to the winner of the tournament, which of the following could have been the winner?
   (A) L or P
   (B) M or N
   (C) O or Q
   (D) any one of M, N, O, or Q
   (E) any player except L or P

4. SPEAKER: The great majority of people in the United States have access to the best medical care available anywhere in the world.

OBJECTOR: There are thousands of poor in this country who cannot afford to pay to see a doctor.

A possible objection to the speaker's comments would be to point to the existence of

(A) a country which has more medical assistants than the United States

(B) a nation where medical care is provided free of charge by the government

(C) a country in which the people are given better medical care than Americans

(D) government hearings in the United States on the problems poor people have getting medical care

(E) a country which has a higher hospital bed per person ratio than the United States

5. It is sometimes argued that we are reaching the limits of the Earth's capacity to supply our energy needs with fossil fuels. In the past ten years, however, as a result of technological progress making it possible to extract resources from even marginal wells and mines, yields from oil and coal fields have increased tremendously. There is no reason to believe that there is a limit to the Earth's capacity to supply our energy needs.

Which of the following statements most directly contradicts the conclusion drawn above?

(A) Even if we exhaust our supplies of fossil fuel, the earth can still be mined for uranium for nuclear fuel.

(B) The technology needed to extract fossil fuels from marginal sources is very expensive.

(C) Even given the improvements in technology, oil and coal are not renewable resources, so we will sometime exhaust our supplies of them.

(D) Most of the land under which marginal oil and coal supplies lie is more suitable to cultivation or pasturing than to production of fossil fuels.

(E) The fuels which are yielded by marginal sources tend to be high in sulphur and other undesirable elements that aggravate the air pollution problem.

6. Statistics published by the State Department of Traffic and Highway Safety show that nearly 80% of all traffic fatalities occur at speeds under 35 miles per hour and within 25 miles of home.

Which of the following would be the most reasonable conclusion to draw from these statistics?

(A) A person is less likely to have a fatal accident if he always drives over 35 miles per hour and always at distances greater than 25 miles from his home.

(B) There is a direct correlation between distance driven and the likelihood of a fatal accident.

(C) The greater the likelihood that one is about to be involved in a fatal accident, the more likely it is that he is driving close to home at a speed less than 35 miles per hour.

(D) If it were not the case that a person were about to be involved in a fatal traffic accident, then he would not have been driving at the speed or in the location he was, in fact, driving.

(E) Most driving is done at less than 35 miles per hour and within 25 miles of home.

Questions 7–11

Coach Nelson is putting together a four-member handball team from right-handed players R, S, and T and left-handed players L, M, N, and O. He must have at least two right-handed players on the team, and all players must be able to practice with each other.

S cannot practice with L.
T cannot practice with N.
M cannot practice with L or N.

7. If L is on the team, what other individuals must also be on the team?

(A) R and T only

(B) R, T, and N

(C) R, T, and O

(D) R only
(E) M and O only

8. If O is not on the team, which of the other players must be on the team?
   (A) No other particular player must be on the team if O is not chosen.
   (B) M only
   (C) R and S only
   (D) R, S, T, and M
   (E) S only

9. If both S and T are chosen for the team, what other individuals must be on the team with them?
   (A) L only
   (B) M only
   (C) M and O only
   (D) O only
   (E) none of the above

10. How many different teams can be formed without R?
    (A) 0
    (B) 1
    (C) 2
    (D) 3
    (E) more than 3

11. If T were to become a left-handed player, how many different teams could be formed?
    (A) 0
    (B) 1
    (C) 2
    (D) 3
    (E) more than 3

Questions 12–16

   I. A cube has six sides, each of which is a different one of the following colors: black, blue, brown, green, red, and white.
   II. The red side is opposite the black.
   III. The green side is between the red and the black.
   IV. The blue side is adjacent to the white.
   V. The brown side is adjacent to the blue.
   VI. The red side is the bottom face.

12. Which statement adds no information that is not already given by the statements above it?
    (A) II

(B) III
(C) IV
(D) V
(E) VI

13. The side opposite brown is
    (A) white
    (B) red
    (C) green
    (D) blue
    (E) black

14. The four colors adjacent to green are
    (A) black, blue, brown, red
    (B) black, blue, brown, white
    (C) black, blue, red, white
    (D) black, brown, red, white
    (E) blue, brown, red, white

15. Which of the following can be deduced from statements I, II, and VI?
    (A) Black is on the top.
    (B) Blue is on the top.
    (C) Brown is on the top.
    (D) Brown is opposite black.
    (E) None of the above can be deduced.

16. If the red side is exchanged for the green side, and blue is swapped for black, which of the following is false?
    (A) Red is opposite black.
    (B) White is adjacent to brown.
    (C) Green is opposite blue.
    (D) White is adjacent to green.
    (E) White is adjacent to blue.

Questions 17–22

   I. Four contestants, P, Q, R, and S, will each receive one of four prizes. They are, in descending order of value: a new car, a vacation to Europe, a stereo system, and a year's supply of dog food.
   II. If P gets the car, then Q gets the dog food.
   III. If Q gets the stereo, then P gets the dog food.
   IV. P will get a more valuable prize than R.
   V. If S doesn't get the car, then P will get the vacation.
   VI. If Q gets the vacation, then R won't get the dog food.
   VII. If Q gets the car, then R gets the vacation.

17. Based on the above information, which of the following conclusions must be false?
    (A) R will get a more valuable prize than Q.
    (B) No two people will get the same prize.
    (C) Q gets the vacation and R gets the dog food.
    (D) P gets a less valuable prize than S.
    (E) Q will get one of the two least valuable prizes.

18. Which of the contestants will get the dog food?
    (A) P
    (B) Q
    (C) R
    (D) S
    (E) none of the above

19. Which of the contestants will get the car?
    (A) P
    (B) Q
    (C) R
    (D) S
    (E) none of the above

20. Which of the following combinations of the above statements are sufficient to deduce that Q will not receive the car?
    (A) I, II, and VI
    (B) II, VI, and VII
    (C) III and V
    (D) VI and VII
    (E) I, IV, and VII

21. Which of the seven statements merely gives information available from previous statements?
    (A) IV
    (B) V
    (C) VI
    (D) VII
    (E) none of the above

22. Which of the contestants will not receive a stereo?
    (A) Q and S only
    (B) P, Q, and R
    (C) P, S, and R
    (D) P, S, and Q
    (E) P and R only

23. A study published by the Department of Education shows that children in the central cities lag far behind students in the suburbs and the rural areas in reading skills. The report blamed this differential on the overcrowding in the classrooms of city schools. I maintain, however, that the real reason that city children are poorer readers than non-city children is that they do not get enough fresh air and sunshine.

Which of the following would LEAST strengthen the author's point in the argument above?
    (A) Medical research which shows a correlation between air pollution and learning disabilities.
    (B) A report by educational experts demonstrating there is no relationship between the number of students in a classroom and a student's ability to read.
    (C) A notice released by the Department of Education retracting that part of their report which mentions overcrowding as the reason for the differential.
    (D) The results of a federal program which indicates that city students show significant improvement in reading skills when they spend the summer in the country.
    (E) A proposal by the federal government to fund emergency programs to hire more teachers for central city schools in an attempt to reduce overcrowding in the classrooms.

24. Some judges have allowed hospitals to disconnect life-support equipment of patients who have no prospects for recovery. But I say that is cold-blooded murder. Either we put a stop to this practice now or we will soon have programs of euthanasia for the old and infirm as well as others who might be considered a burden. Rather than disconnecting life-support equipment, we should let nature take its course.

Which of the following are valid objections to the above argument?

    I. It is internally inconsistent.

II. It employs emotionally charged terms.
III. It presents a false dilemma.

(A) I only
(B) II only
(C) III only
(D) II and III only
(E) I, II, and III

25. PUBLIC ANNOUNCEMENT: When you enroll with Future Careers Business Institute (FCBI), you will have access to our placement counseling service. Last year, 92% of our graduates who asked us to help them find jobs, found them. So go to FCBI for your future!

Which of the following would be appropriate questions to ask in order to determine the value of the preceding claim?

I. How many of your graduates asked FCBI for assistance?
II. How many people graduated from FCBI last year?
III. Did those people who asked for jobs find ones in the areas for which they were trained?
IV. Was FCBI responsible for finding the jobs or did graduates find them independently?

(A) I and II only
(B) I, II, and III only
(C) I, II, and IV only
(D) III and IV only
(E) I, II, III, and IV

STOP

END OF SECTION. IF YOU HAVE ANY TIME LEFT, GO OVER YOUR WORK IN THIS SECTION ONLY. DO NOT WORK IN ANY OTHER SECTION OF THE TEST.

PRACTICE EXAMINATION 5—ANSWER KEY

Section I

1. E	5. E	9. E	13. C	17. C	21. C	25. A	29. B	33. A	37. B
2. C	6. E	10. B	14. D	18. C	22. D	26. D	30. E	34. B	38. D
3. A	7. B	11. B	15. D	19. A	23. B	27. C	31. D	35. D	
4. A	8. C	12. C	16. D	20. E	24. B	28. C	32. D	36. C	

Section II

1. B	5. B	9. E	13. B	17. C	21. C	25. E	29. E	33. A	37. C
2. A	6. C	10. E	14. B	18. B	22. B	26. D	30. A	34. B	38. B
3. C	7. C	11. E	15. B	19. C	23. A	27. C	31. B	35. D	
4. E	8. C	12. D	16. D	20. B	24. C	28. C	32. C	36. A	

Section III

1. D	4. D	7. A	10. B	13. A	16. B	19. D	22. E	25. C	28. E
2. B	5. B	8. C	11. C	14. D	17. A	20. D	23. A	26. D	29. A
3. C	6. C	9. A	12. C	15. D	18. D	21. A	24. D	27. D	30. B

Section IV

1. A	4. B	7. B	10. D	13. A	16. A	19. D	22. E	25. B	28. B
2. C	5. C	8. D	11. D	14. C	17. B	20. C	23. E	26. C	29. D
3. A	6. A	9. C	12. D	15. C	18. C	21. A	24. A	27. E	30. D

Section V

1. C	6. E	11. C	16. D	21. C
2. B	7. A	12. C	17. B	22. D
3. E	8. E	13. B	18. D	23. C
4. E	9. E	14. D	19. E	24. D
5. A	10. D	15. B	20. A	25. A

Section VI

1. B	6. E	11. E	16. B	21. E
2. B	7. C	12. B	17. C	22. D
3. C	8. D	13. A	18. B	23. E
4. C	9. E	14. D	19. D	24. E
5. C	10. B	15. A	20. E	25. E

EXPLANATORY ANSWERS

SECTION I

1. **(E)** If you are now supporting a candidate whom you have attacked only a month before, your position must be embarrassing. Anomalous is the second-best answer, but it means deviating from the norm or, here, irregular. This has appeal since one would like to think that such things as those described in the sentence are deviations from the norm, but the sentence says that these things often occur. Thus, (E) is the best answer. Piquant means sharp, spicy-tasting, or flavorful; succulent means juicy.

2. **(C)** The sentence structure tells us that we are looking for a better and different way of communication than direct censure. You do not really need to know what censure means to answer the question, since it is clearly some form of criticism. Thus, we seek an answer that is an *indirect* form of communication criticism. (C), innuendo, is precisely that. (A) might have some appeal since one might suppose that writing is less direct than speaking to someone face to face; however, writing is not necessarily indirect, only not oral. Furthermore, writing is not necessarily a form of criticism, as censure and innuendo are. (B), (D), and (E) are not really forms of communication. (D) and (E) appeal since they remind you of allusion, which is a form of indirect reference and communication and would therefore be a fairly good answer choice, though still not as good as innuendo, which carries the particular connotation of making an indirect, critical remark.

3. **(A)** If the Congress is uncooperative, the Chief Executive may lack the power to accomplish his program. There is some outside knowledge required here, in that you need to know that power in the government is likely divided between the Congress and the Chief Executive. If the Chief Executive had all the power, there would be no point to worrying about whether the Congress was cooperative or not. (A) means powerless and is thus just the right word. (C) and (D) do not even fit into the sentence and are eliminated.

   (B) and (E) have only a little merit. (E)'s appeal is from a mental extension of the sentence to say something like: "He is equipped to do the program, but is not allowed to do it." This is a fine idea, but not the one that is presented in the problem. (B) has the same slight merit if it is interpreted to mean that he is permitted by the grace of the Congress to do something, as opposed to being able to do it based on his own power. However, this is a derivative meaning and first depends on the idea that the Chief Executive is impotent; thus, (A) remains the better answer.

4. **(A)** Someone with a high opinion of his own importance tends to try to run others' activities. Choice (A) best reflects this attitude. (E) is good for the first blank, but diffusion would not flatter Larry's ego.

5. **(E)** If we accept that Arlene's cooking was delicious, one doesn't generally avoid or console someone for a tasty meal. Thus, (E) is the only logical answer.

6. **(E)** The color is expressing feeling, so something implying feeling should be in the way that the painting relates to the museum-goer. This is a sentence in which none of the answer choices is eliminated by reference to only one of the blanks. The sentence structure shows that the first blank—the way in which the paintings are done—will produce a result described by the second blank. Therefore, the solution to the question is to see how well each answer choice will work in this structure. Painting techniques might be ingenious, (A), but that would not make it fall on the viewer, hence (A) fails. (B) has some merit since too emphatic a technique might insult the viewer, though it is not a strong answer choice. (C) is unacceptable since something that echoes in your mind is very strong, and not very subtle. "Creep up on" would express being subtle, but it is not available. (D) has some merit since a sensitive expression of feeling might be very appealing, although seduce has more meaning than merely sensitivity of feeling. (E) is quite strong for two reasons. First, if the technique is successful, it will "say" something to the viewer. Second, if the expression of feeling is "so" successful, some strong result is appropriate and cry out is a strong result. (E) is preferable to (D) primarily because crying out is a better way to express feeling than seduction. Both of these are preferable to (B) since there is no reason to suppose that emphatic feeling in a painting is universally insulting, and we do know that Van Gogh is revered today. Thus, (E) is the best answer.

7. **(B)** The structure of the sentence tells us that the factories and the workers were regarded in the same way by the monopoly capitalists. Thus, the

first blank must be filled with a word that could apply to both factories and workers in order to express their lack of rights or feelings. It is, of course, correct and natural to say that a factory has no rights or feelings, so the qualifier—without rights or feelings—will primarily apply to the workers.

In (A), the workers are seen as animals, which does not deny their feelings and is an unlikely view of a factory. (B) is strong because in equating the workers and factories to machinery, the workers' rights and feelings are denied. (C) fails since beings likely do have the rights and feelings which the sentence says were denied. (D) and (E) are acceptable since they both conform to the idea that there is something that has no rights or feelings.

The second blank must be filled with a word that relates the use to which we would expect a monopoly capitalist of the early 1900's to put something that had no rights or feelings. The capitalist clearly wishes to increase his profits; thus (B) is superior to (D) or (E). (D)'s use of the word guarantee is deceptive. While the capitalist would certainly like to guarantee his profits, there is no reason to suppose that the workers and factories, no matter how regarded by him, would, in fact, guarantee that he would have profits. Thus, that purpose, while desirable, would not be reasonably expected in this context. Thus, (B) is the best answer choice.

8. **(C)** The original pair, mouth and orifice, have the relationship that a mouth can be described physically as an orifice. Similarly, an ear can be described physically as a projection. All the other answer choices relate a sense to the type of thing sensed, such as a nose sensing odors. Thus, (C) is the best answer.

9. **(E)** A worker earns a bonus and the bonus is an extra, something over and above his regular earnings, a reward, say, for a job well done. (D) has some small attraction since one could conceive of a bonus as a spur to better efforts; however, to use the old image of the stick and the carrot, the spur is a stick to the horse, while the bonus is a carrot to the worker. Thus, (D) fails. (C) has winning in the second position, but that is a goal and not a reward, so (C) fails. (A), (B), and (E) are all attractive since they are all types of rewards or earnings. (A) and (B) are appealing since they continue the theme of monetary reward. However, when there is an overlapping situation, you must have an even more precise relationship. The dividends of the capitalist and the interest of the banker are their regualr receipts, while the similar idea for the worker would be his wages. Thus, (A) and (B) are not as good as (E), where the actor is receiving a reward, a "bonus" of applause. Also, it is a little difficult to tell the difference between (A) and (B). Thus, (E) is the best answer.

10. **(B)** Rigid and flexible are opposites that describe a physical property, and that are also used to describe personalities. (A) is eliminated since it is a pair of synonyms. (E) is eliminated since muscle and tone are not opposites, but an object (muscle) and a typical characteristic of it (tone). (D) is not a real pair of opposites, and therefore fails. This leaves (B) and (C). (C) is an example of something that is relatively unusual. (C) is wrong because it has the noun steel instead of the adjective steely, which would make it quite as good as (B). As written, however, (B) is the best answer.

11. **(B)** We have here another special word, gobble, which means to eat quickly and in large pieces. Guzzling is to drink quickly and in large draughts. A good first approximation of this relationship might have been that these are synonyms with differences of degree. This would eliminate (D) and possibly (E). (A), (B), and (C) all have the idea of the second term being a hurried form of the first, but then we have the additional concept of it being some sort of eating or drinking, and thus the idea of doing it in large pieces/draughts. Hence, (B) is the best answer.

12. **(C)** A sin requires forgiveness and a debt requires release. (A) is wrong since the two terms represent the same idea and do not, therefore, mirror the stem-pair relationship of having the second undo the first. The other answers also lack this idea. Thus, (C) is the only answer that carries out this idea of undoing, or forgiving. It is perfectly proper to speak of forgiving a debt, but it is not the only way of referring to the situation in which the debt is undone.

13. **(C)** The function of an anesthetic is to reduce or even obliterate sensation. The purpose of a muffler is to reduce or even obliterate sound. Note that one would use the meaning of muffler relating to sound and not that of the muffler which goes around the neck. (A) and (B) have no idea of the second word working against the first. (D) and (E) do share some of the idea with (C). In (E) we have, however, a vaccine, which is a preventative measure only, and in (D) we have a curative, or palliative, measure. Actually, a detoxicant is not necessarily correct for a particular poison. (E) is not as good as (C) because of the need to use the vaccine prior to the crisis, while an anesthetic could be used at any time. But even more important than any details of usage, sound is a sensation and the muffling of it is more like the idea of an anesthetic. One could even speak of muffling the pain.

14. **(D)** A holster is the special device which holds the gun in readiness for use. The scabbard is the special device which holds the sword in readiness for use. All the answer choices have the idea of

the first term being in the second one. However, (A), (B), and (C) lack the idea of a weapon, and in (E) the cannon is itself the weapon. Thus, (D) is the best answer.

15. **(D)** A mist is a mild rain in that it is composed of the same material and does the same thing—make you wet—but does so very gently. A breeze is a mild wind and a gale is a strong one. (B) fails since it is a pair of opposites, not a matter of difference in degree. (A), (C), and (E) all have some idea of the two items being the same or similar, but a fog is a cloud, and the foam is not really a kind of sea. (C) is the second-best answer choice since both snow and hail are made of ice. However, while hail might be seen as icier than snow, a rain is not really wetter than mist. More to the point, snow is not necessarily as gentle as a mist or a breeze is. Thus, (D) is the best answer choice.

16. **(D)** A pharmacist prepares drugs, just like a chef prepares foods. None of the other answer choices has the idea of the first term being in charge of the creation and preparation of the second term.

17. **(C)** The author first uses a comparison to the Arabian Nights as a positive example, and then uses music and poetry in the streets as an example of true bliss. At the end he refers to artists having "fair and noble" designs. The focus on reality should not be seen as antithetical to arts, which can be seen as mirrors of reality rather than as "mere" fictions.

(E), perhaps the second-best answer, fails because there is no reluctance to be found in the admiration. The indifference, suspicion, and repulsion in the passage are all for lies and fictions, not art, thus (A), (B), and (D) fail.

18. **(C)** The end of the first paragraph equates experience with failure, an unusual thought that should stand out to your eye. This directly eliminates (B) and (D), and argues for (C). (A) is wrong because it is in discernment that children excel, not in amount of knowledge, which the author feels may even interfere with discernment. (E) means that childhood sets many patterns for the adult that is to come, but here the author is saying that the adult is less able than the child.

19. **(A)** The first sentence says just what (A) says. (D) is incorrect because the reference to Arabian Nights is to show the wonder of reality. (B), (C), and (E) have no basis in the passage.

20. **(E)** The first sentence describes the situation that the author sees as actually going on in the world—delusions are seen as real and reality as delusion—everything is backward. Thus, (E) makes the best sense. Note that he is speaking of the perceptions of the actual reality. (A) is a common meaning of the word fabulous, but not the one used in this

sentence. The whole passage is about how to comprehend reality. Hence, (D) fails while (C) and (B) are entirely unrelated.

21. **(C)** In the last paragraph all the true and sublime are stated to be true now and the emphasis is on the value of properly and truly perceiving the present, hence (C) rather than (A), (B), or (D). (E) is an attempt to lure the unwary into thinking that children and Arabian Nights refer to leisure.

22. **(D)** The issues dealt with in the passage are the good, the true, and the soul—hence, (D). (C) and (A) have little connection to the passage. (B)'s word society connects, but population does not. (E)'s reference to the arts confuses the celebration with the cause for celebration.

23. **(B)** (B) is admittedly a little glib and has a lighthearted tone not entirely in keeping with the passage, but it is the only choice which conveys the meaning of the passage, albeit by using this expression somewhat differently than common usage does. The passage indicates that we can achieve what we see, but we will be limited by our false perceptions of the world if we let ourselves be blinded. The universe's answering to our perceptions is just that—the limits are set by us, not the universe.

(A) plays on the universe-answering idea; however, physical control is not the issue, but rather spiritual matters. (C) is opposite to the theme of the passage and a trap for those who think of any reference to Eastern religion as meaning all is fated. (D) plays with the fast and slow tracks, which we may choose, but it is not physical speed, but mental life which is referred to. Perceiving fully makes us experience more and more quickly. (E) is simply false since the last sentence has posterity, in fact, doing what the poet conceived.

Questions 24–27

Since several of the questions turn on somewhat similar parts of the passage, it is simplest first to discuss them together to some extent. The change in the ranking of the causes of death does not, by itself, indicate that there has been any change in the rates of any particular disease. If pneumonia, for instance, continued at the same rate, a large increase in heart disease, for example, could cause heart disease to become ranked higher than pneumonia. Conversely, a constant rate of heart disease combined with a drastically falling rate of pneumonia could cause the same change in rankings. In fact, any absolute movement of either of the two diseases is compatible with the change in rank order, provided that the other disease rate changes in the proper fashion. However, there is one other significant fact about the changes in the diseases which is mentioned in the passage: the diseases of the old have become the top-ranked causes of death. Either the old are dying much more rapidly or the young are dying much less rapidly. Since we do know, as common knowledge, that the population of the United States has increased significantly over the period 1900–1945, it is clear that the young people are dying less frequently—that is, there is less death than before. Let us now consider the specific problems.

24. **(B)** Since the diseases that are most common now are those of advanced years, this implies (B) rather directly. (A) and (E) are clearly not within the scope of the passage and are thus untenable, based on the passage. Sadly, (D) is not true in the real world, but, more importantly, the descending of tuberculosis on the ranking of causes of death does appear to mean that it is less common, but it does not mean that it is all but eliminated, which is a very strong statement and not at all supported in the passage. (C) has some real merit since fatal accidents are part of the list which is referred to as being typical of the advanced years. Thus, you must determine whether (B) or (C) is best. Both suffer from the difficulty that the paragraph only deals with causes of death, while the answer choices concern total medical practice or total "accident-proneness." In order to distinguish these answer choices, one must ask which of the two is least likely to lead to the mortality statistics cited. Since (B) merely says that many problems are, while (C) compares older and younger persons, in the absence of any statement in the passage about younger persons, (B) is less demanding and thus the best answer.

25. **(A)** The form of the question stem tells us that four of the answer choices will be strongly indicated and one will not be indicated as strongly. The correct answer choice may not be indicated either because it refers to some information that is not in the passage or because the passage makes it clear that the choice is false.

   As developed in the general discussion above, the passage does seem to imply that young persons are suffering from less disease than the elderly. However, despite the fact that mortality statistics are being used, there is no reference to debilitating disease as opposed to other disease. This is probably a true statement in the world, but it is not indicated in the passage. Thus, (A) is the answer we seek. The other answers are all indicated, as developed in the general discussion.

26. **(D)** (D) is known to be true from the data presented and the judgment of the author that the changes in the period 1910–1945 are referred to as being profound.

   (A) fails since nothing is stated about infant mortality. (B) fails for the same lack of reference in the passage. (C) is a typical wrong answer in that it overstates a piece of evidence in the passage. All that is said in the passage is that this data would span the possible early and late practice of certain physicians, but it does not state

that the data is from those physicians. (E) fails, of course, when (D) succeeds.

27. **(C)** As the general discussion above notes, there is some inference that the relative changes in the causes of death were a function of the young dying less frequently rather than of the old dying more frequently. In short, the argument is that more people are living long enough to suffer from diseases that afflict the elderly. This argument is not absolutely dominant, but it is strong enough to support (C). (A) fails since the first decade of the period did not show as profound a change as the last 35 years. (B) fails because of the word steadily. We have no information about how these changes operated between the dates cited. (D) and (C) are arguable, as noted above, but (C) is a better choice.

28. **(C)** Restitution means to return something that one had taken, probably wrongly. Deprivation means to take something away from someone, and there is some idea of the action not being good. None of the other answers speaks at all to the issue of taking or giving. Inflation means getting bigger, like a balloon or prices; a cataclysm is a catastrophe; and the constitution of something is its makeup or its ingredients; anonymity means literally having no name (from the Greek *on-yma* and thus being unknown in one's true self. Although constitution shares a considerable number of letters with restitution, knowledge of prefixes could help you if you needed it. *Con-* means with and *re-* means again. These are not really opposite ideas and thus you should not be tempted by constitution.

29. **(B)** Parsimony is thriftiness. Free spending is a perfect opposite. The others are unconnected. To ape means to imitate without understanding, so acting apishly would be acting imitatively, without understanding. Frugality is a synonym of parsimony, though not as strong. Modish would simply mean fashionable, so the result is not opposite to parsimony.

30. **(E)** Perspicuity means mental sharpness, and mental dullness is a perfect opposite. Perspicacious is the adjective and is somewhat more common than the noun given in the problem. Some of the other answer choices refer to mental attributes, but none to the same attribute.

31. **(D)** Preposterous means directly contrary to reason or good sense, and comes from a root meaning with the back part foremost. Something that is credible is inherently believable and sensible. The connection is not perfect, but preposterous does have the connotation of unbelievability that is directly related to its primary meaning.

   Complaisant means agreeable in the sense of being willing to go along with someone else's plans or ideas. This is not a matter of whether something is believable. Conceited means having an exaggerated opinion of one's own worth. Sincere, like complaisant, has a vague connection to preposterous. Sincere means truthful and with full intention to mean what you say. A sincere statement is perhaps more believable than an insincere one, which is probably meant to mislead. This is not the same as saying that something is inherently believable or not.

32. **(D)** Sanctimony is hypocritical devoutness. Thus, devout refers to the real thing, and sanctimonious describes a false show of religious feeling. Impervious, meaning unable to be breeched or broken through, might appeal to an echo of sanctuary, but that is a different word from sanctimony.

33. **(A)** To extirpate something means to hunt it down and destroy it utterly. To preserve something is an active stance of helping the thing to survive—a perfect opposite. To inseminate is to either fertilize or to put something where it can grow, which only establishes the capacity for growth; to ingratiate is to act so as to obtain the gratitude and favor of someone else, but usually in a petty or unworthy way; daub means to smear with.

34. **(B)** Capricious is whimsical and arbitrary changing, presumably for little or no reason. Constant means to be steady and sure, and always the same. Phlegmatic means to have a slow or apathetic nature, to not be easily excited. Naturally, a phlegmatic person will not be too likely to be capricious since he will not likely do much of anything or change much from his apathy. However, this is a derivative meaning and, while possessing some real merit as an answer choice, is not nearly as good as constant, which addresses the heart of the matter, the changeability. Ignominious means disgraceful and unworthy.

35. **(D)** Casuistry is the misapplication of general ethical principles and often has the connotation of being a deliberate misapplication, and thus a lie or deceit. Verity is not a perfect opposite, but at least it opposes the deceitful aspects of casuistry. This is not a problem that provides many clues for guessing. If you had an echo of its being an ignoble or bad thing, then the first three answer choices would not be attractive. Do not confuse sediment, meaning precipitated deposits at the bottom of a liquid, with sentiment, meaning feeling.

36. **(C)** Contumely is a humiliating insult. Despite the -ly ending, it is a noun and not an adverb. When there is a mixture of word types in the answer choices, you might think twice before relying only on a word ending to make eliminations. There are a number of words which have misleading endings, and some may appear on the test.

Praise is the best opposite to insult. Tractability means the ability to be easily directed onto a particular course or track.

37. **(B)** Sedulous means to be very conscientious in taking care of duty. To be derelict in one's duty is to abandon it and fail to carry it out. Vociferous means loud and assertive; concomitant means typically accompanying; itinerant means traveling; and onerous, from onus, means difficult and burdensome.

38. **(D)** Imperturbable is a good example of a word whose word parts can help you to understand it. The stem portion of this word is perturb, which means disturb, so imperturbable means undisturbable, calm. Thus, agitated, meaning in motion and, by extension, upset or disturbed, is a nearly perfect opposite. Militant means aggressive or combative; cynical is distrustful of other people's motives; conical means shaped like a cone; and flattering means something which puts you in the best light and makes the best of what you have.

SECTION II

1. **(B)** If Gene dashed across the courtyard, he might have run quickly; but since he didn't take time to think of his safety, courageously is better. Quickly only repeats what the dash already says.

2. **(A)** The loss of the *Titanic* is best described as a tragedy or a disaster. Precautions, not reservations, is the second word that is required, making (A) the correct response.

3. **(C)** As the Earth's resources are not limitless, worthless, vanished, or unavailable, only (C) logically completes this sentence.

4. **(E)** A meek spirit may comfort or console people, but it won't delight them. A juvenile spirit is immature and thus is also inappropriate. A youthful spirit, however, may be mature as well as vigorous.

5. **(B)** According to the sense of this sentence, it was merciful, not unintentional, blithe, importunate, or tragic, that the factories remained open.

6. **(C)** It follows that a hush or a quiet about an estate would concern the guards, not a pall, focus, coolness, or talent.

7. **(C)** The sentence structure tells us that one type of book is interesting but another is only good for the blank. The blank, then, is some characteristic of books that are not interesting. Furthermore, this special function of being uninteresting is

carried out near a bedside table, in other words in bed. The likely function is to help one to get to sleep, a notorious effect of uninteresting books; thus soporific, which means something that makes one sleepy, is the ideal answer. All of the other answers are ideas which could apply to books, but not particularly because they are uninteresting or at the side of a bed. Thus, (C) is the best answer.

8. **(C)** In karate the foot is a weapon. In fencing the foil—a type of sword—is a weapon. (B) has an echo of hand to foot in the second position, but this is just flack and has no merit. In (D), the ring is the arena, not any sort of equipment, thus it fails. In (A), which appeals at first because of the relationship between karate and judo, we could have had a relationship based on the fact that karate uses the foot as a weapon and judo uses the hand as a weapon. This would have some appeal even though it is not strictly accurate. However, the term chop does not refer to the weapon, but the movement of the weapon. In fencing, the equivalent of the judo chop would be the thrust or parry. Thus, (A) fails for addressing a different part of the process involved. (E) is probably the second-best answer, though it is quite poor. A bat is a piece of equipment used in the sport of baseball, but this does not say it is better than (C), but only shares some merit with (C). In addition to that equipment aspect, (C) has the idea of weapon, which is important since both karate and fencing are combat sports.

9. **(E)** The incisor and the molar are both teeth. The difference is that they have different functions. The incisor cuts and the molar grinds. The knife cuts and the hammer, being blunt like the molar, bashes and breaks up things, even if it does not quite grind. (A) is attractive since it would result in a completed analogy with four teeth. However, the canines do not cut, but rather rip, and the bicuspids are not molars but work more like the canines. It is still attractive, but does not fit very precisely. (C) is eliminated since both incisors and molars are upper and lower. (D) fails since an incisor and molar will have a much more complex relationship than merely being opposites. Even though incisive can mean sharp in a mental sense, one would not speak of someone being a molar-mind to mean they are foolish. (B) and (E) both present tools which could relate to the original pair's functions. The first word in both (B) and (E) is fine. In (B), however, the second word, file, has little to do with the action of the molars. Hammer, in (E), is not perfect, but is at least the action of a blunt instrument like the molar.

10. **(E)** Both the gourmand and the gourmet are interested in food. The gourmand is interested in quantities of food, while the gourmet is interested in the quality of food. Thus (D) expresses,

in admittedly abstract terms, the relationship between the original pair quite well. The only problem is that it is backward. However, (E) is even better since the difference between the two types of eaters is that the one will eat anything while the other, because he is interested in quality, will be selective. So the sharper difference is the indiscriminate eater versus the selective eater. Wisdom disqualifies (A), and (B) and (C) are totally unrelated. The specific food is irrelevant.

11. **(E)** A tress of hair is a lock of hair. A skein of wool is an amount of wool, probably more than a tress's worth of hair, but at least it is a special word for describing an amount. (D) does not have the relationship of an "amount" word to the thing of which there is an amount. (A), (B), and (C) are all "amount" or group words. (C) is a group word, like a gaggle of geese, and that is not the same as an amount of something. The best distinction between (A), (B), and (E) is that wool is hair and thus a tress is a collection of thin fibers (of probably human hair), and a skein is a collection of thin fibers (of wool). The other words refer to solid objects, which are a piece of something, but tress and skein refer to something consisting of many little parts. Thus, (E) is the best answer.

12. **(D)** Libel and slander are both offensive statements that are presumably incorrect and untrue, even malicious. The difference between them is that libel is written and slander is spoken. (D) perfectly catches that difference in the abstract. (A) has some of the same distinction, but is backward. Both parts of (B) and (E) refer to written work. (C) is irrelevant. Thus, (D) is the best answer.

13. **(B)** A colander is a kitchen utensil that is used to drain water off of or out of something. A sifter separates the wheat from the chaff, although in that case the wheat is the part that falls through, and the waste product, chaff, remains in the sifter. (C), (D), and (E) lack the idea of separation of the useful part of something from the waste product or non-useful part. (A) has some idea of cleaning up, but the broom does not separate dust from, say, the floor in the same way that a sifter and colander do their work. The broom merely rubs the surface and brushes dust away. The sifting action is key to the utility of the colander. Thus, (B) is the best answer.

14. **(B)** A decibel is the unit used to measure sound. Similarly, the volt is used to measure electricity. Both decibel and volt measure the "force" of the sound and electricity, but this need not be considered since none of the other choices presents a measurement and the thing measured. A calorie is not a measure of weight, but of energy. The fact that a decibel is used to measure some

quantities other than sound and that a volt is not the only measure of electricity do not disqualify the choice, but merely make it less than perfect. (B) is still clearly the best answer choice.

15. **(B)** The original pair present opposites, which are positive and negative attributes in terms of intelligence. (E) fails for being synonyms, and (D) has much the same problem. (A) has some idea of mental ability and oppositeness, but even if it had scholarly rather than scholar, the oppositeness is not very precise, and the original pair are very precise opposites indeed. (C) has no opposite meaning. This leaves (B), which has precisely opposite parts and which also has a positive and negative connotation in the same direction as the original pair. Thus, (B) is the best answer.

16. **(D)** A queue is a line of people in a particular order, such as a line waiting to get something. All of the answer choices have the meaning of a grouping of things, but (A) and (B) are merely undifferentiated groupings. (E) has no feel of being a line of anything. (D) and (C) both have some idea of being stretched out, but (D) does this much more than (C). (E) presents the problem of the idea of order that is present in a queue. A file of letters need not be in order, but even if it is, the image of a queue, which is a physical concept, is much more like a string than a file.

17. **(C)** Since the excitation is the force leading to the occurrence of the response, and the inhibition is the force leading to the non-occurrence of the response, the fact that the response does not occur indicates that the inhibition is greater than the excitation. (B) and (D) are outside the scope of the passage, and thus incorrect. (A) fails since once a response does not occur, its latency period is not relevant, nor does it exist. (E) fails when (C) succeeds.

18. **(B)** Since the theory holds that there is always a finite amount of inhibition and that the inhibition can be increased by the right experimental actions, it can be inferred that there is always some possibility of getting the response to fail, given enough time and energy. In other words, continuing support is required, even if there can be occasional lapses.

(A) is incorrect since training can include training to reduce the response or to increase it at any point. After the twists and turns of (C) are plumbed, what it means is that responses might not differ, which is certainly possible. (D) is certainly possible, for the same reason that (B) is not. (E) is the second-best answer choice since the issue of measurement is not directly addressed in the passage. There is a finite amount of the two forces at all times. From that, it can be concluded that it can be measured, though we do not need to meet the claim that it is currently known how to

measure it, but only that it is measurable in principle.

19. **(C)** Latency is, of course, defined in the passage, and the most usual situation would be for the correct answer to be either the passage's definition or some paraphrase of that. Sometimes, as in this case, the correct answer is a somewhat derived concept. If latency is the time that it takes for an action to occur after the stimulus is applied, then it is a measure of the tendency for the action not to occur at all. In addition, the passage itself explicitly says that there is such a connection; thus, (C) is the best answer. The others are all either not specifically related to the passage or wrong.

20. **(B)** The references to the shires and London are detailed and imply a closeness to hand. (A), France, is only mentioned with one reference, and thus is not as good as (B). America, (C), is only supported by a reference to North America, which is insufficiently detailed to override the English references. (D) is nowhere mentioned.

21. **(C)** The only trick here is to remember that the third line of a syllogism does not always have the word thus or its equivalent. The other methods are all in the passage, but not for this sort of reasoning. (See also the instructional materials for the Logical Reasoning questions.)

22. **(B)** While it is true that the use of apples gives the story a pedestrian flavor, this is merely to exemplify the author's view that there is real reasoning even in very ordinary events. The apples are the subject of an analogy between the situation with them and all everyday reasoning, which is likened and explained through that example. (C) has a little merit, but (B) is far better since it goes with the basic ideas of the passage. (D) is attractive, but it is false since the author shows how common logic is, not how foolish. (A) and (E) are merely flack.

23. **(A)** While the answer choice of "philosopher" would be better yet, the scientist's reference to experimental method and logic make (A) the best available choice. All the others may use logic and experiment, of course, but the topic here is science—in the sense of its root, meaning knowing—not art, fiction, economics, or business, nor the distinguishing methods of those fields.

24. **(C)** The passage notes that you establish a natural law as the result of the induction in just those words—hence, (C). (D) and (E) are other meanings of the term natural law, but not the ones used in this particular passage. (A) and (B) have little connection to the passage.

25. **(E)** All the answer choices reflect part of the

passage, but (E) covers the largest portion of the passage, and thus is best. Each of the others can be subsumed under it since (A) is the example used, and (B), (C), and (D) are the methods of everyday reasoning brought out through the use of the example of apples.

26. **(D)** The law of apples is a construct based, as noted in the passage, on experimental verification of an induction. If further verification should show that the law is not perfect, then it must be modified as (D) suggests. (C) is particularly attractive, but the word usually makes it fail, since it is still the case that hard and green apples are usually sour. If (C) had said always, it would have been hard to refuse.

   (A) is subsumed under (D) and is incorrect in supposing that the nature of apples has changed, when it is only that our original understanding of them proved to be inadequate. (B), while attractive in the real world, where tasty apples are all too rare, has little to do with standardized tests. Since (A), (B), and (C) are faulty, (E) does not apply.

27. **(C)** Extensive verification is brought up in the last part of the passage as something that makes an argument or proposed general law more attractive. Proposition I is just flack. There is nothing in the passage that says whether general laws are harder or easier to prove or disprove than any other kind of law. Proposition III is precisely what the passage does say. This is why the friend will find it persuasive for you to show him that the law has been tested in a variety of situations. Proposition II is a bit of precision reading that turns on the word tested. Tested means that something is put to some sort of test; it does not mean that the something passed the test. The reason that II is attractive is that a law or proposal that was not passing its tests would soon be dropped and no longer subjected to tests. Thus, there is a potential for erroneously leaping from the fact that something was widely tested to the conclusion that it passed most of its tests. This is, however, based on an idea not present in the passage.

28. **(C)** A profusion is a great number, even an overabundance. A scarcity is an excellent opposite. A travesty is a bizarre and vastly inferior imitation. Antidote, meaning something which counteracts some poison or disease, might have some appeal if profusion were misinterpreted to be a medical term of some sort.

29. **(E)** Temperate means moderate, but is not a general synonym for moderate. Temperate applies to passions, appetites, and temperature and has a special meaning of not drinking alcohol. This special meaning derives from the temperance movement and supports inebriated as an opposite.

A more general opposite, such as extreme, would be stronger, but is not present. Unlimited has some appeal since it has a non-moderate feel to it, but without limit is not as good as inebriated because temperate is not as general a word as is unlimited. This is a fairly tough choice. Truncated means cut off short.

30. **(A)** Mitigation means amelioration or lessening of some harm or evil. Aggravation means increasing some harm or evil—one would not speak of aggravating one's love for something. Verdancy means greenness, especially with plants. Imposition has some opposite feel to mitigation since mitigating a condition can reduce the burden or even lift the burden. But this is a derived, or two-step, connection, which is only rarely a sound basis for a correct answer.

31. **(B)** Iniquity means a gross injustice, hence evil. There is a definite moral tone. Fairness and rectitude are both strong answers. Fairness is a weaker level of moral correctness than is rectitude. Rectitude means great goodness, and iniquity means great evil. Apostasy is a total abandonment of one's principles or cause.

32. **(C)** A protuberance is something that sticks out. An indentation is the opposite since it is a portion of a surface that recedes or is forced inward. Recession itself has merit, but is a more general word in which one would speak of the entire sea or wave receding as opposed to a portion sticking out. Cadence is rhythmic modulation or the beat of something, usually a voice. A habitation is a place that is lived in or inhabited, such as a home or house.

33. **(A)** Effulgence means a bright shining or radiance. Murk is darkness. Harshness may erroneously appeal if effulgence is confused with indulgence. A mercenary is someone who is hired, usually to fight. Mundane means commonplace or ordinary.

34. **(B)** To ameliorate is to mitigate or make less severe, as in to ameliorate the effects of a disease. Worsen is the precise opposite. Dissemble means to deceive or lie.

35. **(D)** Benign means harmless or well intentioned. Evil is a clear opposite. Sick may appeal because of the association to benign tumors not usually being as serious as malignant tumors. Morose means sad.

36. **(A)** Salutary means healthful and noxious means unhealthful or even poisonous. Objectionable has a negative connotation which opposes the positive connotation of salutary, but there is no specific meaning of health. Moderate has no real connection. Neither does farewell, but it might be

attractive if you thought that salutary had something to do with a salute or greeting. Actually, a salute originally meant a wish for good health, but no longer. Antiseptic is, if anything, similar to the stem word.

37. **(C)** Alienate means, literally, to make an alien of someone, which is the opposite of making friends of them. (A) is an attempt to appeal to the oppositeness of alien and native, but alienate does not mean to go alien.

38. **(B)** A drollery is an amusing statement since droll means amusing. (D) has some appeal since witty has to do with drollness, perhaps. However, there is no necessary idea of a drollery being an aside.

SECTION III

1. **(D)** Since we do not know the value of any of the coins, we cannot know the value of 2, 3, 4, or even of a dozen coins. For that reason, our answer must be (D). We don't even know they are U.S. coins.

2. **(B)** Since the first equation shows only one variable, it makes sense to start our attack there, solving for x. If $x + 7 = 8$, then $x = 1$. Once we know that $x = 1$, we can substitute that value into the second equation:

$$x + y = 6$$
$$1 + y = 6$$
$$y = 5$$

Now that we have determined that $x = 1$ and $y = 5$, we can conclude that Column B is greater than Column A.

3. **(C)** The $\sqrt{9} = 3$. Thus the two columns must be equal. (Note that a printed $\sqrt{}$ sign should be interpreted as a positive root.)

4. **(D)** We can deduce that Jack is taller than Mike. But the information we are given does not allow us to reach any conclusion about the *difference* between their heights. Consequently, we do not know how much taller Jack is than Mike.

5. **(B)** Although we do counsel performing an indicated operation, e.g., multiplication, we have also cautioned against undertaking unwieldy or hopelessly complicated arithmetic or algebra. In this case, it would probably require too much time to perform the multiplication indicated in the right-hand column. A quick glance should show that there will be a n^4 term, some n^3's, some n^2's, some n's and 6. That realization shows that the multiplication is much too involved for the time allowed by the section. It also provides the

answer. We can see that even if we used just the last two expressions, we would have $n^2 + 5n + 6$. The expression in Column A is only $3n + 6$. Since $n > 1$, more n's make Column B greater than Column A.

6. **(C)** Since there are three feet in a yard, the radius of the circle mentioned in Column A is equal to the radius of the circle mentioned in Column B. Circles with radii which are equal must have areas which are equal, so our answer is (C). You did not need to compute the areas and should not have tried until trying this method.

7. **(A)** The negative of a negative number is a positive number. So the negative of negative 4 is a positive 4. Column B is negative while Column A is positive, so Column A must be the larger.

8. **(C)** This is a variation on the standard children's riddle, "Which weighs more, a pound of feathers or a pound of lead?" Of course, they both weigh the same. A pound of any substance is a pound. Surprisingly, however, just such a problem has appeared on the GRE, so we remind students of the importance of carefully reading each question.

9. **(A)** We must begin by determining the greatest integer or whole number less than -10. Since the larger the absolute value (the numerical value) of a negative number, the smaller the actual value of that number, the greatest integer which is less than -10 is -11. That is the largest integer which is still less than -10. When we square -11, we get a positive 121. So Column A is greater than Column B.

10. **(B)** Try to find a way of comparing the fractions without doing extra work. We can reduce $\frac{34}{68}$ to $\frac{1}{2}$. Then, when we square $\frac{1}{2}$, Column A becomes $\frac{1}{4}$ while Column B is $\frac{1}{2}$, so Column B is greater. Any number multiplied by a fraction gets smaller.

11. **(C)** In this case, before performing any multiplication, we must try to cancel like terms. This simplifies the problem to such an extent that no multiplication is really needed:

$$1/2 \times 2/3 \times 3/4 \times 4/5 = x$$
$$1/5 = x$$

And our two columns are equal.

12. **(C)** To discuss this problem clearly, let us add the points T and U. QR and SR are the same for both perimeters, so we don't need to consider them further. The same applies to ST and QU. This leaves the four sides of PUVT. PUVT must be a rectangle since angle P and angle V are right angles. Since PUVT is a rectangle, the opposite sides are equal, which is to say that PT = UV and

UP = VT. Thus the two perimeters are equal.

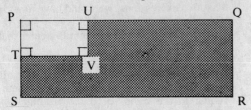

13.   **(A)**   In this problem it is best to do the indicated operation in Column A so that the comparison is easier.

$$-2(-x - 2) = 2x + 4$$

Now we can strip the 2x from both sides of the comparison (technically by subtracting 2x from both sides). Then we are left comparing +4 in Column A with −4 in Column B, so Column A must be greater.

14.   **(D)**   The common information simply makes both x and y positive and greater than 1. This means that both columns are positive. You are always trying to see what connections can be made between the quantities in the two columns. In this case, it is possible for x to equal y. In that case we would have x^2 versus 2x, which is a (D) answer.

   Another approach, which is also quite effective and efficient in this sort of problem, is substitution. When you are considering substitution, you should be choosing numbers that are both easy to compute with and usefully varied. Normally, positive and negative numbers are good to substitute with; but we only have positive numbers, so we want to use numbers at the ends of our available range. Since x and y can be equal, it is easiest to start the substituting with both the same. First try 1.1 for each, which yields (1.1)(1.1) = 1.21 in Column A and 1.1 + 1.1 = 2.2 in Column B. Since B is greater, answer choices (A) and (C) are eliminated.

   A second substitution could be 10, yielding (10)(10) = 100 in Column A and 10 + 10 = 20 in Column B. Since A is larger, that eliminates B as an answer choice, leaving (D).

15.   **(D)**   We cannot assume that the figure is a square:

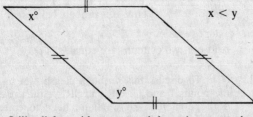

Still, all four sides are equal, but x is not equal to y.

16.   **(B)**   There is no mystical math formula which you are supposed to know in order to solve this problem. It is merely a matter of counting up the possibilities. Thus there are four ways of getting nine as the problem specifies. (8 + 1 is the same thing as 1 + 8.)

17.   **(A)**   This problem asks you to divide feet and inches. You could convert the whole length into inches, getting 93 inches divided by three and giving an answer of 31 inches, or 2 feet 7 inches. Alternatively, you could divide three into seven feet, getting two feet, and then carry the other foot over into the inches as 12 inches. Twelve inches plus the nine inches is 21 inches, which yields seven inches when divided by three. The latter approach is a little more direct, but also has more opportunities for error.

18.   **(D)**   Since all three variables are integers, we know that K is a number that is both a perfect square and a perfect cube (perfect means that a number is the square or cube of an integer). Eight and 27 are not perfect squares and 4 is not a perfect cube. 64 does work, since $8^2 = 4^3 = 64$.

19.   **(D)**   The only formula for the area of a triangle that you need on this test is A = bh/2. The base is the distance from R to S, which is 7 units. The height is the distance from T to the Y axis, which is 5 units. Using the formula we get (7)(5)/2 = 17.5 units.

20.   **(D)**   Since the test will permit only one answer to be correct, give the choices a once-over to try and find some simple answer. (D) is it since 3 can be cancelled from the top and bottom of the fraction to give P/Q. (C) may have some attraction, but it yields $(P/Q)^2$ not P/Q.

21.   **(A)**   Since ACB is a straight line, ∠ACD + ∠DCE + ∠ECB = 180°. You are told that $\overline{DC}$ is perpendicular to $\overline{CE}$, which means that ∠DCE = 90°. If ∠ACD = x°, then the first equation looks like this: x° + 90° + ∠ECB = 180°. Moving x and the 90° to the right leaves ∠ECB = 180° − 90° − x = 90° − x.

22.   **(E)**   Knowing the length of the hypotenuse of a right triangle does not tell you what the sides are as the diagrams below indicate:

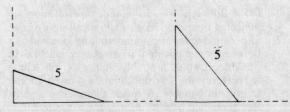

There might be some temptation to think that because the hypotenuse is 5, the other two sides must be 3 and 4. However, 3, 4, and 5 represent a special case of the right triangle not because they are the only solutions with a hypotenuse of 5, but because they are the only way to have the lengths of the sides be integers. The following is an acceptable right triangle with a hypotenuse of 5: $5^2 = (\sqrt{5})^2 + (\sqrt{20})^2$; so the sides could be 5, $\sqrt{5}$, $\sqrt{20}$.

23. **(A)** Taxes are 12% of monthly income. If monthly income is $650, then taxes are 12% × $650 = $78.00.

24. **(D)** In a pie chart, the entire circle represents 100%. The total number of degrees around the center of a circle is 360. Thus 100% = 360°. Clothing, taxes, and transportation total 35%. 35% × 360° = 126°.

25. **(C)** It is important to note that the boy answered all of the questions. This gives you a way of relating the total correct answers and total wrong answers. Before setting up a system of equations, let us try a shortcut. The heart of the matter is that the boy did not get them all right. If he had gotten them all right, he would have scored 100. If he missed one, then he would have lost the 4 plus points AND he would have another point taken off. This means that, compared to 100, he loses 5 points for each of the 25 problems he got wrong instead of right. Since he actually scored 70, he actually lost 30 points. 30 points divided by 5 points per error means he made 6 errors. 25 questions − 6 errors leaves 19 correct. A system of equations would look like this:

Let x = number of questions correct. 25 − x = number of questions wrong.
$$\text{Then } 4x - 1(25 - x) = 70$$
$$4x - 25 + x = 70$$
$$5x = 95$$
$$x = 19$$

26. **(D)** The temptation here is to simply average 40 MPH and 60 MPH and choose the wrong answer, (E). The reason that you cannot just average the speeds is that speed is PER HOUR and the hours are different. The trip took longer at 40 MPH than at 60 MPH. A speed is a fraction with some number of miles on top and some number of hours underneath. If you travelled for one hour at 40 MPH and one hour at 60 MPH, then you would have gone 100 miles in 2 hours and would have averaged 50 MPH. This case is very different.

You should think of what information you need to compute an average rate of speed. You need the total miles and you need the total time. To find the total miles and hours, you have to add together the miles and the hours respectively for the two legs of the trip, and then make the division of miles per hour.

Let the number of miles traveled each way = M

$$\text{The time going} = \frac{\text{distance}}{\text{rate}} = \frac{M}{60}$$

$$\text{The time coming} = \frac{M}{40}$$

$$\text{Total time for round trip} = \frac{M}{60} + \frac{M}{40}$$

$$= \frac{2M + 3M}{120} = \frac{5M}{120} = \frac{M}{24}$$

Average rate =

$$\frac{\text{total distance}}{\text{total time}} = \frac{2M}{\frac{M}{24}} = 48 \text{ miles per hour.}$$

27. **(D)** The total work that is to be done is six tractors times 8 hours = 48 tractor-hours of work. Four tractors will thus take $\frac{48 \text{ tractor-hours}}{4 \text{ tractors}} = 12$ hours.

28. **(E)** In comparing fractions, one important separation is between the fractions which are larger than 1 and those which are smaller. (B), $\sqrt{5}$, is larger than 1. All the others have bottom parts larger than their tops and thus are smaller than 1. (A), (C), and (E) can be compared directly since they all have the same top, 1. When fractions have the same top, the largest bottom will denote the smaller fraction since the same quantity is being divided into more parts. $5\sqrt{5} > 5 > \sqrt{5}$; therefore, (E) is smaller than (A) or (C) or, as previously established, (B). All that remains is to compare (E) to (D). (E) has both a larger bottom and a smaller top than (D) and thus (E) is smaller. Note that, in this case, you did not have to actually compute the values of any of the possibilities.

29. **(A)** Since your money available with which to buy melons is in cents, it is probably easiest to put the price of melons into cents as well. The cost of melons is $\frac{100d \text{ cents}}{30 \text{ melons}}$, which is to say $\frac{100d}{30}$ cents per melon. We know that the purchasing power of our 80 cents will be 80 cents divided by the cost per melon. We now have the cost per melon and can go ahead.

$$\frac{80 \text{ cents}}{\dfrac{100d \text{ cents}}{30 \text{ melons}}}$$

To divide by a fraction, the rule is to invert the fraction and multiply: 80 cents $\times \dfrac{30 \text{ melons}}{100d \text{ cents}} = \dfrac{2400 \text{ melons}}{100d \text{ cents}} = \dfrac{24}{d}$ melons. Those partial to the ratio method might work this way: Let x = the number of melons you can buy for 80 cents. Then $\dfrac{30}{100d} = \dfrac{x}{80}$, 100dx = 2400, and $x = \dfrac{24}{d}$.

30. **(B)** Consecutive odd numbers, where n is an integer, may be represented as

$$2n + 1$$
$$2n + 3$$
$$\underline{2n + 5}$$

Sum = 6n + 9
Always divisible by 3. Thus, only II.

The key is to remember that an odd number is always one more than an even number. Another, similar approach would be to represent the three numbers as x + (x + 2) + (x + 4) = 3x + 6, which is always divisible by 3.

SECTION IV

1. **(A)** The simplest approach is to substitute (−1) for x:
Col. A: $x^3 + x^2 - x + 1 = (-1)^3 + (-1)^2 - (-1) + 1$
$= -1 + 1 + 1 + 1$
$= 2$
Col. B: $x^3 - x^2 + x - 1 = (-1)^3 - (-1)^2 + (-1) - 1$
$= -1 - 1 - 1 - 1$
$= -4$

You might have omitted the x^3 term in evaluating each column since it is the same in each column.

2. **(C)** Setting the edge length as e, we get:

Col. A	Col. B
$e^3 = 27$	$6e^2 = 54$
$e = 3$	$e^2 = 9$
$e = 3$

3. **(A)** You know it cannot be (D) since it is all numbers. In addition, looking, as always, for connections between the columns, you see that the two columns are reciprocals. So knowing one will give you the other. You could calculate Column A, for instance:

$$\frac{\frac{1}{2} + \frac{1}{3}}{\frac{2}{3}} = \frac{\frac{3+2}{6}}{\frac{2}{3}}$$

$$= \frac{\frac{5}{6}}{\frac{2}{3}}$$

$$= \frac{\frac{15}{12}}{1} \quad \text{multiplying numerator and denominator by } \frac{3}{2})$$

$$= \frac{15}{12}$$

But you don't need to do this if you can see that in Column A the top of the fraction $(\frac{1}{2} + \frac{1}{3})$ is bigger than the bottom $(\frac{2}{3})$. That means Column A is > 1, and Column B, its reciprocal, must be < 1, giving answer (A).

4. **(B)** When you square a fraction, you are multiplying it by a fraction, so it gets smaller. Conversely, taking the square root of a fraction or other number between zero and +1 gets larger. Thus:

$$.02 = \sqrt{.0004}$$
$$\sqrt{.02} > \sqrt{.0004}$$

5. **(C)** Since you have squares of the lengths of the sides and a right triangle, the Pythagorean Theorem should leap to mind. Column A is the hypotenuse squared, so we must see if Column B is the sum of the squares of the other two sides. $(AC)^2$ is one side squared and 5CB is the other because CB = 5.

6. **(A)** This is not a computational question. The real issue is noticing how the two figures would fit together. As the diagram below makes clear, the circle is much larger.

7. **(B)** Column B is simply the distance from −1 to +5, which is 6. For Column A we can construct a right triangle in this way:

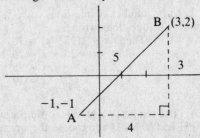

As often is the case, it is a 3–4–5 right triangle, leaving Column A as 5. Thus, (B) is the answer.

8. **(D)** If we had been told the two bottom angles of the triangle, $\angle B$ and $\angle C$, were equal, then we would know x = y by subtraction from the straight line. As it is, the knowledge that $\angle C = \angle A$ does not tell us anything about $\angle B$, which we would need in order to know x.

9. **(C)** Since the heights and bases of the triangle DEC and the parallelogram are the same, $\triangle DEC$ is equal in area to one-half the parallelogram.

Therefore, the area of $\triangle DEC$ equals the combined areas of $\triangle ADE$ and $\triangle EBC$.

10. **(D)** Nothing is tying down B or C, so the joints are flexible and no fixed relationship between $\angle B$ and $\angle C$ is to be found.

11. **(D)** While both sides are positive, since a negative squared is positive, no size information is given. For example a could be -1 and b could be 2 or a could be -1 and b could be 12.

12. **(D)** We only know that both r and t are the same sign, but no magnitudes are known.

13. **(A)** This is one of the rare Quantitative Comparison computational problems. Shaded areas are usually found by subtracting one area from another or by addition. Here, the shaded area is the outer circle minus the inner one.

$$\begin{pmatrix} \text{Area of} \\ \text{shaded} \\ \text{portion} \end{pmatrix} = \begin{pmatrix} \text{Area of} \\ \text{larger} \\ \text{circle} \end{pmatrix} - \begin{pmatrix} \text{Area of} \\ \text{smaller} \\ \text{circle} \end{pmatrix}$$

$$= \pi(10^2) - \pi(7^2)$$
$$= 100\pi - 49\pi$$
$$= 51\pi$$

$$\begin{pmatrix} \text{Area of} \\ \text{smaller} \\ \text{circle} \end{pmatrix} = \pi r^2$$
$$= \pi(7^2)$$
$$= 49\pi$$
$$51\pi > 49\pi$$

14. **(C)** No calculation is needed. Just set it up: $(4)(\frac{1}{100})(\frac{3}{1000})$ versus $(3)(\frac{1}{100})(\frac{4}{1000})$.

15. **(C)** Since PR = PQ, angles PRQ and PQR are equal. Since $\angle PRQ = x$ and $\angle PQR = y$, x = y as well.

AB $\parallel$ DF and BD $\parallel$ FG, but $x° \neq y°$.

16. **(A)** The dimensions of the open box become:

length = $24 - 10 = 14$ in.
width = $18 - 10 = 8$ in.
height = 5 in.
$V = h \cdot l \cdot w$

Hence, $V = 14 \cdot 8 \cdot 5 = 560$ cu. in.

17. **(B)** VT = 32 feet so that ST = $\frac{1}{2}$TV = 16 feet. Thus, in right triangle QST, the legs are $12 = 4(3)$ and $16 = 4(4)$, so that hypotenuse QT = $4(5) = 20$ feet. Add 1 foot for the extension and we get QR = 21 feet.

18. **(C)** Form the proportion $\frac{3\frac{3}{4}}{9} = \frac{7\frac{7}{8}}{x}$, where x is the side in miles. Then $\frac{3}{4}x = \frac{7}{8} \cdot 9$. Multiply both sides by 8.

$$6x = 7 \cdot 9 = 63$$
$$x = 10\frac{1}{2} \text{ miles}$$

Area = $x^2 = \frac{21}{2} \cdot \frac{21}{2} = \frac{441}{4} = 110\frac{1}{4}$ square miles.

19. **(D)** The tens digit of a number has a place value which is ten times the value of the digit. Hence, the number may be represented as $10t + u$.

20. **(C)** Highest point of curve occurred in February, when it reached 600.

21. **(A)** Highest was 600.
Lowest was about 450.

Ratio $= \frac{600}{450} = \frac{4}{3}$

22. **(E)** From July '65 to Sept. '66, the average dropped from 525 to 450, about 75 points, which was the steepest decline.

23. **(E)** 5 is written ten times in the units column of the pages: 5, 15 . . . 95; and ten times in the tens column: 50, 51 . . . 59.

24. **(A)** The key here is to focus on the minute hands alone. The fast clock gains 24 minutes. The slow clock loses 12 minutes. The fast clock reads 12:24. The slow clock reads 11:48.

25. **(B)** The divisors of 28 are 14, 7, 4, 2, 1. The sum of these is 28, making it a perfect number. This does not apply to the other numbers listed.

26. **(C)** Let x = number of minutes per period. There are 4 class periods and 3 passing periods from 9 A.M. to 11:51 A.M., or in 2 hr. 51 minutes. Hence:

$$4x + 3(5) = 120 + 51$$
$$4x + 15 = 171$$
$$4x = 156$$
$$x = 39$$

27. **(E)** Since the perimeter involves 3 fenced-in sides, it is true that $L + 2W = 90$. Also, the area is LW. If we solve the first equation for L, we obtain $L = 90 - 2W$. Now substitute in area = LW, giving area = $W(90 - 2W) = 90W - 2W^2$. Let W = 20 in this equation, giving area = 1000. Hence, A, B, C, D are all true.
Now substitute L = W in the first equation;
$$W + 2W = 90, 3W = 90, W = 30$$
When W = 30, area = $90(30) - 2(30^2)$
$$= 2,700 - 1,800 = 900$$
But this area is less than when W = 20.
Hence, E is not true.

28. **(B)** Discount = $90 - 75 = \$15$
Rate of Discount = $\frac{15}{90} = \frac{1}{6} = 16\frac{2}{3}\%$

29. **(D)** The two semicircles make up the circumference of one circle of diameter 60 yd. Hence, the circumference = $\pi 60$. The sum of the two lengths of the rectangle is 200. Thus, the perimeter is equal to $200 + 60\pi$.

30. **(D)** No matter what happens, x cannot quite equal the sum of the other two sides, or 10. If $\angle P = 90°$, then we have a 45–45–90 right triangle, so $x = 5\sqrt{2}$. Any time you have a range on the GRE, you need concern yourself only with the ends of the range.

SECTION V

Questions 1–3

Arranging the Information

This is clearly a process situation with some element of transformation since one puts in one color of token and gets another. Thus, a labelled-arrow method seems appropriate. The restriction that a player may possess only one token at a time is not essential in making the diagram, but must be kept in mind for the questions.

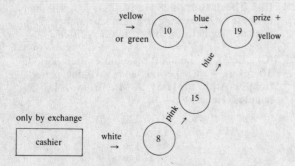

Answering the Questions

1. **(C)** There is no specification about getting a green token. (A) is specified in several ways. (B) is specified since the yellow token which is obtained with the prize can be used to get another prize. (D) is specified since any other color of token may start one enroute to a prize, and a yellow token may be obtained along with a prize. The most salient thing not specified is how to get your first token. However, the question does not present that as an available answer choice, so you must look for something else that is not specified, which is (C).

2. **(B)** After winning a prize, a player is in possession of one yellow token. (Remember, only one token per customer at a time.) With only a yellow token, a player cannot play slots 15, 19, or 8; so (C), (D), and (E) are wrong. (A) is incorrect since the cashier will not exchange a white token for a yellow token. (B) is possible since slot 10 uses yellow tokens.

3. **(E)** Just follow through the diagram. If you have a green token, you can go through the slots 10 and 19, or you can go and exchange the green token for a white one and go through that branch of the procedure, following up by going through the 10, 19 cycle. Thus, you can get whichever color of token you want. You could, of course, stop at any point and keep that token. The phrase all the other colors refers to all the other colors that are mentioned in the problem.

4. **(E)** The main point of the advertisement is that you should not hesitate to buy Cold Springs Water even though it is not imported. According to the ad, you will not be able to taste the difference. Thus, I is an assumption of the ad: "Neither you nor your guests will taste the difference," and it is explicitly mentioned. We know it is an assumption for if there were a taste difference, the appeal of the ad would be seriously undermined. III is an assumption, too—but it is hidden or suppressed. Implicit in the ad is a rebuttal to the objection: "Yes, but it is not imported." Whether it is imported or not can have only to do with status since the ad also states (assumes) that the tastes of Cold Springs and imported waters are indistinguishable. II is not an assumption. Although it is mentioned that Cold Springs is bottled at the source, the ad does not depend on where other imported or domestic waters are bottled. They could be bottled fifty miles away from the source, and that would not affect the appeal of the ad.

5. **(A)** The argument makes the rather outlandish assumption that the physical characteristics of the criminal dictate the kind of crime he will commit. But as unreasonable as that may seem in light of common sense, it *is* an assumption made by the speaker. (We did not make the assumption, he did.) II is not an assumption of the argument, since the paragraph specifically states that the killer was executed—he could not have escaped. III does not commit the blatant error committed by II, but it is still wrong. Although III might be a better explanation for the crimes now being committed than that proposed by our speaker, our speaker advances the explanation supported by I, not III. In fact, the speaker uses phrases such as "looks very much like" which tells us that he assumes there are two killers.

6. **(E)** The ad is a little deceptive. It tries to create the impression that if hospitals are using Dr. John's Milk of Magnesia, people will believe it is a good product. But what the ad actually says is that Dr. John uses the same *ingredient* that hospitals use (milk of magnesia is a simple suspension of magnesium hydroxide in water). The ad is something like an ad for John's Vinegar which claims it has "acetic acid," which is vinegar. I falls into the trap of the ad and is therefore wrong. II is not inferable since there may be treatments other than milk of magnesia for these disorders. Finally, since I is incorrect, III must certainly also be incorrect. Even if I had been true, III might still be questionable since use and recommendation are not identical.

Questions 7–11

Arranging the Information

Since the transfer from clan to clan takes place upon reaching adulthood, a person can be referred to either by the clan into which they were born or by the one in which they are adults. The requirement that only mature Ater may marry simply keeps order. The basic information can be organized in this way

MEN		WOMEN	
BORN	ADULT	BORN	ADULT
1	2	1	3
2	3	2	1
3	1	3	2

Answering the Questions

7. **(A)** Answers (C) and (D) are flack and can be dismissed.

The nephew we are seeking is the son of a sister OR of a brother. Since marriage is permitted only within a clan, the question is whether the nephew can ever be the same clan.

The woman and her brother or sister would have been born into the same clan—the first. Sisters born into the first clan would both become third-clan adults and the son of a third-clan person becomes a first-clan adult and is not able to marry the third-clan adult woman who is the subject of the question. This eliminates (B).

A brother and sister born into the first clan would be in separate clans as adults, the woman moving to the third and the man to second. The brother's son would be born second clan and be a third-clan adult, who is eligible to marry his aunt. Hence, (A). (E) is eliminated by this reasoning also.

8. **(E)** An adult second-clan male was born into the first clan, thus, both parents must be first-clan adults. The father, as an adult first-clan male, must have been born third clan, which gives the answer (E). The mother, as a first-clan adult, must have been born into the second clan.

9. **(E)** Tracing the lineage:

BABY 3 → MOTHER 3 ADULT → 1 BORN → GRANDMOTHER 1 ADULT → 2 BORN → GREATGRANDMOTHER 2 ADULT → 3 BORN.

10. **(D)** Tracing the lineage possibilities:

GRANDDAUGHTER 2 ADULT → 3 BORN → (branch here)

because the subject of the question could be related through either the father or the mother of the granddaughter.

→ FATHER/SON ADULT 3 → BORN 2, AND THUS GRANDFATHER IS A 2 OR → MOTHER/DAUGHTER ADULT 3 → BORN 1, THUS GRANDFATHER IS A 1.

Note that we are concerned only with the adult status of the subject of the question since he is clearly an adult now.

11. **(C)** I is inferable since a sister and brother are born into the same clan and move in different directions, and thus cannot marry each other.

II is inferable since a son will move out of his birth clan and his mother will stay in it. Thus, they cannot marry.

III is not inferable since it is possible for the grandson to be the same clan as the grandmother, and clan membership is the only restriction on who may marry whom. For example:

woman adult 3 → daughter born 3 → adult 2 → grandson born 2 → adult 3, same as grandmother.

Questions 12–16

Arranging the Information

This is similar to an elevator problem or any other sequence or arrival and departure problem. You can refer to the express stops as 1 through 8, with 3 and 6 not used. P gets off earlier than Q, with three on after 8.

10	20	30	40	50	60	70	80	
		xx			xx			3 left
		P < Q						

Answering the Questions

12. **(C)** J is M + 2. At first it seems as though M can get off anywhere except 30th and 60th (10th is not possible). But since there is the two-stop differential, J cannot get off at 10th, 20th, 30th, 50th, (because M can't leave at 30th), 60th, or 80th (because M can't get off at 60th). This leaves only 40th and 70th.

13. **(B)** The seeming addition of information actually does nothing except to specify which were the three who were still on the bus after 80th. There are four passengers and five available exit stops (20th, 40th, 50th, 70th, and 80th), so I and II are both possible. III however is not known for sure since the unused stop could have been any other available stop. Hence, (B).

14. **(D)** Learning that K and L got off before 80th, coupled with the information that P and Q also got off before 80th, means that J, M, and N are still on the bus. Thus, (A), (B), and (C) are true. The original information tells us that (D) must be false.

15. **(B)** If M precedes P, and therefore Q, this couples with the original information that P preceded Q to produce M P Q. Since Q had to wait through at least two available stops, he could not have exited at either 20th or 40th, but used 50th, 70th, or 80th, but the question stem rules out 70th, leaving (B).

    (A) is not necessarily true since the fourth departing passenger may have left at the same time as M, P, or Q.

    (C) is not necessarily true since P could have left as early as 40th. (D) and (E) fail since we do not even know that J left at all.

16. **(D)** We know from the original information that three of the original persons were still on the bus after 80th Street, so the answer cannot be (A) or (B).

    X enters on 20th and leaves at 50th, Y enters at 30th and leaves at 70th, but Z enters at 40th and leaves at 90th, thus adding one to the three otherwise known to be on the bus after 80th. Hence, (D).

Questions 17–23

Arranging the Information

Previewing the question stems and the information set shows that the concern of this question is the schedule of events at the foundation. You really don't care what the names of the courses are, though the fact that three of them begin with E and two with P means that you need at least two letter abbreviations. Probably a syllable is best, so you can recognize the answer choices most easily.

Since the schedule is organized by the months of the year, the diagram should be too:

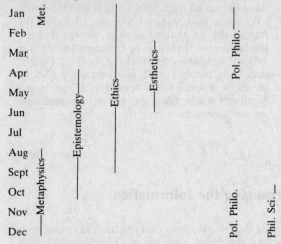

Answering the Questions

Most of these answers will be matters of checking the chart:

17. **(B)** February has the fewest available classes of any of the answer choices available. July also has only two classes, but is not an available answer choice.

18. **(D)** The phrase *a single month* refers to a single calendar month since that is the way that month is used in the problem. October and April both have four lectures each.

19. **(E)** The qualification "without overlap" is the key here. (A), (B), and (C) do not fill the year, and (D) fills the year with an overlap during January to April. (E) fills the year neatly.

20. **(A)** The simplest way to figure this out is just to take any one of the courses and then check the remaining months. Metaphysics covers August through January, leaving February through July. Epistemology covers April through July of that and Esthetics adds March, leaving only February uncovered. Hence, 11 months are needed to hear the three series.

21. **(C)** This is just a matter of counting. Epistemology, Ethics, and Political Philosophy all last longer than six months.

22. **(D)** This question is asking just what it says: how many of the series can be attended, not how many lectures. In September there are three series running and in October two more start, for a total of 5.

23. **(C)** Here the issue is how many different lectures can be heard. Three are available in January, two in February, and three more in March, for a total of 8.

24. **(D)** The question contains a hidden assumption: that the person questioned agrees that his company has, in the past, discriminated. So I is applicable since the speaker may wish to answer neither "yes" nor "no." He may wish to object to the question: "But I do not admit that our company has ever discriminated, so your question is unfair." III is just another way of describing the difficulty we have just outlined. II is not applicable to the question. Since a simple question never actually makes a statement, it would seem impossible for it to contradict itself. A contradiction occurs only between statements or assertions.

25. **(A)** There are two weaknesses in Ms. Rose's argument: she reaches a very general conclusion on the basis of one example and her argument overlooks the possibility that an education can be valuable even if it is not used to make a living. Importantly, Rose may be correct in her criticism of the man she mentions—we need make no judgment about that—but the assumption is nonetheless *unsupported* in that she gives no arguments to support it. (B) plays on the superficial detail of the paragraph—the inversion of customary role models. But that is not relevant to the structure of the argument; the form could have been as easily shown using a woman with a law degree who decided to become a sailor, or a child who studied ballet but later decided to become a doctor. (D) also is totally beside the point. Rose never commits herself to so specific a conclusion. She simply says professional education is a waste; she never claims success is related to quality of education. (E) is wrong because Rose is making a general claim about professional education—the man with the law degree was used merely to illustrate her point. (C) is, perhaps, the second-best answer, but it is still not nearly as good as (A). Her objection is that the man she mentions did not use his law degree in a law-related field. She never suggests that such a degree should be used to make money. She might not have objected to his behavior if he had used the degree to work in a public interest capacity.

SECTION VI

Questions 1–3

Arranging the Information

We are interested in the scores of the various participants in the tournament. We have two groups of three members each and we have a process. Each player will play five games, but these games are not entirely symmetrical since each master will play two other masters and three experts, while each expert will play two experts and three masters.

Since the questions are all conditional, we do not expect to spend much time on the diagram. The questions will be the thing.

EXPERTS—L, M, N
MASTERS—O, P, Q

All play two of the same category and three in the other category.

Scoring depends on classification of the loser. If loser is a master, winner scores 2, loser loses 2. If loser is an expert, the winner scores 1 and the loser loses 1.

Answering the Questions

1. **(B)** Since the most is gained from beating masters, the master will wish to lose to experts so that he can beat masters. His loss of points is the same whether he loses to a master or to an expert—2 games at 2 points each = loss of 4 points. By beating two masters, he will gain back these four points and by winning his match against the third expert, he will end up with a score of +1.

2. **(B)** We are speaking now of minimums. If a minimum number of games is to yield a best result, then it is masters who must be beaten. We have two things to figure out: First, the master's maximum score under the circumstances must be determined; then the expert's score must be worked out.

   If the master has lost two games to the other masters, he has lost 4 points. The best he can do is win his other three games against the experts and gain back 1 point for each victory, yielding a net score of $-4 + 3 = -1$.

   Thus, all the expert has to do is to end up with a net score greater than -1. We figured out the master's score first so that we would know the limits for our work on the expert's score. If the expert wins only one game, he could get +2, but losing four games would be -4, yielding a total of

−2, which is not enough. Winning another game against a master would result in a swing of 3 points—two for beating the master and one for not losing the game as first projected. This would increase the score from −2 to +1, which is enough to beat the master. Hence, (B) is the correct answer.

3. **(C)** Since P has lost to L and did not lose to the winner, the first inference is that L is not the winner, which eliminates answer (A). Here, our reference point is P's score. He has lost to one master (−1) and beaten two masters (+4) and two experts (+2), for a total score of +5. Clearly the final winner must have won all of his games except the one he lost to P. This means that the final winner must have scored at least 6 points total, which means that the winner must have gained at least 7 points in the four games he won. The only way to do that would be to have played and beaten all of the masters and one of the experts (2 + 2 + 2 + 1 = 7). This means that the winner must have been an expert rather than a master since the masters only got to play two masters—hence, answer choice (C).

4. **(C)** There are really two parts to the speaker's claim. First, he maintains that the majority of Americans can get access to the medical care in this country; and, second, that the care they have access to is the best in the world. As for the second, good medical care is a function of many variables: number and location of facilities, availability of doctors, quality of education, etc. (A) and (E) may both be consistent with the speaker's claim. Even though we have fewer assistants (A) than some other country, we have more doctors and that more than makes up for the fewer assistants. Or, perhaps, we have such good preventive medicine that people do not need to go into the hospital as frequently as the citizens of other nations (E). (B) is wrong for a similar reason. Although it suggests there is a country in which people have greater access to the available care, it does not come to grips with the second element of the speaker's claim: that the care we get is the best. (C), however, does meet both because it cites the existence of a country in which people are *given* (that is the first element) *better* (the second element) care. (D) hardly counts against the speaker's claim since he has implicitly conceded that some people do not have access to the care.

5. **(C)** The author's claim is that we have unbounded resources, and he tries to prove this by showing that we are getting better and better at extracting those resources from the ground. But that is like saying "I have found a way of getting the last little bit of toothpaste out of the tube; therefore, the tube will never run out." (C) calls our attention to this oversight. (A) does not contradict the author's claim. In fact, it seems to support it. He might suggest, "Even if we run out of fossil fuels, we still have uranium for nuclear power." Now, this is not to suggest that he would. The point is only to show that (A) supports rather than undermines the author's contention. (B) is an attack on the author's general stance, but it does not really *contradict* the particular conclusion he draws. The author says, "We have enough." (B) says, "It is expensive." Both could very well be true, so they cannot contradict one another. (D) is similar to (B). Yes, you may be correct, the technology is expensive or, in this case, wasteful, but it will still get us the fuel we need. Finally, (E) is incorrect for pretty much these same reasons. Yes, the energy will have unwanted side effects, but the author claimed only that we could get the energy. The difficulty with (B), (D), and (E) is that though they attack the author's general *position*, and though they undermine his general suggestion, they do not *contradict* his *conclusion*.

6. **(E)** Common sense dictates that where one is driving in relationship to his home (within or without a 25 mile radius) has little or nothing to do with the safety factor. Moreover, common sense also says that a person driving under 35 miles per hour is (usually) safer than one driving at 60 miles per hour. The explanation, then, for the fact that most traffic fatalities occur under conditions contrary to those which would be suggested by common sense is that more driving is done under those conditions. Just as common sense indicates, the driving is safer per mile, but there are so many more miles driven under those conditions that there are many fatalities. (A) is obviously inconsistent with common sense. And the directions for the Logical Reasoning section explicitly say that the BEST answer will be one which does not require you to make such assumptions. (B) is incorrect since the statistics mention the location of the accident—how far away from home—not how far the driver had driven at the time of the accident. Even though the accident occurred, say, 26 miles from home, you would not want to conclude the driver had driven 26 miles. (C) compounds the error made by (A). Not only does it take the general conclusion regarding fatalities and attempt to apply it to a specific case without regard to the individual variety of those cases, but it commits the further error of conditioning the speed of driving on the occurrence of an accident. (D) does exactly the same thing and is also wrong.

Questions 7–11

Arranging the Information

LEFT-HANDED   RIGHT-HANDED

M← NOT WITH→ $\begin{cases} \text{L← NOT WITH→ S} \\ \text{N← NOT WITH→ T} \quad \text{4 TOTAL} \end{cases}$

O   R

MUST BE 2

Answering the Questions

7. **(C)** If L is on, that eliminates M and S, and thus choice (E) is out. The elimination of S means that T and R must be on the team since two right-handers are needed, which eliminates (D). The inclusion of T means the exclusion of N, and thus choice (B). Thus, L, O, R, and T are the team, answer choice (C).

8. **(D)** This is a little tricky since you have to remember that the only handedness limitation is that at least two right-handers must be on the team. It is OK if only one left-hander is on the team.

   If O is omitted, then the only way to have two left-handers is to have L and N, since neither of those can go with M. But if L and N are used, then S and T can't be, which leaves only one right-hander, R, and a team of only three players. This means that L and N cannot be right, so the left-hander component must be M only, since M cannot go with L or N. (Note that using only L or N will still leave only three players even though two right-handers will be achieved.)

   If only M is taken from the left-handers, then all three right-handers must be used, hence (D). The key was to start with the information you had—about left-handers—and build on that.

9. **(E)** If S and T are chosen, then L and N are excluded. At first glance, this seems to require M and O also to be chosen, but remember that, as discussed in 8, there can be three right-handers, so any two of M, O, and R could be chosen, which means (E) is correct since none of the answer choices has sufficient flexibility.

10. **(B)** If R is omitted, S and T are chosen. If S and T are chosen, then L and N are out and only M and O are left, which is only one possibility, M, O, S, and T—answer choice (B).

11. **(E)** Changing T to a left-handed player does not eliminate the restriction that T cannot go with N, or any other restriction or condition. If T is left-handed, then S and R must be on the team as the two needed right-handers. S eliminates L and we are left with R, S, and two of the others. Let us count the ways:

    If N is chosen, T and M are out, giving R, S, N and O—1.

    If T is chosen, N is out, but T could be combined with either M or O giving R, S, T, and M/O for two more—3 so far.

    If M is chosen, N is out leaving T and O. R, S, M, and T/O. The combination with T has already been counted, but R, S, M, and O is a fourth possibility, thus answer choice (E).

Questions 12–16

Arranging the Information

Some people can easily either visualize or draw a cube and label the sides accordingly. However, such powers are not necessary to the solution of the problem. Simply note that a cube, like a room, has a top, a bottom, and four sides, and draw the diagram as follows:

TOP   _____

SIDES   _____

BOTTOM   _____

At first it is not clear how this information is to be arranged, since the top and bottom are not clear until the end of the information. If you noticed that the last statement gave the bottom side's color, you could have done that first. If not, just assign one side to the top or bottom and then shift if it turns out to be wrong.

Since question 12 asks about redundancy from the top down, it is best to do the statements in that order, at least until 12 is solved.

Problem 12 is solved by noting that if red and black are opposite sides, all of the other sides are between them, so that statement III must be true, given II, and, thus, (B) is the answer to 12.

Code in I:

TOP   BLACK

SIDES   _____

BOTTOM   RED

As previously noted, III adds nothing new.

Code in IV. Note that these other sides are all in the middle of the diagram, so even though they are not specifically related to red/black, we still do know where in the diagram they go.

TOP   BLACK

SIDES   BLUE   WHITE

BOTTOM   RED

Code in V:

TOP	BLACK		
SIDES	BROWN	BLUE	WHITE
BOTTOM	RED		

From the preceding diagram we can put the last color, green, next to white and between white and brown—since that is the only place left.

TOP	BLACK			
SIDES	BROWN	BLUE	WHITE	GREEN
BOTTOM	RED			

The colors of the sides could be rotated in any way, as long as their relative order is preserved. VI places red on the bottom, so this is the final diagram.

Answering the Questions

12. **(B)** This is analyzed in "Arranging the Information."

13. **(A)** Sides that are separated by one other side are opposite, just as the wall in front of you is one wall away from the wall in back of you (if you are in a box-like room). Thus, white is opposite brown.

14. **(D)** Since green is one of the side colors, the top and bottom—red and black—are adjacent to it, eliminating (B) and (E). From the diagram, we can see that white and brown are adjacent sides, thus (D).

15. **(A)** Since the statements in the question mention specific positions only of red and black, answers (B), (C), and (D) cannot be supported. If red is the bottom (VI) and black is opposite it (II), then black must be the top—(A).

16. **(B)** This problem calls for a readjustment of the diagram, which now becomes:

TOP	BLUE			
SIDES	BROWN	BLACK	WHITE	RED
BOTTOM	GREEN			

This was a tricky but easy question since the statement that is false, (B), was false in the original configuration. The diagram shows that (A), (C), (D), and (E) are all true. (A) is also a little tricky since this very important original relationship is preserved.

Questions 17–22

Arranging the Information

The question stems tell us that the situation is a stable, or fixed, one. You will end up knowing pretty much which contestant won which prize. This conclusion follows from the fact that the questions are all descriptive and do not add any further information before asking you who won the dog food, etc. Knowing that it can be figured out is a help since you may wish to try certain assumptions and see if they work.

Question 21 is a redundancy question, which inclines us to do the propositions in order, though 20 seems to require otherwise.

Question 20 is a form of partial information question, though not as simple to deal with as the usual form in which the propositions are listed and the conclusion is at issue. Here the conclusion is listed and we must see what could lead us to that conclusion. Question 20 is unusual. The question stem gives a specific part of the final diagram which makes it clear that the original setup does tell you that Q does not receive the car. You will probably not see a stem like this on the actual test, and we will not use its piece of information in solving the problem. This is such an unlikely situation that we urge you to not believe it when you think you see it on the test.

This problem could be diagrammed as an information table, provided that you write in all of the back-and-forth connections. Another way of doing this problem would be to make a scorecard with arrows connecting the various boxes indicating how they are connected. This tends to be a bit messy.

The simplest approach would be to search for a general statement as a good starting point and then to consider all of the ramifications of each of the statements. All of the statements except I and IV are specific statements about particular prize–contestant relationships. I is the setup and IV covers the total relationship between P and R.

First, however, let us turn to the partial information question (20). Choices (B), (C), and (D) are highly unlikely since they exclude the situation given in I. Between the other two, (E) has a better case on its face since it includes VII, the only statement to directly address the issue of Q and the car. Under VII, if Q gets the car, which is the most valuable prize, R gets the vacation, which is the second-most-valuable prize. This would mean that P could not have gotten a more valuable prize than R. Since we know that the result of Q getting the car would lead to something impossible, Q does not get the car. Note that IV is not a conditional statement, but a statement of definite fact. Thus, I, IV, and VII are enough by themselves to tell us that Q does not get the car.

Note that we have not established that R doesn't get the vacation, but only that Q does not get the car. If P got the car, then R could have the vacation.

Let's get down to the situation. We have four statements that could bear on the disposition of the car: II, IV, V, and VII, so that looks like a good place to start.

Under IV, R cannot win the car since it is the most valuable, and P must receive a more valuable prize than R.

Under IV and VII together, as described above, Q cannot win the car.

Under V, we see that P cannot get the car. If S gets it, then P doesn't, and if S doesn't get it, then P gets something other than the car. Thus, S gets the car.

Since we have a powerful general principle in IV, we might as well work our way down the list in decreasing order of value. Thus, the vacation is next. VI addresses the vacation directly. If Q gets the vacation, then R won't get the dog food, which means he would get the stereo and P would take the dog food. That, however, is impossible since it would have R getting a more valuable prize than P, which is forbidden by IV. Thus we find that Q did not get the vacation. Similarly, we know that R cannot have it since he must be below P. This leaves only P to have the vacation.

The stereo and dog food must be distributed between R and Q. III refers to one of those possibilities and states that if Q gets the stereo, P will get the dog food, but P is, in fact, getting the vacation, so Q is not getting the stereo. This means that R is getting the stereo and the final allocation is:

S   Car
P   Vacation
R   Stereo
Q   Dog food

There are other routes of deduction that could have been followed. The redundancy issue is discussed in the answer to question 21.

Answering the Questions

17. **(C)** This is largely a matter of checking the final solution. (B) is true from the setup of the situation. (C) contradicts the fact that Q got the dog food and R the stereo.

18. **(B)** This is also a look-up question. (E) is absurd since the whole premise of the situation is that each of the four prizes was awarded to a different contestant.

19. **(D)** Again, our work was done in the arranging. S gets the car.

20. **(E)** This was discussed in "Arranging the Information." I, IV, and VII yield the conclusion that Q will not receive the car.

21. **(E)** Having previewed this question, we would at first be expecting to do the statements in numerical order. However, that did not seem to be the way things were going, especially under the impetus of question 20. Another way of keeping track of the question of redundancy is to see if any of the statements are not used in the working out of the problem. In this case, all of them were used and we could have checked them off as we used them for different deductions. Even more to the point, the kinds of statements given are not likely to be redundant since they are one-way statements

only—if A, then B—which would only be redundant if there were other statements saying, essentially: if A then C; if C then B. There is no such overlap in the statements given. Hence, there is no wasted information.

22. **(D)** This question is just a backhanded way of asking which of the contestants did win the stereo. Since all is known, (A) and (E) are not possible. Since R won the stereo, P, S, and Q did not, answer choice (D).

23. **(E)** The question stem asks us to find the one item which will not strengthen the author's argument. That is (E). Remember, the author's argument is an attempt (to be sure, a weak one) to develop an alternative causal explanation. (A) would provide some evidence that the author's claim—which at first glance seems a bit farfetched—actually has some empirical foundation. While (B) does not add any strength to the author's own explanation of the phenomenon being studied, it does strengthen the author's overall position by undermining the explanation given in the report. (C) strengthens the author's position for the same reason that (B) does: It weakens the position he is attacking. (D) strengthens the argument in the same way that (A) does, by providing some empirical support for the otherwise seemingly farfetched explanation.

24. **(E)** Perhaps the most obvious weakness in the argument is that it oversimplifies matters. It is like the domino theory arguments adduced to support the war in Vietnam: Either we fight Communism now or it will take us over. The author argues, in effect: Either we put a stop to this now, or there will be no stopping it. Like the proponents of the domino theory, he ignores the many intermediate positions one might take. III is one way of describing this shortcoming: The dilemma posed by the author is a false one because it overlooks positions between the two extremes. II is also a weakness of the argument: "Cold-blooded murder" is obviously a phrase calculated to excite negative feelings. Finally, the whole argument is also internally inconsistent. The conclusion is that we should allow nature to take its course. How? By prolonging life with artificial means.

25. **(E)** This advertisement is simply rife with ambiguity. The wording obviously seeks to create the impression that FCBI found jobs for its many graduates and generally does a lot of good for them. But first we should ask how many graduates FCBI had—one, two, three, a dozen, or a hundred. If it had only twelve or so, finding them jobs might have been easy; but if many people enroll at FCBI, they may not have the same success. Further, we might want to know how many people graduated compared with how many enrolled. Do people finish the program, or does

FCBI just take their money and then force them out of the program? So II is certainly something we need to know in order to assess the validity of the claim. Now, how many of those who graduated came in looking for help in finding a job? Maybe most people had jobs waiting for them (only a few needed help), in which case the job placement assistance of FCBI is not so impressive. Or perhaps the graduates were so disgusted they did not even seek assistance. So I is relevant. III is also important. Perhaps FCBI found them jobs sweeping streets—not in business. The ad does not say what jobs FCBI helped its people find. Finally, maybe the ad is truthful—FCBI graduates found jobs—but maybe they did it on their own. So IV also is a question worth asking.

ANSWER SHEET—PRACTICE EXAMINATION 6

Section I

1 Ⓐ Ⓑ Ⓒ Ⓓ Ⓔ	8 Ⓐ Ⓑ Ⓒ Ⓓ Ⓔ	15 Ⓐ Ⓑ Ⓒ Ⓓ Ⓔ	22 Ⓐ Ⓑ Ⓒ Ⓓ Ⓔ	29 Ⓐ Ⓑ Ⓒ Ⓓ Ⓔ	36 Ⓐ Ⓑ Ⓒ Ⓓ Ⓔ
2 Ⓐ Ⓑ Ⓒ Ⓓ Ⓔ	9 Ⓐ Ⓑ Ⓒ Ⓓ Ⓔ	16 Ⓐ Ⓑ Ⓒ Ⓓ Ⓔ	23 Ⓐ Ⓑ Ⓒ Ⓓ Ⓔ	30 Ⓐ Ⓑ Ⓒ Ⓓ Ⓔ	37 Ⓐ Ⓑ Ⓒ Ⓓ Ⓔ
3 Ⓐ Ⓑ Ⓒ Ⓓ Ⓔ	10 Ⓐ Ⓑ Ⓒ Ⓓ Ⓔ	17 Ⓐ Ⓑ Ⓒ Ⓓ Ⓔ	24 Ⓐ Ⓑ Ⓒ Ⓓ Ⓔ	31 Ⓐ Ⓑ Ⓒ Ⓓ Ⓔ	38 Ⓐ Ⓑ Ⓒ Ⓓ Ⓔ
4 Ⓐ Ⓑ Ⓒ Ⓓ Ⓔ	11 Ⓐ Ⓑ Ⓒ Ⓓ Ⓔ	18 Ⓐ Ⓑ Ⓒ Ⓓ Ⓔ	25 Ⓐ Ⓑ Ⓒ Ⓓ Ⓔ	32 Ⓐ Ⓑ Ⓒ Ⓓ Ⓔ	
5 Ⓐ Ⓑ Ⓒ Ⓓ Ⓔ	12 Ⓐ Ⓑ Ⓒ Ⓓ Ⓔ	19 Ⓐ Ⓑ Ⓒ Ⓓ Ⓔ	26 Ⓐ Ⓑ Ⓒ Ⓓ Ⓔ	33 Ⓐ Ⓑ Ⓒ Ⓓ Ⓔ	
6 Ⓐ Ⓑ Ⓒ Ⓓ Ⓔ	13 Ⓐ Ⓑ Ⓒ Ⓓ Ⓔ	20 Ⓐ Ⓑ Ⓒ Ⓓ Ⓔ	27 Ⓐ Ⓑ Ⓒ Ⓓ Ⓔ	34 Ⓐ Ⓑ Ⓒ Ⓓ Ⓔ	
7 Ⓐ Ⓑ Ⓒ Ⓓ Ⓔ	14 Ⓐ Ⓑ Ⓒ Ⓓ Ⓔ	21 Ⓐ Ⓑ Ⓒ Ⓓ Ⓔ	28 Ⓐ Ⓑ Ⓒ Ⓓ Ⓔ	35 Ⓐ Ⓑ Ⓒ Ⓓ Ⓔ	

Section II

1 Ⓐ Ⓑ Ⓒ Ⓓ Ⓔ	8 Ⓐ Ⓑ Ⓒ Ⓓ Ⓔ	15 Ⓐ Ⓑ Ⓒ Ⓓ Ⓔ	22 Ⓐ Ⓑ Ⓒ Ⓓ Ⓔ	29 Ⓐ Ⓑ Ⓒ Ⓓ Ⓔ	36 Ⓐ Ⓑ Ⓒ Ⓓ Ⓔ
2 Ⓐ Ⓑ Ⓒ Ⓓ Ⓔ	9 Ⓐ Ⓑ Ⓒ Ⓓ Ⓔ	16 Ⓐ Ⓑ Ⓒ Ⓓ Ⓔ	23 Ⓐ Ⓑ Ⓒ Ⓓ Ⓔ	30 Ⓐ Ⓑ Ⓒ Ⓓ Ⓔ	37 Ⓐ Ⓑ Ⓒ Ⓓ Ⓔ
3 Ⓐ Ⓑ Ⓒ Ⓓ Ⓔ	10 Ⓐ Ⓑ Ⓒ Ⓓ Ⓔ	17 Ⓐ Ⓑ Ⓒ Ⓓ Ⓔ	24 Ⓐ Ⓑ Ⓒ Ⓓ Ⓔ	31 Ⓐ Ⓑ Ⓒ Ⓓ Ⓔ	38 Ⓐ Ⓑ Ⓒ Ⓓ Ⓔ
4 Ⓐ Ⓑ Ⓒ Ⓓ Ⓔ	11 Ⓐ Ⓑ Ⓒ Ⓓ Ⓔ	18 Ⓐ Ⓑ Ⓒ Ⓓ Ⓔ	25 Ⓐ Ⓑ Ⓒ Ⓓ Ⓔ	32 Ⓐ Ⓑ Ⓒ Ⓓ Ⓔ	
5 Ⓐ Ⓑ Ⓒ Ⓓ Ⓔ	12 Ⓐ Ⓑ Ⓒ Ⓓ Ⓔ	19 Ⓐ Ⓑ Ⓒ Ⓓ Ⓔ	26 Ⓐ Ⓑ Ⓒ Ⓓ Ⓔ	33 Ⓐ Ⓑ Ⓒ Ⓓ Ⓔ	
6 Ⓐ Ⓑ Ⓒ Ⓓ Ⓔ	13 Ⓐ Ⓑ Ⓒ Ⓓ Ⓔ	20 Ⓐ Ⓑ Ⓒ Ⓓ Ⓔ	27 Ⓐ Ⓑ Ⓒ Ⓓ Ⓔ	34 Ⓐ Ⓑ Ⓒ Ⓓ Ⓔ	
7 Ⓐ Ⓑ Ⓒ Ⓓ Ⓔ	14 Ⓐ Ⓑ Ⓒ Ⓓ Ⓔ	21 Ⓐ Ⓑ Ⓒ Ⓓ Ⓔ	28 Ⓐ Ⓑ Ⓒ Ⓓ Ⓔ	35 Ⓐ Ⓑ Ⓒ Ⓓ Ⓔ	

Section III

1 Ⓐ Ⓑ Ⓒ Ⓓ Ⓔ	6 Ⓐ Ⓑ Ⓒ Ⓓ Ⓔ	11 Ⓐ Ⓑ Ⓒ Ⓓ Ⓔ	16 Ⓐ Ⓑ Ⓒ Ⓓ Ⓔ	21 Ⓐ Ⓑ Ⓒ Ⓓ Ⓔ	26 Ⓐ Ⓑ Ⓒ Ⓓ Ⓔ
2 Ⓐ Ⓑ Ⓒ Ⓓ Ⓔ	7 Ⓐ Ⓑ Ⓒ Ⓓ Ⓔ	12 Ⓐ Ⓑ Ⓒ Ⓓ Ⓔ	17 Ⓐ Ⓑ Ⓒ Ⓓ Ⓔ	22 Ⓐ Ⓑ Ⓒ Ⓓ Ⓔ	27 Ⓐ Ⓑ Ⓒ Ⓓ Ⓔ
3 Ⓐ Ⓑ Ⓒ Ⓓ Ⓔ	8 Ⓐ Ⓑ Ⓒ Ⓓ Ⓔ	13 Ⓐ Ⓑ Ⓒ Ⓓ Ⓔ	18 Ⓐ Ⓑ Ⓒ Ⓓ Ⓔ	23 Ⓐ Ⓑ Ⓒ Ⓓ Ⓔ	28 Ⓐ Ⓑ Ⓒ Ⓓ Ⓔ
4 Ⓐ Ⓑ Ⓒ Ⓓ Ⓔ	9 Ⓐ Ⓑ Ⓒ Ⓓ Ⓔ	14 Ⓐ Ⓑ Ⓒ Ⓓ Ⓔ	19 Ⓐ Ⓑ Ⓒ Ⓓ Ⓔ	24 Ⓐ Ⓑ Ⓒ Ⓓ Ⓔ	29 Ⓐ Ⓑ Ⓒ Ⓓ Ⓔ
5 Ⓐ Ⓑ Ⓒ Ⓓ Ⓔ	10 Ⓐ Ⓑ Ⓒ Ⓓ Ⓔ	15 Ⓐ Ⓑ Ⓒ Ⓓ Ⓔ	20 Ⓐ Ⓑ Ⓒ Ⓓ Ⓔ	25 Ⓐ Ⓑ Ⓒ Ⓓ Ⓔ	30 Ⓐ Ⓑ Ⓒ Ⓓ Ⓔ

Section IV

1 Ⓐ Ⓑ Ⓒ Ⓓ Ⓔ   6 Ⓐ Ⓑ Ⓒ Ⓓ Ⓔ   11 Ⓐ Ⓑ Ⓒ Ⓓ Ⓔ   16 Ⓐ Ⓑ Ⓒ Ⓓ Ⓔ   21 Ⓐ Ⓑ Ⓒ Ⓓ Ⓔ   26 Ⓐ Ⓑ Ⓒ Ⓓ Ⓔ

2 Ⓐ Ⓑ Ⓒ Ⓓ Ⓔ   7 Ⓐ Ⓑ Ⓒ Ⓓ Ⓔ   12 Ⓐ Ⓑ Ⓒ Ⓓ Ⓔ   17 Ⓐ Ⓑ Ⓒ Ⓓ Ⓔ   22 Ⓐ Ⓑ Ⓒ Ⓓ Ⓔ   27 Ⓐ Ⓑ Ⓒ Ⓓ Ⓔ

3 Ⓐ Ⓑ Ⓒ Ⓓ Ⓔ   8 Ⓐ Ⓑ Ⓒ Ⓓ Ⓔ   13 Ⓐ Ⓑ Ⓒ Ⓓ Ⓔ   18 Ⓐ Ⓑ Ⓒ Ⓓ Ⓔ   23 Ⓐ Ⓑ Ⓒ Ⓓ Ⓔ   28 Ⓐ Ⓑ Ⓒ Ⓓ Ⓔ

4 Ⓐ Ⓑ Ⓒ Ⓓ Ⓔ   9 Ⓐ Ⓑ Ⓒ Ⓓ Ⓔ   14 Ⓐ Ⓑ Ⓒ Ⓓ Ⓔ   19 Ⓐ Ⓑ Ⓒ Ⓓ Ⓔ   24 Ⓐ Ⓑ Ⓒ Ⓓ Ⓔ   29 Ⓐ Ⓑ Ⓒ Ⓓ Ⓔ

5 Ⓐ Ⓑ Ⓒ Ⓓ Ⓔ   10 Ⓐ Ⓑ Ⓒ Ⓓ Ⓔ   15 Ⓐ Ⓑ Ⓒ Ⓓ Ⓔ   20 Ⓐ Ⓑ Ⓒ Ⓓ Ⓔ   25 Ⓐ Ⓑ Ⓒ Ⓓ Ⓔ   30 Ⓐ Ⓑ Ⓒ Ⓓ Ⓔ

Section V

1 Ⓐ Ⓑ Ⓒ Ⓓ Ⓔ   6 Ⓐ Ⓑ Ⓒ Ⓓ Ⓔ   11 Ⓐ Ⓑ Ⓒ Ⓓ Ⓔ   16 Ⓐ Ⓑ Ⓒ Ⓓ Ⓔ   21 Ⓐ Ⓑ Ⓒ Ⓓ Ⓔ

2 Ⓐ Ⓑ Ⓒ Ⓓ Ⓔ   7 Ⓐ Ⓑ Ⓒ Ⓓ Ⓔ   12 Ⓐ Ⓑ Ⓒ Ⓓ Ⓔ   17 Ⓐ Ⓑ Ⓒ Ⓓ Ⓔ   22 Ⓐ Ⓑ Ⓒ Ⓓ Ⓔ

3 Ⓐ Ⓑ Ⓒ Ⓓ Ⓔ   8 Ⓐ Ⓑ Ⓒ Ⓓ Ⓔ   13 Ⓐ Ⓑ Ⓒ Ⓓ Ⓔ   18 Ⓐ Ⓑ Ⓒ Ⓓ Ⓔ   23 Ⓐ Ⓑ Ⓒ Ⓓ Ⓔ

4 Ⓐ Ⓑ Ⓒ Ⓓ Ⓔ   9 Ⓐ Ⓑ Ⓒ Ⓓ Ⓔ   14 Ⓐ Ⓑ Ⓒ Ⓓ Ⓔ   19 Ⓐ Ⓑ Ⓒ Ⓓ Ⓔ   24 Ⓐ Ⓑ Ⓒ Ⓓ Ⓔ

5 Ⓐ Ⓑ Ⓒ Ⓓ Ⓔ   10 Ⓐ Ⓑ Ⓒ Ⓓ Ⓔ   15 Ⓐ Ⓑ Ⓒ Ⓓ Ⓔ   20 Ⓐ Ⓑ Ⓒ Ⓓ Ⓔ   25 Ⓐ Ⓑ Ⓒ Ⓓ Ⓔ

Section VI

1 Ⓐ Ⓑ Ⓒ Ⓓ Ⓔ   6 Ⓐ Ⓑ Ⓒ Ⓓ Ⓔ   11 Ⓐ Ⓑ Ⓒ Ⓓ Ⓔ   16 Ⓐ Ⓑ Ⓒ Ⓓ Ⓔ   21 Ⓐ Ⓑ Ⓒ Ⓓ Ⓔ

2 Ⓐ Ⓑ Ⓒ Ⓓ Ⓔ   7 Ⓐ Ⓑ Ⓒ Ⓓ Ⓔ   12 Ⓐ Ⓑ Ⓒ Ⓓ Ⓔ   17 Ⓐ Ⓑ Ⓒ Ⓓ Ⓔ   22 Ⓐ Ⓑ Ⓒ Ⓓ Ⓔ

3 Ⓐ Ⓑ Ⓒ Ⓓ Ⓔ   8 Ⓐ Ⓑ Ⓒ Ⓓ Ⓔ   13 Ⓐ Ⓑ Ⓒ Ⓓ Ⓔ   18 Ⓐ Ⓑ Ⓒ Ⓓ Ⓔ   23 Ⓐ Ⓑ Ⓒ Ⓓ Ⓔ

4 Ⓐ Ⓑ Ⓒ Ⓓ Ⓔ   9 Ⓐ Ⓑ Ⓒ Ⓓ Ⓔ   14 Ⓐ Ⓑ Ⓒ Ⓓ Ⓔ   19 Ⓐ Ⓑ Ⓒ Ⓓ Ⓔ   24 Ⓐ Ⓑ Ⓒ Ⓓ Ⓔ

5 Ⓐ Ⓑ Ⓒ Ⓓ Ⓔ   10 Ⓐ Ⓑ Ⓒ Ⓓ Ⓔ   15 Ⓐ Ⓑ Ⓒ Ⓓ Ⓔ   20 Ⓐ Ⓑ Ⓒ Ⓓ Ⓔ   25 Ⓐ Ⓑ Ⓒ Ⓓ Ⓔ

PRACTICE EXAMINATION 6

SECTION I

30 minutes
38 questions

Directions: Each of the questions below contains one or more blank spaces, each blank indicating an omitted word. Each sentence is followed by five (5) lettered words or sets of words. Read and determine the general sense of each sentence. Then choose the word, or set of words, which, when inserted in the sentence, best fits the meaning of the sentence.

1. _____ and piety seem to have been two qualities almost universally shared by the original settlers of the Northeast who faced the almost _____ problems of the weather and disease.
   (A) Candor—insignificant
   (B) Veracity—understandable
   (C) Cowardice—enduring
   (D) Avarice—threatening
   (E) Fortitude—insurmountable

2. A _____ review of the recent performance of *La Bohème* called the production grotesque and the conducting of the orchestra _____ .
   (A) glowing—benign
   (B) scathing—pedestrian
   (C) laudatory—heretical
   (D) premeditated—prejudicial
   (E) concentrated—munificent

3. The young soloist broke a string in the middle of the performance of the Tchaikovsky Violin Concerto and motioned to the concertmaster to hand over his own violin so that she might _____ her performance, demonstrating _____ rare in one so young.
   (A) interrupt—a confidence
   (B) continue—an aplomb
   (C) rehearse—a stage presence

(D) illuminate—a perseverity
(E) renew—an elegance

4. The Supreme Court, in striking down the state law, ruled the statute had been enacted in an atmosphere charged with religious convictions which had _____ the lawmaking process, a _____ of the Constitutional provision requiring the separation of church and state.
   (A) written—bastion
   (B) influenced—harbinger
   (C) infected—violation
   (D) repealed—fulfillment
   (E) sanctified—union

5. Because customers believe that there is a direct correlation between price and value, software manufacturers continue to _____ their prices at _____ rate.
   (A) raise—an astonishing
   (B) inflate—a moderate
   (C) advertise—a rapid
   (D) control—an acceptable
   (E) determine—a shared

6. The _____ performance of the Rachmaninoff Piano Concerto in D Minor, one of the most difficult modern compositions for the piano, _____ the audience and earned the pianist a standing ovation.
   (A) virtuoso—thrilled
   (B) excellent—offended
   (C) miserable—excited
   (D) mediocre—incited
   (E) masterful—disappointed

511

7. Painters and poets are possessed of the same qualities of mind, governed by the same principles of taste, and are consistently in _____ and never in_____ with one another.
   - (A) contention—accord
   - (B) sympathy—disagreement
   - (C) demonstrations—collusion
   - (D) seclusion—danger
   - (E) concordance—agreement

Directions: In each of the following questions, you are given a related pair of words or phrases in capital letters. Each capitalized pair is followed by five (5) lettered pairs of words or phrases. Choose the pair which best expresses a relationship similar to that expressed by the original pair.

8. TRAP : GAME ::
   - (A) novel : author
   - (B) net : fish
   - (C) leash : dog
   - (D) wall : house
   - (E) curtain : window

9. MANSARD : ROOF ::
   - (A) ice : igloo
   - (B) spine : book
   - (C) closet : hallway
   - (D) dormer : window
   - (E) tent : military

10. PASTOR : CONGREGATION ::
    - (A) shepherd : flock
    - (B) teacher : faculty
    - (C) chef : restaurant
    - (D) clerk : market
    - (E) painter : canvas

11. ODE : POEM ::
    - (A) character : novel
    - (B) brick : building
    - (C) ballad : song
    - (D) street : intersection
    - (E) museum : painting

12. TENACITY : WEAK ::
    - (A) apathy : caring
    - (B) pity : strong
    - (C) immorality : wrong
    - (D) frequency : known
    - (E) control : expensive

13. CURATOR : PAINTING ::
    - (A) jailor : sheriff
    - (B) treasurer : secretary
    - (C) archivist : manuscript
    - (D) general : army
    - (E) machinist : metal

14. CREPESCULE : TWILIGHT ::
    - (A) week : calendar
    - (B) temperature : climate
    - (C) dawn : daybreak
    - (D) radiation : sun
    - (E) commutation : voyage

15. AUGUR : PORTEND ::
    - (A) foresee : bode
    - (B) pass : rescind
    - (C) illuminate : obscure
    - (D) flourish : harvest
    - (E) protect : delimit

16. PUERILE : BOY ::
    - (A) subdued : riot
    - (B) marked : recreation
    - (C) flappable : calm
    - (D) intrusive : family
    - (E) juvenile : youth

Directions: Below each of the following passages you will find questions or incomplete statements about the passage. Each statement or question is followed by lettered words or expressions. Select the word or expression that most satisfactorily completes each statement or answers each question in accordance with the meaning of the passage. After you have chosen the best answer, blacken the corresponding space on the answer sheet.

War has escaped the battlefield and now can, with modern guidance systems on missiles, touch virtually every square yard of the earth's surface. War has also lost most of its utility in achieving
5 the traditional goals of conflict. Control of territory carries with it the obligation to provide subject peoples certain administrative, health, education, and other social services; such obligations far outweigh the benefits of control. If the ruled population is
10 ethnically or racially different from the rulers, tensions and chronic unrest often exist which further reduce the benefits and increase the costs of domination. Large populations no longer necessarily enhance state power and, in the absence of high levels

15 of economic development, can impose severe burdens on food supply, jobs, and the broad range of services expected of modern governments. The noneconomic security reasons for the control of territory have been progressively undermined by
20 the advances of modern technology. The benefits of forcing another nation to surrender its wealth are vastly outweighed by the benefits of persuading that nation to produce and exchange goods and services. In brief, imperialism no longer pays.

25 Making war has been one of the most persistent of human activities in the 80 centuries since men and women settled in cities and thereby became "civilized," but the modernization of the past 80 years has fundamentally changed the role and func-
30 tion of war. In premodernized societies, successful warfare brought significant material rewards, the most obvious of which were the stored wealth of the defeated. Equally important was human labor —control over people as slaves or levies for the
35 victor's army, and there was the productive capacity —agricultural lands and mines. Successful warfare also produced psychic benefits. The removal or destruction of a threat brought a sense of security, and power gained over others created pride and
40 national self-esteem.

War was accepted in the premodernized society as a part of the human condition, a mechanism of change, and an unavoidable, even noble, aspect of life. The excitement and drama of war made it
45 a vital part of literature and legends.

17. According to the passage, leaders of pre-modernized society considered war to be
(A) a valid tool of national policy
(B) an immoral act of aggression
(C) economically wasteful and socially unfeasible
(D) restricted in scope to military participants
(E) necessary to spur development of unoccupied lands

18. The author most likely places the word "civilized" in quotation marks (line 28) in order to
(A) show dissatisfaction at not having found a better word
(B) acknowledge that the word was borrowed from another source
(C) express irony that war should be a part of civilization

(D) impress upon the reader the tragedy of war
(E) raise a question about the value of war in modernized society

19. The author mentions all of the following as possible reasons for going to war in a pre-modernized society EXCEPT
(A) possibility of material gain
(B) total annihilation of the enemy and destruction of enemy territory
(C) potential for increasing the security of the nation
(D) desire to capture productive farming lands
(E) need for workers to fill certain jobs

20. Which of the following best describes the tone of the passage?
(A) scientific and detached
(B) outraged and indignant
(C) humorous and wry
(D) fearful and alarmed
(E) concerned and optimistic

There is extraordinary exposure in the United States to the risks of injury and death from motor vehicle accidents. More than 80 percent of all households own passenger cars or light trucks and
5 each of these is driven an average of more than 11,000 miles each year. Almost one-half of fatally injured drivers have a blood alcohol concentration (BAC) of 0.1 percent or higher. For the average adult, over five ounces of 80 proof spirits would
10 have to be consumed over a short period of time to attain these levels. A third of drivers who have been drinking, but fewer than 4 percent of all drivers, demonstrate these levels. Although less than 1 percent of drivers with BACs of 0.1 percent or
15 more are involved in fatal crashes, the probability of their involvement is 27 times higher than for those without alcohol in their blood.

There are a number of different approaches to reducing injuries in which intoxication plays a role.
20 Based on the observation that excessive consumption correlates with the total alcohol consumption of a country's population, it has been suggested that higher taxes on alcohol would reduce both. While the heaviest drinkers would be taxed the
25 most, anyone who drinks at all would be penalized by this approach.

To make drinking and driving a criminal offense

is an approach directed only at intoxicated drivers. In some states, the law empowers police to
30 request breath tests of drivers cited for any traffic offense and elevated BAC can be the basis for arrest. The National Highway Traffic Safety Administration estimates, however, that even with increased arrests, there are about 700 violations for
35 every arrest. At this level there is little evidence that laws serve as deterrents to drinking while intoxicated. In Britain, motor vehicle fatalities fell 25 percent immediately following implementation of the Road Safety Act in 1967. As the British
40 increasingly recognized that they could drink and not be stopped, the effectiveness declined, although in the ensuing three years the fatality rate seldom reached that observed in the seven years prior to the Act.

45   Whether penalties for driving with a high BAC or excessive taxation on consumption of alcoholic beverages will deter the excessive drinker responsible for most fatalities is unclear. In part, the answer depends on the extent to which those with
50 high BACs involved in crashes are capable of controlling their intake in response to economic or penal threat. Therapeutic programs which range from individual and group counseling and psychotherapy to chemotherapy constitute another ap-
55 proach, but they have not diminished the proportion of accidents in which alcohol was a factor. In the few controlled trials that have been reported, there is little evidence that rehabilitation programs for those repeatedly arrested for drunken behav-
60 ior have reduced either the recidivism or crash rates. Thus far, there is no firm evidence that Alcohol Safety Action Project supported programs, in which rehabilitation measures are requested by the court, have decreased recidivism or crash involvement for
65 clients exposed to them, although knowledge and attitudes have improved. One thing is clear, however; unless we deal with automobile and highway safety and reduce accidents in which alcoholic intoxication plays a role, many will continue to die.

21. The author is primarily concerned with
    (A) interpreting the results of surveys on traffic fatalities
    (B) reviewing the effectiveness of attempts to curb drunk driving
    (C) suggesting reasons for the prevalence of drunk driving in the United States

    (D) analyzing the causes of the large number of annual traffic fatalities
    (E) making an international comparison of U.S. and Britain

22. It can be inferred that the 1967 Road Safety Act in Britain
    (A) changed an existing law to lower the BAC level which defined driving while intoxicated
    (B) made it illegal to drive while intoxicated
    (C) increased the number of drunk driving arrests
    (D) placed a tax on the sale of alcoholic drinks
    (E) required drivers convicted under the law to undergo rehabilitation therapy

23. The author implies that a BAC of 0.1 percent
    (A) is unreasonably high as a definition of intoxication for purposes of driving
    (B) penalizes the moderate drinker while allowing the heavy drinker to consume without limit
    (C) will operate as an effective deterrent to over 90 percent of the people who might drink and drive
    (D) is well below the BAC of most drivers who are involved in fatal collisions
    (E) proves that a driver has consumed five ounces of 80 proof spirits over a short time

24. With which of the following statements about making driving while intoxicated a criminal offense versus increasing taxes on alcohol consumption would the author most likely agree?
    (A) Making driving while intoxicated a criminal offense is preferable to increased taxes on alcohol because the former is aimed only at those who abuse alcohol by driving while intoxicated.
    (B) Increased taxation on alcohol consumption is likely to be more effective in reducing traffic fatalities because taxation covers all consumers and not just those who drive.
    (C) Increased taxation on alcohol will constitute less of an interference with personal liberty because of the necessity of blood alcohol tests to determine BACs in drivers suspected of intoxication.

(D) Since neither increased taxation nor enforcement of criminal laws against drunk drivers is likely to have any significant impact, neither measure is warranted.

(E) Because arrests of intoxicated drivers have proved to be expensive and administratively cumbersome, increased taxation on alcohol is the most promising means of reducing traffic fatalities.

25. The author cites the British example in order to
(A) show that the problem of drunk driving is worse in Britain than in the U.S.
(B) prove that stricter enforcement of laws against intoxicated drivers would reduce traffic deaths
(C) prove that a slight increase in the number of arrests of intoxicated drivers will not deter drunk driving
(D) suggest that taxation of alcohol consumption may be more effective than criminal laws
(E) demonstrate the need to lower BAC levels in states that have laws against drunk driving

26. Which of the following, if true, most weakens the author's statement that the effectiveness of proposals to stop the intoxicated driver depends, in part, on the extent to which the high-BAC driver can control his or her intake?
(A) Even if the heavy drinker cannot control intake, criminal laws against driving while intoxicated can deter him or her from driving while intoxicated.
(B) Rehabilitation programs aimed at drivers convicted of driving while intoxicated have not significantly reduced traffic fatalities.
(C) Many traffic fatalities are caused by factors unrelated to the excessive consumption of alcohol by the driver involved.
(D) Even though severe penalties may not deter the intoxicated driver, these laws will punish him or her for the harm caused by driving while intoxicated.
(E) Some sort of therapy may be effective in helping the problem drinker to control the intake of alcohol, thereby keeping him or her off the road.

27. The author's closing remarks can best be described as
(A) ironic
(B) indifferent
(C) admonitory
(D) indecisive
(E) indignant

Directions: Each of the following questions consists of a word printed in capital letters, followed by five (5) lettered words or phrases. Select the word or phrase which is most nearly *opposite* to the capitalized word in meaning.

28. RESIDENT :
(A) factual
(B) constrained
(C) transitory
(D) lofty
(E) merciful

29. PROLIFIC :
(A) worthless
(B) barren
(C) practical
(D) baleful
(E) youthful

30. LAMBAST :
(A) deny
(B) understand
(C) praise
(D) imagine
(E) flatten

31. COURT :
(A) reject
(B) uncover
(C) infect
(D) subject
(E) elect

32. FORGE :
(A) continue
(B) dissolve
(C) quiet
(D) invite
(E) prevent

33. MOTILE :
    (A) confused
    (B) frightened
    (C) immobile
    (D) willing
    (E) nervous

34. LACHRYMOSE :
    (A) sacred
    (B) unknowable
    (C) miraculous
    (D) humble
    (E) joyful

35. QUIESCENCE :
    (A) calamity
    (B) timidity
    (C) persistence
    (D) frenzy
    (E) eternal

36. URBANE :
    (A) deceitful
    (B) rude
    (C) controlled
    (D) faithful
    (E) insincere

37. RUDIMENTARY :
    (A) sophisticated
    (B) illegal
    (C) striking
    (D) redundant
    (E) soft

38. MAGNANIMOUSLY :
    (A) confidently
    (B) precariously
    (C) sentimentally
    (D) abruptly
    (E) grudgingly

STOP

END OF SECTION. IF YOU HAVE ANY TIME LEFT, GO
OVER YOUR WORK IN THIS SECTION ONLY. DO NOT
WORK IN ANY OTHER SECTION OF THE TEST.

SECTION II

30 minutes
38 questions

Directions: Each of the questions below contains one or more blank spaces, each blank indicating an omitted word. Each sentence is followed by five (5) lettered words or sets of words. Read and determine the general sense of each sentence. Then choose the word or set of words which, when inserted in the sentence, best fits the meaning of the sentence.

1. It is _____ that students do not repay their student loans and thereby make it more _____ for future generations of students to obtain them.
    (A) unfortunate—urgent
    (B) regrettable—difficult
    (C) unforgivable—likely
    (D) laudable—practical
    (E) worrisome—imperative

2. Although her initial success was _____ by the fact that she was the daughter of a famous actor, the critics later _____ her as a star in her own right.
    (A) enhanced—acclaimed
    (B) impeded—criticized
    (C) refuted—summarily acknowledged
    (D) superceded—disavowed
    (E) trivialized—accepted

3. Contrary to popular belief, the Mayans were not peace-loving astronomers but _____ warriors, who viewed their gods as cruel and _____ .
    (A) formidable—vengeful
    (B) skilled—benevolent
    (C) reluctant—omnipotent
    (D) docile—patronizing
    (E) amicable—malevolent

4. Despite the fact that she was much _____ , the scientist continued to present her controversial theories to the _____ of the Royal Academy, whose members repeatedly denounced her research.
    (A) admired—chagrin
    (B) revered—benefit
    (C) imitated—foreboding
    (D) chastened—temerity
    (E) maligned—consternation

5. Washington Irving, the father of American literature and creator of such delightful characters as Ichabod Crane and Rip Van Winkle, will be remembered more for the _____ of his prose than for the originality of his tales, which were _____ from popular folklore.
    (A) density—obtained
    (B) vulgarity—stolen
    (C) mediocrity—descended
    (D) charm—borrowed
    (E) pomposity—reduced

6. Although alcoholism has long been regarded as a personality disorder, there is evidence to suggest that alcoholics are often the children of alcoholics and that they are born with a _____ the disease.
    (A) respect for
    (B) predisposition to
    (C) liability for
    (D) deterioration of
    (E) misunderstanding of

7. The latest research indicates that feelings of love occur in the nonverbal part of the brain, which helps to explain why people are often able to _____ such feelings but not _____ them.
    (A) accept—believe
    (B) enjoy—mistake
    (C) experience—explain
    (D) recall—remove
    (E) describe—convey

Directions: In each of the following questions, you are given a related pair of words or phrases in capital letters. Each capitalized pair is followed by five (5) lettered pairs of words or phrases. Choose the pair which best expresses a relationship similar to that expressed by the original pair.

8. PROHIBITED : REFRAIN ::
    (A) innocuous : forbid
    (B) deleterious : embark
    (C) required : decide
    (D) compulsory : comply
    (E) ridiculous : laugh

9. OVERTURE : OPERA ::
    (A) epilogue : movie
    (B) preface : book
    (C) concerto : piano
    (D) footnote : paragraph
    (E) singer : aria

10. RESOLVED : DOUBT ::
    (A) confirmed : suspicion
    (B) announced : candidacy
    (C) included : guest
    (D) suggested : idea
    (E) demolished : opponent

11. EXEMPLARY : REPROACH ::
    (A) erroneous : correction
    (B) accomplished : praise
    (C) fulfilling : control
    (D) planned : implementation
    (E) unimpeachable : criticism

12. MENDICANT : BEGGING ::
    (A) competitor : joining
    (B) legislator : funding
    (C) miser : donating
    (D) prevaricator : lying
    (E) mechanic : selling

13. RAIN : DELUGE ::
    (A) pond : ocean
    (B) desert : camel
    (C) ore : iron
    (D) street : road
    (E) wheat : crop

14. LUBRICANT : FRICTION ::
    (A) balm : pain
    (B) eraser : correction
    (C) solvent : paint
    (D) reagent : chemical
    (E) merchant : business

15. POMPOSITY : BOASTFUL ::
    (A) courage : cowardly
    (B) silence : mature
    (C) forgetfulness : youthful
    (D) conceit : arrogance
    (E) malice : strong

16. THEOLOGY : RELIGION ::
    (A) astronomy : stars
    (B) politics : ethics
    (C) sociology : individuals
    (D) economics : theory
    (E) physics : chemistry

Directions: Below each of the following passages you will find questions or incomplete statements about the passage. Each statement or question is followed by lettered words or expressions. Select the word or expression that most satisfactorily completes each statement or answers each question in accordance with the meaning of the passage. After you have chosen the best answer, blacken the corresponding space on the answer sheet.

Reverse discrimination, minority recruitment, racial quotas, and, more generally, affirmative action are phrases that carry powerful emotional charges. But why should affirmative action, of all
5 government policies, be so controversial? In a sense, affirmative action is like other governmental programs, e.g., defense, conservation, and public schools. Affirmative action programs are designed to achieve legitimate government objectives
10 such as improved economic efficiency, reduced social tension, and general betterment of the public welfare. While it cannot be denied that there is no guarantee that affirmative action will achieve these results, neither can it be denied that there are plau-
15 sible, even powerful, sociological and economic arguments pointing to its likely success.
Government programs, however, entail a cost, that is, the expenditure of social or economic resources. Setting aside cases in which the specific
20 user is charged a fee for service (toll roads and tuition at state institutions), the burdens and benefits of publicly funded or mandated programs are widely shared. When an individual benefits personally from a government program, it is only be-
25 cause she or he is one member of a larger beneficiary class, e.g., a farmer; and most government revenue is obtained through a scheme of general taxation to which all are subject.
Affirmative action programs are exceptions to
30 this general rule, though not, as might at first seem, because the beneficiaries of the programs are specific individuals. It is still the case that those who ultimately benefit from affirmative action do so only by virtue of their status as members of a
35 larger group, a particular minority. Rather, the difference is the location of the burden. In affirmative action, the burden of "funding" the program is not shared universally, and that is inherent in the nature of the case, as can be seen clearly in the
40 case of affirmative action in employment. Often job promotions are allocated along a single dimension, seniority; and when an employer promotes a less senior worker from a minority group, the person disadvantaged by the move is easily identified:
45 the worker with greatest seniority on a combined minority–nonminority list passed over for promotion.
Now we are confronted with two competing moral sentiments. On the one hand, there is the
50 idea that those who have been unfairly disadvantaged by past discriminatory practices are entitled to some kind of assistance. On the other, there is the feeling that no person ought to be deprived of what is rightfully his or hers, even for the worth-
55 while service of fellow humans. In this respect, disability due to past racial discrimination, at least insofar as there is no connection to the passed-over worker, is like a natural evil. When a villainous man willfully and without provocation strikes
60 and injures another, there is not only the feeling that the injured person ought to be compensated but there is consensus that the appropriate party to bear the cost is the one who inflicted the injury. Yet, if the same innocent man stumbled and in-
65 jured himself, it would be surprising to hear someone argue that the villainous man ought to be taxed for the injury simply because he might have tripped the victim had he been given the opportunity. There may very well be agreement that he should be aided
70 in his recovery with money and personal assistance, and many will give willingly; but there is also agreement that no one individual ought to be singled out and forced to do what must ultimately be considered an act of charity.

17. The passage is primarily concerned with
    (A) comparing affirmative action programs to other government programs
    (B) arguing that affirmative action programs are morally justified
    (C) analyzing the basis for moral judgments about affirmative action programs
    (D) introducing the reader to the importance of affirmative action as a social issue
    (E) describing the benefits that can be obtained through affirmative action programs

18. The author mentions toll roads and tuition at state institutions (lines 20–28) in order to
    (A) anticipate a possible objection based on counterexamples
    (B) avoid a contradiction between moral sentiments
    (C) provide illustrations of common government programs
    (D) voice doubts about the social and economic value of affirmative action
    (E) offer examples of government programs which are too costly

19. With which of the following statements would the author most likely agree?
    (A) Affirmative action programs should be discontinued because they place an unfair burden on nonminority persons who bear the cost of the programs.
    (B) Affirmative action programs may be able to achieve legitimate social and economic goals such as improved efficiency.
    (C) Affirmative action programs are justified because they are the only way of correcting injustices created by past discrimination.
    (D) Affirmative action programs must be redesigned so that society as a whole rather than particular individuals bears the cost of the programs.
    (E) Affirmative action programs should be abandoned because they serve no useful social function and place unfair burdens on particular individuals.

20. The author most likely places the word "funding" in quotation marks (line 37) in order to remind the reader that
    (A) affirmative action programs are costly in terms of government revenues
    (B) particular individuals may bear a disproportionate share of the burden of affirmative action
    (C) the cost of most government programs is shared by society at large
    (D) the beneficiaries of affirmative action are members of larger groups
    (E) the cost of affirmative action is not only a monetary expenditure

21. The "villainous man" discussed in lines 59–74 functions primarily as
    (A) an illustration
    (B) a counterexample
    (C) an authority
    (D) an analogy
    (E) a disclaimer

22. According to the passage, affirmative action programs are different from most other government programs in which of the following ways?

    I. the goals the programs are designed to achieve
    II. the ways in which costs of the programs are distributed
    III. the ways in which benefits of the programs are allocated

    (A) I only
    (B) II only
    (C) III only
    (D) II and III only
    (E) I, II, and III

23. It can be inferred that the author believes the reader will regard affirmative action programs as
    (A) posing a moral dilemma
    (B) based on unsound premises
    (C) containing self-contradictions
    (D) creating needless suffering
    (E) offering a panacea

24. The primary purpose of the passage is to
    (A) reconcile two conflicting points of view
    (B) describe and refute a point of view
    (C) provide a historical context for a problem
    (D) suggest a new method for studying social problems
    (E) analyze the structure of an institution

Desertification in the arid United States is flagrant. Groundwater supplies beneath vast stretches of land are dropping precipitously. Whole river systems have dried up; others are choked with sediment washed from denuded land. Hundreds of thousands of acres of previously irrigated cropland have been abandoned to wind or weeds. Several million acres of natural grassland are eroding at unnaturally high rates as a result of cultivation or overgrazing. All told, about 225 million acres of land are undergoing severe desertification.

Federal subsidies encourage the exploitation of arid land resources. Low-interest loans for irrigation and other water delivery systems encourage farmers, industry, and municipalities to mine groundwater. Federal disaster relief and commodity programs encourage arid-land farmers to plow up natural grassland to plant crops such as wheat and, especially, cotton. Federal grazing fees that are well below the free market price encourage overgrazing of the commons. The market, too, provides powerful incentives to exploit arid land resources beyond their carrying capacity. When commodity prices are high relative to the farmer's or rancher's operating costs, the return on a production-enhancing investment is invariably greater than the return on a conservation investment. And when commodity prices are relatively low, arid land ranchers and farmers often have to use all their available financial resources to stay solvent.

If the United States is, as it appears, well on its way toward overdrawing the arid land resources, then the policy choice is simply to pay now for the appropriate remedies or pay far more later, when productive benefits from arid land resources have been both realized and largely terminated.

25. The author is primarily concerned with
    (A) discussing a solution
    (B) describing a problem
    (C) replying to a detractor
    (D) finding a contradiction
    (E) defining a term

26. The passage mentions all of the following as effects of desertification EXCEPT
    (A) increased sediment in rivers
    (B) erosion of land
    (C) overcultivation of land
    (D) decreasing groundwater supplies
    (E) loss of land to wind or weeds

27. The author's attitude toward desertification can best be described as one of
    (A) alarm
    (B) optimism
    (C) understanding
    (D) conciliation
    (E) concern

Directions: Each of the following questions consists of a word printed in capital letters, followed by five (5) lettered words or phrases. Select the word or phrase which is most nearly *opposite* to the capitalized word in meaning.

28. COVERT :
    (A) protracted
    (B) insensitive
    (C) reclining
    (D) open
    (E) taxing

29. SALIENT :
    (A) insignificant
    (B) climactic
    (C) worrisome
    (D) awesome
    (E) radical

30. MORIBUND :
    (A) contentious
    (B) malignant
    (C) pretentious
    (D) detestable
    (E) vital

31. PLIANT :
    (A) humble
    (B) rigid
    (C) tactful
    (D) earnest
    (E) solemn

32. DORMANT :
    (A) authoritative
    (B) elastic
    (C) active
    (D) uninteresting
    (E) endearing

33. PLACATE :
    (A) abet
    (B) enrage
    (C) invite
    (D) witness
    (E) repent

34. EXTRANEOUS :
    (A) outlandish
    (B) tumultuous
    (C) impetuous
    (D) central
    (E) guarded

35. RENOWN :
    (A) suggestiveness
    (B) superficiality
    (C) anonymity
    (D) deviousness
    (E) valor

36. RUE :
    (A) celebrate
    (B) denounce
    (C) engender
    (D) join
    (E) constrain

37. BALEFUL :
    (A) empty
    (B) soft
    (C) timid
    (D) fortunate
    (E) respectful

38. FORTITUDE :
    (A) debility
    (B) instruction
    (C) calamity
    (D) encouragement
    (E) complicity

STOP

END OF SECTION. IF YOU HAVE ANY TIME LEFT, GO
OVER YOUR WORK IN THIS SECTION ONLY. DO NOT
WORK IN ANY OTHER SECTION OF THE TEST.

SECTION III

30 minutes
30 questions

Directions: For each of the following questions two quantities are given, one in Column A
and one in Column B. Compare the two quantities and mark your answer sheet with the
correct lettered conclusion. These are your options:
    A: If the quantity in Column A is the greater;
    B: if the quantity in Column B is the greater;
    C: if the two quantities are equal;
    D: if the relationship cannot be determined from the information given.
Common Information: In any question, information applying to both columns is centered
between the columns and above the quantities in columns A and B. The common information applies to both columns. Any symbol that appears in both columns represents the same
idea or quantity in both columns.
Numbers: All numbers used are real numbers.
Figures: Assume that the position of points, angles, regions and so forth are in the order
shown. Figures are assumed to lie in a plane unless otherwise indicated. Figures accompany-

ing questions are intended to provide information you can use in answering the questions. However, unless a note states that a figure is drawn to scale, you should solve the problems by using your knowledge of mathematics and *not* by estimating sizes by sight or measurement. **Lines:** Assume that lines shown as straight are indeed straight.

	COLUMN A	COLUMN B
1.	$5 - \frac{6}{6}$	$5 - \frac{1}{4}$

2.

x is 4 more than y

x	y

3.

The price of a book increased from $7.95 to $8.95.

the percent increase in the price of the book	12%

4.

M + 2 is the average (arithmetic mean) of x and y.

$\dfrac{x + y}{2}$	M

5.	$(x + y)(x - y)$	$x^2 - y^2$

6.

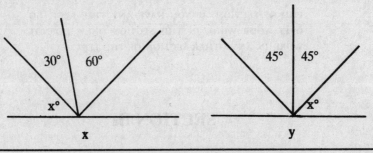

x	y

7.

The population of City X decreased by 5 percent while the population of City Y decreased by 7.5 percent

the loss of population by City X	the loss of population by City Y

8.

The perimeter of square PQRS is $12\sqrt{3}$

side PQ	$3\sqrt{3}$

9.	$\left(\dfrac{3}{7} \times \dfrac{101}{104}\right) + \left(\dfrac{3}{7} \times \dfrac{4}{104}\right)$	$\dfrac{3}{7}$

10.

Point P has coordinates $(-2, 2)$; point Q has coordinates $(2, 0)$.

4	the distance from P to Q

COLUMN A	COLUMN B

11. the least positive integer that is divisible by both 18 and 24 | the least positive integer that is divisible by both 18 and 28

12.

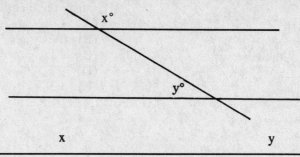

x | y

---

13. For all real numbers P and Q,
$$P * Q = P + Q - PQ.$$

4 * 1 | 4 * 2

---

14. $j > 0, k > 0, m < 0$

(3j)(3k)(3m) | 3(j)(k)(m)

---

15. $x = \dfrac{4y}{5}$

$\dfrac{5}{6}$ | $\dfrac{2y}{3x}$

Directions: For each of the following questions, select the best of the answer choices and blacken the corresponding space on your answer sheet.

Numbers: All numbers used are real numbers.

Figures: The diagrams and figures that accompany these questions are for the purpose of providing information useful in answering the questions. Unless it is stated that a specific figure is not drawn to scale, the diagrams and figures are drawn accurately as possible. All figures are in a plane unless otherwise indicated.

16. $5^2 + 12^2 =$
   (A) 13^2
   (B) 17^2
   (C) 20^2
   (D) 144^2
   (E) 169^2

17. A salesperson works 50 weeks each year and makes an average (arithmetic mean) of 100 sales per week. If each sale is worth an average (arithmetic mean) of $1000, then what is the total value of sales made by the salesperson in a year?
   (A) $50,000
   (B) $100,000
   (C) $500,000
   (D) $1,000,000
   (E) $5,000,000

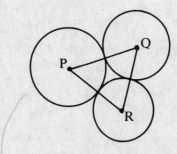

18. In the figure above, the three circles are tangent to each other at the points shown. If circle P has a diameter of 10, circle Q has a diameter of 8, and circle R has a diameter

of 6, then what is the perimeter of triangle
PQR?

(A) 24
(B) 18
(C) 12
(D) 9
(E) 6

19. If $x = 1$ and $y = -2$, then $\dfrac{x^2 - xy}{y} =$

(A) -3
(B) -2

(C) $-\frac{3}{2}$
(D) 2
(E) 3

20. Which of the following numbers does NOT
satisfy the inequality $5x - 2 < 3x - 1$?

(A) 1
(B) 0
(C) -1
(D) -2
(E) -3

Questions 21–25 are based on the following graphs:

SELECTED MOTOR VEHICLE REGISTRATION DATA
FOR TWO CITIES (BY MANUFACTURER)

Distribution of Motor Vehicles Registered
in City X According to Manufacturer
(100% = 8400)

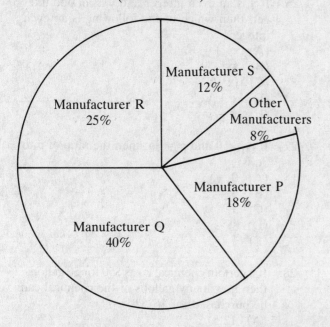

Number of Vehicles Registered in City X
Manufactured by Other Manufacturers

Manufacturer T	212
Manufacturer U	210
Manufacturer V	250

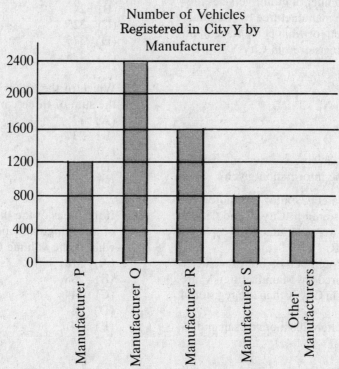

21. In City X, how many of the registered motor vehicles were manufactured by Manufacturer Q?
    (A) 1512
    (B) 1600
    (C) 2400
    (D) 3360
    (E) 6000

22. How many more of the motor vehicles registered in City Y were manufactured by Manufacturer R than were manufactured by Manufacturer P?
    (A) 400
    (B) 688
    (C) 800
    (D) 1200
    (E) 1688

23. Of the following, which is the closest approximation to the percentage of motor vehicles registered in City X that were manufactured by Manufacturer V?
    (A) 45%
    (B) 37%
    (C) 8%
    (D) 3%
    (E) 1%

24. In City Y, the number of motor vehicles registered that were manufactured by Manufacturer R accounted for what percentage of all motor vehicles registered in City Y?
    (A) 4%
    (B) 8%
    (C) 12.5%
    (D) 16%
    (E) 25%

25. Which of the following conclusions can be inferred from the information given?

    I. Approximately 3700 of the motor vehicles registered in City X and City Y combined were manufactured by Manufacturer R.
    II. A greater number of motor vehicles manufactured by Manufacturer V are registered in City X than are registered in City Y.
    III. Approximately 200 more cars manufac-

tured by Manufacturer S are registered in City X than are registered in City Y.
    (A) I only
    (B) III only
    (C) I and II only
    (D) I and III only
    (E) I, II, and III

26. If x is an even integer and y is an odd integer, then which of the following is an even integer?
    (A) $x^2 + y$
    (B) $x^2 - y$
    (C) $(x^2)(y)$
    (D) $x + y$
    (E) $x - y$

27. If $pq \neq 0$ and $p = \frac{1}{3}q$, then the ratio of p to 3q is
    (A) 9
    (B) 3
    (C) 1
    (D) $\frac{1}{3}$
    (E) $\frac{1}{9}$

28. If a certain chemical costs $50 for 30 gallons, then how many gallons of the chemical can be purchased for $625?
    (A) 12.5
    (B) 24
    (C) 325
    (D) 375
    (E) 425

29. Which of the following can be expressed as the sum of three consecutive integers?
    (A) 17
    (B) 23
    (C) 25
    (D) 30
    (E) 40

30. If the areas of the three different sized faces of a rectangular solid are 6, 8, and 12, then what is the volume of the solid?
    (A) 576
    (B) 288
    (C) 144
    (D) 48
    (E) 24

STOP

END OF SECTION. IF YOU HAVE ANY TIME LEFT, GO
OVER YOUR WORK IN THIS SECTION ONLY. DO NOT
WORK IN ANY OTHER SECTION OF THE TEST.

SECTION IV

30 minutes
30 questions

Directions: For each of the following questions two quantities are given, one in Column A and one in Column B. Compare the two quantities and mark your answer sheet with the correct lettered conclusion. These are your options:
   A: If the quantity in Column A is the greater;
   B: if the quantity in Column B is the greater;
   C: if the two quantities are equal;
   D: if the relationship cannot be determined from the information given.
Common Information: In any question, information applying to both columns is centered between the columns and above the quantities in columns A and B. The common information applies to both columns. Any symbol that appears in both columns represents the same idea or quantity in both columns.
Numbers: All numbers used are real numbers.
Figures: Assume that the position of points, angles, regions and so forth are in the order shown. Figures are assumed to lie in a plane unless otherwise indicated. Figures accompanying questions are intended to provide information you can use in answering the questions. However, unless a note states that a figure is drawn to scale, you should solve the problems by using your knowledge of mathematics and *not* by estimating sizes by sight or measurement.
Lines: Assume that lines shown as straight are indeed straight.

	COLUMN A	COLUMN B
1.	$16 \div 4$	$\frac{4}{11} \times 11$
2.	$x = \frac{1}{3}$ of 12 $y = \frac{1}{3}$ of 9	
	x	y
3.	When n is divided by 49, the remainder is 0.	
	the remainder when n is divided by 7	7
4.	$\left(\frac{101}{202}\right)^{11}$	$\left(-\frac{101}{202}\right)^{11}$

COLUMN A	COLUMN B

5.

An apartment building has 5 floors, one of which has only 2 apartments. Each of the other floors has 4 apartments.

3 times the number of floors in the building	the number of apartments in the building

---

6.

$$x^2 - 3x - 4 = (x + m)(x - n)$$

m	n

7.

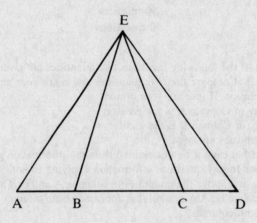

$$AB = CD = \tfrac{1}{2} \times BC$$

area of triangle BEC	sum of the areas of triangles AEB and CED

8.

$\sqrt{\tfrac{3}{16}} + \sqrt{\tfrac{3}{16}} + \sqrt{\tfrac{3}{16}}$	$\sqrt{\tfrac{9}{16}}$

9.

$5\left(\dfrac{x}{5} + \dfrac{y}{5} - \dfrac{7}{5}\right)$	$x + y - 7$

10.

Point P has coordinates (x, y); point Q has coordinates (x − 1, y − 1).

the distance from P to the origin	the distance from Q to the origin

---

11.

the perimeter of a square with an area of 16	the perimeter of a square with a diagonal of $4\sqrt{2}$

12.

$\tfrac{1}{3} \times \tfrac{2}{3}$	(.333)(.666)

13.

When x + 5 is divided by 3, the remainder is 2.

the remainder when x is divided by 2	1

COLUMN A	COLUMN B
14. the smallest number greater than 12 that is divisible by 12 but not by 8	48

---

15.   x, y, and z are fractions between 0 and 1

$x(y + z)$ $xy + z$

Directions: For each of the following questions, select the best of the answer choices and blacken the corresponding space on your answer sheet.

Numbers: All numbers used are real numbers.

Figures: The diagrams and figures that accompany these questions are for the purpose of providing information useful in answering the questions. Unless it is stated that a specific figure is not drawn to scale, the diagrams and figures are drawn as accurately as possible. All figures are in a plane unless otherwise indicated.

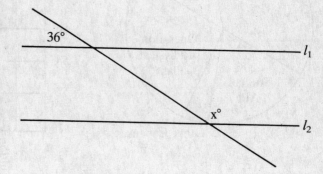

16. Which of the following is equal to 0.00127?
(A) 1.27×10
(B) 1.27×0.10
(C) 1.27×0.01
(D) 1.27×0.001
(E) 1.27×0.0001

17. A prize of $240 is divided between two persons. If one person receives $180, then what is the difference between the amounts received by the two persons?
(A) $30
(B) $60
(C) $120
(D) $210
(E) $420

18. If $3x - 4y = 5$ and $\frac{y}{x} = \frac{1}{3}$, then what is x?

(A) $-5y$
(B) $-5x$
(C) 4
(D) 1
(E) 3

19. In the figure above, if $l_1 \parallel l_2$, what is the value of x?
(A) 36
(B) 54
(C) 90
(D) 144
(E) 154

20. If $\frac{x - 1}{x + 1} = \frac{4}{5}$, then x =

(A) 5
(B) 3
(C) 4
(D) 9
(E) 12

21. In a certain group of people, $\frac{3}{8}$ of the people are men, and $\frac{2}{3}$ of the men have brown eyes. If $\frac{3}{4}$ of the people have brown eyes, then what fraction of the group are women who do not have brown eyes?
(A) $\frac{1}{8}$
(B) $\frac{3}{16}$
(C) $\frac{1}{4}$
(D) $\frac{5}{16}$
(E) $\frac{3}{8}$

Questions 22—25 are based on the following graphs:

BUDGET INFORMATION FOR COLLEGE M IN YEAR N

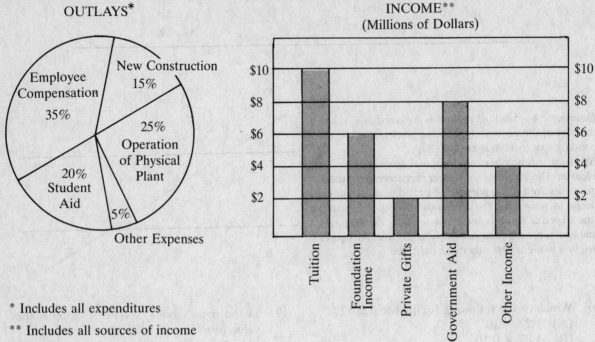

OUTLAYS*

INCOME**
(Millions of Dollars)

* Includes all expenditures

** Includes all sources of income

NOTE: Outlays = Income

22. For the year shown, College M spent how much money on the operation of its physical plant?
    (A) $2,500,000
    (B) $4,000,000
    (C) $7,500,000
    (D) $8,000,000
    (E) $9,500,000

23. For the year shown, what percentage of College M's income came from foundation income?
    (A) 6%
    (B) 20%
    (C) 25%
    (D) 33⅓%
    (E) 60%

24. For the year shown, how much more money was spent by College M on employee com-

pensation than on student aid?
    (A) $16,500,000
    (B) $10,500,000
    (C) $6,000,000
    (D) $4,500,000
    (E) $2,500,000

25. Which of the following can be inferred from the information provided?
    I. In year N, tuition accounted for ⅓ of total income.
    II. In year N, the foundation provided three times as much income as private gifts.
    III. In year N, $4,000,000 spent in student aid came directly from the foundation income.

    (A) I only
    (B) III only
    (C) I and II only
    (D) II and III only
    (E) I, II, and III

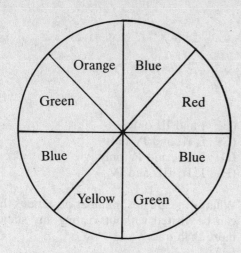

(B) $\dfrac{x - y}{xy}$

(C) xy

(D) $\dfrac{xy}{x - y}$

(E) $\dfrac{xy}{y - x}$

26. The figure above shows a wheel of fortune divided into sections of equal size and painted with the colors indicated. If the wheel has a diameter of 64 centimeters, what is the total area of the wheel that is painted blue (expressed in square centimeters)?

(A) 3π
(B) 24π
(C) 40π
(D) 128π
(E) 384π

27. Right circular cylinder P has a radius of 3 and a height of 4. If the volume of P is equal to the volume of right circular cylinder Q, which has a radius of 2, then what is the height of Q?

(A) 6
(B) 9
(C) 12
(D) 18
(E) 36

28. If $\dfrac{1}{x} - \dfrac{1}{y} = \dfrac{1}{z}$, then z is equal to which of the following?

(A) $\dfrac{y - x}{xy}$

29. In a certain company, the ratio of the number of women employees to the number of men employees is 3 to 2. If the total number of employees is 240, then how many of the employees are men?

(A) 40
(B) 48
(C) 96
(D) 144
(E) 160

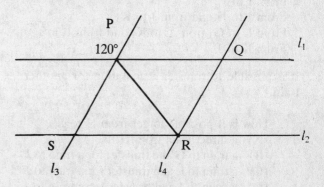

30. In the figure above, $l_1 \parallel l_2$, and $l_3 \parallel l_4$. If PQ = 3 and QR = 3, then what is the length of PR?

(A) $6\sqrt{3}$

(B) $\dfrac{3\sqrt{3}}{2}$

(C) 3

(D) $9\sqrt{5}$

(E) $\dfrac{\sqrt{3}}{2}$

STOP

END OF SECTION. IF YOU HAVE ANY TIME LEFT, GO
OVER YOUR WORK IN THIS SECTION ONLY. DO NOT
WORK IN ANY OTHER SECTION OF THE TEST.

SECTION V

30 minutes
25 questions

Directions: Each of the following questions or groups of questions is based on a short passage or a set of propositions. In answering these questions it may sometimes be helpful to draw a simple picture or chart. When you have selected the best answer to each question, darken the corresponding circle on your answer sheet.

Questions 1–6

A railway system consists of six stations, G, H, I, J, K, and L. Trains run only according to the following conditions:

From G to H
From H to G and from H to I
From I to J
From J to H and from J to K
From L to G; from L to K, and from L to I
From K to J

It is possible to transfer at a station for another train.

1. How is it possible to get from H to J?
   (A) a direct train from H to J
   (B) a train to G and transfer for a train to J
   (C) a train to L and transfer for a train to J
   (D) a train to I and transfer for a train to J
   (E) It is impossible to reach J from H.

2. Which of the following stations CANNOT be reached by a train from any of the other stations?
   (A) G
   (B) H
   (C) I
   (D) K
   (E) L

3. From which of the following stations is it possible to reach I with exactly one transfer?
   I. G
   II. H
   III. J
   IV. K

   (A) I only

(B) I and III only
(C) I, II, and IV only
(D) I, III, and IV only
(E) I, II, III, and IV

4. What is the greatest number of stations that can be visited without visiting any station more than once?
   (A) 2
   (B) 3
   (C) 4
   (D) 5
   (E) 6

5. Which of the following trips requires the greatest number of transfers?
   (A) G to I
   (B) H to K
   (C) L to H
   (D) L to I
   (E) L to K

6. If station I is closed, which of the following trips is impossible?
   (A) G to J
   (B) J to K
   (C) L to K
   (D) L to J
   (E) L to G

7. Since all swans I have encountered have been white, it follows that the swans I will see when I visit the Bronx Zoo will also be white.

   Which of the following most closely parallels the reasoning of the preceding argument?
   (A) Some birds are incapable of flight; therefore, swans are probably incapable of flight.
   (B) Every ballet I have attended has failed to interest me; so a theatrical production which fails to interest me must be a ballet.
   (C) Since all cases of severe depression I have encountered were susceptible to treatment by chlorpromazine, there

must be something in the chlorpromazine which adjusts the patient's brain
chemistry.
(D) Because every society has a word for
justice, the concept of fair play must be
inherent in the biological makeup of the
human species.
(E) Since no medicine I have tried for my
allergy has ever helped, this new product probably will not work either.

8. ERIKA: Participation in intramural competitive sports teaches students the importance of teamwork, for no one
wants to let his or her teammates
down.

NICHOL: That is not correct. The real reason students play hard is that such
programs place a premium on winning and no one wants to be a
member of a losing team.

Which of the following comments can most
reasonably be made about the exchange between Erika and Nichol?
(A) If fewer and fewer schools are sponsor-
ing intramural sports programs now than
a decade ago, Erika's position is undermined.
(B) If high schools and universities provide
financial assistance for the purchase of
sports equipment, Nichol's assertion
about the importance of winning is
weakened.
(C) If teamwork is essential to success in
intramural competitive sports, Erika's
position and Nichol's position are not
necessarily incompatible.
(D) Since the argument is one about motivation, it should be possible to resolve
the issue by taking a survey of deans at
schools which have intramural sports
programs.
(E) Since the question raised is about hidden psychological states, it is impossible to answer it.

9. A cryptographer has intercepted an enemy
message that is in code. He knows that the
code is a simple substitution of numbers for
letters. Which of the following would be the
least helpful in breaking the code?

(A) knowing the frequency with which the
vowels of the language are used
(B) knowing the frequency with which two
vowels appear together in the language
(C) knowing the frequency with which odd
numbers appear relative to even numbers in the message
(D) knowing the conjugation of the verb *to
be* in the language on which the code is
based
(E) knowing every word in the language that
begins with the letter *R*

10. One way of reducing commuting time for
those who work in the cities is to increase
the speed at which traffic moves in the heart
of the city. This can be accomplished by raising the tolls on the tunnels and bridges connecting the city with other communities. This
will discourage auto traffic into the city and
will encourage people to use public transportation instead.

Which of the following, if true, would LEAST
weaken the argument above?
(A) Nearly all of the traffic in the center of
the city is commercial traffic, which will
continue despite toll increases.
(B) Some people now driving alone into the
city would choose to carpool with each
other rather than use public transportation.
(C) Any temporary improvement in traffic
flow would be lost because the improvement itself would attract more cars.
(D) The numbers of commuters who would
be deterred by the toll increases would
be insignificant.
(E) The public transportation system is not
able to handle any significant increase
in the number of commuters using the
system.

Questions 11–16

A travel agent is arranging tours which visit various cities: L, M, N, O, P, Q, R, S, and T. Each
tour must be arranged in accordance with the following restrictions:

If M is included in a tour, both Q and R must
also be included.

P can be included in a tour only if O is also included.

If Q is included in a tour, M must be included along with N or T or both.

P and Q cannot both be included in a tour.

A tour cannot include O, R, and T.
A tour cannot include N, S, and R.
A tour cannot include L and R.

11. If M is included in a tour, what is the minimum number of other cities which must be included in the tour?
    (A) 2
    (B) 3
    (C) 4
    (D) 5
    (E) 6

12. Which of the following cities cannot be included in a tour which includes P?
    (A) M
    (B) N
    (C) O
    (D) S
    (E) R

13. Which of the following is an acceptable group of cities for a tour?
    (A) M, N, O, P
    (B) M, N, Q, R
    (C) M, N, Q, S
    (D) L, M, Q, R
    (E) N, S, R, T

14. Which one city would have to be deleted from the group M, Q, O, R, T to form an acceptable tour?
    (A) M
    (B) Q
    (C) O
    (D) R
    (E) T

15. Which of the following could be made into an acceptable tour by adding exactly one more city?
    (A) L, O, R
    (B) M, P, Q
    (C) M, Q, R
    (D) N, S, R
    (E) R, T, P

16. Exactly how many of the cities could be used for a tour consisting of only one city?
    (A) 2
    (B) 3
    (C) 4
    (D) 5
    (E) 6

Questions 17–22

A child is stringing 11 different colored beads on a string.

Of the 11, four are yellow, three are red, two are blue, and two are green.
The red beads are adjacent to one another.
The blue beads are adjacent to one another.
The green beads are not adjacent to one another.
A red bead is at one end of the string and a green bead is at the other end.

17. If the sixth and seventh beads are blue and the tenth bead is red, which of the following must be true?
    (A) The second bead is green.
    (B) The fifth bead is yellow.
    (C) The eighth bead is green.
    (D) A green bead is next to a yellow bead.
    (E) A blue bead is next to a green bead.

18. If the four yellow beads are next to each other, and if the tenth bead is yellow, which of the following beads must be blue?
    (A) the fourth
    (B) the fifth
    (C) the sixth
    (D) the seventh
    (E) the eighth

19. If each blue bead is next to a green bead, and if the four yellow beads are next to each other, then which of the following beads must be yellow?

    I. the fourth
    II. the fifth
    III. the sixth
    IV. the seventh

    (A) I and II only
    (B) II and III only
    (C) III and IV only
    (D) I, II, and III
    (E) II, III, and IV

20. If the fifth and sixth beads are blue and the ninth bead is red, which of the following must be true?
    (A) One of the green beads is next to a blue bead.
    (B) One of the red beads is next to a green bead.
    (C) Each yellow bead is next to at least one other yellow bead.
    (D) The second bead is yellow.
    (E) The eighth bead is yellow.

21. If the fifth, eighth, ninth, and tenth beads are yellow, which of the following must be true?
    I.   The fourth bead is green.
    II. The sixth bead is blue.
    III. Each green bead is next to at least one yellow bead.

    (A) I only
    (B) II only
    (C) I and II only
    (D) I and III only
    (E) I, II, and III

22. If one green bead is next to a red bead and the other green bead is next to a blue bead, which of the following must be true?
    (A) The second bead is blue.
    (B) The fourth bead is green.
    (C) The fourth bead is yellow.
    (D) The seventh bead is yellow.
    (E) The eighth bead is green.

23. Some philosophers have argued that there exist certain human or natural rights which belong to all human beings by virtue of their humanity. But a review of the laws of different societies shows that the rights accorded a person vary from society to society and even within a society over time. Since there is no right that is universally protected, there are no natural rights.

    A defender of the theory that natural rights do exist might respond to this objection by arguing that
    (A) some human beings do not have any natural rights
    (B) some human rights are natural while others derive from a source such as a constitution
    (C) people in one society may have natural rights which people in another society lack
    (D) all societies have some institution which protects the rights of an individual in that society
    (E) natural rights may exist even though they are not protected by some societies

Questions 24 and 25

The single greatest weakness of American parties is their inability to achieve cohesion in the legislature. Although there is some measure of party unity, it is not uncommon for the majority party to be unable to implement important legislation. The unity is strongest during election campaigns; after the primary elections, the losing candidates all promise their support to the party nominee. By the time the Congress convenes, the unity has dissipated. This phenomenon is attributable to the fragmented nature of party politics. The national committees are no more than feudal lords who receive nominal fealty from their vassals. A congressman builds his own power upon a local base. Consequently, a congressman is likely to be responsive to local special interest groups. Evidence of this is seen in the differences in voting patterns between the upper and lower houses. In the Senate, where terms are longer, there is more party unity.

24. Which of the following, if true, would most strengthen the author's argument?
    (A) On 30 key issues, 18 of the 67 majority party members in the Senate voted against the party leaders.
    (B) On 30 key issues, 70 of the 305 majority party members in the House voted against the party leaders.
    (C) On 30 key issues, over half the members of the minority party in both houses voted with the majority party against the leaders of the minority party.
    (D) Of 30 key legislative proposals introduced by the president, only eight passed both houses.
    (E) Of 30 key legislative proposals introduced by a president whose party controlled a majority in both houses, only four passed both houses.

25. Which of the following, if true, would most weaken the author's argument?
    (A) Congressmen receive funds from the national party committee.
    (B) Senators vote against the party leaders only two-thirds as often as members of the House.
    (C) The primary duty of an officeholder is to be responsive to his local constituency rather than party leaders.
    (D) There is more unity among minority party members than among majority party members.
    (E) Much legislation is passed each session despite party disunity.

STOP

END OF SECTION. IF YOU HAVE ANY TIME LEFT, GO OVER YOUR WORK IN THIS SECTION ONLY. DO NOT WORK IN ANY OTHER SECTION OF THE TEST.

SECTION VI

30 minutes
25 questions

Directions: Each of the following questions or groups of questions is based on a short passage or a set of propositions. In answering these questions it may sometimes be helpful to draw a simple picture or chart. When you have selected the best answer to each question, darken the corresponding circle on your answer sheet.

Questions 1–6

A geneologist has determined that M, N, P, Q, R, S, and T are the father, the mother, the aunt, the brother, the sister, the wife, and the daughter of X, but she has been unable to determine which person has which status. She does know:

P and Q are of the same sex.
M and N are not of the same sex.
S was born before M.
Q is not the mother of X.

1. How many of the seven people—M, N, P, Q, R, S, and T—are female?
    (A) 3
    (B) 4
    (C) 5
    (D) 6
    (E) 7

2. Which of the following must be true?
    (A) M is a female.
    (B) N is a female.
    (C) P is a female.
    (D) Q is a male.
    (E) S is a male.

3. If T is the daughter of X, which of the following must be true?
    (A) M and P are of the same sex.
    (B) M and Q are of the same sex.
    (C) P is not of the same sex as N.
    (D) R is not of the same sex as S.
    (E) S is not of the same sex as T.

4. If M and Q are sisters, all of the following must be true EXCEPT
   (A) N is a male.
   (B) M is X's mother.
   (C) Q is X's aunt.
   (D) T is X's daughter.
   (E) S is not X's brother.

5. If S is N's grandfather, then which of the following must be true?
   (A) R is N's aunt.
   (B) X is P's son.
   (C) M is X's brother.
   (D) Q is S's husband.
   (E) P is N's aunt.

6. If M is X's wife, all of the following could be true EXCEPT
   (A) S is X's daughter.
   (B) P is X's sister.
   (C) Q is X's sister.
   (D) R is X's father.
   (E) N is X's brother.

7. AL: If an alien species ever visited Earth, it would surely be because they were looking for other intelligent species with whom they could communicate. Since we have not been contacted by aliens, we may conclude that none have ever visited this planet.
   AMY: Or, perhaps, they did not think human beings intelligent.

   How is Amy's response related to Al's argument?
   (A) She misses Al's point entirely.
   (B) She attacks Al personally rather than his reasoning.
   (C) She points out that Al made an unwarranted assumption.
   (D) She ignores the detailed internal development of Al's logic.
   (E) She introduces a false analogy.

8. If quarks are the smallest subatomic particles in the universe, then gluons are needed to hold quarks together. Since gluons are needed to hold quarks together, it follows that quarks are the smallest subatomic parti-

cles in the universe.

The logic of the above argument is most nearly paralleled by which of the following?
(A) If this library has a good French literature collection, it will contain a copy of *Les Conquerants* by Malraux. The collection does contain a copy of *Les Conquerants;* therefore, the library has a good French literature collection.
(B) If there is a man-in-the-moon, the moon must be made of green cheese for him to eat. There is a man-in-the-moon, so the moon is made of green cheese.
(C) Either helium or hydrogen is the lightest element of the periodic table. Helium is not the lightest element of the periodic table, so hydrogen must be the lightest element of the periodic table.
(D) If Susan is taller than Bob, and if Bob is taller than Elaine, then if Susan is taller than Bob, Susan is also taller than Elaine.
(E) Whenever it rains, the streets get wet. The streets are not wet. Therefore, it has not rained.

9. In the earliest stages of the common law, a party could have his case heard by a judge only upon the payment of a fee to the court, and then only if his case fit within one of the forms for which there existed a writ. At first the number of such formalized cases of action was very small, but judges invented new forms which brought more cases and greater revenues.

Which of the following conclusions is most strongly suggested by the paragraph above?
(A) Early judges often decided cases in an arbitrary and haphazard manner.
(B) In most early cases, the plaintiff rather than the defendant prevailed.
(C) The judiciary at first had greater power than either the legislature or the executive.
(D) One of the motivating forces for the early expansion in judicial power was economic considerations.
(E) The first common law decisions were inconsistent with one another and did not form a coherent body of law.

Questions 10–15

A farmer has three fields, 1, 2, and 3, and is deciding which crops to plant. The crops are F, G, H, I, and J.

F will grow only in fields 1 and 3, but in order for F to grow it must be fertilized with X.

G will grow in fields 1, 2, and 3, but in order for G to grow, fertilizer X must not be used.

H will grow in fields 1, 2, and 3, but in order for H to grow in field 3, it must be fertilized with Y.

I will grow only in fields 2 and 3, but in order for I to grow in field 2 it must be sprayed with pesticide Z, and in order for I to grow in field 3, it must not be sprayed with Z.

J will grow only in field 2, but in order for J to grow, H must not be planted in the same field.

All crops are planted and harvested at the same time. More than one crop may be planted in a field.

10. It is possible to grow which of the following pairs of crops together in field 1?

    I. F and G
    II. G and H
    III. F and H
    IV. H and J

    (A) I and II only
    (B) I and III only
    (C) II and III only
    (D) I, II, and III only
    (E) II, III, and IV only

11. It is possible for which of the following groups of crops to grow together in field 2?
    (A) F, G, and H
    (B) F, H, and I
    (C) G, H, and J
    (D) G, I, and J
    (E) H, I, and J

12. Which of the following is a complete and accurate listing of all crops that will grow alone in field 2 if the only pesticide or fertilizer used is Y?
    (A) F
    (B) F and H
    (C) G and H
    (D) G, H, and J
    (E) G, H, I, and J

13. Which of the following pairs of crops will grow together in field 3 if no other crops are planted in the field and no fertilizers or pesticides are applied?
    (A) F and H
    (B) F and I
    (C) G and H
    (D) G and I
    (E) H and J

14. What is the maximum number of different crops that can be planted together in field 3?
    (A) 1
    (B) 2
    (C) 3
    (D) 4
    (E) 5

15. Which of the following is a complete and accurate list of the crops that will grow alone in field 2 if X is the only pesticide or fertilizer applied?
    (A) H, J
    (B) I, G
    (C) I, H
    (D) I, J
    (E) J, G

Questions 16–21

A group of six players, P, Q, R, S, T, and U, are participating in a challenge tournament. All matches played are challenge matches and are governed by the following rules:

A player may challenge another player if and only if that player is ranked either one or two places above her.

If a player successfully challenges the player ranked immediately above her, the two players exchange ranks.

If a player successfully challenges the player two ranks above her, she moves up two ranks, and both the loser of the match and the player ranked below the loser move down one rank.

If a player is unsuccessful in her challenge, she and the player immediately below her exchange ranks, unless the unsuccessful challenger was already ranked last, in which case the rankings remain unchanged.

The initial rankings from the highest (first) to the lowest (sixth) are P, Q, R, S, T, U.

Only one match is played at a time.

16. Which of the following is possible as the first match of the tournament?
    (A) P challenges Q.
    (B) Q challenges R.
    (C) R challenges P.
    (D) S challenges P.
    (E) T challenges Q.

17. If S reaches first place after the first two matches of the tournament, which of the following must be ranked fourth at that point in play?
    (A) P
    (B) Q
    (C) R
    (D) T
    (E) U

18. All of the following are possible rankings, from highest to lowest, after exactly two matches EXCEPT
    (A) P, R, Q, T, S, U
    (B) P, R, Q, S, U, T
    (C) R, P, Q, U, S, T
    (D) Q, P, S, R, T, U
    (E) Q, P, S, R, U, T

19. If exactly two matches have been played, what is the maximum number of players whose initial ranks could have been changed?
    (A) 2
    (B) 3
    (C) 4
    (D) 5
    (E) 6

20. If after a certain number of matches the players are ranked from highest to lowest in the order R, Q, P, U, S, T, what is the minimum number of matches that could have been played?
    (A) 2
    (B) 3
    (C) 4
    (D) 5
    (E) 6

21. If after the initial two matches two players have improved their rankings and four players have each dropped in rank, which of the fol-

lowing could be the third match of the tournament?
    (A) R challenges P.
    (B) R challenges Q.
    (C) Q challenges U.
    (D) U challenges P.
    (E) T challenges Q.

22. A recent survey by the economics department of an Ivy League university revealed that increases in the salaries of preachers are accompanied by increases in the nationwide average of rum consumption. From 1965 to 1970 preachers' salaries increased on the average of 15% and rum sales grew by 14.5%. From 1970 to 1975 average preachers' salaries rose by 17% and rum sales by 17.5%. From 1975 to 1980 rum sales expanded by only 8% and average preachers' salaries also grew by only 8%.

Which of the following is the most likely explanation for the findings cited in the paragraph?
    (A) When preachers have more disposable income, they tend to allocate that extra money to alcohol.
    (B) When preachers are paid more, they preach longer; and longer sermons tend to drive people to drink.
    (C) Since there were more preachers in the country, there were also more people; and a larger population will consume greater quantities of liquor.
    (D) The general standard of living increased from 1965 to 1980, which accounts for both the increase in rum consumption and preachers' average salaries.
    (E) A consortium of rum importers carefully limited the increases in imports of rum during the test period cited.

23. Since all four-door automobiles I have repaired have eight-cylinder engines, all four-door automobiles must have eight-cylinder engines.

The author argues on the basis of
    (A) special training
    (B) generalization
    (C) syllogism
    (D) ambiguity
    (E) deduction

24. Two women, one living in Los Angeles, the other living in New York City, carried on a lengthy correspondence by mail. The subject of the exchange was a dispute over certain personality traits of Winston Churchill. After some two dozen letters, the Los Angeles resident received the following note from her New York City correspondent: "It seems you were right all along. Yesterday I met someone who actually knew Sir Winston, and he confirmed your opinion."

The two women could have been arguing on the basis of all the following EXCEPT
(A) published biographical information
(B) old news film footage
(C) direct personal acquaintance
(D) assumption
(E) third party reports

25. The protection of the right of property by the Constitution is tenuous at best. It is true that the Fifth Amendment states that the government may not take private property for public use without compensation, but it is the government that defines private property.

Which of the following is most likely the point the author is leading up to?
(A) Individual rights that are protected by the Supreme Court are secure against government encroachment.
(B) Private property is neither more nor less than that which the government says is private property.
(C) The government has no authority to deprive an individual of liberty.
(D) No government that acts arbitrarily can be justified.
(E) The keystone of American democracy is the Constitution.

STOP

END OF SECTION. IF YOU HAVE ANY TIME LEFT, GO OVER YOUR WORK IN THIS SECTION ONLY. DO NOT WORK IN ANY OTHER SECTION OF THE TEST.

PRACTICE EXAMINATION 6—ANSWER KEY

Section I

1.	E	10.	A	19.	B	28.	C	37.	A
2.	B	11.	C	20.	A	29.	B	38.	E
3.	B	12.	A	21.	B	30.	C		
4.	C	13.	C	22.	B	31.	A		
5.	A	14.	C	23.	A	32.	B		
6.	A	15.	A	24.	A	33.	C		
7.	B	16.	E	25.	C	34.	E		
8.	B	17.	A	26.	A	35.	D		
9.	D	18.	C	27.	C	36.	B		

Section II

1.	B	10.	A	19.	B	28.	D	37.	D
2.	A	11.	E	20.	E	29.	A	38.	A
3.	A	12.	D	21.	D	30.	E		
4.	E	13.	A	22.	B	31.	B		
5.	D	14.	A	23.	A	32.	C		
6.	B	15.	D	24.	E	33.	B		
7.	C	16.	A	25.	B	34.	D		
8.	D	17.	C	26.	C	35.	C		
9.	B	18.	A	27.	E	36.	A		

Section III

1.	C	7.	D	13.	A	19.	C	25.	D
2.	A	8.	C	14.	B	20.	A	26.	C
3.	A	9.	A	15.	C	21.	D	27.	E
4.	A	10.	B	16.	A	22.	A	28.	D
5.	C	11.	B	17.	E	23.	D	29.	D
6.	D	12.	D	18.	A	24.	E	30.	E

Section IV

1.	C	7.	C	13.	D	19.	D	25.	C
2.	B	8.	A	14.	B	20.	D	26.	E
3.	B	9.	C	15.	B	21.	A	27.	B
4.	A	10.	D	16.	D	22.	C	28.	E
5.	B	11.	C	17.	C	23.	B	29.	C
6.	B	12.	A	18.	E	24.	D	30.	C

Section V

1.	D	6.	A	11.	B	16.	E	21.	E
2.	E	7.	E	12.	A	17.	D	22.	D
3.	B	8.	C	13.	B	18.	B	23.	E
4.	E	9.	C	14.	C	19.	E	24.	E
5.	B	10.	B	15.	C	20.	D	25.	C

Section VI

1.	C	6.	A	11.	D	16.	C	21.	D
2.	C	7.	C	12.	D	17.	C	22.	D
3.	D	8.	A	13.	D	18.	E	23.	B
4.	D	9.	D	14.	C	19.	E	24.	C
5.	C	10.	C	15.	A	20.	B	25.	B

EXPLANATORY ANSWERS

SECTION I

1. **(E)** The keys here are the parallelisms or continuations required by each blank. For the first substitution you need something that is parallel to piety, another virtue. On this ground you can eliminate both (C) and (D). Then, in the second blank you will need an adjective describing serious problems such as weather and disease, and only (E) does this.

2. **(B)** The key to this question is the parallel or continuation set up by the structure of the entire sentence. It is possible that the sentence can be completed in one of two ways. Either the review was good, in which case the adjective completing the second blank must suggest something positive, or the review was bad, and the second element must also suggest something negative. At first, therefore, (C) looks like a possibility based on the first element, but it fails because it does not complete the needed parallel. (B) does complete the parallel. As for the remaining choices, you can eliminate them on one or two grounds because their substitutions are not idiomatic, e.g., what does it mean to say that the conducting was benign?

3. **(B)** There are two ways of attacking this question. First, the initial substitution must make sense in terms of the situation described. It is possible to eliminate (A), (C) and (D) on this basis. For example, since the violinist is already performing, it makes no sense to say that she is rehearsing her performance. You might make an argument for "renew" in choice (E), even though that is stretching things to the limit. In any event, you can eliminate (E) on the second ground that it fails to carry through the continuation indicated by the action.

4. **(C)** There are two points of attack here. First, you need a word to parallel the idea of a charged atmosphere. What happened to the law? It was infected with religious overtones. Second, you need a parallel to this. As a consequence, what did the law do to the required separation of state and church? It violated it—and this was the reason the law was struck down.

5. **(A)** You should almost be able to complete the sentence even without looking at the choices. Since there is a perceived correlation between price and value, you would expect that sellers would raise prices. This suggests either (A) or (B) as the correct choice. (B), however, fails to carry through the continuation or parallel. Given the correlation, the price increase would not be moderate but very great.

6. **(A)** Parallelism or continuation is the key here. Notice that we must use adjectives with positive overtones—the audience gave the performance a standing ovation. So we can eliminate (C) on the basis of the first element. And we eliminate (B) and (E) on the basis of the second substitution. (A) is the only choice to carry through the positive notion.

7. **(B)** The structure "in . . . and never in . . ." requires a set of contrasting words (because of the negative). In the greater context of the entire sentence, we see that artists and poets think alike, so (B) provides the pair we are looking for.

8. **(B)** The part of speech of the word "trap" is ambiguous. It might be either a verb or a noun. The issue is settled, however, by consulting choice (A). There the first element is "novel," a word that cannot be a verb. So we formulate the relationship as a trap is used to catch game. So, too, a net is used to catch fish. Notice also the "echo" relationship. Both activities are very similar: hunting: fishing.

9. **(D)** The relationship is that of example to category. A mansard is a type of roof, and a dormer is a type of window. Further, there is a confirming "echo": both are architectual features.

10. **(A)** The pastor is charged with the care of the congregation, just as the shepherd is charged with the care of the flock. And there is the interesting and very powerful "echo" between pastor and shepherd and congregation and flock.

11. **(C)** As in question 9, the relationship is again that of example to general type. An ode is a kind of poem, and a ballad is a kind of song. And again there is an "echo," for there is a kinship between poem and song.

12. **(A)** The relationship here is one of opposition. Playing with the part of speech, we might say that

someone who is tenacious is not weak, and someone who is apathetic is not caring.

13. **(C)** The curator is in charge of caring for paintings, and the archivist has the same relationship to manuscripts. And there is an echo of kinship between the curator and the archivist and between paintings and manuscripts.

14. **(C)** "Crepescule" means twilight, so the stem words are synonyms, just as dawn and daybreak are synonyms. And you will notice the "echo" between twilight and daybreak.

15. **(A)** Again, the relationship is based on similarity. To augur is to predict the future, and portend is to indicate what is to come. To foresee is to predict, and to bode is to indicate what is to come. And there is a very strong "echo" here, since all words have to do with knowing or predicting the future.

16. **(E)** Puerile means childish or immature, or, reflecting its root, boyish. Juvenile means youthful or young. Making suitable adjustment for the part of speech in question, you can see the analogy. Additionally, there is a very strong "echo" between puerile and juvenile, which can be used to convey negative meaning.

17. **(A)** The passage describes the attitude of premodernized society toward war as accepted, even noble, necessary. Coupled with the goals of war in premodernized societies, we can infer that leaders of premodernized society regarded war as a valid policy tool. On this ground we select (A), eliminating (B) and (C). As for (D), although this can be inferred to have been a feature of war in premodernized society, (D) does not respond to the question: What did the leaders think of war, that is, what was their attitude? (E) can be eliminated on the same ground and on the further ground that "necessity" for war was not that described in (E)

18. **(C)** The author is discussing war, a seemingly uncivilized activity. Yet the author argues that war, at least in premodernized times, was the necessary result of certain economic and social forces. His use of the term "civilized" is ironic. Under other circumstances, the explanations offered by (A) and (B) might be plausible, but there is nothing in this text to support either of them. (D), too, might under other circumstances be a reason for placing the word in quotation marks, but it does not appear that this author is attempting to affect the reader's emotions; the passage is too detached

and scientific for that. Finally, (E) does articulate one of the author's objectives, but this is not the reason for putting the one word in quotations. The explanation for that is something more specific than an overall idea of the passage.

19. **(B)** This is an explicit idea question, and (A), (C), (D), and (E) are all mentioned at various points in the passage as reasons for going to war. (B), however, is not explicitly mentioned. Indeed, the author states that control and exploitation, not annihilation and destruction, were goals.

20. **(A)** The tone of the passage is neutral—scientific and detached. As for the remaining choices, (B) and (D) can be eliminated as overstatements. (E) is a closer call. While it is true that the author expresses concern about war, it cannot be said that hope is a *defining* feature of the passage. A better description of the prevailing tone is offered by (A) As for (C), the one ironic reference ("civilized") does not make the entire passage humorous.

21. **(B)** This is a main idea question. The author begins by stating that a large number of auto traffic fatalities can be attributed to drivers who are intoxicated. He then reviews two approaches to controlling this problem, taxation and drunk driving laws. Neither is very successful. The author finally notes that therapy may be useful, though the extent of its value has not yet been proved. (B) describes this development fairly well. (A) can be eliminated since any conclusions drawn by the author from studies on drunk driving are used for the larger objective described in (B). (C) is incorrect since, aside from suggesting possible ways to reduce the extent of the problem, the author never treats the causes of drunk driving. (D) is incorrect for the same reason. Finally, (E) is incorrect, because the comparison between the U.S. and Britain is only a small part of the passage.

22. **(B)** This is an inference question. In the third paragraph, the author discusses the effect of drunk driving laws. He states that after the implementation of the Road Safety Act in Britain, motor vehicle fatalities fell considerably. On this basis, we infer that the RSA was a law aimed at drunk driving. We can eliminate (D) and (E) on this ground. (C) can be eliminated as not warranted on the basis of this information. It is not clear whether the number of arrests increased. Equally consistent with the passage is the conclusion that the number of arrests dropped because people were no longer driving while intoxicated. (C) is incorrect for a further reason, the justification for (B). (B) and (A) are fairly close since both describe the RSA as a

law aimed at drunk driving. But the last sentence of the third paragraph calls for (B) over (A). As people learned that they would not get caught for drunk driving, the law became less effective. This suggests that the RSA made drunk driving illegal, not that it lowered the BAC required for conviction. This makes sense of the sentence " . . . they could drink and not be stopped." If (A) were correct, this sentence would have to read, " . . . they could drink the same amount and not be convicted."

23. **(A)** This is an inference question. In the first paragraph, the author states that for a person to attain a BAC of 0.1 percent, he or she would need to drink over five ounces of 80 proof spirits over a *short period of time*. The author is trying to impress on us that that is a considerable quantity of alcohol for most people to drink. (A) explains why the author makes this comment. (B) is incorrect and confuses the first paragraph with the second paragraph. (C) is incorrect since the point of the example is that the BAC is so high most people will not exceed it. This is not to say, however, that people will not drink and drive because of laws establishing maximum BAC levels. Rather, they can continue to drink and drive because the law allows them a considerable margin in the level of BAC. (D) is a misreading of that first paragraph. Of all the very drunk drivers (BAC in excess of 0.1), only 1 percent are involved in accidents. But this does not say that most drivers involved in fatal collisions have BAC levels in excess of 0.1 percent, and that is what (D) says. As for (E), the author never states that the only way to attain a BAC of 0.1 percent is to drink five ounces of 80 proof spirits in a short time; there may be other ways of becoming intoxicated.

24. **(A)** This is an application question. In the second paragraph, the author states that increased taxation on alcohol would tax the heaviest drinkers most, but he notes that this would also penalize the moderate and light drinker. In other words, the remedy is not sufficiently focused on the problem. Then, in the third paragraph, the author notes that drunk driving laws are aimed at the specific problem drivers. We can infer from this discussion that the author would likely advocate drunk driving laws over taxation for the reasons just given. This reasoning is presented in answer (A). (B) is incorrect for the reasons just given and for the further reason that the passage never suggests that taxation is likely to be more effective in solving the problem. The author never really evaluates the effectiveness of taxation in reducing drunk driving. (C) is incorrect for the reason given in support of (A) and for the further reason that the author never raises the issue of personal liberty in conjunction with the BAC test. (D) can be eliminated because the author does not discount the effectiveness of anti-drunk driving measures entirely. Even the British example gives some support to the conclusion that such laws have an effect. (E) is incorrect, for the author never mentions the expense or administrative feasibility of BAC tests.

25. **(C)** This is a question about the logical structure of the passage. In paragraph 3, the author notes that stricter enforcement of laws against drunk driving may result in few more arrests; but a few more arrests is not likely to have much impact on the problem because the number of arrests is small compared to those who do not get caught. As a consequence, people will continue to drink and drive. The author supports this with the British experience. Once people realize that the chances of being caught are relatively small, they will drink and drive. This is the conclusion of answer (C). (A) is incorrect since the passge does not support the conclusion that the problem is any worse or any better in one country or the other. (B) is incorrect since this is the conclusion the author is arguing against. (D) is wrong because the author is not discussing the effectiveness of taxation in paragraph 3. (E) is a statement the author would likely accept, but that is not the reason for introducing the British example. So answer (E) is true but nonresponsive.

26. **(A)** This is an application question which asks us to examine the logical structure of the argument. In the fourth paragraph, the author argues that the effectiveness of deterrents to drunk driving will depend upon the ability of the drinker to control consumption. But drunk driving has two aspects: being drunk and driving. The author assumes that drunk driving is a function of drinking only. Otherwise, he would not suggest that control on consumption is *necessary* as opposed to *helpful*. (A) attacks this assumption by pointing out that it is possible to drink to excess without driving. It is possible that stiff penalties could be effective deterrents to drunk driving if not to drinking to excess. (B) is incorrect because the author himself makes this point, so this choice does not weaken the argument. (C) is incorrect since the author is concerned only with the problem of fatalities caused by drunk driving. It is hardly an attack on his argument to contend that he has not solved all of the world's ills. Then (D) can be eliminated since the author is concerned to eliminate fatalities caused by drunk driving. He takes no position on whether the drunk driver ought to be punished,

only that he or she ought to be deterred from driving while intoxicated. (E) is not a strong attack on the argument since the author does leave open the question of the value of therapy in combating drunk driving.

27. **(C)** This is a tone question which focuses on the final sentence of the paragraph. There the author states again that the problem is a serious one and that we must find a solution. Since he admonishes us to look for a solution, (C) is an excellent description. (A) can be eliminated since there is no irony in the passage. (B) can be eliminated since the author is concerned to find a solution. (E), however, overstates the case. Concern is not indignation. Finally, (D) may seem plausible. The author does leave us with a project. But to acknowledge that a problem exists and that a clear solution has not yet been found is not to be indecisive. The author is decisive in his assessment of the problem.

28. **(C)** The part of speech of the stem word is ambiguous, but that issue is settled by choice (A), which is an adjective. Something which is resident lives in a particular area or, more figuratively, belongs to a particular institution in a permanent fashion. So a good opposite would be transitory.

29. **(B)** Prolific means producing in great quantity, as a prolific writer, so a good opposite would be barren, which means unable to produce at all.

30. **(C)** To lambast is to heap criticism upon, to scold, or to denounce severely. So a good opposite would be to praise.

31. **(A)** The part of speech of the stem word is ambiguous. It might be a verb or it might be a noun. The issue is settled by choice (A). Here court is a verb. As a verb, to court means to solicit or to try to get. So a possible opposite is to reject.

32. **(B)** To forge has the literal meaning of shaping metal. The more figurative meaning is to create or to shape anything. For example, to forge a union means to create that unity. So a good opposite would be to "un-create" or dissolve.

33. **(C)** This is pretty much just a vocabulary item. Motile means having the power of motion or able to move, so a good opposite is immobile.

34. **(E)** Here is another vocabulary item. Lachrymose means tearful or sad, so a good opposite is found in (E), joyful.

35. **(D)** Quiescence refers to a state of quiet or rest. A good opposite would be one referring to a state of motion, even violent motion, such as frenzy.

36. **(B)** Urbane means elegant and refined, so a good opposite would be rude.

37. **(A)** Rudimetary means basic, simple, undeveloped, so a good opposite is sophisticated.

38. **(E)** One meaning of magnanimous is generous, and the word suggests nobility of spirits. So a good opposite would be grudging, suggesting a pettiness of spirits.

SECTION II

1. **(B)** For the first substitution, we need a choice that passes some judgment about the students who do not repay their loans; on that ground we can eliminate (D) The remaining choices seem acceptable on the basis of the first element. For the second element, we need a choice that will show a logical connection between the failure of some students to repay loans and the later availability of loan money for others. Choice (B) is best since it shows that the failure of some students to pay back what they owe will adversely affect the availability of money for other studens desiring loans later.

2. **(A)** The "Although . . . ," structure requires a contrast between the thoughts in the first clause and those in the second clause; (A) nicely provides this contrast. The other choices can be eliminated on various grounds. (B) can be eliminated on the basis of the second element, for it makes no sense to say that the critics criticized her as a star in her own right. (C) can be eliminated on the first element since you would not say that initial success was "refuted." And you can eliminate (D) and (E) for similar reasons.

3. **(A)** There are two keys to this question. First, the "Contrary to . . . ," structure sets up a contrast between peace-loving and something else. Additionally, you will want a pair of words that will apply to both the warriors and the gods, bringing them into a parallel relationship. (A) does this by first contrasting peace-loving astronomers with formidable warriors, then establishing a parallel between the formidable warriors and the vengeful gods.

4. **(E)** You can eliminate (B), (C) and (D) on the basis of their second elements. They really make

no sense when substituted into the second blank. And you can probably see that (E) is a good answer because it both provides the needed contrast indicated by the introductory word "Despite" and supplies a second element that could be used to describe the feeling of the Academy. (A), perhaps, is an arguably correct choice, yet if you examine (A) closely, you will see that it fails. Although "admired" is syntactically acceptable for the first blank, it really does not make a meaningful statement. It does not explain the perseverance of the scientist.

5. **(D)** All but one of the choices can be eliminated on the basis of the first substitution. Notice that the question refers to the "delightful" characters of Irving. Only "charm" is consistent with such a judgment. Additionally, only "borrowed," of all the possible second elements, provides the logical contrast required by the second part of the sentence: more for this than for that.

6. **(B)** The "Although" that introduces the sentence requires a contrast in the second portion of the sentence; only (B) provides this. The contrast between personality disorder and physical disease must be established.

7. **(C)** The two blanks stand in logical contrast to each other; on this ground you should be able to eliminate (B) and (D), for those two choices fail to supply a contrast. The other three choices do provide a contrast. (C), however, is the best choice because it provides a logical contrast between the experienced or felt emotion and the ability to articulate or express it in words.

8. **(D)** A good attack strategy is to formulate a sentence expressing the relationship between the stem words. Remember that you can take some liberties here, changing the parts of speech if you wish or reversing the word order. Here you might have used the sentence "One should refrain from doing that which is prohibited." Similarly, "One should comply with that which is compulsory." Notice also that there is a confirming "echo" between first elements of each pair and the second elements of each pair. Compulsory is the opposite of prohibited and comply is somewhat opposite to refrain.

9. **(B)** The relationship here is one of order of elements. The overture is the opening portion of an opera and the preface is the opening portion of a book.

10. **(A)** To resolve a doubt is to eliminate it, just as confirming a suspicion eliminates it by making it a certainty. There is also an "echo" here, since re-

solve and confirm are similar, and doubt and suspicion are similar.

11. **(E)** This relationship might be expressed as "That which is exemplary is beyond reproach." So, too, that which is unimpeachable is not subject to criticism.

12. **(D)** Here the relationship is one of defining characteristic. The mendicant is a beggar and the prevaricator is a liar.

13. **(A)** This relationship is simply one of degree: A deluge is a big rain and an ocean is a big pond.

14. **(A)** The relationship here is that of agent to effect. The effect of a lubricant is to reduce friction, and the effect of a balm is to reduce pain. Notice also that there is an "echo" here. Friction and pain are somewhat similar in that friction is something that "afflicts" a machine as pain afflicts a body. And a lubricant is something like a "medicine" or balm that solves the problem.

15. **(D)** Here the relationship is that of defining characteristic. Boastfulness is one way of describing the essence of pomposity, just as arrogant is a way of describing the essence of conceit. Notice also the presence of an "echo" between pomposity and conceit and boastful and arrogance.

16. **(A)** The relationship here is fairly easy to describe, for theology is the study of religion and astronomy is the study of stars.

17. **(C)** This is a main idea question. The author begins by posing the question: Why are affirmative action programs so controversial? He then argues that affirmative action is unlike ordinary government programs in the way it allocates the burden of the program. Because of this, he concludes, we are torn between supporting the programs (because they have legitimate goals) and condemning the programs (because of the way the cost is allocated). (C) neatly describes this development. The author analyzes the structure of the moral dilemma. (A) is incorrect since the comparison is but a subpart of the overall development and is used in the service of the larger analysis. (B) is incorrect since the author reaches no such clear-cut decision. Rather, we are left with the question posed by the dilemma. (D) is incorrect since the author presupposes in his presentation that the reader already understands the importance of the issue. Finally, (E) is incorrect since the advantages of the programs are mentioned only in passing.

18. **(A)** This is a logical structure question. In the second paragraph, the author will describe the general structure of government programs in order to set up the contrast with affirmative action. The discussion begins with "Setting aside . . . ," indicating the author recognizes such cases and does not wish to discuss them in detail. Tolls and tuition are exceptions to the general rule, so the author explicitly sets them aside in order to preempt a possible objection to his analysis based on claimed counterexamples. (B) is incorrect since the overall point of the passage is to discuss this dilemma, but the main point of the passage will not answer the question about the logical substructure of the argument. (C) is incorrect since tolls and tuition are not ordinary government programs. (D) is incorrect since the author never raises such doubts. Finally, (E) misses the point of the examples. The point is not that they are costly but that the cost is born by the specific user.

19. **(B)** This is an application question. In the first paragraph, the author states that affirmative action is designed to achieve social and economic objectives. Although he qualifies his claim, he seems to believe that those arguments are in favor of affirmative action. So (B) is clearly supported by the text. (A) is not supported by the text since the author leaves us with a question; he does not resolve the issue. (C) can be eliminated on the same ground. The author neither embraces nor rejects affirmative action. (D) goes beyond the scope of the argument. While the author might wish that this were possible, nothing in the passage indicates such restructuring is possible. Indeed, in paragraph 3, the author remarks that the "funding" problem seems to be inherent. Finally, (E) can be eliminated on the same ground as (A). Though the author recognizes the unfairness of affirmative action, he also believes that the programs are valuable.

20. **(E)** In paragraph 2, the author mentions that government programs entail both social and economic costs. Then the cost of the specific example, the passed-over worker, is not a government expenditure in the sense that money is laid out to purchase something. So the author is using the term "funding" in a nonstandard way, and he wishes to call his reader's attention to this usage. (E) parallels this explanation. (A) is incorrect since it is inconsistent with the reasoning just provided. (B) is incorrect, for though the author may believe that individuals bear a disproportionate share of the burden, this is not a response to the question asked. (C) is incorrect for the same reason: It is a true but nonresponsive statement. Finally, (D) fails for the same reason. Though the author notes that affirmative action programs are similar to other government programs in this respect, this is not an explanation for the author's placing "funding" in quotation marks.

21. **(D)** This is a logical structure question. In the final paragraph, the author analyzes another, similar situation. This technique is called arguing from analogy. The strength of the argument depends on our seeing the similarity and accepting the conclusion of the one argument (the "villainous man") as applicable to the other argument (affirmative action). (A) is perhaps the second best response, but the author is not offering an illustration, e.g., an example of affirmative action. To be sure, the author is attempting to prove a point, but attempting to prove a conclusion is not equivalent to illustrating a contention. (B) is incorrect since the author adduces the situation to support his contention. (C) is incorrect for the author cites no authority. Finally, (E) can be eliminated since the author uses the case of the villainous man to support, not to weaken, the case.

22. **(B)** This is an explicit idea question. In paragraph 1, the author mentions that affirmative action is like other government programs in that it is designed to achieve certain social and economic goals. So statement I cites a similarity rather than a difference. Statement III can also be eliminated. In paragraph 3, the author states that the relevant difference is not the method of allocating benefits. The salient difference is set forth in the same paragraph, and it is the difference described by statement II.

23. **(A)** This is an inference question. In the first paragraph the author asks why affirmative action is so controversial. In the final paragraph, he reveals the answer: the moral dilemma. The wording of the passage, e.g., "we are confronted with . . . ," indicates that the author expects his reader will share this tension. So the passage is addressed to those who think affirmative action has value but who also believe it is unfair to nonminority persons. As for (B), the author believes that affirmative action is based on sound premises, achieving a legitimate social goal, but that the world is built so that we encounter this conflict. As for (C), it is not the programs themselves that contain contradictions. Rather, it is our value structure that creates the conflict. As for (D), the author believes the reader will regard the programs as creating suffering, but not that the suffering is needless. It may very well be the cost that must be paid. (E) is easily eliminated since the author expresses reservations about the program.

24. **(E)** This is a main idea question, but one which asks about the main idea in the abstract. The discussion thus far makes clear the justification for (E). The author has a sense of this moral dilemma, which he believes will be shared by his readers, and he wants to explain why we experience this as conflict. As for (A), though the author develops a dilemma, he does not suggest that it is possible to slip between the horns of the dilemma. As for (B), he offers no refutation, so we will eliminate this as incorrect. As for (C), any historical references are purely incidental to the overall development of the thesis. And as for (D), though the analysis of affirmative action may suggest to the reader a method of analyzing other social problems, the focus of the passage is a particular problem—not methodology.

25. **(B)** This is a main idea question. The author's primary concern is to discuss the problem of desertification. So choice (B) is correct. A natural extension of the discussion would be a proposal to slow the process of desertification, but that is not included in the passage as written, so (A) must be incorrect. (C), (D), and (E) are each incorrect because we find no elements in the passage to support those choices. Even admitting that the author intends to define, implicitly, the term "desertification," that is surely not the main point of the passage. The author also dwells at length on the causes of the problem.

26. **(C)** This is an explicit idea question. In the first paragraph, the author mentions (A), (B), (D), and (E) as features of desertification. (C), however, is one of the *causes* of desertification.

27. **(E)** This is a tone question. We can surely eliminate (B), (C), and (D) as not expressing the appropriate element of worry. Then, in choosing between (A) and (E), we find that (A) overstates the case. The author says we solve the problem now or we solve it later (at a higher cost). But that is an expression of concern, not alarm.

28. **(D)** Covert means undercover or concealed, so a good opposite would be open.

29. **(A)** The literal meaning of "salient" is projecting forward or jutting out, and it has come to have the related (and more figurative) meaning of standing out from the rest as obvious or important. A good opposite, then, would be insignificant.

30. **(E)** Moribund means dying, so a good opposite would be a word referring to life or good health, such as vital.

31. **(B)** Pliant means bending, as found in the composite word "compliant." A good opposite, therefore, is rigid.

32. **(C)** Dormant means sleeping or inactive, and a fairly clear opposite is active.

33. **(B)** Placate is related to placid, and to placate means to calm down. So a good opposite would be a word meaning to stir up—as here to stir up anger is to enrage.

34. **(D)** Extraneous means coming from outside, foreign or alien to something else. The word is also used to mean not pertinent, so a good opposite would be central: That which is extraneous to an inquiry is surely not central to it.

35. **(C)** Renown means fame, so a good opposite would be a word describing the complete lack of fame, anonymity.

36. **(A)** To rue means to regret, to wish that something had not occurred. A good opposite is celebrate, since it means to commemorate something, and in so doing, to regard the thing or event commemorated with a positive, perhaps even joyous, attitude.

37. **(D)** Baleful means evil, destructive, or unfortunate, so a good opposite is fortunate.

38. **(A)** Fortitude is now used to mean strength of character, but its older and more literal meaning referred to physical strength. Hearing this associated and deeper meaning buried in the word will allow you to select debility, or weakness, as the best opposite.

SECTION III

1. **(C)** With a problem that indicates a very simple manipulation, as this one does, the easiest way to arrive at a comparison is often just to do the operation. In this case, Column A is $5 - 1 = 4$, and Column B is $5 - 1 = 4$.

2. **(A)** A question like this just tests your understanding of the centered statement. If x is 4 more than y, then x must be larger than y. So Column A is larger than Column B.

3. **(A)** Contrast this question with question 1. Notice that the manipulation here would be more dif-

ficult, for to find the percent increase you would create a fraction with the change as the numerator and the original amount as the denominator:

$$\frac{\text{change}}{\text{original amount}} = \frac{\$1.00}{\$7.95}$$

But converting this fraction to a decimal and then to a percent is tiresome. Instead of actually performing the calculation, you should look for an alternate way of making the comparison. In this case, you are asked to compare $\frac{1}{7.95}$ to 12%. $\frac{1}{7.95}$ is very close to $\frac{1}{8}$ (slightly more, since 7.95 is less than 8, and the smaller the denominator the larger the value of the fraction). And $\frac{1}{8}$ is exactly $12\frac{1}{2}$%. So $\frac{1}{7.95}$ must be more than $12\frac{1}{2}$%, and that is enough to justify the conclusion that Column A is larger than Column B.

4. **(A)** Since M + 2 is the average of x and y, $\frac{(x + y)}{2} = M + 2$. This means that Column A could be rewritten as M + 2. Since Column B is M and Column A is 2 larger than M, Column A must be larger.

5. **(C)** With a question of this type, a good strategy is to do the indicated algebraic manipulation. If we do the multiplication indicated in Column A, we have $(x + y)(x - y) = x^2 + xy - xy - y^2 = x^2 - y^2$. The two expressions are equivalent, so the two columns are equal.

6. **(D)** Remember that figures in this section are not necessarily drawn to scale. Because of that, we cannot make a comparison based upon measuring. Moreover, since the size of the unlabeled angles is unknown, we cannot deduce any conclusion about the size of angles x and y.

7. **(D)** Remember that "percent" means "per one hundred," and it is just a convenient ratio to work with. But because it is only a ratio, percent itself gives you no information about the actual numbers involved. Although City Y experienced a greater *percentage* decrease than City X, we cannot reach any conclusion about the actual number of persons involved.

8. **(C)** A square has four equal sides, so its perimeter is just 4 times the length of one side. Conversely, the perimeter divided by 4 gives you the length of each side. In this case, the perimeter is $12\sqrt{3}$, so the length of each of the four sides is $12\sqrt{3} \div 4$ $3\sqrt{3}$.

9. **(A)** Here is another question with a difficult manipulation, so we look for another way to make the comparison. Here it is possible to factor out $\frac{3}{7}$ from both terms of the left-hand expression, yielding $\frac{3}{7}(\frac{101}{104} + \frac{1}{104}$ which is equal to $\frac{3}{7}\frac{105}{104})$. At this point a comparison is possible. Since $\frac{105}{104}$ is larger than 1, $\frac{3}{7} \times \frac{105}{104}$ must be slightly larger than $\frac{3}{7}$, so Column A must be larger than Column B.

10. **(B)** Since no drawing is provided, you might find it easiest to reach a comparison by sketching the coordinate system:

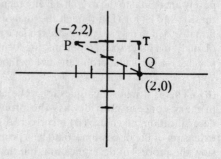

You could now find the distance from P to Q by using the Pythagorean Theorem: $PT^2 + TQ^2 = PQ^2$. There is no need to work out the actual length, however, because you can make your comparison with an approximation. Notice that the length of PT is 4. This means that PQ, which is the hypotenuse of the right triangle, is longer than 4, so Column B must be larger.

11. **(B)** One way to make the comparison is to find the largest common factor for each of the pairs. 18 and 24 have a common factor of 6: $6 \times 3 = 18$ and $6 \times 4 = 24$. Since the smallest number evenly divisible by both 3 and 4 is $3 \times 4 = 12$, the smallest number divisible by 18 and 24 is $6 \times 12 = 72$. On the other side, 18 and 28 have a common factor of 2: $2 \times 9 = 18$ and $2 \times 14 = 28$. the smallest number divisible by both 9 and 14 is $9 \times 14 = 126$, so the smallest number evenly divisible by both 18 and 28 is $2 \times 126 = 252$. Thus, Column B is larger. Alternatively, you might have realized that since 18 is not a factor of either 24 or 28, it's "easier" to find a number divisible by 18 and 24 than by 18 and 28. By "easier" we mean that if you kept trying number after number, you would get to the one divisible by 18 and 24 before you got to the one divisible by 18 and 28.

12. **(D)** Remember that figures are not necessarily drawn to scale. You cannot conclude, without further information, that the two lines in the figure are parallel to each other. Without that information, you should not attempt to arrive at any conclusion regarding the relative sizes of x and y.

13. **(A)** This question defines a certain operation "*". All you need to do is substitute the numbers provided in the two columns into the definition. Since $P * Q = P + Q - PQ$, to find $4 * 1$, you substitute 4 for P and 1 for Q: $4 + 1 - (4)(1) = 1$. To find $4 * 2$, substitute 4 for P and 2 for Q: $4 + 2 - (4)(2) = -2$. You can see that Column A is larger.

14. **(B)** You might find it useful to perform the algebraic operations indicated: $(3j)(3k)(3m) = 9jkm$ and $3(j)(k)(m) = 3jkm$. But that alone does not answer the question. You need to consider the centered information. Notice that j and k are positive while m is negative. This means that both columns are negative numbers (positive × positive × negative yields a negative number). Consequently, Column A is even smaller than Column B since it is 9 times that negative number rather than 3 times that negative number.

15. **(C)** One way of arriving at the comparison is to rewrite the centered information, $\frac{x}{y} = \frac{4}{5}$, as $\frac{y}{x} = \frac{5}{4}$.

    Column B is asking for the value of $\frac{2}{3}(\frac{y}{x})$ (which is equivalent to $\frac{2y}{3x}$). In other words, Column B is two-thirds of $\frac{y}{x}$, and since $\frac{y}{x}$ is $\frac{5}{4}$, Column B is $\frac{2}{3}$ of $\frac{5}{4} = \frac{10}{12} = \frac{5}{6}$. So the two columns are equal.

16. **(A)** One way of attacking a question like this with easily performed operations is to do the arithmetic: $5^2 = 25$, $12^2 = 144$, and $25 + 144 = 169$. Then look for an equivalent answer choice: $13^2 = 169$. Alternatively, you might have remembered that one set of "magic" Pythagorean numbers is 5, 12, 13, that is, a triangle with sides of 5, 12, 13 is a right triangle so $5^2 + 12^2 = 13^2$.

17. **(E)** This is essentially a bookkeeping problem, and all you need to do is multiply the numbers to find the total value of sales: 50 weeks × 100 sales per week = 5000 sales; 5000 sales × $1000 per sale = $5,000,000.

18. **(A)** Given the diameter of a circle, we know the radius, since the radius is just half the diameter:

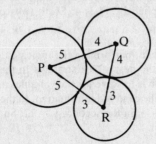

So the perimeter of the triangle formed by the radii of the circles is 24.

19. **(C)** With a question of this type, the best approach is to substitute the values provided into the expression:

$$\frac{x^2 - xy}{y} = \frac{1^2 - (1)(-2)}{-2} = \frac{1 - (-2)}{-2} = \frac{3}{-2}$$

20. **(A)** Here we suggest that you manipulate the inquality until you have a single x on one side:

$$5x - 2 < 3x - 1$$
$$2x - 2 < -1$$
$$2x < 1$$
$$x < \frac{1}{2}$$

Subtract 3x from both sides:
Add 2 to both sides:
Divide both sides by 2:

So x is less than ½, which means that 1 is not a possible value of x.

21. **(D)** The pie chart shows the distribution of motor vehicles in City X according to their manufacturer: 40% were manufactured by Q. Since the total number of motor vehicles registered is 8400, the number registered that were manufactured by Q is 40% of 8400 = 3360.

22. **(A)** This question is based on the information for City Y, which is given in the bar graph. Consulting that portion of the chart, we find that there were 1600 motor vehicles registered in City Y manufactured by R and 1200 manufactured by P: $1600 - 1200 = 400$. So there were 400 more vehicles manufactured by R registered in City Y.

23. **(D)** Notice that this question specifically asks for an approximation. If you look at the small table that summarizes the information for City X and manufacturers T, U and V, you will see that each of those manufacturers accounted for approximately the same number of registrations. The three together accounted for 8% of all City X registrations, as shown in the pie chart. This means that Manufacturer V accounted for about ⅓ of the 8%, or about 3%, so (D) is the best approximation.

24. **(E)** To answer this question, you will first need the total number of registrations in City Y. Adding the various values we have 1200 + 2400 + 1600 + 800 + 400 = 6400, of which 1600 were from Manufacturer R. And 1600/6400 = ¼ = 25%.

25. **(D)** Here we test each statement. As for I, we calculate the number of R-manufactured registrations in City X by multiplying the total of 8400 by 25%, which is R's share of the total, and that result is 2100. Then we add that to the 1600 registrations shown for City Y and the result is 3700. So I is true. As for II, although we do know how many V-vehicles there are in City X, we cannot reach any conclusion about the number of such vehicles in City Y, for the "other" category is not further broken down for City Y. So II cannot be inferred from the information supplied. As for III, the number of S-vehicles in City X is 12% of 8400 or 1008. And the number in City Y is only 800, so there are 208 more in City X, or approximately 200, so III is inferrable from the graph.

26. **(C)** To answer this question, you might try substituting values for x and y, or you might just think generally about the properties of the numbers they describe. As for (A), if x is even, then x^2, which is x times x, must also be even; but since y is an odd number, the entire expression is odd. As for (B), x^2 is even, and since y, an odd number, is subtracted from x, the result must also be an odd number. As for (D) and (E), an even number plus (or minus) an odd number is odd. (C) is the correct choice, for x^2 is even, and an even number multiplied by an odd number generates an even result.

27. **(E)** Here we might manipulate the equation that is given. Since $p = \frac{1}{3} q = $. Then set up a direct proportion:

$$\frac{p}{q} = \frac{1}{3}$$

Cross Multiply: $\left(\frac{1}{3}\right) \frac{p}{q} = \frac{1}{3} \left(\frac{1}{3}\right)$

Multiply by $\frac{p}{3q} = \frac{1}{9}$

28. **(D)** A direct proportion will easily solve the problem. Since the cost remains constant, the more chemical purchased the greater the cost, and vice versa:

$$\frac{\$50}{30} = \frac{\$625}{x}$$

Cross-multiply: $50x = 18,750$
Divide by 50: $x = 375$

29. **(D)** The best way to the solution here might be just to try various combinations. For example, for 17 you might try $4 + 5 + 6$, which is 16, and then $5 + 6 + 7$, which is 18. So there is no set of three consecutive integers that will do the trick. When you get to (D), you will find that $9 + 10 + 11 = 30$.

For the mathematically inclined, you can express the sum of three consecutive integers as follows: Let x be the first of the three integers; the second integer is one more, or $x + 1$; and the third is one more than that, or $x + 2$. So the sum of any three consecutive integers is $x + x + 1 + x + 2 = 3x + 3$. For a number to be the sum of three consecutive integers, it must be 3 more than some other number that is divisible by 3. Or, in different words, for a number to be the sum of three consecutive integers, if you subtract 3 from it, what is left will be divisible by 3. Of the available choices, only the number 30 fits this description.

30. **(E)** The information given can be rendered in equation form. Let x, y, and z represent the three sides, x being the shortest and z being the longest. Given the information about the area of the faces: $xy = 6$, $xz = 8$, and $yz = 12$. Now treat these as simultaneous equations. Since $xy = 6$, $x = \frac{6}{y}$. Substitute this value for x in the second equation, and you have $z\left(\frac{6}{y}\right) = 8$, so $z = 8\left(\frac{y}{6}\right) = \frac{4y}{3}$. Now put this value for z in the third equation: $y\left(\frac{4y}{3}\right) = 12$, so

$4y^2 = 36$, $y^2 = 9$, and $y = +3$ or -3. Since we are dealing with distances, y cannot be negative, so $y = +3$. From here on in, the solution is easy. If $y = 3$, then $x = 2$; and if $x = 2$, then $z = 4$. So the three sides are 2, 3, and 4, and the volume of the solid is $2 \times 3 \times 4 = 24$.

SECTION IV

1. **(C)** The arithmetic operations indicated here are very simple, so the best approach to the comparison is to perform the indicated operations. For Column A, 16 divided by 4 is 4. For Column B, $\frac{4}{11}$ multiplied by 11 is 4. So th two columns are equal.

2. **(B)** Again, performing the indicated operations may be the best attack strategy. In this case, the operation is to solve for the variables in the equations in the centered information. In the first equation, $x = 4$; in the second, $y = 12$. So Column B is greater.

3. **(B)** This type of question appears with some regularity in various guises. The heart of the question is the centered information that 49 is one of the factors of n. Then the key to the comparison is recognizing that since 7 is a factor of 49, 7 must also be a factor of n. Thus, when n is divided by 7 (just as when it is divided by 49), there is no remainder. So Column A is 0 while Column B is 7. So Column B is larger.

4. **(A)** Since the operations indicated here are much too cumbersome to be performed, you should look for a shortcut. The key is to recognize that since the fraction in Column A is positive, the final result of performing the operation indicated would also be a positive number. Since the fraction in Column B is negative, the final result of raising the fraction to an odd power will be negative. Thus, the positive quantity in Column A must be larger.

5. **(B)** This question is really not so much a matter of mathematics as just common sense. Indeed, you can probably solve it easily just by counting on your fingers (or multiplying and adding). First, Column A must be 15 since 5 x 3 = 15. As for Column B, since there is one floor with 2 apartments and 4 floors with 4 apartments, the total number of apartments in the building is 18. So Column B is larger.

6. **(B)** When you look at the centered information, you should have the strong suspicion that the solution to the entire comparison will be found by factoring the expression on the left side of the centered equation. This is a correct intuition. If we factor $x^2 - 3x - 4$, we get $(x + 1)(x - 4)$. (You can check this by multiplying $(x + 1)(x - 4)$.) Since one of the factors uses addition $(x + 1)$, and the other uses subtraction, $(x - 4)$, we can match them up with m and n in the expression to the right of the equals sign in the centered equation: m must be 1 while n must be 4. So column B is larger.

7. **(C)** The key to the question is the realization that all three triangles share a common altitude. Drop a line from point E, perpendicular to ABCD:

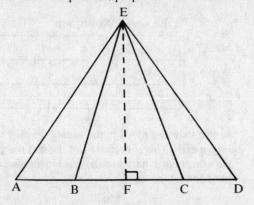

Since the three triangles have a common altitude, whatever difference there might be in their areas must be solely a function of the lengths of their bases. Since AB and CD are half of BC, triangles AEB and CED must have areas equal to half that of BEC. Consequently, the area of triangle BEC is equal to the sum of the areas of triangles AEB and CED.

8. **(A)** Here the key is the proper manipulation of the radicals. Column B is easily manipulated, for you need only to extract the square root, which is $\frac{3}{4}$. In Column A, do not make the mistake of adding the fractions beneath the radicals as you would ordinary fractions. Column A is not equal to Column B; instead, Column A is equal to $3\sqrt{\frac{3}{16}}$. We can extract the square root of $\frac{1}{16}$, which is $\frac{1}{4}$, giving us $\frac{3}{4}\sqrt{3}$ in Column A. Now we can see that Column A is larger, since $\sqrt{3}$ is about 1.7.

9. **(C)** The easiest approach to this question is to do the multiplication indicated in Column A. The fives cancel, so the result is $x + y - 7$ and the two columns are equal.

10. **(D)** This question is a little tricky, but it can be answered using a principle we have used several times earlier: With a variable such as x or y, be alert for possible values such as zero or negative numbers. For example, if $x = 1$ and $y = 1$, then point Q is the origin. But if $x = 0$ and $y = 0$, then point P is the origin (and Q is farther away). Similarly, if $x = \frac{1}{2}$ and $y = \frac{1}{2}$, then Q has coordinates of $(-\frac{1}{2}, -\frac{1}{2})$, and P and Q would be at the same distance from the origin.

11. **(C)** Whenever you have a question dealing with a square, remember that a number of special relationships exist. First, since a square has four equal sides, you can find the length of each side if you know the perimeter. Also, if you know the length of a side, you know the area. In Column A, a square with an area of 16 has a side of 4 and therefore has a perimeter of 16. In Column B, the diagonal of the square cuts the square into two, isoceles right triangles: 45°–45°–90°. In such triangles, the hypotenuse is equal to length of either of the two shorter sides multiplied by $\sqrt{2}$. Conversely, the shorter sides are each equal to one-half the length of the hypotenuse multiplied by $\sqrt{2}$. So if the diagonal of a square (the hypotenuse of the right triangle) is $4\sqrt{2}$, the side of the triangle (which is also the side of the square) is $\frac{1}{2}(4\sqrt{2})(\sqrt{2}) = 4$. And a side of 4 means a perimeter of 16, so the two squares have the same perimeter.

12. **(A)** You might get away with doing the manipulation indicated here. After all, multiplying .333 by .666 is not too unmanageable; and multiplying $\frac{1}{3}$ by $\frac{2}{3}$ and converting that to a decimal will not take forever. The results will show that Column A is larger. But there is an easier approach: .333 and .666 are approximately, but not exactly, $\frac{1}{3}$ and $\frac{2}{3}$, respectively. But how do they differ from the exact decimal equivalents for $\frac{1}{3}$ and $\frac{2}{3}$? The answer is that the actual decimals obtained by dividing 1 by 3 and 2 by 3 are *repeating* decimals. In other words, $\frac{1}{3}$ is really .3333... and $\frac{2}{3}$ is really .6666..., which is to say that $\frac{1}{3}$ is really larger than just .333 and $\frac{2}{3}$ is really larger than just .666. So Column A must be larger than Column B.

13. **(D)** Sometimes just substituting numbers is enough to find the pattern needed to answer the question. For example, possible values of x are 6 ($6 + 5 \div 3 = 3$, remainder 2) and 9 ($9 + 5 \div 3 = 4$, remainder of 2). One of these is even and the other odd, which means that when x is divided by 2 you might get a remainder of 0 (in which case Column A is greater) or you might get a remainder of 1 (in which case the columns are equal).

14. **(B)** Here again, trial and error is probably faster than trying to devise an elaborate mathematical proof. What are the first few numbers divisible by 12?: 12, 24, 36, 48, 60, etc. And which is the first one larger than 12 that is not divisible by 8? The answer, as you can see by checking our list, is 36.

15. **(B)** As we suggest, a good starting point is performing the operations indicated in one or both columns, in this case, the operations indicated in Column A: $x(y + z) = xy + xz$. Since there is an xy in Column A and the same term in Column B, we can just eliminate those—they won't make any difference. So our comparison is really just xz versus z. Since x and z are both fractions, xz (which is taking a fraction of a fraction) must be smaller than z, so Column B is larger.

16. **(D)** This question is nothing more than a test of your ability to move decimal points. All of the answer choices are expressed as variations of 1.27. To change 0.00127 to 1.27 times some number, you must move the decimal point three places to the right. In "official" notation, $0.00127 = 1.27 \times 10^{-3}$. $10^{-3} = 0.001$, so $0.00127 = 1.27 \times 0.001$.

17. **(C)** The key to this question is careful reading. If the $240 prize is divided between two people, and if one person receives $180, then the other person receives $60. The difference in the amounts received is $180 - 60 = 120$.

18. **(E)** One way of solving this problem is to treat the equations as simultaneous equations, isolating a variable in one, substituting into the other, and then solving for that variable. One way of doing this is to isolate y in the second equation. Since $\frac{y}{x} = \frac{1}{3}$, $y = \frac{x}{3}$. Substitute this value of y into the other equation:

$$3x - 4\left(\frac{x}{3}\right) = 5$$
$$3x - 4\,\frac{x}{3} = 5$$
$$\frac{9x - 4x}{3} = 5$$
$$5x = 15$$
$$x = 3$$

19. **(D)** Once it is established that the two lines are parallel, it is possible to calculate the value of all the angles in the figure. The 36° angle and angle x are supplementary angles, that is, they total 180°, so angle x must be 144°.

20. **(D)** With a question of this type, a good strategy is to cross-multiply:

$$5(x - 1) = 4(x + 1)$$

Multiply: $5x - 5 = 4x + 4$
Solve for x: $x = 9$

21. **(A)** A table will help us organize the information:

	Brown	Not-Brown	Total
Men			
Women			
Total			

Filling in the information given:

	Brown	Not-Brown	Total
Men	$\frac{1}{4}$		$\frac{3}{x}$
Women			
Total	$\frac{3}{4}$		

Notice that we enter $\frac{1}{4}$ in the square for men with brown eyes. This is because $\frac{3}{4}$ of the $\frac{3}{4}$ of the people who are men have brown eyes. Finally, we complete the table:

	Brown	Not-Brown	Total
Men	$\frac{1}{4}$	$\frac{1}{8}$	$\frac{3}{8}$
Women	$\frac{1}{2}$	$\frac{1}{8}$	$\frac{5}{8}$
Total	$\frac{3}{4}$	$\frac{1}{4}$	1

22. **(C)** To answer this question, you must first determine the total number of dollars in the budget. This can be done by adding together the various sources of income shown in the bar graph: $10 + $6 + $2 + $8 + $4 =$30 (millions of dollars). From the pie chart, we learn that 25%, or $\frac{1}{4}$, of this $30 million was allocated to operation of the physical plant; $\frac{1}{4}$ of $30 million is $7,500,000.

23. **(B)** We already have a start on this question given what we learned in the previous explanation. Income from the foundation accounted for $6 million of the total of $30 million, and $\frac{6}{30} = \frac{1}{5}$ = 20%.

24. **(D)** Given a total budget of $30 million and the distribution shown in the pie chart, the question is answered: 35% of $30 minus 20% of $30 = $4,500,000.

25. **(C)** As for I, we know that total income was $30 million, of which $10 million came from tuition, so statement I is inferrable. As for II, the foundation generated $6 million in income while private gifts generated only $2 million, so it is inferrable that the foundation generated three times as much income as private gifts. III, however, is not inferrable. Although we know the sources of income and the categories of expenditures, we cannot conclude that money from the foundation did or did not go directly into student aid.

26. **(E)** The wheel is divided into eight equal sectors, 3 of which are painted blue. So $\frac{3}{8}$ of the wheel's area is blue. What is the area of the wheel? Since it is a circle with a diameter of 64 centimeters, it has a radius of 32 centimeters and an area of $\pi \times 32 \times 32 = 1024\,\pi$ square centimeters. And $\frac{3}{8}$ of $1024\,\pi$ is $384\,\pi$.

27. **(B)** The formula for finding the volume of a right circular cylinder is πr^2 times the height of the cylinder. Here we have cylinders of equal volume so the πr^2 times the height of the one must be equal to the other:

$$\pi (3^2) \times 4 = \pi (2^2) \times h$$
$$36\,\pi = 4\,\pi \times h$$
$$h = 9$$

28. **(E)** With a question like this, you should perform the indicated operations. First subtract $\frac{1}{y}$ from $\frac{1}{x}$, using the common denominator of xy. The result is $\frac{y - x}{xy} = \frac{1}{z}$. Now cross-multiply and divide. The result is $z = \frac{xy}{y - x}$.

29. **(C)** Here is a question involving ratio *parts*. Since the ratio of women to men employed by the company is 3 to 2, there are five (3 + 2) ratio parts, that is, the total number of employees is divisible by 5, of which 3 parts or $\frac{3}{5}$ are women and 2 parts or $\frac{2}{5}$ are men. And $\frac{2}{5}$ of 240 = 96.

30. **(C)** When you look at this question and see the 120° angle, one of the first things that should come to mind is the possibility that the other angles will be 60° or 30°. If that is correct, then the key to the question will either be an equilateral triangle or the special case of the right triangle, the 30°–60°–90° triangle. As it turns out, the key here is a simple equilateral triangle. The information given is sufficient to establish that all sides are parallel and equal. This means that angles S and Q are 60°. Then the line PR divides angles P and R, which are both 120 degrees, into 60° angles. As a result, PRS turns out to be an equilateral triangle with side 3, so PR = 3.

SECTION V

Questions 1–6

Arranging the Information

This is a fairly simple "connective" set. A "connective" set is a problem set in which one event is somehow connected with another event, e.g., X causes Y, or Y leads to Z. The connection can be expressed by an arrow. We begin with the first condition:

G   H

Adding the second condition:

G   H   I

And the third:

G   H   I   J

And the fourth:

G   H   I   J   K

And the fifth:

L   G   H   I   J   K

And the sixth:

L   G   H   I   J   K

Of course, there is no necessity that the stations be oriented exactly this way on the page, so long as the relative connections are specified. An equivalent diagram is:

L   G   H

K   J   I

Once the diagram is drawn, answering the questions is merely a matter of using the picture.

Answering the Questions

1. **(D)** The diagram shows that it is possible to get from H to J only via I. (A) is incorrect since the direct connection between J and H runs only from J to H, not vice versa. As for (B), while it is possible to get from H to G, there is no connecting train between G and J. (C) is incorrect because there is no train from H to L. Finally, (E) is incorrect for there is a route from H to J, via I.

2. **(E)** Notice that there are no arrows in the diagram which point toward L. This means that it is possible only to leave L. It is not possible to arrive at L. As for (A), one can arrive at G from L or H. (B) is incorrect since one can arrive at H from either G or J. (C) is incorrect since there is a connection between H and I and between L and I. Finally, (D) is incorrect since K can be reached from either L or J.

3. **(B)** Consulting the diagram, we see that I can be reached from either H or L. H, however, can be reached from either G or J. Thus, one can go from G and J via H and reach I with only one transfer. So the correct answer must be I and III only, (B). As for II, there is only a direct connection between H and I—so a transfer is not possible. And as for IV, the trip from K to I goes via J and H, so two transfers are required.

4. **(E)** All six stations can be visited, without revisiting any station, if we begin at L. The trip then proceeds: L to G to H to I to J to K.

5. **(B)** To get to K from H, we must go via I and J, and that is a total of two transfers. As for (A), the trip from G to I is accomplished by transferring only at H. As for (C), the trip from L to H is accomplished by going via G, again requiring only one transfer. As for (D), though the trip from L to I would reqiure two transfers if the L–G–H–I route is selected, note that the trip can be made directly from L to I without *any* transfers. (E) is incorrect because a direct route is available from L to K.

6. **(A)** If I is closed, the only transfer point from H to J is closed, and that means that it is not possible to get from G to J. (B) is incorrect since there is a direct link between J and K. (C) is incorrect since there is a direct link between L and K. (D) is incorrect since the L to K to J route remains unimpaired. (E) is incorrect since there is a direct link from L to G.

7. **(E)** The sample argument is a straightforward generalization: All observed S are P. X is an S. Therefore, X is P. Only (E) replicates this form. The reasoning in (A) is: "Some S are P. All M are S. (All swans are birds, which is a suppressed assumption.) Therefore, all M are P." That is like saying: "Some children are not well behaved. All little girls are children. Therefore, all little girls are not well behaved." (B), too, contains a suppressed premise. Its structure is: "All S are P. All S are M. (All ballets are theatrical productions, which is suppressed.) Therefore, all M are P." That is like saying "All little girls are children. All little girls are human. Therefore, all humans are little girls." (C) is not a generalization at all. It takes a generalization and attempts to explain it by uncovering a causal linkage. (D) is simply a *non sequitur*. It moves from the universality of the *concept* of justice to the conclusion that justice is a *physical* trait of man.

8. **(C)** The dispute here is over the motivation to compete seriously in intramural sports. Erika claims it is a sense of responsibility to one's fellows; Nichol argues it is a desire to win. But the two may actually support one another. In what way could one possibly let ones fellow players down? If the sport was not competitive, it would seem there would be no opportunity to disappoint them. So the desire to win contributes to the desire to be an effective member of the team. Nothing in the exchange presupposes anything about the structure of such programs beyond the fact that they are competitive, that is, that they have winners and losers. How may such programs exist, how they are funded, and similar questions are irrelevant, so both (A) and (B) are incorrect. (D) is close to being correct, but it calls for a survey of *deans*. The dean is probably not is a position to describe the motivation of the *participants*. Had (D) specified participants, it too would have been a correct answer. Of course, only one answer can be correct on the GRE. Finally, (E) must be wrong for the reason cited in explaining (D); it should be possible to find out about the motivation.

9. **(C)** To break the code, the cryptographer needs information about the language which the code conceals. (A), (B), (D), and (E) all provide such information. (C), however, says nothing about the underlying language. The code could even use all even or all odd numbers for the symbol substitutions without affecting the information to be encoded.

10. **(B)** The question is one which tests the validity or strength of a causal inference. Often such arguments can be attacked by finding intervening causal linkages, that is, variables which might interfere with the predicted result. (A) cites such a variable. If the traffic problem is created by commerical traffic which will not be reduced by toll increases, then the proposed increases will not solve the problem. (C), too, is such a variable. It suggests that the proposal is essentially self-defeating. (D) undermines the claim by arguing that the deterrent effect of a price increase is simply not significant, so the proposal will have little, if any, effect. (E) attacks the argument on a different ground. The ultimate objective of the plan is to reduce commuting time. Even assuming a drop in auto traffic because some commuters use public transportation, no advantage is gained if the public transportation system cannot handle the increase in traffic. (B), however, does very little to the argument. In fact, it could be argued that (B) is one of the predicted results of the plan: a drop in the number of autos because commuters begin to carpool.

Questions 11–16

Arranging the Information

This is a "selection" set, that is, we must select cities for the tours according to the restrictions set forth in the problem set. There are many different ways of summarizing the information, and we each have our own idiosyncratic system of notational devices. There are, however, some fairly standard symbols used by logicians, and we will employ them here. We summarize the information in the following way:

1. M → (Q & R)
2. P → O
3. Q → (M & N) v (M & T) v (M & N & T)
4. P ≠ Q
5. ~ (O & R & T)
6. ~ (N & S & R)
7. L ≠ R

Some clarifying remarks about this system are in order. We are using the capital-letter designation of each city to make the statement that the city will be included on the tour, e.g., "M" means "M will be included on the tour." The → stands for "if..., then...."; the "&" stands for "and"; the "v" stands for "or"; the / stands for "not." We use parentheses as punctuation devices to avoid possible confusion. So the first condition is to be read, "If M, then both Q and R," that is, "If M is included on the trip, then both Q and R must be included on the trip." Notice that the parentheses were necessary, for the statement

$$M → Q \& R$$

might be misinterpreted to mean "If M is included on the tour, then Q must also be included. In addition, R must be included on the trip." That would be punctuated with parentheses as:

$$(M → Q) \& R$$

As for the second condition, we note simply that if P is included, O must also be included.

As for the third condition, some students will find it easier to write this condition out rather than to use the notational system. That is fine.

Statement 3 is to be read, "If Q, then M and N, or M and T, or all three," which is, of course, equivalent to the statement included in the initial conditions of the problem.

The fourth condition is similar to the second in that we use a nonstandard symbol, " ≠ ". The same information could be written as ~ (P & Q) or P → ~ Q. This last notation is equivalent to Q → ~ P, for logically P → / Q is the same as Q → / P.

The fifth and sixth conditions are to be read, respec-

tively, "It is not the case that O and R and T are included" and "It is not the case that N and S and R are
included." And finally, condition seven is summarized
using the " ≠ ", which we have already discussed.

We now have the information ready for easy reference, and we turn to the individual questions.

Answering the Questions

11. **(B)** If M is included on the trip, we know that we
must also include Q and R. And if Q is included
on the trip, we must include N or T (or both, but
we are looking for the *minimum* number of other
cities). No other cities need be included. So, including M requires both Q and R plus one of the
pair N and T. So a total of three *additional* cities
are needed.

12. **(A)** By condition 4, Q cannot be included with
P. Unfortunately, that is not an available answer
choice, so we will have to dig a little deeper. If Q
cannot be included on the tour, then we conclude
that M cannot be included, for condition 1 requires
that Q be included on any tour on which M is a
stop.

13. **(B)** This question requires only that we check each
of the choices against the summary of conditions.
(A) is not acceptable because we have M without
Q. (C) is not acceptable because we have M without R. (D) is not acceptable because we have L
with R (in violation of condition 7) and because
we have Q without either N or T. (E) is not acceptable because we have N, S, and R together, in
violation of condition 6. The group in (B), however, meets all of the requirements for an acceptable tour.

14. **(C)** By deleting O, we have the tour M, Q, R,
and T. This satisfies condition 1, since Q and R
are included with M. And this satisfies condition 3
since we have M and T. No other condition is violated, so the group M, Q, R, T is acceptable. (A)
is incorrect, for eliminating M leaves Q in the group
(without M), in violation of condition 3. Similarly,
eliminating Q leaves M on the tour without Q,
violating condition 1. (D) is incorrect because it
also violates condition 1. (E) is incorrect for this
would leave Q on the tour without the (M & N) or
(M & T) combination required by condition 3.

15. **(C)** To make the group M, Q, R into an acceptable tour, we need only to add N or T. This will
finally satisfy both conditions 1 and 3 without violating any other requirement. (A) is incorrect, for

adding another city will not remedy the violation
of condition 7 (L ≠ R). (B) is incorrect, because
satisfying the conditions requires the addition of
O (condition 2), R (condition 1), and either N or
T (condition 3). (D) is incorrect since the addition
of another city will not correct the violation of condition 6. Finally, (E) is incorrect because the addition of O to satisfy condition 2 would then violate
condition 5 (O, R, and T on the same tour).

16. **(E)** Here we must test each lettered city. M cannot constitute a tour in and of itself, for condition
1 requires that Q and R be included on any tour
that includes M. P, by condition 2, cannot constitute a tour of a single city. Finally, by condition 3,
Q's inclusion requires more cities. The remaining
cities, L, N, O, R, S and T, however, can be used
as single-city tours.

Questions 17–22

Arranging the Information

This set is a linear ordering set. At first glance, the
set appears to be very complex, involving as it does the
positioning of 11 items. But a closer examination shows
the questions are not that difficult, since the particular
restrictions considerably simplify the problem. For example, we know that a red bead is on one end, and we
also know that all three red beads are together. So there
are only two possible arrangements for the red beads:

1	2	3	4	5	6	7	8	9	10	11
R	R	R								

or

1	2	3	4	5	6	7	8	9	10	11
								R	R	R

In fact, each additional condition on the placement of
the beads tends to simplify matters for us because it
eliminates possible arrangements.

With a linear ordering set, we begin by summarizing
the information:

Color	Number	
Blue	2	B = B
Red	3	G ≠ G
Green	2	R = R = R
Yellow	4	G or R = ends
	11	

We have made a note of the number of beads of each
color, and we have summarized the particular conditions: Blue is next to blue (B = B); green is not next to
green (G ≠ G; red is always next to red (R = R= ends).

Answering the Questions

17. **(D)** From the given information and our own deductions based on the restrictions that all red beads be together and that one end be red and the other green, we set up the following diagram:

```
1  2  3  4  5  6  7  8  9  10  11
               B  B        R
G              B  B        R   R   R
```

This leaves the four yellow beads and the one remaining green bead to be positioned. The only restriction on the placement of these five beads is that the green bead may not be next to the other green bead, that is, the remaining green bead cannot be in position 2. This eliminates (C), since the green bead might be in position 8, though it could also be in positions 3, 4, and 5. This also eliminates (B), since position 5 might be filled by a green bead. (A) is clearly incorrect since that is the one remaining position which cannot be occupied by the other green bead. (E) is incorrect since the green bead could be placed in position 3 or 4, separated from the blue beads by one or more yellow beads. We do know, however, that at least one green bead, the one in position 1, will be next to a yellow bead, for a yellow bead is needed to separate the green beads. Of course, the other green bead may also be next to a yellow bead, but that is not necessary. In any event, the fact that the green bead must be separated from the other green bead is sufficient to show the correctness of (D).

18. **(B)** The question stem stipulates

```
1 2 3 4 5 6 7 8 9 10 11
          Y    Y = Y = Y = Y
```
and we fill in YYY Y

since the last position cannot be yellow. This then allows us to deduce

```
1  2  3  4  5  6  7  8  9  10  11
               Y  Y  Y  Y  G
```

since the three red beads are together and one of them must be on the end of the string. Then, since the two blue beads must be together, we know that only two different arrangements are possible:

```
1 2 3 4 5 6 7 8  9  10  11
R R R G B B Y Y  Y      G
```

OR: R R R B B G Y Y Y Y   G

Under either arrangement, the fifth bead must be blue.

19. **(E)** The question stem stipulates that each blue bead be next to a green bead. Because the blue beads are next to each other, this means the blue and green beads are arranged as a bloc: GBBG. According to the stipulation in the question stem, the four yellow beads are also arranged as a bloc: YYYY. And we know from the initial presentation of restrictions that the three red beads are a bloc: RRR. The only open question is which end of the string is green and which is red. So there are only two possible arrangements:

```
1   2 3 4 5 6 7 8 9 10 11
G   B B G Y Y Y Y R R  R
```

OR: R   R R Y Y Y Y Y G B B   G

Under either arrangement, positions 5, 6, and 7 are occupied by yellow beads.

20. **(D)** The question stem stipulates

```
1  2  3  4  5  6  7  8  9  10  11
               B  B        R
```

and, given the restriction on the reds and the further restriction on the end beads, we can deduce

```
1  2  3  4  5  6  7  8  9  10  11
G              B  B        R   R   R
```

The only restriction which remains to be observed is the separation of the green beads. This means that the remaining green bead may or may not be next to a green or a blue bead. What is established, however, is that position 2 must be yellow, not green.

21. **(E)** The question stem stipulates

```
1  2  3  4  5  6  7  8  9  10  11
               Y        Y  Y  Y
```

and we deduce

```
1  2  3  4  5  6  7  8  9  10  11
R  R  R        Y        Y  Y  Y  G
```

on the basis of the restrictions regarding the placement of the red beads and the colors of the end beads. Further, there is only one open pair left for the blue beads, 6 and 7, which means bead 4 will be green:

```
1   2   3   4   5   6   7   8   9   10   11
R   R   R   G   Y   B   B   Y   Y   Y    G
```

So all three statements are true.

22. **(D)** Since we do not know on which end to place the red beads (nor the green bead), we have the possibility

```
1   2   3   4   5   6   7   8   9   10   11
R   R   R   G                      B    G
```

and its mirror image

```
1   2   3   4   5   6   7   8   9   10   11
G   B                      G   R   R    R
```

We know also that the two blue beads are together, and this means the yellow beads must form a bloc:

```
1       2  3  4  5  6  7  8  9  10 11
R       R  R  G  Y  Y  Y  Y  B  B  G
```

OR: G   B B Y Y Y Y G R R   R

In either case, the seventh bead must be yellow.

23. **(E)** The argument assumes that a right cannot exist unless it is recognized by the positive law of a society. Against this assumption, it can be argued that a right may exist even though there is no mechanism for protecting or enforcing it. That this is at least plausible has been illustrated by our own history, e.g., minority groups have often been denied rights. These rights however, existed all the while—they were just not protected by the government. (A) is incorrect, for the proponent of the theory of natural rights cannot deny that some human beings do not have them. That would contradict the very definition of natural right on which the claim is based. (B) is incorrect because it is not responsive to the argument. Even if (B) is true, the attacker of natural rights still has the argument that there are no universally recognized rights, so there are no universal (natural) rights at all. (C), like (A), is inconsistent with the very idea of a "natural" right. (D) is incorrect because it does not respond to the attacker's claim that no one right is protected universally. Consistency or universality within one society does not amount to consistency or universality across all societies.

24. **(E)** The author is arguing that political parties in America are weak because there is no party unity. Because of this lack of unity, the party is unable to pass legislation. (E) would strengthen this contention. (E) provides an example of a government dominated by a single party (control of the presidency and both houses), yet the party is unable to pass its own legislation. (A) provides little, if any, support for the argument. If there are only 18 defectors out of a total of 67 party members, that does not show tremendous fragmentation. (B) is even weaker by the same analysis: 70 defectors out of a total of 305 party members. (C) is weak because it focuses on the minority party. (D) strengthens the argument less clearly than (E) becuase there are many possible explanations for the failure, e.g., a different party controlled the legislature.

25. **(C)** Here we are looking for the argument that will undermine the position taken by the paragraph. Remember that the ultimate conclusion of the paragraph is that this disunity is a weakness and that this prevents legislation from being passed. One very good way of attacking this argument is to attack the value judgment upon which the conclusion is based: Is it good to pass the legislation? The author assumes that it would be better to pass the legislation. We could argue, as in (C), that members of the Congress should not pass legislation simply because it is proposed by the party leadership. Rather, the members should represent the views of their constituents. Then, if the legislation fails, it must be the people who did not want it. In that case, it is better not to pass the legislation. (A) does not undermine the argument. That members receive funding proves nothing about unity after elections. As for (B), this seems to strengthen rather than weaken the argument. The author's thesis argues that there is greater unity in the Senate than in the House. (D) would undermine the argument only if we had some additional information to make it relevant. Finally, (E) does not weaken the argument greatly. That some legislation is passed is not a denial of the argument that more should be passed.

SECTION VI

Questions 1–6

Arranging the Information

This set is based upon family relationships. At the outset we note that of the seven people related to X, two are males (father, brother) and five are females (mother, aunt, sister, wife, and daughter). We can summarize the additional information:

P = Q (same sex)
M ≠ N (not same sex)
S > M (born before)
Q ≠ mother (Q is not X's mother.)

There is a further deduction to be drawn. There are only two male relatives. Of the four individuals, P, Q, M, and N, three are of the same sex and one is of the opposite sex. Since there are only two males in the scheme, this means that the three of the same sex are female. So P, Q, and either M or N are females; either M or N is male.

Answering the Questions

1. **(C)** The answer to this question is evident from the analysis above.

2. **(C)** This question is also answerable on the basis of our previous analysis. As for (A) and (B), though we know that of M and N one is male and the other is female, we have no information to justify a judgment as to who is the female. Nor is there any information to support the conclusions in (D) and (E).

3. **(D)** We have established that P and Q are females, and that either M or N is female. So M or N is male, and of the remaining three relatives, S, R, and T, one is male as well. If T is the daughter of X, this establishes that she is female and, further, that either R or S is the remaining male. (A), (B) and (C) are incorrect since the additional stipulation of this question does not add anything to the analysis of sexual distribution above. (E) is incorrect since it asserts that S is the male, but there is nothing to support that conclusion. (D), however, is necessarily true. Of the pair R and S, one must be male and the other female, so they are not of the same sex.

4. **(D)** In the scheme of relations, there is only one possible pair of sisters: the mother and the aunt. It will not do to argue that X might have married his sister, especially when an ordinary sister relationship is available. In any event, if M and Q represent the mother and the aunt, since Q is not the mother, M must be X's mother, so (B) and (C) are both true. Further, since M must be female, N must be male, and (A) is true. Then, since M is X's mother, and since S was born before M, S could not be X's brother and (E) is true. As for (D), M,

Q, and N (a male) are eliminated as daughters, but this still leaves several possibilities.

5. **(C)** There is only one available grandfather-grandchild relationship: S must be X's father and N his daughter. If N is female, then M is male and must be X's brother. So (C) is necessarily true. As for the remaining choices, (A) is possible though not necessary. (B) is also possible since P might be X's mother. (D) is not possible since Q is female. Finally, (E) is possible since P is a female and might be X's sister and so N's aunt.

6. **(A)** Since M was born after S, if M is the mother of X's daughter, S cannot be the daughter. (Again, it will not do to argue about stepdaughters, for that is clearly outside the bounds of the problem.) The remaining choices, however, are possible. As for (B) and (C), no restriction is placed on P and Q. And as for (D), R is not further defined. As for (E), we do know that N is male if M is female, and N could be X's brother.

7. **(C)** Amy points out that Al assumes that any extraterrestrial visitors to Earth, seeking intelligent life, would regard human beings here on Earth as intelligent, and therefore contact us. Amy hints that we might not be intelligent enough to interest them in contacting us. This is why (C) is the best answer. (A) is wrong. Amy does not miss Al's point: She understands it very well and criticizes it. (B) is wrong since Amy is not suggesting that Al is any less intelligent than any other human being, just that the aliens might regard us all as below the level of intelligence they are seeking. (D) is more nearly correct than any other choice save (C). The difficulties with it are threefold: One, there really is not all that much internal development of Al's argument, so (D) does not seem on target; two, in a way Amy does examine what internal structure there is—she notes there is a suppressed assumption which is unsound; finally, even assuming that what (D) says is correct, it really does not describe the point of Amy's remark nearly so well as (C) does. Finally, (E) is incorrect because Amy does not offer an analogy of any sort.

8. **(A)** Let us assign letters to represent the complete clauses of the sentence from which the argument is built. "If quarks . . . universe" will be represented by the letter P, the rest of the sentence by Q. The structure of the argument is therefore: "If P then Q. Q. Therefore, P." The argument is obviously not logically valid. If it were, it would work for any substitutions of clauses for the letters, but we can easily think up a case in which the argument will not work: "If this truck is a fire en-

gine, it will be painted red. This truck is painted red; therefore, it is a fire engine." Obviously, many trucks which are not fire engines could also be painted red. The argument's invalidity is not the critical point. Your task was to find the answer choice that paralleled it—and since the argument first presented was incorrect, you should have looked for the argument in the answer choices which makes the same mistake: (A). It has the form: "If P then Q. Q. Therefore, P." (B) has the form: "If P, then Q. P. Therefore, Q," which is both different from our original form and valid to boot. (C) has the form: "P or Q. Not P. Therefore, Q." (D) has the form: "If P, then Q. If Q, then R. Therefore, If P, then R." Finally, (E) has the form: "If P then Q. Not Q. Therefore, not P."

9. **(D)** The author explains that the expansion of judicial power by increasing the number of causes of action had the effect of filling the judicial coffers. A natural conclusion to be drawn from this information is that the desire for economic gain fueled the expansion. (A) is not supported by the text since the judges may have made good decisions —even though they were paid to make them. (E) is incorrect for the same reason. (C) is not supported by the text since no mention is made of the other two bodies (even assuming they existed at the time the author is describing). (B) is also incorrect because there is nothing in the text to support such a conclusion.

Questions 10–15

Arranging the Information

The primary task here is to organize the information. And for that we will use a matrix:

	F	G	H	I	J
1	YES(X)	YES(~X)	YES	NO	NO
2	NO	YES(~X)	YES	YES(Z)	YES(~
3	YES(X)	YES(~X)	YES(~Y	YES(~Z)	NO

Once the information has been organized, the questions are readily answerable.

Answering the Questions

10. **(C)** With regard to statement I, F and G cannot grow together since F requires the presence of X

and G requires the absence of X. H can grow with or without X, so G and H can grow together, and F and H can grow together. So II and III are possible. IV, however, is not possible since J does not grow in field 1 at all.

11. **(D)** Since F does not grow at all in field 2, (A) and (B) can be eliminated. Then, since J will not grow with H, both (C) and (E) can be eliminated. Combination G, I, and J, however, is consistent with all conditions.

12. **(D)** Notice that this question asks for a list of all crops which could grow *alone*. F cannot, since F simply does not grow in field 2. G grows in field 2 so long as X is not applied to the field, so G is part of the correct answer. I will not grow since it requires Z. Finally, J will grow since the question stipulates the crops will grow alone. So the correct answer consists of G, H, and J.

13. **(D)** Neither F nor H will grow in field 3 unless certain fertilizers or pesticides are added, so we can eliminate choices (A), (B), and (C). (E) can be eliminated on the further ground that J simply does not grow in field 3.

14. **(C)** J does not grow in field 3, so that reduces the number of possible crops to four. But F and G cannot grow together, which further reduces the number to three. So the maximum number of crops which can be planted together is three—F, H, and I or G, H, and I.

15. **(A)** Consulting the chart, we see that F does not grow there at all. G will not grow in the presence of X, and I will only grow in the presence of Z. So only H and J will grow under the stipulated conditions.

Questions 16–21

For this set no diagram is needed since the relationships are inherent in the system of arithmetic, that is, five is one more than six, etc. You may find it useful to make a marginal note or two, e.g., "challenge +1 or +2."

16. **(C)** The setup for this group of questions is fairly long, but once the rules of the game are understood, this question is easy. (A) and (B) are incorrect, for a challenge must issue from a player of lower rank. (D) and (E) are incorrect, for a challenge can be issued only to a player at most two ranks superior.

17. **(C)** Since S begins in fourth position, S can reach first in two plays by issuing and winning two challenges. This can be done in two ways. S can first challenge Q and then P, or S can first challenge R and then P. Either way, R must be in fourth position.

18. **(E)** This arrangement could come about only after a minimum of *three* matches: P versus Q, S versus R, and U versus T, with the challenger prevailing in each case. The other rankings are possible after only two matches:

    (A) R versus Q and T versus S
    (B) R versus Q and U versus T
    (C) R versus P and U versus S
    (D) Q versus P and S versus R

19. **(E)** If U challenges and defeats S, the bottom half of the ranking changes from STU to UST; and if R challenges and defeats P, the top half of the ranking changes from PQR to RPQ. So in just two matches, all 6 players could be displaced from their initial rank.

20. **(B)** For P to be moved down to third place, at least two matches must have been played (Q challenging and defeating P and then R challenging and defeating Q, or R challenging and defeating P with Q in turn challenging and defeating P). The UST ordering of the bottom half of the ranking could be obtained in one match, with U challenging and defeating S.

21. **(D)** For one player to improve and two to drop in a single match, a player must have challenged and defeated a player two ranks superior. For such challenges to have the stipulated results, it must have been player 3 challenging and defeating player 1, and player 6 challenging and defeating player 4. So the rankings at the end of two matches will be RPQUST. The third match could pit U against P.

22. **(D)** You must always be careful of naked correlations. Sufficient research would probably turn up some sort of correlation between the length of skirts and the number of potatoes produced by Idaho, but such a correlation is obviously worthless. Here, too, the two numbers are completely unrelated to one another at any concrete cause-and-effect level. What joins them is the very general movement of the economy. The standard of living increases; so, too, does the average salary of a preacher, the number of vacations taken by factory workers, the consumption of beef, the number of color televisions, and the consumption of rum. (D) correctly points out that these two are probably connected only this way. (A) is incorrect for it is inconceivable that preachers, a small portion of the population, could account for so large an increase in rum consumption. (B) is wildly implausible. (C), however, is more likely. It strives for that level of generality of correlation achieved by (D). The difficulty with (C) is that it focuses upon *total* preachers, not the *average* preacher; and the passage correlates not *total* income for preachers with rum consumption, but *average* income for preachers with consumption of rum. (E) might be arguable if only one period had been used, but the paragraph cites three different times during which this correlation took place.

23. **(B)** This is a relatively easy question. The argument is similar to "All observed instances of S are P; therefore, all S must be P." (All swans I have seen are white; therefore, all swans must be white.) There is little to suggest the author is a mechanic or a factory worker in an automobile plant; therefore, (A) is incorrect—and would be so even if the author were an expert because he does not argue using that expertise. A syllogism is a formal logical structure such as "All S are M; all M are P; therefore, all S are P," and the argument about automobiles does not fit this structure—so (C) is wrong. by the same token, (E) is wrong since the author generalizes—he does not deduce, as by logic, anything. Finally, (D) is incorrect because the argument is not ambiguous, and one could hardly argue on the basic of ambiguity anyway.

24. **(C)** The key phrase here—and the problem is really just a question of careful reading—is "who actually knew." This reveals that neither of the two knew the person whom they were discussing. There are many ways, however, of debating about the character with whom one is not directly acquainted. We often argue about the character of Napoleon or even fictional characters such as David Copperfield. When we do, we are arguing on the basis of indirect information. Perhaps we have read a biography of Napoleon, (A), or maybe we have seen a news film of Churchill, (B). We may have heard from a friend, or a friend of a friend, that so and so does such and such, (E). Finally, sometimes we just make more or less educated guesses, (D). At any event, the two people described in the paragraph could have done all of these things. What they could not have done—since they finally resolved the problem by finding someone who actually knew Churchill—was to have argued on the basis of their own personal knowledge.

25. **(B)** Here we have a question which asks us to draw a conclusion from a set of premises. The author points out that the Constitution provides that the government may not take private property. The irony, according to the author, is that government itself defines what it will classify as private property. We might draw an analogy to a sharing practice among children: You divide the cake and I will choose which piece I want. The idea behind this wisdom is that this ensures fairness to both parties. The author would say that the Constitution is set up so that the government not only divides (defines property), it chooses (take what and when it wants). (A) is contradicted by this analysis. (C) is wide of the mark since the author is discussing property rather than liberty. While the two notions are closely connected in the Constitution, this connection is beyond the scope of this argument. (D) is also beyond the scope of the argument. it makes a broad and unqualified claim that is not supported by the text. (E) is really vacuous and, to the extent that we try to give it content, it must fail for the same reason as (A).